T0136451

Battles and Leaders of the Civil War

VOLUME 5

Battles and Leaders of the Civil War

VOLUME 5

Edited by Peter Cozzens

University of Illinois Press
Urbana and Chicago

For Issa

First Illinois paperback, 2007
© 2002 by the Board of Trustees
of the University of Illinois

∞ This book is printed on acid-free paper.

Library of Congress Cataloging-in-Publication Data
Battles and leaders of the Civil War. Volume 5 /
edited by Peter Cozzens.
p.   cm.
Supplement to the four vol. work: Battles and leaders
of the Civil War / edited by Robert Underwood Johnson
and Clarence Clough Buel. 1887–1888.
Includes bibliographical references and index.
ISBN 0-252-02404-4 (cloth : alk. paper)
1. United States—History—Civil War, 1861–1865—Campaigns.
2. United States—History—Civil War, 1861–1865—Personal narratives.
3. Generals—United States—History—19th century.
4. Generals—United States—Biography.
I. Cozzens, Peter, 1957– .
E470.B33   2002
973.7'3—dc21   2001002656

PAPERBACK ISBN 978-0-252-07450-9

CONTENTS

MAPS

ILLUSTRATIONS

ACKNOWLEDGMENTS

I never would have completed—nor contemplated doing—a work of this magnitude without the help of my wife, Issa Maria, who tirelessly transcribed dozens of marginally legible articles—and even enjoyed reading some of them.

I would like to express my deepest gratitude to T. Michael Parrish, for whom a project of this sort had long been a desideratum. When I first mentioned to Mike my own interest in undertaking the work (not knowing he had considered doing the same), Mike not only gave me encouragement and superb advice, but also shared with me materials he already had gathered. Mike is a scholar in the truest sense, both knowledgeable and generous with that knowledge.

Several librarians and archivists were also especially helpful in providing me access to obscure periodicals and newspapers. Gary Arnold of the Ohio Historical Society made available to me *The Ohio Soldier*. The staff of the periodicals department of the Philadelphia Free Library provided me with copies of articles from the *Philadelphia Weekly Times,* and the periodicals staff of the Wheaton, Illinois, Public Library filled the countless interlibrary loan requests that my mother kindly submitted on my behalf.

In its July 1883 issue, *The Century Magazine* featured two articles on John Brown's Harper's Ferry raid. The first was written by Alexander R. Boteler, a former United States congressman and colonel on the staff of Stonewall Jackson. Boteler had witnessed much of the raid and later spoken to a captive John Brown. The second article was a Northern abolitionist's lengthy rejoinder to Boteler.

Both pieces were so well received that assistant editor Clarence Clough Buel suggested a series on the Civil War, juxtaposing clashing viewpoints in the manner of the Harper's Ferry articles. Associate editor Robert Underwood Johnson embraced the idea warmly, as did *Century*'s editor in chief, Richard Watson Gilder, who assigned Buel and Johnson the project.[1]

As Johnson later explained, "the plan was, first of all, so far as possible, to give an account of the campaign or battle from the commander of each side, or, if he were not living, from the person most entitled to speak for him or in his place, after which papers on pivotal or specifically interesting phases of the engagement were sought for from the officers most concerned. All this was then supplemented by articles giving the life and color of the service or of particular events."[2]

Gilder had convinced a skeptical Century Company president to back the war series as a money-making venture, rather than for its historical worth. In that regard Gilder proved quite prescient. The first installment of *Century*'s war series appeared in November 1884. Each monthly issue thereafter carried two or three articles by major personalities under the rubric of "Battles and Leaders of the Civil War." Within a year, the magazine's monthly circulation had climbed from 127,000 to 225,000 copies, pushing *Century* past *Harper's* as the best-selling magazine in America. By the time the "Battles and Leaders" series ended in November 1887, ninety-nine feature articles and dozens of letters and shorter pieces, called "Memoranda of the Civil War," had appeared.[3]

Not only did the series prove a grand commercial success, but it also had provided the reading public with a superb library of historically significant writings by many of the leading participants in the Civil War. Capitalizing on both these elements, in 1888 Johnson and Buel published a four-volume collection of war reminiscences, retaining the title *Battles and Leaders of the Civil War*. It too proved a smashing success. A remarkable 75,000 sets were sold. Although the ninety-nine *Century* feature articles were at the heart of the endeavor, they represented but a small part of the nearly four hundred articles that comprised the books. For the remainder, Johnson and Buel drew on articles previously published in other magazines and newspapers, among them two Philadelphia papers, the *Weekly Press* and the *Weekly Times;* the *North American Review;* and *Southern Bivouac,* as well as a number of submissions not carried in the *Century Magazine* series.[4]

Because *Century* was an illustrated magazine, a hallmark of the series had been high-quality illustrations done by former combat artists and by *Century's* own staff of talented illustrators. The same was true of the books. For the project, *Century* editors gathered nearly a thousand pictures, many of which had appeared in the magazine series. The illustrations proved so popular with the public that Johnson and Buel released a one-volume edition of *Battles and Leaders,* called the *Century War Book,* which featured two or more illustrations from the four-volume work on each page.[5]

As Stephen Sears observed in his introduction to *The American Heritage Collection of Civil War Art,* "the achievement of assembling and publishing the great volumes of *Battles and Leaders* was of massive importance." The historian Stephen Davis concurred: "As the most comprehensive single collection of writings by leading participants in the Civil War, *Battles and Leaders* is both extremely valuable to historians and highly entertaining to general readers. Few historiographical landmarks have proven so versatile. . . . The largest and most scrupulously edited compilation of war-related articles by major military figures of the Civil War, the greatest contribution of *Battles and Leaders of the Civil War* has been as an indispensable source of information."[6]

I agree wholeheartedly with the judgments of Sears and Davis. But while worthy of high praise, *Battles and Leaders* was not alone in its field. Several other superb series of participant accounts appeared concurrently with the *Century* series. The best was the "Annals of the War: Chapters of Unwritten History," which ran in Alexander K. McClure's Philadelphia *Weekly Times.* A prominent editor and Pennsylvania Republican, who as state assistant adjutant general had placed seventeen Pennsylvania regiments in the field during the Civil War, McClure had a keen interest in the legacy of the conflict. In 1877 he began devoting the front page of his newspaper to war articles, many by former officers only slightly less prominent than those who later contributed to *Century Magazine.* McClure sought to balance contributions between Northern and Southern veterans and alternated articles weekly on the basis of wartime allegiance. McClure was less interested in stirring controversy than were Johnson and Buel, who often coerced generals into contributing material on subjects they would rather have forgotten, as was the case with James Longstreet's articles on Gettysburg and John Pope's missive on Second Bull Run. Consequently, articles in the "Annals of the War" series were generally less partisan and more accurate. The "Annals of the War" both predated and outran the *Century* series, ending with the eight hundred fifty-sixth article on July 7, 1888. Several dozen articles from the first two years were collected in a single volume of the same title, which McClure published in 1879.[7]

A second Philadelphia paper, the *Weekly Press*, started in 1886 by Isaac R. Pennypacker, tried to compete with McClure's *Weekly Times* with a series of its own. Called "Pennsylvania in the War," it featured the contributions of both Northern and Southern veterans and was comparable in quality to "Annals of the War." The *Weekly Press* series lasted until 1889 and consisted of more than one hundred articles. Notable contributors included Confederate generals Evander M. Law and Lafayette McClaws.

Shortly after the start of the *Century* war series, Martha J. R. N. Lamb's *Magazine of American History, with Notes and Queries* announced its own gathering of Civil War articles, to begin the following year. The only periodical in the nation then devoted to American history, Lamb's journal published forty-four war articles between July 1885 and December 1886. Among the better-known contributors were Union generals William Farrar "Baldy" Smith, Egbert L. Viele, and Henry M. Cist, Confederate general Thomas Jordan, and a historian and former Southern colonel, Charles C. Jones Jr. Many of the articles were enhanced with original illustrations and maps.[8]

Several postwar newspapers published for the benefit of Union veterans also carried eyewitness accounts. Foremost among these was the *National Tribune,* a weekly paper that eventually reached a circulation of over 300,000. In August 1881, two years after founding the *Tribune,* publisher George E. Lemon told readers he would "be glad at all times to hear from any of our soldier or sailor friends who have matters of historical interest, incidents, or amusing anecdotes of the war to relate." The response was overwhelming. Over the next forty-five years, the *Tribune* would run several thousand Civil War articles, letters, and reminiscences contributed by veterans. Few ex-Confederates responded, but among the prominent former Federals to contribute their reminiscences were Generals Oliver O. Howard, John Pope, William Starke Rosecrans, and William P. Carlin.

Worthwhile eyewitness accounts also were featured regularly in the *Ohio Soldier,* a weekly veterans' newspaper published during the 1880s in Dayton, Ohio, and in *Blue and Gray,* a veterans' magazine published in Philadelphia.[9]

Some twenty-five years after the *Century* series ended, William Randolph Hearst announced that his monthly *Hearst's Magazine* would commission eyewitness accounts of Civil War battles on the fiftieth anniversary of a particular event. The magazine's short life, and the dwindling number of living veterans, limited contributions to fewer than a dozen. But among these were fine pieces by Generals Joshua L. Chamberlain, James O'Bierne, and Michael V. Sheridan, and a former Confederate naval officer, Arthur L. Sinclair.

The articles that appeared in the *Weekly Times, Weekly Press, Magazine of American History, National Tribune, Ohio Soldier,* and *Blue and Gray* have one thing in common: they are largely unknown to modern readers. Similarly forgotten are the scores of participant accounts that appeared in diverse other postwar publications, such as *Scribner's Magazine, Atlantic Monthly, Galaxy, McClure's, Overland Monthly, United Service,* and *Cosmopolitan,* to name but a few.

A significant but generally unknown fact is that *Century Magazine* continued to feature participant accounts of the war for three decades after the publication of *Battles and Leaders* in book form. These generally dealt with themes overlooked or given short shrift in the original *Century* war series, particularly prisoner-of-war narratives, naval accounts, and analytical pieces on the war's legacy. Among the prominent contributors during these years were former Confederate generals Edward Porter Alexander, Stephen Dill Lee, and Joseph Wheeler, and former Federal generals Jacob D. Cox and Don Carlos Buell.

• • •

In assembling articles for this volume, I have tried to choose some of the best of the obscure articles that appeared in the decades following the Civil War. I cannot claim to have selected articles according to any precise criteria. I collected several hundred articles of genuine merit covering a broad range of war-related topics, so that my choices for publication have been necessarily based somewhat on personal taste.

Like Johnson and Buel, I have tried to ensure that each article is broadly accurate, and I have sought out controversial pieces. Unlike Johnson and Buel, I have given preference to lively, well-written accounts over the dry and cumbersome pieces that occasionally found their way into the *Century* series. A few of my selections, most notably Henry M. Kieffer's "'Little Jim,' the Pride of the Regiment," I confess are eccentric.

In keeping with the composition of the original *Battles and Leaders* volumes, I have chosen articles primarily from *Century Magazine* and the Philadelphia *Weekly Times*. Whenever possible, I have tried to complement selections with the maps and illustrations that accompanied the original magazine or newspaper accounts. In the case of articles that first appeared without maps or pictures, I selected illustrative material from the *Century* series or from other period works. All maps and illustrations are contemporaneous.

With the exception of George Armstrong Custer's irresistible piece on his balloon rides over the Peninsula, I have eschewed articles—no matter how worthy—that have been reprinted in recent decades or that ran in magazines that have themselves been reprinted. Thus there are no articles from either *The Southern Historical Society Papers* or *Confederate Veteran*. With such a rich store of untapped material to draw from elsewhere, I trust this will not prove a liability.

Among the articles in *Battles and Leaders of the Civil War: Volume 5* is a wealth of fresh material on major events and undying controversies of the war, written by as lustrous an array of contributors as Johnson and Buel managed to gather for their original *Century* series, as well as by some whom they were unable to engage in the project. Major General Winfield S. Hancock, one of the North's most illustrious corps commanders, refused to write for Johnson and Buel. Yet he appears here as the author of an important and lengthy rejoinder to Major General Oliver O. Howard's compelling article on Gettysburg. They spar angrily over one of the lingering controversies of Gettysburg: Who was responsible for deciding upon the Cemetery Ridge line of defense, the position that eventually won the battle for the North?

Another controversial figure in the Gettysburg drama to speak in the present volume is Confederate Major General Henry Heth, whose foraging expedition into the Pennsylvania town precipitated the battle. In a spirited critique of Robert E. Lee's performance at Gettysburg, Heth argues that the burden of the defeat should rest largely on the shoulders of cavalry commander "Jeb" Stuart.

Best known for his heroic defense of Little Round Top, Major General Joshua Chamberlain appears here as the author of a long-neglected article on the Battle of Fredericksburg, as fresh and dramatic a piece of writing as any of his widely known works on Gettysburg and Appomattox.

The roster of notable contributors goes on: Major General William S. Rosecrans presents his version of the Tullahoma and Chickamauga campaigns, in which he led the Union Army of the Cumberland; Lieutenant General James Longstreet speaks out from postwar poverty to offer his first public utterances on the war, its leaders, and the Southern failure; Ulysses S. Grant pens an incisive critique of the Second Bull Run campaign exculpating Fitz John Porter from blame for the Union defeat; General Joseph E. Johnston discusses his surrender to William T. Sherman; Sherman himself describes his conference with Lincoln and Grant at City Point, which helped shaped the nature of his subsequent negotiations with Johnston.

Also of immeasurable value for the new information they reveal are a host of articles by less well known, but nevertheless important, war figures. Confederate Major General "Prince John" Magruder provides a clear account of one of the war's earliest engagements, the little-known Battle of Big Bethel, at which he led the Southern forces. Dabney Maury, himself a talented Confederate commander, paints a vivid portrait of the enigmatic Nathan Bedford Forrest, with whom he served through much of the war, and in a second article offers an equally fine portrayal of the early fighting at Vicksburg. Brevet Major General John W. Fuller presents his experiences at the vortex of the Confederate attack at the Battle of Atlanta.

I hope the reader will share my enthusiasm for these and the other fine articles appearing here, as well as my conviction that *Battle and Leaders of the Civil War: Volume 5* is a stirring and worthy continuation of the great war series begun by Robert Underwood Johnson and Clarence Clough Buel over a century ago.

Notes

1. Stephen Davis, "A Matter of Sensational Interest: The Century 'Battles and Leaders' Series," *Civil War History* 27, no. 4 (1981): 339.
2. Robert Underwood Johnson, *Remembered Yesterdays* (Boston, 1923), 189–90.

3. Davis, "Matter of Sensational Interest," 342–44; Stephen Davis and J. Tracy Power, "Battles and Leaders of the Civil War," in *Dictionary of Literary Biography, Volume Forty-seven: American Historians, 1886–1912,* ed. Clyde N. Wilson (Detroit, 1986), 376.

4. Davis and Power, "Battles and Leaders of the Civil War," 344–45.

5. Davis, "Matter of Sensational Interest," 347–48.

6. Stephen W. Sears, ed., *The American Heritage Century Collection of Civil War Art* (New York, 1974), 11; Davis and Power, "Battles and Leaders," 373, 376.

7. Alexander K. McClure, *Colonel A. K. McClure's Recollections of Half a Century* (Salem, Mass., 1902), 399; Richard A. Sauers to T. Michael Parrish, August 25, 1985, courtesy of T. Michael Parrish; Davis, "Matter of Sensational Interest," 340–41; John Pope to Manning F. Force, July 22, 1885, Force Papers, University of Washington.

8. Dumas Malone, *Dictionary of American Biography,* 23 vols. (New York, 1933), 10:556.

9. Richard A. Sauers, *"To Care for Him Who Has Borne the Battle": Research Guide to Civil War Material in the National Tribune,* Volume 1: 1877–84 (Jackson, Ky., 1995), xv–xviii.

Wishing to allow the authors of the articles gathered here to speak posthumously for themselves, I have not edited the pieces for accuracy in details, nor have I done much more than silently correct misspelled names, complete partial references to persons with bracketed insertions, break up paragraphs of unwieldy length, or correct egregious errors of punctuation and grammar. The footnotes that appear in a few of the chapters are my additions.

PART 1

Prelude to War

1

Recollections of the John Brown Raid
Alexander R. Boteler, Colonel, C.S.A.

STORER COLLEGE, at Harper's Ferry, West Virginia, a flourishing institution "for the education of colored youth of both sexes," owes its existence to
the philanthropic gentleman of New England whose name it has taken. At its
fourteenth annual commencement on May 30, 1881, Frederick Douglass, who
is undoubtedly the most gifted orator of his race, delivered a eulogistic address
on old John Brown, in which he claimed for him "the honor" of having originated the war between the Northern and Southern sections of our Union, sum-
ming up his conclusions on this point in the following expressive language: "If,"
said he, "John Brown did not end the war that ended slavery, he did, at least,
begin the war that ended slavery. If we look over the dates, places, and men for
which this honor is claimed, we shall find that not Carolina, but Virginia—not
Fort Sumter, but Harper's Ferry and the arsenal—not Major [Robert] Anderson, but John Brown began the war that ended American slavery, and made this
a free republic. Until this blow was struck, the prospect for freedom was dim,
shadowy, and uncertain. The irrepressible conflict was one of words, votes, and
compromises. When John Brown stretched forth his arm the sky was cleared—
the time for compromises was gone—the armed hosts of freedom stood face
to face over the chasm of a broken Union, and the clash of arms was at hand."

These words, uttered with an emphasis belonging to a strong conviction of
their truth, will be accepted by the public as an authentic but somewhat tardy
confession of one who, as a confidential coadjutor of Brown in his conspiracy
against the South, is understood to have been fully acquainted with his plans and
purposes; and the avowal thus frankly made by him is sufficiently confirmed by
the contemporaneous facts to which it refers. For, when a complete and impartial history of our late civil war shall be written, it will be seen that the "John
Brown Raid," at Harper's Ferry, in the latter part of 1859, was indeed the beginning of actual hostilities in the Southern States; that then and there the first shot

was fired and the first blood was shed—the blood of an unoffending free Negro, foully murdered while in the faithful discharge of his duty! It will be further seen that there and then occurred the first forcible seizure of public property; the first attempt to "hold, occupy, and possess" a military post of the government; the first outrage perpetrated on the old flag; the first armed resistance to national troops; the first organized effort to establish a provisional government at the South, in opposition to that of the United States; the first overt movements to subvert the authority of the constitution and to destroy the integrity of the Union.

Looked at in the light of subsequent events these facts, with their antecedent and attendant circumstances, are so significant that few now can fail to see and none need hesitate to say that "the abolition affair at Harper's Ferry," in the fall of 1859, was an appropriate prelude to that gigantic war which was so soon to follow it, and which, conducted on a scale commensurate with the magnitude of the work to be accomplished, effectually completed what old John Brown so fatally began—a work concerning which friends of Brown now boast that "Lincoln with his proclamations, Grant and Sherman with their armies, and Sumner with his constitutional amendments, did little more than follow in the path which Brown had pointed out." (F. B. Sanborn, in "Atlantic Monthly," April, 1875.) But whatever difference of opinion yet exists as to who fired the first hostile gun in the South—John Brown or General [Pierre G. T.] Beauregard—one thing is certain: If it had not been for a comparatively small class of factious and implacable politicians in both sections—the active abolitionists of the North and the secessionists *per se* of the South—there would have been no fratricidal civil war, especially if it had depended on the aforesaid extremists to go to the front and do the fighting. But it is enough for us to know what was actually done during a maddened and misguided epoch and what our obvious duty is in these improving times of reestablished peace, and, it is to be hoped, restored fraternity.

Passing by the question, then, as to whether the Harper's Ferry outbreak was "a legitimate consequence of the teachings of the Republican Party," as was claimed at the time of its occurrence by some of the prominent leaders of that party; disregarding also the kindred inquiry as to whether the forcible extinction of slavery in the South was the logical consummation of a foregone conclusion in the North, where it had long been labored for by a constantly increasing faction who, professing to be governed in their political action by a "higher law" than the Constitution, were willing to "let the Union slide" for the sake of abolition, and who, likewise, on that account, opposing all compromises, persistently urged war at a time when many patriots, North and South, were nobly striving to avert that calamity—I will confine myself here to outlining some of the scenes and incidents that occurred, partly under my personal observation, at the time of Brown's hostile incursion, for which he and his deluded followers paid the forfeit of their lives, and from which the people of the unfortunate town selected for his midnight raid may date the beginning of the end of their former prosperity.

On the morning of the raid, Monday, October 17, 1859, I was at my home near Shepherdstown (ten miles west of Harper's Ferry), and had hardly finished breakfast when a carriage came to the door with one of my daughters, who told me that a messenger had arrived at Shepherdstown, a few minutes before, with the startling intelligence of a Negro insurrection at Harper's Ferry!

She could give no particulars, except that a number of armed abolitionists from the North—supposed to be some hundreds—had stolen into "the Ferry" during the previous night, and, having taken possession of the national armories and arsenal, were issuing guns to the Negroes and shooting down unarmed citizens in the streets. Ordering my horse, I started at once for Harper's Ferry, by way of Shepherdstown, where I found the people very much excited. Their first feeling, on hearing the news, had naturally been one of amazed and, with some, of amused incredulity, which, however, soon gave place to an intense and pardonable indignation.

The only military organization of the precinct—a rifle company, called The Hamtramck Guards—had been ordered out, and as I rode through town the command was nearly ready to take up its line of march for the Ferry, while a goodly number of volunteers, with every sort of firearm, from old Tower muskets which had done service in colonial days to modern bird guns, were joining them. I observed, in passing the farms along my route, that the Negroes were at work as usual. When near Bolivar—a suburb of Harper's Ferry—I saw a little old "darky" coming across a field toward me as fast as a pair of bandy legs, aided by a crooked stick, could carry him. From the frequent glances he cast over his shoulder and his urgent pace, it was evident that the old fellow was fleeing from some apprehended danger, and was fearfully demoralized.

I hailed him with the inquiry: "Well, Uncle, which way?"

"Sarvint, marster! I'se only gwine a piece in de country for ter git away from de Ferry."

"You seem to be in a hurry," said I.

"Yes, sah, I is dat an' it's 'bout time ter be in a hurry when dey gits ter shootin' sho 'nuff bullets at yer."

"Why, has any one been shooting at you?"

"No, not exactly at me, bless de Lord! kase I didn't give 'em a chance ter. But dey's been a-shootin' at pleanty folks down dar in de Ferry, an' a-killen of 'em, too."

"Who's doing the killing?"

"De Lord above knows, marster! But I hearn tell dis mornin' dat some of de white folks allowed dey was abolitioners, come down for ter raise a ruction 'mong de colored people."

And on inquiring if any of the colored people had joined them, "No-sahree!" was his prompt and emphatic answer, at the same time striking the ground with his stick, as if to give additional force to the denial.

I insert this colloquy simply because it tends to illustrate the fears and feelings of the Negroes at Harper's Ferry as well as in the surrounding region, at the time of Browns's abortive attempt to secure their aid. Somewhat relieved by the assurance that the Negroes had nothing to do with the trouble, I continued on my way to Harper's Ferry, arriving a little before noon.

It is necessary here to give a summary of the day's doings up to the time of my arrival at the Ferry, together with a preliminary explanation of Brown's plans and preparations. From facts which are fully admitted by his friends, it is now known that for more than five and twenty years Brown had cherished the idea of making slavery "insecure" in the States where it existed by a pre-concerted series of hostile raids and servile insurrections, and that at least two years previous to his raid on Harper's Ferry he had selected it as a suitable place for the initial attack. His three principal reasons for choosing the Ferry as his *point d'appui* were: (1) The presence of a large slave population in what is known as "the Lower Valley," which is that fair and fertile portion of the great valley of Virginia embraced within the angle formed by the Potomac and Shenandoah rivers before their confluence at Harper's Ferry; (2) the proximity of the Blue Ridge range of mountains, where, in their rocky recesses and along their densely wooded slopes, he would be comparatively safe from pursuit and better able to protect himself from attack; (3) because of the location at Harper's Ferry of the United States armories and arsenal, in which were always stored many thousand stands of arms without sufficient guard to protect them.

His plan was to make the Blue Ridge Mountains his base of operations, and descending from them at night with his armed marauders, to attack the unprotected villages and isolated farm-houses within his reach, wherever and whenever his incursions would probably be least expected.

These raids were to be made on the Piedmont side of the Blue Ridge, as well as in the Valley—his forces acting as infantry or cavalry, according to circumstances, and to have no scruples against taking the horses of the slave-holders and other needed property.

As many of the slaves as could be induced to abandon their homes were to be armed and drilled, and, by recruiting his "army of occupation" in this way, he expected soon to raise a large body of blacks, reinforced by such white men as he could enlist, with which he believed he could maintain himself successfully in the mountains, and, by a predatory war, so harass and paralyze the people along the Blue Ridge, through Virginia and Tennessee into Alabama, that the whole South would become alarmed and slavery be made so insecure that the slaveholders themselves, for their own safety and that of their families, would be compelled to emancipate their Negroes. It was, also, part of his plan to seize the prominent slave owners and hold them prisoners either "for the purposes of retaliation," or as hostages for the safety of himself and his band, to be ransomed only upon the surrender of a specified number of their slaves, who were to be given their freedom in exchange for that of their masters.

When Brown went to Europe in 1848, to sell Ohio wool, it is said that he inspected fortifications on the Continent, "with a view of applying the knowledge thus gained, with modifications of his own, to mountain warfare in the United States"; and though not much given to books, he read all he could get that treated of insurrectionary warfare. Plutarch's account of the stand made for years by Sertorious, the Spanish chieftain, against the combined power of the Romans, it is said, was frequently referred to by him in conversation with his friends, as also the war against the Russians by Schamyl, the Circassian chief; that against the United States by Osceola, in the Everglades of Florida; and that so successfully fought by Toussaint L'Ouverture and Dessalines, in St. Domingo. He likewise regarded his own bloody experiences in Kansas as so many practical lessons on the skirmish line; and he also believed himself to be an appointed agent of Deity in the work he intended to do.

He allowed few of his friends besides his immediate followers to know his plans; but there were certain pseudo-philanthropists in the North who knew all about them, and who now boast that, with a full knowledge of his intentions, they "were indifferent to the reproach of having aided him" with means for their execution. While the self-sacrificing bravery of Brown has a claim to our respect and admiration, however much we may condemn his unlawful and treacherous attack, Southern people can feel only abhorrence and contempt for the cowardly conspirators who encouraged his design without having the manliness to share its dangers.

John Brown's first appearance south of Mason and Dixon's line was on June 30, 1859, at Hagerstown, in Maryland. Coming from Chambersburg, in company with a man named [Jeremiah G.] Anderson, who was one of his "lieutenants," they remained overnight there, "passing themselves off for Yankees, going through the mountains in search of minerals." On July 3, he appeared at Harper's Ferry, under the assumed name of Smith, with his two sons—Watson and Oliver—and "Lieutenant" Anderson, passing that night at a small tavern in Sandy Hook, a hamlet on the left, or Maryland, bank of the Potomac, about a mile below the Ferry. The next day, July 4, a farmer, whom I knew very well, met them on a mountain road above the Ferry, when, in reply to his remark: "Well, gentlemen, I suppose you are out hunting minerals?" Brown said, "No, we are not; we are looking for land." He said they were "farmers from the western part of New York," whose crops had been so "cut off" by the frosts, that they had concluded to settle farther south.

Subsequent conversations directed Brown's attention to a small tract further up the road, about five miles from the Ferry, belonging to the heirs of Dr. Booth Kennedy, and a few weeks later he rented a portion of it, including "the improvements," which consisted of a plain two-storied log-house with a high basement, and a small outhouse or shop which was also of logs; for which, with the right to firewood and pasture for a horse and cow, he paid, in advance, thirty-five dollars, taking the property until the first of March following. The place was admirably adapted to the purposes of concealment, being somewhat remote from other settlements, surrounded by dense forests, with its house some dis-

John Brown (*Century*)

tance back from the rarely traveled public road in front of them, and almost entirely hidden from view by undergrowth.

Having thus secured a suitable hiding-place, his men began to gather there— coming from the North, one or two at a time, at intervals, and generally in the night. Meanwhile, there also arrived quietly from the same quarter—great precautions being used to conceal their destination as well as their contents—a number of boxes filled with guns, pistols, pikes, powder, and percussion caps, together with fixed ammunition, swords, bayonets, blankets, canvas for tents, tools of all kinds, maps and stationary; so that few camps were ever more fully supplied for an active campaign than was Old John Brown's mountain aerie.

Sunday night, October 16, was fixed for the foray; and at eight o'clock that evening, Brown said to his companions: "Come, men, get on your arms; we will proceed to the Ferry." They took with them a one-horse wagon, in which were placed a parcel of pikes, torches, and some tools, including a crowbar and sledge hammer, and in which also Brown himself rode as far as the Ferry.

Brown's actual force, all told, consisted of only twenty-two men including himself, three of whom never crossed the Potomac. Five of those who did cross were Negroes, of whom three were fugitive slaves. Ten of them were killed in

Virginia; seven were hanged there, and five are said to have escaped, viz., two of those who crossed the river, and the three who did not cross. Six of the white men were members of Brown's family, or connected with it by marriage, and five of these paid the forfeit of their lives to the Virginians. Owen Brown is the only one of the whole party who now survives.

The following is a list of the party with their respective titles, according to commissions given them under authority of the provisional government, which Brown intended to establish in the South, the constitution for which had been adopted by "a quiet convention," held in Canada for the purpose, over which Brown presided: John Brown, commander in chief; John Henry Kagi, adjutant, second in command, and secretary of war; Aaron C. Stevens, captain; Watson Brown captain; Oliver Brown, captain; John E. Cook, captain; Charles Plummer Tidd, captain; William H. Leeman, lieutenant; Albert Hazlett, lieutenant; Owen Brown, lieutenant; Jeremiah G. Anderson, lieutenant; Edwin Coppic, lieutenant; William Thompson, lieutenant; Dauphin Thompson, lieutenant; *Shields Green; Dangerfield Newby; John A. Copeland; Osborn P. Anderson; Lewis Leary;* Stewart Taylor; Barclay Coppic, and Francis Jackson Merriam. The three last named were left at the Kennedy farm as a guard, and did not cross the river; the five names italicized were colored men, and the only persons among the actual invaders who did not hold commissions—all compliments of that kind having been monopolized by the white men of the party, as a practical commentary on their professions of fraternity and equality. The army so fully officered beforehand, was not yet raised. According to certain general orders, issued by Brown, October 10, a week before his raid, his forces were to be divided into battalions of four companies, which would contain, when full, seventy-two men including officers in each company, or two hundred and eighty-eight in the battalion. Each company was divided into bands of seven men under a corporal, and every two bands made a section under a sergeant.

When Brown's party arrived opposite the Ferry at the entrance to the Baltimore and Ohio Railroad bridge over the Potomac—alongside of which there was, as now, a wagon road—two of the number (Cook and Tidd) were detailed to tear down the telegraph wires, while two more (Kagi and Stevens), crossing the bridge in advance of the others, captured the night watchman, whose name was [William] Williams, and who was entirely too old to make any effective resistance. Leaving Watson Brown and Stewart Taylor as a guard at the Virginia end of the bridge, and taking old Williams, the watchman, with them, the rest of the company proceeded with Brown and his one-horse wagon to the gate of the United States armory, which was not more than sixty yards distant from the bridge. Finding it locked, they peremptorily ordered the armory watchman, Daniel Whelan, who was on the inner side of the gate, to open it, which he as peremptorily refused to do. In his testimony before the U.S. Senate committee, of which Mr. [James M.] Mason of Virginia was chairman, Whelan described this scene so graphically that I here quote a part of it, as follows:

"Open the gate!" said they. I said, "I could not if I was stuck," and one of them jumped up on the pier of the gate over my head, and another fellow ran and put his hand on me and caught me by the coat and held me. I was inside and they were outside, and the fellow standing over my head upon the pier. And then, when I would not open the gate for them, five or six ran from the wagon, clapped their guns against my breast, and told me I should deliver up the key. I told them I could not, and another fellow said they had not time now to be waiting for a key, but to go to the wagon and bring out a crowbar and a large hammer and they would soon get in.

After telling how, with their crowbar and sledge, they broke the fastenings of the gate, Whelan went on to testify: "They told me to be very still and make no noise, or else they would put me to eternity. . . . After that, the head man of them, Brown, said to me: 'I came here from Kansas, and this is a slave State. I want to free all the Negroes in this State; I have possession now of the United States armory, and if the citizens interfere with me I must only burn the town and have blood.'"

Edwin Coppic and Hazlett were next sent across the street to break into the United States arsenal, which stood within another inclosure and where there was no guard whatever; while, at the same time, Oliver Brown and William Thompson occupied the bridge over the Shenandoah near the arsenal, and Kagi, with John Copeland, went up the Shenandoah to the government rifle works, about half a mile above, where there was another superannuated and unarmed watchman to encounter, whom they likewise captured, and then they took possession of "the works."

Harper's Ferry, Looking East (*Century*)

It was now near midnight. Brown's next step was to dispatch Stevens, Cook, and others, six in all, to the country to capture my lifelong friend and college mate Colonel Lewis W. Washington, and also to kidnap his Negroes. In capturing Colonel Washington, they also seized the historic dress sword which had been given by Frederick the Great to George Washington, with the memorable words: "From the oldest soldier to the greatest," together with one of a pair of pistols presented by La Fayette to General Washington, and some other valuable arms. They brought Colonel Washington to Harper's Ferry in his own carriage, and his Negro men in his four-horse farm wagon—stopping on their way at the house of another farmer, Mr. [John H.] Allstadt, whom they likewise took prisoner, together with his son and menservants, all of whom were taken under guard to Brown at the armory, arriving there before daylight.

In the meantime, the eastbound passenger train on the Baltimore and Ohio Railroad arrived at the Ferry after midnight, and was detained there until daylight by Brown's order, his son Watson stopping the train as it approached the station. The passengers at a loss to comprehend the cause of the delay, some of them supposing it to be a strike of railroad hands, and others thinking it was an emeute among the armorers. While they were yet in ignorance of the real cause, an incident occurred at about 1:30 A.M. which served sufficiently to show, at least, the murderous character of insurgents.

Haywood Shepherd, one of the most respectable free Negroes in the county and the regular railroad porter, employed to look after the luggage of passengers, had occasion to see the night watchman, Williams, whose post of duty was on the bridge.

After calling him once or twice and getting no response, he walked out upon the bridge. But he had gotten only a short distance from the entrance of the bridge, when he was confronted by two strange men, who pointing their guns at him, commanded him to halt. The poor fellow was naturally frightened, and, either mistaking the purport of the order, or else confused by the suddenness of the summons, turned around to go back to the railroad office, when he was fired upon by Watson Brown and Stewart Taylor, one of their balls inflicting a mortal wound. Haywood died between twelve and one o'clock the next day.

This was the first victim of the foray, and there is suggestive significance in the fact that it was an inoffensive free Negro, and that his assassination was as cowardly as it was cruel and uncalled for. This firing was the first intimation that any of the citizens of the Ferry had—except, of course, the captured watchman—that there was an enemy in their midst. Several persons living near the bridge were awakened by it, some of whom got up and looked out of their windows to ascertain the cause. But as they heard nothing more, and it was too dark to distinguish objects a few feet from them, they concluded that the noise had been occasioned by midnight revelers shooting off their pistols in sport, and they returned to their beds.

One of these awakened citizens, however, Dr. [John] Starry, was not so easily contented to lie down again without looking a little further into the matter, as he had heard a cry of distress following the shots, and his professional instincts prompted him to go to the relief of the sufferer. The wounded Negro had managed to make his way back to the office of Mr. [Fountaine] Beckham, the railroad agent, where the doctor found him lying upon the floor, writhing in agony. After doing what he could to make him more comfortable, and having learned from him the circumstances under which he had been shot, the doctor started out to investigate more fully the situation.

When he had watched the movements of the raiders for some time and from different points of observation, he was enabled to form an idea of what they had done and were then doing, though not of their ulterior designs; for he thought that their only object was robbery. With this idea in his mind he determined to arouse Mr. [Archibald M.] Kitzmiller, the chief clerk, who, in the absence of Colonel Alfred H. Barbour, the superintendent, had official charge of the armories. So, getting out his horse, he made his way to Kitzmiller's house, which was in quite a different part of the town; and having informed him of the condition of things at the armory, he rode on to Bolivar and elsewhere, arousing the people as he went. By this time it was broad daylight, and some of the citizens were appearing in the streets. Such of them, in the lower part of the town near the government works, as had occasion to pass down Shenandoah and High streets, were surprised to see them picketed near their intersection, and, as may be supposed, their surprise was not diminished on being rudely told they were prisoners and being unceremoniously marched to a building in the armory yard which Brown had appropriated as headquarters for himself and as a "calaboose" for his captives, of whom some thirty or forty altogether were thus taken and held by him.

One of the citizens by the name of [Thomas] Boerley—a well-to-do grocer, and an Irishman by birth—when walking quietly along not far from his residence, happened to get within range of a picket—a black fellow who called himself Dangerfield Newby—whereupon the Negro raised his rifle and without a word of warning shot him dead, with as little compunction as if he had been a mad dog.

It was now about seven o'clock, by which time most of the people of the town had been warned of the raid and its real object. Accordingly, messengers were sent for assistance to the neighboring towns, while prompt and effective steps were taken by the citizens of the Ferry to resist the insurgents, whose force was supposed to be far greater that it really was, from the fact of Brown's making an ostentatious display of sentinels outside of the armory buildings while keeping up from their interiors a desultory fire upon the citizens, when any of them appeared in sight.

There was unavoidable delay in the preparations for a fight, because of the scarcity of weapons; for only a few squirrel guns and fowling pieces could be found. There were then at Harper's Ferry tens of thousands of muskets and rifles of the most approved patterns, but they were all boxed up in the arsenal, and the arsenal was in the hands of the enemy. And such, too, was the scarcity of ammunition that, after using up the limited supply of lead found in the village stores, pewter plates and spoons had to be melted and molded into bullets for the occasion.

By 9:00 A.M. a number of indifferently armed citizens assembled on Camp Hill and decided that the party, consisting of half a dozen men, should cross the Potomac a short distance above the Ferry, and, going down the towpath of the Chesapeake and Ohio Canal as far as the railway bridge, should attack the two sentinels stationed there, who, by the way, had been reinforced by far more of Brown's party. Another small party under Captain Medler was to cross the Shenandoah and take position opposite the rifle works, while Captain [John] Avis, with a sufficient force, should take possession of the Shenandoah bridge, and Captain Roderick, with some of the armorers, should post themselves on the Baltimore and Ohio Railway west of the Ferry just above the armories.

These movements and dispositions were made with commendable promptness under the general direction of Colonels Robert W. Baylor and John T. Gibson—the former being the ranking officer by right of seniority. Thus was cut off Brown's retreat to the mountains in Maryland across the Potomac, or to those in Virginia across the Shenandoah. Shortly after the first of the above-mentioned parties had crossed the Potomac and driven the enemy's sentinels from the Maryland end of the bridge to its Virginia entrance, the Jefferson Guards, under Captain [J. W. Rowen], and the Botts Greys, under Captain Lawson Botts, arrived at the Ferry from Charlestown; and the former company being immediately sent over the river at the Old Furnace, to reinforce those who had crossed before them into Maryland, as soon as they had reached the railway bridge charged across it, killing one of the insurgent sentinels and capturing another (William Thompson), whom they confined in the railway hotel facing the bridge.

Cook and Tidd, of Brown's party, were at this time in Maryland, having been sent early in the morning to the Kennedy farm with Colonel Washington's farm wagon and some of his servants to bring down the boxes of Sharp rifles, Ames pistols, pikes, etc., to a schoolhouse about a mile above the ferry, which was intended to be a convenient depot of supplies for the raiders in the event of their falling back into Maryland. So, of course, as the bridge was no longer in possession of the insurgents, they were unable to rejoin their companions now cooped up in the armories and rifle works. Just after the Botts Greys reached the ferry, a man reported to its captain that he had come from the Gault House (a small tavern situated near the arsenal at the junction of the two rivers commanding the mouth of the bridge and a view of the armory yard), where there was but one man, its proprietor (George Chambers), who was maintaining an unequal skirmish with the raiders, had but one load left for his gun, and wanted reinforcements.

Captain Botts called for twenty volunteers to go with him, and more than twice the number stepped out from the ranks. They had great difficulty in getting to the tavern, being obliged, in order to avoid a raking fire from the raiders, to make a detour around the base of the hill under Jefferson's Rock, and along the bank of the Shenandoah, and then to climb up a wall thirty feet high so as to enter the house by a cellar window, reaching their destination just as Chambers fired his last shot, which wounded the insurgent Stevens.

About the same time, Mr. George Turner, who had the respect and esteem of the entire community, was killed. He was a graduate of West Point. When he heard that his friend, Colonel Lewis Washington, had been forcibly abducted by a band of ruffians, and was a prisoner in their hands, he started at once for the Ferry. As he rode into the upper part of the town, some one handed him a shotgun for his protection. Dismounting from his horse, he walked down High Street, which runs parallel with and only a few paces from the long range of buildings in the armory grounds. When he had approached within some fifty yards of the corner of High and Shenandoah streets, the same Negro—Dangerfield Newby—who had killed Boerley, saw him coming, and, taking deliberate aim, shot him dead. But the assassin himself was soon made to bite the dust. For one of the armorers, by the name of Bogert, a few minutes afterward got the opportunity of a shot at him from an upper window of Mrs. Stephenson's house at the corner of High and Shenandoah streets, and killed him on the spot. I saw his body while it was yet warm as it lay on the pavement in front of the arsenal yard, and I never saw, on any battlefield, a more hideous musket wound than his. For his throat was cut literally from ear to ear, which was afterward accounted for by the fact that the armorer, having no bullets, had charged his musket with a six-inch iron spike.

As already mentioned, it was a little before noon when I reached Harper's Ferry on the day of the raid. By that time Brown and those of his party who were with him in the armory buildings were completely hemmed in. The bridges over both rivers, north and east, together with the western or upper end of the armory grounds, were in possession of the citizens, who occupied every *coign of vantage* from which they could get a fair shot at the insurgents, who, on their part, fighting from under cover of the buildings, were equally on the alert, to retaliate in kind, so that there was a lively little skirmish going on when I got there, which I watched for some time from an open space on High Street overlooking the lower part of the armory yard. Seeing that there was no probability of the escape of the insurgents, surrounded as they were on all sides—with the volunteer citizens on both flanks, the Potomac in their front, and in their rear the town, which was becoming rapidly filled with people from every portion of the county, and ascertaining, also, that no attempt would be made to take the armories by assault before the arrival of the volunteers from Martinsburg and Shepherdstown—I returned to the upper part of the town, where I had left my horse, and rode around toward the rifle works, getting there in time to see the assault made on them which drove Kagi and his party pell-mell out of the rear of the building into the Shenandoah River, where a very exciting scene occurred; for, as soon as the insurgents were recognized attempting to cross the river, there was a shout among the citizens, who opened a hot fire upon them from both banks.

The river at that point runs rippling over a rocky bed, and at ordinary stages of the water is easily forded. The raiders, finding their retreat to the opposite shore intercepted by Medler's men, made for a large flat rock near the middle of the stream. Before reaching it, however, Kagi fell and died in the water, apparently without a struggle. Four others reached the rock, where, for a while, they made an ineffectual stand, returning the fire of the citizens. But it was not long before two of them were killed outright and another prostrated by a mortal wound, leaving Copeland, a mulatto, standing alone and unharmed upon their rock of refuge.

Thereupon, a Harper's Ferry man, James H. Holt, dashed into the river, gun in hand, to capture Copeland, who, as he approached him, made a show of fight by pointing his gun at Holt, who halted and leveled his; but, to the surprise of the lookers-on, neither of their weapons were discharged, both having been rendered temporarily useless, as I afterward learned, from being wet. Holt, however, as he again advanced, continued to snap his gun, while Copeland did the same.

Reaching the rock, Holt clubbed his gun and we expected to see a hand to hand fight between them; but the mulatto, showing the white feather, flung down his weapon and surrendered. Copeland, when he was brought ashore, was badly frightened, and well he might be in the midst of the excited crowd who surrounded him, some of whom began to knot their handkerchiefs together, with ominous threats of "lynch law." But better counsels prevailed, and he was taken before a magistrate, who committed him to jail to await his trial.

When I returned to my former place of observation on High Street, the expected reinforcements from Martinsburg and Shepherdstown had arrived, as also a small body of cavalry under Lieutenant Hess, the latter of who (dismounted) were, with the Shepherdstown company, posted on Shenandoah Street near the armory gate at the lower or eastern end of the grounds, while the men from Martinsburg and those under Roderick prepared to charge the raiders from the upper or western end.

The charge, which I witnessed, was spirited and made in the face of the concentrated fire of Brown's party, who were forced to retreat into the engine house near the armory gate, where nine or ten of the most prominent of the prisoners had been previously placed by Brown as hostages for his own safety and that of his companions. Watson Brown was wounded when his charge was made, also several of the citizens, among whom was a gallant young man by the name of George Wollet, whom I particularly noticed among the foremost of the Martinsburg men until he was disabled by a shot in his wrist. A young lawyer, also from Martinsburg, George Murphy, was wounded in the leg, and an old gentleman of the county, Mr. Watson, who was seventy-five years of age, had the stock of his gun shattered as he raised it to his shoulder to shoot. Thomas P. Young, of Charlestown, who was permanently disabled during the day, got his wound, too, I think, in this charge; but of this I am not so certain.

Brown, having now barricaded himself and prisoners in the engine house—a small but substantial building of brick, still standing—said to Phil, one of Alstadt's kidnapped servants, "You're a pretty stout-looking fellow; can't you knock a hole through there for me?" at the same time handing him some mason's tools with which he compelled him to make several loopholes in the walls through which to shoot. He also fastened, with ropes, the large double door of the house so as to permit its folding leaves (which opened inward) to be partly separated so that he might fire through that opening.

These arrangements having been hurriedly made, Brown and his men opened an indiscriminate fire upon the citizens. While they were thus shooting at every one they saw, without regard to his being armed or not, Mr. Fountaine Beckham, station agent, who was then mayor of the town, happened to walk out upon the depot platform near his office; when, incautiously exposing himself, he was instantly shot down, though it was evident he was unarmed, as he had his hands in his pockets at the time. This was the fourth victim of the foray. When Mr. Beckham's friends upon the platform saw him fall dead in their presence—shot through the heart without a word of warning—killed without having taken any part in the fight, notwithstanding the special provocation he had received that morning in having his favorite servant murdered by the men who had now caused his own death—their rage became uncontrollable, and they impulsively rushed into the railroad hotel to take summary vengeance on the prisoner, Thompson, who was confined there. But the lady of the house, Miss Christine C. Fouke, a most estimable woman, placing herself in front of the prisoner, declared that as long as he was under the shelter of her roof she would protect him, with her life, from harm—which for a time saved the prisoner from death. But the respite was a brief one, for the maddened crowd soon brought him forth upon the platform where he was immediately shot, and his body thrown over the parapet of the bridge into the river below.

One of the raiders, Leeman, was discovered trying to escape across the river; and having been fired on and wounded, an excited volunteer from Martinsburg waded out to where he was in the water and killed him, it was said, after he had surrendered.

Shortly after, the charge was made which brought Brown to bay in the engine house; and while I was yet standing at the point on High Street whence I had witnessed the fight, where there was an unobstructed view across the river, I heard the hum of a ball as it went singing by me, and presently it was followed by another which passed in unpleasant proximity to my head. There were several persons with me at the time who were armed and who, discovering by the smoke that the shots, so evidently meant for ourselves, had come from a clump of small trees on the mountainside across the river, fired a volley in that direction which silenced the unseen marksman. I refer to this trifling incident only because it was mentioned by [John E.] Cook in his confession, as follows:

"I saw," said he, "that our party were completely surrounded, and as I saw a body of men on High Street firing down upon them, though they were about half a mile distant from me, I thought I would draw their fire upon myself; I therefore raised my rifle and took the best aim I could and fired. It had the desired effect, for the very instant the party returned it. Several shots were exchanged. The last one they fired at me cut a small limb I had hold of just below my hand, and gave me a fall of about fifteen feet, by which I was severely bruised, and my flesh somewhat lacerated."

It was now near nightfall, and the gathering gloom of a drizzly evening began to obscure surrounding objects, making it so difficult to distinguish them that, as if by common consent on both sides, active operations were suspended.

At this time a conference was held by three or four of the principal officers in command, to which two or three civilians, including myself, were invited— the object of the consultation being to determine whether or not to take the engine house by assault at once, or to wait until morning.

It was represented to us by the prisoners whom Brown had released, when he selected out of their number nine or ten to be held as hostages in the engine house, that, if an attempt should be made to carry it by storm at night, it would be impossible to distinguish the hostages from the insurgents; and that Brown would probably place the former in front of his own party as a protection, and thereby cause them to receive the brunt of the attack.

It was also urged that the raiders were then as securely imprisoned in their place of refuge as if incarcerated in the county jail, and could be taken in the morning without much risk to our friends. Before deciding the question under consideration, it was thought proper, at any rate, to send Brown a summons to surrender, and a respectable farmer of the neighborhood, Mr. Samuel ——— was selected to make the demand—a duty which he undertook very willingly, although it was not unattended with danger, as the usages of ordinary warfare had been more than once disregarded, during the day, by the belligerents on both sides. Mr. ——— was a man of indomitable energy, undoubted courage, and of such a genial disposition as to make him a general favorite; but he was somewhat eccentric and so fond of using *sesquipedalia verba* that, occasionally, he was betrayed thereby into those peculiarities of speech which characterized the conversation of Mrs. Malaprop.

Tying a white handkerchief to the ferrule of a faded umbrella, he went forth upon his mission with a self-imposed gravity becoming his own appreciation of its importance.

Marching up to the door of the engine house, he called out in stentorian tones,

"Who commands this fortification?"

"Captain Brown, of Kansas," was the answer, from within the building.

"Well, Captain Brown, of Kansas," continued Mr. [S.], with his voice pitched in the same high key, "I am sent here, sir, by the authorities in command, for to summon you to surrender; and, sir, I do it in the name of the Commonwealth of old Virginia—God bless her!"

"What terms do you offer?" inquired Brown.

"Terms!" exclaimed [S.]. "I heard nothing said about them, sir, by those who sent me. What terms do you want?"

"I want to be allowed," said Brown, "to take my men and prisoners across the bridge to Maryland and as far up the river as the lock house (which was about a mile above) where I will release the prisoners unharmed, provided no pursuit shall be made until I get beyond that point."

To which [S.] replied by saying:

"Captain, you'll have to put that down in writing."

"It's too dark to write," answered Brown.

"Pshaw!" said [S.]; "that's nonsense—for you needn't tell me that an old soldier like you hasn't got all the modern conveniences. So, if you don't write your terms down, in black and white, I won't take 'em back to those who sent me."

Thereupon, a light was struck in the engine house, and presently a piece of paper was handed out to [S.], on which Brown had written what he wished to have accorded him.

The proposed terms were, of course, inadmissible; and after the paper containing them had been read by two or three of us, it was handed to Lawson Botts, who threw it contemptuously upon the floor, and placing his foot on it, said:

"Gentlemen, this is adding insult to injury. I think we ought to storm the engine house and take those fellows without further delay."

But the representations of the released prisoners, already mentioned, caused the contemplated assault to be postponed for the night.

The next morning the first thing I learned was that Colonel Robert E. Lee and Lieutenant J. E. B. Stuart (both of whom subsequently gained fame as Confederate leaders) had arrived about midnight with a small body of marines from Washington, and that Colonel Lee had assumed command of all the forces assembled in the place. Having the pleasure of his acquaintance, I lost no time in calling upon him, when he informed me that he intended at once to take Brown and his party. Accordingly, at about seven o'clock, a detachment of marines—three of whom had heavy sledge hammers—were marched up to the west end of the "watch-house" which hid them from the insurgents, and which was under the same roof as the engine house, being separated from it only by a brick partition. Colonel Lee himself (who was not in uniform) took a position outside of the armory gate, within thirty paces of the engine house, but protected from those within it by one of the heavy brick pillars of the railing that surrounded the inclosure.

All now being in readiness, Colonel Lee beckoned to Stuart, who, accompanied by a citizen displaying a flag of truce, approached the engine house.

A parley the ensued between Stuart and Brown, which was watched with breathless interest by the crowd.

Although from the position I occupied (which was, probably, some sixty paces from the engine house) I could not hear the conversation between them, I often afterward heard it detailed by Stuart, when sharing his tent or sitting with him by his camp fire, and therefore am enabled to confirm the correctness of the report of it, made by my friend and former comrade, Major John Esten Cooke, in a graphic account given by him. Stuart began by saying,

"You are Ossawattomie Brown, of Kansas?"

"Well, they do call me that sometimes, Lieutenant," said Brown.

"I thought I remembered meeting you in Kansas," continued Stuart. "This is a bad business you are engaged in, Captain. The United States troops have arrived, and I am sent to demand your surrender."

"Upon what terms?" asked Brown.

"The terms," replied Stuart, "are that you shall surrender to the officer commanding the troops, who will protect you and your men from the crowd, and guarantee you a fair trial by the civil authorities."

"I can't surrender on such terms," said Brown; "you must allow me to leave this place with my party and prisoners for the lock house on the Maryland side. There I will release the prisoners, and as soon as this is done, you and your troops may fire on us and pursue us."

"I have no authority to agree to such an arrangement," said Stuart, "my orders being to demand your surrender on the terms I have stated."

"Well, Lieutenant," replied Brown, "I see we can't agree. You have the number on me, but you know we soldiers are not afraid of death. I would as leave die by a bullet as on the gallows."

"Is that your final answer, Captain?" inquired Stuart.

"Yes," said Brown.

This closed the interview. Thereupon Stuart bowed, and as he turned to leave made a sign, previously agreed upon, to Colonel Lee, who immediately raised his hand, which was the signal of assault. Instantly the storming party under Lieutenant [Israel] Green, consisting of a dozen marines, sprang forward from behind the angle of the wall that had concealed them, and the sledge hammers on the door of the engine house sounded with startling distinctness, and were re-echoed from the rocky sides of the lofty mountains that rose in all their rugged majesty around us.

As yet, to our surprise, there was no shot fired by the insurgents, nor any sound heard from within the engine house. Unable to batter down its doors, the men with the sledges threw them aside, at a sign from Stuart, and withdrew behind the adjoining building. Then there was a brief pause of oppressive silence, as some twenty-five or thirty more marines were seen coming down the yard with a long ladder that had been leaning against one of the shops. Nearing the engine house they started into a run, and dashed their improvised battering ram against the door with a crashing sound, but not with sufficient force to effect an entrance. Falling back a short distance they made another run, delivering another blow, as they did so a volley was fired by the conspirators, and two of the marines let go the ladder—both wounded and one of them mortally. Two others quickly took their places, and the third blow, splintering the right-hand leaf of the door, caused it to lean inward sufficiently to admit a man. Just then Lieutenant Green, who had been standing close to the wall, sword in hand, leaped upon the inclining door-leaf, which, yielding to his weight, fell inside and he himself disappeared from our view in the interior of the building. There was a shot, some inarticulate exclamations, and a short struggle inside the engine house, and then, as our rescued friends emerged from the smoke that filled it, followed by marines bringing out the prisoners, the pent-up feelings of the spectators found appropriate expression in a general shout.

As Colonel Lewis Washington came out I hastened to him with my congratulations, and to my inquiry:

"Lewis, old fellow, how do you feel?"

He replied, with characteristic emphasis:

"Feel! Why, I feel as hungry as a hound and as dry as a powder horn; for, only think of it, I've not had anything to eat for forty-odd hours, and nothing better to drink than water out of a horse bucket!"

He told me that when Lieutenant Green leaped into the engine house, he greeted him with the exclamation: "God bless you, Green! There's Brown!" at the same time pointing out to him the brave but unscrupulous old fanatic, who, having discharged his rifle, and seized a spear, was yet in the half-kneeling position he had assumed when he fired his last shot. He said, also, that the cut which Green made at Brown would undoubtedly have cleft his skull, if the point of his sword had not caught on a rope, which of course weakened the force of the blow; but it was sufficient to cause him to fall to the floor and relax his hold upon the spear, which, by the way, I took possession of as a relic of the raid.

Within the engine house one of Brown's party was found lying dead on the floor and another (Watson Brown) was stretched out on a bench at the right-hand side of the door, and seemed to be in a dying condition. John Brown himself had been brought out and was then lying on the grass; but so great was the curiosity to see him that the soldiers found some difficulty in keeping back the crowd, and Colonel Lee consequently had him removed to a room in an adjoining building, strictly guarded by sentinels, where, shortly afterward, I had an interview with him, the particulars of which have remained distinctly impressed upon my memory.

On entering the room where he was I found him alone, lying on the floor on his left side, and with his back turned toward me. The right side of his face was smeared with blood from the sword-cut on his head, causing his grim and grizzly countenance to look like that of some aboriginal savage with his war paint on.

Approaching him, I began the conversation with the inquiry: "Captain

Brown, are you hurt anywhere except on your head?"

"Yes, in my side—here," said he, indicating the place with his hand.

I then told him that a surgeon would be in presently to attend to his wounds, and expressed to hope that they were not very serious. Thereupon he asked me who I was, and on giving him my name he muttered as if speaking to himself: "Yes, yes—I know—member of Congress—this district."

I then asked the question: "Captain, what brought you here?"

"To free your slaves," was the reply.

"How did you expect to accomplish it with the small force you brought with you?"

"I expected help," said he.

"Where, whence, and from whom, Captain, did you expect it?"

"Here and from elsewhere," he answered.

"Did you expect to get assistance from whites here as well as from the blacks?" was my next question.

"I did," he replied.

"Then," said I, "you have been disappointed in not getting it from either?"

"Yes," he muttered, "I have—been—disappointed."

I then asked him who planned his movement on Harper's Ferry, to which he replied: "I planned it all myself," and upon my remarking that it was a sad affair for him and the country, and that I trusted no one would follow his example by undertaking a similar raid, he made no response. I next inquired if he had any family besides the sons who had accompanied him on his incursion,

John Brown after His Capture (*Century*)

to which he replied by telling me he had a wife and children in the State of New York at North Elba, and, on my then asking if he wished them to know how he was, he quickly responded: "Yes, I would like to send them a letter."

"Very well," said I, "you will doubtless be permitted to do so. But, Captain," I added, "probably you understand that, being in the hands of the civil authorities of the state, your letters will have to be seen by them before they can be sent."

"Certainly," said he.

"Then with that understanding," continued I, "there will, I'm sure, be no objections to your writing home; and although I myself have no authority in the premises, I promise to do what I can to have your wishes in that respect complied with."

"Thank you—thank you, sir," said he, repeating his acknowledgment for the proffered favor and, for the first time, turning his face toward me.

In my desire to hear him distinctly I had placed myself by his side, with one knee resting on the floor; so that, when he turned, it brought his face quite close to mine, and I remembered well the earnest gaze of the gray eye that looked straight into mine. I then remarked:

"Captain, we too have wives and children. This attempt of yours to interfere with our slaves has created great excitement, and naturally causes anxiety on account of our families. Now, let me ask you: Is this failure of yours likely to be followed by similar attempts to create disaffection among our servants and bring upon our homes the horrors of a servile war?"

"Time will show," was his significant reply.

Just then a Catholic priest appeared at the door of the room. He had been administering the last consolations of religion to [Luke] Quinn, the marine, who was dying in the adjoining office; and the moment Brown saw him he became violently angry, and plainly showed, by the expression of his countenance, how capable he was of feeling "hatred, malice, and all uncharitableness."

"Go out of here—I don't want you about me—go out!" was the salutation he gave the priest, who, bowing gravely, immediately retired. Whereupon I arose from the floor, and bidding Brown good morning, likewise left him.

In the entry leading to the room where Brown was, I met Major [W. W.] Russell, of the Marine Corps, who was going in to see him, and I detailed to him the conversation I had just had. Meeting the major subsequently he told me that when he entered the apartment Brown was standing up—with his clothes unfastened—examining the wound in his side, and that as soon as he saw him he forthwith resumed his former position on the floor; which incident tended to confirm the impression I had already formed, that there was a good deal of vitality left in the old man, notwithstanding his wounds—a fact more fully developed that evening after I had left Harper's Ferry for home, when he had his spirited and historic talk with [Governor Henry A.] Wise, [R. M. T.] Hunter, and [Clement L.] Vallandigham.

Between the time of his raid and his execution I saw Brown several times, and was sitting near him in the courtroom when sentence of death was pronounced upon him, during which he was apparently the least interested person present. Of course, I did not witness his execution, as I had seen quite enough of horror at Harper's Ferry, little dreaming of those, ten thousand times more terrible, which I was yet to witness as among the results of the John Brown raid.

2

Mob Violence in Baltimore
John C. Robinson, Major General, U.S.A.

No PERSON of northern birth who happened to be a resident of one of the border slave states in the early part of 1861 could fail to observe, that although many of the people loved the Union and deprecated anything tending to its disruption, yet a very large portion of the population talked loudly about Southern rights, were avowed secessionists, or secretly sympathized with treason and rebellion. This feeling was greatly intensified after threats of secession had become a reality, and nowhere was it more strongly manifested than in the State of Maryland.

In the month of January 1861, the writer of this paper being absent on sick leave from his regiment, stationed at the time in the territory of New Mexico, received an order to report for duty at Fort Columbus in New York harbor, which was then used as the general recruiting depot of the army. The superintendent and commander was Major Theophilus H. Holmes, of the Eighth Regiment of Infantry, a native of North Carolina, and the second officer in rank was Captain Edward Johnson, of the Sixth Regiment of Infantry, a native of Kentucky. As my rank entitled me to precedence over Johnson, I saw at once that my assignment was not pleasing to either of those gentlemen, both of whom soon after resigned their commissions in the army and entered the Confederate service as general officers.

In February I received an order from the headquarters of the army assigning me to the command of Fort McHenry near Baltimore. The very day I received this order [President-elect Abraham] Lincoln arrived in New York on his way to Washington. He was accompanied by his wife and children, his secretaries, John G. Nicolay and John Hay, Judge David Davis, Ward. H. Lamon, N. B. Judd, and Elmer E. Ellsworth, the first victim of the rebellion on rebel soil, also by Colonel [Edwin V.] Summer, Major [David] Hunter, and Captain [John]

Pope, of the army. I was invited to join the party, and went with it to Washington. The journey of Mr. Lincoln was a continued ovation from Springfield to Harrisburg, where he was received by the Pennsylvania legislature and addressed a large assemblage of people. At all places on the route the crowds were gathered in great numbers to see and hear him. Early in the evening while he was at dinner, at Harrisburg, Governor [Andrew G.] Curtin, Colonel Lamon, and Mr. Judd came in, said a few low words to him, escorted him to a carriage, drove away, and early the next morning he arrived in Washington. It was so quietly done that only four or five persons knew anything of it.

The presidential train started the next morning at the appointed hour and attracted the usual crowds at the Harrisburg depot, and all stations on the route. At Cockeysville it was met by a committee of reception from Baltimore, composed of political friends of the President elect, who were greatly disappointed when informed that he was not aboard the train, but had preceded the party to Washington. Some of the gentlemen became much excited and quite indignant, saying that great preparations had been made, and that Baltimore had intended to give him the grandest reception of any city on the whole route. They felt that the Republicans of Baltimore had been slighted and insulted. They did not know at that time, but afterward learned the truth, that men, who had sworn that Abraham Lincoln should never be inaugurated president of the United States, were prepared to give him a very different reception.

Brigadier General John C. Robinson (U.S. Army Military History Institute)

When the train stopped in Baltimore it was instantly besieged by the crowd. Men forced their way in at the doors of the cars and thrust their heads through the windows, shouting: "Where is he?" "Trot him out." "Let us see him," etc. All this in a very different tone and style from the deferential and affectionate greeting that had been extended to him in all other places.

It was with great difficulty the party succeeded in making the change from the cars to the carriages which were to convey them across the city. The crowd of people far exceeded any seen there before. Mr. Lincoln's secret passage through Baltimore was ridiculed at the time, and there are many who still believe it was unnecessary; but subsequent events have proved that had he been one of the party who crossed the city that day he would not have lived to become the idol of the people, and the saviour of the nation, for from the nature of the attack contemplated, few if any of the number would have escaped uninjured.

At the date of Mr. Lincoln's inauguration the country was in a very defenseless condition. Both army and navy had been so scattered as to be unavailable, and the arsenals in the Northern states had been stripped of arms and ammunition. A few companies of artillery garrisoned some of the Atlantic forts, and in the District of Columbia, Colonel Charles P. Stone, acting by authority of Judge [Joseph] Holt, then secretary of war, and Lieutenant-General [Winfield] Scott, general in chief of the army, had enlisted a battalion of volunteers, but they had not been mustered into service.

On February 26 I assumed the command of Fort McHenry, where I found Lieutenant S. H. Reynolds, of the First Regiment of Infantry, and Lieutenant A. T. Smith, of the Eighth Infantry, and a garrison of 100 recruits. Reynolds was relieved from duty at the post, and afterward resigned and entered the Confederate service.

Fort McHenry is situated on what is called Whetstone Point, between the northwest branch and the main branch of the Patapsco River, which forms the harbor of Baltimore. It was a work of five bastions, built of brick, without casemates or bomb proofs, and surrounded by a dry ditch. It had a water battery on the south, and a demi-line in front of the sally-port. The armament consisted of about forty old thirty-two pounders, mounted *en barbette,* for which there was no suitable ammunition. The carriages were old, and many of them rotten. In case of an attack, these guns were of no more use than so many Quaker guns. On the parade ground there was piled a large number of eighteen-pound shot, and a quantity of eight-inch shells.

The officers at the post were on friendly and visiting terms with some of the leading families of Baltimore, but when secession became the harbinger of war, they found many of these acquaintances were intensely Southern in their feelings, and ready to unite with the seceding states in their efforts to destroy the Union.

In the month of March recruiting for the rebel service was secretly commenced in Baltimore under the superintendence of Louis T. Wigfall (Senator from Texas), and many men were enlisted and forwarded to Charleston.

The first regiment to respond to the call of the President was the Sixth Massachusetts militia, commanded by Colonel Edward F. Jones. This regiment left Boston on the evening of April 17, reached New York in the morning, and Philadelphia the afternoon of the next day. The train bearing this command arrived at the President Street depot in Baltimore about noon on April 19, the anniversary of the Battle of Lexington. It was the intention of Colonel Jones to march his regiment across the city to the Washington branch of the Baltimore and Ohio Railroad, but as soon as the train arrived in Baltimore, the engine was switched off, horses attached to the cars, and they were hurried off to Camden station. A little more than half the regiment reached the station without molestation, but as soon as it became generally known that a Yankee regiment was passing through the city on its way to Washington, a mob collected in Pratt Street, and piled anchors, stones, and other obstacles on the track, and prevented the remaining cars from proceeding.

Colonel Jones says: "After leaving Philadelphia I received intimation that our passage through the City of Baltimore would be resisted. I caused ammunition to be distributed, and went personally through the cars and issued the following order, viz.—'The regiment will march through Baltimore in column of sections, arms at will. You will undoubtedly be insulted, abused, and perhaps assaulted, to which you must pay no attention whatever, but march with your faces square to the front, and pay no attention to the mob even if they throw stones, bricks, or other missiles, but if you are fired upon, and any one of you is hit, your officers will order you to fire. Do not fire into any promiscuous crowd, but select any man whom you may see aiming at you and be sure you drop him.'"

When it was ascertained that the cars could not proceed, they were vacated, and the soldiers formed in line on the sidewalk. Captain [Albert S.] Follansbee, of Lowell, being the ranking officer present, assumed the command and attempted to march through the crowd, when they were attacked by the yelling, hooting mob, with brick bats, stones, pieces of iron, and other missiles. The command "double quick" was give. This the mob interpreted as evidence of fear, that the soldiers dared not fire, or, that they had no ammunition. Then the assault was redoubled, numerous pistol shots were fired into the ranks, and one soldier fell dead. Patience ceased to be a virtue, and officers gave the order to fire. The firing now became general on both sides. Three soldiers, Sumner H. Needham, of Lawrence, Addison O. Whitney and Luther Ladd, of Lowell, were killed, and about forty others were wounded. The number of citizens killed and wounded is not known. At this juncture, the mayor of the city, Mr. George William Brown, made his appearance, placed himself by the side of Captain Follansbee at the head of the leading company, and exerted himself to the utmost to quiet the affray. The city police, also, soon after arrived on the ground, and forming in line across the street allowed the soldiers to pass through and kept back the infuriated mob. At Camden station, where the cars were taken for Washington, the assault was renewed. Colonel Jones says of this: "As the men

The Sixth Massachusetts Volunteer Infantry Passing through Baltimore
(*Magazine of American History*)

went into the cars, I caused the blinds to the cars to be closed and took every precaution to prevent any shadow of offense to the people of Baltimore; but still the stones flew thick and fast into the train, and it was with the utmost difficulty that I could prevent the troops from leaving the train and avenging the death of their comrades. After a volley of stones, some one of the soldiers fired and killed Mr. [Robert W.] Davis, who, I have since ascertained by reliable witnesses, threw a stone into the car; yet that did not justify the firing at him, but the men were infuriated beyond control." This Mr. Davis was a prominent citizen of Baltimore, and it is claimed by his friends that he was a quiet spectator and had taken no part in the affray. His death, under the circumstances, was considered by us a very unfortunate event.

While this tragedy was being enacted in the streets and at Camden station, a regiment of Pennsylvania volunteers, commanded by Colonel [William F.] Small, arrived at the President Street depot *en route* to Washington, but as they had been sent forward without arms, they were sent back to Philadelphia on the same train that brought them.

It is impossible to describe the intense excitement that now prevailed. Only those who saw and felt it can understand or conceive any adequate idea of its extent. Meetings were held under the flag of the state of Maryland, at which speeches were inflammatory secession harangues, and it was resolved that no soldier should be allowed to pass through Baltimore for the protection of the national capital. Secessionists and sympathizers with rebellion had everything their own way. The national flag disappeared. No man dared to display it, or open his mouth in favor of the Union. The governor of Maryland, who had been a strong Union man, was overawed, weakened, and induced to call out the state militia. The Maryland Guards were immediately under arms, and batteries of artillery, with horses in harness, were paraded in the streets.

On the morning of the twentieth I went to the city in citizen's dress, and as I walked past a battery paraded in front of the post office, I was recognized by Captain Woodhull, who immediately joined me and asked if I was armed. "Why do you ask that?" I inquired. "Because," was his reply, "you are not safe here, and had better return to the fort." I told him I had some purchases to make, and when that was done I would follow his advice. He remained with me until I was ready to leave town. By order of the city government, to prevent the passage of other troops, the bridges over the Gunpowder and Bush rivers, on the Philadelphia, Wilmington, and Baltimore Railroad, and the bridge near Cockeysville, on the Northern Central Railroad, leading to Harrisburg were burned, which severed all connection by rail with the northern states.

The conspiracy extended to the neighboring towns, and it seemed that for hours of the night mounted men from the country were crossing the bridges of the Patapsco. Marshal [George P.] Kane, chief of the police force, telegraphed to Bradley T. Johnson, at Frederick: "Street red with Maryland blood—Send expresses over the mountains of Maryland and Virginia for the riflemen to come without delay—Fresh hordes will be down on us tomorrow—We will fight then and whip them or die." Threats were made to capture Fort McHenry. Baltimore at that time was as much in rebellion as Richmond or Charleston.

A few years ago, a prominent Baltimore paper denied that there was ever any intention to attack Fort McHenry. It is a sufficient answer to this, to state that in the spring of 1862, the Maryland delegation in Congress, headed by the Honorable Reverdy Johnson, addressed a letter to President Lincoln, in which they said, "It was mainly owing to the determined stand taken by Captain Robinson that Fort McHenry was saved to the government."

The officers at Fort McHenry knew its defenseless condition. They also knew its importance. If it was lost, Maryland would probably secede and the Capital would be cut off. The officers determined to hold it at all hazards, and immediately set to work with the means at hand to prepare for its defense. Sandbags were filled, timber was procured, and a splinter proof built for the side of the magazine toward the city. A quantity of eight-inch shells were filled with powder, and paper fuses calculated to burn about thirty seconds attached to them; gutters were manufactured and placed on the slope for the purpose of rolling these shells into the ditch in case of an assault, a brass field piece was placed in the angle commanding the approach from the town, and another was placed on the parade ground, pointed toward the sally-port and loaded with canister for the benefit of any party that might succeed in forcing the gates. An old mortar was found and a bed improvised for it. As long as it would stand fire, shells could have been thrown into Monument Square, or the heart of the city. It was, however, honeycombed, and probably would not have lasted long. Requisitions had previously been made out and forwarded for ordnance and ordnance stores and other supplies, to which no answer had been received, but subsistence stores were purchased in Baltimore and carted to the fort. At the first intimation of trouble, the orders already given were duplicated, so that rations enough were on hand to meet the emergency.

At about 9 o'clock on the evening of the twentieth, Police Commissioner [John W.] David called at the fort, bringing the following letter from the president of the police board:

> Office Board of Police
> Baltimore April 20, 1861
> 8 o'clock P.M.

> Captain Robinson, U.S.A.
> Commanding Fort McHenry.

> Dear Sir
> From rumors that have reached us, the board are apprehensive that you may be annoyed by lawless and disorderly characters approaching the walls of the Fort to night. We propose to send a guard of perhaps 200 men to station themselves on Whet-stone Point, of course entirely beyond the outer limits of the Fort, and within those of the city. Their orders will be to arrest and hand over to the civil authorities any evil disposed and disorderly persons who may approach the fort. We should have confided this duty to our regular police force, but their services are so imperatively required elsewhere, that it is impossible to detail a sufficient number of them to your vicinity, to insure the accomplishment of our object. This duty has therefore been entrusted to a detachment of the regular organized militia of the state, now called out pursuant to law and actually in the service of the state of Maryland. The commanding officer of the detachment will be instructed to communicate with you. Permit me here to repeat the assurance I verbally gave you this morning that no disturbance at or near your post shall be made with the sanction of any of the constituted authorities of the city of Baltimore, but that on the contrary all their powers shall be exerted to prevent any thing of the kind, by any parties.
> I have the honor to be Very respectfully
> Your ob'd't Servt. Charles Howard Pres't.
> (By order of the Board of Police)

> P.S. There may perhaps be a troop of volunteer Cavalry with the detachment. These will of course be under the orders of the officer in command.
> Yours &c
> Charles Howard
> Pres't.

I did not question the good faith of Mr. Howard, but Commissioner Davis verbally stated that they proposed to send the Maryland Guards to help protect the fort. Having made the acquaintance of some of the officers of that organization and heard them freely express their opinions, I declined the offered support, and then the following conversation occurred:

Commandant—"I am aware, sir, that we are to be attacked tonight. I received notice of it before sundown. If you will go outside with me you will see we are prepared for it. You will find the guns loaded and men standing by them. As for the Maryland Guards, they cannot come here. I am acquainted with some of those gentlemen and know what their sentiments are."

Commissioner Davis—"Why, Captain, we are anxious to avoid a collision."

Commandant—"So am I, sir. If you wish to avoid a collision, place your city military anywhere between the city and that chapel on the road (about three-quarters of a mile from the fort), but if they come this side of it I shall fire on them."

Commissioner Davis—"Would you fire into the city of Baltimore?"

Commandant—"I should be sorry to do it, sir, but if it becomes necessary in order to hold this fort, I shall not hesitate for one moment."

Commissioner Davis (very excitedly)—"I assure you, Captain Robinson, if there is a woman or child killed in that city there will not be one of you left alive here, sir."

Commandant—"Very well, sir. I will take the chances. Now I assure you, Mr. Davis, if your Baltimore mob comes down here tonight you will not have another mob in Baltimore for ten years to come, sir."

Fortunately that night the steamer *Spaulding,* that had been carrying troops to Fortress Monroe, came into the harbor and anchored under the guns of the fort and sent up to the city for coal, which was supplied by a lighter. A report was spread in Baltimore that this ship had brought a reinforcement of eight hundred men. All the tents to be found at the post were pitched on the esplanade, as if for accommodation of the newly arrived troops. All communication with the city was cut off; a picket guard was placed at the hospital gate, and no one was allowed to go out or come in except officers and a trusty messenger. All civilians were stopped there until an officer could be sent for to ascertain their business. It was ten days before the public knew that no reinforcement had been received. By that time there was a reaction; the reign of terror was over, and Baltimore became a quiet city.

One day word came in that there was a stranger at the picket who wanted to see the commanding officer. When I met him he wished to see me privately, and when out of view of the guard he informed me that he was the bearer of a letter from the secretary of the navy, that as he did not know what might happen to him in Baltimore he had concealed it in a queer place. He then removed his hat, and lifting his wig, drew out the letter from between it and his bald crown. It was rather oily, but, nevertheless, a document I was glad to receive. About the time the excitement commenced Lieutenant [Thomas] Grey arrived at the post with a skeleton company of the Second Artillery. He was soon after sent on disguise through Baltimore with a letter to the secretary of the navy, calling his attention to the fact that the United States receiving ship *Allegheny* was lying at Baltimore, and suggesting to him that under the circumstances she would be much safer under the guns of Fort McHenry. On reading the letter the secretary started from his chair, saying no one in his own department had reminded him of this thing, and immediately gave orders for the removal of the ship. Captain Hunter, who commanded her, obeyed the order, reported to me the position of the vessel, returned to the city and resigned from the navy.

Soon after the attack on the Massachusetts troops, Brevet Colonel Benjamin Huger, of the ordnance corps, who was in charge of Pikesville Arsenal, and living in Baltimore, resigned his commission in the army. Meeting him afterwards and expressing regret at the course he had taken, he replied: "I never did anything with so much regret in my life. I was brought up in the army, my father was in the army, my son is in the army, and I hoped to end my days in the army, but *the country has gone to hell!* My friends in South Carolina are constantly writing to me, urging and begging me to resign and come home, and I can't stand it any longer. But one thing I assure you, old fellow, I never will fight against the old flag."

On June 25, 1862, at the Orchard, the first battle of the Seven Days' fighting on the Peninsula, the First Brigade of [Major General Philip] Kearny's division under my command was directly opposed by the division of Major General Ben Huger. This is not an isolated case. There were other officers who, feeling compelled to leave our service, did so with the same determination as Huger, but after they reached home within the limits of the Confederacy they found the pressure too strong, and were almost forced to draw their swords against the flag they had sworn to defend. Were they not virtually conscripted as well as the men they commanded?

The first demonstration of returning loyalty was on Sunday morning, April 28, when a sailing vessel came down the river crowded with men, and covered from stem to stern with national flags. She sailed past the fort, cheered and saluted our flag, which was dipped in return, after which she returned to the city.

The tide had turned. Union men avowed themselves, the Stars and Stripes were again unfurled, and order was restored. Although after this time arrests were made of persons conspicuous for disloyalty, the return to reason was almost as sudden as the outbreak of rebellion. The railroads were repaired, trains ran regularly, and troops poured into Washington without hindrance or opposition of any sort.

Thousands of men volunteered for the Union army. Four regiments of Maryland troops afterwards served with me and constituted the Third Brigade of my division. They fought gallantly the battles of the Union, and no braver soldiers ever marched under the flag.

In the summer of 1882 the national encampment of the Grand Army of the Republic was held in the city of Baltimore and received a welcome never exceeded in any Northern city. The escort was composed of military companies of

Maryland and Virginia. The blue and the gray mingled. Union and Confederate soldiers walked the streets arm in arm, red, white and blue bunting covered the buildings on all the business streets, and the starry banner of the Union floated from every flagstaff. In May last the Society of the Army of the Potomac held its annual meeting in Baltimore. Hundreds of the soldiers who had marched through Baltimore to Washington in 1861 received a cordial and hearty welcome to that city in 1885.

PART 2

The War in 1861

3

The First Battle of the War: Big Bethel

John B. Magruder, Major General, C.S.A.

IN THE AUTUMN of 1859 I was placed in command of the Artillery School of Practice at Fort Leavenworth, Missouri, where, against many obstacles, I was successful in establishing a valuable school for improvement in that arm of the service. In November 1860, the secretary of war, after expressing his entire satisfaction with my management of this military school of practice, selected me to go abroad and to inspect and report upon the modern improvements, equipment, and drill of artillery, especially in the light artillery branch of the service.

In obedience to these instructions I sailed from New York for Havre on November 10, 1860. I received from the French officers the most courteous attention, and from the imperial government every facility for the accomplishment of my purpose. Having inspected the French military establishments and a portion of their army, I traveled through Italy, and on my arrival at Florence, en route to Berlin, Vienna and St. Petersburg, I received late in the winter of 1861, orders from General Scott, commander in chief of the American army, to return home immediately and report for duty. Information reached me at the same time that war was imminent between the North and the South. I returned to the United States immediately and found my own command stationed in Washington City. Here I was on duty about a month previous to the secession of Virginia—my native state. During this interval I had several interviews with the late President Lincoln, whom I found kind, considerate, and conciliatory. On the last of these occasions the president, with whom I was alone at the White House, conversed with me for an hour or two on the state of public affairs. President Lincoln said that "independently of all other reasons he felt it to be a constitutional obligation binding upon his conscience to put down secession." At the same time he said he bore testimony to the honor, good faith, and high character of the Southern people, whom he said he "knew well."

Major General John B.
Magruder (*Century*)

I availed myself of this opportunity to state to the president that I had always been a soldier of the Republic, that I had borne the Stars and Stripes triumphantly over many a battlefield, that under its folds I had been willing to meet death among the storming parties and on the forlorn hope. That now I would be happy to render it in the defense of the country against a foreign foe. I stated also that I did not own a slave in the world and had no property in the South, that the ties which connected me with the old army were dearer to me than anything on earth except those which bound me to my own family, and I implored the president not to attempt coercion as I felt convinced that in the event of war the people of my state, Virginia, would resist it as long as it was possible to do so. I asked the president to remember that the people of the South also had consciences, that they had been educated in this belief from the very commencement of the government, and therefore no precipitate measures should be adopted against them. I said frankly to the president that while this was the most unhappy moment of my life I felt that I could not fight against my own people, among whom I was born and raised, who believed they were right and whom I knew to be honorable and sincere; that I considered it the most ignoble part of all for me to go to Europe on service, as it had been intimated I might do, and with folded arms coolly look on without taking part in a struggle which involved not only the lives of the bravest and best men in the country on both sides, but was fraught with danger to our highest interests and dearest liberties that, therefore, for me there was but one course to pursue, which was to share the fate of Virginia, whatever that might be; but I said, "Mr. President, as long as I have the honor of holding a commission in the army of the United States, there is no officer upon whose loyalty, fidelity, and devotion you can more fully depend."

President Lincoln answered, "I know it, sir, and that my family and myself can sleep in safety when a Southern gentleman is on guard." I stated to Mr. Lincoln that should I be compelled by the course of public events to resign, I would do so most respectfully but openly, and that he, Mr. Lincoln, should be immediately informed of the fact. The hour having arrived for the meeting of the cabinet, in whose room this interview took place, it terminated with expressions of respect and kindness on both sides. Very soon after Virginia seceded. I resigned my commission in the army of the United States and immediately sent the information to President Lincoln. My resignation was promptly accepted.

I then repaired to Richmond and offered my services to my native state, to act in any capacity the authorities might think proper. I received an appointment of colonel in the Virginia state troops, and the building known as the Baptist Seminary, having been assigned to me as a barrack, I organized, equipped, and drilled some eight or ten batteries for the field. I was then placed in command of the District of Henrico (Richmond) for a few days, and about May 24, 1861, was ordered to command, fortify, and defend Yorktown, at the mouth of the York River. On my arrival at Yorktown I found but one gun mounted and not a trace of a work to defend the place from approach by land. In two days I organized my command, consisting of several regiments, made arrangements for supplies of rations and ammunition, designed a plan for fortification, set the engineers to work, and taking with me the high sheriff of the county, Major George Wray, and a company of active fox-hunting cavalry, under command of Captain Jefferson Phillips, proceeded toward Fortress Monroe, a United States fort of great strength, from which I knew troops would soon be sent to interfere with my plan of fortifying Yorktown.

Having made myself in a short time thoroughly acquainted with the roads, I selected Great Bethel (a spot which derived its name from a wooden church called Bethel) as a point at which I would give battle to the enemy. This place offered some natural advantages for defense, but could be easily flanked by a road passing over a bridge about two miles to its right and by a ford a quarter of a mile to its left. In consequence of the dangerous facilities they offered to an invading force, I proceeded to destroy the bridge on the right and caused heavy timber to be felled across the road, thus rendering it impracticable, and carefully reconnoitered the ford on the left. I believed that with one piece of artillery, supported by a company of infantry, it could be safely defended. I then returned rapidly to Yorktown, and on June 6 I dispatched all my disposable force, consisting of two battalions of Virginia infantry, the First North Carolina Regiment, under command of Colonel D. H. Hill, two batteries of artillery, under Colonel George W. Randolph, with some sixty Virginia cavalry, to take post at Great Bethel. I ordered Colonel Hill to construct rifle pits, and arriving in person

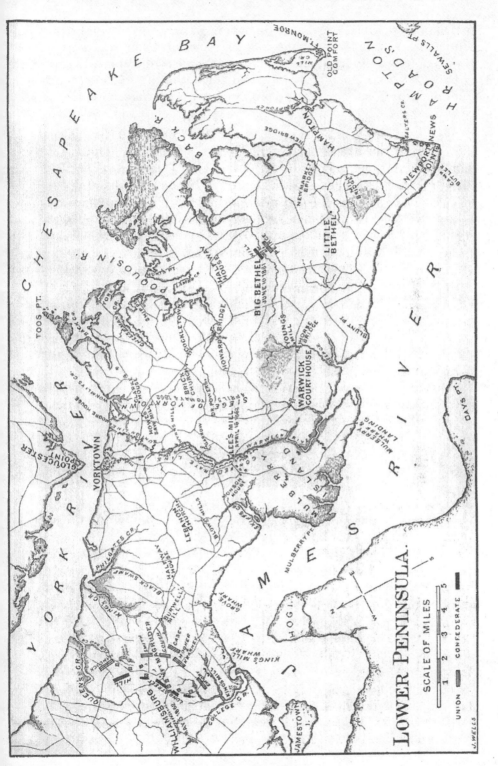

Lower Peninsula of Virginia (*Century*)

on June 8, extended the line of defense and caused the work to be pushed forward rapidly to completion. On the same day some skirmishing took place between our reconnoitering parties and those of the enemy, the latter being driven back. On Sunday, June 9, the Rev. Mr. George F. Adams, of the Baptist Church, came out to us from Hampton, and proposing to have divine service, protected by the shade of some fine oak trees, the work was stopped, and I ordered the troops to be assembled for that purpose. The sermon was most eloquent and impressive. The officers and soldiers, without exception, united in prayer to God, and the effect of the psalms and hymns which arose from that devoted band was most striking in its sublime solemnity. The service over, we learned that the enemy was advancing from Fortress Monroe in force; but it was supposed by those who gave the information that their object was to fortify, by a *tete dupont*, the only remaining bridge over Back River, between Fortress Monroe and Great Bethel. This bridge being of great use to me, as it enabled me to cross at a convenient point this deep and muddy creek, and harass with my sharpshooters the enemy's troops and trains on their passage from Fortress Monroe to Newport News, a work erected by the enemy on the James River, I determined, if possible, to seize the bridge next morning and defend it, sending scouts, however, that night in advance to ascertain if the enemy stopped at the bridge to fortify it or merely passed it. In the former case, I intended to attack; in the latter, to fall back to my position at Great Bethel.

The forward movement from Great Bethel was ordered to take place the next morning at 2 o'clock, but the troops were not put en route till some hours later. After marching some two or three miles we were informed by a respectable elderly lady who met the column in the road, and who was flying from her house in a state of great distress and agitation, that the enemy had crossed the bridge over Back River in great force and robbed her of everything she had, and driven her from her home. This intelligence induced me to march my forces and place them at their respective positions at Great Bethel. Proceeding to the right of the line I addressed separately each body of troops, informing them of the battle about to commence and counseling coolness, steadiness, and closeness of fire. When I had reached the center, intending to address the remainder of my troops, I discovered the head of the enemy's column advancing by the road leading to my position and about 300 yards in front of it. I directed one of Randolph's pieces to be moved a little to the left and to be discharged at the head of the enemy's column. This was done, Colonel Randolph (afterward secretary of war of the Confederate States) pulling the lanyard. This shot enfiladed the enemy's advancing line and caused great destruction. Nothing daunted, however, the enemy formed line of battle, his right occupying a wood in front of our left and his left an open space in front of our right, the distance between the two forces being about 250 yards. It was soon seen that he outnumbered us by three or four to one. As soon as his line of battle was formed he opened on us a tremendous fire of infantry and artillery. The distance not being, however, correctly estimated by them, all of the artillery shots and most of the infantry passed over our heads, while the fire of our men told with deadly effect. Colonel Randolph, who had been an officer of the United States navy, had equipped and drilled his artillery in the most perfect manner. The officers and men were gentlemen of the first standing and of the best social position in Virginia—generally from Richmond. In no army in Europe or in the country could there be found more intelligent officers, more bold or dashing drivers, or more skillful cannoneers.

This artillery occupied the center of the line of battle where I was posted for most of the time during the struggle. Being served with the greatest rapidity it soon became evident that no troops could stand before it; the enemy therefore determined, if possible, to carry the position by assault. In front of our right flank there was a very weak detached rifle pit, at the near extremity of which was a field piece supported by a small detachment of infantry. The enemy charging this work in great force, the piece was withdrawn and our infantry retired to an inner line which had been provided for such an emergency.

At this time I learned that my flank was threatened by a road the enemy had discovered on my left at the ford. I detached troops to my right under Major John B. Cary, in command of a company of his battalion, to reinforce those already at the ford, thus securing both of these points. The battle increased in violence—the enemy being more determined to carry the position. I therefore deemed it necessary to retake the works, which had been carried and occupied by the enemy, and, after an address to a portion of the Virginia troops led by Major Thompson Brown, of the artillery, the officer who had previously occupied them, he charged upon and retook them. About the same time Colonel D. H. Hill, of the First North Carolina, sent an officer of his regiment and a force

The Battle of Big Bethel (*Campfire and Battlefield*)

to accomplish the same purpose, but though they advanced rapidly and in gallant style the works were recovered by the Virginians before their arrival on the ground. The right flank being thus reestablished in its original position the enemy now made a still more serious and desperate attack on our left, and upon that portion of the line defended by the First North Carolina Regiment, under Colonel Hill.

From my position in the center I saw that the enemy's fire came from the left, wounding some men around me. I cast my eyes in that direction and seeing no one in the trenches assigned to the North Carolinians, was under the impression for a moment that the line there was undefended. In an instant, however, the First North Carolina sprang up to its feet as one man and, pouring into the enemy several concentrated discharges at seventy or eighty yards distance, repelled the attack with great havoc—killing eighty men on the spot, including their brave and enterprising leader, Major [Theodore] Winthrop.

The battle in front continued a short time longer, when the enemy retired, leaving his killed and some of his wounded upon the field of battle. I kept my cavalry formed ready to pursue without a moment's loss in case of success. Colonel Hill, at his own request, was allowed to send one of his companies to the wood in front to learn if the enemy there had not prepared an ambuscade. As soon as it returned the cavalry was dispatched, but it was found the main body of the enemy had retreated some time before the battle terminated. Closely pressed by the cavalry, a few prisoners were taken, though many of the enemy threw away their arms, and others were reported to have been drowned in crossing the creek.

The enemy's force, as published afterward in the New York *Herald*, was six regiments with one battalion, exclusive of artillery and cavalry, and as the regiments were then full, this force must have been from 5,000 to 6,000 men.[1] Our force was about 1,500 men of all arms. The losses of the enemy in killed and wounded could not have been less than 500, probably more. Our loss was one killed and seven wounded.[2]

Had the enemy succeeded they must have gotten possession of Yorktown, and the road to Richmond thus early in the war would have been open to them. The officers and men of all arms behaved with distinguished courage and steadiness. Being a Virginian, I took great pains to do justice to the North Carolina regiment, which had left their homes to defend the soil of Virginia. It is now well known that all the troops behaved well, as my report shows, but that Randolph's artillery played, perhaps, the most important part in this well-fought battle.

The time gained by this battle enabled us to erect works at Yorktown and on

---

1. Approximately 4,400 Federal troops were engaged at Big Bethel.

2. Federal losses at Big Bethel totaled eighteen killed, fifty-three wounded, and five missing, including Major Winthrop, on detached service from the staff of the commander of the Department of Virginia, Major General Benjamin F. Butler—Editor.

the James River, and to connect them by damming up the Warwick River, and thus with 11,000 men to hold [Major General George B.] McClellan with his 120,000 men in check until General Joseph E. Johnston could move with his army from 75 miles west of Richmond to about the same distance east of the city, where we jointly held him at bay for one month, so that the authorities at Richmond had time to concentrate the Confederate forces and afterward to organize that army which, after seven victories around Richmond, forced the enemy, under General McClellan, to raise the siege of the Confederate capital and retire in discomfiture to their ships in the James River, at Harrison's Landing.

4

With Generals Bee and Jackson at First Manassas

William M. Robbins, Major, Fourth Alabama Infantry

ON THE AFTERNOON of July 18, 1861, the army of [Brigadier General Joseph E.] Johnston—about ten thousand strong—which had been for some weeks manoeuvering up and down the [Shenandoah] Valley in front of [Major General Robert] Patterson and was then lying around Winchester, was hastily put in motion and marched off southeastwardly, going we knew not whither. Most of the men belonged to the class which may be described as "young bloods," sons of planters, reared in ease and affluence—intelligent, merry hearted, high spirited, full of romance and enthusiasm. They had volunteered at the first call, not only from devotion to the cause, but love of adventure, and there was nothing they were so eager for as to get into a battle, being somewhat tinctured with the idea that they "could whip at least three Yankees apiece," and were rather afraid that the war might come to an end before they got a chance to prove it. In spite of their confidence in their general, they had been a good deal chagrined and disgusted at what they deemed his overwary strategy in not delivering battle to the enemy under Patterson. They were therefore greatly delighted to hear the general order which General Johnston caused to be read to each regiment as soon as we got well out of Winchester that summer evening. That order was about in these words: "Beauregard is attacked by overwhelming odds at Manassas. Your commanding general has full confidence in your zeal and devotion and asks every man to step out lively. You are going on a forced march over the mountains to reinforce your companions in arms and save the country." Loud cheers welcomed the tidings. The prospect of an early encounter with the enemy loomed up ahead and stimulated the impatient spirits of the men to their best exertions. Heat, dust and night-fall soon made the rapid march disagreeable enough, but it was pushed without check till we reached the Shenandoah. This river, about waist deep, was waded at dawn of July 19, amidst songs, jokes, and general hilarity. The Blue Ridge was passed at Ashby's Gap, and at evening of the same day the head of the column arrived at Piedmont Station on the Manassas Gap Railroad, whence Johnston's forces were sent forward in detachments by rail as fast as transportation could be furnished.

So much has been said about Johnston's troops appearing on the field in the nick of time after the battle had been long raging that the impression extensively prevails that none of them were there at its beginning. This is a great mistake. Three brigades—[Brigadier General Thomas J.] Jackson's, [Colonel F. S.] Bartow's and nearly all of [Brigadier General Barnard E.] Bee's—were at hand when

Brigadier General Barnard
E. Bee (*Century*)

the battle opened and bore an important part in it all day. The Fourth Alabama and other regiments of Bee's Brigade reached the Junction at noon of the twentieth and were among the very earliest in the conflict next day. It was only the comparatively minor number of Johnston's men under [Brigadier General Edmund] Kirby Smith and [Colonel Arnold] Elrey that leaped from the train when they heard the battle in progress, and, hastening down the Warrenton Pike, came in so luckily on the right rear of the Federals and caused that panic which gave the victory to the Confederates.

I have spoken of the eagerness of our inexperienced but enthusiastic soldiers to see and participate in the battle. This feeling did not diminish, but rather grew in intensity on this occasion, up to the time of actual engagement, and how much longer I cannot say; but one thing is certain—all of us by the time the day was over felt sufficiently amused. Thousands of soldiers on both sides know all about the experiences of a first battle, and anything said on the subject would be but an old tale to them; but those who never took a hand, and especially the young who have come up since the war would no doubt like to know how a battle looks and seems to a new soldier—its thrill, its thunder, its grandeur, its horror, and no less its odd, absurd, and even grotesque features. I do not feel competent to paint an adequate picture and description of these things. I doubt if any pen can fitly paint them. A few hints of how this battle opened and proceeded—as the writer saw it—must suffice. The Fourth Alabama were busy with breakfast not far from the junction when the sudden boom of a gun in the direction of the railroad bridge over Bull Run drew our eyes that way and we saw for the first time the little dense round sphere of white vapor, high up in the air, produced by the bursting of a shell. This was quickly followed by others, the design of the Federals being to draw all attention to that part of the line while they were executing their shrewd flanking movement on our left. However, our regiment, with others of Bee's Brigade, was at once moved at double-quick towards the Confederate left, to a position that had been allotted to us at one of the upper fords. But we had scarcely reached the designated point when we were again ordered to go at a rapid run for about two miles still further up the stream to meet the Federals—our commanders having just at that moment discovered that they had crossed the stream at Sudley's Ford, entirely beyond the Confederate left, and were pouring down in heavy force on that flank. All depended on presenting a quick front to this unexpected movement. So we went—a few battalions only—across the fields at our highest speed, and soon reached the plateau of the Henry House, around which the battle was afterward mainly fought. But Bee did not permit us to stop there. He marked that as the most favorable position for the Confederate line to form its new front on, but he knew his brigade alone could not hold it and he also saw that the enemy would reach it, unless checked and delayed by some means before an adequate force of Confederates could get there to oppose them. To gain the needed time it was necessary to risk the sacrifice of the two and a half regiments then with him by a bold movement still further to the front. He could not hesitate. So he ordered the Fourth Alabama, Second Mississippi and Eleventh Mississippi (two companies) to move half a mile further forward to the next ridge to engage the enemy and delay them as long as possible. Down the slope we rushed, panting, breathless, but still eager because ignorant of the desperate crisis which had doomed us to probable destruction to save the whole army. As we passed the little rivulet below the Stone House, the duel of the artillery began and the shells of friend and

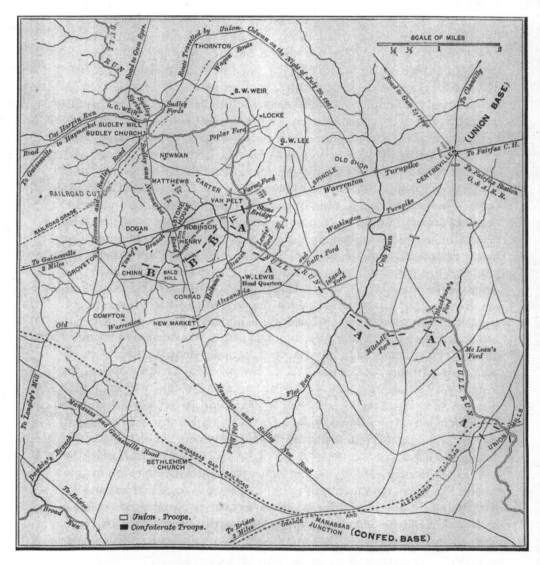

The Battlefield of First Bull Run (*Century*)

The Federal Advance from Sudley Springs (*Life of General Sherman*)

foe shrieked wildly above our heads. Mounting the hill and entering the copse of timber north of the Stone House, we began to hear a sharp crackling of musketry ahead of us—a collision between the Federals and some small bodies of Confederates we had not known were there before, among them [Major C. R.] Wheat's Louisiana Tigers, wearing the zouave uniform.

As we emerged from the little wood we caught sight of these Tigers, utterly overwhelmed and flying pell-mell, most of them running off to our right and toward the stream (Bull Run). This and their zouave uniform, which we had never before seen, but had heard some of the enemy wore, for a minute caused us to mistake these "Tigers" for Federals, and as they were flying in disorder, some of our men set up a loud yell and shout of victory, supposing the enemy were already routed and retreating, whereupon one ardent fellow of the Fourth Alabama, with his finger on the trigger and anxious to pull down on somebody before they all got away, burst out with: "Stop your darned hollerin' or we won't get a shot!" But the mistake was discovered just in time to prevent our firing on friends. A little way further up the hill beyond the timber and we struck the enemy and no mistake. Their long advancing line, with the Stars and Stripes waving above it (which made some of us feel sorry), began to peer over the crest, eighty yards in our front, and opened a terrific fire, which at first went mostly over us. It is proper to mention that the Mississippians, who had come with us, were halted at the edge of the wood behind us, and so did not get into the hot conflict that ensued, the whole brunt of which thus fell upon the Fourth Alabama alone. On receiving the enemy's first fire we lay down and waited till we could see their bodies to the waist, when we gave them a volley which was very effective, firing uphill. The Federals fell back and disappeared behind the crest. After some interval they advanced another and longer line; but the result was the same as before, only they held on longer this time and their fire hurt us badly.

A third time they came on in a line which extended far beyond both our flanks, and now the conflict became bloody and terrible to us, their balls coming not only from the front but from the right and left oblique, cutting down our colonel (Egbert Jones) and stretching lifeless many a familiar form so recently full of hope and gayety. Then war began to show us his wrinkled front. But we thought of what they would say at home if we flinched and how ashamed we should feel if after all the big talk about whipping the enemy we let them whip us at the first chance. We could see, too, that they were as awkward at the business and enjoyed it as little as ourselves. Besides, it looked like they could hardly help killing every one of us if we got up and tried to run away. It seemed our safest chance to hug the ground and pepper away at them; and so from sheer desperation, as much as anything, we kept to it, until after awhile, to our great joy, the enemy fell back once more behind the crest, and their fire lulled. Our general, seeing we would be certainly overwhelmed at the next onslaught, gave us the order to retire, which we did before another attack. We had been at it over an hour and had really rendered great service in gaining time for the Confederate army to change front and form the new line. But nearly one third of the Fourth Alabama had gone down in the effort and were left on the ground, including the colonel, mortally wounded. I should not omit to mention that the Seventh and Eighth Georgia, of Bartow's brigade, also came into our advanced position far to our right during our contest, and had a bloody collision with another column of the Federals, and though these Georgians were recalled some time before we were, they contributed materially to the delay of the Federal advance.

The two Mississippi regiments of our (Bee's) brigade had also retired before us, so that the Fourth Alabama was going back alone. In this movement a bloody episode occurred to us. Retiring by the same route along which we had come, when we reached the little rivulet running near the stone house, we saw a regiment, in column by companies, marching down that rivulet toward us. Their flag was furled on the staff and so was ours. By the quarter we had just come from they thought us probably Federals, but were not sure. As for us, we felt the enemy had got so far around in rear of the place of our recent fight; their uniform also resembled that of the Sixth North Carolina, belonging to our brigade, and we hastily took them for that regiment coming to our aid. Thus encouraged we halted, faced about and reformed our line, intending with this supposed reinforcement to take another tilt with the enemy we had been fighting if they should pursue us as we expected. The unknown regiment also halted and deployed into line of battle at right angles with ours and less than 100 yards from our left flank. Their colonel signaled us with his handkerchief for the purpose of communicating and learning who we were as it afterward appeared; but we never dreamed that was his purpose and made no haste to respond, feeling confident we knew him, and thinking of course he knew us. All this took place in a few moments. Having quickly rearranged our line, our flag was then unfurled and displayed—the Stars and Bars! Instantly a blaze of fire flashed along the line of our supposed friends (a New York regiment it really was), and an enfilading hailstorm of bullets tore through the Fourth Alabama from left to right, killing many and disabling more, among the rest Lieutenant Colonel [Evander M.] Law and Major Scott, leaving our regiment without field officers.

What does the reader suppose we did? We did not stay there. The position was too bad and the surprise too sudden. True, the enemy's fire was once returned with considerable effect; but it is only frank to say that we resumed, without delay, our movement back to the main Confederate line, whither Bee had intended us to go when he first ordered us to retire. Having arrived there, even after all they had suffered, the Fourth Alabama still had pride enough left to rally again, and under the command of a captain fell in on the right of the line and fought to the end of that terrible day. I will not now attempt to detail all the incidents that befell this regiment in these later hours of the battle. I will give one, however, which will always be of special historic interest.

The position of our regiment being now on the right of the Confederate line as drawn up on the plateau of the Henry House, and the leading design of the Federals during the entire day being to turn the Confederate left, the heaviest fighting gradually veered toward that flank. No one who was there can ever forget how the Federal musketry crashed and rolled in fresh outbursts as new troops poured in against our centre and left. Farther and farther round its awful thunder seemed to encroach, as if it would never be stayed till it should rend and tear that part of our line to atoms. Our brigade comrades of the Sixth North Carolina, separated from us in the manoeuvres of the day, had rushed in single-handed and attempted to check it, but had been smitten as with fire by its overwhelming power and their gallant Colonel [C. F.] Fisher, with many of his men, were no more. Jackson, with brigade, was struggling desperately, and at length successfully, to arrest the Federal columns; but immovable as Jackson and his

Going into Action under Fire (*Century*)

men stood, the surging tides of the enemy were beating upon him with such a mighty momentum that it seemed as if he must give way. Just then the battle had entirely lulled in our front on the right. Our Brigadier, General Barnard E. Bee, at this moment came galloping to the Fourth Alabama and said: "My brigade is scattered over the field and you are all of it I can now find. Men, can you make a charge of bayonets?" Those poor battered and bloody-nosed fellows, inspired by the lion-like bearing of that heroic officer, responded promptly: "Yes, general, we will go wherever you lead and do whatever you say." Bee then said, pointing toward where Jackson and his brigade were so desperately battling: "Yonder stands Jackson, like a stone wall! Let us go to his assistance." Saying that Bee dismounted and led the Fourth Alabama (what remained of them) to Jackson's position and joined them on the right of his brigade. Some other reinforcements coming up a vigorous charge was made, pressing the Federals back. In this charge Bee fell mortally wounded. Bartow fell nearly at the same time and within a stone's throw of the same spot. Before the Federals recovered from the impression made by this partial repulse they saw Kirby Smith's men advancing down the Warrenton Pike upon their right rear, as before stated, and his unexpected appearance in that quarter struck them with an overpowering panic and caused their precipitate retreat from the field. The battle ended so suddenly that the Confederates could not understand and could scarcely believe it. When afterwards the doings of that day were recounted among us the above expression, uttered by General Bee concerning Jackson, was repeated from mouth to mouth throughout the Confederate army, and that is how he came to be known everywhere as Stonewall Jackson.

Rallying the Troops of Bee, Bartow, and Evans (*Century*)

In conclusion, as I have set down with an endeavor at entire frankness the achievements, the mistake and the misfortunes that day of the regiment to which I myself belonged (the Fourth Alabama), I may be pardoned for adding a word about how we looked back upon our experience after it was over as a curious illustration of the absurd notions of inexperienced soldiers. Our ideal was that we were to whip whatever we came across—no matter about numbers; many or few, we must put them to flight. To turn the back before any enemy would be disgraceful. Having, therefore, shown our backs to the enemy twice that day, as I have narrated, once under orders and once without, we of the Fourth Alabama, upon the whole, felt humiliated and rather ashamed of ourselves on reviewing what had occurred. It was some days after the battle that to our surprise we began to hear from our comrades of the army and to read in the papers that our regiment was thought to have distinguished itself greatly. Then we began to hold up our heads again and to recall the fact that we had lost more than any other regiment in the army. Finally, we got hold of Northern newspapers and found where our gallant and generous adversary, [Brigadier General Samuel P.] Heintzelman, giving an account of what he termed our stubborn resistance in that opening conflict, which I have described, had praised us extravagantly, saying: "That Alabama regiment was composed of the most gallant fellows the world ever saw." This restored us once more to our equanimity, and we concluded that if we had not come up to our previous ideas of our invincibility, maybe we had not done so badly after all, and perhaps our sweethearts at home would not scorn us a poltroons. One other profound impression, however, was left on the minds, at least of some of us, by the events of that day, and especially when we came to gather up the mangled remains of so many of our late merry-hearted and beloved comrades—an impression which was not changed by all we saw in the succeeding four years, nor by the lapse of time since, and that was—talk as men may about great warlike deeds, heap plaudits on heroes and worship military glory how they will—war is from hell!

5

Folly and Fiasco in West Virginia
William B. Taliaferro, Major General, C.S.A.

ON JUNE 1, 1861, I received orders to turn over the command of the post of Gloucester Point to Major P. R. Page and report to Richmond for other duty.

On reaching that city I was referred to Brigadier General [T. T.] Fauntleroy, late colonel of the United States Second Dragoons, a gallant old soldier, who was charged under General [Robert E.] Lee with the organization and distribution of troops, for assignment to a command.

He informed me that it was the purpose of the government to organize an expedition to the northwestern part of the state, across the Alleghenies, in aid of the small force already there, in order to give countenance to the secessionists of that region, suppress the Union sentiment, which was more developed there than in any other part of the state, to repel any attack of the Federals from that quarter, and to effect such other ulterior objects as were practicable, and he assigned me to the command of one of the regiments destined for that service.

I was ordered to Camp Lee, just without the corporate limits of the city, commanded by Colonel William Gilham, who had been an officer of the United States Army, and was professor and commandant of cadets of the Virginia Military Institute. This camp was established at the Agricultural Fair Grounds, and the several houses and cattle sheds, supplemented by a few tents, all surrounded by a close wooden paling, made it a capital rendezvous for troops. I there found my regiment, just organized of the independent companies daily reporting. It was the Twenty-third Virginia, and it is but a just tribute to the brave men who composed it to say that in the course of the war no regiment ever experienced harder service, performed it with more cheerfulness, or achieved for itself a more honorable record.

I was almost an entire stranger to men and officers. The companies were from a different section of the state from that in which I lived, being drawn chiefly from the Piedmont. A lieutenant colonel, James L. Crenshaw, had been assigned to the regiment, who had selected as temporary adjutant Lieutenant William B. Pendleton. This officer was a graduate of the military institute, and I retained him in his position, for which he was well-qualified by his intelligence and activity. He proved a gallant soldier, and was subsequently, as my adjutant general, permanently disabled by severe wounds received at the Battle of Slaughter's Mountain.

Colonel Samuel Y. Fulkerson, who had resigned a circuit judgeship to offer his services to the state, had been assigned to the command of another regiment, just organized of companies from southwestern Virginia, and his regiment was among those designated to take part in the northwestern expedition. He had served in the Mexican War as a lieutenant in a Tennessee regiment. He was a man of sterling worth, of marked decision of character, and of high soldierly qualities. His loss to the Confederate service was sincerely deplored, when, at the head of his brigade, he fell mortally wounded in the seven days' fighting around Richmond. The regiment was the Thirty-seventh Virginia. The other field officers were Lieutenant Colonel [R. P.] Carson and Major [Samuel] Williams. Lieutenant Campbell, son of ex-Governor Campbell, was adjutant.

The affair at Philippi, Barbour County, in western Virginia, and the retreat of Colonel [George P.] Porterfield from that place, which occurred at that time (June 3), gave impulse to the expedition. This unfortunate occurrence caused a great sensation in Richmond and produced a severe shock to the sentiment of Southern invincibility. Porterfield was loudly censured and fell under the ban of public opinion, which could not comprehend a condition of circumstances which could make it necessary for Virginians to retire before an enemy. The severity of this public censure was undeserved, as was shown by the finding of a court of inquiry, composed of Lieutenant Colonel, afterwards General, [John] Pegram, Captain, afterwards General, [Julius A.] De Lagnel, and myself, which was accorded him.

Major Robert S. Garnett, a Virginian, who had distinguished himself in the Mexican War, in which he served upon the staff of General [Zachary] Taylor, had been appointed, after his resignation of his commission in the United States Army, adjutant general to General Lee, commander in chief of the Virginia army. He was highly estimated by that officer and by all who had known him in the old service. He was selected by President Davis for the command of the troops destined for the northwest, created brigadier general of the Confederate Army, and on June 8 assigned to the command. Colonel Fulkerson and myself were ordered to report to him, and received orders from him to hold our regiments in readiness to take the cars for Staunton, where the troops of his command would rendezvous and receive their field transportation.

Brigadier General Robert
S. Garnett (*Century*)

The regiment was marched into the city and then past the executive mansion. The men presented a fine appearance and were in high spirits. We carried the Virginia flag, on the blue field of which was stitched a legend from the bible. One of the ladies of Richmond, whose name is embalmed in the memory of thousands of Confederate soldiers for her tender and efficient ministrations to the wounded and the sick, and should be repeated and honored as long as that of Florence Nightingale, Miss Sally Thompson, had presented us the legend, and begged that we would attach it to our flag.

Ex Governor [Henry A] Wise, who had been made a brigadier general by President Davis, arrived at this time in Staunton, en route for the Kanawha Valley. His arrival was the remote cause of a ludicrous incident which came very near opening our campaign with an unpleasant tragedy. Lieutenant Colonel Crenshaw, who had gone with me to pay our respects to Governor Wise on the evening of his arrival, invited his staff surgeon, Dr. Peter Lyons, to accompany us to our camp, with a promise of sardines, cigars, and other comforts with which he was provided. We reached camp about 9:00 P.M. and were halted by the first sentinel we approached, who ordered one of us to advance and give the countersign.

Unfortunately, although having the envelope which contained the countersign, which had been handed us by the adjutant, we had not opened it and it was too dark to read it. We replied, "Commanding officer without the countersign; call the sergeant of the guard." "That won't do," said the sentinel. "Now mark time; them's my orders." We remonstrated against this indignity to which he contemplated subjecting his field officers in the presence of a stranger, as well as against the exercise involved in the execution of his command on a hot summer night, but he was inflexible. "Mark time," he replied, "or I will certainly shoot you," and suiting the action to the word, cocked his musket and leveled it at us. We tried threats, but he was not to be intimidated; he knew nothing, and would neither permit us to advance or retire, insisting upon "doing his duty," which was to shoot us if we did not mark time.

He was master of the situation, and as we looked down the musket barrel we marked time until the perspiration rolled from our foreheads. We were relieved by the sergeant of the guard, who relieved the sentinel, but not until we had whetted our appetites for the expected repast by abundant exercise.

I supposed the man was a lunatic and sent for his company officers to make inquiries. It turned out that he had been instructed at Camp Lee by cadets of the military institute, who required all who failed to have the countersign to mark time for their amusement until the guard officer appeared. He was very much alarmed when told of the deception which had been practiced upon him by his youthful instructors.

We left Staunton with some companies of the Thirty-seventh and a battery of light artillery from Danville, commanded by Captain [L. M.] Shumaker, who had been a lieutenant in a Virginia regiment of volunteers in Mexico. We had a large wagon train, ample for the promiscuous baggage with which raw troops are sure to encumber themselves, but we had a poor supply of tents, some of which were made of canvas, but most of striped bed-ticking. Our first day's march took us to Buffalo Gap, of the North Mountain, twelve miles west of Staunton, from which place General Garnett pushed on ahead of us to Huttonsville, in Randolph County, west of the Allegheny and Cheat mountains, to which locality Porterfield's command had fallen back.

I shall not undertake to describe the incidents of the march across these grand mountains and along the exquisite valleys which we pursued until we overtook him. The Bull Pasture, Cow Pasture, and other spurs of the Alleghenies, the main chain of the great Appalachian range, the double-bodied monster Cheat, were in turn surpassed, the men expressing with wild cheers and exclamations of delight their admiration of the magnificent panorama unfolded to their view, and we finally debouched into the narrow, but lovely valley of the Tygart.

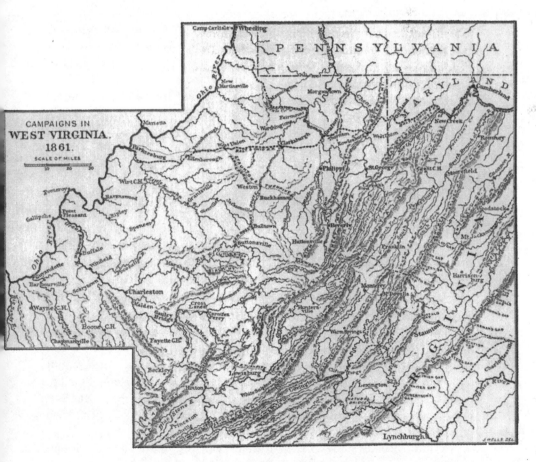

West Virginia, 1861 (*Century*)

Our little command was magnified by the estimation of the primitive people of these mountains into a large army, and they began to fear that their substance would be destroyed. I stopped one day at a roadside inn to dine. We were given a good dinner of mountain trout and mutton, with an abundance of pancakes and maple syrup. Asking for the bill the old landlady apologized for her exorbitant charge by saying that "since the troops came along the road she had been afraid she would be eaten out and had determined to double her rates," and deprecatingly remarked that she had formerly charged four-pence ha'-penny for a dinner, but that now it was nine pence. The Federal nomenclature of coins had not reached these regions. She meant six and a quarter and twelve and a half cents, which she expressed in the old Virginia equivalent. Alas! poor woman—her fears were too soon realized. Within a few weeks her house lay between the lines held for months by the contending forces, and becoming the scene of frequent skirmishes, it was riddled with bullets and made desolate forever.

Passing through Beverly, the county seat of Randolph County, we overtook General Garnett at Laurel Hill, in Barbour County, where he had established himself with the main portion of his command. It was a small army, consisting of a few regiments of infantry, two batteries of light artillery, and a squadron of cavalry. But the authorities at Richmond believed it sufficient for a nucleus, about which would concentrate a large force from the secession element in that region. Laurel Hill, a few miles west of Beverly, was known as a mountain pass, but was not worthy of that designation. The northwest Virginia troops consisted of Lieutenant Colonel [William L.] Jackson's command (subsequently the Thirty-first Virginia Regiment), Lieutenant Colonel [G. W.] Hansborough's Battalion, [Lieutenant Colonel J. M.] Heck's and Major [A. G.] Reger's commands, occupying Laurel Hill, Rich Mountain Pass, and a point known as Leadsville.

Colonel Jackson had been lieutenant governor of the state. He was a man of good talent, genial disposition, and of deserved influence in his quarter of the commonwealth. He belonged to the family of which Stonewall Jackson was a scion, and his soldierly qualities elevated him to the rank of brigadier general during the war. Major Francis M. Boykin, a gallant soldier, was attached to Jackson's regiment.

We were encamped near a little hamlet called Bealington, some two or three miles northwest of us, separated from us by a stream and some timber. Our position, on the crests of the hills, was protected by a ditch, with the bank thrown outward, conforming to the outline of the hills we occupied, and by a few simple epaulements for the artillery. We were joined by the Twenty-first Virginia Regiment and some other troops under the command of Lieutenant Colonel Pegram. This officer, with his regiment, after remaining several days at Laurel Hill, was detached and sent to reinforce Lieutenant Colonel Heck at Rich Mountain Pass, where he assumed command.

General Garnett's staff consisted of Major Williams, whom I have mentioned as engineer officer; Colonel [W. E.] Starke, of New Orleans, a volunteer aide;

Captain James L. Corley, adjutant general; Lieutenant Lee, ordnance officer; and Lieutenant [W. D.] Humphries.

Colonel Starke, a Virginian by birth, was a gentleman of high character, agreeable manners and decided military talent. He subsequently commanded a Virginia regiment and ultimately a Louisiana brigade; distinguished himself in the war as a brigadier and fell gloriously at Sharpsburg, commanding the famous Stonewall Division.

Captain Corley was a native of South Carolina, a graduate of West Point, who had resigned from the army on the secession of his native state. He resembled Colonel Starke in his affability and chivalry, and his soldierly qualities, which were conspicuously displayed in the subsequent events of General Garnett's unhappy campaign, entitled him to high rank among the general officers of the Confederacy. Governed by a high sense of duty, however, he yielded to the solicitations of the president and General Lee and accepted the position of chief quartermaster of the Army of Northern Virginia, the responsible duties of which office he performed with credit to himself and benefit to the army until the close of the war.

A regiment from Georgia, commanded by Colonel [J. N.] Ramsey, now joined General Garnett. The appearance of this regiment created a great sensation in our little command. It was a very full regiment, the companies of which were old volunteer organizations, called by their original distinctive names— such as Gate City Guards, etc. They were beautifully equipped, and the material composed of young and active men, handsomely uniformed, was superb. The regiment was preceded by a full drum corps, and the clangor of their kettle drums and screams of their fifes were unsubdued even by the shouts and loud cries of welcome with which they were saluted.

They were fancy volunteers of the cities and had left their homes apparently rather for a gay holiday than for real war. All the paraphernalia of a volunteer summer encampment accompanied them. Cards, wines, liquors and potted luxuries, as well as "red gold for the winning," abounded. Discipline was their only want, but in that they were sadly deficient. The field officers, as well as company officers, had been elected directly by the men. Promotions were to be made by a like suffrage, and discipline and consequent efficiency were impossible. These men, possessing all the elements of good soldiers, but careless, reckless, and uncontrolled, became a terror to the country in which they were encamped. Unrestrained by their officers and far from homes and the influence of social life and public opinion, they abandoned themselves to all manners of deviltry, more, however, from the life of excitement than from any really evil intent. These same men, subsequently, organized into a battalion, under Major Harvey, an accomplished officer, at that time one of the captains, became one of the most efficient and best disciplined organizations in the Confederate service.

The enemy now made his appearance in our vicinity. Our foraging parties had to be accompanied by detachments of troops and the excitement and so-

Awkward Volunteers (*St. Nicholas*)

licitude of immediate hostilities was for the first time realized. In the first week in July, the enemy appeared near Bealington. The pickets of the opposing forces extended on each side of the creek, near the village, and occasional interchanges of musketry firing occurred between them, but with little result. Our entrenched camp was well selected for defense and gave us a commanding view of the country around wherever it was cleared.

About July 6 the enemy made quite a decided demonstration at Bealington, designed to cover their movements against Rich Mountain. I was ordered with my regiment to the front, but waited most of the day without any effort being made by them to cross the creek and attack us. We were to be relieved by the Thirty-seventh about 6:00 P.M., and as the relieving regiment marched up and we were in the act of retiring we were saluted by a salvo which suddenly burst forth from a battery of field pieces, which were posted beyond the creek and concealed from our view by the woods which we occupied, and at the same time by a smart fusillade from small arms. It was the first time the regiment had been under fire, and their conduct on the occasion filled me with mortification.

To new troops nothing is so demoralizing as a shelling, especially if it occurs in a wood. The whistling of musket balls and the peculiar note of the minie projectiles as they rush madly past on their errand of death is a frightful sound to the recruit who for the first time hears it, and it requires a stout heart or a reckless spirit to disregard it. Still, there is something of excitement in the very sound which seems to brace and nerve men to withstand it. But the effect produced upon raw troops by artillery is much more marked, although the actual danger is not comparable to that from small arms. The rushing sound of shot and shells, their crashing through the branches of trees, the scattering of boughs, the crackling of the timber, the explosion of the shells above and the flying fragments that are hurled around, united with the fear that the fuse of some unexploded shell which has fallen near will renew its life and belch out its death-dealing fragments, all tend to create a consternation which the deadlier, but less noisy small-arm projectiles are never so apt to produce.

The first shells thrown at our position seemed to have acquired our exact range. Singularly, nobody was hurt, but the men scattered from the line and rushed in every direction to the protection of the fallen logs with which the wood was filled.

Then, as is often, if not always, the case under such circumstances, they began to fire their pieces without waiting for orders, as if to give vent to their panic by firing as rapidly and making as much noise as possible. The Thirty-seventh had just marched up and occupied the crest of the hill, at the base of which we had formed. They behaved well, but their firing, which was entirely sympathetic, was terribly wild. Luckily their shot passed over our heads. We were, of course, in imminent peril, for we were between the fire of friends and foes, and no effort which I could make could induce the men to stop firing or reform the line of battle.

This firing continued until it seemed to die out of its own accord. Gradually the men regained their composure when they saw that little damage had been done by the shells and but few hurt by the bullets, and at last they listened to the commands and expostulations of their officers, fell in, and reorganized the regiment.

The affair lasted from thirty to forty-five minutes. The enemy seemed to be satisfied that we had a large force, as they might well imagine from the firing, and having developed our strength, retired; not, however, until they had experienced some loss, as they afterwards admitted, from our desultory firing.

Shortly after the affair at Bealington I was summoned with the other officers commanding regiments to General Garnett's headquarters, where we were informed of the unfortunate result of the attack upon our position at Rich Mountain and the consequent necessity of our falling back to a more eligible position, nearer our base of supplies and within easy reach of reinforcements.

It was manifest that we must select some position upon the Staunton and Parkersburg Turnpike; but what point had been decided on by General Garnett I have never known, if, indeed, he had determined it in his own mind. My impression is that he would have selected the point on the crest of the Cheat Mountain, where the turnpike crosses, known as White's, which was afterwards for a long time occupied by the Federal forces, and which afforded, as far as my observation had extended, the best position for defense and for menace which that region presented. He complained bitterly of the failure of the government to send him reinforcements and of the want of sympathy with our cause which that country exhibited. He declared that he had been led to believe that a large force would join us from the counties west of us, but that hardly a man had been added to his army from that quarter, and he openly expressed his censure of the authorities for relying upon a public opinion which they had not sufficiently sounded before sending an insufficient force into the country.

We received orders to make immediate preparations for the retreat—to destroy our tents and all extra baggage; to throw into the wells we had dug the surplus commissary stores, and burn in small fires, so as to give no intimation to the enemy of our intention, everything else that could not be transported.

These orders were executed as speedily as possible. Our tents were struck and destroyed after nightfall, our wagons packed, and about 10:00 P.M., sad and dejected, we began our retreat. The road winding among the mountains sometimes brought the head of the column back parallel with the line of march of the rear, and apparently in an opposite direction. In the darkness and rain, which fell heavily, the front of our command mistook the rear for an advancing enemy marching on the same road to meet them, and opened fire upon their supposed assailants.

This unfortunate circumstance caused considerable confusion and delay, but luckily little or no damage. Every precaution was taken after that to prevent the firing of a gun; the men were assured that no enemy could be either in front or rear, and the weary march was resumed. The road was muddy and slippery with the rain, and the difficulty of closing up the wagon trains and artillery, of keeping the cavalry back from riding down the infantry, of preserving proper distances between the sub-divisions, of preventing the intermixture of men of different commands, and of preserving the continuity of the line of march in the darkness and vapor which surrounded us, can be more easily understood than described.

At daybreak we were halted within four miles of Beverly, and after an hour's rest were again put in motion; but to our surprise, instead of pursuing our road to that town, through which we would necessarily have to pass in the direct line of retreat, we were turned sharply to the left, over a country road leading into the county of Tucker.

We were soon apprised of the cause of this change of direction. We were informed that Colonel William C. Scott, who had been sent with his regiment, the Forty-fourth Virginia, to reinforce General Garnett, had reached Beverly the day before, had marched on the Rich Mountain road to the assistance of Colonel Pegram, but, failing to unite with his forces before the disaster which overtook us at that point, determined to retire without uniting his own with the immediate command of General Garnett, and had accordingly, after destroying the stores at Beverly, begun his retrograde movement, blocking the road with trees cut across it to retard the pursuing enemy, but at the same time as efficiently impeding our progress.

There is no doubt that we could have passed the point of intersection with the Rich Mountain road before the Federal troops from that point could have intercepted us, and we could in that event certainly had made good our retreat without the loss of our trains, even in the event that the road had not been blocked, and it was unwise, perhaps, not to have attempted it under any circumstances, taking the chances of removing the obstructions, for we could have blocked the road behind us if we succeeded in obtaining a reasonable start of our pursuers, and put them to as much trouble to our rear as we had in our front. However, General Garnett thought it unwise to hazard the experiment and we were marched north, in the direction of Maryland. It is due to Colonel Scott to state that he afterwards insisted that the road had not been blocked and that General Garnett had been misled and deceived by the regiments which reached him.

The bright sunlight uplifted the spirits of the command, and the upsetting, at a farm house near the road, of a number of beehives, whose disturbed and plundered inhabitants made fierce war upon all who passed, created an amusing diversion, which surprisingly restored gaiety to the jaded troops.

The road was a bad country highway, little traveled by wheels—rocky, ungraded and muddy, and progress over it was difficult and slow. There were rumors all day that the Federal cavalry were close behind us and that we would have a fight before night. Our cavalry had been instructed to impede the progress of the enemy by blocking the roads, and our men were often reminded of the fact, but the infantry had lost confidence in the cavalry, and believed that they would get out of the way without notifying them of the enemy's approach, so that little reliance was placed in the assurance that time would be afforded by the check given by the mounted men to enable the infantry to take position.

We bivouacked that night at Kalar's Ford of the Cheat River—a wet, uncomfortable halting place, and made the best of the situation by cooking rations.

About 8:00 A.M., Saturday, July 13, the command was again put in motion.

The Thirty-seventh regiment, Colonel Fulkerson, Colonel Jackson's regiment, and Lieutenant Colonel Hansborough's battalion, which had joined us on the march, with a section of Captain Shumaker's light battery, commanded by that officer, and a squadron of cavalry under Captain [George W.] Smith, formed the advance, General Garnett accompanying the division. Then came the wagon train and then the rear subdivision, consisting of the First Georgia and Twenty-third Virginia regiments, accompanied by a section of Shumaker's Battery, commanded by Lieutenant [Adolphus C.] Lanier and a cavalry detachment in charge of Captain [G.] Jackson, a graduate of West Point, and an ex-officer of the United States Army. The roads were even in worse condition than they had been the previous day, owing to heavy rains which fell during the night, and the train was, from the circumstance and the jaded condition of the teams, still more unmanageable.

The report soon reached us that the enemy was close upon our track, and the men became impatient and restless from the delays occasioned by the stalled wagons. They began to look back over their shoulders as they marched along and showed signs of demoralization. I determined to correct and check this feeling if possible, and coming upon an open field I turned the head of my regiment from the road and marched it into the unprotected opening. Then I formed it into a close column and made an address to the command. The men responded with cheers. I could see they were touched on the point of honor. The symptoms of demoralization vanished, and from that moment no troops ever behaved better in action or responded more cheerfully or gallantly to every call made upon them in the long progress of the war.

The rumors of the near approach of the enemy were confirmed by the reports of Captain Jackson, and dispositions were made to meet them and endeavor to save the train. Colonel Ramsay, with the Georgia regiment, was ordered to take position near a crossing of the river to oppose the enemy in front, and directed to place some of his companies in the woods on his right to ambush and enfilade the line of the enemy's march. The trains, with the Twenty-third Virginia, were ordered to proceed with all rapidity, and after that regiment, which had attached to it the section of artillery, had moved a reasonable distance beyond the Georgians, I was directed to select a good position, and pushing on the trains, to remain until the Georgians, in turn, had overtaken the retreating train and selected another defensive point. It was thus hoped that by retiring one regiment upon the other the enemy might be sufficiently checked to save the trains. These orders were given as from Colonel Garnett by his adjutant, Captain Corley.

We had only passed the Georgians a short distance when the enemy's skirmishers made their appearance and fire was opened on both sides. I had moved, with my regiment, about three-quarters of a mile, when a good position on a hill was selected, commanding a river bottom, through which the road ran. The Georgians, who opposed the enemy in front, after giving us time to make this disposition, retired without loss; but the companies which had been detached for the ambuscade, by some mistake or accident, became separated from their regiment, and, being entangled in the woods, were permanently cut off from rejoining their command. They had the good fortune, however, to escape capture, and making their way through the mountains, after several days of severe toil and extraordinary hardships, ultimately rejoined us in the valley of the south branch of the Potomac.

The enemy had not come up in force and we had little difficulty in retarding their movements until we reached Carrick's Ford, some miles distant from our camp of the preceding night. This ford was deep and broad; the banks on the opposite side of the river were high, and the hills rising above them, skirted with undergrowth, commanded the approach to the ford. Captain Corley had at once detected the importance and strength of the position, and we found him waiting to point it out to us.

The enemy was now closely pressing us, but the depth of the water in the river rendered it difficult to pass the train. Some of the teamsters in their hurry drove out of the roadway and plunged their horses into deep holes, or ran their wagons upon unseen boulders. The confusion was frightful. The soldiers waiting on the bank were shouting to the teamsters, drive on; the drivers, urging and whipping their horses; the wagon masters and quartermasters wrangling and freely distributing imprecations upon men and animals; the half-drowned horses struggling to pull, and the men, over their middles in water, struggling to push the loaded wagons.

Most of the wagons were rescued from the dangers of flood and field which menaced them, but several, and among them my own headquarters wagon, were abandoned, the teamsters cutting the traces and escaping with the horses. It was an uncomfortable sight to me to see my property abandoned to the mercy of the flood, if it escaped that of the enemy, and as I crossed the river I rode close to my wagon; but I could only gaze on my trunk, mess chest, and roll of bedding. They were too heavy to be removed, and with a half-muttered aspiration that my clothes might prove uncomfortable to the future owner, I pushed through the surging water, bereft of all my property except the clothes I wore.

My regiment was formed rapidly, in good order and without confusion, upon the hills overlooking the ford, the section of artillery properly parked, and we waited the arrival of our pursuers.

We had not long to wait. In a few minutes the skirmishers made their appearance. The distinctive gray uniform of the Confederate army had not at that time been adopted; most of our men were clad in blue clothes, and at first we mistook the approaching troops for the companies of Georgians who had been separated from their command. But we were soon undeceived by a few unfriendly shots. Lieutenant [James E. M.] Washington, a brave youth from South Carolina, one of the descendants of Colonel William Washington, of Revolutionary fame, a cadet at West Point at the breaking out of hostilities, who was attached as supernumerary officer to the light section, full of enthusiasm and unable to restrain his feelings, leaped upon his gun, and swinging his cap in the air gave a hearty cheer for President Davis.

The action and the cheer were electrical. The men with one voice took up the shout, and a Rebel Yell was uttered which, although, perhaps, the first, would have done credit to any veteran regiment at the close of the war. The battle opened at that early period, the affair rose to the dignity of an action, and it was called the Battle of Carrick's Ford. If the loss of life is to be considered and not the number of troops engaged, as a means of ensuring its title to that distinction, it is as worthy of the name as the affairs at Palo Alto and Contreras, which are described in our histories as two of the great battles in the War with Mexico. The men behaved admirably; as a matter of course, they fired wildly, as all new men will. The attack was heavy, but the men displayed a composure which surprised me. One man informed me his musket was out of order, and asked me what to do. I directed him to take a seat upon a log, unscrew the musket and endeavor to correct the trouble. He coolly did so and soon resumed his place in the line. Our loss was heavy. Some of my best men were killed and wounded; but these casualties produced no demoralizing effect upon the men. There were no stragglers to the rear, and there seemed to be a determination on the part of every man to gain a name for the regiment which would be respected.

The fire of the enemy's artillery was heavy, but they overestimated the height of our position, and their pieces were too much elevated. They brought down the boughs of the trees among us, but I do not think a man was hurt by shot or shell. The lesson taught at Bealington of the inefficiency of artillery, compared with musketry, was repeated, greatly to the benefit of my command. Our own guns were served well, under the direction of Lieutenants Lanier, Brown, and Washington, and, I think, with good effect. The enemy were unable to cross the river in the face of this fire and twice retired, but again renewed the attack with violence. The river, however, still remained between us and afforded us the protection of its rapid current, which would have greatly impeded and embarrassed any assailants, however enterprising and determined they may have been.

I was ordered to retire the artillery, through a message sent me from General Garnett, which was done; but the rifled six-pounder, which had been disabled, was spiked and abandoned. Our ammunition was by this time nearly exhausted; the trains had been afforded the opportunity of a long start; our own situation was becoming precarious, as we were a great distance from the rest of the command, and I thought it not improbable that some crossing of the river below or above us would bring the enemy upon our rear, for they were doubtless provided with guides to direct their movements.

Under these circumstances I determined to withdraw the regiment. We had lost about thirty men, half of them killed, and I was forced to leave the dead and severely wounded in the hands of the enemy. It is an agreeable duty to relate that they were cared for in a generous and humane manner and the survivors paroled, and in a short time permitted to return to their homes. This generous policy on the part of General McClellan, had it been adopted by the government afterwards, would not only have deprived the war of many of its horrors, but might have been the means of exerting a decided influence upon its earlier termination.

The men were marched quietly off without disorder, manifesting no impatience to retire, but rather a reluctance to resume their weary march. After marching about half a mile I was met by Colonel Starke, who informed me that General Garnett was a short distance in front, across the next ford, and directed me to bring my regiment to that point, when I would receive his instructions.

We crossed the ford and found the general on the river bank. There were quantities of drift wood washed up by former floods along the line of the river. These the general pointed out, remarking that they would form capital shelter for skirmishers. He directed me to march the regiment up the hill and halt it some two hundreds off and then detail ten riflemen to be sent back to him and to be posted by him behind the driftwood. I detailed a company, commanded by Captain [R. A.] Tompkins, and returned with it, asking him to use the whole company. This he refused to do, but selected ten men under Lieutenant [Emmett E.] De Priest and sent the company back.

Before my leaving General Garnett, the firing had begun from the opposite bank and I urged him to retire. I pointed out to him a man in dark clothes, evidently a citizen, who was firing at me, as I believed, with a country rifle, and I urged him to shelter himself from this fire. He disregarded my admonitions, and directing me to return to my regiment, busied himself in posting the riflemen. Very soon afterward Colonel Starke notified me that General Garnett wished me to move as rapidly as I could and overtake the main body. I was overtaken a few minutes afterwards by Lieutenant De Priest with his party, who informed me of the general's death. He fell just as he gave the skirmishers orders to retire, and one of them was killed by his side.

My regimental surgeon, Dr. William A. Carrington, who had lingered in the discharge of his duty in aiding the wounded at Carrick's Ford, had been surrounded and captured before he could make his escape. His high character and fine intelligence, added to the easy manners which he had acquired from a long service on the sea, made him a very pleasant companion in the field. His professional knowledge and experience were highly valuable to us; but it was perhaps fortunate that he was captured, as he was permitted to attend the wounded and sick who were made prisoners. The service sustained a serious loss in his death, which occurred in the early part of the war. Remaining himself with the sick and wounded who could not be moved, he wrote me by his paroled men an account of his capture and of the death of General Garnett. General Garnett fell as a soldier would like to die, "decorated with a death wound in the breast." He was shot through the right breast, the ball passing out at the back, and life was extinct when he was found. A generous sympathy was shown by General McClellan, and every respect paid to his remains. Major [John] Love, his former room-mate at the Military Academy, was gratefully mentioned by Dr. Carrington for his kind offices to the remains of his former friend.

I endeavored at first to conceal the death of their commander from the men, fearing the dispiriting influence it would naturally produce, but it was impossible to do so. The sad news was whispered from ear to ear, and spread over the whole command. We were miles behind our main body, and the reaction, after the excitement of the late conflict, was telling sadly upon the troops. The train had had a good opportunity of making headway, but the roads were bad and the teamsters demoralized, and abandoned wagons, mess chests, baggage, blankets, and accoutrements were strewn along the way.

It was all important to overtake our friends, but we knew nothing of their movements. The head of the army had perished, and we had no information of the whereabouts of the next officer in rank, Colonel Ramsay, or of his knowledge of this succession to the command. Colonel Starke and Captain Corley had ridden ahead to communicate the intelligence of the loss of their chief, but we had heard nothing of the assistance, which, under the circumstances, should have been sent us, for we required rest and the intervention of fresher troops between us and the enemy. The country became, unfortunately, open, and an enterprising body of cavalry could have harnessed us, cut off our stragglers, and perhaps have destroyed us. I looked painfully back for their coming, but fortune befriended us and they did not appear.

We had marched some miles from Carrick's Ford, and the country was again, to my great relief, offering advantageous positions for defense, when we saw the head of a column advancing towards us. It proved to be Colonel Jackson's regiment, which had been sent by Captain Corley to reinforce us. They had left the main body but a short distance, but the mountain ridge had intercepted our view of their advance. We were received by them with hearty cheers as the heroes of a bloody fight. Captain Corley reported to me that Colonel Ramsay was sick and that the command of the troops devolved upon me.

It is by no means a desirable honor to be suddenly invested with the responsibility of a retreating army, no matter how small it may be; and exhausted as I was by the fatigues of the march and the recent combat I was by no means ambitious of succeeding to the command. However, I accepted the situation and endeavored to make the best of it. The little army was in bad condition; it was suffering from an exhausting march, had lost its commander, was pursuing a road which led it into a state north of the Confederacy, and was further menaced by an enemy in front, as it was reported, who had to be beaten before it could expect to regain a friendly country, while at the same time it was pursued by a victorious army in its rear. These were disagreeable conditions and tended to depress and dispirit officers and men. The report was that a considerable force lay in our front at the Red House in Maryland, which point they were obliged to pass in order to enter the South Branch Valley of the Potomac, up which, with the intervening barrier of mountains on our right flank, lay our hope of subsistence and escape.

The little army, jaded and worn down, stretched out necessarily much more than it would have done had it been fresh, and to the country people whom we passed it seemed a large body of men. We marched all night along the road leading up Horseshoe Run, and in the morning reached Red House. The night march was trying in the extreme; the jaded teams could with difficulty be urged along, and the embarrassment of halting wagons was insufferable. We had taken the best care of our ammunition wagons, but about midnight one of them became irretrievably stalled on a narrow mountain road and blocked the passage of the whole command in the rear. So narrow was the interval between the wheels and the mountain precipice that men could hardly pass, and after ineffectual efforts to extricate it it was hurled down the gorge and the march resumed. At Red House we were enabled to procure a few bullocks, which were slaughtered and eaten with ravenous appetites, albeit cooking utensils played no part in the preparation of our feast. Our halt there was protracted to some hours before it was resumed.

We reached Greenland in Hardy County, Virginia, that evening. The march through these mountains of Hardy was greatly lightened and relieved by the superb floral displays which they presented; the gorgeous treasures of the rhododendron that flushed the mountain sides and lay massed in heaps of purple beauty in the deep gorges beneath our feet seemed to charm the men and inspired them with a new energy.

No enemy now pursued us, but of that we were ignorant, as our cavalry had deserted us and we had only to rely upon the vigilance of our rear guard of infantry; but our faces were turned south and we were entering a sympathetic country. Our difficulty was not so much to obtain supplies as to cook them, and the commissaries and quartermasters were sent forward to have provisions cooked and brought to the roadside to await our coming. The inhabitants cheerfully complied with our demands, and wagon loads of bread and cooked meats were kindly given or sold by the generous people. Colonel Ramsay recovered from his indisposition and resumed command.

We entered the county of Pendleton, and as we advanced south the sympathy for the Southern cause was more and more developed. The troops, notwithstanding their relief from the anxiety of impending attack, were in a deplorable condition; they were ragged, almost shoeless, footsore and hungry, and it was next to impossible to maintain the integrity of the several organizations. The lameness of our horses for the want of shoes to replace those cast in the night march was another serious inconvenience. Gold pieces were offered for horseshoes, but this tempting reward rarely produced them at Franklin, the county seat of Pendleton County. We were received with cordial hospitality, and many of us again enjoyed the unaccustomed luxury of knife, fork, and napkin. The Georgians, who had been cut off and separated from the command several days before, rejoined us at Franklin.

On the evening of the seventh day of our unhappy retreat our eyes were gladdened by the sight of the tents of our friends near the village of Monterey,

the county seat of Highland County. This immediate prospect of long anticipated security and repose, of certain supplies of food, of new clothes and clean-
liness, with the natural satisfaction of having surmounted and overcome all the
dangers which had menaced them, flashed upon the minds of the wearied troops
by this sudden vision of white canvas, found expression in prolonged cheers.

It may perhaps be useless to speculate on the policy which originated or the
military management which directed the operations of this unfortunate northwestern campaign. The event demonstrated that the government was misled by
its erroneous estimate of the secession sentiment of that country. There were
certainly numbers of true and loyal men who sympathized with their native state
in her determination to resist Federal encroachment upon her rights or the
coercion or subjugation of sovereign Commonwealths, and these men suffered
cruel insult and injury for their opinions' sake, and many vindicated as among
the most gallant soldiers that their state could boast upon the bloodiest battlefields their devotion to her cause; but the great mass and bulk of the people
was opposed to secession, and the force of public opinion was strong against a
resort to arms; the views of George W. Summers, a distinguished citizen of the
Kanawha Valley, that of neutrality and opposition to the occupation of the country by the arms of either contestants, prevailed, and the people were suspicious
of the movements of the Confederate forces in their territory as apt to invite
invasion and convert their territory into the permanent theater of hostilities. It
was natural that the government, from political considerations, should desire
to bring over to the support of the Southern cause this region, and the experiment of sending a force there by way of a reconnaissance to test and develop,
and, if possible, to create a sympathetic public opinion may have been wise, but
the test was too soon applied and the discovery of a hostile feeling was soon
made, and then the presence of our troops became rather the occupation of a
hostile country than the protection of our own soil.

There was nothing in the resources of the country to compensate for the
military disadvantages of holding it. The Baltimore and Ohio Railroad was too
far west to be used by us as a base, and it was palpably obvious that a force in
possession of that great artery possessed advantages over an adversary, one west
of the Cheat and perhaps Allegheny mountains, which would place the latter
constantly in jeopardy, if not at the mercy of the former. The bridges and tun-
nels of the railroad should have been destroyed west of Harper's Ferry the day
after the Virginians occupied that point when there was ample force to accomplish it, but when General Garnett was sent to West Virginia it was too late to
undertake it.

What the instructions to General Garnett were, or how far his dispositions
were directed and his movements controlled by the authorities at Richmond, I
have no means of knowing. He was either the victim to a political mistake of
the government or, if absolute military discretion was permitted him, which is
doubtful, he committed a grave error. His troops were pushed too far west, and

it was a violation of the most simple principles of strategy to subdivide his command and subject it to the danger of being beaten in detail. The enemy possessed equal, if not better means of information, of his movements than he did of theirs, and concentration was essential to his safety. The occupation of Rich Mountain, Laurel Hill, and Leadsville, at the same time with a command divided, was playing into the hands of his adversary, and General McClellan seized the opportunity which the mistake afforded him. Our troops should have been drawn back to the line of the Staunton and Parkersburg turnpike and concentrated.

It would be unjust and ungenerous to criticize the conduct of this gallant officer who was the first of his rank who fell a sacrifice to our cause, and there is much to be said in extenuation of his course and that of the government. It was important to preserve the autonomy and integrity of the state. The Unionists were rebels to the state authority, and the pretension of the transfer of the state government to the western counties, although recognized afterwards by the Congress and the Executive of the United States, was an absurd farce. To correct this sentiment and its influence, the occupation of the section was important, and it was justifiable to run some risk, but unfortunately General Garnett permitted, or was forced to permit the political considerations to take precedence over military considerations.

6

Missouri's Unionists at War
The Honorable Montgomery Blair

THE MAP OF the country shows the strategic importance of Missouri to the Union. It is the great central state of the Union on the west bank of the Mississippi and extends from north latitude thirty-six degrees to forty degrees thirty minutes, and contains nearly 70,000 square miles of territory. With this vast territory wrenched from the Union, secession would not only have been an accomplished fact, but it would have carried with it to the Southern Confederacy all the territory lying south and west of it, and have founded that "Empire across the continent to the Pacific and down through Mexico and around the great gulf and over the isle of the sea," contemplated by the secessionists as proclaimed by Mr. [Robert B.] Rhett, of South Carolina, in November 1860. Without this territory the scheme of secession was impracticable, and the vision of the slave empire which lured it on would seem to be a delusion. This circumstance and the bearing of slavery on the political relations of the state made the question of the abolition of slavery as the condition of the admission of the state into the Union—or the Missouri Question, as it has since been called—a question of Union or disunion in 1860. It was, moreover, at this key point of the great conflict that the first blow was struck for the Union.

These conditions entitle the transactions by which this great commonwealth was saved to the Union to more of the public attention than they have hitherto attracted; for it is the effect on the great result and the ability, patriotism, and courage displayed in an achievement, rather than the numbers engaged or the blood spilled, which measures the importance in history, and the events, civil and military, which fixed the relations of Missouri to the Union. A brief resume may, therefore, be interesting to readers.

The chiefs of the secession conspiracy, seeing that Missouri was the pivotal state, turned their attention to that state and organized their forces there at a very early stage of the plot. As early as 1847 Claiborne F. Jackson, who, as governor in 1861, attempted to carry the state out of the Union, was furnished by them with the resolutions, since known as The Jackson Resolutions, which he introduced into the legislature, asserting the principle announced ten years later, by

Governor Claiborne F. Jackson (*Century*)

the Supreme Court of the United States in the Dred Scott decision, to prepare the way for secession.

The significance of this movement was fully comprehended by the friends of the Union in Missouri, and resolutions drawn by me, denouncing it, were adopted by them at St. Louis on July 8, 1848, and on his return from Washington, Senator [Thomas Hart] Benton thoroughly exposed its traitorous object in a speech delivered from the capitol steps in Jefferson City. By combining with the Whigs and using the party prestige, of which the disunionists had possessed themselves, they ejected Colonel Benton from the Senate, and although elected from the First District to the House of Representatives in 1852, by changing the district and combining with the Know Nothings in 1854, they excluded him finally from public life. This result, however, was partly due to his declining years, which, with his previous defeats, had impaired his great spirit, so that he did not confront the adversaries of the Union as he was wont to do, and contrary to the whole tenor of his life, he had advised compromise with them and submission to the repeal of the Missouri Compromise. The leadership of the Unionists in Missouri, thus abdicated by Benton, was taken by Frank P. Blair, who declared against the compromise proposed by his old leader. He regarded the repeal to be what the sequel shows it to have been, a declaration of war against the Union, and the Unionists of St. Louis sustained him in that view of it, and elected him to the legislature. He alone of the eighteen candidates who ran upon this same ticket with Colonel Benton in 1854 was elected. He was also elected to Congress by them in 1856, by a decisive majority, over the gentleman who had defeated Colonel Benton in 1854, and he was reelected in 1858 and 1860.

Early in December 1860, soon after the call of the secession convention in South Carolina, a private meeting of the leading Union men in St. Louis was held. Messrs. Oliver D. and Giles F. Filley, James O. Broadhead, Franklin A. Dick, Barton Able, Charles M. Elleard, William McKee, B. Gratz Brown, F. H. Mantir, Samuel T. Glover, Benjamin Farrar, Samuel Simmons, Peter L. Foy, and Frank P. Blair were present.

Mr. Blair briefly summed up the situation. The state authorities in Missouri had been purposely constituted to follow South Carolina in secession. Missouri was necessary to the success of the movement, and the arsenal at St. Louis, containing 60,000 stand of arms, 150,000 ball cartridge, 90,000 pounds of powder, and a number of field pieces and siege guns, and with shops and machinery of immense value, would secure the state to the Southern Confederacy. Moreover, these arms and military stores comprised nearly all that the United States government held in the West. Hence it was a prize likely to be decisive, not only of the attitude of Missouri but of Kentucky, and to exert great influence on southern Illinois and Indiana. It would, therefore, certainly be seized by the Missouri authorities if not prevented by the Union men of St. Louis, nor would Major [William H.] Bell, the commanding officer at the arsenal, put any obstacle in the way of the seizure—for he was in full sympathy with the South.

Major General Frank P.
Blair Jr. (*Century*)

Mr. Blair, therefore, advised that the Union men should immediately take arms and form a military organization. This was not only indispensable to protect the public interests which the authorities in Washington were betraying, but the personal safety of the Union men, and especially of their German fellow citizens, depended on it. Mr. Blair's views and proposition were warmly supported and enlarged upon by Mr. Glover, and were generally assented to by those present. A form of enrollment was drawn up by Mr. Mantir, and within a few days what was afterward known as the parent company, seventy-three in number, of which Frank P. Blair was captain, was organized and armed with muskets chiefly paid for by the Filleys; and within a few weeks eleven other companies were organized and armed. All the arms, except 200 stand obtained from the governor of Illinois, were paid for by a few Union men of St. Louis.

This force was called the Union Legion. Only about fifty of the men in it, all of whom belonged to the parent company, were native Americans; the others were all citizens of German birth, who were especially obnoxious to the secessionists. The command of the legion was given to a council, of which Mr. Blair was president. Union clubs in the various wards of the city, and a general committee of safety of which Oliver D. Filley was president, was formed to cooperate with the military organizations. The drilling of these companies, which immediately began in all parts of the city, and the activity of the subsidiary civilian organizations, and the determined character of the men concerned in them signified to the governor in the most unmistakable manner that any attempt by him to seize the arsenal would be repelled by force.

The effect was to arrest his actions for the time. This was contrary to the advice of Colonel Thomas Grimsley, a man of great courage and strong passions who, in a letter dated January 1861 (found in Jefferson City on the capture of that place), urged the governor to order him to seize the arsenal, telling him he had a thousand men under arms ready to obey the order. Fortunately, the governor had committed the work to [Major General Daniel M.] Frost, then in command of the militia at St. Louis, a man of less daring and military judgement—as the event proved—than Grimsley; although he was a graduate of West Point and had seen military service. Indignant at Grimsley's interference, Frost, in a letter to the governor of January 24 (afterward captured), pronounced Grimsley "an unconscionable jackass, who only desires to make himself notorious. The arsenal," he says, "will be everything for our state, and I intend to look after it very quickly." But he thought he had done everything to secure it that was necessary for the present by the arrangement he reports as having been made by him with Bell, the United States officer in command there. By that arrangement Bell had agreed to hold the arsenal subject to Governor Jackson's order, regarding it as belonging to the state, and to resist and to call on Frost to help him resist any attempt on the part of the Union men to take it, or on the part of the government to remove the arms. Jackson's apologetic letter to the St. Louis secessionists shows plainly that he did not concur in Frost's reasoning, but that he did not dare to take the responsibility of overruling him and of bringing on a collision of arms.

In that letter he excuses himself by saying "that Missouri ought to have gone out of the Union last winter when she could have seized the public arms and public property and defended herself." This means that he would have seized the arsenal last winter, when Colonel Grimsley, on behalf of the St. Louis secessionists, had so strongly urged him to do so, if the state had then gone out of the Union, as he (Jackson) thought at the time it ought to do. But this was not the true reason for his failure, for he had not hesitated to seize the United States arsenal at Liberty, although the state had not gone out of the Union. Hence it is plain that the excuse here offered for not seizing the St. Louis arsenal—that the state had not gone out of the Union—was not the true reason, and that the only reason why he did not clutch the greater as he had the lesser prize, was that the Union men of St. Louis were in arms to defend it. But while prepared for defense, the Union men studiously avoided giving the secessionists any pretext for disturbing the peace, lest they might avail themselves of it to attempt to take possession of the arsenal.

It is scarcely possible at this day fully to appreciate the courage, patriotism,

and good judgment displayed by the men who thus confronted the armed conspiracy in Missouri and prevented the seizure of the St. Louis arsenal, or to estimate the virtue of that service to the Union. The letters of Jackson, Frost, and
Grimsley, above cited, demonstrated singular accuracy of their judgment as to
the design of the enemy, and how timely and effective was the action taken by
them to frustrate it.

I will note a few circumstances to illustrate the firmness displayed. The small
band who performed this service represented but 17,000 of the 163,000 votes cast
at the preceding election in the state, and but 11,000 of the 27,000 votes cast in
the city of St. Louis, and nineteen-twentieths of the men composing it were citizens of foreign birth. This circumstance, which would of itself have unnerved
men of less hardy fiber, with them served only to enforce the necessity of their
action. It is true that a majority of their opponents were not disunionists in
principle, and soon afterward rallied for the Union, but at this critical juncture
their insane hatred of "Black Republicanism" allied them to secession, and made
them reject with great unanimity the proposition made by the Republicans on
January 11, at Washington Hall, to abandon old part organizations and unite in
Union clubs to resist secession. It would be incredible that the common sense
of multitudes of true men could be so benumbed as not only to veil from them
the conspiracy against the Union, which was then flagrant, but make them in
effect co-workers in it, did not these benumbed intellects still insist that Lincoln made the war.

The disunionists who were then rushing through the legislature the convention bill to take the state out of the Union were greatly encouraged by the rejection of the Republican overtures to form a Union party on January 11. It was
upon the abhorrence of Black Republicanism which had caused that rejection,
and with which the leaders of the various opposing parties had united in endeavoring to fill the hearts of the people, that the secessionists counted to force
the state out of the Union.

But notwithstanding the rejection of their overtures the Republican leaders persisted in making them and in endeavoring to conciliate and consolidate
the Union men, and the removal of Bell from command at the arsenal and the
arrival there of [Captain Nathaniel] Lyon and his company of regulars greatly
aided in the work of conciliation. By these means and by conceding to [John]
Bell and [Edward] Everett, and [Stephen A.] Douglas, leaders whose friends cast
less than one-fourth of the votes—three-fourths of the tickets in St. Louis—they
finally succeeded in creating the Unconditional Union Party in St. Louis, which
at once extended itself throughout the state.

Messrs. Filley, Broadhead, Glover, [J. J.] Witzig, and Blair, of the committee
of safety, were the chief authors of the new party. And it was formed not only
against the wishes of most of the leaders of those claiming to be especial friends
of the Union, but in spite of the general feeling of the Republicans who wished
a straight Republican ticket for St. Louis. To one of these who said: "I don't

Ferrying Proslavery Voters from Missouri to Kansas (*Century*)

believe in breaking up the Republican Party to please these tender-footed Unionists," Mr. Blair replied: "Let us have a country first, and then we will talk about parties." By this means Black Republicanism, the specter with which the secessionists confidently expected to drive the state out of the Union, suddenly disappeared, and the Unconditional Union Party as suddenly rose to confront and confound them.

And there never was a more effective or far-reaching stroke of genius in political history than this movement, and the declaration made by Mr. Blair at its inauguration, that "the city of St. Louis would remain in the Union whether the state went out or not" was the deathknell of secession in the state.

The secessionists soon saw the effect of this master stroke of policy, and that it would inevitably defeat them before the people unless they could counteract it by some measure which would assure them of St. Louis. With this object they attempted to hurry through the legislature a bill to enable the governor to control the election in St. Louis by the military. And it ought to be remembered now that it was in the special message of the rebel governor of Missouri, sent to the legislature in hot haste to enable him to force the state out of the Union, that it was first attempted in this country to give an executive control of an election by the use of the military under color of keeping the peace at the polls. The rebel

Senate of Missouri passed the bill, but it could not be reached in the House until the election was over.

The letter of Jackson, already stated, shows that secession was a foregone conclusion of the conspirators, without regard to the will of the people. "The military bill," as it was called, was introduced as soon as the legislature met in January, to carry out their purpose. Even [Brigadier General William S.] Harney at one time could see that this was the object of this bill, for in his proclamation he characterized it as "indirect secession."

But there was no indirection about it. It not only undertook to throw off the allegiance of the people of Missouri to the Federal government, but to make that declaration effective, appropriated money and put the lives and liberties of the people at the mercy of the governor. Many of the secessionists did not see the necessity of such usurpation and were unwilling to submit to it to accomplish their purposes, and therefore opposed and prevented the passage of the act at the winter secession. Jackson himself recognized this bill as direct secession, for in the letter of April 28 [on secession], wherein he says: "She (the state) ought to have gone out last winter," and he would then have "seized the public arms and public property." It is to this bill he refers as the act by which it was then proposed to secede.

It is also clear that it was not until it was found that the bill could not be passed during the winter that the convention bill referring the question of secession to the people was adopted. It was confidently believed that the people would vote it as the convention bill, but it was not intended to leave the matter to their uncontrolled will. To this end Jackson, as he says in his letter, took every responsibility and did everything he could do by virtue of his power as governor to force it so.

Among other things, the militia at St. Louis was reorganized and the rank and file made up from Democratic Minutemen organizations, and all who upheld the authority of the Federal government were excluded from command by an order of February 4, declaring this to be "insubordination in advance." Frost was charged with the duty of taking the St. Louis arsenal, and promised to do so quickly, and gave secret orders to his command to turn out for that purpose on a signal to be given by the cathedral bells.

Mr. Blair was not informed of this plot [or] of the preparation to execute it, by the letters we have now before us, but he knew the men he had to deal with and their long cherished schemes. He knew, also, of their military preparation, and had even got hold of a copy of Frost's order fixing the signal for action. All this, with the disloyalty of Bell, who commanded the arsenal, he communicated through me to General [Winfield] Scott, urged the removal of Bell, the reinforcement of the arsenal, and especially that a reliable man should be put in command there.

General Scott was sensible to the peril, but at a loss where to get the force and the commander needed. With rare exceptions, the officers of the army were hostile to the Republican Party and, whilst not justifying secession, thought the Republicans culpable for having provoked it, and were therefore in the beginning reluctant to aid or cooperate with them. We shall presently see the disaster, consequent upon this state of feeling, in the conduct of General Harney and others, whose loyalty to the Union was not doubted.

Mr. Blair wanted then at St. Louis an officer who was in sympathy with the Republicans, upon whose cooperation he would have to rely. After much inquiry, I learned from the Hon. Marcus L. Parrott of Kansas that Captain [Nathaniel] Lyon, of the Second Infantry, [was] then in command of his company at Fort Scott in that state, and I immediately applied to General Scott to order him and his company to St. Louis. Lyon was notified of the application and urged to get ready to move promptly on receipt of orders. He did so and reached St. Louis on February 6. Bell was also removed. Captain [Thomas W.] Sweeney had been ordered from Newport, Kentucky, with a small squad of recruits, and arrived at the arsenal a few days in advance of Lyon.

These movements produced great commotion in the rebel quarters, and on several occasions the indications were that immediate action was intended. Immediately after Sweeney's arrival, and again shortly after Lyon's arrival, the Union Legion turned out and remained on duty at the arsenal through the night in the expectation of attack, and again on April 20, after the capture of Sumter and the riot in Baltimore and the seizure of the Liberty Arsenal, which was suggested by Frost in his letter to the governor of the fifteenth, the Union Legion was assembled and remained at their various armories throughout the day and night.

In response to the president's proclamation for 75,000 men, Mr. Blair telegraphed the secretary of war on April 17, tendering the quota for Missouri of four regiments from St. Louis, Jackson having indignantly refused to comply with the requirements from the state. Mr. Blair's offer was accepted and Lieutenant [John M.] Schofield was ordered to muster the four regiments into the service. But General Harney, commanding the military district, refused to allow them to be armed or to enter the arsenal grounds.

On April 19, Colonel Blair sent a special messenger to Washington with a letter to me giving information of Harney's action and asking for his removal from the command of the department. Without waiting for action on this application, Lyon decided, on the twenty-first, to disobey Harney's order and directed Mr. Blair to introduce the men and officers into the arsenal grounds that night.

Within a few days Harney was removed, and left for Washington on April 24, and Lyon was invested with full command. The four regiments of which Blair, [Henry] Boernstein, [Franz] Sigel, and [Nicholas] Schuettner were respectfully chosen colonels, were immediately mustered into service. The command of this brigade was tendered by the officers to Colonel Blair, and Lyon urged him to accept it, preferring, he said, to serve under him, but Colonel Blair declined and the command was finally transferred upon Lyon.

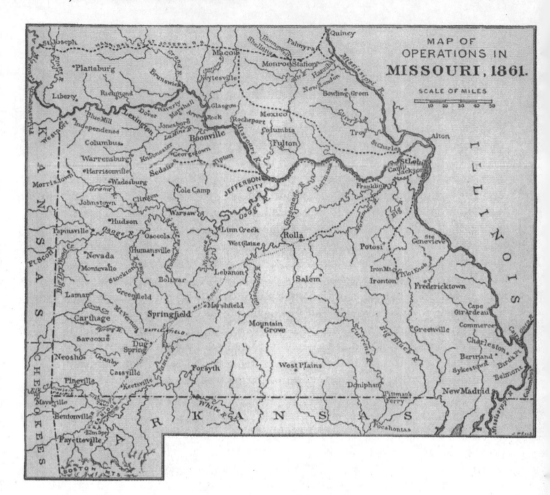

Missouri, 1861 (*Century*)

Before offering it to Lyon, however, Colonel Blair tendered it to William T. Sherman, then a resident of St. Louis. Colonel Blair desired to secure his services to the country, not only because of his recognized military ability, but the sake of his relations to society in the city which, in the then condition of sentiment were of much greater importance than his military skill. But Sherman refused the command. This Colonel Blair attributed to the operations upon him of those social influences which he had in offering him the command to reach and control for the government.

Nothing could better illustrate the difficulties which Mr. Blair and his associates had met and had yet to meet than this refusal by Sherman to accept the responsibility of commanding them, for this was a light responsibility compared with that which they had assumed. They had armed and organized, with ropes around their necks, to defend the Union and protect the property of the United States against both state and national authority without official sanction of any kind for their action. But even when that perilous stage had passed, and they had been mustered into the service of the United States, they were still under such odium in the higher social and army circles as not to be able to obtain Sherman's services as their commander.

It need not be said that it was either for want of courage or want of heart for the Union that Harney opposed so strenuously the organization of this force, or that Sherman declined taking the command of it. Their total incapacity to comprehend the true political situation created an intense prejudice in their minds against this clan of politicians to which Colonel Blair and his associates in arms belonged. For this reason they believed the charge against Colonel Blair and his associates that they, for their personal and partisan prejudices alone, were jeopardizing the peace of the state. And the fact that Sherman, in his autobiography, speaks of General Blair as a political general shows that prejudice was so bitter that it survived the war and defied all fact and reason.

The false clamor against Colonel Blair for organizing this force had been exposed and the soundness of his military judgment had been fully vindicated by the letters of Sherman and Frost; Sherman himself had recognized the timeliness of his movement in his eulogy on General Lyon; Colonel Blair's disinterestedness had been shown by offering the command first to General Sherman and then to Lyon, instead of taking it himself, and he had served throughout the war, and for a great part of the time under Sherman himself, without at any time exerting political influence to secure command, but on the contrary, had received it from Secretary [of War Edwin M.] Stanton, who certainly had no political partiality for him. And yet it is plain not only from Sherman's speaking of him as a political general, but from his failure either in his eulogy on Lyon or to say of the various reports of military operations in which General Blair took part, to do him justice, that the prejudice aimed at the object survived to the end.

In his letter of April 15, above referred to, suggesting the seizure of the Liberty arsenal, Frost urges the governor to send to Louisiana for the mortars and siege guns which had now become necessary to take the St. Louis arsenal, because numerous batteries and earthworks had recently been erected for its defense; and it is likely, he adds, that the defenses would be made still stronger, for the president cannot but be aware of the strategic importance of St. Louis, militarily and politically, by reason of its control over the commerce of the Mississippi and over the relations of the state to the Union. He also urges the governor to proclaim Lincoln's efforts to sustain the Union to be gross violations of the Constitution; to call the legislature together to enable him to oppose those efforts by force, and to order a military camp at once to be formed near St. Louis with that object.

All of these suggestions were adopted. On April 22 the governor issued his proclamation to convene an extra session of the legislature on May 2. The militia were ordered into camp on the third, and on that day a camp was established within the limits of St. Louis which was named by Frost for the governor, Camp Jackson. The streets in it were significantly named from Davis, Beauregard, and other rebel leaders. The militia companies, which were somewhat thinned by the withdrawal of Union men, were rapidly filled up by the large numbers of young men from the city and the state. On May 8 the steamer *Swan* brought the arms, cannon, and ammunition taken from the United States arsenal at Baton Rouge, for which the governor had sent, in pursuance of Frost's advice, and were transported during the night under a guard of city police (governed by state appointments) from the boat to Camp Jackson. The encampment was limited by law to six days, but the military bill, which was expected to pass at once, would extend the time indefinitely, and Frost acted as if it were already in force, for he was about organizing another regiment from arrivals in camp on May 9 and 10.

To meet the emergency which he saw approaching and Colonel Blair had suggested, I had drawn, and the president had made, the following order:

Adjutant General's Office
Washington, D.C., April 20, 1861

Captain Nathaniel Lyon,
Second Infantry, Commanding,
St. Louis, Missouri

The president of the United States directs that you enroll in the military service of the United States the loyal citizens of St. Louis and vicinity not exceeding, with these heretofore enlisted, 10,000 in number, for the purpose of maintaining the authority of the United States and for the protection of the peaceable inhabitants of Missouri. And you will, if deemed necessary for that purpose by yourself and by Messrs. Oliver D. Filley, John How, James O. Broadhead, Samuel T. Glover, J. J. Witzig, and Francis P. Blair Jr., proclaim martial law at St. Louis. The additional force hereby authorized shall be discharged in part or in whole, if enlisted, as soon as it appears to you and the gentlemen above-named that there is no danger of an attempt on the part of the enemies of the government to take military possession of the city of St. Louis or put the city in the control of a combination against the government of the United States; and while such additional force remains on the service, the same shall be governed by the rules and articles of war and such special regulations as you may prescribe, and shall, like the fore heretofore directed to be enrolled, be under your command. I am, sir, very respectfully, your obedient servant.
L. Thomas, Adjutant General.

Four of the additional regiments, called the Home Guards, authorized by this order were mustered into service on May 7 and 8, and a fifth on the eleventh. They were commanded by Colonels [Henry] Almstedt, [Herman] Kallmann, [John] McNeil, R. Gratz Brown, and [John T. Fiala].

Brigadier General Daniel
M. Frost (*Century*)

It was not necessary that Lyon should see Frost's letter of April 15 to apprise
him that Camp Jackson, with its outfit of mortars, arms, and ammunition from
Baton Rouge, was an open menace to the arsenal, or to determine him to deal
with it as such. Accordingly, on the ninth he submitted to the committee with
whom he was directed to consult by the president a proposition to capture the
camp the next day, and the committee unanimously concurred with him. His
preparation during the night and the march of his troops from Jefferson Barracks, ten miles below, commenced before daylight next day, gave notice of his
purpose to Frost. Frost sought to avert the blow by earnestly protesting that
nothing was further from his thoughts than any design against the property or
rights of the United States—so far from it, he said, he had proffered protection
both to Major Bell and to General Harney, etc.

Lyon replied, when his troops had entirely surrounded the camp, by demanding an unconditional surrender within thirty minutes. He forbore charging Frost with falsehood, but contented himself with proving it upon him by
pointing to his open communication with the Confederate authorities; to his
reception from them of the arms and ammunition they had taken from the
United States arsenal at Baton Rouge, and to the hostile attitude of the governor and legislature.

Lyon had four volunteer regiments and Third and Fourth Home Guards and
some of the regulars. Frost had but two organized regiments, the First and Second state militia; the disparity of numbers did not admit to his resisting, and
he surrendered at once.

An excited crowd had followed the Union troops to the camp, and when the return march with their prisoners began, assailed them with abuse and every sort of missile, and finally fired upon them. This was borne with patiently until a captain of the third regiment and several of his men were killed. This company then fired into the crowd and killed fifteen persons.

The wildest excitement followed. Up to this time the Confederacy had carried everything before it. Farms, arsenals, customs houses, public buildings, and public treasure had been seized throughout the South without resistance. They had been seized by those whom the people were accustomed to see in the exercise of power and so long associated with authority that it was not easy to regard them as rebels and usurpers, and they still represented that power of slavery which had consolidated the south politically. These influences had so stultified President [James] Buchanan and his able attorney general that whilst they held secession to be unlawful they held it to be equally unlawful to resist it, and the national arm, which was thus paralyzed under his administration, seemed to be equally powerless under his successor.

Hence the capture of Camp Jackson, which was its first blow, was a surprise to everyone. The effect upon the public men at the North was cheering, and it would have been salutary in Missouri and have silenced and intimidated the secessionists and emboldened the Union men, but that, simultaneously almost, General Harney got back to St. Louis and resumed the command of the department.

On reaching Washington he had employed Mr. Edwin M. Stanton, afterwards secretary of war, as his counsel, and Mr. Stanton had prepared for him a letter for publication, addressed to Colonel O. Fellow, of St. Louis, professing the most ardent loyalty. With this letter Stanton had prevailed upon [Secretary of War Simon] Cameron to restore Harney to command, without my knowledge and without the consent of the president.

His return to St. Louis completely changed the day from one of disaster to the secessionists into a day of exaltation and triumph. Immediately on his arrival he promised them to disband the Home Guard, and at once repaired to the arsenal to carry out that purpose and, sending for Colonel Blair, announced it to him. Colonel Blair told him emphatically that his order would not be obeyed, and at once concerted measures for his arrest if he should attempt to carry out his purpose. Harney then carried off to the city the regular troops to assure the citizens of protection against the volunteers, and immediately the city reverberated with indignation against the capture of Camp Jackson.

A meeting of citizens was called at the mayor's office, on the eleventh, in which many of the principal Union men participated. The capture was denounced in unmeasured terms as an outrage, and Messrs. [Hamilton R.] Gamble (afterwards Union governor), [James E.] Yeatman, and [Henry] Turner were appointed a committee to proceed to Washington to remonstrate with the president against it, and to procure the removal of Lyon from command of the arsenal on that ground that he was a mere tool of Frank Blair. Accordingly the committee made this representation and recommendation, and were warmly supported by Attorney General [Edward] Bates.

Harney's return to command also reassured Jackson and his associates at Jefferson City. They had been terror-stricken by the capture of Camp Jackson, had burned the railroad bridge across the Osage River to prevent Lyon from capturing them, had rushed through the military bill and appropriated three millions of dollars, including the school fund, to arm their followers, and Jackson had fled with his family from Jefferson City on May 11. But their panic subsided when they found out that Harney had returned, and they proceeded diligently to organize the rebellion under the military bill. Sterling Price was appointed major general under that bill, and the most oppressive measures were resorted to throughout the state to subject or drive out the Union men. Letters and fugitives attesting this poured in so rapidly from all quarters that Harney was forced to expostulate with Jackson.

To gain time, Jackson sent his major general, Price, to explain, deny, or promise anything to Harney, and succeeded so well that on May 21 Harney actually entered into a written agreement with him formally committing the peace of the state to Price's keeping, subordinating himself entirely to Price, and agreeing to respond to his call for troops to quell disturbances. And this, it must be borne in mind, was done while Price was in actual rebellion against the government of the United States, having repudiated his allegiance to that government by taking the commission under which he was acting under the military bill, and which Harney himself had pronounced to be in effect a secession ordinance. It seems incredible that any loyal officer could have been a party to such a machination. Yet Harney was not only himself true, but [Brigadier General Ethan Allen] Hitchcock, his principal adviser, was also loyal, and so also were General Sherman, James E. Yeatman, Governor Gamble, Attorney General Bates, and others who advised or approved what Harney did.

The explanation is that these gentlemen belonged to the old Whig and American Party and shared in the bitter prejudice and jealousy towards Colonel Blair that breaks out long years afterwards in Sherman's book, when he is spoken of as a political general. Their political views were superficial. They did not see that the slave party was the aggressive party and that slavery was being used to force disunion, and accepted as true the false pretexts of the secessionists that Colonel Blair and his associates were the disturbers of society, his associates being Abolitionists and he a mere politician seeking advancement through the anti-slavery feeling. How little they comprehended the political situation and how intense must have been their prejudice and personal jealousy is shown by their being betrayed into alliance with the rebellion.

Mr. Lincoln had more insight into the politics of the day, and fortunately, although himself a Whig and strongly prepossessed towards his old Whig associates, was not so blinded by party prejudice and personal jealousy as to surrender the defenders of the Union because they charged him with being a tool of Frank Blair; on the contrary, on May 16, after patiently hearing them, he ordered Lyon to be commissioned a brigadier general, and made an order removing Harney and installing Lyon in command. This last order, however, was not to be delivered unless Colonel Blair held it to be necessary to do so. And on the sixteenth the president explained his motive for doing it, to be withheld if possible, in the following note:

Waohington, D.C., May 18, 1861

Hon. F. P. Blair:

My Dear Sir: We have a good deal of anxiety here about St. Louis. I understand an order has gone from the War Department to you, to be delivered or withheld at your discretion, relieving General Harney from his command. I was not quite satisfied with the order when it was made, though on the whole I thought it best to make it; but since then I have become more doubtful of its propriety. I do not write now to countermand it, but to say I wish you would withhold it, unless in your judgment the necessity to the contrary is very urgent. There are several reasons for this. We had better have him a friend than an enemy. It will dissatisfy a good many who otherwise would be quiet. More than all, we first relieve him, then restore him, and now, if we relieve him again, the public will ask, "Why all this vacillation?" Still, if in your judgment it be indispensable, let it be so.
Very truly yours,
A. Lincoln
(Private)

This letters shows that the committee and Mr. Bates had made an impression on the president (and we shall presently see that they followed up with fatal results) even while he knew that it was impossible for men whose lives were at stake to be satisfied with the command of one whose intimates were against them, and that "it was better to mortify Harney than to endanger the lives of multitudes and the position of Missouri in the present conflict," which were the grounds upon which he was removed, as stated, in my letter of the seventeenth, accompanying the order.

On the thirtieth, Colonel Blair wrote the president that he had been obliged to deliver the order relieving Harney from command. In that letter, Colonel Blair reviews and contrasts in a striking manner the administration of Harney and Lyon; he recited the facts, showing that under Harney the Union cause rapidly declined, and the rebellion rose correspondingly; that in violation of Price's agreement with Harney the rebels had continued to organize and arm throughout the state under the military bill; that [Lieutenant Governor Thomas C.] Reynolds had gone to Arkansas to urge invasion from that quarter, and negotiations had been opened through [James S.] Rains, a major general under Price, with [John] Ross, the Cherokee chief, to send 15,000 Indian warriors into the state;

that when informed by Colonel Blair of these and other similar facts, Harney would communicate with Price, at his headquarters in Jefferson City, get a denial of the facts from him, hand it to Colonel Blair as satisfactory and as what he expected.

Harney's credulity was strikingly illustrated by his thus accepting such a denial of a statement made by [John S.] Phelps, the present governor of the state, of facts transpiring at Springfield, where Phelps lived. But Harney and his advisors had relations personally so friendly with the secessionists and so unfriendly with their opponents (Hitchcock, particularly, his chief advisor, was hostile to the Blairs, because of their intimacy with Benton and [John C.] Frémont, with whom he was at war) that they could not discredit their solemn protestations or duly weight the authentic facts which Colonel Blair adduced against them.

Lyon, on the other hand, who had no previous acquaintance with the secessionists or with Colonel Blair, accepted the facts as they were and read the rebel intent in their acts, not in their words, and, "Seeing," as Colonel Blair says, "that the most formidable preparations were made by the state authorities to commence war on the United States, he struck them a decisive blow at Camp Jackson, and intended to follow it up by marching upon Springfield. Had this been done, the rebellion would have been crushed in Missouri. This was the policy of General Lyon, and in this policy I sustained him." He adds: "We are well able to take care of this state without assistance from elsewhere, if authorized to raise a sufficient force within the state, and after that work is done we can take care of the secessionists from the Arkansas line to the Gulf, along the west shore of the Mississippi."

How Colonel Blair's action was regarded at Washington, and what Mr. Bates proposed and afterwards accomplished in regard to Lyon, appears from my letter, dated Washington, June 4, as follows:

Dear Frank: Yours to the president came to hand and has been read by him. He is persuaded that you were right, and Cameron sustains you. I learned from Henry Turner, who came on to sustain Harney, that Hitchcock was his guide. I showed Cameron also letters from [Thomas T.] Gannt, Glover, Dr. Silas Reed, and Dick Howard—the letters well-written and saying that nothing but the supposition that you consented to the bargain between Harney and Price satisfied anybody with it. Bates was satisfied to let things remain as they are, but wishes [Major General George B.] McClellan's authority extended over Missouri. To this there can be no objection. I hope, indeed, that McClellan may be induced to visit St. Louis and order some of the Illinois troops to be quartered in Missouri at once, so that there may be a suppression of the rebellion there. I have no doubt of your information being correct, and that there will be an invasion from Arkansas. McClellan, from what I can hear from him, will sympathize strongly with your people, and from his position and high character in the West it would remove all idea from the minds of those Union men of Missouri, who do not like you, that the movements of the troops were dictated by partisanship. It is not so much disunion as hostility to the Republicans which gives Jackson unique power. Now, while I am anxious that the Union feeling in the state should come to the Republicans, and it will eventually do so, you must be careful at present, as far as possible, not to arrest the Union feeling by making it visibly your property. I see that you have acted with this before you in giving Lyon the position of general and not taking it yourself.

It is full justification and vindication of you, that Harney, after denouncing the military bill as unconstitutional, proceeded to treat with Price while acting under its authority, who did not, of course, keep faith, but proceeded at once to play out the game intended by the bill itself.

Jackson and Price knew that Harney had been superseded because he permitted them to proceed unmolested in organizing the rebellion, but with the hope of gaining time by parleying with his successor. They asked for an interview with Lyon and to enter into a correspondence with him. On June 8, Lyon acceded to their request for an interview, and exempted them from arrest for four days to visit him in St. Louis. Accordingly they came and had an interview with him and Colonel Blair, and proposed that Missouri should be neutral ground, that it should be left to Jackson to protect all citizens, that the home guards should be disbanded, and that no United States troops should march through or be posted in the state. This was simply Harney's agreement over again, which, in allowing neutrality by the state authorities, admitted their right of secession, and in practice allowed the Union men to be subjected by the rebels or driven out of the state.

Lyon would entertain no such proposition nor have any correspondence on the subject, but told his visitors bluntly that Harney had been deceived and he did not mean to be; that the United States was bound to protect the people of

The Opening Gun at Boonville (*Camp-fire and Cotton-field*)

Missouri against the conspiracy existing within and without the state to wrest it from the Union, and in performance of that duty had the right to use force wherever it was necessary.

This direct and plain talk forced the conspirators to throw off their mask. They hurried off on a locomotive, only stopping on the way to burn the bridges behind them. On reaching Jefferson City, Jackson immediately declared war against the United States in a proclamation which, after stating that he had made the most humiliating propositions in a vain effort at conciliation, he called for 50,000 men to resist the "invasion of the state by the unconstitutional despotism enthroned at Washington."

Lyon had lost no time in pursuing Jackson and Price, and overtook them at Boonville on June 17. They had 4,000 men and he had but 2,000, but after a short engagement he routed them and captured large numbers of their followers. They fled towards the southwest with a part of their force, and would have been captured if Lyon had had the necessary transportation to enable him to pursue them.

To supply this Colonel Blair urged him to impress teams and wagons of a large body of Mormon emigrants, which would have been ample for the purpose, but he declined to do so, saying that our officers were so hampered by red tape at Washington that he could not venture to adopt the suggestion. The result was that, having in the meantime been again superseded in the command of the department and being obstructed at every step, he did not reach Springfield until July 13, nearly a month after the Battle of Boonville, and was sacrificed at Wilson's Creek on August 10.

Missouri had, however, long before been safely anchored in the Union. The capture of Camp Jackson, the flight of Jackson from the seat of government at Jefferson City, then defeat at Boonville and flight thence to the southwest, put an end to their authority in the state and fixed it firmly in the Union. This was generally recognized after the Battle of Boonville, and it was then proposed by the leading Union men that Colonel Blair should be made military governor by the president. But he disapproved of this, and the convention was reassembled on the call of its duly authorized committee, and by it the state offices were declared vacant, and Hamilton R. Gamble was chosen governor, owing his place entirely to Lyon, whom he had gone to Washington to have removed. From thenceforth the state authority gave a vigorous support to the Union and to the Federal authorities. It was to the comprehension by the Union leaders at St. Louis that the question of secession in Missouri was to be decided by arms, and to their prompt actions accordingly that this result was due.

Mr. Bates, to gratify the Camp Jackson remonstrants, caused Lyon to be superseded by including Missouri in McClellan's command. My letter above quoted shows that no objection was made to this on behalf of Lyon. It was only when McClellan found it impossible to exercise the command and asked to be relieved from it that I addressed to Mr. Bates as follows:

Washington, June 19, 1861

Hon. Edward Bates.

Dear Sir: At my solicitation Governor [Salmon P.] Chase yesterday called on General Scott in reference to relieving our friends in Missouri from the annoyance of being subjected to an officer whose attention must necessarily be, to a great extent, directed to another field of operations, showing McClellan's letter, in which he confesses he does not understand the course of policy proper to be pursued in Missouri, and says that he is embarrassed in the matters in his more immediate charge by having Missouri added to his division. General Scott declined to detach Missouri from McClellan's division on the ground of your objection to it. I conjure you to withdraw that objection. Lyon is an older officer than McClellan. He has seen much more service in the field, and has, in his conduct of affairs in Missouri, exhibited good judgment as a commanding officer. There is indeed, so far as I can discover, no sufficient reason for subjecting his operations in Missouri to any intermediate supervisor. When the disturbances in Missouri shall have been suppressed and it becomes necessary to combine the movements of the forces in the West upon the South—for which purpose alone I understand you to desire to have Missouri added to the Ohio division—it may then be restored to it. But while the operations are so distinct as at present, McClellan's attention being exclusively limited to almost one field and Lyon's entirely to another, it is surely unnecessary to place the older officer under the younger. Hoping you will concede this to men who are your tried friends, and that you will not cooperate with those whose evident design is to embarrass them, to deprive them of the credit of their success, whilst subjecting them to all the discredit of defeat if they meet it, I remain yours truly.
    M. Blair.

But Mr. Bates still persisted in his opposition to Lyon, notwithstanding the estimates of his best friends. This made it necessary to assign the command to someone else. Frémont had been appointed major general through my own and my father's efforts, against the opposition of the leading members of the cabinet. His appointment was objected to because he had been, and was, therefore, likely again to be, a presidential aspirant, and in that case he would be certain to use his position as a general to advance his presidential views, seek to make controversies with the administration, and be of no use in the field. The reports of his explorations, and especially [Secretary of War William L.] Marcy's report of his military operations in California, had impressed the people with the conviction that Frémont possessed extraordinary genius, courage, and energy; and believing that to these qualities, then so much needed in the service, he added the patriotism to forego aspirations so prejudicial to it, my father declared on his behalf that he would not entertain them, and Frémont accepted the appointment with full knowledge that this pledge was the condition upon which it had been obtained.

With such views of Frémont's character and capacity it was natural that we should endeavor to have him assigned to the command of the Missouri military department when Lyon was proscribed and McClellan could no longer exercise the command. And accordingly we procured his assignment to that command, which was greatly extended by adding Illinois and all the states and territories east of the Rocky Mountains, and Frémont's powers were also greatly enlarged.

The opposition to Lyon had overruled Colonel Blair's request to allow Lyon to receive into the service all who offered in Missouri, although coupled with the same assurance that if this were done the Union men of Missouri would take care of the state without outside help. This power was freely accorded to Frémont, and he was ordered to Missouri when Lyon's victories had firmly fixed the state in the Union and created great enthusiasm for the service. But although ordered to proceed to St. Louis immediately and earnestly pressed from day to day to go, it was nearly three weeks before he started. In this part of my testimony before the Committee on the Conduct of the War I say:

> As soon as he (Frémont) was appointed, I urged him to go to his department. I did so both on my own judgment and because the president expressed to me, every day he delayed, a growing solicitude for Lyon's command. Frémont, however, after his appointment, went to the city of New York and remained for some time; I forget how long. It seemed to me a very long and unaccountable delay. The president questioned me every day about his movements. I told him so often that Frémont was off, or was going next day, according to my information, that I felt mortified when allusion was made to it, and dreaded a reference to the subject. Finally, on the receipt of a dispatch from Lyon by my brother, describing the condition of his command, I felt justified in telegraphing General Frémont that he must go at once. But he remained until after Bull Run, and even then, when he should have known the inspiration that would give the rebels, he traveled leisurely to St. Louis. He stopped, as I learned, for the night on the mountains and passed the day at Columbus.

On his arrival he found ample means already at his disposal, and he had ample time and unlimited power to add to it, to enable him to send succor to General Lyon, who was confronting a force under Price, Rains, and [Brigadier General Benjamin] McCulloch at Springfield at least three times as large as his own. But although pressed to go to St. Louis by the president for that purpose especially, and pressed by Lyon most earnestly after he got to St. Louis, he did not send him a man or hold out any hope that he would reinforce him at any time.

When Lyon learned that it was Frémont's determination not to reinforce him at all he saw that the only chance of saving his army was to beat the enemy by a sudden and unexpected attack. To retreat in the face of an overwhelming fore or to remain where he was without hope of succor involved its certain loss. Accordingly, on August 10, he made a sudden and furious attack upon the enemy and drove them before him. Greatly outnumbering him, they repeatedly turned upon him with fresh troops, but were always defeated and finally routed, and burned some of their wagons. McCulloch excused the rebel retreat in a subse-

Major General John C.
Frémont (*Century*)

quent publication by saying their ammunition was exhausted. Lyon won this
unequal combat and secured unmolested retreat for his army at the cost of his
own life. His victory would have been complete and he could have pursued and
destroyed the invaders utterly ([Brigadier General Joseph B.] Plummer's testimony before the Committee on the Conduct of the War) with two additional
regiments, and if he had survived no additional force would have been required.

Frémont had on his arrival at St. Louis forty-four regiments under his com-
mand, and Governor [Oliver P.] Morton of Indiana sent him five additional
regiments within a few days afterwards and in full time to have succored Lyon.
Many of these regiments were disposable and could easily have been sent to
Lyon. Among others it appears by the testimony of [Major] General John M.
Palmer, who commanded one of the regiments, that there were at the time six
Illinois and one Iowa regiment in North Missouri, "who were doing nothing,"
he says, "but guarding railroads and eating their rations."

The pretense afterwards made that he failed to reinforce Lyon because he had
to elect between reinforcing him and [Brigadier General Benjamin M.] Prentiss at Cairo, and deemed Cairo the more important position, is answered by the
fact that he sent to Cairo but one of the seven regiments mentioned by General
Palmer. But the fact that Frémont made no better use of any force, then or afterwards entrusted to him, either in Missouri or elsewhere than he made of these,
points to the true cause of the disasters in Missouri dating from his advent.

When Price and McCulloch found they were not pursued after their defeat at Wilson's Creek and that Lyon's army was withdrawn from Springfield, they turned and marched undisturbed through Missouri, captured [Colonel James A.] Mulligan at Lexington, and were sweeping on to St. Louis, where Frémont was engrossed in fortifying the town and in organizing a presidential movement for himself, based on fat contracts for cattle and horses and war materials of all kinds and an emancipation proclamation.

Congress was convened on the Fourth of July, and Colonel Blair left his regiment to take his seat, and remained in Washington till Congress adjourned, on August 6. On returning to St. Louis, Frémont's incapacity and corruption was made known to him, and he promptly reported the facts to the president and recommended his removal from command, and followed this recommendation with formal charges and specifications. Frémont sought to get these charges withdrawn through the intervention of friends in the East, and Mrs. [Jesse Benton] Frémont hurried on to Washington to effect that object by threatening Colonel Blair's father with a challenge to his son from Frémont. These efforts were unavailing. The influence by which Frémont's appointment and assignment to command in Missouri had been made, and the lifelong intimacy between Mrs. Frémont's father, Colonel Benton, and his father, made it a painful duty for Colonel Blair to expose the blunder made in committing a great public trust to him. But he could not conceal the facts from himself and his sense of duty left no choice but to state them unreservedly to the president and endeavor to repair the wrong done. But, although his statements were unquestioned and were abundantly confirmed by official reports, and the charges and specifications were of the gravest character, yet the members of the cabinet who had been most strongly opposed to Frémont's appointment when his capacity and integrity were not questioned now interposed to prevent his removal from command, and his trial on the charges preferred against him, when his incapacity and corruption were confessed. The explanation of this is that Frémont had allied himself with the jobbers, and they had set him up as a presidential candidate, and, adopting the common artifice of making corrupt practice with ultra opinion, they had mounted him on an emancipation proclamation.

The president had written to him requesting him to modify his proclamation. Frémont declined to do so, and the president had published an order making the required modification himself. It was with no intention or expectation of saving slavery that the president had thus interposed. In the debate with Douglas in 1858 he had applied the words of Scripture—"the house divided against itself cannot stand"—to the antagonism of slavery with free government, and saw that the war of secession would test the question whether slavery or the government should stand. But great numbers had opposed the Republican Party, not because they dissented from its principles, but because its success would lead to attempts at disunion.

It was a genuine Union sentiment, not wisely directed, which had made the Republican Party a minority party. Secession had demonstrated that it was the true Union party, and to press this truth home was the obvious policy of all who were loyal to it. Frémont's backers thought that the way to make him strong for the party nomination was to make slavery the paramount consideration and that war what the secessionists charged it to be, not a war for the Union, but an antislavery war. By this means they expected to enlist in his cause the earnest antislavery men of the party, whom they supposed to be its controlling element. The president's action in his proclamation was anticipated, and they took issue with him and charged him with surrendering the cause of freedom to border state proslavery influence.

To remove Frémont summarily from command, bring him to trial, and cashier him on Colonel Blair's charges would, under such circumstances, it was argued, serve only to make him formidable as an antislavery martyr. I contended that the people were not so weak as to be thus deceived, would appreciate the patriotism and statesmanship which dictated the president's course, and would see that Frémont was but a self-seeking charlatan.

The president, as was his habit, to bring out the same result in time by a less pronounced method, took a middle course. He would not give Frémont the advantage of martyrdom. [Brigadier General Justus] McKinstry, his quartermaster and accomplice, he caused to be tried and turned out of the army. Frémont was suffered to remain in command in Missouri until November 2. Colonel Blair's charges drove him out of St. Louis on September 27, but not until Price had commenced his retreat.

Price moved slowly, but the more slowly he moved the more slowly Frémont followed. It took him until October 13 to get to Tipton, the terminus of the railroad, only thirty miles beyond Jefferson City. There Cameron, the secretary of war, found him, and, although he had been sent by the president empowered to remove him and was satisfied he ought to remove him, he would not take the responsibility of doing so.

It took Frémont three weeks more to get to Springfield, where the order for his removal found him. Aware of its coming, he prepared to receive it by issuing orders as if for an impending battle, knowing that the enemy was not within fifty miles of him, the purpose being to impress the country with the idea that the president, through mere jealousy of his prowess, had snatched from him a crowning victory. Frémont was then transferred to Stonewall Jackson's bailiwick, which was not like St. Louis, a great contract center, where his only occupation was to dispose of millions of the public money, but was the theater of constant and sharp fighting and where he was to be a subordinate to be ordered into the fray. In that field he soon discovered that his occupation was gone, and asked to be relieved from the command assigned to him in the impending battles of the Second Bull Run, and never asked or received another command.

Explanation is often asked of the part taken by the Blairs in making Frémont the candidate for the Republican Party for the presidency in 1856 and afterwards a major general in the army. It is due to my brother to say that he had no part in conferring these great honors upon him. He did not share in the favorable opinion entertained of Frémont by my father and myself. He recognized Colonel Benton's graphic hand in those famous reports of his explorations which had made Frémont's name a household word throughout the country, and regarded the extravagant eulogies which Colonel Benton lavished upon him in his public speeches and private talk as the overflowings of an overweening affection, and habitually laughed at the colonel's weakness on this point. He was silenced but not convinced when his father cited the report of Frémont's brilliant military career in California, made by Governor Marcy—one of Colonel Benton's most bitter opponents—in proof of Frémont's genius.

And it was this report, which so impressed my father, which had overcome the unfavorable opinion I had formed of Frémont's capacity from my own intercourse with him. It is a paper of extraordinary power. Frémont's achievements, as given in it, have been compared, and not unfavorably, with those of Julius Caesar for celerity of movement and the accomplishment of great results with small means. From this report I derived every effective fact presented in the campaign life I wrote of Frémont, and it was the whole basis of my recommendation of him for a major generalship and to the command in Missouri. The reader may conceive of my astonishment when upon subsequently stating these facts to Governor Marcy's brother-in-law, he informed me that the governor had not written a word of the report in question, and that he had the original in his possession in the handwriting of Colonel Benton and President [James K.] Polk's autograph letter to the governor directing him to adopt it as his own.

7

Avenging First Bull Run: The Port Royal Expedition

Egbert L. Viele, Brigadier General, U.S.V.

PROBABLY NO EVENT of the late gigantic Civil War so stirred the loyal hearts of the country with joy and thankfulness as the unexpected, absolute, and decisive victory in Port Royal harbor, South Carolina, on November 8, 1861. A great armada, surpassed by few expeditions of like character in the history of war, passed out into the ocean from Hampton Roads on October 29, in a grand pageant, to a destination utterly and entirely unknown to the thirty thousand soldiers and sailors who composed its military and naval forces, but followed by the prayers of millions for its success—millions who for long days and weeks and months had lived in doubt and despondency. The consternation and alarm aroused throughout the land by the disaster at Bull Run could only be counterbalanced by some great and overwhelming victory; but where the blow would fall, or through what special channels the much-desired victory could be won, was as yet an unsolved problem.

A gun from the flagship *Wabash*, at a few minutes past five o'clock of that lovely October morning, gave the signal for starting. Not a cloud was to be seen in all the broad expanse of the blue sky, and scarcely a breeze ruffled the surface of the water. Both shores of the magnificent harbor were lined with spectators. From one side came blessings, from the other curses—for those serene waters constituted the dividing line between the two section of the country arrayed in deadly warfare. A scene so remarkable in grandeur and effect has seldom been witnessed. The fleet consisted of seventy-seven vessels, including its men of war, transports, steam tugs, and sailing craft. It was under the command of Commodore Samuel Francis Du Pont. It sailed in three parallel lines the steam frigate *Wabash*, the flagship of the expedition, leading the men of war and gunboats—the *Baltic, Oriental, Empire City, Atlantic, Ericsson, R. B. Forbes, Ocean Express, Vanderbilt, Illinois, Golden Eagle, Great Republic, Ocean Queen, Phila-*

Brigadier General Egbert
L. Viele (*Century*)

The Federal Fleet Passing Hampton Roads (*Magazine of American History*)

delphia, Roanoke, Locust Point, Zenas Coffin, Matanzas, Star of the South, Potomac, Ben Deford, Parkersburg, Winfield Scott, Belvidere, Union, Daniel Webster, Alabama, Aeriel, Marion, Cahawba, Mayflower, Mohican, O. M. Pettit, Mercury, Osceola, the United States coast steamer *Vixen,* the *Augusta, Bienville, Curlew, Florida, Isaac P. Smith, Mohican, Ottawa, Pawnee, Pocahontas, Penguin, Pembina, Seminole, Seneca, Unadilla,* and many others. The vessels were scattered all through that memorable morning over an area of more than twenty miles. The night before this another scene, also of a remarkable character, had taken place, known to but few, but which resulted in a change of the whole scheme of the undertaking, and brought about events entirely unanticipated by those who had originally planned it.

Months of preparation had been given to this expedition, to insure a completeness and a potentiality that would make defeat impossible. A careful review of the situation of the country at that time developed the fact that so long as the disaffected states could have free access to the sea and the benefits of commerce with foreign nations, while the servile labor was devoted to the production of the great staple upon which depended all their financial hopes, it would be next to impossible for any force, however large, to suppress the insurrection and restore the Union in its integrity.

Therefore it became a matter of the most vital importance to suppress foreign intercourse with the people of the South. In order to do this a complete system of blockade must be secured on the seaboard, then controlled and held along the entire coast south of Hampton Roads by the states that had seceded. Along this coast the government had, during a long series of former years, expended enormous sums of money in the construction of permanent works of defense, in accordance with the most approved principles of military engineering. They had been regarded as almost impregnable at the time of their construction against any then known ordnance or projectiles. To attack any of those great forts by sea was deemed a most hazardous undertaking. Nothing but the most consummate strategy and the boldest skill could hope for success against them. The nature of the undertaking proposed in the organization of an expeditionary force against the Southern coast will therefore be comprehended at a glance. If, however, there was one thing more than another that might be deemed positively essential to success, it would appear that absolute secrecy as to its destination was paramount. So important was this element of secrecy regarded by the government, that from the first it was assumed to be a *cabinet secret,* to be confided only to the ranking military and naval commanders. How inviolable the secret was regarded by at least one of the cabinet members the sequel will show.

The first movement toward the formation of this expedition had been the selection of a large area of ground at Hempstead Plains, Long Island, for the encampment and drill of the military portion of it. Twenty or thirty wells were sunk in the plain at convenient intervals. The accumulation of quartermaster and commission stores began, and two regiments, the Third New Hampshire and Eighth Maine, had arrived, when in obedience to orders from General [Winfield] Scott, commander in chief of the army, I assumed command of the camp—[Brigadier] General T. W. Sherman being military commander of the expedition. Twenty thousand soldiers were to constitute the military part of the force. Scarcely had the two regiments pitched their tents when one of those periodical stampedes that were constantly occurring at Washington took place, and a telegram directed the immediate transfer of these regiments to the capital, notwithstanding the expense in preparing the ground at Hempstead, digging wells, and accumulating material—which was all thrown away, merely to add two raw regiments (one of whom had only received their muskets three days before) to the forces at Washington; and this on the strength of some cock-and-bull story by a contraband that the enemy was about to attack Washington in force, when he had no more intention of going there than he had of visiting the moon. Thus the camp of the First Brigade, E. C. was transferred to the water-soaked clay of Capitol Hill—where the Eighth Maine (nearly all six-footers) caught the mumps and measles to a man. In the pure atmosphere of the pine woods where they came from these diseases of childhood had never prevailed. After receiving the addition of the Forty-sixth, Forty-seventh, and Forty-eighth New York regiments, the brigade was removed to Annapolis, which was the final rendezvous, and from this place were embarked on transports which, with the naval fleet, ultimately assembled at Hampton Roads. While at Annapolis the

A Dinner of Hardtack, Coffee, and Rice (*St. Nicholas*)

brigade encamped in the old graveyard of Count de Grasse's French contingent of the Revolution, where the men slept in the hallows of the sunken graves of the Frenchmen who died there while in camp.

The expedition was now composed of about 20,000 soldiers and 5,000 sailors, all the largest transport vessels, such as the *Vanderbilt, Atlantic* and *Baltic,* in fact, all the available vessels that could be obtained and some of the finest men-of-war in the service; the frigate *Wabash* as the flagship, and Commodore Du Pont, an old and experienced naval officer, to command the naval part of the expedition. He had with him the two Rogers, [Commanders] John and Raymond, and [Fleet-Captain C. H.] Davis, as associate commanders. The land forces were under the command of [Brigadier] General T. W. Sherman, and were divided into three brigades, the first commanded by [Brigadier General] Egbert L. Viele, the second by [Brigadier General] Isaac J. Stevens, the third by [Brigadier General] Horatio [Gouverneur] Wright. These eight officers were called together on board the flagship the night before the proposed departure of the expedition, to listen to the final instructions of the government and learn the destination of the force. The council assembled in the inner cabin of the *Wabash*. The outer door was securely fastened, and a marine placed ten paces from it, with strict orders to allow no listeners to approach. Commodore Du Pont then unfolded the carefully prepared instructions, and read them in a low tone that could not be heard beyond the immediate circle of those assembled.

To my utter astonishment the destination of this formidable armada was stated to be Bull's Bay, South Carolina, and Fernandina, Florida, two compara-

Commodore Samuel F. Du Pont (*Magazine of American History*)

tively insignificant places; but more than this, the supposed secret destination had been imparted to me more than a month before in the city of Washington, as coming from a woman who was on terms of the closest intimacy with one of the members of Mr. Lincoln's cabinet. He was a widower, and this woman, who possessed unusual attractiveness of appearance and manners, was a constant *habitué* of the secretary's house, receiving his guests at receptions, accompanying him on occasional visits to the camps, and evidently a favored friend. She was a Southern woman by birth and sympathies; but when I learned, as coming from her, the destination of this great assailing force—which had been officially withheld from me—I treated the idea with ridicule, not only from the insignificance of the destinations named, but from the natural supposition that it was impossible for such a woman to know anything about it. What, then, was my amazement, not to say consternation, when Du Pont communicated in whispered tone to the council of commanders this same destination. I could hardly believe my own sense of hearing. What hope was there for the Union cause if the great secrets of the government, the plans of her army and navy commanders, could be thus thrown to the winds of heaven—or communicated as these were directly to Jefferson Davis, as will be seen? As a matter of course I made known the fact to the officers present that this supposed secret was no longer a secret. A long conference ensued, lasting into the hours of the early morning. A close and careful examination of the charts furnished by the coast surveys exhibited the remarkable character of Port Royal as a harbor, and after receiving from Commodore Du Pont, in answer to a question if this harbor would suffice as a safe place of rendezvous, the assurance that his fondest anticipations had never contemplated the occupation of so spacious a harbor, and that it would be sufficient without any other, it was earnestly urged upon the council to adopt Port Royal as the destination. The council adjourned, however, without coming to a decision: but in reassembling next morning, Port Royal was unanimously chosen. Sealed orders were then prepared for every vessel, not to be opened until each one was out of sight of land.

Port Royal is fifteen miles northeast from the entrance of Savannah River, and has the most capacious harbor on the southern coast south of Hampton Roads. The entrance itself is a broad inlet from the Atlantic, between two of the large sea islands that are formed along the entire extent of the coast. The island of Hilton Head is on the south and Edding Island on the north. The whole of this region has great historic interest. In fact Port Royal was the first settled spot on the North American coast. The first colony was sent out from France in the year 1562 under Jean Ribault, who, landing in Florida, afterward sailed northward, and discovering this harbor was so struck with its capaciousness that he called it Port Royal. The old chronicles describe it as "a place where all the argosies of Venice could ride upon its bosom." The first colony did not flourish, and another that was sent out from France was no more successful, and therefore in 1567 the French abandoned the idea of forming a permanent settlement here. Nearly a century afterward a colony from Scotland led by Lord Cadross formed a settlement here, and in 1670 William Sayle was sent out as governor. An English writer described it as a harbor where the whole royal navy might ride with safety, and as being admirably adapted "for a squadron of ships in time of war." It is not surprising that strenuous efforts were made by the South for its defense.

This destination was *our* secret, and was committed only at the last moment to the president at Washington. Nevertheless a dispatch from Jefferson Davis was found afterward at Fort Walker, one of the captured forts, informing the commander that Port Royal had been selected for the attack. The woman in the case had evidently been on alert, and a preparation to meet us was made that would have destroyed a less thoroughly organized and equipped force. How much the cause of the Union suffered through all the bitter struggle from such similar breaches of trust will probably never be known.

The three leading principles that govern a true plan of military operation are *secrecy, celerity* and *audacity.* The Port Royal expedition started out handicapped with the absence of the first of these, and the elements combined to deprive it of the second. Scarcely had the great fleet lost sight of the American cost when a storm commenced to gather that threatened for a time to disperse if not destroy it. The weather was unsettled from the first, the wind veering to all points of the compass. On the fifth day, or rather on the night of the fourth day, November 1, the powers of the winds and waves culminated in one of the

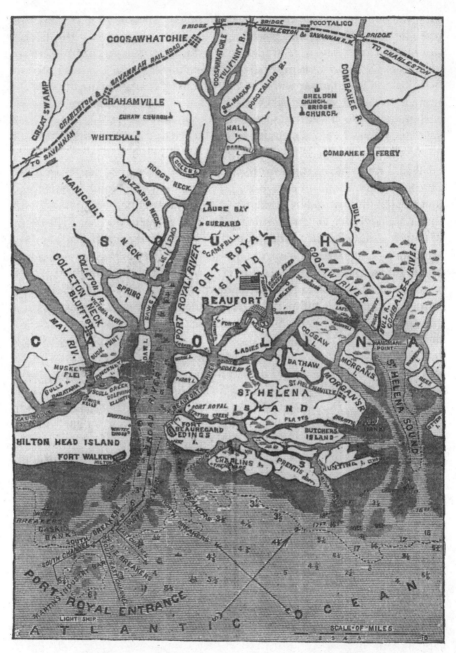

The Harbor of Port Royal (*Magazine of American History*)

most fearful storms ever known on the Atlantic coast. The exigencies of the case had caused the drafting into the service of every description of craft—ocean steamers, coasters, sailing vessels, ferry boats, river steamers, many of them of light draft, and all were compelled to breast the fury of the gale. The steamer *Baltic*, of the old Collins line of European steamers, had in tow the steamer *Vanderbilt*. The steamer *Illinois* had in tow the ship *Golden Eagle*. Nearly all parted their hawsers during the night the long hours of which will never be forgotten by those who passed through them in wakeful uncertainty.

When the morning dawned the fleet was scattered in every direction. The *Peerless*, the *Osceola*, the *Governor*, and the *Union* were wrecked. Several others were saved only by throwing overboard their guns or cargoes. The *Belvidere* found safety in putting back to Hampton Roads. It was almost a miracle that so many escaped. Nevertheless on Monday, November 4, the seventh day after starting, the fleet was at anchor off Port Royal, ready for active work. First the channel had to be sounded and buoys placed to mark the entrance. A little more enterprise and daring on the part of Commodore [Josiah] Tatnall, who commanded the insurgent fleet inside the harbor, would have made this operation a very hazardous and difficult one. Once the channel was defined it was not a difficult matter to enter, but it was fortunate for the fleet that the storm had subsided. On the morning of the fifth, the light draft gunboats passed over the bar, followed the next day by all the men of war.

And now another dilemma presented itself. The *Ocean Express*, a large sailing ship that was in tow of the *Baltic*, and had parted her hawser during the night of the storm, contained all the small ammunition of the force as well as the heavy ordnance. This vessel had failed to put in an appearance off Port Royal, and it was feared that she was lost. At any rate, Sherman refused his assent to the commencement of hostilities until this vessel was heard from, or, if lost, until more guns and more ammunition could be procured from the North. As we had stripped the arsenals of all their available ordnance, it looked as if the expedition would have to be abandoned at the moment of success. It having been suggested to Commodore Du Pont that when the forts were taken he, if found necessary, could dismantle some of his war vessels and send the guns on shore, he at once acquiesced, and it being further decided that the bayonet could supply the absence of small ammunition, Sherman reluctantly assented, and the order was given out for commencing the bombardment the next morning. During the night the *Ocean Express* arrived off the harbor, and Sherman's mind was greatly relieved.

The planning of the bombardment, the manning of the ships, and the effective work done by the fleet, will pass into history as one of the most successful achievements of the kind, as it marked an era in naval warfare. It was the first time that the powerful auxiliary of steam was brought to play such a decided part in war operations. It was grander and more audacious under [Admiral David G.] Farragut at New Orleans, but it was superb under Du Pont at

Port Royal. The two works to be encountered, Forts Walker and Beauregard, situated on either side of the harbor, were in themselves models in their construction; admirably designed, well mounted with guns of heavy caliber, and manned by as gallant a set of men as ever fought for any cause of country. They were well drilled and disciplined and were all sanguine of victory; a telegram from Jefferson Davis had given them the true destination of the fleet; they knew its power to a ship, and its strength to a man. I doubt if even the smallest particular was unknown to them, thanks to the reliable sources of information they possessed at Washington. Notwithstanding all this they prepared to meet the odds that were pitted against them with calm determination. The manner in which they served their guns to the last while a hurricane of shot and shell poured in upon them elicited the unqualified admiration of every soldier and sailor. It was all of no avail. Du Pont had planned the attack with the utmost precision. Every vessel had its designated place. The fleet sailed in the form of an ellipse, each ship to deliver its fire at each fort as it passed abreast of it. Three times this circle of death passed in its relentless course. Three times the gallant men at the works received and returned the fire of every vessel. The vessels engaged were the *Wabash, Ingraham, Pawnee, Seminole, Bienville, Pocahontas, Mohican* and *Augusta;* the gunboats, *Ottawa, Seneca, Unadilla* and *Pembina.* It

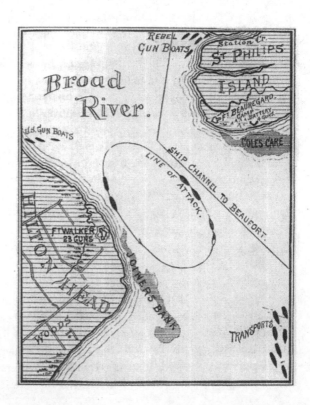

The Union Fleet Passing
Fort Walker (*Magazine of
American History*)

Fort Walker after the Battle (*Magazine of American History*)

was a powerful array. For four hours the terrible duel was maintained, and then after a well directed broadside from the *Wabash,* all was over! The resistless force of numbers prevailed and the forts so desperately and courageously defended were abandoned, their occupants making an undisturbed and safe retreat to the mainland, which by the way, could have been prevented had even a single gunboat been sent to intercept the crossing of the river. Why this was not done is one of those things that will probably never be explained. Commodore Du Pont told me he had ordered three gunboats to perform this duty. When Fort Walker was taken possession of a scene presented itself that beggars description. Such havoc and ruin! Such utter destruction probably never overtook a fortification. Certainly no work was ever more valiantly defended.

One of the sad incidents of this engagement was the fact that while [Brigadier] General T. F. Drayton, of Charleston, South Carolina, commanded the forces at Fort Walker, his brother, Captain Percival Drayton, also a South Carolinian, was the commander of the *Pocahontas,* one of the Union vessels in the attack. General Drayton's residence at Hilton Head was riddled with shells, some of them in all probability coming from Captain Drayton's vessel. This was truly a fratricidal combat.

Thus was accomplished the most important step taken up to that time in subduing the rebellion. It was a serious blow to the South, effecting as it did the complete blockade of all the Atlantic seaports through which the European enemies of America had so successfully introduced the sinews of war. It gladdened the hearts of the loyal people of the North, and sent a thrill of joy throughout the vast camps where the legions were gathered for the defense of the Union. But the question will never be answered how often and by whom was the cause of the Union betrayed to its enemies?

PART 3

Leaders, Civilian and Military

8

Life in the White House with President Lincoln

John Hay, Private Secretary to President Lincoln

THE DAILY LIFE of the White House during the momentous years of [Abraham] Lincoln's presidency had a character of its own, different from that of any previous or subsequent time. In the first days after the inauguration there was the unprecedented rush of office seekers, inspired by a strange mixture of enthusiasm and greed, pushed by motives which were perhaps at bottom selfish, but which had nevertheless a curious touch of that deep emotion which had stirred the heart of the nation in the late election. They were not all ignoble; among that dense crowd that swarmed in the staircases and the corridors there were many well-to-do men who were seeking office to their own evident damage, simply because they wished to be a part, however humble, of a government which they had aided to put in power and to which they were sincerely devoted. Many of the visitors who presented so piteous a figure in those early days of 1861 afterwards marched, with the independent dignity of a private soldier, in the ranks of the Union army, or rode at the head of their regiments like men born to command. There were few who had not a story worth listening to, if there were time and opportunity. But the numbers were so great, the competition was so keen, that they ceased for the moment to be regarded as individuals, drowned as they were in the general sea of solicitation.

Few of them received office; when, after weeks of waiting, one of them got access to the president, he was received with kindness by a tall, melancholy looking man sitting at a desk with his back to a window which opened upon a fair view of the Potomac, who heard his story with a gentle patience, took his papers and referred them to one of the departments, and that was all; the fatal pigeonholes devoured them. As time wore on and the offices were filled the throng of eager aspirants diminished and faded away. When the war burst out

Abraham Lincoln in October 1861 (*Century*)

an immediate transformation took place. The house was again invaded and overrun by a different class of visitors—youths who wanted commissions in the regulars; men who wished to raise irregular regiments or battalions without regard to their state authorities; men who wanted to furnish stores to the army; inventors full of great ideas and in despair at the apathy of the world; later, an endless stream of officers in search of promotion or desirable assignments. And from first to last there were the politicians and statesmen in Congress and out, each of whom felt that he had the right by virtue of his representative capacity to as much of the president's time as he chose, and who never considered that he and his kind were many and that the president was but one.

It would be hard to imagine a state of things less conducive to serious and effective work, yet in one way or another the work was done. In the midst of a crowd of visitors who began to arrive early in the morning and who were put out, grumbling, by the servants who closed the doors at midnight, the president pursued those labors which will carry his name to distant ages. There was little order or system about it; those around him strove from beginning to end to erect barriers to defend him against constant interruption, but the president himself was always the first to break them down. He disliked anything that kept people from him who wanted to see him, and although the continual contact with importunity, which he could not always relieve, wore terribly upon him and made him an old man before his time, he would never take the necessary measures to defend himself. He continued to the end receiving these swarms of visitors, every one of whom, even the most welcome, took something from him in the way of wasted nervous force. [Senator] Henry Wilson once remonstrated with him about it: "You will wear yourself out." He replied, with one of those smiles in which there was so much of sadness, "They don't want much; they get but little, and I must see them." In most cases he could do them no good, and it afflicted him to see he could not make them understand the impossibility of granting their requests. One hot afternoon a private soldier who had somehow got access to him persisted, after repeated explanations that his case was one to be settled by his immediate superiors, in begging that the president would give it his personal attention. Lincoln at last burst out: "Now, my man, go away! I cannot attend to all these details, I could as easily bail out the Potomac with a spoon."

Of course it was not all pure waste; Mr. Lincoln gained much of information, something of cheer and encouragement, from these visits. He particularly enjoyed conversing with officers of the army and navy, newly arrived from the field or from sea. He listened with the eagerness of a child over a fairy tale to [Brigadier General James A.] Garfield's graphic account of the Battle of Chickamauga; he was always delighted with the wise and witty sailor talk of John A. Dahlgren, Gustavus V. Fox, and Commander Henry A. Wise. Sometimes a word fitly spoken had its results. When R. B. Ayres called on him in company with Senator [Ira] Harris, and was introduced as a captain of artillery who had taken part in a recent unsuccessful engagement, he asked, "How many guns did you take in?" "Six," Ayres answered. "How many did you bring out?" the president asked maliciously. "Eight." This unexpected reply did much to gain Ayres his merited promotion.

The president rose early, as his sleep was light and capricious. In the summer, when he lived at the Soldiers' Home, he would take his frugal breakfast and ride into town in time to be at his desk at 8:00 A.M. He began to receive visits nominally at 10:00 A.M., but long before that hour struck the doors were besieged by anxious crowds, through whom the people of importance, senators and members of Congress, elbowed their way after the fashion which still survives. On days when the cabinet met, Tuesdays and Fridays, the hour of noon closed the interviews of the morning. On other days it was the president's custom, at about that hour, to order the doors to be opened and all who were waiting to be admitted. The crowd would rush in, thronging the narrow room, and one by one would make their wants known. Some came merely to shake hands, to wish him Godspeed; their errand was soon done. Others came asking help or mercy; they usually pressed forward, careless, in their pain, as to what ears should overhear their prayer. But there were many who lingered in the rear and leaned against the wall, hoping each to be the last, that they might in tete-a-tete unfold their schemes for their own advantage or their neighbors' hurt. These were often disconcerted by the president's loud and hearty, "Well, friend, what can I do for you?" which compelled them to speak, or retire and wait for a more convenient season.

The inventors were more a source of amusement than annoyance. They were usually men of some originality of character, not infrequently carried to eccentricity. Lincoln had a quick comprehension of mechanical principles, and often detected a flaw in an invention which the contriver had overlooked. He would sometimes go out in to the waste fields that then lay south of the Executive Mansion to test an experimental gun or torpedo. He used to quote with much merriment the solemn dictum of one rural inventor that "a gun ought not to rekyle; if rekyled at all, it ought to rekyle a little forrid." He was particularly interested in the first rude attempts at the afterwards famous mitrailleuses; on one occasion he worked one with his own hands at the arsenal, and sent forth peals of Homeric laughter as the balls, which had not power to penetrate the target set up at a little distance, came bounding back among the shins of the bystanders. He accompanied Colonel Hiram Berdan one day to the camp of his sharpshooters and there practiced in the trenches his long-disused skill with the rifle. A few fortunate shots from his own gun and his pleasure at the still better marksmanship of Berdan led to the arming of that admirable regiment with breech loaders.

At luncheon time he had literally to run the gauntlet through the crowds who filled the corridors between his office and the rooms at the west end of the house occupied by the family. The afternoon wore away in much the same manner as the morning; late in the day he usually drove out for an hour's airing; at 6:00 P.M. he dined. He was one of the most abstemious of men; the pleasures of the table had few attractions for him. His breakfast was an egg and a cup of coffee; at luncheon he rarely took more than a biscuit and a glass of milk, a plate of fruit in its season; at dinner he ate sparingly of one or two courses. He drank little or no wine; not that he remained always on principle a total abstainer, as he was during a part of his early life in the fervor of the Washingtonian reform; but he never cared for wine or liquors of any sort, and never used tobacco.

There was little gaiety in the Executive house during his time. It was an epoch, if not of gloom, at least of a seriousness too intense to leave room for much mirth. There were the usual formal entertainments, the traditional state dinners and receptions, conducted very much as they have been ever since. The great public receptions, with their vast rushing multitudes pouring past him to shake hands, he rather enjoyed; they were not a disagreeable task to him, and he seemed surprised when people commiserated him upon them. He would shake hands with thousands of people, seemingly unconscious of what he was doing, murmuring some monotonous salutation as they went by, his eye dim, his thoughts far withdrawn; then suddenly he would see some familiar face—his memory for faces was very good—and his eye would brighten and his whole form grow attentive; he would greet the visitor with a hearty grasp and a ringing word and dismiss him with a cheery laugh that filled the Blue Room with infectious good

John Hay after the War
(*Century*)

nature. Many peopled armed themselves with an appropriate speech to be delivered on these occasions, but unless it was compressed into the smallest possible space it never got utterance; the crowd would jostle the peroration out of shape. If it were brief enough and hit the president's fancy, it generally received a swift answer. One night an elderly gentleman from Buffalo said, "Up our way, we believe in God and Abraham Lincoln," to which the president replied, shoving him along the line, "My friend, you are more than half right."

During the first year of the administration the house was made lively by the games and pranks of Mr. Lincoln's two younger children, William and Thomas; Robert, the eldest, was away at Harvard, only coming home for short vacations. The two little boys, aged eight and ten, with their Western independence and enterprise, kept the house in an uproar. They drove their tutor wild with their good-natured disobedience; they organized a minstrel show in the attic; they made acquaintance with the office-seekers and became the hot champions of the distressed. William was, with all his boyish frolic, a child of great promise, capable of close application and study. He had a fancy for drawing up railway timetables, and would conduct an imaginary train from Chicago to New York with perfect precision. He wrote childish verses, which sometimes attained the unmerited honors of print. But this bright, gentle, studious child sickened and died in February 1862. His father was profoundly moved by his death, though he gave no outward sign of his trouble, but kept about his work the same as ever. His bereaved heart seemed afterwards to pour out its fullness on his youngest child. "Tad" was a merry, warm-blooded, kindly little boy, perfectly lawless, and full of odd fancies and inventions, the "chartered libertine" of the Executive Mansion. He ran continually in and out of his father's cabinet, interrupting his gravest labors and conversations with his bright, rapid, and very imperfect speech—for he had an impediment which made his articulation almost unintelligible until he was nearly grown. He would perch upon his father's knee, and sometimes even on his shoulder, while the most weighty conferences were going on. Sometimes escaping from the domestic authorities, he would take refuge in that sanctuary for the whole evening, dropping to sleep at last on the floor, when the president would pick him up and carry him tenderly to bed.

Mr. Lincoln's life was almost devoid of recreation. He sometimes went to the theater, and was particularly fond of a play of Shakespeare well acted. He was so delighted with Hackett in *Falstaff* that he wrote him a letter of warm congratulation which pleased the veteran actor so much that he gave it to the New York *Herald,* which printed it with abusive comments. Hackett was greatly mortified and made suitable apologies; upon which the president wrote him again in the kindliest manner, saying: "Give yourself no uneasiness on the subject. . . . I certainly did not expect to see my note in print; yet I have not been much shocked by the comments upon it. They are a fair specimen of what has occurred to me through life. I have endured a great deal of ridicule, without much malice; and have received a great deal of kindness, not quite free from ridicule. I am used to it."

This incident had the usual sequel: the veteran comedian asked for an office, which the president was not able to give him, and the pleasant acquaintance ceased. A hundred times this experience was repeated: a man whose disposition and talk were agreeable would be introduced to the president; he took pleasure in his conversation for two or three interviews, and then this congenial person would ask some favor impossible to grant, and go away in bitterness of spirit. It is a cross that every president must bear.

Mr. Lincoln spent most of his evenings in his office, though occasionally he remained in the drawing room after dinner, conversing with visitors or listening to music, for which he had an especial liking, though he was not versed in the science, and preferred simple ballads to more elaborate compositions. In his office he was not often suffered to be alone; he frequently passed the evening there with a few friends in frank and free conversation. If the company was all of one sort he was at his best; his wit and rich humor had free play; he was once more the Lincoln of the Eighth Circuit, the cheeriest of talkers, the riskiest of story tellers; but if a stranger came in he put on in an instant his whole armor of dignity and reserve. He had a singular discernment of men; he would talk of the most important political and military concerns with a freedom which often amazed his intimates, but we do not recall an instance in which this confidence was misplaced.

Where only one or two were present he was fond of reading aloud. He passed many of the summer evenings in this way when occupying his cottage at the Soldiers' Home. He would there read Shakespeare for hours with a single secretary for audience. The plays he most affected were *Hamlet, Macbeth,* and the series of histories; among these he never tired of *Richard the Second.* The terrible outburst of grief and despair into which Richard falls in the third act had a peculiar fascination for him. I have heard him read it at Springfield, at the White House, and at the Soldiers' Home.

> For heaven's sake, let us sit upon the ground,
> And tell sad stories of the death of kings:—
> How some have been deposed, some slain in war,
> Some haunted by the ghosts they have deposed;
> Some poisoned by their wives, some sleeping killed;
> All murdered:—For within the hollow crown
> That rounds the mortal temples of a king
> Keeps Death his court; and there the antic sits,
> Scoffing his state, and grinning at his pomp—
> Allowing him a breath, a little scene
> To monarchize, be feared, and kill with looks;
> Infusing him with self and vain conceit—
> As if this flesh, which walls about our life,
> Were brass impregnable—and humored thus,
> Comes at the last, and with a little pin
> Bores through his castle walls and—farewell, King!

He read Shakespeare more than all other writers together. He made no attempt to keep pace with the ordinary literature of the day. Sometimes he read a scientific work with keen appreciation, but he pursued no systematic course. He owed less to reading than most men. He delighted in Burns; he said one day after reading those exquisite lines to Glencairn, beginning, "The bridegroom may forget the bride," that "Burns never touched a sentiment without carrying it to its ultimate expression and leaving nothing further to be said." Of Thomas Hood he was also excessively fond. He often read aloud "The Haunted House." He would go to bed with a volume of Hood in his hands, and would sometimes rise at midnight and traversing the long halls of the Executive Mansion in his night clothes would come to his secretary's room and read aloud something that especially pleased him. He wanted to share his enjoyment of the writer; it was dull pleasure to him to laugh alone. He read Bryant and Whittier with appreciation; there were many poems of Holmes's that he read with intense relish. "The Last Leaf" was one of his favorites; he knew it by heart, and used often to repeat with deep feeling:

The mossy marbles rest
On the lips that he has pressed
   In their bloom,
And the names he loved to hear
Have been carved for many a year
   On the tomb;

giving the marked Southwestern pronunciation of the words "hear" and "year."
A poem by William Knox, "Oh, why should the Spirit of Mortal be Proud?" he
learned by heart in his youth, and used to repeat all his life.

   Upon all but two classes the president made the impression of unusual power
as well as of unusual goodness. He failed only in the case of those who judged
men by a purely conventional standard of breeding, and upon those so poisoned
by political hostility that the testimony of their own eyes and ears became un-
trustworthy. He excited no emotion but one of contempt in the finely tempered
mind of Hawthorne; several English tourists have given the most distorted pictures of his speech and his manners. Some Southern writers who met him in
the first days of 1861 spoke of him as a drunken, brawling boor, whose mouth
dripped with oaths and tobacco, when in truth whiskey and tobacco were as alien

John G. Nicolay after the
War (*Century*)

to his lips as profanity. There is a story current in England, as on the authority of the late Lord Lyons, of the coarse jocularity with which he once received a formal diplomatic communication; but as Lord Lyons told the story there was nothing objectionable about it. The British minister called at the White House to announce the marriage of the Prince of Wales. He made the formal speech appropriate to the occasion; the president replied in the usual conventional manner. The requisite formalities having thus been executed, the president took the bachelor diplomatist by the hand saying, "And now, Lord Lyons, go thou and do likewise."

The evidence of all the men admitted to his intimacy is that he maintained, without the least effort or assumption, a singular dignity and reserve in the midst of his easiest conversation. Charles A. Dana says, "Even in his freest moments one always felt the presence of a will and an intellectual power which maintained the ascendancy of the president." In his relations to his cabinet "it was always plain that he was the master and they were the subordinates. They constantly had to yield to his will, and if he ever yielded to them it was because they convinced him that the course they advised was judicious and appropriate." While men of the highest culture and position thus recognized his intellectual primacy there was no man so humble as to feel abashed before him. Frederick Douglass beautifully expressed the sentiment of the plain people in his company: "I felt as though I was in the presence of a big brother and that there was safety in his atmosphere."

As time wore on and the war held its terrible course, upon no one of all those who lived through it was its effect more apparent than upon the president. He bore the sorrows of the nation in his own heart; he suffered deeply not only from disappointments, from treachery, from hope deferred, from the open assaults of enemies, and from the sincere anger of discontented friends, but also from the worldwide distress and affliction which flowed from the great conflict in which he was engaged and which he could not evade. One of the most tender and compassionate of men, he was forced to give orders which cost thousands of lives; by nature a man of order and thrift, he saw the daily spectacle of unutterable waste and destruction which he could not prevent. The cry of the widow and the orphan was always in his ears; the awful responsibility resting upon him as the protector of an imperiled republic kept him true to his duty, but could not make him unmindful of the intimate details of that vast sum of human misery involved in a civil war.

Under this frightful ordeal his demeanor and disposition changed—so gradually that it would be impossible to say when the change began; but he was in mind, body, and nerves a very different man at the second inauguration from the one who had taken the oath in 1861. He continued always the same kindly, genial, and cordial spirit he had been at first; but the boisterous laughter became less frequent year by year; the eye grew veiled by constant meditation on momentous subjects; the air of reserve and detachment from his surroundings increased. He aged with great rapidity.

This change is shown with startling distinctness by two life masks—the one made by Leonard W. Volk in Chicago, April 1860, the other by Clark Mills in Washington, in the spring of 1865. The first is of a man of fifty-one, and young for his years. The face has a clean, firm outline; it is free from fat, but the muscles are hard and full; the large mobile mouth is ready to speak, to shout, or laugh; the bold, curved nose is broad and substantial, with spreading nostrils; it is a face full of life, of energy, of vivid aspiration. The other is so sad and peaceful in its infinite repose that the famous sculptor Augustus Saint-Gaudens insisted, when he first saw it, that it was a death mask. The lines are set, as if the living face, like the copy, had been in bronze; the nose is thin, and lengthened by the emaciation of the cheeks; the mouth is fixed like that of an archaic statue; a look as of one on whom sorrow and care had done their worst without victory is on all the features; the whole expression is of unspeakable sadness and all-sufficing strength. Yet the peace is not the dreadful peace of death; it is the peace that passeth understanding.

9

Reminiscences of General Grant
James Harrison Wilson

I WAS WITH [Major General William T.] Sherman the night before he began his march to the sea, in camp near Gaylesville, in the northeastern corner of Alabama, to which point he had followed [General John Bell] Hood from Atlanta in his countermovement towards Tennessee. I had recently arrived from the Valley of Virginia, whence I had been sent by [Lieutenant General Ulysses S.] Grant to reorganize and command the Western cavalry. After disposing of the business of the day we spent the evening, indeed most of the night, in front of a comfortable campfire, chatting about the incidents of the recent campaigns and considering details of those yet to come. One by one the staff officers had withdrawn to their tents, for Sherman was an owl, always ready to make a night of it, and they saw that he was well under way towards it upon that occasion.

A dark and solemn forest surrounded us, and a dead silence had fallen upon the sleeping army; not a sound except that of the measured tread of the sentinel in front of the general's tent disturbed the quiet of the night. Twelve o'clock had come and gone, and one o'clock was at hand, when there came a pause in the conversation; then a moment of reflection on the part of Sherman, whose

General Sherman's Field Headquarters (*St. Nicholas*)

deeply lined face and brilliant, sleepless eyes I see now as plainly as I did then, turned towards and lighted up by the red glare of the blazing logs, and bright with intelligent and energetic life. Then came a quick, nervous upward glance at me, and then the following remark: "Wilson, I am a great deal smarter man than Grant; I see things more quickly than he does. I know more about law, and history, and war, and nearly everything else than he does; but I'll tell you where he beats me and where he beats the world. He don't care a damn for what he can't see the enemy doing, and it scares me like hell!"

And this vigorous and graphic speech is the best description of the fundamental characteristics and differences of the two men I have ever heard. It shows not only a profound self-knowledge on the part of Sherman, but a profound, comprehensive, and discriminating estimate of the personal peculiarities of General Grant; for it is true that the latter was never scared by what the enemy might be doing beyond his sight. He gave his best attention to learning the position, strength, and probable plans of his adversary, and then made his own plans as best he might to foil or overthrow him, modifying or changing them only after it became clearly necessary to do so, but never lying awake of nights trying to make plans for the enemy as well as for himself; never countermanding his orders, never countermanding his troops, and never annoying or harassing his subordinate commanders by orders evolved from his imagination. He never worried over what he could not help, but was always cool, level-headed, and reasonable, never in the least excitable or imaginative. He always had the nerve to play his game through calmly and without any external exhibition of uneasiness or anxiety; and this was constitutional with him, not the result of training nor altogether of reflection. It was his nature, and he could not help it. The sanguine and nervous elements were so happily modified, blended, and held in check by the lymphatic element of his temperament that he could do nothing in a hurry or a heat, and, above all, it was impossible for him to borrow trouble from what he did not know to be certain, or could not change.

While this equable temper guided him smoothly through many dangers, it also kept him out of many difficulties of a personal as well as of an official nature. It made it easy for him to command an army of discordant elements, filled with jealousies, and led by generals mostly from civil life, quite ready to quarrel with each other, or with anyone else, for that matter, excepting himself, while another commander less happily organized would have been constantly in hot water.

The value of such a temperament in war can scarcely be estimated by one not acquainted with the troubles which come from a vivid and excitable imagination. It was this temperament, together with a modest reasonableness and capability, an openness to good counsels, and a freedom from offensive obsti-

Major General James H. Wilson (*Century*)

nacy of opinion, in reference to what should be done in a campaign, which caused so many experienced and judicious officers to say, as they frequently did, that they would rather take their chances in a great war or in a desperate campaign with Grant, even in his old age, than with any of his great subordinates.

But Grant had another noticeable characteristic, in a measure flowing from his temperament, which was of immense value, and ultimately gave the greatest confidence to the armies commanded by him, I refer, of course, to his constancy or steadfastness—that quality which was blood of his blood and bone of his bone, which came to him perhaps from generations of wild and warlike ancestry, and which caused him to fight all his campaigns and battles through to the end, whether it took three days, three weeks, all summer, or a whole year. It was that quality which made it natural and easy for him to say at Belmont, when his little army was surrounded, "We must fight our way out as we fought our way in"; which made him exclaim, on seeing the well-filled haversack of a dead rebel at Donelson, "They are trying to escape; if we attack first and vigorously we shall win"; which made him try every possible way of reaching a solid footing for his army in the Vicksburg campaign, and finally run the batteries with his transports, ferry his army across the Mississippi at Bruinsburg, cut loose from his line of communications, swing out into the Confederacy, beat and disperse the army confronting him, break up the railroads and sit down calmly and resolutely behind the fortifications of Vicksburg, resolved to take it by siege or starvation if not by assault. It was that quality which carried him through the perils and difficulties of Chattanooga and Missionary Ridge, and which finally brought him the rank of lieutenant general, and gave him command of all the loyal armies. And finally it was that quality which caused him to fight his way, inch by inch, through the Wilderness and to continue the fighting day after day, from the morning of May 5 till the evening of the twelfth, holding on to all the ground he gained, never halting, never yielding, but inexorably pressing forward, no matter what the discouragements nor what the difficulties to be overcome.

Such persistency was never before shown by an American general. The Army of the Potomac had never before been compelled to fight more than two days consecutively. Its commanders had always hesitated even in the full tide of victory, as at Antietam or Gettysburg, or had fallen back as at Fredericksburg or Chancellorsville, after the second day's fighting, and before any decisive advantage had been gained by either side. It had never been compelled to fight its battles through before, but now all this was changed. And there is no sort of doubt that this change marked the final epoch of the war, inasmuch as it convinced both the officers and men of the Army of the Potomac, and indeed of all the Union armies, that there would be no more yielding, no more retreating, no more rest from fighting and marching till the national cause had everywhere triumphed over its enemies!

Neither is there any sort of doubt that [General Robert E.] Lee and his valiant army also recognized the advent of Grant as the beginning of the end. They were from the first amazed at the unshakable steadiness and persistency with which he held his army to its work, and they saw at once the doom of the Confederacy and the end of all their hopes. This is plainly shown by the defensive attitude which they maintained thenceforth to the end of the war. The only *riposte* Lee ever made against Grant was on the evening of the second day's fighting in the Wilderness, when the rebels by a happy stroke turned the right flank of the Sixth Corps and threw it into great confusion.

There is reason for supposing, notwithstanding statements to the contrary, that Grant's nerves were severely shaken by this unexpected and untoward reverse. He was in a strange army, surrounded almost entirely by strangers, and naturally enough for a short time amidst the darkness and confusion felt uncertain as to the purposes of the enemy, the extent of the disaster, and the capacity of his own army to recover from it. In all that host there were only three general officers who had served with him in the West—[Brigadier General John] Rawlins, his able and courageous chief of staff, [Major General Philip H.] Sheridan, and myself. [Major General George G.] Meade, whose headquarters were near by, and all the infantry corps and division commanders, were comparatively unknown to him, and what is worse, precedent, so far as there was any precedent, in that army, seemed to require them under such circumstances to retire, and not advance.

I was with Sheridan and [Major George A.] Forsyth, his chief of staff, that night, near Old Chancellorsville. Forsyth and I lay till dawn listening to what seemed to us to be the roar of distant musketry; orders had been received during the night by the cavalry to cover the trains, and from our position, and what we knew of the precedents, as well as of the temper of the army, we feared that the next day would find us on the way to the north side of the Rappahannock, instead of on the road to Richmond. Sheridan shared this apprehension. Before dawn he gave me orders to move as soon as I could see with my division towards Germanna Ford, and ascertain if the enemy, after turning the right flank of the Sixth Corps, had interposed between the army and the river or penetrated towards the rear.

By sunrise I had covered the whole region in the direction indicated, and having ascertained that the noise of the night before was the rumbling of the trains on the Fredericksburg Turnpike, and that the enemy had withdrawn without discovering the magnitude of his advantage, I rode rapidly to General Grant's headquarters, for the two-fold purpose of reporting the result of my reconnaissance and of ascertaining how the general had stood the alarm and trials of the night before. I felt that the Army of the Potomac had not been beaten and that it would be fatal for it to withdraw at that stage of the campaign, and yet I feared that the pressure upon General Grant might be so great as to induce him to yield to it.

I found him at his camp on a knoll covered with scrub pine, where he had spent the day and night, just ready to mount and move out. I dismounted at the foot of the knoll, and throwing my bridle to my orderly, started rapidly towards the general, who not only saw me coming, but saw also the look of anxious inquiry in my face, and, without waiting to receive my report or to question or be questioned, called out in cheerful and reassuring tones: "It's all right, Wilson; the army is already on the move for Richmond! It is not going back, but forward, until we beat Lee or he beats us." I saw at a glance that, however severely tried, Grant had recovered his equilibrium, and that his courage was steadfast and unshaken. My anxieties were relieved, and after expressing my gratification at the orders he had given, and saying what I could in support of the policy announced, I remounted my horse and galloped back to my division. I imparted the result of my reconnaissance and of my interview with General Grant promptly to Forsyth and Sheridan, both of whom received it with unmistakable delight and satisfaction. It is not too much to say that a great load was lifted from our minds. We saw that the gravest crisis of Grant's life was safely past, and we felt that our success was now solely a question of pluck and persistency on the part of the army. We knew that the commanding general would do his duty to the bitter end, and we could not doubt what the end would be.

Grant has been severely criticized for the rude and disjointed battles fought by the Army of the Potomac during this memorable campaign, and much of this criticism is well founded, though not so well directed. If Grant had been a great tactician, which he was not, or had more closely supervised the carrying out of his own orders, instead of depending upon Meade and his corps and division commanders for all the details and their execution, it is probable that many valuable lives would have been spared; but it must not be forgotten, after all, that whenever everything else fails and the resources of strategy and tactics are exhausted, the fundamental fact remains that that army or that nation generally prevails, or has the greatest capacity for war, which stands killing best. In the words of the rebel [Lieutenant General Nathan B.] Forrest, "War means fight, and fight means kill." Lee and his army of veterans had to be taught that there was nothing left for them but to fight it out; that no matter how many Union soldiers they killed, their places would be promptly filled; that no matter how many assaults they might repulse, new assaults would follow, until finally there would be no safety left for their steadily decreasing numbers except in fight or surrender. And this was the result which followed! Even the unsuccessful and unnecessary assaults at Spotsylvania, Cold Harbor, and Petersburg contributed to this result, for they taught the rebels to beware of meeting in the open field soldiers who could make such assaults and withstand such bloody repulses without being disgraced or seriously discouraged thereby.

But General Grant's temperament gave him other good qualities besides the one so graphically described by Sherman. It made him modest, patient, and slow to anger, and these virtues contributed to his earlier successes almost as much as the rapid and sturdy blows which he dealt the enemy confronting him. They kept him from putting on airs, assuming superiority, or otherwise offending the sensibilities and self-respect of either the officers or men who constituted the rank and file of the army, and while these were negative virtues, they were unfortunately not possessed by all the regular army officers who found themselves in command of volunteers at the outbreak of the rebellion. Notwithstanding Grant's extraordinary success at Donelson and his excellent behavior at Shiloh, there was a great outcry against him not only in the army, but throughout the Northwest. He was charged with leaving his command without authority, neglect of duty, and incompetence, and there is no doubt that the administration not only lent ear to these charges, but authorized [Major General Henry] Halleck to supersede Grant in the field, and assured [Major General John A.] McClernand that he should have command of an expedition for the purpose of opening the Mississippi River.

I joined the staff of General Grant as an officer of engineers, in October 1862, and found him just starting on the Tallahatchee or Grenada (Mississippi) campaign. Before leaving Washington I became satisfied that the chief honors of his command would be given to McClernand, if the president and secretary of war could manage it without a public scandal; and I lost no time, after returning from a short tour of duty with [Major General James B.] McPherson, then commanding the left wing of Grant's army, in making known to Major Rawlins the information upon which I had reached my conclusion. Grant had gone to Memphis, but Rawlins and I followed him shortly, and when fitting opportunity presented itself the former laid my information before the general, and considered it with him.

At that time Vicksburg had come to be regarded as the great strategic point in the Western theater of war, and consequently its capture was looked upon as of the first importance to the Union cause. It also became abundantly evident that McClernand had not only been promised the command of the expedition for that purpose, but there was reason for believing that he and his friends were using all the means in their power to foster and spread the discontent with Grant, and if possible to relegate him to a subordinate position.

Grant's conduct at this juncture was cautious and prudent. Rawlins and others urged him to make short work of it, and relieve McClernand, or at least to assert his own authority, and rebuke the pretensions of his lieutenant in a manner which could not be misunderstood, but he declined, contenting himself with modestly asking General Halleck if there was any reason why he should not himself go in chief command of that part of the army to be employed in the movement against Vicksburg. Later on, when McClernand showed his resentment and bad temper, and indirectly claimed independence of Grant's control, Rawlins again urged a decided rebuke of his insubordination, but Grant still declined, saying, quietly but firmly: "I can't afford to quarrel with a man whom I have to command."

McClernand, it will be remembered, was a politician of influence and distinction, had been a leading and influential member of Congress, was a townsman of Mr. Lincoln, a War Democrat of pronounced and ardent loyalty to the government, and above all he had shown himself to be a brave, energetic, and fairly skillful division commander, and, notwithstanding his extraordinary vanity and captiousness, was of entirely too much consideration to admit of being relieved for any light or trivial or uncertain cause; and so Grant bore with him modestly and patiently till, in his estimation, forbearance was no longer possible.

In this I encouraged him whenever occasion offered, and appreciating my motives, it was his custom to instruct me with nearly all of the orders and instructions for McClernand's corps. At the battle near Port Gibson, where the enemy was first met after our passage of the Mississippi, McClernand behaved with his accustomed gallantry and sound judgment, and as I had been near him throughout the action, I thought I saw an opportunity in it for bringing about a better understanding between him and General Grant. Accordingly, when the latter arrived upon the field I explained the situation to him, and suggested that he should congratulate and thank McClernand in person for his good management and success. But much to my surprise he declined to do this, merely remarking that McClernand had done no more than his duty, and that it would be time enough to thank and congratulate him when the action was over and good conduct and subordination had become habitual with him.

From that day forward the breach between them widened, notwithstanding the bravery of McClernand's corps at the battle of Champion's Hill, and of [Brigadier General Michael K.] Lawler's brigade of the same corps at Big Black. McClernand's temper seemed to grow worse and worse. He alienated the only friends he had at headquarters by violent language and threatened insubordination. Finally, "for falsely reporting the capture of the enemy's works in his front," for the publication of a bombastic order of congratulation to his corps, and for failing to send a copy of the same to army headquarters, Grant relieved him from command, while in the trenches before Vicksburg, and ordered him to proceed to such a point in Illinois as he might select, reporting thence to the War Department for orders.

I mention this circumstance with no intention of passing censure upon McClernand, nor even of judging between him and his commanding general, but merely for the purpose of illustrating Grant's patience and forbearance, and calling attention to the fact that when he was ready to act, his action was vigorous and effective; and that notwithstanding his patience he was inexorable and unrelenting towards one who he thought had intended to do him official and personal injury. In this he was not unlike the most of mankind so far as the feeling of resentment was concerned, but it will be observed that he acted even in this case with caution and prudence, inasmuch as he took no action and raised no questions to be settled by the president or secretary of war till substantial success had so strengthened him in the popular mind that his position was unassailable.

And so it was throughout his military career. He never quarreled with those he had to command, but bore with their shortcomings long and patiently. Such as proved themselves incompetent or inefficient from any cause were quietly but surely eliminated, while those who were so imprudent as to criticize him or his generalship in such a way as to attract his notice were more summarily and promptly disposed of as his power increased and as his own supremacy became assured. In reference to all official matters he was a man of but few words, either in speech or writing, hence whatever he did in this direction was done decently and in order, and apparently upon the theory that "He who offends by silence offends wisely; by speech rashly." While it is certainly true, as a general rule, that Grant was impatient of even friendly criticism from subordinates, and did not like unfriendly criticism from any quarter, it would give an entirely erroneous impression of him and his peculiarities, if the foregoing statement were not qualified by a brief explanation of his relations with Rawlins, Sherman, and McPherson.

When I reported at his headquarters at Grand Junction, I found Major (afterwards Major General) John A. Rawlins in charge as assistant adjutant general. He received me warmly and cordially, explained frankly but impressively the character of General Grant, including its defects as well as its strong array of virtues, described the staff by whom he was surrounded, and gave me a brief account of the army and its subordinate commanders, concluding the conversa-

Captain John A. Rawlins, 1861 (*Century*)

tion by proposing that we should form an "alliance offensive and defencive" in the performance of our duties towards General Grant and the cause in which we were all engaged. We soon became fast friends, with no reserve or concealments of any kind between us. Shortly afterwards the forces serving in that region were organized into the Army of the Tennessee, and divided into corps; whereupon Rawlins was designated as adjutant general and I as inspector general of the army, each with the rank of lieutenant colonel. The duties of these positions brought us still more closely together, and if possible established our relations on a still firmer footing with each other and with General Grant. I mention this fact merely to show that I was in a position to know all that took place at headquarters, and especially to learn the characteristics and influence of the men by whom Grant was surrounded and with whom I was thrown in daily contact.

Rawlins was a man of extraordinary ability and force of character, entirely self-made and self-educated. When he was twenty-three years of age he was burning charcoal for a living. By the meager gains from this humble calling he had paid his way through the [Military] Academy, where he had acquired most of his education. He had studied and practiced law, rising rapidly in his profession and acquiring a solid reputation for ability as a pleader and as a public speaker. He had come to be a leader of the [Stephen A.] Douglas wing of the Democratic party, and was a candidate for the Electoral College on that ticket in 1860, before he had reached his thirtieth year. Immediately after the rebels fired upon Sumter, he made an impassioned and eloquent speech at Galena, in which he declared for the doctrine of coercion, and closed with the following stirring peroration: "I have been a Democrat all my life; but this is no longer a question of politics. It is simply union or disunion, country or no country. I have favored every honorable compromise, but the day for compromise is past. Only one course is left for us. We will stand by the flag of our country and appeal to the God of Battles!"

Amongst the audience was Ulysses S. Grant, late captain Fourth United States Infantry, but then a clerk in his father's Galena leather store. He was not a politician, still less a partisan, but he had hitherto called himself a Democrat, and had cast his only presidential vote four years before for James Buchanan. He had listened attentively to Rawlins's speech, and had been deeply impressed by it and by the manly bearing of the orator, with whom he had already formed an acquaintance, and that night on his way home he declared himself in favor of the doctrine of coercion, telling a friend that he should at once offer his services to the government through the adjutant general of the army. The story of his fruitless efforts to secure recognition at first, and of his final success in getting into the volunteer army through Governor Yates, who appointed him colonel of the Twenty-first Illinois Infantry, and also of his appointment to the rank of brigadier general of volunteers through the recommendation of the Hon. E. B. Washburne and his colleagues of the Illinois delegation in Congress, is well known, and needs no repetition here; but it is not so well known that the very first day after

Grant's assignment by seniority to the command of a brigade, he wrote to Mr. Rawlins and offered him the place of aide de camp on his staff, or that with equal promptitude after receiving notice, only a few days later, of his appointment as brigadier general, he wrote again to Rawlins, offering him the position of assistant adjutant general, with the rank of captain.

When it is remembered that Rawlins was at that time not only entirely ignorant of everything pertaining to military affairs, but had never even seen a company of artillery, cavalry, or infantry, it will be admitted at once that he must have had other very marked qualities to commend him so strongly to a professional soldier, and this was indeed the case. Having been a politician himself, he knew many of the leading public men from Illinois and the Northwest; being a lawyer, he had carefully studied the relations between the states and the general government, and had arrived at clear and decided notions in reference to the duties of the citizen towards both. He was a man of the most ardent patriotism, with prodigious energy of both mind and body, of severe, upright conduct, rigid morals, and most correct principles. He was not long in learning either the duties of his own station or the general principles of army organizations; and what is still more important, he also learned, with the promptitude of one having true genius for war, the essential rules of the military art, so that he became from the start an important factor in all matters concerning his chief, whether personal or official, and was recognized as such by Grant, as well

Brigadier General Ulysses S. Grant, 1861 (*Century*)

as by all the leading officers in the army with which he was connected. He did not hesitate when occasion seemed to call for it to express his opinion upon all questions concerning Grant, the army he was commanding, or the public welfare; and this he did in language so forcible and with arguments so sound that he never failed to command attention and respect, and rarely ever failed in the end to see his views adopted.

It cannot be said that Grant was accustomed to taking formal counsel with Rawlins, but owing to circumstances of a personal nature, and to the fearless and independent character of the latter, this made but little difference to him. Grant himself was a stickler neither for etiquette nor ceremony, while Rawlins never permitted either to stand between him and the performance of what he conceived to be a duty. Grant was always willing to listen, and even if he had not been he could not well have failed to hear the stentorian tones in which Rawlins occasionally thought it necessary to impart his views to a staff or general officer, so that all within earshot might profit thereby.

I never knew Grant to resent the liberties taken by Rawlins, and they were many, but to the contrary their personal intimacy, although strained at times and perhaps finally in some degree irksome to Grant, remained unbroken to the end of the war, and indeed up to the date of Rawlins's death, in 1869. When the history of the Great Rebellion shall have been fully written, it will appear that this friendship was alike creditable to both and beneficial to the country, and that Rawlins was, as stated by Grant himself, "more nearly indispensable to him than any other man in the army." Indeed nothing is more certain than that he was altogether indispensable; and that he was a constant and most important factor in all that concerned Grant, either personally or officially, and contributed more to his success at every stage of his military career that any or all other officers or influences combined.

Both Sherman and McPherson were very intimate with Grant, and were held in the highest estimation by him; both were fully trusted, and both acted towards him with the most perfect loyalty; and yet neither of them, although both were men of extraordinary brilliancy, ever exerted a tithe of the influence that was exerted by Rawlins. Sherman was especially outspoken in giving his views, whether asked for or not; but having once freed his mind, verbally, or by letter, as in the case of the Vicksburg campaign in opposition to the turning movement as it was finally made, he dropped his contention there, and loyally and cheerfully, without hesitation or delay, and equally without grumbling or criticism, set vigorously about performing the duty assigned to him. It is but fair to add that Sherman always had decided views. He was then, as now, a man of great abilities and great attainments, not only in the art of war, but in nearly everything else. In short, to use his own words, he was "a great deal smarter man than Grant," and knew it, and perhaps Grant knew it also, and yet there was never any rivalry or jealousy between them. In view of all this, and especially in view of the marked differences and idiosyncrasies of the two men, it must be admitted that there is nothing in the life of either which reflects more honor upon him than his friendship for and confidence in the other.

McPherson, who was also serving with Grant when I joined him, and enjoyed his confidence and affectionate regard, was also an officer of rare merit. Like Sherman, he was a graduate of the Military Academy, and was justly noted for the brilliancy of his intellect and his high standing and attainments in the military profession. He was much younger than Sherman, but, unlike him, had never been in civil life since his original entry into the service at West Point. He was cheerful, modest and unassuming, but vigorous and active in the performance of every duty, and while he was justly regarded by all as a general of excellent judgment and great promise, and while it is also certain that he enjoyed Grant's confidence and esteem to the highest degree, it is equally certain that Grant rarely if ever consulted him on questions of policy, or even as to the details of the movements or dispositions of the army. It is still more certain that McPherson did not, during the Vicksburg campaign nor at any time subsequent, volunteer his opinions. He neither furnished brains nor plans, as was at one time so commonly supposed in army circles to be the case, but confined himself strictly to the duty of commanding his corps, and doing cheerfully and ably whatever he was ordered to do by those in authority over him. He made no protests, wrote no letters of advice, and indulged in no criticisms whatever. He was an ideal subordinate, with a commanding figure and a lofty and patriotic character, and endeared himself, by his frank and open nature and his chivalric bearing and behavior, to his superiors and equals as well as to his subordinates. Grant loved him as a brother, and lost no opportunity to secure his promotion or to advance his fortunes, but never leant upon him for either advice or plans. He sent orders as occasion required, never doubting that they would be understood, and loyally and intelligently carried out according to the requirements of the case and the best interests of the service.

As a rule these orders were general in their terms, and especially designed to leave McPherson free to regulate and arrange the details according to his own judgment. So perfectly in accord were Grant and McPherson, so well placed was Grant's confidence in his admirable lieutenant, that there was never a shade of disappointment or ill feeling on the part of either towards the other. It is almost needless to add that Grant and Rawlins were of one mind in reference to both Sherman and McPherson, and indeed in reference to nearly everybody else. They judged from the same standpoint and from the same facts, knowledge of which necessarily in many cases reached Rawlins first, producing a profound impression on his vigorous and alert mind, and with gathered force upon that of his chief. It is proper to add that I never knew an army which was so little affected by jealousies, ill feeling, and heart-burnings as was the Army of the Tennessee under Grant; and I cannot imagine an army headquarters or administration where prejudice had so little influence or where the public business was conducted on higher principles than at those of General Grant.

Merit and success were the sole tests by which subordinate commanders were judged. I say merit and success, but I wish to emphasize the statement that merit even without success was sure to receive the recognition it deserved. In this respect Grant's conduct was a model which cannot be too highly commended. His patience and deliberation caused him to judge fairly of every action before meting out praise or blame. With the former he was lavish and generous; with the latter no one could be more sparing. If the circumstances did not justify success, or if the orders given were misunderstood, or if contingencies were not properly provided for, he would always say: "It was my fault, not his; I ought to have known better," or "I should have foreseen the difficulty," or "I should have sent so and so," or "I should have given him a larger force."

It is not to be wondered at that, with such consideration for his subordinate commanders, Grant should have become exceedingly popular with them, from the highest to the lowest. And yet it should not be forgotten that he was free from and above all claptrap, and utterly despised to cheap arts of advertisement and popularity so easily mastered by the military charlatan. He was at that period of his life the embodiment of modesty and simplicity, and showed it not only in his relations with those above and below him, but in his retinue and equipage, whether in camp or on the march. This is well illustrated by the fact that he crossed the Mississippi at Bruinsburg, without a horse, and with no baggage whatever except a toothbrush and a paper collar. He rode forward to the battle near Port Gibson on an orderly's horse, and knocked about the field and country like any private soldier till his own horse and camp equipage, which did not cross till after the main body of the army, had rejoined him. Throughout this wonderful campaign he shared every hardship and every peril, and what is more, never for a moment forgot the comfort or hardships of those about him.

Having been engaged the second night in rebuilding the bridges over the north fork of the Bayou Pierre, in order that the army might not be delayed in following up its advantages, after completing my task, and seeing the advanced division well started on the march, I went to the little log cabin by the roadside where the general and staff had bivouacked. It was between two and three o'clock in the morning, and after reporting to the general, as he always desired should be done under such circumstances, that the bridge was completed and the column moving, I turned in for sleep and rest, and was soon unconscious of everything around me. Breakfast was ready and eaten before daylight, and Grant and the rest of the staff moved out as soon as they could see the road and the marching soldiers; but as it was my second night without sleep he would not permit me to be disturbed, but directed the cook to put up my breakfast, and left an orderly to keep it for me, and to show me the road he and the staff had taken. I rejoined him, after a rapid ride of fifteen miles, about noon that day, shortly after which, hearing that Grand Gulf had been abandoned and was in Admiral [David D.] Porter's possession, he started with Rawlins, myself, Mr. [Charles A.] Dana, assistant secretary of war, and a few orderlies, to that place.

Arriving after dark we went at once on board the admiral's flagship, where he kept us busily engaged writing dispatches and orders till 11:00 P.M. We then went ashore, remounted our horses, and rode rapidly through the dark by a strange and circuitous road to Hankinson's Ferry, to which point the army had been directed. The distance covered that night was between twenty and twenty-five miles, and for the day between forty-five and fifty. We rejoined the army at a double log plantation house about a mile from the ferry, just as dawn began to appear. Hastily unsaddling our horses, we threw ourselves flat upon the porch, using our saddles for pillows and our horse blankets for covering. General Grant did not even take time to select a soft plank, but lay down at the end of the porch so as to leave room for the rest of us as we came up. In an incredibly short space of time we were all asleep, and yet he and the rest were up and about their respective duties shortly after sunrise.

The army was rapidly concentrated, provisions were brought forward, and in a few days operations were again renewed and the country was electrified by the series of brilliant victories which followed. Grant's conduct throughout the campaign was characterized by the same vigor, activity, and untiring and unsleeping energy that he displayed during the two days which I have just described. It is difficult, I should say impossible, to imagine wherein his personal or official conduct from the beginning of the turning movement by Bruinsburg, till the army had sat down behind Vicksburg, could have been more admirable or more worthy of praise. His combinations, movements, and battles were models which may well challenge comparison with those of Napoleon during his best days. Withal he was still modest, considerate, and approachable. Victory brought with it neither pride nor presumption. Fame, so dear to every honorable and patriotic soldier, had now come to him and his praise resounded throughout the north. Cavil and complaint were silenced. His shortcomings ceased to be matters for public condemnation; and when Vicksburg and the army defending it also fell before his well-directed blows, no name in all the land brought so much pleasure to the minds of the loyal and patriotic people as did that of Ulysses S. Grant. President Lincoln hastened to write him a cordial and magnanimous letter, saying in regard to the forecast of the campaign, "I now wish to make a personal acknowledgment that you were right and I wrong." It is worthy of remark that whatever were Lincoln's opinions during the campaign he kept them to himself, and, so far as General Grant then knew, did not in any way try to influence him or his movements. It is also worthy of remark that notwithstanding the heartiness and magnanimity of the letter just referred to, a new source of anxiety had arisen in Lincoln's mind in regard to General Grant, and the nature and extent of this anxiety will best appear from the following anecdote.

Amongst the most sagacious and prudent of General Grant's friends was J. Russel Jones, Esq., formerly of Galena, at that time United States marshal for the northern district of Illinois, and also a warm and trusted friend of the president. Mr. Jones, feeling a deep interest in General Grant, and having many friends and neighbors under his command, had joined the army at Vicksburg and was there on the day of its final triumph. Lincoln, hearing this, and knowing his intimacy with Grant, sent for him, shortly after his return to Chicago, to come to Washington. Mr. Jones started immediately and traveled night and day. On his arrival at the railway station at Washington he was met by the president's servants and carriage, taken directly to the White House, and at once shown into the president's room. After a hurried but cordial greeting the president led the way to the library, closed the doors, and when he was sure that they were entirely alone addressed him as follows: "I have sent for you, Mr. Jones, to know if that man Grant wants to be President."

Mr. Jones, although somewhat astonished at the question and the circumstances under which it was asked, replied at once: "No, Mr. President."

"Are you sure?" queried the latter.

"Yes," said Mr. Jones, "perfectly sure; I have just come from Vicksburg; I have seen General Grant frequently and talked fully and freely with him, about that and every other question, and I know he has no political aspirations whatever, and certainly none for the presidency. His only desire is to see you reelected, and to do what he can under your orders to put down the rebellion and restore peace to the country."

"Ah, Mr. Jones," said Lincoln, "you have lifted a great weight off my mind, and done me an immense amount of good, for I tell you, my friend, no man knows how deeply that presidential grub gnaws till he has had it himself."

10

The Real Stonewall Jackson
Daniel Harvey Hill, Lieutenant-General, C.S.A.

So MUCH HAS been said and written about the military career of [Lieutenant General Thomas J.] "Stonewall" Jackson that I design to confine myself mainly to personal recollections of him, and to the relation of incidents and anecdotes which I know of my own knowledge to be true. By the way, I have never heard or seen an anecdote of him which had any marks of authenticity about it. A letter writer from the Rio Grande said of General [Zachary] Taylor, after the battles of Palo Alto and Resaca, "We call him old Rough and Ready." No one in the army had ever heard it before; but it struck the popular fancy, it won him tens of thousands of votes for the Presidency, and it has gone down to history.

In like manner a letter writer from the field of the First Manassas gave Jackson the cognomen of Stonewall, and told a very pretty story about [Brigadier General Barnard E.] Bee pointing to him, and saying, "There stands Jackson like a stone wall." Not only was the tale a sheer fabrication, but the name was the least suited to Jackson, who was ever in motion, swooping like an eagle on his prey. But the name spread like wildfire, and has reached the uttermost limits of the globe. The story of how Jackson told the Yankee gunner at Port Republic to point the other way is very romantic, but is also false. So the pretty incident of his standing sentinel for his weary brigade is touching, but is monstrously absurd, and reflects but little credit on Jackson as a soldier. The efficient guarding of a whole brigade in the presence of an enemy requires more than the vigilance of one man, even though that man were Jackson himself; yet the grotesque story has been often repeated by press and pulpit.

There was a nuisance in the service known as the army correspondent. He was generally the hanger-on of some officer's headquarters, and managed to escape conscription by vigorous and unremitting puffing of his chief. As the knight of the quill never ventured into the fight, and only snuffed the battle afar, he knew nothing accurately of battles, but managed to pick up a few real or supposed incidents from the wounded and from stragglers. These, enlarged, beautified, and embellished, constituted the sensational letters from the front. He often, however, managed adroitly to give a sly laudation of himself by tell-

Lieutenant General Daniel H. Hill (*Century*)

ing about what he heard [General Robert E.] Lee say, or what he saw Jackson and [Lieutenant General James] Longstreet do. Of course the letter writer must have been under fire if with these generals. Many of the sensational anecdotes had their origin in this species of self-exaltation; but most of them were made out of whole cloth, to give spice and piquancy to army correspondence.

I knew Stonewall Jackson from 1846 till 1863, was often thrown into intimate relations with him, had many hundreds of conversations with him, heard his opinions upon a vast variety of subjects, saw him in many different positions— a lieutenant of artillery, a lieutenant general, a college professor, a church deacon, a Sabbath-school teacher, etc.—and the estimate I formed of him in these different walks of life and phases of character was in many respects different from that usually accepted.

In the winter of 1846–47 the greater part of the regular troops of the United States army were taken from General Taylor, marched to the mouth of the Rio Grande, and shipped to Vera Cruz, the new base of operations selected by General [Winfield] Scott. While waiting there for shipping, I strolled over to the tent of Captain George Taylor of the artillery, and as we were conversing, a young officer was seen approaching "Do you know Lieutenant Jackson?" asked Captain Taylor. "He will make his mark in this war. I taught him at West Point; he came there badly prepared, but was rising all the time, and if the course had been four years longer, he would have been graduated at the head of his class. He never gave up anything, and never passed over anything without understanding it." Lieutenant Jackson was rather reserved and reticent for a time, but soon proposed a walk on the beach, during which he became more sociable. One remark he made is still most distinctly remembered, "I really envy you men who have been in action; we who have just arrived look upon you as veterans. *I should like to be in one battle.*" His face lighted up, and his eyes sparkled as he spoke, and the shy, hesitating manner gave way to the frank enthusiasm of the soldier.

Some years after the Mexican War, a vacancy occurred in the chair of Natural and Experimental Philosophy in the Virginia Military Institute. It was offered to Professor (afterward Lieutenant-General) A. P. Stewart, who declined. Colonel F. H. Smith, the superintendent, applied to me for the name of a suitable army officer to fill the chair. Captain Taylor's eulogy upon Lieutenant Jackson at once recurred to my mind, and he was recommended. There was a meeting of the board of visitors held in Richmond, and Mr. [John S.] Carlisle of West Virginia, a relative of Lieutenant Jackson, was present, and cordially endorsed the recommendation given him. He was elected without any other testimonial than that given on the banks of the Rio Grande. Lieutenant Jackson resigned from the army, and accepted the position tendered him. Thus a chance conversation on the utmost verge of Texas was the means of transferring him to the Valley of Virginia, and of identifying him with those stubborn fighters of Scotch-Irish descent who first gave him reputation at Bull Run, and who will be known in history as the heroes of the Stonewall Brigade.

Jackson was not a religious man when he came to Lexington. His uncle, Mr. Alfred Neal of Parkersburg, West Virginia, told me that Jackson had never been under serious impressions as boy or youth, but had always been distinguished for great tenderness of conscience, and for a scrupulous discharge of what he believed to be duty. In Mexico he was noted for his faithfulness as a company officer, his strict compliance with orders in his own person, and his rigid notions of discipline. But he had no particular regard for religion, and was even the bearer of a challenge from Captain [John B.] Magruder to [Brigadier General Franklin] Pierce. Soon after the Mexican War, he brought charges of an immoral act against his commanding officer. The wife of this officer was a most charming lady, and a great favorite throughout the army. If the crime charged against her husband were proved, her peace of mind would be gone forever. An officer, who afterward became chief of staff to General [Braxton] Bragg, went to Jackson to get him to withdraw the charges, lest the wife should learn of her husband's unfaithfulness. Jackson shed tears, and said that the thought of inflicting pain upon her was agony to him, but his conscience compelled him to prosecute the case. This tenderness of conscience was the only religious element in him, so far as I could judge, when he entered upon his duties as a professor in the Virginia Military Institute.

Jackson had been baptized in the Episcopal Church, but not confirmed. His

Lieutenant General Thomas J. Jackson (*Century*)

leanings, however, were toward that church. One day I read him the definition of sin given in the Assembly's *Shorter Catechism*. Its brevity and comprehensiveness impressed him very much. Knowing his great admiration for sententiousness, I read him the answers to several other questions. He became so much interested that he borrowed the little book, which he said he had never seen nor heard of before. He kept it a week or more, and on returning it said that he had read it very carefully, that it was a wonderful production, a model of fine English, as well as of sound theology. I then gave him the *Confessions of Faith of the Presbyterian Church*. This, too, he had never seen. He kept it a much longer time than the catechism, and compared the footnotes with his Bible. He professed himself pleased with everything except predestination and infant baptism. His scruples about the latter did not last very long. In the last years of his life he was regarded as a fatalist; but his repugnance to predestination was long and determined.

John B. Lyle of Lexington, one of the holiest of men, was instrumental in first arousing a religious interest in Jackson's mind. But even after he had become an earnest Christian, and wished to connect himself with the church, he had no special predilection for Presbyterianism. This was determined by a potent influence, unconscious, I doubt not, to himself. He fell in love with the daughter of a Presbyterian clergyman. Had he known it he would have resisted a bias in his denominational connection from such a cause. But I have always believed that her faith wore new attractions in his eyes, after he had given her his heart. In this love affair, as in all other things, his simple, earnest nature was displayed. I remember but as yesterday his coming to my room, and, turn the conversation as often as I might, his bringing it back to this young lady. At length he said: "I don't know what has changed me. I used to think her plain, but her face now seems to me all sweetness." I burst out laughing, and replied, "You are in love; that's what is the matter!" He blushed up to the eyes, and said that he had never been in love in his life, but he certainly felt differently toward this lady from what he had ever felt before. They were engaged soon after, but a rupture took place, and the engagement was broken off. I don't think I ever saw any one suffer as much as he did during the two or three months of estrangement. He was excessively miserable, and said to me one day, "I think it probable that I shall become a missionary, and die in a foreign land."

The lovers' quarrel was settled. They were married, and in one short year Jackson followed his wife and newborn babe to their last resting place. His grief was profound and of long continuance. More than a year after the death of his wife, he told me that on visiting her grave, which he did daily, he felt an almost irresistible desire to dig up the body and once more be near the ashes of one he had loved so well.

When Jackson first came to the Virginia Military Institute he was a dyspeptic and something of a hypochondriac. His health was bad, but he imagined that he had many more ailments than he really did have. He had been at a water cure establishment in the North, and the prescription had been given him to live on stale bread and buttermilk, and to wear a wet shirt next to his body. He followed these directions for more than a year after coming to Lexington. Boarding at a public hotel, these peculiarities attracted much attention, and he was much laughed at by the rude and coarse. But he bore all their jests with patience, and pursued his plan unmoved by their laughter. In like manner he carried out strictly the direction to go to bed at nine o'clock. If that hour caught him at a party, a lecture, a religious exercise, or any other place, he invariably left. His dyspepsia caused drowsiness, and he often went to sleep in conversation with a friend, and invariably, without exception, went to sleep at church. I have seen his head bowed down to his very knees during a good part of the sermon. He always heard the text of our good pastor, the Reverend Doctor [William S.] White, and a few of his opening sentences. But after that all was lost.

I remember a witticism at his expense which caused a good deal of amusement. The faculty of the two colleges was specially invited to attend the lecture of a celebrated mesmerist. Many of the citizens of the town were also present. The lecturer, after doing some surprising things, wished to try his hand upon one of the professors. Major Jackson went forward to the stage, but his will was too strong for that of the mesmerizer, and the operator failed to affect him. The operator showed so much chagrin and mortification at his failure that the audience became very much amused, and their fun ran over when a witty daughter of Governor [James] McDowell said in a stage whisper, "No one can put Major Jackson to sleep but the Rev. Dr. White!" I believe that Jackson never entirely overcame this drowsiness in church, though in military service his health improved, and drowsiness wore off to some extent.

A remark of the Rev. Dr. White that "in our country the man who can speak multiplies himself by five" made a great impression upon Jackson, and he resolved to become a speaker. Like most of the graduates of West Point, he was totally unskilled in oratory. He had never made a speech in his life, and was remarkably diffident. But he had determined to succeed, and his iron will prevailed. I well remember his first effort. On anniversary occasions of the literary societies of Washington College, the students were in the habit, at the close of their exercises, of calling upon invited spectators for a speech, and would continue their noisy demonstrations until the persecuted guest rose to make some reply. At the time referred to, many gentlemen were called upon, and among the rest Major Jackson. He rose with a determined aspect, and never did resolution sit more grandly upon his brow when charging a battery than it did on that night. But his health was poor and his nerves unstrung, and he betrayed much embarrassment. The town paper, in describing the exercises, referred to the *nervous* speech of Major Jackson, coarsely and unfeeling putting the word nervous in italics. Jackson, however, persevered. He joined the Franklin Debating Society, an institution that had been in existence over fifty years, and had enrolled in its membership some of the ablest men in Virginia. He succeeded in making an impressive, but never a ready or an eloquent, speaker. On one occasion Dr. White called upon him to pray in public. He was so much confused that Dr. White told him, some days afterward, that he would never require so unpleasant a task of him again. He replied that it was a cross to him to pray in public, but that he had made up his mind to bear it, and did not wish to be excused. He persevered, and became very fluent and easy in public prayer. I think that his conduct in this case was partly due to a determination which he had made in early life to conquer every physical, mental, and moral weakness of his nature. As an illustration of this, he once told me that when he was a small boy it was necessary to put a mustard plaster upon his chest, and his guardian mounted him on a horse to go to a neighbor's house, so that his mind might be diverted and the plaster kept on. He said that the pain was so dreadful that he fainted soon after dismounting. I asked if he had left it on in order to obey his guardian. He answered, no; it was owing to a feeling that he had from early childhood not to yield to trials and difficulties.

Doctor [Robert L.] Dabney thinks that he was naturally timid, and that nothing but his iron will made him brave. I think that this is a mistake. The muscles of his face would twitch convulsively when a battle was about to open, and his hand would tremble so that he could not write. The men often noticed working of his face, and would say, "Old Jack is making mouths at the Yankees." But all this only indicated weak nerves, and not timidity. I think that he loved danger for its own sake, and, though his nervous system was weak, he gloried in battle, and never shrank from its dangers or its responsibilities. Like Paul, he kept his body under, and would not let any appetite control him or any weakness overcome him. He used neither tobacco, nor coffee, nor spirits; he would go all winter without cloak or overcoat in the mountains of Virginia, giving no other reason than that he "did not wish to give way to cold." These peculiarities were laughed at, and he was regarded as a marvel of eccentricity. But there was nothing erratic in it. This self-denial and self-control explain his wonderful success. He had conquered himself, and was thus made fit to be a conqueror. The contest with self begun in childhood, and perfected in manhood, culminated in those splendid victories which electrified the world. No self-indulgent man was ever truly great, however lavishly nature may have showered upon him her bounties. How many splendid opportunities have been lost through the wine-bibbing or pleasure-seeking of some officer of rank! How often a blow might have been struck, but was not, because the commander had not, like Jackson, learned to master his weakness! Every page of history points to such instances, and the experience of every man in his own life confirms them.

"Let us go on" was the key to his marvelous success. "I would not have succeeded against [Major General Nathaniel] Banks," said he to the writer, "had I not pressed him from the moment I struck his out-posts at Front Royal. Soon after crossing the north fork of the Shenandoah, I found my cavalry halted, and a formidable body of the enemy drawn up to receive them. I knew that delay would be fatal. I ordered a charge. They hesitated"—here he paused, and at length added—"but they *did* charge, and routed the enemy." (He himself led the charge, and hence his pause.) "I pressed them rapidly all night. They frequently halted and fought us for a time, but the darkness was too great to permit much execution on either side. But for the panic created by this rapid pursuit, I would have been beaten at Winchester. Banks is an able man, and his troops fought well, under the circumstances. His retreat was skillfully conducted. Had my cavalry done their duty, he would have been destroyed; but they fell to plundering, and did not carry out my orders." And here he spoke freely of cavalry leaders. "[Brigadier General Turner] Ashby never had his equal in a charge; but he never had his men in hand, and some of his most brilliant exploits were performed by himself and a handful of followers. He was too kind-hearted to be a good disciplinarian. [Major General James Ewell Brown] 'Jeb' Stuart is my ideal of a cavalry leader; prompt, vigilant, and fearless."

His fondness for Stuart was very great, and it was cordially reciprocated. Their meeting after a temporary absence was affectionate and brotherly in the extreme. No welcome was ever more hearty and cordial than that given by Jackson to Stuart after his return from his celebrated raid around [Major General George B.] McClellan, a few weeks subsequent to the battle of Sharpsburg. They both laughed heartily over a picture Stuart picked up in Pennsylvania headed, "Where is Stonewall Jackson?" "Well, Stuart, have you found your hat?" inquired the general. This was an allusion to the narrow escape from capture of the great cavalry leader with the loss of that important article of head-gear. Stuart laughingly replied, "No; not yet." The general laid aside his old Valley suit, and appeared at the battle of Fredericksburg in a magnificent uniform presented to him by Stuart. "Ah, General," said one of his impudent rebel boys, as he rode along the line, "you need not try to hide yourself in those clothes; we all know you too well for that." The love of the rank and file for him at that time was almost idolatrous, and it steadily increased till the close of his career. A more grandly impressive sight was never witnessed than that of the greeting of his men on that bright morning at Fredericksburg as he passed in his gay clothing on his fiery war steed. These hardy veterans, all of them ragged, and many shoeless, sprang to their feet from their recumbent position, and waved enthusiastically their dingy hats and soiled caps; but refrained from their wonted cheers lest they should draw the fire of the enemy's artillery upon their beloved chief.

Jackson was not a popular professor. He had rigid notions of discipline, and was uncompromising in his enforcement of the rules of the institute. He was unbending, uncongenial, intolerant of neglect of duty, inattention to studies, carelessness at drill, etc. This, combined with his eccentricities, made him a mark for the witticisms and the mischief of the cadets. They played tricks upon him, they made sport of him, they teased him, they persecuted him. All in vain. He turned neither to the right nor to the left, but went straight on his own ways.

As he was passing by the tall institute building one day, a vicious and cow-

A Virginia Military Institute Cadet (*Century*)

ardly cadet, who hated him, let drop a brick from the third-story window. It fell close by his feet, and his escape was almost miraculous. He did not deign to look up, and stalked on with contemptuous indifference. He brought charges against a cadet for some misdemeanor, and got him dismissed. The cadet was a daring and reckless character, and challenged him, accompanying the note with the message that if the professor failed to give him satisfaction in that way, he would kill him on sight. Jackson brought the challenge to me, and asked my advice in regard to swearing the peace against the cadet. I vehemently opposed it on the grounds that the cadets would always regard him as a coward, and that he would be annoyed by their contemptuous treatment. He heard me through patiently, thanked me for my advice, went straight to a magistrate and swore the peace against the cadet. There was a perfect hoot of derision in the town, in Washington College, and in the institute. A military man, who had distinguished himself on the plains of Mexico, had taken an oath that he was in bodily fear of a mere stripling. But the end was not yet. The officer of the law was afraid to serve the writ on the young desperado, who easily kept out of his way. Jackson had rooms in the institute building. He went in and out as usual, both day and night. The dismissed cadet told his comrades that he would attack Jackson at a certain hour one day, but he did not. The time was changed to that night, to the next day, to the next night. But the attack never came, and the boys discovered that the blusterer was afraid of the man who had sworn the peace against him, and they turned their derision from the professor to their comrade. The explanation of his conduct was this: Jackson had let it be known that as a Christian he felt it to be his duty to avoid a difficulty, and therefore had gone to an officer of the law for protection. That failing, he had felt it to be a duty to protect himself, and had prepared himself for a personal affray. The cadet had seen the flash of that blue eye, and knew that the result of a collision would be fatal to himself.

I have thought that no incident in the life of Jackson was more truly sublime than this. He was unmarried, a comparative stranger, with but few friends. He was ambitious, covetous of distinction, desirous to rise in the world, sensitive to ridicule, tenacious of honor—yet, from a high sense of Christian duty, he sacrificed the good opinion of his associates, brought contempt upon his character as a soldier and a gentleman, and ran the risk of blighting his prospects in life forever. The heroism of the battlefield, yea, the martyr courage of the stake, are nothing to this.

Jackson was truly a modest man. He would blush like a schoolgirl at a compliment. He was easily confused in the presence of strangers, especially if they were ladies. It is well known that the noisy demonstrations which the troops always made when they saw him were painfully embarrassing to him. This was usually attributed to his innate modesty, but that was not the sole cause. It had its origin in a higher source. In the last interview I ever had with him, he said: "The manner in which the press, the army, and the people seem to lean upon certain persons is positively frightful. They are forgetting God in the instruments he has chosen. It fills me with alarm." Did this fear foreshadow his own sad fate at the hands of his own men, who almost idolized him? "These newspapers with their trumpery praise make me ashamed," said General Lee to me at Petersburg. What a lesson is here to flatterers!

But the admiration for Jackson was by no means confined to his own soldiers and to his own section. The Federal prisoners always expressed a great desire to see him, and sometimes loudly cheered him. This was particularly the case at Harper's Ferry, where the whole line of eleven thousand prisoners greeted him with lusty shouts. Citizens say that the hostile troops always spoke of him with marked respect. While he was making his stealthy march around [Major General John] Pope's rear, as still as the breeze, but eventually as dreadful as the storm, a Philadelphia paper remarked, "The prayerful partisan has not been heard from for a week, which bodes no good." "Where is Jackson?" I asked an Irish prisoner, who was astonished beyond measure to find a rebel grasp upon his shoulder. With the apt readiness of his people, he replied, "Faith, and that's jist the trouble all the time, shure."

It is an interesting subject to investigate the cause of this popularity with friend and foe. Jackson went from the professor's chair to the officer's saddle. He carried with him the very elements of character which made him odious as a teacher; but I never saw him in an arbitrary mood.

I think it was Jackson's reticence more than anything else that gave offense. His next in command knew no more than the private soldier what he intended to do. I think that this must have had a palsying effect at times on his next in command. I was for some weeks in this embarrassing position. The ultimate end of the movement was unknown to me, and it was almost impossible to coordinate the secondary movements with the chief one without knowing what that was to be.

I happened to be present upon two occasions when subordinate officers spoke to him in a manner that few superior officers would have tolerated. One of these subordinates was a magnificent soldier; the other was not. But he was patient with both. Why, then, was he hated in one sphere, and almost adored in another? I think it was owing mainly, if not entirely, to his success. When his Romney expedition turned out badly in the winter of 1861–62, he was as unpopular with the troops at Winchester as he was with the cadets at Lexington. He had about him some of those qualities which the man of the people and the man for the people must have. He had not the grace and suavity of Marlborough, the easy fascination of Napoleon, the imposing dignity of Washington. His bearing was awkward, his address unprepossessing, his conversational powers limited save when warmed up, his manner cold and ungenial to strangers. Success threw a halo of glory around all this, and endeared even his ungainly qualities to his men. The successful general is always popular.

Jackson's men loved him, then, for his victories, and not for his piety and purity of character. It is true that this love was mingled with a good deal of awe, because of his communings with Heaven; but his prayers, unaccompanied by heavy and telling blows, would have been looked upon as tokens of weakness.

11

Recollections of Nathan Bedford Forrest
Dabney H. Maury, Major General, C.S.A.

NATHAN BEDFORD FORREST died in Memphis, Tennessee, on October 29, 1877. He was born in Bedford County, Tennessee, July 12, 1821. His parents were plain people of moderate means, and his opportunities for education were limited, so that throughout his eventful life he had to encounter the embarrassments of this early disadvantage. By the time he reached forty years of age he had acquired a large fortune, and established for himself a character for energy, courage, financial ability, and integrity unsurpassed by that of any man in his state.

When the war began he threw himself into it with all his force. He organized and equipped a regiment of horse, and in the very outset of his career was distinguished above all others in the Western armies by his will, self-reliance, and instinctive aptitude for war. From first to last he acquired but little acquaintance with mere tactical details, and it is probable that he could never at any time in his whole career direct with accuracy the maneuvers of any body of troops under his orders according to tactics. But he knew how to find subordinate officers who could impart the necessary instruction in detail, while he directed the quiet movements which ensured the grand success. Napoleon himself did not know better when or how to strike his enemy, and he reduced his comprehension of the whole theory of war to one pithy apothegm: "War means to fight, and to fight means to kill."

It is thought by some that had Forrest been thoroughly educated, he would have been a greater general than he was, and probably that is just. But there abounded in his makeup so much good sense, so much energy, so much fertility of resource, as made us feel he was born for war, and that his native gift raised him above the aid of education. His intuition led him directly to the essence of every question, and while he perceived the true objects of war no less quickly and clearly, and pursued them with no less vigor than [Stonewall] Jackson did, he had vastly more fertility of resource than that great captain ever evinced, and when main force and direct attack failed of success he often won it by stratagem and finesse.

When the War between the States broke out, long-range arms had been generally adopted by the great military nations, and the first manifest result was a demand for material changes in the organization and formation of troops and in the composition of armies. It was evident to practical men that the role of

Lieutenant General
Nathan B. Forrest
(*Harper's New Monthly
Magazine*)

the cavalry arm of the service was thenceforth to be extended, that the day of double-rank cavalry and sword-in-hand charges had passed, that in the future the mounted troops would play a more important and independent part in wars, and that the most active forces of all campaigns would be mounted upon horses for transportation and equipped like the best infantry to fight on foot. The Crimean War had furnished us with the first practical illustrations of a necessity for cavalry to abandon its traditions. We had seen the Russian cavalry repulsed by the Highlanders with their Minie rifles from a line of battle, and we had seen the bootless blunder of the Light Brigade against the Russian guns.

The vigorous intellect of Forrest, unclouded by precedents or the dogmas of military critics, perceived the career opened to mounted riflemen, and he became the great exponent of the power of that arm. In thin-ordered formations, with a tactic of few commands and simple evolutions, he threw his lines with unparalleled rapidity on the point of attack, and succeeded as often by the surprise as by the vim of his onslaught. For four years he was the chief cause of apprehension and of fierce disaster to every enemy who invaded the territory of Tennessee, Mississippi, Alabama, or Georgia. His banners were the first given the breeze of war and the last furled in token of surrender.

It is beyond my ability and the scope of this paper to attempt to relate the history of this wonderful man. I propose only to record some recollections and traditions of him which may illustrate his character and peculiar power. It was my privilege to be often associated with him in the war and to enjoy unusual opportunities of observing some of the most remarkable evidences of his great ability. I leave it to some great military critic, equal to the importance of the work, to prepare such a history of his campaigns as will illustrate for military students the great examples he has left them. The incidents and recollections I am presenting may not be accurate as to date and order of sequence, and are entirely based on my memory of them as related by him or his comrades, or as having been observed by myself. Therefore, I ask indulgence for all inaccuracies.

I first saw him in April 1862, a few miles outside the defenses of Corinth. He was already famous and was then in the very prime of his powers. In stature he was over six feet, with a physical development of great strength and activity. His eyes were light gray, his cheek bones were high, his hair brown and straight, his complexion generally pallid. But those who have seen him in the heat of battle can never forget the martial beauty and grandeur of the man. A bright hectic color then glowed in his cheeks and his eyes gleamed with the light of his fierce spirit, and I have heard men say, who were by him then, that nothing could surpass or eradicate the impression of his aspect.

In the spring of 1863 Forrest was in Middle Tennessee, commanding a brigade in the cavalry corps of [Major General Earl] Van Dorn. By one of his bold and skillful movements he captured a Federal brigade commanded by [Colonel John] Coburn, and duly reported the capture of the men, horses, arms, and equipage to General [Braxton] Bragg, commanding the army, who ordered that all of the property and accoutrements should be turned in to the ordnance officer and quartermaster of the army. But inasmuch as Forrest's men acted on the principle that the spoils of war belong to the victors, General Bragg's supply officers received no contributions from this important capture, and Van Dorn was instructed to inquire into the matter and enforce obedience to the order.

Accordingly he sent for Forrest and rather sternly asked him why he had not turned in the arms, etc., captured with Coburn's brigade. Forrest replied: "General Van Dorn, I am not in the habit of being spoken to in that way, and I won't allow it; and when the time comes that your rank won't interpose, you shall answer to me for this, sir." "General Forrest, my rank shall never stand between me and any man who feels aggrieved by me, and I am at your service now, sir."

Forrest paused a moment, passing his hand across his forehead, and said: "General Van Dorn, there are enough Yankees for you and I to fight without fighting each other; and you and I can afford to let this matter stop right here. I am sorry I spoke to you as I did, and I hope you will forget it." Van Dorn said: "General Forrest, I am very glad to hear you speak so, and assure you I shall never again think of your words. No man will ever question your readiness to fight any man or anything. But, general, so long as you are under my command you must obey my orders."

And thus ended the most remarkable collision that ever occurred between two of the bravest men in the world—each confident in his own courage and well-knowing that of his antagonist. They were almost the only two men living who were brave enough to settle a controversy like this. Van Dorn then turned to Forrest and said: "General, I have more work for you now," and sent him off in pursuit of the raiding column of Colonel [Abel D.] Streight, which had passed down into North Alabama and was moving toward Rome, Georgia. These gallant spirits never again met in life, for in a few days afterward Van Dorn was murdered.

The writer was commanding the Department of East Tennessee at the time, and was cautioned to be on the alert to intercept Streight, who would pass out of Georgia through Tennessee and back into Kentucky. But scarcely had the cavalry of the department been set in motion toward its southern borders, when Streight and his brigade, over 1,200 men, came to Knoxville on their way as prisoners to Richmond.

Forrest had followed them like a bloodhound. He pressed them by day and by night and finally brought Streight to a parley at a point about two days' march from Rome. By this time Forrest's command had been diminished by the severity of his pursuit to about 400 men and but three cannon of his one battery had been able to keep up with the column.

The conference between the two leaders occurred within sight of a cut off in the road, which enabled the battery captain to keep his guns moving continually in sight. They would march along the road, over the edge of the hill, turn into the cut off, march back by it into the road again, and thus move along as a continuous column of artillery.

While negotiating with Streight, Forrest stood with his back to the artillery, so as to afford the other a full view of it. At last Streight said: "In the name of God how many guns have you got? There go fifteen I have counted already." "Well, I reckon they are about all that have kept up," said Forrest, looking around carelessly.

Impressed by the futility of further attempts to escape from a force so superior to his own, Streight finally agreed to surrender, stacked his arms, and by Forrest's direction moved his men away from the line of stacks. Then the Confederate force, which, leaving out the horse-holders, numbered only about 300 men, were moved forward by Forrest and took possession of the arms. Streight was a gallant fellow, and was greatly mortified at having been outwitted, and charged Forrest with unfair dealing. "Oh, no, Colonel," said Forrest, laughing, "all's fair in war, you know." Streight and his men were sent on to Richmond, whence their brave leader effected for himself and for many of them one of the boldest and most successful escapes ever made from prison.

This expedition was perhaps the greatest military achievement of Forrest's life; it was one which evoked in an eminent degree all of his capacities for war, and of which he was most fond of relating the incidents. One of them which he used to tell with much enjoyment illustrated the heroism and cleverness of a young Alabama girl, and is worthy of perpetuation. While pressing close upon the retreating enemy and riding at the head of the column, Forrest was met by a little girl of about twelve years [Emma Sanson, age sixteen], who told him to stop, "For just a little way on is a bridge where the Yankee soldiers are all ready to shoot at you if you go there."

Forrest halted and asked her if there was no other way to get across that river than by the bridge. "Yes," she said, "two miles above is a ford where you can cross; and if you will take me up behind you I'll show you the way to it."

Accordingly he rode up to a stump, from which the little girl mounted behind him, and then guided him to where the road turned down to the ford. "Now, you had better stay here and let somebody go to the turn of the road and see if there are any soldiers there," said she.

Forrest and several others at the head of the column dismounted and moved to where the road turned into full view from the riverbank beyond the ford,

General Forrest and Emma Sanson (*Harper's New Monthly Magazine*)

when they were at once fired upon by a volley from the enemy, who had been sent to defend the crossing. The little guide, unobserved by any of them, kept along with Forrest on this reconnaissance, and what was his surprise and alarm and amusement when the bullets began to whistle, to see the little thing dart in front of him, spread out her little frock in either hand, and call out to him: "Get behind me, general! Get behind me!" He snatched her up and bore her back to a safer place.

Another illustration of the pluck of our women, which pleased him greatly, was afforded by an old lady in north Georgia just after the defeat of our army at Missionary Ridge. Forrest with his horsemen was covering the retreat, and took his stand upon every vantage ground and held it till the enemy would deploy in force and drive him off, when he would gallop on to seize and hold the next ridge he might find defensible. Generally he would be among the last to retire, and was galloping on to overtake his command, when he was hailed by a brave, old matron, who called loudly to him, as he hastened by her house: "Stop! Why don't you stop and fight, you great, big, cowardly thing you? Oh! If old Forrest was only here, he'd make you stand and fight!"

The State of Mississippi owes a heavy debt of gratitude to Forrest, for he saved her three different times from the enemy's occupation during the war, and wrought earnestly for her restoration and development after peace was proclaimed. In 1863 [Major General Samuel D.] Sturgis, at the head of a column of cavalry and infantry, estimated at 12,000 men, moved down into Mississippi to ravage and occupy that fine region known as the prairie country, which lies along the Mobile and Ohio Railroad.

The evils which would have followed the success of this enterprise are incalculable, whether estimated as to its effect upon the people of Mississippi alone, or as to the consequences to the cause of the Confederacy itself. Forrest, fortunately, was within sound of the call for help which went up from all parts of the state, and moved at once to encounter the enemy—his whole force numbering about 2,000 horsemen. With these he fell upon Sturgis's column on the Tishomingo Creek, a few miles from Tupelo.

His onslaught was so sudden and fierce and unexpected that the advance of Sturgis was thrown into confusion, was routed and driven back upon the main body, which in turn became disordered, fell back upon the trains, and finally broke up in absolute disorder and fled in a panic, without any semblance of organization, back to its base at Memphis—where the commander arrived, among the other fugitives, in very sorry plight.

The pursuit had been unremitting from the moment of the first attack. It was Forrest's way to press a beaten enemy; he never gave time to rally or to rest. When he was on the warpath and had struck an effective blow, it was sure to be followed up until there was nothing more to strike. The upper counties of Mississippi were for days traversed by the stragglers from Sturgis' command, many of whom were captured by Confederate soldiers who happened to be at their homes on furlough from their commands, and by the old men and youths exempt from service because of age; and even by that noble class of able-bodied Southern men who claimed exemption under the twenty-Negro bill, but who could sometimes do valiant service on a thoroughly routed and panicked enemy. Some time elapsed before another expedition could be organized to invade and lay waste the region of Mississippi, in which was Forrest's home, and over which he hovered with his protecting wings for four long years.

In 1864 [Major General William] Tecumsah Sherman conceived the project of conquering Mississippi and Alabama by a combined expedition under his personal direction. The scheme was worthy of the erratic brain of Sherman, and its execution was what might have been expected from it under him. The co-operative columns were to move from Memphis and Vicksburg respectively, to meet at Meridian, whence they would move on together to Selma and Mobile. The column from Vicksburg was of infantry, artillery, and cavalry, in all about 23,000 effectives, and under General Sherman himself. The column from Memphis was of cavalry, with perhaps a battery or two, was estimated at 7,000 or 8,000 men, and was commanded by [Brigadier General William Sooy] Smith.

Sherman moved out in brave array and kept the direct road from Vicksburg to Meridian, unopposed by any force except the cavalry of [Brigadier General] Wirt Adams, about 1,000 strong, who checked and impeded his march materially, but could not do more, until he came near Morton Station, where [Lieutenant General Leonidas] Polk with about 15,000 infantry was in position and offered him battle. This Sherman declined, and turning off toward the southeast marched upon Enterprise, a railroad village on the Mobile and Ohio Railroad, where he remained some days awaiting news from his cooperative cavalry.

General Smith with the cavalry column moved from Memphis, and marched southeast toward the appointed rendezvous at Meridian, without any check till he came near Okaloosa. Forrest was in that vicinity, and was ordered to retire before the enemy until he should effect a junction with the main body of the Confederate cavalry, under [Major General] Stephen D. Lee, when the whole force would fall upon Smith. Disregarding these orders, Forrest advanced upon the enemy and gave him battle in the open country about Okalona. The ground was a greatly undulating prairie, with occasional clumps of timber, and was altogether favorable for the movements of large bodies of cavalry. Forrest's whole force numbered 2,000 horsemen—the enemy about four times that number.

In the course of the action, Colonel [Jeff. E.] Forrest, a younger brother of the general, was killed. He was a daring officer, of excellent character, highly respected by the whole command and dearly loved by his brother. On hearing of his fall the general rode forward to where he lay, took him in his arms and kissed his dead face, then mounted his horse, ordered the charge to be sounded and led his body guard in person right into the enemy's ranks. His onset broke up their lines, and the defeat soon became a rout, which ended only at Memphis.

The body guard, or headquarters' company of his command was made up of the most daring men in the army. On one occasion, a year or so before the war ended, Forrest and I were seated on the portico of the headquarters at Meridian, when this company passed by on its way to water. I remarked: "General, you have the finest company of men and horses there I ever remember to have seen." "Yes," he said, "it is a fine company, and that is the eighth captain who has commanded it—all the other seven have been killed in battle."

The fact was, he with his body guard often took part in the fight, and generally at the critical moment, as at Okalona, when his opportune charge decided one of the most desperate battles he ever fought. He lost eleven field officers in the fight, killed or severely wounded. But he not only destroyed the cavalry column which was to cooperate with Sherman, but struck a panic into that general himself, who, on hearing of Forrest's victory, hastily abandoned his enterprise and ran back to Vicksburg with all speed. And thus did Forrest again save Mississippi.

It was after this, I think, that he captured Fort Pillow, and as so much has been said about "his ruthless butchery" of the garrison there, I will give my recollection of his own statement to me about it. I said to him one day: "I hear you shot some of your own men at Fort Pillow, how was that?" "Well," he said, "I'll tell you how that was. The boys had promised their wives and sweethearts to bring them a calico frock the first chance they got at a Yankee store, and while we were fighting our way up to the breastworks of Fort Pillow, I noticed the firing ceased all at once on the left of my line, and rode down that way to see what was the matter, and there was the sutler's store just broken open, and as I rode up one of the boys came out with his arms full of dry goods. I was so mad I dropped him with my pistol; right behind him came another, and he was a captain, and he, too, was loaded with plunder, and I shot him, too. They all went on with the fighting after that."

"Well," I said, "how about your shooting the Negroes after they had surrendered?" "Oh!" said he, "there has been a great deal of exaggeration and misrepresentation about that, and I'll tell you how that was. When we got into the fort the white flag was shown at once, and the Negroes ran out down to the river; and although the flag was flying, they kept on turning back and shooting at my men, who consequently continued to fire into them crowded on the brink of the river, and they killed a good many of them in spite of my efforts and those of their officers to stop them. But there was no deliberate intention nor effort to massacre the garrison as has been so generally reported by the northern papers."

In 1864 the writer was placed by the president of the Confederacy in command of the Department of Mississippi and Alabama, pending the arrival from the Trans-Mississippi Department of Lieutenant General [Richard] Taylor and the troops which he was to bring over with him. [Admiral David G.] Farragut was bombarding my forts in Mobile Bay, a large force was threatening North Alabama, and a large column under [Major General A. J.] Smith, estimated at

Forrest's Men Spill into Fort Pillow (*Harper's New Monthly Magazine*)

25,000 men of all arms, was preparing to move from Memphis into Mississippi down the Mississippi Central Railroad.

Forrest, with about 4,500 effective horsemen, was in north Mississippi, and I wrote him that I charged him with the entire responsibility of keeping the enemy out of all that portion of the state; that I should not assume to hamper him with any instructions, but left him full discretion in the premises; that I could not reinforce him with a man, but I would promptly help him to all the supplies he might need; and that finally I would be responsible for all the failures or disasters he might meet with, and he should have full credit for all the successes he might accomplish.

This sort of treatment from his commanding officer was not usual, and untrammeled all of his great powers. Smith soon moved out and began his progress very slowly, because of heavy rains and bad roads, down the Central Road from Grand Junction toward Grenada. Forrest held one brigade in front of the enemy, while he lay with the other over on the Mobile and Ohio Road, resting his men and horses. From there he telegraphed me in cipher: "I am unable to check the enemy's march, he is too strong; but, with your permission I will pass behind him to Memphis and destroy his depots of supply, and he will then be compelled to retreat." I replied: "Go as you propose, but don't be gone long, for I have only you to depend on to save that part of the state.

Not hearing from him for some days, and the enemy's column still continuing to advance, I became very uneasy and was only relieved by receiving a telegram from the operator at Senatobia on Saturday evening: "General Forrest's command has just passed at a gallop, bound for Memphis." Next morning the same operator telegraphed: "Heavy firing since daybreak in vicinity of Memphis." That relieved us all, the work was done—Mississippi was safe again!

After informing me of his plan and receiving my consent to its execution, he had remained about West Point, where supplies for men and beast were abundant, preparing the command of about 2,000 horses for the tremendous feat he performed with it. When the enemy had reached Oxford with his advance and pushed the brave [Brigadier General James R.] Chalmers, who had been constantly opposing him, backwards over the Youghony, Forrest darted across from West Point, fell furiously upon the advanced force, drove it out of Oxford, telegraphed Chalmers to come up at once, left him to occupy Oxford, and at 4:00 P.M. Friday evening, with 2,000 horsemen and four guns, he set out for Memphis.

The distance was ninety-eight miles; steady rains had soaked the roads until they were knee-deep in mud and all the streams were up to their banks, and he had to bridge three rivers to get his artillery and ordnance wagons over. He directed in person the building of three bridges, which were constructed of such materials as were found at hand; he had to tear down some neighboring houses to find the timber; but he got his guns safely over and rode into Memphis in the early dawn of Sunday morning!

The commanding general of the city escaped in a very scanty raiment out of the back door as his morning visitors entered by the front; and, like Joseph, he left his coat behind him. Seven of his staff officers were less fortunate and were made prisoners. One bright young Mississippi colonel gave a very funny account of how he searched the Grayoso House for prisoners: "We dismounted on the floor of the office, ran up the stairway and along the broad hall above where the first-class boarders were lodged, arousing the occupants of those luxurious chambers by the startling raps of saber hilts and pistol butts upon the mahogany doors. At every summons the door flew open and the occupants appeared accoutered as they were just when they sprang from their beds. Sometimes it was a man, sometimes a woman—sometimes both. One beautiful young lady sprang out of bed, threw her arms around my neck, and cried, 'For God's sake, don't kill me, sir.' 'Not for the world, madam,' said I, gently returning her embrace and leaving her regretfully for a less charming enemy."

The whole city was now aroused. The news that Forrest was in town spread like wildfire. The aching Confederate hearts bounded with joy and pride. The renegades and the Federals took such shelter as they could find. The few troops in the city, bravely commanded, threw themselves into a strong building from which they boldly defied all attempts at assault; and Forrest, not being prepared to carry on any operations involving delay, he left them in their stronghold and drew his men out of the city. In the course of the evening a flag came out borne by a staff officer of the general who so narrowly escaped capture in the morning, who now desired to make arrangements for the release of his captured officers and for the return of his own uniform.

Forrest described this ambassador as "a pretty saucy sort of fellow," who informed him that his commander intended to intercept him on his return. "Well," replied Forrest, "you tell him from me that I am going back the same way I came, and if he meets me on that road, I'll give him the worst licking he has ever had." He did this in *finesse*. For he did intend to return by the road he came, but he believed by telling the enemy so that all efforts would be made to intercept and pursue him on the other road, as the result proved. But, he said that after the major had gone off he began to think, "the blockheads may actually take me at my word." Consequently he lost no time on his return march, but got back to Oxford in about the same time his advance march had been made in.

He was neither pursued nor molested on his return, and had the satisfaction of having again saved Mississippi by his bold conception and rapid execution of an enterprise no other man living would have ventured upon. For no sooner did the commander of the Federal column hear, "Forrest is in Memphis," than he is said to have tossed his hands in the air, and exclaiming: "My God! all our stores are gone up!" ordered an immediate return to Memphis. This had become imperative, because the long continued rains had damaged the supplies with the column to such an extent that its progress could not be continued without fresh victuals and ammunition from the depots. Really Forrest's command had destroyed very little in Memphis and occasioned very little real loss of any sort to the enemy, and he had met with no loss himself, while causing in this extraordinary manner the abandonment of a very formidable campaign.

One of Forrest's most efficient and favorite associates was [Brigadier General Frank C.] Armstrong—himself a man of extraordinary ability, and with the peculiar qualifications of a great cavalry commander. Recently he related to me an illustration of Forrest's imperturbability under the most alarming circumstances. They were operating against [Major General David S.] Stanley in Tennessee. Armstrong in advance had struck the enemy's pickets and was pushing them rapidly before him. Forrest was riding with him. A battery and a rear guard of a regiment had stopped to water.

So rapidly had Armstrong been pressing the force before him that a gap of one or two miles was presented to Stanley, who swooped down upon this rearmost party and occupied the road behind Armstrong's division. A courier or staff officer at full speed bore the news of this disastrous condition of affairs to Forrest, and the excited messenger arriving within hail, bawled out his tidings thus: "General Forrest, Stanley has cut into the road behind you; has captured the battery and all of the rear guard, and is now moving along the pike right behind you to attack you in rear."

This was very startling. Armstrong says he felt all was up with his whole division, and so did Forrest; but to his surprise and amusement, without showing the slightest disconcertment, he heard Forrest shout out so that it was heard by most of the command: "Is he? Damn him! That's just where I've been trying to get him all day. Face about Armstrong, and go for him, and we'll give him hell!" Sure enough, the line was faced about, passed through the line of horses, met the enemy, drove him from the road, recaptured the battery and rear guard, and secured about one hundred cavalry prisoners. And to this day the whole of the men present with him believe that Forrest had laid a trap for the enemy into which he had fallen.

In the winter of 1865 and 1866 I was in the employment of an express company in New Orleans, and was sent over to Mobile on duty, which occupied me there several days. On the evening of my return to New Orleans, [Rear Admiral Raphael] Semmes, under a guard of marines, preceded me over the gang-plank of the steamer, bound to New Orleans and thence to New York, to be tried for piracy. The officer in command of the guard was quite a gentleman, expressed his regret for his unpleasant duty, and his hope that the admiral would feel that no unnecessary duress or surveillance would be exercised over him.

Accordingly, the prisoner and myself held a full and uninterrupted conference over the prospect before us, and we were both agreed that his arrest was but the commencement of a wholesale disregard of our paroles. Having recently seen in the papers allusions to the "massacre of Fort Pillow," I expected Forrest would be the next man arrested; and having to visit Memphis on business for my company, I tried to find Forrest and tell him what was on foot, and advise him to take care of himself. He was, however, down on his plantation, forty miles off, hard at work. So I wrote him a full account of Semmes' arrest and of his view and my own opinion of what we might all expect, and told him if I were in his place "I would not remain one night longer in this country." A warm friend and comrade of the general found a trusty messenger, a young captain who had served under him, to bear my letter and also letters of credit to enable him to procure funds abroad.

Having to leave Memphis next day, some weeks elapsed before I heard about Forrest's manner of receiving our well-intentioned mission. He simply remarked: "This is my country, and I'll be damned if anybody shall run me out of it; and I will stay here on my plantation and attend to my business peaceably so long as they will let me alone."

On the first convenient occasion which took him to Memphis, he made a personal call on the general commanding, in order, as he expressed it, "to know at once what your government means to do about my case." The general replied: "I do not know, General Forrest, what you refer to, and have received no orders especially relating to you." "Well," he said, "I hear they are about to make arrests of paroled officers because of their acts during the war—that Admiral Semmes is now in arrest and to be tried on charges of piracy, and that there is talk of arresting me, so I thought I would call and let you know I am now quietly engaged at work on my plantation; am trying to support my family, as every peaceable citizen should, and am strictly obeying the obligations of my parole. But I desire to know whether your government is going to regard that parole or not, and have come to hear about it from you, and I will say that if I am not to be protected by it, I have only to sound the call to have thousands of my old men serve me and we can guerrilla it around here for ten years and all your forces can't prevent it. And, general, there is another thing I'll mention—your government might hang me forty times and it would not be even with me."

He was assured there was no known purpose to interfere with him, and the general good-naturedly advised him to make himself easy, and go on attending to his business as heretofore, and he would not be molested in any way. Forrest was probably the only man living who would not have put himself beyond danger of arrest under those circumstances and at that time.

When Mobile was besieged I had been assured that Forrest, with all the available forces of the department, would be sent to my succor, and was very confident of holding the place till he would be in position to strike the besieging army. Within a few days after the attack on my works began I heard of the disasters which had befallen the little army of Forrest and knew that nothing was left to me but to make time and to save my garrison after having protracted the defense to the utmost. On April 12, 1865, I marched out of the city of Mobile with the rear guard (300 Louisianians, commanded by Colonel Robert Lindsay, now of Shreveport) and notified the enemy that no opposition would be made to its peaceable occupation by his forces.

We marched to Meridian, where were soon assembled the principal commanders of the department and the relics of the armies of the Confederacy. Among these was Forrest. General [Robert E.] Lee had then surrendered. The capitulation of General Joseph Johnston soon followed, and by the terms which that able man procured for his comrades in arms and his countrymen made us feel that amid the general ruin of our fortunes there was yet hope left for us that the laying down of our arms would be the end of the war. Each day brought us news of some fresh misfortune to our cause, and sad, indeed, were our conferences with each other. Forrest alone seemed undismayed. There was nothing forced or unnatural in his cheerfulness. It was the equipoise resulting from the combination of the great qualities which composed his mind and character, which could not be disturbed by any course of human events, and which imparted sustaining power to his comrades of that dark hour.

Soon after meeting him I said: "I heard you were wounded at Selma the other day; were you hurt much?" "Oh, no!" he said; "I'll tell you how that was. Armstrong's division was trying to hold [Major General James H.] Wilson's column in check until reinforcements could get to him, and [Brigadier General Daniel W.] Adams and I had gone to the telegraph office to dispatch orders, when a boy came running in and said: 'The Yanks are a-coming.'"

We ran to the door and sure enough a large squad of them were galloping right for us. Our horses were hitched to the fence near by, and we ran for them and mounted. Dan Adams had a smarter horse than mine, and he got off all right. But a big, yellow-haired Dutchman, on a very fine horse, overtook me and began cutting at me with his saber. The sword was not sharp, but he hit me with it, sometimes on the head and sometimes on my arm, and all the time I was dodging his cuts and trying to get out my pistol, but somehow it had got hitched, so that I couldn't draw it for a long time, and I kept getting madder and madder all the time, so that when at last I got it out I just dropped my reins and caught the Dutchman by the hair and drew him toward me and fired two loads right into his heart. He bruised me a little, that's all.

By May 14, 1865, all of Forrest's command and of mine had been paroled, and we were endeavoring to get to our ruined homes. Forrest went direct from where his forces had been bivouacked, near Canton, across the state to a plantation on the Mississippi, and went to work. Several years later he organized a railroad company to construct a road from Memphis to Selma. He was not effectually supported by those on whose aid he had counted, and the great panic of 1873 and other causes combined against him and for the first time he was defeated.

I saw him about the climax of his troubles and he seemed quite depressed in health and spirits. He said to me: "General, I am broke every way—broke in health, broke in fortune, broke in spirit." And as I observed his changed appearance, how his form had lost its robustness and erectness and his general appearance of declining vitality, I feared his race was nearly run. Even his iron frame could not meet the demands of his energy and will, and he closed his extraordinary career at an age when most men begin to achieve their greatest works.

PART 4

The Eastern Theatre in 1862

12

In the Air above Yorktown
George Armstrong Custer, Major General, U.S.V.

NO DELAY was submitted to in pushing the preparation for the siege of Yorktown to a speedy completion. [Brigadier General William F. "Baldy"] Smith's division was posted near the left of the line, and opposite Lee's and Wynn's Mills.

An engineer of admitted ability himself, he exercised an intelligent supervision over the construction of the works to be thrown up on his front. Working parties of immense strength were kept in employment by reliefs day and night. Work was carried on in the trenches during the night, their close proximity to the enemy's batteries rendering it impracticable during the hours of daylight. In the daytime other parties were employed constructing gabions and fascines, filling sandbags, and completing earthworks which were far enough advanced to afford protection against the enemy's fire. The nearest work to any point of the enemy's line thrown up by the Army of the Potomac was a small rifle pit, whose plan and construction was assigned the writer. The enemy had a battery erected opposite what was then known as Garrow's Chimneys, near which point General Smith proposed to erect quite an extensive work, to be occupied by artillery and infantry.

So annoying had the enemy's artillery and sharpshooters become that working parties were continually interrupted in their labors. As a counter-annoyance it was decided to throw up a simple rifle pit on a point of timbered land separated from the enemy's battery only by the Warwick [River], which at this point had by artificial means been widened so as to extend about 150 yards from bank to bank. In marking out the rifle pit the utmost caution had to be exercised to prevent the enemy from becoming apprised of the design. No word was spoken above a whisper, as the voices of the enemy could be distinctly heard while engaged in ordinary conversation; even the breaking of twigs under their feet, as they moved about in the woods, could be heard.

Brevet Captain George A. Custer (left), April 1863 (*Century*)

Fortunately the soil was sandy and loose, thus rendering unnecessary the use of the pick, the slightest blow of which might have been carried to the enemy's ears. The shovel, less objectionable, and at the same time more efficient, was used to advantage. It was surprising how rapidly 100 men, each wielding a shovel, threw up the intended work. Never, perhaps, did a working party labor more earnestly or steadily. Conversation of course was out of the question; each man knew that the enemy's battery, supported by his sharpshooters, was within easy range, and no one knew how soon the enemy might discern what was going on; it was of course the purpose of all engaged to push the work forward as rapidly as possible, at least until it would afford cover from the enemy's guns, which by daylight would certainly open upon them.

The work, though insignificant, performed its part well. Before daylight it was so far advanced as to be ready for its occupants. Two companies of [Colonel Hiram] Berdan's sharpshooters were quietly conducted to it, and when daylight dawned the enemy found fronting them, and almost under their guns, a small but most troublesome garrison, entirely protected from their fire. The sharpshooters took particular delight in their little stronghold, as it afforded them a fine opportunity to exercise their peculiar accomplishment, an opportunity they were not slow to improve. And from the date of their occupation of the work, their accurate and destructive fire compelled the enemy to cease his annoyance to the working parties on his front, and virtually deprived him of any further practical use of what was then termed the "one-gun battery."

In addition to the duties devolving upon me as an assistant to Lieutenant [Nicolas] Bowen, and which were strictly those pertaining to his corps, there was one other duty to which General Smith assigned me, which was of so peculiar a character as to deserve particular mention. It was neither more nor less than making balloon ascensions, at stated times, to observe the enemy, and detect if possible any changes in the number of his works or location of his troops.

Strong doubts have been expressed as to the practical utility of balloons in war. Much depends upon the character of the country and the proximity of the opposing lines to each other. The large majority of the army, without giving it a personal test, condemned and ridiculed the system of balloon reconnaissances. One powerful reason inducing the opinion was that the ascensions were generally made by the professional aeronauts, Professor [Thaddeus S. C.] Lowe and his assistants, and they frequently reported having seen "clouds of dust," "a heavy column of troops moving," "new earthworks being erected," "a large encampment on the right," "great activity along the enemy's works," all of which might have been true; but there were no means of verifying it nor of refuting it so long as only professionals made the ascensions. And it was a common remark in the army, when referring to any report made as the result of a balloon reconnaissance, that "it was to the interest of the aeronauts to magnify their statements and render their own importance greater, thereby insuring themselves what might be profitable employment; and they could report whatever their imagination prompted them to, with no fear of contradiction."

Whether it was with any such impression, or from other motives, that General Smith determined to send an officer to make ascensions, is not known, nor is it material. I was directed by the general to make a reconnaissance in a balloon, an order which was received with no little trepidation; for although I had chosen the mounted service from preference alone, yet I had a choice as to the

The Army of the Potomac Marching on Yorktown (*Campfire and Battlefield*)

character of the mount, and the proposed ride was far more elevated than I had ever desired or contemplated. It was a kind of danger that few persons have schooled themselves against, and still fewer possess a liking for. The balloon was usually allowed to ascend 1,000 feet, and was there retained by ropes or guys extending to the ground, and held by men detailed for that purpose.

What tended to diminish admiration for this style of warfare was an incident in which [Major] General Fitz John Porter was the leading character. He had ascended in one of the balloons alone, and after reaching a perilous height the rope restraining the ascent, which had become weakened by contact with the acid used in inflating the balloon, broke, and General Porter, much against his will, found himself being rapidly carried not only upward, but over in the direction of the enemy. Thousands of soldiers who had witnessed his ascent, and had seen the accident, now watched his course with breathless interest. Fortunately General Porter had, prior to starting, informed himself regarding the valve cord, by which the gas is allowed to escape and the balloon lowered.

With his wonted coolness and presence of mind, he pulled this cord, opened the valve, and soon found his ascent changed to descent; but owing to his inexperience with balloons, he allowed too much gas to escape, and the descent became not only rapid, but dangerous. Fortunately the branches of a tree were encountered, and the balloon caught and secured, the general narrowly escaping what seemed likely to prove a serious disaster.

I was told to take with me in my balloon ascent a field glass, compass, pencil, and notebook. With these I was supposed to be able, after attaining the proper elevation, to discover, locate, and record the works and encampments of the enemy. The balloon was kept but a short distance from General Smith's headquarters, fastened to the earth by numerous ropes, like a wild and untamable animal.

Thither I proceeded, my mind not entirely free from anxious doubts as to how the expedition would terminate. The person in charge, having been previously notified, had everything in readiness for the ascent. Previous to this time I had never even examined a balloon except from a distance. Being interested in their construction, I was about to institute a thorough examination of all its parts, when the aeronaut announced that all was ready. He inquired whether I desired to go up alone, or he should accompany me. My desire, if frankly expressed, would have been not to go up at all; but if I was to go, company was certainly desirable. With an attempt at indifference, I intimated that he might go along.

The basket in which we were to be transported was about two feet high, four feet long, and slightly over half as wide, resembling in every respect an ordinary willow basket of the same dimensions, minus the handles. This basket was attached to the cords of the balloon. Stepping inside, my assistant, after giving directions to the men holding the four ropes, told me to take my place in the basket. I complied, and before being fully aware that such was the fact, found that we were leaving *terra firma,* and noiselessly, almost imperceptibly, were ascending toward the clouds.

The assistant was standing upright, supporting himself by the iron band placed for that purpose about two feet above the top of the basket. I was urged to stand up also. My confidence in balloons at that time was not sufficient, however, to justify such a course, so I remained seated in the bottom of the basket, with a firm hold upon either side. I first turned my attention to the manner in which the basket had been constructed. To me it seemed fragile indeed, and not intended to support a tithe of the weight then imposed upon it. The interstices in the sides and bottom seemed immense, and the further we receded from the earth the larger they seemed to become, until I almost imagined one might tumble through. I interrogated my companion as to whether the basket was actually and certainly safe. He responded affirmatively; at the same time, as if to confirm his assertion, he began jumping up and down to prove the strength of the basket, and no doubt to reassure me. Instead, however, my fears were redoubled, and I expected to see the bottom of the basket giving way, and one or both of us dashed to the earth. These fears, I afterward found, were absurd; the basket was supported by a number of small but powerful steel bands, rendering it capable of sustaining an immense burden.

Gradually I became more familiar with the car, by which title the basket was dignified, and was able to cease estimating our altitude and turn to the contemplation of the magnificent scenery which lay spread out beneath and around us as far as the eye could extend. To the right could be seen the York River, following which the eye could rest on Chesapeake Bay. On the left, and at about the same distance, flowed the James River, afterward destined to play so important a part in the termination of the great struggle which was then but in its infancy. Between these two rivers extended a most beautiful landscape, and no less interesting than beautiful; it was being made the theatre of operations of armies larger and more formidable than had ever confronted each other on this continent before. It had been the scene of former military operations, which though less extensive were probably not less important in their results. Yorktown, which could be seen far in the distance, as it rested on the right bank of the York river, had witnessed the surrender of a disciplined and tried army of veterans, commanded by the brave and distinguished officers, to an army its inferior in equipment, discipline, and experience, equal if not superior, however, in courage, but surely stronger in the justness of the cause for which it contended. Going back even beyond the days of the American Revolution, much could be recalled of great historic interest with which the peninsula was intimately and inseparably connected. Jamestown, noted as the first settlement made by the whites, was located but a few miles from the ground then occupied by the opposing armies. Here too occurred the incidents upon which is based the familiar story of Pocahontas and her generous conduct toward John Smith.

A Federal Observation Balloon on the Peninsula (*Century*)

I endeavored to locate and recognize the different points of interest, as they lay spread out over the vast surface upon which the eye could rest. The point over which the balloon was held was probably one mile from the nearest point of the enemy's line. In an open country balloons would be invaluable in discovering the location of the enemy's camp and works. Unfortunately, however, the enemy's camps, like our own, were generally pitched in the woods to avoid the intense heat of a summer sun; his earthworks along the Warwick were also concealed by growing timber, so that it would have been necessary for the aeronaut to attain the highest possible altitude and then secure a position directly above the country to be examined.

With the assistance of a good field glass, and watching opportunities when the balloon was not rendered unsteady by the different currents of air, I was enabled to catch glimpses of canvas through openings in the forest, while camps located in the open space were as plainly visible as those of the Army of the Potomac. Here and there the dim outline of an earthwork could be seen more than half concealed by the trees which had been purposely left standing on their front. Guns could be seen mounted and peering sullenly through the embrasures, while men in considerable numbers were standing in and around the entrenchment, often collected in groups, intently observing the balloon, curious, no doubt, to know the character or value of the information its occupants could derive from their elevated post of observation.

After noting such of my observations as were deemed important, I signified my desire to descend. The aeronaut gave the signal to those in charge below, and we were gradually lowered to the ground, the motion of the balloon being so noiseless and easy that it was only perceptible to us by the change in the relative position of objects located on the ground's surface. Proceeding to General Smith's headquarters, I submitted my report of the reconnaissance, and was then informed by the general that I would be required to repeat my aerial expeditions from time to time; an announcement that was not received with the reluctance attending the reception of the first order to this effect. Subsequently I made ascensions almost daily, principally to ascertain if any change in the enemy's position was observable.

The obstruction which the forests offered to a satisfactory view of the enemy's camp suggested the idea that by making the ascension during the hours of darkness the camp fires of the enemy might afford a more positive index of his strength and position than the faint glimpse previously obtained of his canvas tents. Upon imparting this suggestion to General Smith, I was authorized to try the proposed plan, which I did the succeeding night. It being summer, however, but few fires were maintained, so that my reconnaissance immediately after darkness had cast its shadow over the two contending hosts resulted in adding but little to the information already possessed. Resolved to give the experiment another test before condemning it, I determined to ascend just at reveille, which was a short time before daylight, and thus have an opportunity to observe the mess fires which must necessarily be kindled before dawn.

The result fulfilled my expectations. The campfires of the enemy could be plainly seen at many points of their line, and an approximate idea of the enemy's strength at various points could be formed, while fires were clearly distinguishable in many localities where it had been impossible to detect the presence of the enemy by observations during the day.

So satisfied was General Smith with the information derived in this manner, that ascensions were frequently ordered to be made thereafter in the morning before daylight. Upon the evening of May 3 [1862], the division commander directed me to make two ascensions during the night, one immediately after dark, the other just before reveille. Nothing unusual was observed during the first ascent; the second was made about 2:00 A.M.; heavy fires were visible in the vicinity of Yorktown, resembling the burning of ordinary dwelling houses, while at brief intervals the flash and report such as attend the discharge of heavy ordnance was observable. In watching these unusual occurrences, and reasoning upon their probable causes, no attention was given to time until the sounding of reveille in the camps along the line of the Army of the Potomac, and the springing up of innumerable fires, warned me of the near approach of daylight. Suspicions were then excited by the fact that the fires usually observable along the enemy's line were entirely wanting.

As yet no idea of evacuation had occurred to me. Remaining in my position until the dawn of day enabled me to inspect the works of the enemy which were visible, the entire absence of their usual occupants surprised me. A second and more careful examination convinced me that the works of the enemy were deserted. Descending as rapidly as possible, I hastened to General Smith's headquarters to report my information to him. It was scarcely daylight. I met the general at the opening of his tent; he had been aroused by a couple of contrabands who had just come through the Union picket lines and reported that the enemy had evacuated his entire line, and was retreating toward Williamsburg.

The general, just awakened from a sound slumber, could scarcely believe the report, and seeing me approach hastily, repeated the substance of the contrabands' statement, as if in doubt concerning its correctness. I then reported to him the result of my observations that morning, all of which confirmed the contrabands' story. A dispatch containing this report was at once sent over the military telegraph to [Major General George B.] McClellan; at the same time the troops were ordered under arms.

General McClellan telegraphed in reply directing General Smith to advance his command and determine the truth or falsity of the reported evacuation, at the same time informing him that a similar report had been made on the right of the line. Smith's three brigades, led by [Brigadier General Winfield S.] Hancock, [Brigadier General William T. H.] Brooks, and [Colonel Francis L.] Vinton, were soon in readiness to advance.

Brooks's men were the first to enter the enemy's works in front of Smith's position. The enemy had stripped his entrenchments on the right of all their armament, and left nothing behind of value. On the left it was different. He had been unable to remove vast quantities of ordnance and military stores, all of which fell into the hands of his opponent. Compelling the enemy to evacuate without much bloodshed or loss of life was made the cause of considerable outcry against General McClellan by his enemies in the North.

As soon as it was definitely determined that the Confederates had withdrawn their forces, [Brigadier General George] Stoneman's cavalry and flying artillery were sent in pursuit to harass the movements of the enemy, and if possible bring him to bay until the army could overtake and attack him. [Brigadier General Joseph] Hooker's division was ordered to support Stoneman by moving on the Yorktown and Williamsburg road, while Smith's division was ordered forward by the Lee's Mill and Williamsburg road.

About two miles from Williamsburg, and near the junction of these two roads, the Confederates had erected in the fall of 1861 a system of detached earthworks, consisting of thirteen redoubts, the principal and center one, Fort Magruder, being a large, well constructed, but irregular work, with two bastioned fronts. A few rifle pits had also been thrown up, and the heavy timber in front had been slashed so effectually as to bar the progress of any organized body of troops, infantry skirmishers alone being able to overcome the obstacles. This line the enemy concluded to hold in order to delay the pursuit and give time

The Peninsular Campaign (*Century*)

for the removal of his artillery and trains. Here it was that Stoneman's cavalry and artillery were repulsed on the afternoon of May 4, and compelled to retire.

Later in the day Smith's division reached the ground, [Brigadier General Edwin V.] Sumner, as senior officer present, assumed command, and in obedience to the positive orders of General McClellan, who had been detained at Yorktown superintending the embarkation of [Brigadier General William B.] Franklin's division, an immediate attack of the enemy's position was ordered.

It was then after sundown, and before the troops could be got in motion, utter and complete darkness had set in. The courier from General McClellan had arrived too late to render any organized plan of attack practicable. General Sumner realized this fact, but, too good a soldier to disobey or evade an order, he determined to carry out his instructions. All the principal officers who had reached the front, including Generals [Brigadier General Erasmus D.] Keyes, Baldy Smith, Hancock, Brooks, and others, were assembled mounted, forming a group about General Sumner, who had chosen his headquarters for the expected engagement. After giving what few directions the limited time rendered practicable, General Sumner, that splendid type of a veteran soldier, concluded with the remark, "Gentlemen, at the third tap of the drum the entire command will advance to the attack." Unfortunately the almost impenetrable darkness prevented any attempt at an organized or concentrated movement, and produced almost inextricable confusion the moment the line commenced the advance.

Fearing that the troops might fire into each other, and no correct knowledge being had of the location of the enemy's works, the order for the attack was countermanded, and the different regiments bivouacked for the remainder of the night. By daylight on the morning of May 5 Hooker's division, which during the fourth had exchanged positions with that of Smith, found itself confronting the enemy's works on Smith's left. General Sumner reconnoitered the enemy's position early on the morning of the fifth. Captain [Charles S.] Stewart and Lieutenant [Francis V.] Farquhar, both of the Engineer Corps, in examining the enemy's left in front of Smith, had discovered that the redoubt on the extreme left of the enemy's line, and which covered a very important crossing, was unoccupied.

This intelligence was conveyed to General Sumner, who directed Smith to occupy this work with one brigade. Hancock's brigade was selected for this ser-

Fort Magruder and Other Confederate Earthworks (*Century*)

vice. By permission of General Smith, the writer of this tendered his services to General Hancock for that day, which tender was accepted, and in this way a personal association with the Battle of Williamsburg was enjoyed which otherwise would not have been probable.

Hooker attacked the enemy's position on his front at 7:30 A.M., and for a while was successful in his efforts. Had Hancock's movement on the right been made simultaneously with the attack of Hooker on the left, it is strongly probable that the battle would have been decided against the Confederates, and at but little cost to their opponents, as it was evident on that day, and has been confirmed since, that the severest fighting done by the army during that engagement was by troops who had retreated beyond Williamsburg, and were brought back to the battlefield at the double quick. Hooker, whose temperament was such that he could contend against heavy odds with the same fervor and determination as when opposed by equal or inferior numbers, forced the fighting, and succeeded in silencing the guns of the enemy's principal work, Fort Magruder. Had he been supported or his flanks protected, he could have cleared his entire front of all resistance. The enemy not having anything to occupy his attention on his left, and believing the principal efforts of his antagonist to be directed against his right, concentrated all his strength against Hooker, extending his line so as to overlap Hooker's left.

In his official report of the battle Hooker very pertinently states that "Being in pursuit of a retreating army, I deemed it my duty to lose no time in making the disposition of my forces to attack, regardless of their number and position, except to accomplish the result with the least possible sacrifice of life. By so doing my division, if it did not capture the army before me, would at least hold them in order that some others might. Besides I knew of the presence of more than 30,000 troops not two miles distant from me, and that within twelve miles (four hours' march) was the bulk of the Army of the Potomac. My own position was tenable for double that length of time against three times my number."

Although General Hooker was somewhat in error regarding the actual number of troops which might have supported him, there is no doubt that his reasoning was correct and his plan would undoubtedly have won had it been executed. It was by the adoption of similar principles that the closing battles near Richmond were, under [Major General Philip H.] Sheridan's leadership, made Federal victories, instead of defeats or drawn battles. Hooker, finding himself pressed by superior numbers, repeatedly asked for reinforcements. [Brigadier General Philip] Kearny with his famous division was ordered to Hooker's support at 10:30 A.M., but owing to the almost impassable condition of the roads, was unable to reach the battlefield until late in the afternoon, by which time Hooker, after repulsing several desperate assaults, found his supply of ammunition exhausted and his ranks terribly thinned by the enemy's fire.

Kearny quickly occupied with his division the line held by Hooker, while the weary but not disheartened troops of the latter were withdrawn and held in reserve until the battle ended. Kearny with his accustomed vigor attacked the enemy, and with success; but darkness prevented him from rendering his victory decisive. His loss was severe, yet not so heavy as that of Hooker, whose total loss in this engagement was 1,575.

In obedience to his orders, Hancock conducted his brigade to the unoccupied redoubt on the enemy's left. Before reaching it, it was necessary to cross a narrow dam over which it was barely possible to march infantry in column of fours. Half a regiment stationed in the redoubt could have held the crossing against an entire division. It was certainly a great oversight upon the part of the enemy to leave so important an approach not only unguarded, but unwatched. Meeting with no opposition, Hancock, after crossing his brigade, bore to the left in the direction of Fort Magruder, the center of the enemy's line. Two of the enemy's redoubts, located between Fort Magruder and the crossing, were found occupied. Against these Hancock directed his attack, and with the assistance of his battery of artillery he soon drove the enemy from the redoubts and occupied them with a portion of his brigade. Fort Magruder was still beyond the fire of his battery, posted near the captured redoubt. A position in advance of the latter was obtained from which a well directed fire was poured into Fort Magruder, giving great annoyance to the occupants of the fort.

Hancock's orders prevented him from advancing beyond the position he then held. The strength of his force, however, would not have justified him in proceeding against Fort Magruder unless closely supported by at least twice his own numbers. His position was such, however, that with a reasonable force at his command Fort Magruder, and consequently the enemy's entire line, was untenable the moment he chose to advance. Fully impressed with the importance of the point he held, Hancock, as early as 11:00 A.M., sent a staff officer back to represent the situation of affairs and to request reinforcements. The request was delivered to General Smith, the division commander, who, heartily approving of Hancock's views, urged General Sumner, then senior officer on the field, to grant the request. General Sumner, anxious regarding Hooker's position on the left, declined, and instead directed Hancock to hold his ground, but not to advance.

Again Hancock sent a staff officer, urging in stronger terms the importance of promptly reinforcing him in order that he might at once decide the battle by driving the enemy from their works. From his position to Sumner's headquarters by the circuitous route necessary to be taken was several miles. Hancock awaited the reply to his second appeal with unfeigned anxiety. It came, and instead of acceding to his request, it directed him to relinquish the vantage ground already gained, and which furnished the key to the enemy's position, and to retire to the redoubt covering the crossing over the dam. It was 2:00 P.M. when the last messenger arrived.

Those who have seen Hancock when affairs with which he was connected were not conducted in conformity with his views can imagine the manner in which he received the order to retire. Never at a loss for expletives, and with feelings wrought up by the attendant circumstances, Hancock was not at all loth to express his condemnation of the policy which from his standpoint was not only plainly unnecessary, but in the end must prove disastrous. His was a difficult position to occupy so far as he personally was concerned. After receiving the order to withdraw, rendered more imperative from the fact of its being a reply to his request for authority and troops to enable him to advance, his first duty as a soldier was to obey. His judgment rebelled against such a course and urged him to remain and make one more effort to secure the adoption of his views. The responsibility was great, but he assumed it, trusting to events to justify his course. Another staff officer was sent back, bearing a most urgent appeal from Hancock for assistance, and more fully explaining the importance of his position. Taking out his watch, Hancock, in conversation with the writer, remarked, "It is now two o'clock. I shall wait till four: if no reply reaches me from headquarters, I will then withdraw."

The moments flew by until an hour had elapsed since the departure of the last messenger, and still no reply from headquarters. Hancock's impatience, of which he has ever seemed to have an inexhaustible supply, increased with each passing moment. But little was going on in his front save the usual sharpshooting between skirmishers at long range, yet each discharge of a musket seemed to add to the anxiety of him whose imperturbability had never rendered him remarkable. A fourth staff officer was dispatched at a gallop to hasten, if possible, the expected and long-hoped-for message from "Old Bull," as General Sumner was familiarly termed by the entire army. Messenger after messenger was ordered upon this errand, until the hour hand marked the hour of four, and still no orders came. It was hard for the young brigade commander to relinquish the victory which he justly believed was within his grasp.

He had said he would withdraw at 4:00 P.M., but when the hour arrived it found him still anxious and eager to carry out his first plan of battle, and with a faltering hope, he said, "I will wait a half hour longer; if no orders reach me during that time, I must retire."

He was then without a staff officer, aides, adjutant general, and all having been hurried back for orders and reinforcements. Hancock had scarcely uttered the last resolve to defer his withdrawal half an hour, when the firing in the woods on his front and right suddenly became brisk and indicated a change in affairs. The battery and two of Hancock's regiments had been thrown about half a mile to the front of the last redoubt captured from the enemy, preparatory to withdrawing; and not desiring to provoke an attack from the enemy, Hancock, through the writer, directed the battery commander to retire to the crest on which the redoubt was located and take position on the left of near the redoubt.

While receiving the order from Hancock the enemy displayed a fresh force on his front and near the woods which extended from near Fort Magruder along Hancock's right flank to a point considerably in rear of the latter's right. The firing from the skirmishers became heavier. The order for the battery to retire had been given none too soon. By the time it had withdrawn to the designated position at least a brigade of the enemy's infantry could be seen forming in column of regiments within easy range of Hancock's guns. At the same time a considerable force of cavalry dashed from the woods and charged toward the most advanced regiment of Hancock's, which at that time was assembling its skirmishers and preparing to rejoin the main line near the redoubt.

At this date, and without any guide but memory, it is believed the regiment referred to was the Fourth Wisconsin infantry, commanded by Major Cobb.[1] Seeing the enemy's cavalry approach as if preparing to charge, [Colonel] Cobb rapidly formed his regiment into a hollow square, and opened an oblique fire upon the cavalry. The latter advanced at the charge, and approached quite near to the square; but seeing no evidence of fright or tendency to flee upon the part of the infantry, and finding the fire of the latter becoming quite destructive, they wheeled their horses and sought safety under cover of the woods. [Colonel] Cobb then prepared to rejoin General Hancock with his command, but by this time the enemy's column of infantry were prepared to attack, and advanced toward the ground occupied by the Wisconsin troops who were already in motion, and received the first fire from the enemy while marching to the rear.

They might have been excused if they had broken in disorder and trusted their safety to the speed of their running, being fresh troops and this their first battle. Instead, however, they faced about, and with almost marvellous courage and obstinacy returned the fire of the enemy; and although outnumbered ten to one, and forced to give way both by orders and superior force, they retired in good order, contesting the ground step by step, delaying the enemy's advance, and contributing to a great degree to the victory which was to follow, if not actually saving the day; slightly disorganizing the enemy's organization, and delaying the latter until Hancock could complete his dispositions for receiving the attack.

In the excitement attending the first preparation for the attack the guns of the battery were badly handled. In loading one of them the ball was rammed down before the powder. This so enraged Hancock that he ordered the battery to be withdrawn and moved to the rear. It is probable also that this order was partly precautionary, as the prospect then seemed most unfavorable for a successful issue to the Federal arms. If the attack should terminate in a rout, the Union troops would be compelled to retreat over an open space nearly two miles in extent, then cross the narrow passage over the dam which would only permit infantry to cross by fours. Looking to a retreat, it was perhaps prudent to send the battery in time.

The intention of the enemy was now plainly evident. Their column of at-

---

1. It was the Fifth Wisconsin infantry, commanded by Colonel Amasa Cobb.

tack advanced boldly across the open space in Hancock's front, giving the Federal troops an opportunity, for the first time, of hearing the Southern yell, which ever afterward was made an important auxiliary in every charge or assault made by the Confederates. Hancock's troops were hastily formed in a single line, extending along the crest upon which the enemy had located one of his redoubts, but which Hancock had carried in the early part of the day. Hancock's men were so disposed that the redoubt occupied about the center of his line.

Into this redoubt the [Fifth] Wisconsin was hurried after its first struggle with the enemy. Between the termination of the struggle and the opening of the enemy's final attack upon Hancock's main line there was a brief interval during which there was little or no firing. The enemy were advancing rapidly and confidently. Hancock, deprived of the assistance of every member of his own staff, none having returned from the division commander, busied himself by riding along the line encouraging his men and urging them to do their duty in the fast approaching struggle. "Aim low, men—aim low," was his oft-repeated injunction; and, "Do not be in a hurry to fire until they come nearer."

The enemy was somewhat disconcerted at the cool manner in which their opponents quietly awaited the onset, and this determined manner undoubtedly operated strongly upon the Confederate troops in causing them to disregard the injunction of their division general, [Major General Daniel H.] Hill, who in a speech to them just prior to beginning the assault had told them that the Federals possessed better firearms at long range than they, and their only hope of victory depended upon the bayonet. "Depend upon it, men," said he, "the Yankees cannot stand cold steel." This was the reason the Confederates advanced, after their encounter with the Wisconsin troops, without firing. Gradually losing confidence in the assurances of General Hill, they opened a scattering fire upon the Federals, but as this fire was delivered while advancing, the aim was necessarily defective, and produced little or no damage. Although the enemy had advanced nearly 1,000 yards across an open and nearly level plain, within easy range of the guns of Hancock's men, the latter permitted them to approach undisturbed.

At first this was a necessity, as the Wisconsin troops, while contending against the advance of the enemy, were directly between them and Hancock's line, and prevented them from taking part; this obstacle no longer existed after the enemy had approached within 300 yards of the crest on which the Federals had determined to make a stand. The Wisconsin troops having joined the main force, and taken position within the redoubt, the opening fire of the enemy was made the signal for Hancock's men to return the fire, while the exultant yell of the Southerner met with an equally defiant response from his countryman of the North.

Hancock, realizing to the fullest extent his precarious situation, strove in every possible manner to inspire his troops with confidence. To him the coming contest was destined to become more than an ordinary victory or defeat: if the former, all would be well, and no unhappy criticisms would follow him; if defeat—and defeat under the circumstances implied the loss or capture of most if not all of his command—then death upon the battlefield was far preferable, to the sensitive and high-minded soldier, to the treatment which would be meted out to him, who in violation of positive orders had repeatedly declined to withdraw his command, but had remained until obedience was no longer practicable, and his command was threatened with annihilation. It was probably with thoughts of defeat, and its personal consequences of a court martial for disobedience of orders, that at the moment when the fighting on both sides became terribly in earnest, and the firing loudest, Hancock, galloping along his lines hat in hand, the perfect model of a field marshal that he has since proven himself to be, in tones which even the din of battle could not drown, appealed to his troops, saying, "Men, you must hold this ground, or I am ruined."

It was but the utterance of the thought that was passing through his mind at that moment, and it neither checked nor added to the ardor with which Hancock deports himself in battle. His brilliant, dashing courage, displayed upon scores of battlefields since the one here referred to, has shown that he requires no personal motive to inspire him to deeds of heroism. The Confederates, with courage which has never been surpassed by the troops upon either side, boldly advanced, delivering their fire as rapidly as possible, and never ceasing to utter their inspiring battle cry. The Federals, favored by circumstances, were enabled to deliver a far more effective fire than their assailants.

About forty yards in front of Hancock's line, and parallel to it, was an ordinary rail fence. The advanced line of the Confederates reached this fence; and had they been less brave, or had they been the veterans of either army, who four years later had been thoroughly schooled into the idea that breastworks and courage were almost inseparable adjuncts in the art of war, it is probable that their advance would never have crossed the fence, but, protected by the questionable cover of the rails, would have made a stand, and from there returned the terribly destructive fire their enemies were pouring into their ranks. The fence seemed to offer no obstacle, however, to the assaulting column, which still advanced, as it had started, in four heavy lines. But thirty paces now separated the contending forces, and neither exhibited signs of wavering. The Confederates were losing ten to one of the Federals, the latter, unlike the former, delivering their fire from a halt, and with deliberate aim. The Wisconsin men, being still more favorably situated and protected behind the earthen parapet of the redoubt, and probably smarting under the recollection of their treatment at the hands of the Confederates a few moments previous, gladly improved their opportunity to retaliate upon their late victors.

When within twenty paces of the Federal troops, the fire of whose guns remained unabated, the Confederates, whose ranks had been terribly thinned, and who, from their long and rapid march across a heavy and yielding soil, added to their constant yelling since the opening of the attack, were much exhausted, now exhibited signs of faltering. The Federals, who but a moment before regarded vic-

tory as most doubtful, observed this hesitation, and gave forth cheers of exultation. Hancock, who had been constantly seen where the danger was most imminent, and who, with one exception, was the only mounted officer along the
Federal line, saw that victory was within his grasp and determined to resume the
offensive. With that excessive politeness of manner which characterizes him when
everything is being conducted according to his liking, Hancock, as if conducting guests to a banquet rather than fellow beings to a life-and-death struggle, cried
out in tones well befitting a Stentor: "*Gentlemen*, charge with the bayonet."

The order was responded to with a hearty cheer from the entire line, and
immediately the men—no, the *gentlemen*—brought their bayonets down to the
position of the charge, and moved forward to the encounter. The Confederates,
already wavering, required but this last effort upon the part of their opponents
to relinquish the contest. Not waiting to receive the charge, they began their
retreat, which soon terminated in a rout. The Federals, less exhausted than their
late assailants, were able to overtake and capture large numbers of the Confederates. They also captured one battle flag, being, it is believed, the first battle flag
captured from the enemy by the Army of the Potomac. One of the French princes
serving on General McClellan's staff, the Duc [Louis Philippe] d'Orleans, arriving on the battlefield at this moment, was made the bearer of the captured
colors to army headquarters.

13

Our First Battle, Bull Pasture Mountain [McDowell]

Alfred E. Lee, Captain, U.S.V.

MAJOR GENERAL [John C.] Frémont assumed command of the Mountain Department on March 29, 1862, at Wheeling, West Virginia, relieving Brigadier General [William Starke] Rosecrans. The new department comprised the
following territorial divisions: District of the Cumberland, containing all territory east of the Alleghenies and west of the Department of the Potomac, commanded by Brigadier General R. C. Schenck; the Cheat Mountain District, comprising all west of the Alleghenies, south of the railroad lines, north of the valley
of the Gauley, and east of the Weston and Summerville road, commanded by
Brigadier General R. H. Milroy; the Railroad District, comprising all north and

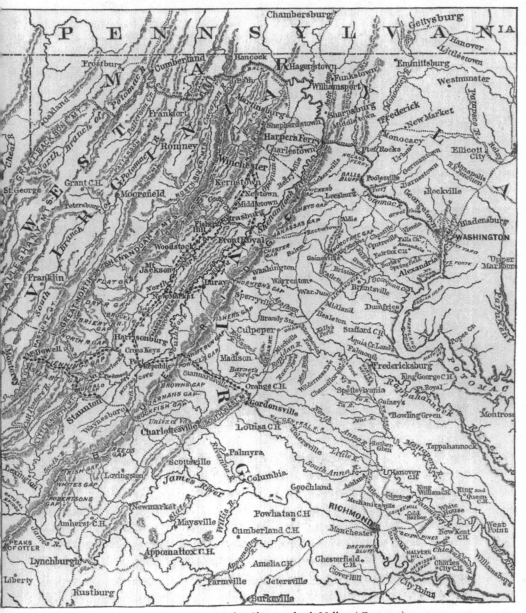

Jackson's Campaign in the Shenandoah Valley (*Century*)

west of the railroad lines, commanded by Brigadier General B. F. Kelly; the District of the Kanawha, comprising all the valleys of the Kanawha and Guyandotte rivers and the mouth of the Big Sandy, commanded by Brigadier General J. D. Cox; the districts of the Big Sandy Valley and Gap, commanded respectively by Colonels [James A.] Garfield and [Samuel P.] Carter.

Contemplating this interesting field, General Frémont laid out for himself a far reaching and somewhat dazzling plan of operations. After collecting his forces, he proposed to move up the South Branch Valley, cross the mountains to Staunton, march thence, in conjunction with [Major General Nathaniel P.] Banks, against the Virginia and Tennessee Railroad at Salem, establish a new base at Gauley, call forward General Cox to Newberne, and then, having "destroyed the connection between Knoxville and the (Confederate) army in eastern Virginia, and perhaps seized some rolling stock, advance rapidly toward Knoxville, turning the (Confederate) position at Cumberland Gap." After taking Knoxville, Frémont proposed to establish a "third base of operations" at Nicholasville, and thus place his army "in a position to cooperate in any way in the general plan of operations for the prosecution of the war."

This ambitious and glowing scheme was approved at Washington, but with a final modification which contemplated the ultimate closing of Frémont's columns toward Richmond rather than at Knoxville. To carry out these designs Frémont had, according to his own estimate, 19,000 effective men. To this force should be added the German Division, about 8,000 strong, under Brigadier General [Louis] Blenker, which was to be transferred from the Army of the Potomac, and assigned to Frémont's command. General Milroy had passed the winter at Monterey—a mountain station near the headwaters of the South Branch of the Potomac—and he had with him there about 3,500 men. General Schenck's force—to which the Eighty-second Ohio regiment, with which the writer was identified, was attached—was concentrated at Moorefield, in the South Branch Valley, and numbered about 3,000. Blenker's division quitted its camps at Fairfax Court House for its new field of operations early in April, but was fully a month in reaching its destination. Blenker was unfamiliar with the country, became confused with his maps, and seems to have lost his way. Though the weather was very inclement, his men marched without tents or other sufficient camp equipage, and were constantly exposed to snow and rain. On April 15 the division crossed the swollen Shenandoah at Berry's Ferry, in boats, one of which was swamped, drowning sixty men. To prevent further mishaps, and accelerate the movement of Blenker's command, the secretary of war directed Rosecrans to hunt it up, take temporary charge of it, and conduct it over the mountains.

The division was in a most wretched state of discipline and equipment. Many of the regiments were armed with old fashioned smoothbore muskets, and the whole command was deficient in necessary wagon transportation. The men suffered greatly for want of shoes, blankets, and overcoats, and also for want of food. Many were sick by reason of exposure and privation and the number increased daily. The animals in the trains were in a starved condition, and fresh horses had to be procured before the batteries could be moved from Martinsburg. The division reached Petersburg on May 9, but in an exceedingly unfit condition for active service.

Early in April, General Milroy, after routing a Confederate force which attacked him near Monterey, pushed across the mountains to McDowell. About the same time General Cox, in pursuance of Frémont's orders, moved in the direction of Lewisburg and Peterstown. Concurrently with these operations, General Schenck was directed to advance toward Franklin, so as to join Milroy, and cooperate with Banks in the Shenandoah Valley.

Owing to the bad condition of the roads, Schenck's forces at Moorefield did

A Federal Picket Exposed
to the Elements (*Century*)

not break camp until April 25, on which date they moved up the South Branch to Petersburg. Here the river, swollen by the rain and very swift, was found to be three feet deep at its shallowest point, making it necessary to construct a temporary foot bridge for the infantry, which was done with farm wagons, ballasted down with stones. The artillery and cavalry managed to get over by fording. The movement was resumed on May 3. Above Petersburg, the road, at best a primitive one, barely practicable for artillery and wagon trains, grew worse and worse as the column proceeded up the river, and penetrated the mountainous country from which the South Branch issues.

The few people who dwelt in these elevated districts seemed to be as heartily and universally loyal as those in the lower valley had been unfriendly and rebellious, and they welcomed Schenck's soldiers with every demonstration of joy. They were generally poor, as was the soil they cultivated, and of course there were very few slaveholders among them. As the column neared Franklin, on the fifth, a courier arrived from Milroy with the news that [Major General Thomas

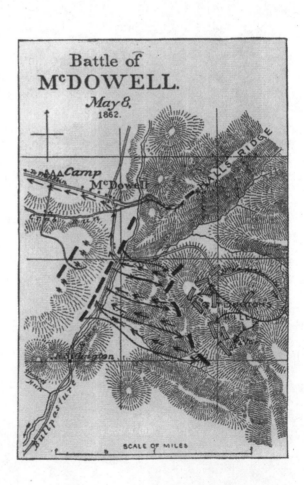

The Battle of McDowell
(Bull Pasture Mountain)
(*Century*)

T. "Stonewall"] Jackson, anticipating Frémont's advance, was coming over the range to meet him.

"There's work ahead, boys!" said Colonel [James] Cantwell, of the Eighty-second Ohio, as he rubbed his mustache in a manner peculiar to him. The brave colonel knew from his own previous experience what "work ahead" meant, but there were few of his boys who, as yet, had ever heard so much as a picket shot fired at an enemy. They were quite ready for the work, however, and rather eager for it, although the colonel's manner did not indicate that he thought it was going to be in the nature of amusement.

At Franklin, an old weather-beaten hamlet in a gorge of the mountains, a temporary supply depot was established, and on May 7 the column pushed on, through a rough and thinly settled country, toward Staunton. On May 8, at 10:00 A.M., the command, having marched most of the night, arrived at McDowell, a village on the Staunton Turnpike, thirty-four miles southwest of Franklin. The village lies at the foot of Bull Pasture Mountain, on the upper slopes of which were descried (for the first time by Cantwell's men) the gray battalions of the Southern Confederacy. The Confederates in sight were the brigades of [Brigadier General] Edward Johnson's division, which were moving into position and forming a line sheltered by rocks and trees, and fronted by clearings extending well down the mountain.

Jackson had present with him, and near at hand, his own and Johnson's divisions, numbering in all about 10,000 men. Defeated (March 23) by Shields at Kernstown, and then by Banks up the valley to Harrisonburg, he had been reinforced by [Brigadier General Richard S.] Ewell's division from Gordonsville. Leaving that division to hold Banks in check, he had now turned to intercept and overwhelm Frémont's advance before it could arrive within reaching distance of our forces in the Valley. Milroy had arrived at McDowell some days before, and had thrown forward part of his force beyond Shaw's Ridge, in the direction of Staunton. This force had fallen back upon the main body, which was preparing to resist Jackson's further progress. Schenck, who was the ranking officer, had brought with him about 1,300 infantry, a battalion of Connecticut cavalry, and [Captain William L.] De Beck's Battery [K, First Ohio Light Artillery]. He saw, at once, that our position at McDowell was not tenable, but after consultation with Milroy, he resolved to put a bold face on matters, and assail the enemy. Under cover of this attack he proposed to get all the wagon trains well out of the way, with a view to withdrawing, during the night, his entire force from its perilous position.

About the middle of the afternoon the Third Virginia, and the Twenty-fifth, Thirty-second, Seventy-fifth, and Eighty-second Ohio regiments moved to the attack, the Twenty-fifth and Seventy-fifth holding the right, the Thirty-second and Eighty-second the left, and the Third Virginia, moving by the turnpike, the center. Passing beyond the village, the Eighty-second crossed the Bull Pasture River and ascended a steep, timbered bluff, known as Hull's Ridge, where there was neither road nor path. A six-pounder of [Captain Aaron C.] Johnson's [Twelfth Ohio Independent] Battery was dragged up after the regiment by hand, and directly opened fire with considerable effect from the summit, from whence the enemy's position, though in plain view, could not be reached by musketry.

Intervening between ourselves (the Eighty-second Ohio) and Bull Pasture Mountain (the cleared part of which was known as Setlingen's Hill), lay a deep valley, along which the turnpike mounted the Shenandoah range. To get at our antagonists it was necessary to descend to the bottom of this valley, and climb the heights on its opposite side. Colonel Cantwell, therefore, started his men on the double-quick down the mountain, himself leading them on foot. The entire movement had to be executed in full view of the enemy, and it quickly brought us within range of his musketry. With a great shout the regiment rushed down the turnpike, reaching which, the men scarcely stopped to take a breath, before they began clambering up the steep slope of Bull Pasture Mountain.

And now the crash of their Enfields began to resound through the gorge! And, in spite of all the battles which have since intervened, how the bang of those muskets reverberates even yet in the living ears that heard them! The enemy's bullets, fired down the mountains, flew over us in myriads, but were not heeded. The Confederate fire seemed only to add to the exhilaration and *elan* of our charge. Up through the slanting meadows went the blue lines, with colors flying and Enfields crashing! No flinching! forward! Some soldiers fall, and lie motion-

The Eighty-second Ohio
Charging up Setlingen's
Hill (*McClure's*)

less upon the grass, but there is no time to pay any attention to that! On the right the Twenty-fifth, Seventy-fifth, and Thirty-second Ohio come up in splendid style, their muskets crashing too! Up, still up go the steady lines, until they arrive within short range of the Confederates. The action is so violent all along the front that Jackson hurries up his reserves. Our men want to go at the enemy with the bayonet, and some of them even make a rush for that purpose, but are called back. It is not deemed prudent to advance the line farther against such superior odds, but the fight goes on unabated until the sun sets, and darkness hides the combatants from each other.

Happening to look to the rear, I saw some men lying on the grass. My first impression was that they had lain down to avoid being hit. But they were motionless. The truth flashed over me—they were dead! I had scarcely noticed, before, that anybody had been hurt, except that a bullet had struck the musket of a man next [to] me, and glancing had wounded him in the wrist.

As darkness came on the firing slackened, and at length ceased. The troops were then recalled. The wounded had all been carried to the rear, but there lay the dead, and it seemed too bad to leave them behind. So two of us picked up one of the bodies, and endeavored to bear it away with the retreating line. But we had not realized until then how fatigued we were! The slain soldier was a young German, who had received a bullet full in the forehead. We laid him down gently by the stump of a tree, with his face upturned to the moonlight, and there we left him. A few minutes later I found myself trying to quench, in a muddy pool at the turnpike, the fever and thirst begotten of the extraordinary exertion and excitement.

"Men, remember that you are from Ohio!" had been General Schenck's admonition prior to the battle. We did not forget it. Jackson telegraphed to Richmond: "God blessed our arms with victory at McDowell yesterday." He would not have coveted many such victories. His loss afterward admitted was seventy-one killed and 390 wounded. Our total loss was 256.

The enemy did not pursue. He did not even seem to anticipate our retreat. Returning to the village, our troops halted unmolested for supper and brief rest. Leaving their campfires burning, they then set forth, preceded by the artillery and trains, on the road toward Franklin. The wounded who could hobble along did so, and those who could not were carried in the ambulances. We marched all night, stopping seldom, and on May 10 the column arrived again at Franklin. Halting in the valley above the town the troops, half dead with fatigue and loss of sleep, stacked their arms, and lay down to rest. Suddenly a great cheer was heard in the direction of the town, and a horseman was seen galloping up the valley, swinging his hat. One regiment after another took up the cry as he passed it, and as he approached ours we heard him shouting at the top of his voice: "The *Monitor* has sunk the *Merrimac!* Hurrah!"

We had scarcely digested this welcome information when the enemy's cavalry appeared up the valley, and the troops were hurried into position covering

the approaches to the town. Then came more news: "General Frémont is coming, with Blenker's division!"

Verily we had fallen upon eventful times! The *Merrimac* sunk, Blenker coming, and the Confederate cavalry bearing down upon us! However, the enemy,
having arrived within hearing of the racket caused by the *Merrimac* news,
seemed to be intimidated by the shouting. His squadrons displayed themselves
very handsomely, with arms glittering and banners flying, but for the time being they kept at a respectful distance. A few shots from our batteries made the
distance still more respectful.

Blenker's division came up according to announcement. At the same time
Jackson's cavalry, with infantry supports, began to feel Frémont's lines, and for
a few hours brisk skirmishing ensued. Meanwhile the woods on the mountains
took fire from the musketry, or the campfires of the combatants, and at night
the contour of the peaks and ridges was outlined against the sky in lambent flame.

On May 14 Jackson withdrew all his forces from Frémont's front, and rapidly disappeared again beyond the Shenandoah Mountain. We were destined to
renew his acquaintance, however, further along.

14

An Undeserved Stigma:
Fitz John Porter at Second Bull Run

Ulysses S. Grant, General, U.S.A.

On NOVEMBER 27, 1862, a court-martial was convened in the city of
Washington, for the trial of Major General Fitz John Porter, of the volunteer
force. The court consisted of nine members and a judge advocate—the judge
advocate general of the army.

The charges against General Porter were:

First. Disobedience of orders under the Ninth Article of War.

Second. Misbehavior before the enemy under the Fifty-second Article of War.

Under the first charge there were three specifications of which the court
found Porter guilty. These were, substantially:

First. Disobedience to the order of August 27 [1862], requiring him to march
from Warrenton Junction at one o'clock on the morning of the twenty-eighth
and be at Bristoe Station by daylight.

Second. Disobedience on August 29, while in front of the enemy, to the joint order to [Major General Irvin] McDowell and Porter, directing them to march toward Gainesville and establish communication with the other corps.

Third. Disobedience on August 29, while in front of the enemy, to what is known as the 4:30 P.M. order, requiring Porter to attack the enemy's flank and rear.

Under the second charge the specifications upon which Porter was tried and convicted were, in substance:

First. Shameful disobedience to the 4:30 P.M. order on August 29, while in sight of the field and in full hearing of its artillery; and retreat from advancing forces of the enemy, without attempting to engage them or to aid the troops who were fighting greatly superior numbers, and who would have secured a decisive victory and captured the enemy's army, but for Porter's neglect to attack and his shameful disobedience.

Second. Failure of Porter all that day to bring his forces on the field when within sound of the guns and in presence of the enemy, and knowing that a severe action of great consequence was being fought, and that the aid of his corps

Ulysses S. Grant, Late in Life (*Century*)

was greatly needed; and his shameful falling back and retreat from the advance of unknown forces of the enemy without attempting to give them battle.

Third. Shameful failure of Porter on the same day, while a severe action was being fought, to go to the aid of [Major General John] Pope's troops, when he believed that they were being defeated and were retiring from the field; and his shameful retreat away and falling back under these circumstances, leaving the army to the disasters of a presumed defeat; and failure, by an attempt to attack the enemy, to aid in averting a disaster which would have endangered the safety of the capital.

These are the accusations that were made against General Porter for his part and failure in the battles generally known as those of the Second Bull Run campaign. The court found him guilty of the charges and specifications. If he was so guilty, the punishment awarded was not commensurate with the offense committed. I believe lawyers have taken exception to the formation of the court and to some of its technical rulings; but neither at the time nor since has General Porter attempted to evade the consequences of his acts by any special pleading, or by taking advantage of any technical error in the composition of the court, or the method of its being ordered, but has relied entirely upon his innocence of all the charges and specifications, and would not be satisfied with an acquittal on any other ground than that of his entire innocence.

It will be seen from the foregoing that General Porter's alleged misconduct was embraced in three separate cases of disobedience of orders: one on August 27, and two on August 29; and in having retreated unnecessarily from the enemy, by that act endangering other portions of the army with which he was co-operating.

It will be seen that, though these offenses were alleged to have been committed in August 1862, he was continued in the command of an army corps until some time in November following, taking an active part in the battles of the day following the date of the last charge, and in command of the defenses of Washington on the west bank of the Potomac, and also at the Battle of Antietam, some weeks later. It would look at first very singular that an officer, so wantonly derelict in the performance of his duty as General Porter was alleged to have been on August 27 and 28, should have continued in so important a place as the command of an army corps, when so much was at stake as there was on August 30, and in the defenses of Washington, and in the later battles in Maryland, when the invasion of the North was threatened. These facts would indicate to an unprejudiced mind that the charges against Porter were an afterthought, to shift the responsibilities of failure from other shoulders and to place them upon him.

In regard to his disobedience of the order of August 27, he is alleged to have without justification deferred his march from Warrenton Junction to Bristoe Station from 1:00 A.M. until 3:00 A.M. of August 28. It was about 10:00 P.M. of August 27 when Porter received the following order:

Major General Fitz John Porter (*Century*)

Headquarters Army of Virginia,
Bristoe Station, August 27, 1862,
6:30 P.M.

General: The major general commanding directs that you start at 1:00 A.M., and come forward with your whole corps, or such part of it as is with you, so as to be here by daylight tomorrow morning. [Major General Joseph] Hooker has had a very severe action with the enemy, with a loss of about 300 killed and wounded. The enemy has been driven back, but is retiring along the railroad. We must drive him from Manassas, and clear the country between that place and Gainesville, where McDowell is. If [Major General George W.] Morell has not joined you, send word to him to push forward immediately; also send word to [Major General Nathaniel] Banks to hurry forward with all speed to take your place at Warrenton Junction. It is necessary, on all accounts, that you should be here by daylight. I send an officer with this dispatch, who will conduct you to this place. Be sure to send word to Banks, who is on the road from Fayetteville, probably in the direction of Bealton. Say to Banks, also, that he had best run back the railroad trains to this side of Cedar Run. If he is not with you, write him to that effect.

By command of Major General Pope,

George D. Ruggles,
Colonel and Chief of Staff
Major General F. J. Porter, Warrenton Junction.

P.S. If Banks is not at Warrenton Junction, leave a regiment of infantry and two pieces of artillery as a guard till he comes up, with instructions to follow you immediately. If Banks is not at the junction, instruct Colonel [Robert E.] Clary to run the trains back to this side of Cedar Run, and post a regiment and section of artillery with it.

By command of Major General Pope.

George D. Ruggles,
Colonel and Chief of Staff.

His troops had been marching all day, were very much fatigued, some of them only having just arrived in camp and had their supper, when the order to march at 1:00 A.M. was received. The night, as shown in the testimony before the court which tried Porter, and as confirmed by the evidence given in what was known as the Schofield Board, was extremely dark; the road very narrow, with numerous cuts and streams passing through it; bounded by woods on both sides in many places, with no place where the open country could be taken for the march of troops; and blocked up with about 2,000 army wagons, many of them mired in the narrow road, so that the officer who conveyed this order to General Porter was over three hours, on horseback, in making the distance of ten miles. Porter was expected, with fatigued troops, worn with long marches, on scanty rations, to make a march on a very dark night, through a blockaded road, more rapidly than a single aide de camp, unencumbered, had been able to get through on horseback.

When he received the order, he showed it to his leading generals, and, apparently with one accord, they decided that the movement at that hour was

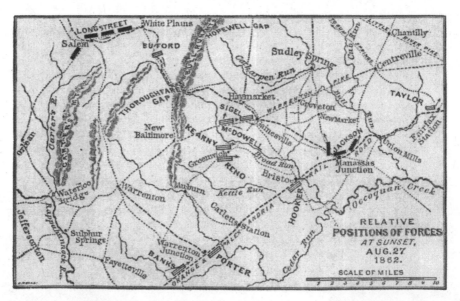

Relative Positions of Forces at Sunset, August 27, 1862 (*Century*)

impossible; further, that no time could possibly be gained by so early a start, and that if they should start at that hour and get through to Bristoe Station at the time designated, the troops would not be fit for either fighting or marching on their arrival at that point. Porter replied, however, "Here is the order, and it must be obeyed"; but, after further consultation, he decided, as did his generals, that a postponement of two hours in starting the march would enable them to get through as quick as if the men were kept on foot and under arms while the road was being cleared, and that the men would be in a much better condition for service on their arrival at their destination. He was entirely justified in exercising his own judgment in this matter, because the order shows that he was not to take part in any battle when he arrived there, but was wanted to pursue a fleeing enemy. He did not leave the commanding general in ignorance of his proposed delay, nor of the reasons for it, but at once sent a request that the general commanding should send back cavalry (he had none himself) and clear the road near him of encumbrances, so that the march might be unobstructed.

It is shown that a literal obedience to the order of August 27 was a physical impossibility. It is further shown that General Porter was desirous of obeying it literally, so far as was practicable, but was prevailed upon by his leading generals—against whom a suspicion of disloyalty to their commander, or to the cause, has never been entertained—to do what his own judgment approved as the best thing to do—to make a later start with a view of arriving at his destination as early as it was possible for him to arrive there, and to give to his jaded and worn troops two hours more of needed rest. If the night had been clear and the road an open one, there would not have been as much justification for the exercise of his discretion in the matter; but there is no doubt but that he would have arrived at Bristoe Station just as early, and with his troops in much better condition, if he had started at early dawn instead of at the hour he did, and the intervening time had been used in clearing the road for his troops when they did march. Where there were open spaces along the line of the road, they were either marshy, filled with stumps of trees, and impossible to march over, or were crowded with army wagons, so that the track of his army was limited to the encumbered narrow road between the two points designated in the order, which could be cleared only by the wagons being moved ahead, as requested of Pope.

Much of the testimony before the court and before the army board might be quoted to confirm what is here stated; but as this is all accessible to the reader, I will not lengthen this statement by quoting it.

I question very much whether there was an engagement during the war, or a series of engagements continuing over as much time as was consumed in the battles about Bull Run in August 1862, when not only one, but a number of generals, did not exercise their discretion, as Porter did on this occasion, and with far less justification. The commanding general who gave the order desired to have the troops at a certain point by daylight, and he gave his orders so as to accomplish that result. Under the circumstances, his order required of the troops an impossibility. That was as evident to Porter, and those with him, before the attempt was made as it was after.

It is a little singular that anyone high in rank, connected with the Army of Virginia, should be in ignorance of the arrival of at least a portion of [General Robert E.] Lee's army, by the very route designated by Pope, many hours before the 4:30 P.M. order was published. Porter was not in ignorance of that arrival. Between 12:00 P.M. and 1:00 P.M., on arriving at his advanced position, Porter was shown by McDowell a dispatch from [Brigadier General John] Buford, sent at 9:30 A.M. on August 29, stating that from seventeen to eighteen regiments of the enemy had passed through Gainesville three-quarters of an hour before, or at 8:45 A.M., on their way to reinforce Jackson, so that the head of the column must have been not only in supporting distance of Jackson, but at the place of deployment by 10:00 A.M.; and now it is known by others, as it was known by Porter at the time, that [Major General James] Longstreet, with some 25,000 men, was in position confronting Porter by 12:00 P.M. on August 29, four hours and a half before the 4:30 P.M. order was written.

While at the head of their united forces, between 12:00 P.M. and 1:00 P.M., and while Porter was preparing to attack the enemy in his immediate front, McDowell, then in command, showed Porter the "joint order" and also Buford's dispatch. It was evident from this dispatch, corroborated by the enemy's movements in their immediate front, that the main forces of the enemy, which the joint order said were far distant, had not only arrived, but had formed a junction with Jackson and deployed in their front. Porter knew of this from another fact—he had prisoners from that force—Longstreet's troops. The object of moving toward Gainesville had been thus defeated, and any further advance, if practicable, would only the more widely separate them from Pope's forces then checked at Groton, at least two miles distant, and with which they were ordered to establish communication. McDowell, as he had the right, at once withdrew his troops, leaving Porter with 10,000 to confront Longstreet's 25,000, while he went by a circuitous route to a point between Porter and Pope, to establish the communication enjoined.

Thus left alone, facing superior numbers advantageously posted, and ignorant of the needs of Pope, if indeed he had any, Porter had necessarily to bide McDowell's arrival on his right. In the meantime his duty was manifestly to engage Longstreet's attention and prevent him from moving against Pope, especially while McDowell was out of support of both Pope and Porter. Porter all that day did not hear of McDowell, or of what was taking place in front of Pope, though he kept the former well-informed of affairs with him, and presumed that his dispatches were sent to the latter. He, however, engaged Longstreet's attention by demonstrations nearly harmless to himself, and so successfully as to cause Longstreet to take [Brigadier General Cadmus M.] Wilcox's division from in front of Pope, in order to strengthen the line confronting Porter, who, at the time, was aware of this movement of forces coming from the right to his front, and notified McDowell of it. Thus Porter, without sacrifice of men, and without endangering any interests, did more for Pope's relief than if he had gone directly to that general's assistance. To have done so would probably have sacrificed his corps without any benefit, and jeopardied the safety of Pope's army.

So far as I have investigated the case—and I have studied it, I think, pretty thoroughly—I see no fact to base the charge of retreat upon. I do not see that any argument to prove this is necessary, because any reader of history may be defied now to find where and when General Porter retreated during the time specified.

In my judgment, this disposes of the charges, and consequently of all specifications under them, except the alleged disobedience of the 4:30 P.M. order.

In regard to the charge of disobedience of the 4:30 P.M. order, which is the principal one and the one that has most deeply impressed the mind of the general public, there are evidences which look to me important and conclusive, showing that the court-martial which tried General Porter found him guilty under a mistaken idea of the actual facts, now accessible to anyone in search of the truth, and which Porter knew to be the facts at the time. As maintained by the prosecution, to the apparent satisfaction of the court, the situation of the belligerent forces were in numbers and position about as here given [Diagram One].

The 4:30 P.M. order of August 29 required Porter to attack the enemy's right flank and to get into his rear, if possible. This enemy, in the mind of the commanding general, and, no doubt, of the court, was Jackson's force of 22,000 men. Porter was supposed to occupy, with 10,000 troops, the position assigned to him in the diagram given. The court also seems to have been satisfied that the order

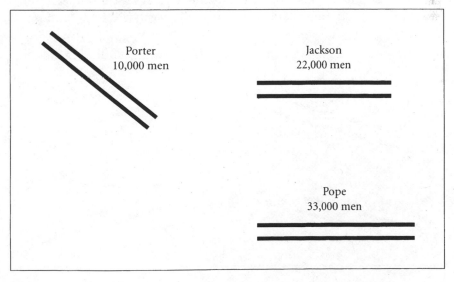

Diagram One, Apparent Situation (*North American Review*)

to make this attack was received by Porter from 5:00 P.M. to 5:30 P.M., leaving him abundance of time to obey the order.

That the commanding general believed the positions as given in the foregoing diagram to be the positions of the different commands, is shown from the fact that in his joint order of that morning he stated that "the indications are that the whole force of the enemy is moving in this direction at a pace that will bring them here by tomorrow night or the next day"—that is, the evening of the thirtieth or the morning of August 31—and from the fact that in the 4:30 P.M. order he stated that "the enemy is massed in the woods in front of us," thus ignoring the presence of Longstreet. This is confirmed in his map number five, furnished to the government. If these had been the facts of the case, there would have been no justification whatever for Porter's failing to make the attack as ordered; but, instead of the facts being as supposed by the commanding general and the court which tried General Porter, they were as shown by the following diagram [Diagram Two]. This Porter knew on indisputable evidence.

As shown by this diagram, Porter was not in a position to attack the right flank of Jackson, because he was at least three miles away, and not across his flank, as shown in the first diagram. With Longstreet's presence, to have obeyed that order he would have been obliged, with 10,000 men, to have defeated 25,000 men in a chosen position, before he could have moved upon the flank of the enemy, as the order directed. But, even if the position of Lee's army had been thirty-six to forty-eight hours distant, as asserted in the joint order to McDowell and Porter, it would have been impossible for Porter to have obeyed the 4:30 P.M. order, because it did not contemplate a night attack, and was not received by Porter until about dark. To have obeyed it would have required some little preparation, movement of troops, and distribution of orders, so that it would have been some time after dark before he could have moved from the position

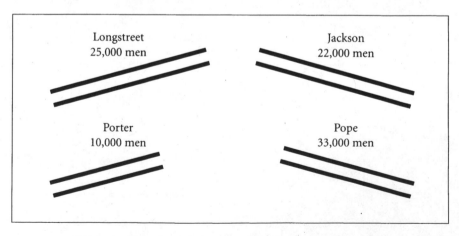

Diagram Two, Actual Situation (*North American Review*)

he was then occupying, and at least as late as 9:00 P.M. before he could have reached Jackson's flank to engage it. His efforts to execute the order, notwithstanding its apparent inappropriateness, demonstrate this assertion.

I consider that these facts, with many more that were brought to the knowledge of the Schofield Board, fully exonerate General Porter of the charge of disobedience of what is known as the 4:30 P.M. order, and also of the imputation of lukewarmness in his support of the commanding general.

General Porter has now for twenty years been laboring under the disabilities and penalties inflicted upon him by the court-martial of 1862, all that time contending for a restoration to his position in the army and in society, and always, as stated in the beginning of this article, on the ground of his entire innocence. The investigation of the Schofield Board has, in my judgment, established his innocence of all the offenses for which he was tried and convicted. The sufferings of twenty years, under such findings, for himself and family and friends, is something it is now impossible to set right. Twenty years of the best part of his life have been consumed in trying to have his name and his reputation restored before his countrymen. In his application now before Congress, he is asking only that he may be restored to the rolls of the army, with the rank that he would have if the court-martial had never been held. This, in my judgment, is a very small part of what it is possible to do in this case, and of what ought to be done. General Porter should, in the way of partial restitution, be declared by Congress to have been convicted on mistaken testimony, and, therefore, to have never been out of the army. This would make him a major general of volunteers until the date might be fixed for his muster out as of that rank, after which he should be continued as a colonel of infantry, and brevet brigadier general of the United States Army from the date of the act, when he could be placed upon the retired list with that rank.

In writing what I have here written, I mean no criticism upon the court which tried General Porter, nor upon the officers under whom or with whom he served. It is easy to understand, in the condition of the public mind as it was in 1862, when the nation was in great peril, and when the Union troops had met with some severe reverses, how the public were ready to condemn—to death if need be—any officer against whom even a suspicion might be raised. For many years, and till within a year, I believed that the position and number of the troops on both sides were as stated in the first diagram given here, and that the order to attack was received at an hour in the day sufficiently early to have made the attack feasible; and, under that impression, it seemed to me that the enemy, unless through very bad generalship on the Union side, could not have been able to escape while a superior force confronted him and 10,000 men flanked him. A study of the case not only has convinced me, but has clearly and conclusively established, that the position and numbers of the armies were as given in the second diagram.

If a solemn and sincere expression of my thorough understanding of and belief in the entire innocence of General Porter will tend to draw the public mind to the same conviction, I shall feel abundantly rewarded for my efforts. It will always be a pleasure for me, as well as a duty, to be the instrument, even in the smallest degree, of setting right any man who has been grossly wronged, especially if he has risked life and reputation in defense of his country. I feel, as stated on a previous occasion, a double interest in this particular case, because, directly after the war, as general of the army, when I might have been instrumental in having justice done to General Porter, and later as president of the United States, when I certainly could have done so, I labored under the firm conviction that he was guilty; that the facts of the receipt of the 4:30 P.M. order were as found by the court, and that the position of the troops and numbers were as given in the first of these diagrams. Having become better informed, I at once voluntarily gave, as I have continued to give, my earnest efforts to impress the minds of my countrymen with the justice of this case, and to secure from our government, as far as it could grant it, the restitution due to General Fitz John Porter.

15

A Witness to Mutiny at Antietam
George W. Smalley

As THIS PAPER concerns itself with journalism, I avoid entering into military details or fighting old battles over again. What I shall attempt is to give some brief notion of what a war correspondent's life was like, and how he collected and transmitted his news.

Mr. Charles A. Dana was in 1861 managing editor of the *Tribune,* with Mr. Sydney Howard Gay as his first lieutenant. Mr. Horace Greeley was, of course, editor in chief, but with him the younger men on the paper came little into contact. If you were outside the office, in the field, you were not absolutely obliged to know of his existence. Any reminder of it was apt to come in the shape of a criticism, always useful to the beginner. Mr. Dana had the reputation of a masterful manager. I can only say that I found him, so long as he remained on the paper, considerate, helpful, just, and even friendly, though he knew that the door by which I entered the office had been opened by Wendell Phillips, for whom he had none too much liking. New as I was to journalism, Mr. Dana gave me a free hand. There is nothing which is more likely to bring out of a man the

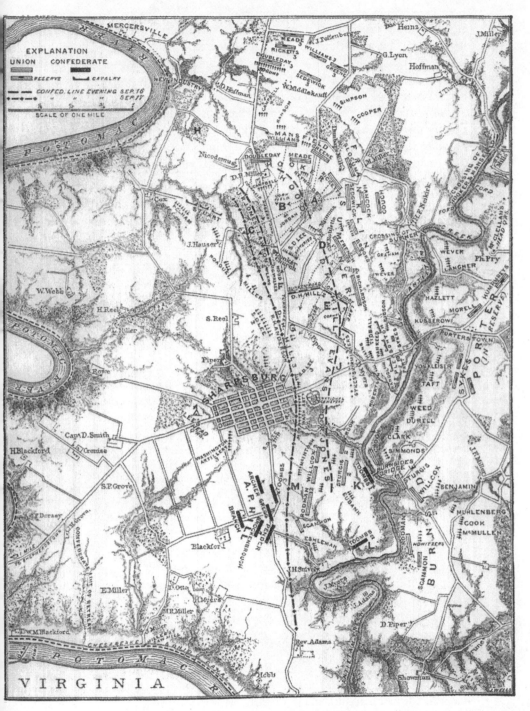

The Field of Antietam (*Century*)

best there is in him. He understood journalism and he understood human nature, and I always thought it, and still think it, a happy circumstance that I
learned my first lessons in journalism under a chief who, being himself at the
head of his profession, found time to show much kindness to a subordinate
whose foot was on the lowest round of the ladder.

In one sense it may almost be said that the history of war correspondence as
it is now understood, begins with the Rebellion; by which I mean that modern
methods were then first applied, and that the transmission of war news was undertaken for the first time *in extenso* by telegraph. My experiences in journalism
began with the war, or, rather, began in November 1861, with a trip to South Carolina, of which the main object was to look into the Negro question a little. The
gallant [Rear Admiral Samuel F.] Du Pont had taken Port Royal, troops had been
landed there, a military post established, and the blacks were pouring in. [Ma-
jor General Benjamin F.] Butler had announced in Maryland the doctrine of contraband, which so impressed itself on the public mind that, for the next year or
so, the blacks went by the name of contrabands. The war was of course still a war
for the Union and not for freedom, but the pressure of the Negro question grew
daily heavier. I stayed in Port Royal, or in that part of the country, until the spring
of 1862; returned to New York, and was sent to join [Major General John C.] Frémont in Virginia, and made the Shenandoah Valley campaign with him. Then I
saw part of the ill-fated enterprise of [Major General John] Pope on the Rappahannock ending in the second peril to Washington. Finally I rode out of Washington one afternoon to have a look at the army of which [Major General George
B.] McClellan had again taken command, in August 1862. Expecting to be away
overnight, I took with me a luggage, a toothbrush and a mackintosh. I was gone
six weeks, and saw the campaign which ended, after a fashion, at Antietam. The
presence of correspondents with the army had been forbidden by [Secretary of
War Edwin M.] Stanton and [Major General Henry] Halleck, but of course there
never was a time when they were really excluded, or never a very long time. General Pope sent for me one evening to his headquarters—by that time in a tent,
and no longer, too rashly announced at the beginning, in the saddle—and told
me in his friendly way that he had received a peremptory order from the War
Office to allow no correspondents to remain in his camp. I said I would leave at
once, to which he replied, "I don't see that you need go till you get the order,"
adding that he had not made up his mind whether or when to issue it. But he
did issue it, and we were all supposed to obey.

At Washington when it was known that McClellan was once more in command, some of us thought it discreet, considering his known dislike to the publication of any war news except such as he himself or his staff supplied, to drop
the journalist and join some friendly headquarters volunteer aides de camp.
[Major General John] Sedgwick, the good soldier who was killed at Spotsylvania, offered me an appointment, or rather an opportunity, which I gladly accepted. He advised me to put on some sort of uniform, which might prevent

Major General George B. McClellan (*Century*)

inconvenient questions being asked. The army moved forward sooner than was expected, and having once joined General Sedgwick, I had no time to turn back nor any wish to. We all knew that the position was such as must before long compel McClellan, the most unready of commanders, to measure himself again with [General Robert E.] Lee. And so it was that on a sunny September afternoon, the fifteenth, I found myself looking across the valley through which flowed the Antietam [Creek], to the heights of Sharpsburg, crowned with the Confederate forces. Nobody called them Confederates in those days. Rebels, or, for short, Rebs, was all that a Northern soldier's lips could shape themselves to utter. General McClellan, in his usual accommodating spirit, waited all next day to allow the enemy to collect his forces.

On the afternoon of the sixteenth I heard that [Major General Joseph] Hooker, "Fighting Joe," had been ordered across the creek to turn the enemy's left. I did not know General Hooker nor anybody on his staff, but I thought I might as well go along, and I went. Nobody seemed to mind. I rode with the staff, and was asked no questions. General Hooker, never lacking in resolution, pushed a regiment or two of cavalry straight forward as far as they could go, and went with them. That was his idea of a reconnaissance. Following with the staff, we all had the pleasure of learning, a few minutes later, what a cavalry stampede to the rear was like, and of taking part in it. But Hooker was in great glee. He had found out what he wanted to know, and had ascertained pretty well where the enemy were. The night was drawing in. He took his own position, which was as close as it could well be to the opposite lines, found a barn to serve as headquarters for the night, and turned in. Most of us slept outside. I had no servant with me, and slept with my horse's bridle round one arm. By five next morning the Battle of Antietam began. By nine, Hooker had been driven back, and sent for more troops. [Major General Joseph K. F.] Mansfield came, and Sumner came, and Hooker himself, with what was left of his divisions, again went forward. It was his way to keep well to the front, too far forward, no doubt, and one result of these tactics was that most of his staff were presently killed or wounded. There came a moment when not one was near him, not even an orderly. They were down or away on duty. He looked rather sharply at me, and asked me who I was. I told him. "Will you take an order for me?" and without waiting for an answer, sent me off to find a certain brigade and order them forward. Then he stopped me. "Order every regiment you can find to advance. It is time to end this business." I went off on this errand, and when I rejoined Hooker he was in the thick of what looked a pretty hot fight. Almost immediately a bullet struck him in the foot. He had to be helped from his horse, taken to the rear on an extemporized ambulance, and finally to quit the battlefield altogether. With his departure the attack on the Confederate left died suddenly away, and was never renewed to much purpose.

During this lull in the battle, which nobody could believe to be the end of it, occurred an incident which even at this distance of time I narrate with some hesitation. But it throws light on General McClellan's character, on the opinion held of him by his own staff, on the state of discipline in the Northern army at this time, and on the extreme looseness of a military organization in which such an incident could occur, and so I give it. I shall neither mention any name nor indicate in any way the identity of the officer chiefly concerned.

When it became evident that the attack on the Rebel left had been repulsed, and that the fighting in that part of the field was over for the time, I rode back across the creek in the direction of General McClellan's headquarters. It was expected he would order forward his reserves under [Major General] Fitz John Porter, but he did not. Precious minutes and priceless hours ebbed away and nothing was done. I was looking about for a remount, as my horse had a couple of bullets in him and could not be depended on, when an officer on General McClellan's staff whom I knew [Lieutenant James Wilson] detached himself from the group at a little distance and came over to me. He said: "I hear you were with Hooker when he was wounded?"

"Yes."

"Do you know whether he is disabled?"

I said that he had been hit hard, could not sit his horse, and had been carried off on an ambulance; since then I had not seen him.

"Do you know where he is?"

"Yes; at a red house-farm in an open field on the right, this side of the creek."

"Will you take a message to him?"

By this time I began to think the interrogatory both curious and serious, and I answered, "That depends on what the message is."

My friend and I were by ourselves, well out of earshot of the staff, but within view, and I saw that the staff or some of them were watching what went on. He came a little closer, lowered his voice, and said:

"Most of us think that this battle is only half fought and half won. There is still time to finish it. But McClellan will do no more. What I want you to do is to see Hooker, find out whether he can mount his horse, and if he can, ask him whether he will take command of this army and drive Lee into the Potomac or force him to surrender."

It was perhaps the most astounding request ever made by a soldier to a civilian. What he suggested was nothing less than an act of mutiny in the face of the enemy, and I told him so.

"I know that as well as you do," was the answer. "We all know it, but we know also that it is the only way to crush Lee and the rebellion and save the country."

I pointed out that if Hooker were to be approached on such a subject, it ought to be by him or by one of his comrades in the plot—for it was a plot—and that, if they meant business, they ought to be ready to take the risk. I added that I thought it more than likely that General Hooker's answer to such a proposal would be to order the man who made it, whoever he was, under arrest.

"It need not be a proposal," he replied. "All we want you to do is to sound Hooker and let us know what his views are. The rest we will do ourselves." I asked him if he meant to give me a written message.

"Certainly not. Such things are not put into writing."

"But why should Hooker believe me, or compromise himself in a conversation with a man he never saw till this morning?"

He said it was known I had acted as Hooker's aide, and urged sundry other reasons. I still declined, but he still pressed it. Hooker, he declared, had won the confidence of the army, and McClellan had lost it. It was no time to stand on trifles. He regarded what he proposed to me as a patriotic duty, and so on. Finally, as I persisted in refusing to be the bearer of any such message, he asked if I would see Hooker, and bring them word whether he could, in any circumstances, take the field again that day. To this I saw no objection, and rode off. I found General Hooker in bed, and in great pain. He asked eagerly for news of the battle. When I told him that the attack on both wings had failed, that no movement had been made for the last two hours, and that General McClellan seemed to have no intention of making any, he became angry and excited, and used language of extreme plainness.

I had noticed in the morning that he had a very copious vocabulary. It was directed, for the most part, against the enemy, whose sharpshooters followed him all over the field, in which his tall figure in full uniform and his white horse were by far the most conspicuous targets. Once his staff got the benefit of this flow of energetic speech, when two or three of them joined in the suggestion that the proper place for a corps commander was not in the skirmish line, and that he could not prudently remain under so hot a fire. Now it was turned upon McClellan, with whose excessive caution and systematic inertness in the crisis of a great battle he had no patience. This outburst gave me an opportunity of putting the question I wanted to, and I asked him whether his wound would permit him to mount his horse again that day. He pointed to his swollen and bandaged foot. "No; it is impossible."

"Or to take command of your corps again in any way—in a carriage, if one could be found?"

"No, no; I cannot move. I am perfectly helpless."

All at once whether from the way in which I had put my question, or from my manner, it seemed to flash upon him that there was something behind it. He broke out: "Why do you ask? What do you mean? Who sent you here?"

He was in such torment from his wound and the fever it had brought on that I thought it best not to fence with his questions and his suspicions. I told him it was true that some friends of his who knew how well he had done his work in the morning were anxious to learn whether, in an emergency, he could resume his duties; that the position was critical; that his troops would fight under him as they would under nobody else; in short, I admitted that I came to find out what his real condition was, and that I thought a good deal depended on his answer. He groaned and swore and half raised himself on his bed. The effort was too much; the agony brought a cry to his lips: "You see what a wreck I am; it is impossible, impossible." Even to his courage there were things which were impossible. Again he asked from whom I came, but I answered that my errand was done, that it was only too plain that his wound crippled him, that the whole army knew what a misfortune it was, and that I must return to my friends and report the facts. The paroxysm of pain had passed, but left him exhausted. He said good-bye faintly, asked me to come again next day, which I knew I could not, and I took my leave.

The account I had to give of General Hooker's condition of course put an end to all schemes at headquarters, and the sun went down upon an indecisive day. General McClellan's irresolution on that memorable afternoon was to cost the country treasure and blood that might have been spared; but it was decreed that the fight should be fought out once for all, and Destiny chooses her own ways and instruments. There is a sequel, almost a counterpart, to this story, but it comes later.

After [Major General Ambrose] Burnside's failure on the left and [Major General William B.] Franklin's check on the right there was no more serious fighting that day. It was supposed that General McClellan must renew the attack next morning. After what I had heard I did not believe he would, and I determined to try at once to get an account of the battle through to New York. To send one by a messenger involved, first, a delay while it was being written,

Major General Joseph Hooker (*Century*)

and secondly, the difficulty of finding a messenger who could be trusted. I had a colleague with me, but there were reasons why he could not be sent. Then, and ever after, I found it sound policy to start either for the office or for the nearest telegraph office as soon as an important battle was over. Some men had to be seen first and some arrangements made in the event of further fighting; and there was the question of dinner, not unimportant to a man who had been mostly in the saddle since five that morning, with no time to think of food. It was nine o'clock in the evening when I got away. Frederick was the nearest town where one might reasonably hope to get a long dispatch on the wires, and Frederick was thirty miles distant, and the horse I had borrowed was anything but fresh. There was a good road, and a good chance of encountering some of those parties of stragglers and marauders who are always hanging on the rear of an army; not, I think, much real danger, and nothing happened.

I rode into Frederick by early daylight of September 18, and found my way to the telegraph office. The clerk on duty said he would take a short dispatch, but that the wires, like everything else, were in the hands of the military authorities, and he would not undertake to say when the dispatch would reach New York, or that it would ever get there at all. They were times when you had to take all chances. I sat in the office and wrote a dispatch of rather more than a column, handing it in to the clerk in sections. The length made it, to his mind, still more doubtful whether it would be forwarded, but he was good-natured and promised to do his best. I heard afterward that it had been wired straight to the War Office in Washington, and was the first narrative of the battle which reached the secretary of war, except a brief dispatch from General McClellan announcing his victory. Secretary Stanton took it to President Lincoln, who, with his cabinet, had the reading of it. They behaved handsomely, however, and allowed it to go on to the office in New York, and it appeared in the *Tribune* on Saturday morning. The battle had been fought on Thursday.

Meantime, having much more to say and no chance of saying it by telegraph from Frederick, I was trying to get a special train to Baltimore. The railroad, like the telegraph, had become a military possession, and there was no one who could, or would, take the responsibility of sending off a train. Money was no temptation, as it would have been to the railroad people. The best I could do was to get a military permit to go by the first military train. I went to the station to make sure of not missing it, and sat on a log and wrote. About 2:00 P.M. the train started. I thought I should have time between Frederick and Baltimore to finish my story of the battle, but once in the train I went to sleep. It was nearly thirty-six hours since I had closed an eye, and excitement is apt to be fatiguing. It is doubtful whether I should have fared better at the telegraph office in Baltimore than in Frederick if I had had a dispatch ready. As it was not ready, I stepped into the New York express, which in those days was lighted by a small oil lamp at each end of the car. Sitting, it was impossible to see. I stood under the lamp and wrote most of the night, finishing, I think, about midway between Philadelphia and New York. The editor had been notified that an account might be expected too late for the regular morning edition.

When I walked into the office it was near five o'clock Saturday morning. Antietam was perhaps the greatest battle which had then been fought, and the first great victory which the North had won; not a complete victory, but a victory, inasmuch as Lee withdrew across the Potomac into Virginia. There was, naturally, a great interest in the event. The office, usually deserted at that hour, was alive; the composing room crowded; the presses manned and waiting. Not long after 6:00 A.M. a second edition appeared, with a letter on Antietam about six-columns long. It was, I imagine, one of the worst pieces of manuscript which had ever puzzled the intelligent typesetter and proofreader; the whole of it in pencil, and most of it written in the train. Mr. Gay, the kindly and cultured man of letters who had become managing editor in the spring in succession to Mr. Dana, asked me if I should be ready to return by the afternoon train. I said yes, and went; but my return visit to the army proved to be a short one, as within a few weeks Mr. Gay proposed to me to enter the office as an editorial writer, and this I did.

16

The Reserve at Antietam

Thomas M. Anderson, Lieutenant Colonel,
Ninth U.S. Infantry

THE ANTIETAM articles in the June [1886] *Century* have renewed the old question as to why [Major General George B.] McClellan did not press his advantage on the afternoon of September 17 [1862].

At the Battle of Antietam I commanded one of the battalions of [Brigadier General George] Sykes's division of regulars, held in reserve on the north of Antietam Creek near the Stone Bridge. Three of our battalions of infantry were on the south side of the creek, deployed as skirmishers in front of Sharpsburg.

At the time [Major General] A. P. Hill began to force [Major General Ambrose] Burnside back upon the left, I was talking with [Lieutenant Colonel Robert C.] Buchanan, our brigade commander, when an orderly brought him a note from Captain [Matthew M.] Blunt, who was the senior officer with the battalions of our brigade beyond the creek. The note, as I remember, stated in effect that Captain [Hiram] Dryer, commanding the Fourth Infantry, had ridden into the enemy's lines, and upon returning had reported that there was but one Confederate battery and two regiments in front of Sharpsburg, connecting the wings of [General Robert E.] Lee's army. Dryer was one of the coolest and bravest officers in our service, and on his report Blunt asked instructions.

We learned afterwards that Dryer proposed that he, Blunt, and [Captain W.

Harvey] Brown, commanding the Fourth, Twelfth, and Fourteenth infantries, should charge the enemy in Sharpsburg instanter. But Blunt preferred asking for orders. Colonel Buchanan sent the note to Sykes, who was at the time talking with General McClellan and [Major General] Fitz John Porter, about 150 yards from us. They were sitting on their horses between [Captain Elijah D.] Taft's and [Captain Stephen H.] Weed's batteries a little to our left. I saw the note passed from one to the other in the group, but could not, of course, hear what was said.

We received no orders to advance, however, although the advance of a single brigade at the time (sunset) would have cut Lee's army in two.

After the war, I asked General Sykes why our reserves did not advance upon receiving Dryer's report. He answered that he remembered the circumstance very well and that he thought McClellan was inclined to order the Fifth Corps but that when he spoke of doing so Fitz John Porter said: "Remember, General! I command the last reserve of the last Army of the Republic."

17

My Story of Fredericksburg
Joshua L. Chamberlain, Brevet Major General, U.S.V.

DECEMBER OF 1862 found the Army of the Potomac not in the best of cheer. After the hard-fought battle of Antietam, [Major General George B.] McClellan thought chiefly to recruit his army, and moved but slowly to follow the discomfited [General Robert E.] Lee. Before we had left that field President Lincoln came to look over the pitiable scene and the heroic men who had made it, its dead, and themselves immortal.

Being a guest at our Fifth Corps headquarters, we had the opportunity to discern something more of that great spirit than was ordinarily revealed in those rugged features and deep, sad eyes. The men conceived a sympathy and an affection for him that was wonderful in its intensity. To cheer him and them, a grand review of the battered army was given. Lincoln was a good horseman, and this showed him to new advantage. He took in everything with earnest eyes. As the reviewing cavalcade passed along our lines, where mounted officers were stationed in front of their commands, he checked his mount to draw McClellan's attention to my horse, whose white-dappled color and proud bearing made me almost too conspicuous on some occasions.

Impatience at McClellan's slowness and irresolution, or some other influence at Washington, prompted the removal of this commander and the substitution of [Major General Ambrose] Burnside: and, as somehow a consequence of this, the removal of [Major General] Fitz John Porter from command of the Fifth Corps and the appointment of [Major General Joseph] Hooker to the place. Whatever justification there was for these changes, the sundering of long-familiar ties brought a strain on the heart strings of many men, but it must be remarked in their honor that no murmuring or lack of loyal and cheerful obedience ever betrayed their sorrow. Things were not brightened when Burnside, in taking command, modestly but unwisely intimated his unfitness for it. There was a tendency to take him at his word—especially among the high-ranking generals—and the men could not help knowing it.

For another change, the army was reorganized in three grand divisions: the Right, consisting of the Second and Ninth corps, commanded by [Major General Edwin V.] Sumner; the Center, the Third and Fifth corps, commanded by Hooker; and the Left, the First and Sixth corps, commanded by [Major General William B.] Franklin.

We were soon aware of a decided division of opinion about the best plan for the prosecution of the campaign. Burnside proposed to give up the pursuit of Lee's army, then gathered mainly in the vicinity of Culpeper, and to strike for Petersburg and Richmond. [Major General Henry] Halleck, general in chief, did not approve of this, as it exposed Washington to a back stroke from Lee. Nor did the president. Burnside then offered a compromise plan: to cross the fords of the Rappahannock above Fredericksburg and seize the heights around that city, making his line of supplies the railroad between Fredericksburg and Aquia Creek on the Potomac. Halleck still disapproved, and the president only reluctantly assented. But to the astonishment of both, Burnside, instead of crossing at the upper fords, moved down the north bank of the river and took position directly confronting Fredericksburg.

Burnside's intention was now manifest—to cross the Rappahannock at this front. This would require the service of pontoons, and the demand for them went promptly to Washington. This, of course, displeased the authorities there, a direct assault on Fredericksburg being no part of the plan approved; and there was a long wait for pontoons. In turn, this gave Lee time to confront our purpose with his usual promptitude and skill. He seemed to have had perfect knowledge of Burnside's movements and plans. He lost no time in seizing the crests and wooded slopes which surround Fredericksburg, where he strongly posted his infantry, covered by breastworks and rifle pits. The ground afforded every advantage for his artillery, both for cover and efficiency, and enabled him to dispose his whole line so as to bring a front and flank fire upon any possible assault of ours. His chief of artillery said to [a] scrutinizing [Lieutenant General James] Longstreet: "Our guns are so placed that we can rake the whole field as with a fine-tooth comb. A chicken could not live on that field!" Other batteries

Waiting to be Reviewed by the President (*St. Nicholas*)

were so directed as to sweep every pontoon bridge we could lay. At the base of the principal crest behind the city some of Lee's best troops manned a breast-high stone wall, before which after-history lays direful memories.

At last, on November 25, the pontoons began to arrive. It requires skill and level heads to lay a pontoon bridge. But our brave engineers found their skill baffled and the level of their heads much disturbed by the hot fire from the well-manned rifle pits on the opposite shore, and from the sharpshooters in the houses above them, and had to give up the task. Then our nearest batteries opened a terrific fire on those offensive shelters and their occupants, under which some of the houses were set afire, the smoke and flame giving a wild background to the tense and stirring scene. In the tumult and shadow of this some daring men of the Seventh Michigan and the Nineteenth Massachusetts forged to the front, manned the forsaken boats, and pushed across, driving all before them. [Major General Oliver O.] Howard's division soon crossed over and seized and held that portion of the town.

I may present an incident of this bombardment which impressed me at the time, and has stood vividly in memory ever since. I was near one of our upper batteries—I think [Lieutenant Samuel N.] Benjamin's of the Second Regular

[Artillery]—observing the effect of the fire, when a staff officer of Sumner's rode up and, pointing across, bent low in his saddle and said with softened voice, "Captain, do you see that white shaft over yonder in the green field above those houses?" "I do, sir," was the reply. "That is the tomb of Washington's mother," rejoined the staff officer. "Let your guns spare that!" "They will, sir!" was the answer, as if the guns themselves knew. I turned away, thoughtful of many things.

Next morning the bridges were laid without opposition; Lee doubtless thought his guns would do better work when crowds of men were crossing. Two bridges were in front of our right, Sumner's ground; one for us, in Hooker's front, just opposite the lower city—one being thought enough, as we were not expected to make our principal crossing there; two a mile or more below, in Franklin's front. Lee's dispositions for an offensive-defensive battle were such that it became necessary for us to cover his entire front with artillery for possible chances; so 149 guns were put in position on the north bank of the Rappahannock.

The plan of battle was now made known to us. Sumner was to make an attack and secure a lodgment in the upper and central portion of the town; Franklin was to make the main assault a mile or two below, turn Lee's right, and take his main position in flank. To support Franklin in this, two divisions of our Third Corps were sent him, thus giving him sixty thousand effective men. Hooker, with the rest of our grand division, was to move up to the north bank, near the middle pontoon bridge, ready to cross there or to go to the support of either right or left as should be needed.

The Bombardment of Fredericksburg, December 11, 1862 (*Century*)

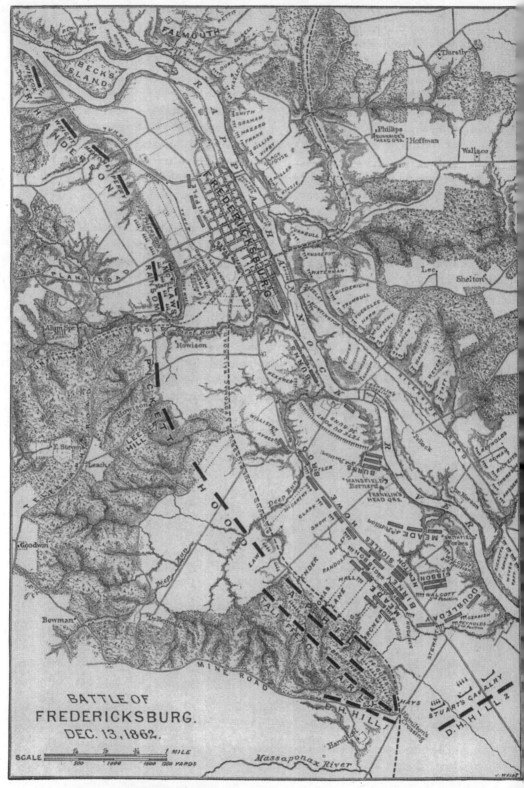

The Battle of Fredericksburg (*Century*)

So we were held in reserve. It may be thought that we were glad to be kept out of the fight, at least for the present. But I take occasion to say that in forming for a great fight it is not regarded as a very special favor to be held in reserve. The holding is, most likely, not for long; and it holds in itself peculiar stress and strain. Waiting and watching, intent and anxious, stirred by the pulse of manhood and the contagion of comradeship, conscious of strength to help, but forbidden to strike, all this wears sorely on every generous spirit. And that other not unmanly impulse—if the worst is coming, let us meet it—may have its part, too, in the drama. It is really less trying to go in first and deliver your blow in the flush of spirit and strength, with the feeling that if the worst come you will be reenforced or relieved, than to be held back till some dire disaster calls when the life-and-death grapple clinches, and you must recover the lost ground or die trying. Or, on the other hand, to be called to advance in triumph over a field already carried—something then is lacking to the manly sense of service rendered according to strength.

Our division, [Brigadier General Charles] Griffin's, of the Fifth Corps, was massed near the Lacy house, opposite the city. We could plainly see the fierce struggle of our Second and Ninth corps to surmount those flaming crests behind the city. Lines first steadily moving forward in perfect order and array, the flag high poised and leading; checked and broken somewhat on each successive rise under the first range of shot and shell; no musket replying—for this would have been worse than useless—but bright bayonets fixed, ready at the final reach to sweep like a sharp wave crest over the enemy's rock-like barrier. Right on! Then, reaching the last slope before and beneath the death-delivering stone wall, suddenly illumined by a sheet of flame, and in an instant the whole line sinking as if swallowed up in earth, the bright flags quenched in gloom, and only a writhing mass marking that high-tide halt of uttermost manhood and supreme endeavor. Then a slow back-flowing, with despairing effort here and there to bear back broken bodies of the brave glorified by the baptism of blood. Again and again the bold essay repeated by other troops, with similar experience, and thickening ridges of the fallen marking the desperate essays.

There we stood for an hour, witnessing five immortal charges. Tears ran down the cheeks of stern men, waiting, almost wishing, to be summoned to the same futile, glorious work. We harkened intensely for the sound of Franklin's guns. Now was heard the exclamation of some veteran commander of ours unable to endure the agony of suspense: "For God's sake, where is Franklin! Where are the 60,000 that were so quickly to decide this day!"

We had heard for a little while the boom of guns and a dull roar through the woods below, but all had died away, and a strange boding silence in that quarter desolated our hearts. The rumor came that [Major General George G.] Meade's division alone had cut through the stubborn lines of Lee's right flank but, unsupported, had been driven back; and thereafter a brave onset by [Brigadier General John] Gibbon's division had met quickly a similar fate—and nothing more seemed attempted; or if so, but in vain.

Now came the call for the reserves! Burnside, despairing of the left and seeing the heroic valor on the right, at last exhausted in unavailing sacrifice, ordered in the Fifth Corps, Griffin's division to lead. First came the silent departure of our first and second brigades, whose course our eyes could not follow.
We waited in tremulous expectation. Not in fear, for that has little place in
manhood when love and duty summon; but eager to do our best and make the
finish. Few words were spoken among officers, however endeared to each other
by confidences deepened by such pressure of life on the borders of death as war
compels; the sense of responsibility silenced all else. Silence in the ranks, too;
one little word, perhaps, telling whom to write to. Griffin gave us a searching,
wistful look, not trusting his lips, and we not needing more. Now rang forth the
thrilling bugle cry, "Third brigade, to the front!"

We pushed for the nearby middle pontoon bridge. The enemy's cannoneers
knew the ranges perfectly. The air was thick with the flying, bursting shells;
whooping solid shot swept lengthwise our narrow bridge, fortunately not yet
plowing a furrow through the midst of us, but driving the compressed air so close
above our heads that there was an unconquerable instinct to shrink beneath it,
although knowing it was then too late. The crowding, swerving column set the
pontoons swaying, so that the horses reeled and men could scarcely keep their
balance. Forming our line in the lower streets, the men were ordered to unsling
knapsacks, and leave them to be cared for by our quartermaster. We began the
advance. Two of our regiments had failed to hear the last bugle calls in the din
and roar around, and did not overtake us: we were thus the right of the line. Our
other two brigades, we heard, had gone to the relief of [Brigadier General Samuel D.] Sturgis's division of the Ninth Corps. We were directed straight forward,
toward the left of the futile advance we had seen so fearfully cut down. The fences
soon compelled us to send our horses back. The artillery fire made havoc.
Crushed bodies, severed limbs, were everywhere around in streets, dooryards, and
gardens. Our men began to fall, and were taken up by the faithful surgeons and
hospital attendants, who also bring courage to their work.

Soon we came out in an open field. Immediately, through the murky smoke,
we saw to our right a battery swing into position to sweep our front. It opened
on us. "God help us now! Colonel, take the right wing; I must lead here!" calmly spoke our brave Colonel [Adelbert] Ames to me, and went to the front, into
the storm.

Now we reached the lines we were to pass for the farther goal. We picked our
way amid bodies thickly strewn, some stark and cold; some silent with slowly
ebbing life; some in sharp agony that must have voice, though unavailing; some
prone from sheer exhaustion or by final order of a hopeless commander. The
living from their close-clung bosom of earth strove to dissuade us: "It's no use,
boys; we've tried that. Nothing living can stand there; it's only for the dead."

On we pushed up slopes slippery with blood, miry with repeated unavailing tread. We reached that final crest, before that all-commanding, counter-

A Defiant Federal
(*Century*)

manding stone wall. Here we exchanged fierce volleys at every disadvantage, until the muzzle flame deepened the sunset red, and all was dark. We stepped back a little behind the shelter of this forlorn, foremost crest, and sank to silence, perhaps—such is human weakness—to sleep.

It was a cold night. Bitter, raw north winds swept the stark slopes. The men, heated by their energetic and exciting work, felt keenly the chilling change. Many of them had neither overcoat nor blanket, having left them with the discarded knapsacks. They roamed about to find some garment not needed by the dead. Mounted officers all lacked outer covering. This had gone back with the horses, strapped to the saddles. So we joined the uncanny quest. Necessity compels strange uses. For myself it seemed best to bestow my body between two dead men among the many left there by earlier assaults, and to draw another cross-wise for a pillow out of the trampled, blood-soaked sod, pulling the flap of his coat over my face to fend off the chilling winds, and, still more chilling, the deep, many-voiced moan that overspread the field. It was heart-rending; it could not be borne. I rose at midnight from my unearthly bivouac, and taking our adjutant for companion went forth to see what we could do for these forsaken sufferers. The deep sound led us to our right and rear, where the fiercest of the fight had held brave spirits too long. As we advanced over that stricken field, the grave, conglomerate monotone resolved itself into its diverse, several elements: some breathing inarticulate agony; some dear home names; some begging for a drop of water; some for a caring word; some praying God for strength to bear; some for life; some for quick death. We did what we could, but how little it was on a field so boundless for feeble human reach! Our best was but to search the canteens of the dead for a draft of water for the dying; or to ease the posture of a broken limb; or to compress a severed artery of fast-ebbing life that might perhaps so be saved, with what little skill we had been taught by our surgeons early in learning the tactics of saving as well as of destroying men. It was a place and time for farewells. Many a word was taken for faraway homes that otherwise might never have had one token from the field of the lost. It was something even to let the passing spirit know that its worth was not forgotten here.

Wearied with the sense of our own insufficiency, it was a relief at last to see through the murk the dusky forms of ghostly ambulances gliding up on the far edge of the field, pausing here and there to gather up its precious freight, and the low-hovering, half-covered lantern, or blue gleam of a lighted match, held close over a brave, calm face to know whether it were of the living or the dead. We had taken bearings to lead us back to our place before the stone wall. There were wounded men lying there also, who had not lacked care. But it was interesting to observe how unmurmuring they were. That old New England habit so reluctant of emotional expressions, so prompt to speak conviction, so reticent as to the sensibilities—held perhaps as something intimate and sacred—that habit of the blood had its corollary of afterglow in this reticence of complaint or murmur under the fearful sufferings and mortal anguish of the battlefield. Yet never have I seen such tenderness as brave men show to comrades when direst need befalls. I trust I show no lack of reverence for gracious spirits nor wrong to grateful memories, when confessing that this tenderness of the stern and strong recalls the Scripture phrase, "passing the love of women."

Down again into our strange companionship of bed! The uncanny quest for covering was still going on around, and coming near. Once a rough but cautious hand lifted the dead man's coat-flap from my face, and a wild, ghoul-like gaze sought to read whether it was of the unresisting.

All night the winds roared. The things that caught their beat were such as were rooted to earth, or broken and shivered by man's machinery. One sound whose gloomy insistence impressed my mood was the flapping of a loosened window blind in a forsaken brick house to our right, desolate but for a few daring or despairing wounded. It had a weird rhythm as it swung between the hoarse-answering sash and wall. To my wakened inner sense it struck a chord far deepening the theme of the eternal song of the "old clock on the stairs": "*Never—forever; forever—never!*" I still seem to hear, in lonely hours with the unforgotten, that dark refrain sounding across the anguished battlefield.

Wakened by the sharp fire that spoke the dawn, as I lifted my head from its restful though strange pillow, there fell out from the breast pocket a much-worn little new testament, written in it the owner's name and home. I could do no less than take this to my keeping, resolved that it should be sent to that home in the sweet valley of the Susquehanna as a token that he who bore it had kept the faith and fought the fight. I may add that sparing mercy allowed the wish to be fulfilled, and this evidence gave the stricken mother's name a place in the list of the nation's remembered benefactors.

Soon came a storm of bullets from front and flank to rout us from our slight shelter in the hollow between the two outermost crests of the manifold assault. This not sufficing, the artillery took up the task, trying to rain shell down upon us and sweep solid shot through our huddled group. We had to lie flat on the earth, and only by careful twisting could any man load and fire his musket against the covered line in front. Before long we saw two or three hundred of the enemy creep out from the right of their stone wall and take advantage of a gully-bank where the ground fell away from our left, to get a full flank fire on us.

The situation was critical. We took warrant of supreme necessity. We laid up a breastwork of dead bodies, to cover that exposed flank. Behind this we managed to live throughout the day. No man could stand up and not be laid down again hard. I saw a man lift his head by the prop of his hands and forearms, and catch a bullet in the middle of his forehead. Such recklessness was forbidden. We lay there all the long day, hearing the dismal "thud" of the bullets into the dead flesh of our life-saving bulwarks. No relief could dare to reach us: reenforcement we did not wish. We saw now and then a staff officer trying to bring orders, and his horse would be shot from under him the moment he reached the crest behind us. We had to take things as they came, and do without the rest.

Night came again, and midway of it the order to remove and take respite within the city. Our wounded were borne to shelter and care back near the pontoon bridge. We got our bodies ready to go, but not our minds. Our dead lay there. We could not take them where we were going, nor would we leave them as they lay. We would bury them in the earth they had made dear. Shallow graves were dug with bayonets and fragments of shell and muskets that strewed the ground. Low headboards, made of broken fence rails or musket butts, rudely carved under sheltered match light, marked each name and home.

We had to pick our way over a field strewn with incongruous ruin; men torn and broken and cut to pieces in every indescribable way, cannon dismounted, gun carriages smashed or overturned, ammunition chests flung wildly about, horses dead and half dead still held in harness, accouterments of every sort scattered as by whirlwinds. It was not good for the nerves, that ghastly march, in the lowering night! We were moved to the part of the town first occupied by Sumner's troops, and bivouacked in the streets, on the stone flagging. Little sleep that night, or rest next morning. Troops of all commands were crowded in without pretension of military use or position. Consequently the Confederates began to bombard their own town. Toward night rumors came through prisoners that Stonewall Jackson was coming down from the right upon our huddled mass to crush us where we were or sweep us into the river. No doubt he could have done it. But we afterward learned that Lee did not favor the proposition, not feeling quite sure of the issue. He thought we might fight with our backs to walls as he had seen us fight before them, in the open. Rumor came also that Burnside, in his desperation, had ordered a new assault on the stonewall front, and proposed to lead his Ninth Corps in person. But, as we afterward learned, Lincoln, hearing of this, wired, forbidding it.

Just after midnight of this miserable day we were summoned—three regiments of us—to set forth on some special service, we knew not what or where, something very serious, we must believe. Some extensive operations were contemplated—we were aware of that from the decided manner and movements of officers and men of all commands. But we were soon assured as to our part. We were bound for the extreme front, to form a picket line to cover the center of the field while the army was to take some important action. Colonel Ames commanded our line, the regiment coming under my charge. The last order came in low tones, "Hold this ground at all hazards, and to the last!" A strange query crossed our minds: Last of what? No dictionary held that definition. As a general term, this reached the infinite!

So we went to work, silently, but intently. Groping about, we laid hold of some picks and spades strewn rather hurriedly around a little to our rear earlier in the night. The men were told to settle themselves into the ground, and let it hold them for a good turn; each two, or each for himself, to throw up a little earthwork, elbow like, behind which the morning's test might be withstood for a while. We were so near the enemy's rifle pits that we could hear something of their conversation, from which it appeared that they were about as anxious as we were. We spoke only in whispers. The night was pitch dark. To be sure of the proper direction of our line I had to feel my way along by such tokens as instinct and prudence could provide. Hearing the gravel going at a lively rate a little out of what I thought conformity to instructions, I approached the sound and said in a very confidential tone to the invisible performer, "Throw to the other side, my man; that's where the danger is!" "Golly!" came back the confident answer, "don't ye s'pose I know which side them Yanks be? They're right onto us now." I was rebuked and instructed, but must preserve my dignity as a Confederate on "grand rounds." "Dig away then, but keep a right sharp lookout!" I said—then obeyed my own suggestion and "dug away" as calmly as my imperfect lookout would permit.

We were pretty well buried, and braced for the coming dawn, when a strange clatter came up from the left rear, and a gasping voice called, "Where is the commander of these troops?" I acknowledged that responsibility. "Get yourselves out of this as quick as God will let you! The whole army is across the river!" was the message—heard, no doubt, by the whole hostile picket line. This was a critical moment. Something must be said and done quickly. "Steady in your places, my men!" I ordered. "One or two of you arrest this stampeder! This is a ruse of the enemy! We'll give it to them in the morning!" This was spoken with no suppressed nor hesitating tone, but pitched for the benefit of our astonished neighbors in double darkness in our front. My men caught the keynote of my policy, trusted my discretion, and held themselves quiet. I stepped back to the staff officer, and rebuked him severely for his rashness, pointing out to him the state of things, vexed at having to moderate even my stress of voice. He explained. He had had such a time getting over that field and up to this front line he had almost lost his wits. I could understand this; and told him to follow for himself his message to us, and I would not report his misdemeanor.

I sought out Ames, and we made up a manner of withdrawal; to keep up appearances; to hold the line for a time, with pretended zeal but redoubled caution; then to withdraw under a new form of tactics: every even-numbered man to resume his digging and make it lively; every odd-numbered man to step softly to the rear and form line under the second officer of the company; this half of the regiment to move back a hundred yards or so and halt in line of battle, faced to the front, and hold there till the other half, formed in like manner, should come up and pass them to a like distance; then the reciprocal movement to be repeated till we got well to the rear. These tactics proved to be wise, for the enemy, after a short, puzzled hesitation, came out from their entrenchments and followed us up as closely as they deemed safe, the same traits of human nature in them as in us causing a little "nervousness" when moving in darkness and in the presence of an alert enemy, also moving.

Thus we made our way over that stricken field, with stooping walk and muskets at a "trail." It had been a misty night, with fitful rains. Just as our first reach was attained, the clouds broke apart in rifts here and there. Through one of these came a sudden gleam from the weird, waning moon, which struck full upon our bright musket barrels, and revealed us clearly to our watchful pursuers. A bullet or two sang past us. "To the ground, every man of you," went the quick order, and only a scattering volley sent its baffled greeting over our heads. We had to watch now for favoring clouds.

It was a dreary retreat down those wreck-strewn slopes. It was hard enough to be stumbling over torn-up sods, groups of the dead or forms of the solitary dying, muskets dropped with quick relax, or held fast with death's convulsive clutch, swords, bayonets, cartridge boxes, fragments of everything, everywhere, but when a ghastly gleam of moonlight fell on the pale faces, fixed and stark; and on open eyes that saw not but reflected uttermost things, it sent a shiver through us.

Reaching the pontoon bridgehead just at dawn, we found that the bridge floor had been muffled by sods and brush, that our expected night tread might not disclose our passing to the pressing foe. We gathered what we could of what had belonged to us, taking those of our wounded that had not gone before. But the piteous spectacle of others not of our command but belonging to us by the bond of a great brotherhood so moved our large-hearted surgeon, Doctor Hersom, that he begged permission to stay among them. This he did at the cost of being taken prisoner with dire experience of suffering for himself. Sorrowfully but proudly we left him for his ministry of mercy.

So we crossed again that bridge we had passed three days before with strange foreboding but unswerving resolution, little dreaming that we should be put to shame, but now little imputing to ourselves the blame. While waiting for the pontoons some of us had frequently ridden along the bank in full view of the Confederates across the river and through field glasses studied the construction of their works with curious interest and the natural common-sense inference that we would never be called upon to assault just where Lee had prepared for and wished us.

Over the river, then, we marched, and up that bank, whence we now looked back across at Fredericksburg, and saw the green slopes blue with the bodies of our dead. It was raining drearily when I brought the regiment to rest by the dismal wayside. General Hooker came riding slowly by. We had not seen him during the terrible three days. Indeed, he had no business to be where we were. We supposed he and our corps commander, [Major General Daniel] Butterfield, were somewhere controlling and observing their commands. Hooker caught sight of me sitting in the rain leaning back against a tree, and gave kindly greeting. "You've had a hard chance, Colonel; I am glad to see you out of it!" I was not cheerful, but tried to be bright. "It was a chance, General; not much intelligent design there!" "God knows I did not put you in!" came the rather crisp reply. "That was

Christmas Eve around the Campfire (*Scribner's*)

the trouble, General. You should have put us in. We were handled in piecemeal, on toasting forks." It was plain talk. And he did not reprove me.

But the general's remark led to wide inferences. It disclosed perhaps the main cause of this great disaster. The commander of the Center Grand Division "did not put his men in!" They were sent by superior orders, in detachments, to support other commands, or as a "forlorn hope" at various times and places during the unexpected developments—or rather the almost inevitable accidents—of the battle. It should not have been a disaster; Franklin with his 60,000 men should have turned Lee's right; whereas he attacked with only two divisions, and one at a time; and did not follow up with his whole force their splendid initiative. When Franklin failed, it was rashness to expect Sumner to carry the formidable heights behind the city, made impregnable by Lee's best skill and valor. That front might have been held still under menace, while Sumner, reinforced perhaps by the main body of Hooker's Grand Division, might have concentrated upon Lee's left, above the city, and flanked the formidable bastions crowning the heights that entrenched his front with all that earth and manhood could do.

That the battle was not fought according to Burnside's intention, and that his plan was mutilated by distrust and disharmony among his subordinate commanders, does not exonerate him. It is part of the great trust and place of a chief commander to control reluctant and incongruous elements and to make subordinates and opponents submit to his imperial purpose.

Burnside attempted a vindication somewhat on these lines; but too late. He prepared an order removing from command several of his high-ranking but too little subordinate generals, and made ready to prefer charges against them for trial by court-martial. But Lincoln again interposed his common-sense advice, and the matter was passed over. Not long after, at his own request, Burnside was relieved from command of the army, and magnanimously resumed his place with his old Ninth Corps.

18

Lee at Fredericksburg
J. Horace Lacy, Major, C.S.A.

AS A GENERAL-STAFF officer thrown into relations confidential and intimate with our Confederate leaders, I had exceptional advantages for observation from behind the scenes of the incidents and actors in what was certainly one of the grandest dramas ever enacted upon the trembling stage of human affairs.

On December 1, 1862, I was sent by Major General Gustavus W. Smith, upon whose staff I was serving, as bearer of dispatches to General Robert E. Lee. I informed General Lee that I had leave of absence for several days, and he kindly invited me to remain as his guest at his headquarters. I felt highly honored by the invitation, but the experience of one meal was enough. Rye coffee, heavy biscuits, and poor, tough beef I thought would hardly compensate for the honor of dining with the commander in chief. The night of the tenth I spent in Fredericksburg with my brother, the Reverend B. T. Lacy, D.D. (afterwards corps chaplain for [Major] General [Thomas J.] Stonewall Jackson), at the house of a dear friend and connection, where a company of young ladies had gathered to listen to my brother, a noted *raconteur*. It was very late before we retired.

Before daylight I was awakened by the sound of three unshotted guns, which I had been informed at headquarters was the battle signal. "I gat up and gat" without much regard to the order of my going. As I left the house the heavy roar of the cannonade and the rattle of musketry told that the fight had begun and the Federals were laying down their pontoons. [Brigadier General William] Barksdale's Mississippi brigade was entrenched along the banks of the Rappahannock. A terrible artillery fire was opened from the Stafford Heights, to protect and cover the parties who were laying down the bridges. Taking only a bird's-eye view of the situation, I double-quicked it out of the doomed town. The streets were swept by a hail storm of grape and shrapnel. Chimneys came toppling down. Houses were in flames—a plank fence behind which I was retreating was suddenly swept away, and then, as the soldier said, "the first thing I knew, I didn't know nothing."

When I returned to consciousness I found myself lying prone on the frozen earth in a little gully. The crepuscular dawn of that cold gray morning was then more illumined by flashes fitfully bursting through sulphurous smoke than by that morning radiance which poets love to sing. Closely hugging the ground, I at length proceeded deliberately to investigate my condition. I felt certain that I was desperately wounded. Putting my hands upon my throbbing temples, I saw even in the dim light that they were red with blood. I soon found, however, that my head was about in its normal condition, and the thought occurred that I had probably been knocked down by the wind from a solid shot and that the blood was from my hands, torn by contact with the ice and splinters when I fell. Perceiving a lull in the storm, I arose and made a beeline for the western hills and the Army of Northern Virginia.

I first came upon a Georgia regiment. Their campfires were still burning brightly, and the men had just finished breakfast. Recognizing my uniform, they kindly invited me to the fire. A dispute was evidently going on as to whether [Major General Ambrose] Burnside would attack Lee in that position. Finally a lieutenant was called up to hold the stakes, and two very dirty soldiers, clad in Georgia butternut homespun, wagered fifty dollars in "Confed" on, as they

Chatham, opposite Fredericksburg (*Century*)

stated it, whether "Burnside would be such a damned fool as to make a real sure-enough attack on 'Mas Bob,' when anybody must know he had the dead wood on him."

Just then the long roll sounded for five miles around the semicircle of hills that look down on Fredericksburg. Sauntering up slowly, and with deliberate and indifferent talk about the small commonplaces of their monotonous camp life, the butternuts took their muskets from where they were stacked and lazily formed the line of battle. At that moment a woman young and pretty, with two little girls clinging to her skirts and a baby pressed to her bosom, suddenly met that serried line. With streaming eyes and impassioned utterance she cried, "Southern soldiers, my husband is somewhere in your army, my home is in flames down there; will you let those people follow me as I pass your lines to find shelter for myself and little children with a friend?" Then with erect front, the response, as the ranks parted to let her pass, was the wild battle cry of the Army of Northern Virginia, which, caught up by each regiment, brigade, and division, rose high above the roll of drums, and sweeping around that semicircle of hills, was not heard with indifference by the distant foe.

Ascending the heights, I soon reached what was called the headquarters battery of General Lee. Afar across the valley and river in the gray light of the early morning could be seen the white porches of my home, Chatham, made historic by Federal army correspondents as the "Lacy House." The porches were filled with officers and gaily dressed women, and from half a score of brass bands rang out across the valley "Yankee Doodle" and "Hail, Columbia!" The commanding officer of the battery asked me if I would permit him to scatter the unbidden guests at my home. At his request I asked General Lee to authorize the fire of the heavy guns, which would have laid Chatham in the dust. With a smile he refused, and asking me to walk with him, we withdrew a short distance. He then motioned me to sit by him on the trunk of a large tree.

Confederate Artillery on Marye's Heights (*Century*)

Looking across at Chatham through his field glass he said,

Major, I never permit the unnecessary effusion of blood. War is terrible enough, at its best, to a Christian man; I hope yet to see you and your dear family happy in your old home. Do you know I love Chatham better than any place in the world except Arlington! I courted and won my dear wife under the shade of those trees. By the way, not long since I was riding out with my staff, and observing how your grand old trees had been cut down by those people, I saw that a magnificent tulip poplar at the head of the ravine, north of the house, was still standing, and, with somewhat of your rhetoric, I said to [Majors Charles S.] Venable and [Walter H.] Taylor: "There is nothing in vegetable nature so grand as a tree. Grappling with its roots the granite foundations of the everlasting hills, it reaches its sturdy and gnarled trunk on high, spreads its branches to the heavens, casts its shadow on the sward, and the birds build their nests and sing amid its umbrageous foliage. Behold, the monarch stripped of its attendants and guards awes the vandal by the simple majesty of his sublime isolation." Pocketing my field glass, and riding on, I heard mingled with laughter a request from the young gentlemen that I would bring my glass to bear once more on the monarch of the forest. I looked, and even while I had been talking the axe of the vandal was laid to the root, and the monarch had fallen.

Then, moved by emotion unusual to his calm and equable nature, he continued, "I had 300 acres of woodland at Arlington. Serving the United States Government for many years on the frontier, I marked with my own hand each tree that was to be used for timber or fuel. They tell me all my trees are gone—

yours are all gone"; then rising from the log, with a fire and a passion rarely witnessed in him, and with all the majesty of his sublime presence, he said: "Major, they have our *trees;* they shall never have the *land!*"

Three years after the close of the war I was a visitor at the home of General Lee, then president of Washington and Lee University. After dinner the general retired, and I was invited to see Mrs. Lee in her chamber. She was a great sufferer and confirmed invalid, incapable of motion save in a roller chair, which it was the chief delight of him who had so long directed great armies to move from room to room, bending over her with the grace of a Sidney and the devotion of a youthful lover.

I told Mrs. Lee the story which I have so imperfectly attempted to reproduce. Need I tell any woman who reads these pages that tears streamed down that patient, furrowed face, or that a light and joy from beyond the stars beamed through those tears, as she knew that the thoughts of her great husband wandered far away from the clash of arms to the memories of their youthful love and courtship under the shade of her ancestral oaks, for Chatham was originally the property of a near relative. As I concluded the sentence, "They shall never have the land," hearing a slight noise, I turned and saw the general, who had silently entered, in dressing gown and slippers. The great buckshot drops slowly rolled down that face, whose calm was never broken by the earthquake shock of battle. Slowly and silently he retired, and I could but feel the deepest compunction that words of mine should have sent another pang through that great heart. For then, looking up from the hell of carpetbag Reconstruction, we verily thought that trees, land, country, liberty, all had gone forever.

The entire day at Fredericksburg was passed by me on the commanding height to which I have already alluded. Nearly 150 guns poured a continuous cannonade upon the city. Yet Barksdale's gallant Mississippians for hours held the river bank, inflicting terrible loss upon those engaged in laying down the bridge. Nine times the enemy were driven back; a heavy detachment of infantry crossing in boats under protection of the cannonade at length forced them to fall back, which they did, fighting from house to house and street to street, and late at night were with difficulty recalled, like dogs that have tasted blood and are forced to quit the quarry.

The next day, December 12, passed without anything I need dwell upon. That night I spent at the tent of my friend Colonel H. Coalter Cabell, and slept between Lieutenant Tom Tucker, son of my father's classmate and dearest friend, Judge Beverly Tucker of William and Mary College, and Captain [H. L. P.] King. The next day Tucker received a wound which lamed him for life, and of King, the record was written in blood: "Dead on the field of glory." Such is war.

The morning of December 13 opened warm and sultry. With the first flash of dawn I was again at the headquarters battery. A white fog covered the valley, through which the spires and chimneys of the town, and the more distant Stafford Heights loomed vague and indistinct.

About 9:00 A.M. this curtain of mist was suddenly lifted by a freshening western breeze. Then to the thousands of spectators along those heights was revealed probably as splendid a spectacle as ever greeted mortal vision. Just then I again heard a cheer, which swept around the semicircle of hills. A horseman came riding up at full speed, with cap in hand and bowed head, and a youth in a gray roundabout followed hard after. That horseman was Stonewall Jackson, and that youth I have since come to know as the aide de camp, Captain (now the Reverend) I. P. Smith, the husband of my eldest daughter.

Soon after, a courier brought me an order from General Smith to return immediately to Richmond. I had to walk along our lines six miles to the nearest point to which the railroad came. I well remember the sole came entirely off one boot. Just in front of me along that whole line came the roar of the great battle. Above the thunder of the artillery and rattle of musketry, I could hear the deep huzzas of the Federals, the shrill battle cry of the Confederates, and the "shouting of the captains." Wearied and exhausted, I reached the train which was being rapidly crowded with the wounded.

When the train reached Richmond, I was met by a member of our staff who informed me that my servant, baggage, and horses were on another train; and in two minutes I was speeding southward. When we reached Goldsboro, North Carolina, our ears were saluted with the familiar sound of battle in which it was my duty immediately to take part. Then was forced upon me the solemn reflection: How far-reaching were the issues of the great sectional contest! How wide, wasting, ruthless, and devastating was this war!

PART 5

The Western Theatre in 1862

19

Desperation and Heroism at the Battle of Valverde

Franklin Cook, First Lieutenant, Fifth U.S. Infantry

THE BARGAIN by which the Stars and Stripes were displaced by the Stars and Bars over all the forts, garrisons, and arsenals in the State of Texas was consummated in the spring of 1861. Fort Bliss, located in the extreme northwest corner of the state, had always been under the jurisdiction of the commander of the Department of New Mexico, but was nevertheless included in the surrender and peacefully handed over to the Texas commissioners on their arrival in April without any demurring on the part of the United States officials.

Acting upon the belief that they were only to be opposed by men who were either afraid to fight or had no heart in the cause in which they were enlisted, a mere handful of Texans moved up the Rio Grande from Fort Bliss in July for the purpose of attempting the capture of Fort Fillmore, forty-five miles above. This fort was garrisoned by a considerable force of all Regular troops and commanded by Major Isaac Lynde, Seventh United States Infantry, who, on the approach of this small force of Texans, abandoned Fillmore and retreated in the direction of Fort Stanton. The victors, highly elated at this unexpected piece of good luck, pursued the fleeing soldiers and made them prisoners as they were overtaken straggling along the road alone and in small squads, until at last the major, with the main body, was overhauled and captured at San Augustine Springs, twenty-five miles from the fort, he making the least possible show of resistance.

Colonel Edward R. S. Canby was in command of the Department of New Mexico, with his headquarters at Santa Fe. He, no doubt, intended to hold Fort Fillmore, making it his frontier post, and thought he had stationed a sufficiently strong garrison there to hold it for the present against any force which the enemy could bring against it, not counting on his subordinate to surrender it to a force so much inferior to his own. Canby, not having a sufficient number of men at his command to attempt its recapture, determined for the time being to forfeit all that portion of his department south of the Jornada del Muerto and strongly fortify Fort Craig, the next military post northwest of it, concentrate his forces there or near there, to be prepared to dispute any forward movement of the enterprising enemy, who, after his success at Fillmore, settled down at Fort Bliss and Mesilla to await reinforcements from below.

All remote posts and outlying stations in New Mexico were at once ordered to be abandoned and their garrisons to take stations along the Rio Grande, within easy distance of Craig or at the fort itself when all had arrived. The total number of effective men who could be thrown into this fortress in case of emergency was still not more than 1,000, a number totally inadequate to successfully cope with the force which it was expected that the enemy would bring against it. That is, they might be able to hold the strong fort, but they were too few to repel the invaders and prevent the country from being overrun by the lawless enemy.

Authority was obtained from Washington to raise some regiments of New Mexican volunteers, and the governor called out the militia of the territory to repel invasion. The volunteers were enlisted, armed, and equipped as rapidly as possible. The whole were assembled in the vicinity of Craig and set to drilling, in the hope to make tolerable soldiers of them by the time their services would be actually needed. Vain hopes, however, as the sequel proved.

A Southern Military District was created with headquarters at Craig, and Colonel Benjamin S. Roberts, Third Cavalry, was assigned to the command. Throughout the fall and early winter of 1861–62 Colonel Roberts kept himself well informed of the movements of the enemy at Fort Bliss and Mesilla by means of spies. They were receiving reinforcements occasionally and it became certain that they would move up the river as soon as they thought themselves strong enough to warrant the risk. There being no regular artillery in the department it was necessary to supply the deficiency by making a detail of picked men from several companies till the number required to work six pieces of cannon was obtained. Captain Alexander McRae, Third Cavalry, was assigned to the command, with Lieutenants Lyman Mishler, Fifth Infantry, and Joseph McC. Bell, of the volunteers, as subordinates. The twenty-four pounder howitzers at the fort were also manned and place under the command of Lieutenant R. H. Hall, Tenth Infantry.

The walls of the fort were strengthened and a long ditch dug around the whole, lunettes at the northern and southern angles commanded the ditches, and knolls in the vicinity of the fort had earthworks erected on them, which in case of an attack would have made a most formidable means of defense. Companies were assigned to defend each earthwork, to which they would repair at all alarms, which soon began to occur nightly and sometimes as often as three or four times in a single night. In short, pending the expected attack, everything

at the fort was put and kept in the best possible condition. Drilling and reconnoitering by day and by night, both officers and men slept in their clothing, with
their arms by their sides ready for use at a moment's warning.

The men being nearly all of the Regular Army were rather pleased than otherwise at the prospect of a struggle with the Texans, for they felt a little chagrined
at the poor record which the Regulars at Fillmore had made, and they wanted
an opportunity to wipe out the stain and also revenge themselves on the Texan
troops for their audacity. For myself I had been treacherously surrendered to
these same troops a little less than a year before in Texas, had escaped from them,
and with a good deal of danger and suffering succeeded in getting North. They
had held me a prisoner for about four months and I had experienced considerable ill usage at their hands. It was, therefore, with keen satisfaction that I anticipated a meeting with them again, this time, however, associated with comrades who did not propose to surrender the arms in their hands to the first rabble
who demanded them; on the contrary, intended to keep and use them until the
enemy had demonstrated his ability to take them or until he had surrendered
to them.

About January 1 [1862] it was known that the main body of the Texans were
encamped at Mesilla and a forward movement was soon to be made. Scouting
parties from each side often met and exchanged a few shots, but did little damage to each other. February 1 brought Colonel Canby and staff, when he assumed
the command, and soon thereafter it was known that Brigadier General H. H.
Sibley, Confederate States Army, had arrived at Mesilla with reinforcements, had
taken command of the Texan forces numbering 1,500, had broken camp at
Mesilla and was slowly moving up the river toward us. We had been sufficiently vigilant before, but we were doubly so now, and owing to this a surprise was
utterly impossible by any foe, however active.

The enemy doubtless was well informed of the state of the defenses at Craig,
also, the vigilance and discipline of the garrison, for he made no attempt to
surprise us, while he gave our stronghold a wide berth in his passage up the
country. When he reached the little town of Paraje, six miles south of the fort,
he crossed the river and proceeded to make a detour of some dozen miles or
more, so as to avoid passing too near the fort. In doing this it was necessary to
cut a new road through a very rough country, composed chiefly of sand drifts
and lava beds. This work was exceedingly laborious and difficult and they were
some four or five days making the passage, all this time suffering much for water,
for there was none to be found except in the river and this, from the roughness
of the country, could only be approached at a few points, and these Canby kept
well-guarded.

Opposite Craig, on the east side of the river, is a long range of high bluffs composed mostly of rough, broken, volcanic rocks. Beyond these the country is less
rocky, but rough and uneven, for a mile or so, gradually rising by a series of ter-
race-like sand drifts, until it reaches the height of the surrounding country.

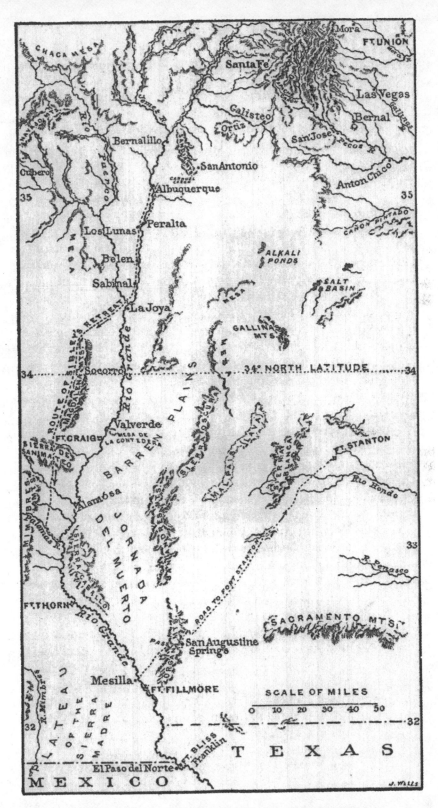

New Mexico Campaign and Sibley's Retreat (*Century*)

Along the summit of these sand drifts the Texans were toiling on February 20. Canby was aware of their sufferings from thirst, and feared that they might attempt to get to the river by occupying the rocky bluffs opposite the fort, in which case they could easily throw shell across and annoy us a good deal. Besides, if he once got there it would be almost impossible for us with our small force to dislodge him. So Canby crossed in force and occupied the bluffs himself. When they were secured he sent forward a strong line of skirmishers under Captain H. R. Selden, Fifth Infantry, who advanced to within a few hundred yards of the enemy and opened fire on him; but he did not accept the challenge or return the fire, except with his artillery, which, posted on the summit of the sand hills, kept up a furious cannonade for several hours, directing his fire chiefly at those who occupied the rocky bluffs, and although he must have fired some two or three hundred shots, the only damage done was to slightly wound one man on the cheek, he being hit by a piece of flying lava splintered from a rock by the concussion of a shot. Our men slept among the rocks that night and all avenues of approach to the river were strongly guarded.

It was evident from the direction in which the enemy were steering that he contemplated striking the river again on the twenty-first at Valverde, six miles above the fort; indeed, this was the nearest point where the river was accessible from that side without great difficulty, if at all. Early on the morning of the twenty-first, therefore, our two batteries, with small supporting columns of infantry, were dispatched to Valverde. The Texan advance and our artillery with their supporting columns must have arrived there nearly simultaneously; at any rate there were few, if any of the enemy, who succeeded in getting to the water until after the battle was over.

The general course of the Rio Grande is south, but just at Valverde it makes a sharp bend to a right angle and for one-half a mile or more runs due east, when it is again bent to the south by meeting some high rocky bluffs. Between these two bends in the river the Texan advance attempted to approach the water, but were immediately fired upon and driven back by our batteries, which were posted on the opposite side, one near each bend. Shortly after this the Texan battery arrived, took position on the opposite side, and for an hour or more a sharp artillery duel was carried on, but without a great deal of damage being done or any very decided advantage gained by either side.

Captain Selden's column of infantry, about 800 strong, consisting of detachments of the Fifth and Seventh Infantry, with two good companies of Colorado volunteers, had spent the night among the rocks of the bluffs opposite the fort. They were withdrawn about 8:00 A.M. and ordered to repair in haste to Valverde, where they arrived about 9:30 A.M., and soon afterwards the main body of the enemy were seen some two miles distant winding their way around the bluffs, their bright gun barrels glistening in the bright morning sun, while they toiled along through the sand drifts approaching the scene of conflict.

If you take a point over half a mile up the river from where it bends to the

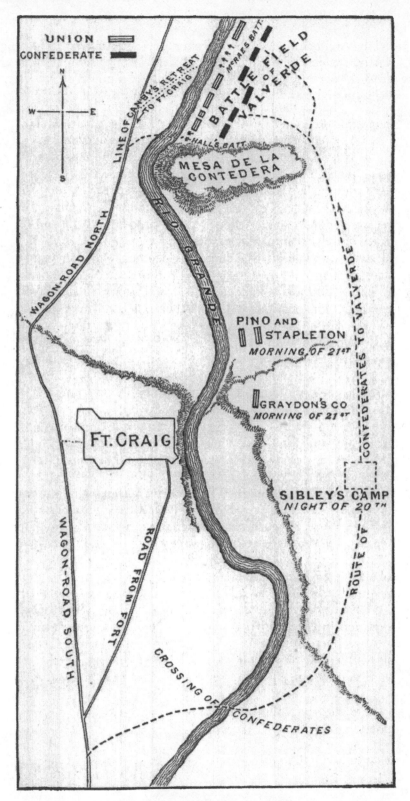

Fort Craig and Valverde (*Century*)

eastward and an equal distance down, then connect these two points by a straight line, you will enclose the whole space where the Battle of Valverde was fought, won, and lost. Four-fifths of this space was covered by a growth of large cotton-wood trees and in parts a thick underbrush. On the side towards the fort there were fewer trees and no underbrush. When Selden's command arrived, and while the men were marching past the bend in the river, the Texan battery opened on them with a plenteous shower of grape and canister; but the guns of the Texans were trained too high, and as the men were covered with leaves and twigs cut from the trees above them not a man was hit by a shot. Two or three strong columns of New Mexican volunteers and militia were sent to the scene, but as they had little or nothing to do with the fighting but little need be said of them.

Colonel Canby remained at the fort, giving the command of the forces at Valverde to Colonel Roberts, who directed Selden to take his command to the ford above the bend in the river, and crossing, deploy them as skirmishers, move forward and clear the woods of the enemy. McRae's battery crossed after Selden, went into battery in a position just inside the bend, and threw shell into the woods ahead of the skirmish line as it advanced. The enemy threw out a line of skirmishers, which, however, quickly retired before ours. The two flanks of our line moved forward at a quicker rate than the center, so this, by the time we had advanced four or five hundred yards, made our line a semi-circle. The right of our line came upon the Texas battery with its support, one thousand strong, posted behind a rough, hastily-constructed breastwork made by piling togeth-er rocks and cottonwood logs. The Texans were too strongly posted to be at once dislodge by our small force, so a halt was sounded. The men were directed to cover themselves as well as possible and continue to fire as often as they could see anything to shoot at.

The Texans could not work their guns, the men being obliged to take ref-uge behind the breastwork to avoid our fire. Their battery horses were all killed or taken out of range. The enemy had all the advantage here, for it was rare that we could get a fair shot at one of them, while we could not so well cover our-selves. Their bullets whistled about our ears and several of our men were killed and wounded. A sergeant of Captain [P. W. L.] Plympton's company of the Sev-enth Infantry, with six men, came up and reported to me, having lost their com-mand. While the sergeant was calling my attention to his waist-belt, which a moment before had been torn in two by a Minie bullet, I heard a dull noise not unlike that produced by throwing a small pebble forcibly into deep water, when he suddenly threw his arms about me, exclaiming: "Lieutenant, you are shot!" and falling to the ground instantly expired. The bullet had passed through the brave fellow's heart.

I have spoken of the semi-circular form of our line. My company was on the extreme right. The adjutant, Lieutenant [A. L.] Anderson, being on the left and wishing to communicate some order to me, instead of going around by the rear of the line rode directly across from wing to wing, and in so doing passed within twenty yards of the Texan breastwork, all the time not only exposed to their fire, but also to that of our own men. Strange to say, both he and his horse escaped until he reached the spot where I was standing, when his horse was struck in the hip by a bullet and began to struggle furiously, and in doing so tramped upon a poor fellow lying at the roots of a tree with a shot through his body. The wounded man cried out piteously: "Oh, keep him off me for I am wounded!" And while we were endeavoring to protect the man another shot struck the animal in the head and killed him.

While the bullets were falling around us the thickest I could not help smiling at a young German of my company who was struck by a shot in the left shoulder, but not very badly hurt. He looked at the hole in his coat for a moment, and then when he saw the blood come trickling through it, seemed to grow very angry, and instead of leaving the field or calling for help, he shouted out towards to enemy: "Wot for you do dat? Damn you, I pay you for dat," and he went on loading and firing with great rapidity, all the time scolding and swearing at the enemy, now in English, and then in German!

This state of affairs continued for an hour or more, when suddenly we discovered a large body of troops coming in on our right. It took but a glance to see that they were Texans, that our right flank was turned and the sooner we got back out of that situation the better for us. Retreat was at once sounded and executed in good order, although the enfilading fire to which we were now subjected caused us here to sustain our heaviest loss. The bullets literally rained about us. Zip! zip! was the sound you heard continually, while the numberless little clouds of dust rising from the earth all about told where the shots had struck. Calls for assistance from our wounded comrades constantly greeted our ears. Many times I heard the prayer, "Oh, I am wounded and cannot walk; don't leave me to be taken prisoner!" We succeeded in carrying away the most of our wounded. Reaching the river again we were ordered to lie down behind a sand bank, expecting that the enemy would soon advance in his turn, but he did not come immediately.

A man of my company named Huston now came to me to inquire the location of the hospital. I told him it was two miles down the river and then inquired what he wanted of it; he said that he was wounded and pointed to his forehead to indicate the spot. I looked for his wound, but only succeeded in finding a small swelling, which looked as though it might have been produced by a slight blow. I heard no more of him until the next day, when I found him in a dying condition in the hospital at the fort. The bullet had entered from behind and passing directly through his head lodged just beneath the skin of his forehead, producing the swelling I had noticed; still, after leaving me he had been able unaided to walk the two miles to the hospital wagons.

When our skirmish line was first formed its right was near the bend in the river where it changes its course to the eastward, and if this flank had been instructed to keep to the river as it advanced—the balance of the line to have been governed by it—no such a disaster as the turning of our right could have happened. Instead of this being done, as the line advanced it drew away from the river, and by the time it had encountered the enemy's breastwork there was an unprotected interval between our right and the river of at least one-fourth of a mile. The enemy were quick to take advantage of this error, and sent the column through and turned our flank and made us retreat. Hall's battery commanded this interval, of course, but the underbrush was so thick that the movement of the enemy was not detected until too late to prevent it.

The morning had been fine and quite warm, so we all came away without our overcoats, but about noon the weather changed; it became very cold, a frozen sleet falling for nearly all the afternoon; we suffered extremely from cold. About 3:00 P.M. Colonel Canby and staff arrived. He assumed command and at once proceeded to make new dispositions, at which we were all well pleased, for we had been standing still in one position now for some two hours and were all very impatient there-at. Colonel [Kit] Carson's regiment was stationed below the bend in the river facing eastward. To his left was [Colonel Miguel E.] Pino, the militia commander, with his forces. Hall's battery, which remained all day in one position, was moved to the front across the river. McRae's battery was moved one-fourth of a mile up the river and advanced a little. In its front was a small cleared space of perhaps two acres, beyond which the woods were thick, but the enemy could be seen moving among the trees in considerable force, and it was known that he had some movement which was soon to be made. McRae began to shell them, and at this moment the report came that Hall's battery was threatened. Canby fearing that, in case of a charge upon Hall, Pino's regiment of militia would not stand its ground (there being but two small companies of Regulars with it) detached three companies of the Fifth Infantry—B, D, and F—under Captain [Benjamin] Wingate, to go in double-quick to its relief.

This was a fatal error, for no sooner had these troops been sent away than a body of the enemy, 1,000 strong, was seen to emerge from the woods into the clearing in front of McRae, making directly for him. He double-loaded his guns with grape and canister and fired as rapidly as possible on the advancing foe, but the distance was so short that the pieces were aimed too high and did no execution. Right on they came in spite of opposition, yelling like so many denizens of the infernal regions who had just made their escape. Armed with double-barreled shotguns, six-shooters, and bowie knives, they waited until at short range, when they discharged their shotguns at the artillerists with murderous effect. Then when their guns were empty they threw them away and mixed with the men at the cannon in a hand-to-hand encounter, using their pistols and knives.

Our men did all that flesh and blood could do to save their battery, but the odds was more than four to one against them, and therefore in a fight of this kind but one termination was possible. Those who were not killed or wounded were driven with their supporters into the river together. Many were shot in the water while crossing and their bodies were carried away by the current. Those who escaped, when they reached the other side, reformed their ranks and marched away towards the fort, their own guns hurling shot and shell after them to expedite their movements.

When Canby saw that McRae's battery was to be charged by the enemy he sent a hasty order for Wingate to return, but by the time that officer got the order he had all that he could attend to in repulsing a squadron of cavalry that was charging him. They came on at a gallop with drawn sabers, making the woods resound with their customary demoniac yells. They, no doubt, expected to scare the bluecoats into taking to their heels for safety, but that battalion happened to be made up of the kind of material that does not do that sort of fighting. They stood their ground until the enemy was within fifty yards of them when the captain's voice rang out clear and sharp, "Fire!" and the report which followed was as if one man had pulled all the triggers at once.

When the smoke cleared away we looked for one moment at the heap of dead and wounded horses and men, but saw no enemy to oppose us. A second order to return now came from Canby, almost instantly followed by another saying that the battery was gone and for us to fall back across the river as quickly as possible. Wingate, instead of obeying this order, wheeled his battalion into line facing towards the captured battery and was about to charge in and attempt its recapture when he was hit and mortally wounded by a stray shot.

Colonel Kit Carson's regiment of New Mexicans was looked upon as being the best of the newly raised troops, being officered largely by old soldiers and having a good sprinkling of Americans in their ranks. This regiment, as I have said, was posted to the left of Hall's battery (but Pino's intervened), facing eastward, consequently was in an excellent position to have charged the men who captured McRae's battery. They were eyewitnesses to that charge, and also the cavalry charge which was repulsed by Wingate, for this happened almost in front of them. They were ordered to fire on the advancing cavalry, and a few of them obeyed, but the greater part of them turned and fled across the river, many of them throwing away their guns, still loaded, that their flight may not be impeded.

Colonel Carson and some of his officers did their best to make the men stand their ground, but all to no purpose. Especially noticeable and praiseworthy was the conduct of the chaplain of the regiment, Padre Taladrid, a Catholic priest, who, forgetting his peaceful calling, beat his panic-stricken countrymen over their heads and shoulders with an iron ramrod, while he swore at them in Spanish in a most unclerical, but soldier-like manner, calling them all sorts of cowards and threatening them with eternal punishment for running away. But they were more afraid of those Texans than they were of him or his threats. They all rushed pell-mell into the river and crossed, Pino's militia having preceded them, this scare and flight all being caused by the mere knowledge that McRae's battery was taken and not because any enemy threatened them.

If Wingate had not been hit and had been able to make his intended attempt to recapture the guns, there was a fair chance of success attending him. His battalion was only about 150 strong, but it was composed of good, reliable, and determined men, and if this force had come unexpectedly on the Texans just as they had succeeded in driving the artillerymen and their supporters into the river, at short range to have delivered their fire and then charged with their bayonets, it could hardly have failed to have taken those dearly-bought cannon from the Texans—for its must be remembered that these latter, now that they had discharged and thrown away their shotguns and emptied their six-shooters, had very slim means of defense. But this was not to be.

Wingate's fall placed Lieutenant Cook in command of the battalion, who immediately began to retreat, and it was high time, if he wished to escape capture, for these men were now the only Union troops on this side of the river. Soon a body of the Texan infantry, four or five times their number, came bearing down upon them. Still there was no undue haste in their retreat. They moved steadily to the rear towards the river, loading as they went. When the pieces were all loaded the order to "About face" would be given and their fire would be delivered. Then they would again move to the rear, stubbornly contesting every foot of ground. The enemy evidently did not care to come into too close quarters with these men, for their fire was well-directed, and at every volley a score or more of the Texans were seen to fall.

The enemy's fire was generally too high, and although his missiles came in showers they, for the most part, cut the air harmlessly above our heads. We came to the river just at the bend where the water was to the depth of the shoulders and the current very swift and strong. Here we halted until the wounded captain had been gotten safely across, then the men locked arms and gained the opposite bank just as their foes reached the river on the other side, to whom we gave a parting volley and then marched away towards the fort with our ranks all reformed and feeling much like men who were running away from troops whom we had whipped.

Captain McRae, when he saw that his battery was lost beyond all hope, drew his pistol and calmly seated himself on one of his guns, defending it until he was shot dead. He was a native of the old North State and had been strongly importuned by his family and friends to throw up his commission and go with his state into secession. But resisting alike their threats and blandishments he preferred to remain true to the government that had educated and protected him and which he had sworn to defend.

Lieutenant Mishler, emulating his superior's example, stood by his gun until shot dead by a Texan major, whom Mishler also took along with him for company to the "misty shore." Lieutenant Bell, the other artillery officer, escaped with several bullet holes in his clothing. Orderly Sergeant Knox, of the battery, saved many lives and rendered the captured guns of little use to the captors by firing his pistol into the ammunition wagon and blowing it up, thus destroying the ammunition and his own life together.

Much adverse criticism of Canby's management was indulged in by some.

He was blamed for remaining at the fort so many hours walking about and smoking his cigar, with the thunder of the contending artillery sounding in his ears. I think that the true solution of this is to be found in his perfect and well-merited confidence in Colonel Roberts. This able officer had done more towards preparing for the present occasion than anyone else, and Canby (whom all knowing him will agree was the soul of justice and generosity) wished to give his faithful subordinate a chance to carry out his plans, unhindered and unembarrassed by a superior.

He was also blamed for changing Roberts' plans when he did come, but if he had been allowed five minutes more to have perfected those changes the battery would not probably have been taken when it was. The change in position, the assault and capture occurred in an almost incredibly short space of time, much shorter than one who did not witness it could readily be induced to believe. It was like a chess player who moves a piece to an exposed square, intending to support it there the next move, but to his chagrin sees it snatched instantly away by his adversary's knight, which, unperceived by him, had commanded that square. If all the facts were fully known and given their proper weight, I think Canby would be fully acquitted of any blame of a serious nature.

Roberts himself did not escape censure from some quarters. He was charged among other things with disobeying his instructions in bringing on an engagement when he was specially ordered by Canby not to do this, but merely to keep the Texans away from the water. The fallacy of this is apparent. How was he to obey one part of this without disobeying the other, if (as certainly was the case) the Texans were determined to get to the river at any cost?

The mistake at Valverde was made when the river was crossed by a force of reliable men numbering less than one-third as many as the foe whom they went to attack. If that deep, wide, rapidly flowing river had been in McRae's front instead of his rear when his battery was charged, what a difference it would have made in his favor! Besides, there never was the slightest advantage to be gained by crossing the river to attack the enemy and everything to be lost! Our infantry and artillery, posted on our own side of the river and as well protected as the means there at hand would permit, could have kept the enemy from the water till doomsday with an extremely small amount of danger to themselves. Why this place was not adopted is a question I have often asked, but have never had answered and probably never shall.

It was said that before the assaulting party of Texans were started on their perilous charge they were called to the commissariat and plied with whiskey until they were in a state of semi-intoxication, so as to render them the more desperate and regardless of danger. It was an undoubted fact that Sibley, their general, had got the start of them in that respect by some hours, for I have since been told by one of his own men that on this occasion Sibley supported himself by holding on to a wagon wheel, telling them to "go in boys and give them hell!"

A flag of truce was sent the next morning and under it our dead, amounting to about 115, were procured and brought into the fort. Owing to the extremely cold weather and to the shameless fact that they had all been stripped of their clothing by their adversaries, they were all frozen stiff, with their limbs in all manner of positions, making them look in the wagons like loads of very knotty gnarled wood. A large room was prepared to receive them, and when they were all in it presented a picture, once seen, never to be forgotten. Every face there was once as familiar to me as "household words," but with their features distorted, their bodies mangled, dirt-begrimed and bent into every conceivable shape, they were almost unrecognizable. Oh, it was a sickening spectacle! and what an instance of "man's inhumanity to man." A separate coffin was made for each and an inscribed board placed at the head of each grave.

Later in the day, on the twenty-second, a deputation from Sibley came in and demanded the surrender of the fort, which was of course refused. Canby told them that if they were as short of clothing as their actions seemed to indicate, and in the future any of his men were unfortunate enough to fall beneath their arms, he would engage to give them a new suit of clothing for every dead body which they would bring him the clothing on in which the victim fell. General Sibley, probably not fancying the look of things about Craig, concluded not to attempt its capture now, but to commit a greater mistake by proceeding on up the country, leaving this still unconquered force in his rear to follow him up whenever they chose to do so. Foolish man, as the sequel proved him.

20

The Shiloh Campaign
Pierre G. T. Beauregard, General, C.S.A.

PART 1

I had always hesitated and persistently declined giving to the public an account of this period of the war. That duty, it seemed to me, devolved upon one not so directly and intimately connected as I was with the events to be there recorded. But, with a few exceptions, the statements—most of them intentionally erroneous—published of late on the subject to be treated here, tended to such an extent to distort the truth of history, and so many strictures have been passed upon me in that connection, that, putting aside all personal feeling, I deem it incumbent on me to prepare a concise but complete and correct narrative of the whole Shiloh campaign, from the time of my arrival in General Albert Sidney Johnston's department, in February 1862, up to and including the Battle of Shiloh—April 6 and 7—and the retreat of the Confederate forces from Corinth.

In a work entitled *Military Operations of General Beauregard*, which was but lately offered to the public, are contained all the details of what was accomplished at that time; as also the causes which brought about the results there depicted. It was "written from notes and documents authenticated by me," and "is offered as a guide to the future historian" of the War between the States.[1] But books are not read by the many, and seldom reach the circulation attained by leading periodicals of this and other countries. Hence my determination to revive the matter in these pages.

• • •

Colonel Roger A. Pryor, of Virginia, a member of the Military Committee of the lower house of the Confederate Congress, called on me at my headquarters in Centreville, on January 22, 1862; and, speaking in his own name, in that of his colleagues of the committee, and also of the different representatives of the Mississippi valley states, at that time in Richmond, told me, substantially, that [Brigadier General Felix] Zollicoffer's defeat, which had just occurred at Spring Mill [Mill Springs], in eastern Kentucky, necessitated prompt and energetic measures on the part of the government, and that it was a very general desire, in which President [Jefferson] Davis joined, that I should be sent at once to the Mississippi Valley, where much discouragement existed, and where, it was believed, my presence might restore confidence and lead to more active and safer operations in the future.

This overture, and the gratifying manner in which it was made, took me by surprise. My answer at first was uncertain. I could not deny my services to the cause, wherever I might be ordered; but the idea of cutting short my relations with an army I had so materially assisted in organizing and leading to victory, made me hesitant and forbade a ready assent on my part. I asked for time to reflect. After reflection and on the assurance, otherwise made, that General Albert Sidney Johnston, in whose military department I was about to go, had under him, at different places, an aggregate of at least 70,000 men of all arms, which would allow early concentration of his forces and consequent aggressive movements on our part, I finally yielded consent, and so informed Colonel Pryor.

The concluding passage of the order of the War Department directing the transfer referred to, bore the date January 26, and read as follows: "He (the president) therefore desires that you proceed at once to report to General A. S. Johnston, at Bowling Green, Kentucky, and thence proceed, as promptly as

---

1. Alfred Roman, *The Military Operations of General Beauregard*, 2 vols. (New York, 1884).

General Pierre G. T.
Beauregard (*Century*)

possible, to assume your new command at Columbus, which is threatened by a powerful force, and the successful defense of which is of vital importance."

I was only able to leave Manassas on February 2. I had previously sent several suggestions to the War Department, through Colonel Thomas Jordan, my chief of staff, with a view to perfect the organization of the troops I was soon to command, for the efficiency of which, as I had been led to believe, much had yet to be done.

I had never met General A. S. Johnston prior to my arrival at Bowling Green. He welcomed me in his department with that simple, dignified, and earnest manner so characteristic of him, and which, I well remember, made a profound impression upon me.

He informed me of the position and strength of the enemy, and did the same as to his own forces. [Brigadier General Don Carlos] Buell's command was then at Bacon Creek, on the Louisville and Nashville Railroad, not farther than forty miles from Bowling Green, and consisted of fully 75,000 men. [Brigadier General Ulysses S.] Grant was near Cairo, and had 20,000 men with him, ready to move either against Fort Henry or Fort Donelson, as might best serve his purpose. [Brigadier General John] Pope commanded not less than 35,000 men, in the state of Missouri, and was, just then, seriously threatening [Major General Leonidas] Polk's position. [Major General Henry] Halleck, the commander in chief of the above enumerated Federal forces, was still at St. Louis, his department headquarters, and had, at the time referred to, subject to his general orders, an aggregate of 125,000 men of all arms.

General Johnston, on the other hand, had but 45,000 effectives of all arms in his large department. They were distributed as follows: 14,000, with General Johnston, at Bowling Green; some 5,500 at Forts Henry and Donelson; about 8,000 at or near Clarksville; and 15,000, under General Polk, in West Tennessee and West Kentucky. These were barely organized and very poorly armed. Such, in fact, was the case with most of [Brigadier Generals Charles] Clark's and [Gideon] Pillow's forces at Clarksville and Hopkinsville, to say nothing of the others. There were men, by the tens of thousands, in Kentucky, in Tennessee, and in the adjoining states, ready at any day to enlist under the Southern banner, and who were actually burning with the desire to do so; but the government had no arms to give them. None had been procured, as yet, from Europe, and none could be manufactured at home—that is to say, in any number approaching sufficiency for the requirements of the hour. General Johnston also told me that the works on the Cumberland and Tennessee rivers, upon which so much depended for the safety of these streams, were defective in more than one respect, and could not be relied on; that Major [Jeremy F.] Gilmer, his chief engineer, had been sent to them with a view of improving their effectiveness, if possible, before it was too late.

I was deeply disturbed when thus made acquainted with the real condition of affairs in General Johnston's department. His surprise was equal to my disappointment when I assured him of the War Department's estimate of his strength. My first impulse was to return at once to Virginia, so powerless did I feel in the presence of the frightful odds existing against us. But General Johnston urged me to remain, and in a manner so earnest, that I acceded to his request and concluded not to leave him in the hard strait in which he was placed. My opinion has ever been that the War Department had not dealt justly toward General Johnston, and had sacrificed him to its own improvidence and neglectful state of unpreparedness.

On February 5, I inspected, with General Johnston, all the works erected at and around Bowling Green. They were unquestionably strong; but besides having consumed too much time and labor, which could have been more wisely expended at other points—notably at Forts Henry and Donelson—it was evident to me that they could be turned on the right, a few miles above, should a vigorous and well-directed attack by made upon them in that quarter. It appeared to me that it would have been sufficient, and far better, to limit the Bowling Green works to a *tete de pont* north of the Barren River, and to one fort only south of the same stream. I so stated to General Johnston, who made no direct reply, but said that, in case of an advance of the enemy, on his flanks, he would withdraw his forces from Bowling Green, as he had no army of relief to call to his assistance.

I gave General Johnston my views as to the best plan for holding Fort Henry, then seriously menaced by General Grant, and which was absolutely necessary to insure the command of the Tennessee River. I told him that, owing to the defective location of Forts Henry and Donelson at about the middle—and at a reentering angle—of our defensive line, weakened by the intersection of the two rivers on which the forts were built; owing also to the saliency of our flanks at Bowling Green and Columbus, which facilitated the turning of the first—Bowling Green—thus compelling it to fall by its own weight, and rendering the second—Columbus—clearly untenable, should Henry succumb, I thought it not only advisable, but of absolute necessity, to abandon Bowling Green without further delay, using it hereafter as a point of observation merely, and to concentrate at once all our available troops upon Henry and Donelson, and thus force General Grant to give us battle there, with every chance of success in our favor, and hardly any hope by him of obtaining assistance elsewhere. The adoption, I said, and above all the vigorous execution of such a plan, would not only restore to us the full control of the Tennessee, but insure likewise the possession of the Cumberland, and eventually secure a much better position to our troops as to the defense of Nashville.

My views were not adopted. General Johnston agreed to their correctness, in a strategic point of view, but feared that a failure to defeat General Grant, as proposed, would jeopardize the security of our positions at other points, and might possibly cause our forces to be crushed between Grant and Buell. His opinion was that, situated as we then were, we should endeavor to gain time, and thus be enabled to save the large stock of supplies and ammunition which the government, with its usual want of foresight, had gathered at Bowling Green, Clarksville, and Nashville.

In differing with me on that occasion, as he did, General Johnston clearly lost sight of the following facts: that General Buell had no pontoon train at his disposal; that he could not have crossed the Cumberland between Nashville and Donelson; that we would have had ample time to withdraw our forces from the Tennessee and Cumberland, and take a position in rear of the new line formed at Duck River; that we could even have retreated as far as Nashville, before falling against General Buell, who would have had a march longer march to make; that, in war, success always depends on prompt and vigorous concentration of masses against fractions, and that we then held the interior lines.

Fort Henry fell. Its resistance did not last over a day. Impartial history will not hold [Brigadier General Lloyd] Tilghman responsible for the fall of a work which was known, from the first, to be untenable, and which was attacked by a strong land and naval force. The railroad bridge, only about twelve miles south of Fort Henry, was now burned by the Federal gunboats, and that line of communication between General Johnston and his forces at Columbus, western Kentucky, was cut off, as had been apprehended, leaving, as the shortest route available, the line of railroad by Nashville, Decatur, Corinth, and Jackson.

The day following—February 7—I again urged the carrying out of the plan of concentration delineated above, which, in my opinion, was imperative at that juncture, and clearly practicable when we consider that the investment of Fort Donelson was only begun on February 13, and the work surrendered on the morning of the sixteenth. Our troops, transferred by rail and by water, could have reached Donelson on the tenth, at the latest; whereas General Buell's forces, with rough roads of fully 125 miles before them, could not possibly have operated a junction with General Grant before February 17. On the morning of the thirteenth, General Grant was at the head of 15,000 men. He was only reinforced (by 10,000 men) on the evening of that day. We could have had, to oppose him on the tenth—say even on the twelfth—10,000 men, out of the 14,000 with General Johnston at Bowling Green; 8,000 men under [Brigadier General John B.] Floyd at Russellville; 3,000 more at Clarksville; and these, with 5,700 more, already at Donelson, would have aggregated a force of nearly 27,000 men. That force, under General Johnston, or even under myself—for I would have willingly marched on with them to Donelson—would have assured us victory over General Grant's 15,000 men; and not only would Fort Donelson have thus been held—for some time to come, at any rate—but we would also have regained Fort Henry before the advent of General Buell. It must be borne in mind that there had been no conflict, worthy of the name, at Donelson prior to February 15, and that it was brought on by the advance of our own forces, the enemy having, at first, clearly given way to the impetuous attack made upon him. It is, therefore, but fair to conclude that, with the reinforcements we could have brought to bear against General Grant at that time, the fight would have unquestionably resulted in something more than a mere appearance of victory on the part of the Confederates.

But General Johnston adhered to his own views, as expressed in a memorandum drawn up by [Major General William J.] Hardee and myself, on February 7, and given in full in *Military Operations of General Beauregard*. It was then determined that, Fort Henry having fallen, and Fort Donelson not being tenable, "*preparations* should at once be made for the removal" of the army of Bowling Green to Nashville; that "the troops at Clarksville would cross over to the south of the Cumberland, leaving behind them a force sufficient to protect the manufactories and other property" established there by the government; that "from Nashville, should any further retrograde movement become necessary," it would "be made to Stevenson, and thence according to circumstances."

"It was also determined that the possession of the Tennessee River by the enemy . . . separates the army at Bowling Green from the army at Columbus, Kentucky, which must henceforth act independently of each other until they again be brought together." That, should the line of communication of the army at Columbus be threatened by an overwhelming force, concentrating from various points on the Ohio, "the main body of that army would fall back to Humboldt, and thence if necessary to Grand Junction, so as to protect Memphis from either point, and still have a line of retreat to the latter point, or to Grenada, Mississippi, and if necessary to Jackson, Mississippi."

The evacuation of Bowling Green was only begun on February 11. I left the next day; but, before doing so, again expressed my views on the condition of affairs around us, in a letter to General Johnston, dated Bowling Green February 12, 1862, wherein the following passages occur:

> It also becomes evident that, by the possession of that river (Tennessee), the enemy can concentrate rapidly, by means of his innumerable transports, all his disposable forces on any point along its banks, either to attack Nashville in rear, or cut off the communications of Columbus by the Mississippi River with Memphis, and by the railroads with the Memphis and Charleston Railroad.
>
> Should the enemy determine on the former plan of operations, your army, threatened also in front and on the right flank by Buell's large army, will be in a very critical condition, and may be forced to take refuge on the south side of the Tennessee River. But should Halleck adopt the second plan referred to, the position at Columbus will then become no longer tenable for an army inferior in strength to that of the enemy, and must fall back to some central point, where it can guard the main railroads to Memphis, i.e., from Louisville and from Charleston. Jackson, Tennessee, would probably be the best position for such an object, with strong detachments at Humboldt and Corinth, and with the necessary advance guards.
>
> Columbus must either be left to be defended to the last extremity by its proper garrison, assisted by [Commodore J. S.] Hollins's fleet of gunboats, and provided with provisions and ammunition for several months, or abandoned altogether, its armament and garrison being transferred, if practicable, to Fort Pillow, which, I am informed, is naturally and artificially a strong position about fifty miles above Memphis.
>
> Island Number Ten, near New Madrid, could also be held by its garrison, assisted by Hollins's fleet, until the possession of New Madrid by the enemy would compel that position to be evacuated. I am clearly of the opinion that to attempt at present to hold so advanced a position as Columbus, with the movable army under General Polk, when its communication can be so readily cut off by a surprise force acting from the Tennessee River as a new base, would be to jeopardize, not only the safety of that army, but necessarily of the whole Mississippi valley. Hence I desire, as far as practicable, specific instructions as to the future movements of the army of which I am about to assume command. If it be necessary for the safety of the country to make, with all my forces, a desperate stand at Columbus, I am ready to do so.

General Johnston's answer was given me verbally, at Edgefield, opposite Nashville, on February 14. He said his views had undergone no change since our last conference at Bowling Green, except as to the abandonment of Columbus, and that he would abide by the decision of the War Department in that respect. His line of retreat, he also said, when forced to withdraw from Nashville, would be along the Nashville, Stevenson, and Chattanooga Railroad.

I left Nashville on the fifteenth, and on my arrival at Corinth the next day, found two telegrams awaiting me—one from General Johnston, and one from Colonel [William W.] Mackall, his chief of staff. Both announced the fall of Fort Donelson. General Johnston's read as follows:

Nashville, February 16, 1862

At 2:00 A.M. today, Fort Donelson surrendered. We lost all.

Colonel Mackall's dispatch began with the same words, but ended thus: "We lost all the army except half of Floyd's brigade, which crossed the river. The head of our column is about reaching Nashville."

I was much grieved at this news, but not taken by surprise. The fall of Donelson, without an effort in season to come to its succor, was almost inevitable. In a letter written by me to Colonel Roger A. Pryor on February 14, 1862, I said: "We must give up some minor points, and concentrate our forces to save the most important ones, or we will lose all of them in succession. The loss of Fort Donelson—(God grant it may not fall!)—would be followed by consequences too lamentable to be now alluded to."

It were scarcely possible to depict the feeling of consternation, anxiety, and distrust that spread over the entire section of country comprised within the bounds of General Johnston's department at the announcement of these disastrous events. The people were panic-stricken. The army was all but demoralized. A clamor, as loud as it was unfair, arose from almost every neighboring city, town, or hamlet against the general commanding our forces in the West. Cries of his incompetency—or his disloyalty, even—were uttered by many. He withstood the storm with firmness and manliness, and was uncomplaining. But those who understood the depth and scope of his nature and had studied the course of action followed at Richmond toward our forces in the West, at that time and later on, were not long in discovering on whose shoulders to lay most of the blame that so weighted him down.

On the same day, February 16, in answer to a dispatch of mine, asking if any direct orders had been issued to General Polk with regard to the troops at and around Columbus, Colonel Mackall, A.A.G., sent me this telegram: "You must do as your judgment dictates. No orders for your troops have issued from here." And General Johnston, in another telegram, dated February 18, said: "You must now act as seems best to you. The separation of our armies is now complete."

I was then at Jackson, Tennessee, where Colonel Jordan, my chief of staff, had just arrived after an inspection tour at Columbus. His report, coupled with that of Captain [D. B.] Harris, my chief engineer, about the exaggerated extension of the lines there, the defective location of the works, and the faulty organization of the troops, strengthened my own opinion as to the inability of Columbus to withstand a serious attack, and rendered more imperative still the

Colonel Nathan B. Forrest Leading His Cavalry out of Fort Donelson (*Harper's New Monthly Magazine*)

necessity of its early evacuation. General Polk, who had considered the situation in a different light, and who believed in the defensive capacity of the place, was at first averse to the movement. He changed his mind, however, upon my showing him the saliency of Fort Columbus and the weak points of its construction, and cheerfully carried out my instructions, when, on February 19, the War Department having given its consent to the evacuation, he was ordered to prepare for it without delay.

The supplies and materials kept in reserve were to be forwarded by railroad to Grenada and Columbus; the remaining ones, to Union City, Humboldt, Madrid Bend, New Madrid, and Memphis. The heaviest guns were to be sent to Island Number Ten, to the batteries already erected at Madrid Bend, and to New Madrid. Guns of a lighter caliber, for the land defenses of the latter place, were also ordered there. Immediate steps were to be taken to prepare for the removal of the other guns to Madrid Bend and Fort Pillow. The greatest precautions were to be observed while carrying on this work, which was to be done at night only, if possible. Columbus was to be held until the batteries at Island Number Ten and at Madrid Bend were reported ready for the defense of the river.

The batteries at the head of Island Number Ten and at Madrid Bend were not intended for permanent occupation; but Fort Pillow was, and was being strengthened, as much as practicable, for that purpose. Captain Harris, who was already an efficient engineer at the time of which I write, and who made such a brilliant record afterward at Charleston, at Savannah, as also at Drewry's Bluff and Petersburg, had received most minute instructions from me as to the planning, laying out, and construction of these batteries, including the details of their parapets, embrasures, traverses, and magazines. He had been ordered, besides, to repair to Fort Pillow as soon as he could, with a view to reducing it to a garrison of about 3,000 men, thus remedying as far as possible the error originally committed there of preparing that work for a force of from nine to ten thousand men.

The evacuation of Columbus was begun on February 25. That it was a military necessity none will now deny, except some blind partisan who may take upon himself to criticize and condemn, without adequate knowledge upon the subject, and without assigning any reason or proof in support of his assertion. If it were a mistake to have evacuated Columbus at that time, the responsibility should rest as much upon General Johnston, who agreed to it, as upon myself, who suggested the movement, but only ordered it after being authorized to do so by the War Department. I was ready to defend Columbus *to the last extremity* if so ordered by the commanding general, and had so expressed myself in my letter to him, dated Bowling Green, February 12, 1862, already referred to in this article. I knew, however, it would be disastrous in the extreme to attempt such a defense, situated as we then were. General Johnston, who understood the crisis far better than those who presume to interpret him today, required no persuasion to adopt this course, and did so, not as a concession to me, but clearly because he was convinced of its advisability. "To defend Columbus" at that time, "with a reduced garrison, and withdraw Polk and his army for active movements"[2] was never even hinted at by General Johnston in any of our conferences on the subject, and was, I may add, a physical impossibility, as no *reduced garrison* could have defended Columbus, when it is considered that the works at that place were made for a garrison of at least 13,000 men, armed with 140 (mostly heavy) guns. Evidently no army at all would have been left to General Polk for *active movements* in the field.

At that time (February 25) I had not yet formally assumed command of the military district assigned to me. My health was impaired, and had been, even before my leaving Bowling Green, on the twelfth, and, in fact, prior to my departure from Centreville, Virginia. My endeavors, however, to become acquainted with every point included in my new command, had been incessant; and General Polk, though not actually relieved from his duties as commander of his district, had kindly allowed me not only to advise him, but also, in a great measure, to direct his own as well as the movements of the forces directly under him. General Johnston favored the course I was then pursuing, as can be seen by the following telegram, dated Murfreesboro, February 21, from Colonel Mackall, A.A.G., speaking in General Johnston's name: "If not well enough to assume

---

2. Beauregard here quotes from William P. Preston, "Albert Sidney Johnston at Shiloh," *The Century Magazine*, February 1885, 618.

command, I hope that you, now having had time to study the field, will advise General Polk of your judgment as to the proper disposition of his army, in accordance with the views you entertain in your memorandum, unless you have changed your views. I can't order him, not knowing but what you have assumed command, and your orders conflict."

Meanwhile, General Johnston, threatened by General Buell's large army, had been compelled to withdraw from Nashville, his rear guard marching out of that city late on the evening of February 23. His line of retreat, as already agreed upon, was toward Stevenson, northeastern Alabama. He had with him, at that time, an aggregate of some 17,000 men.

It was at this most critical juncture of our affairs that, taking advantage of the latitude given me by General Johnston's telegram of February 18, and knowing how important it was that we should adopt prompt measures to improve the situation and instill new confidence in the people, I came to the conclusion to abandon at once the "passive-defensive," which had led us, so far, to disaster only, and to inaugurate instead the entirely opposite system of aggressive warfare, as the best chance—if not the only hope—of recovering some of our lost ground.

The prospect was far from encouraging. General Johnston was retreating toward northeastern Alabama and Georgia. The distance between his sorely tried troops and those who were still under General Polk was daily increasing instead of diminishing. General Grant, on the other hand, emboldened by his recent successes at Henry and Donelson could, almost unimpeded, move at once, either upon the rear of Columbus and thus strike it a deathblow; or he could ascend the Tennessee River as far as Hamburg or Eastport, seize the Memphis and Charleston Railroad, thereby completely separating the two Confederate armies, turning West Kentucky and West Tennessee; and, finally, taking Memphis, Fort Pillow, New Madrid, Island Number Ten, and Columbus, which would have given him possession of the entire Mississippi valley.

The only forces I could control at the time were about 15,000 men under General Polk, stationed at the various Mississippi river defenses; some 2,000 more, at or near Iuka, under [Brigadier General James R.] Chalmers; and 3,000 already at Corinth, with Brigadier General [Daniel] Ruggles; aggregating 20,000 men of all arms, not thoroughly organized, and very poorly armed and equipped.

My plan was to operate with my movable forces, not on the defensive line adopted by General Johnston, as agreed upon at Bowling Green on February 7, but on an entirely new line, starting from Island Number Ten and extending to Corinth, through Union City, Humboldt, and Jackson—thus throwing my forces across the Louisville and Memphis, and the Memphis and Charleston railroads; covering Memphis, and covering the railroad center at Corinth, with as strong a force as possible at Iuka, and a smaller one at Tuscumbia, in order to secure my railroad communication with the east. Holding the Mobile and Ohio Railroad, as I then did, I could have thus concentrated rapidly, with a view either to face the enemy, in an attempt on his part to threaten the Louisville and Memphis Railroad, or even, if circumstances favored me, to directly attack him, should he try to land along the bend of the Tennessee River at any point between Coffee Landing and Eastport.

To carry out such a plan more troops were needed, and I was not ignorant of the difficulty to be met with in my effort to procure them. Time, also, was a very important factor to be considered, for it was apparent to me that, should the enemy be bold and push forward his advantages, we could not hope to be a successful barrier in his way.

I resolved to send messengers at once to the governors of Tennessee, Alabama, Mississippi, and Louisiana, with a circular addressed to each of them, in which I endeavored to explain the inevitable result to us of additional disasters to our arms, and asking each of them to forward to me, with the utmost celerity, from 5,000 to 10,000 men, already armed and equipped, their services not to be taken advantage of for more than ninety days, which, I believed, would be sufficient to enable us, by timely and vigorous action, to recover our losses, and insure the defense of the Mississippi River. I also made an appeal to [Major General Braxton] Bragg, asking him for such troops as he could send from Mobile and Pensacola, assuring him, at the same time, of the additional assistance he would afford me were he able to accompany them. I called likewise on [Major General Mansfield] Lovell, at New Orleans. To [Major General Earl] Van Dorn, then in Arkansas with some 20,000 men, I sent a most pressing message, inviting him to join me, via New Madrid or Columbus, with as large a portion of his forces as possible. In my letter to him I said:

> By the fall of the Tennessee and Cumberland rivers, the forces under General Polk (now to be under me) are entirely cut off from those under General A. S. Johnston, and must henceforth depend upon themselves alone for the defense of the Mississippi River and contiguous states: the fall of Columbus, and of Island Number Ten, must necessarily be followed by the loss of the whole Mississippi River. The fate of Missouri necessarily depends on the successful defense of Columbus and of Island Number Ten: hence, we must, if possible, combine our operations not only to defend those positions, but also to take the offensive as soon as practicable, to recover some lost ground.

I also sent a messenger (Lieutenant, afterward Brigadier General, S. W. Ferguson) to General Johnston, in order to obtain his cooperation to my plan if he could give it. He was then at Murfreesboro, actively engaged with his retreat from Nashville, on the Stevenson and Chattanooga Railroad.

My messengers were all members of my personal and general staff. They left my headquarters, at Jackson, Tennessee, on February 22.

I advised the War Department of what I had done, and asked for whatever instructions it might deem expedient to give me. It neither sanctioned nor disapproved the course I had followed.

General Johnston readily acceded to my request, and took up a new line of march toward Decatur, through Shelbyville, Fayetteville, and Huntsville. Left to his own discretion by the War Department, as to whether to comply with my demand or not, General Bragg concluded to give his assent, and furnished me with some 10,000 men of all arms. General Lovell did all he possibly could under the circumstances. The governors of the four states already mentioned used every exertion in their power to respond to my urgent call upon them. I could get no immediate answer from General Van Dorn, whose whereabouts just then were not very definite. He showed, however, much willingness to assist me, when free to do so, but did not reach the scene of operations in time.

Columbus was evacuated on March 2. The enemy did not show the vigilance and boldness which it was reasonable to expect he would, and thus indirectly facilitated our work. After the evacuation, about 7,000 men of General Polk's forces were placed under General McCown, at New Madrid, some sixty miles below Columbus and not more than ten miles from Island Number Ten. The main body of General Polk's command was collected at Humboldt, which was central to Memphis, Jackson, Grand Junction, Henderson, Corinth, and Fort Pillow. A rear guard of two regiments and about 500 cavalry were stationed at Union City, in the direction of Lexington; the cavalry to be well in advance from Hickman to Paris. The movements of the enemy were watched by mounted parties, provided with pieces of light artillery, who had been ordered to patrol the west bank of the Tennessee, and inform me of anything unusual that might attract their attention.

Reports, in the main reliable, having soon reached me, that the enemy was preparing a great offensive demonstration from Cairo, Paducah, and Fort Henry, while General Pope was on his march to New Madrid, it became plain to me that danger threatened us from the Tennessee River, which, if well founded, might completely separate General Johnston's army from the forces under General Polk, and thus place the former, as well as the latter, at the mercy of the overwhelming masses which would undoubtedly be thrown against them. It was at this precise moment that I fixed upon Corinth as the best point of concentration on our part, and as the natural Confederate base for any offensive operations of our forces. To say that anyone—including General Johnston and myself—had thought of Corinth, and could have designated it as the strategic point of the Shiloh campaign before the enemy had given evidence of any hostile movement from or near Pittsburg Landing, on the Tennessee River, is sheer folly, and scarcely needs contradiction to be so pronounced. But to say, furthermore, as has been the case, that General Johnston "sent me," when we last parted, at Edgefield, opposite Nashville, on February 14, or at any time before, or at any time after, "with instructions to concentrate all available forces near Corinth— a movement previously begun"[3]—is not only absolutely imaginary, but a most positive attempt to pervert the truth of history. General Johnston never made

---

3. Here Beauregard again quotes from Johnston's *Century* article, page 618.

even the slightest allusion to Corinth in any of our conferences about his future plans of operations or mine. I never received a word of instructions from him about concentrating there, or elsewhere. He only agreed to form a junction with me after General Ferguson had seen him, in my name, with the request that he should change his line of retreat and shorten the distance between our two armies, instead of increasing it, as he was actually doing, when met by my messenger at Murfreesboro on February 22 or 23. It was wholly at my suggestion and urgent request that he marched his army to Corinth. In fact, he believed it to be "a hazardous experiment," situated as he then was, as he states himself, in his letter of March 18 to President Davis.

On March 2 I dispatched another messenger to him—Colonel (then Captain) [John M.] Otey, of my staff, with the following letter:

> Dear General: I send you herewith inclosed a slip showing the intended movements of the enemy, no doubt against the troops in western Tennessee. I think you ought to hurry up your troops to Corinth by railroad, as soon as practicable, for there or thereabouts will soon be fought the great battle of this controversy.

General Johnston's answer, through Colonel Mackall, his adjutant, was dated from Fayetteville, March 5, 1862, and ran thus:

> General: Your letter of the second instant has been received by General Johnston. He replies: The army advancing, has reached this place; on arriving at Decatur, he will decide on the promptest mode.

I had now fair reason to hope that all our forces, including General Johnston's small army, and the troops forthcoming from Tennessee, Alabama, Mississippi, and Louisiana, would soon be collected at the point selected by me, and that, should the Federal commander show too much boldness on the west bank of the Tennessee, we could successfully check his course before allowing him to further develop his ulterior plans. Pittsburg Landing, it seemed to me from a critical study of the map and of the reported movements of the enemy, would be one of the points selected by him to effect a landing. General Ruggles, by my order, caused a regiment—the Eighteenth Louisiana—to be sent there as a corps of observation. The attempted landing of a Federal force, supported by two gunboats, which was repulsed the next day by that regiment, proves that I was not mistaken.

On March 6, General Bragg's forces began to arrive. They were pushed on to Corinth, as originally decided upon; and General Bragg was instructed by me to lose no time in organizing into brigades and divisions his own and all the troops then coming in from various points. I also directed him to inspect the position at Monterey, midway between Corinth and Pittsburg Landing, with a view to adopt it, instead of Corinth, as our chief point of concentration, should the enemy evince a serious intent to select Pittsburg—and not Eastport—for a permanent disembarkment. General Bragg was of opinion that Corinth offered greater facilities for transportation, and it therefore remained, as at first intended by me, the grand central point for the rallying and concentration of all the Confederate forces.

I deem it unnecessary, for the purposes of this paper, to dwell upon the difficulties I experienced at that time, through the want of field officers, for the complete organization of the troops that were being conveyed from the states already referred to in response to my call upon them. The indifference and apparent unwillingness of the War Department, as evidenced in that connection, was a great source of perplexity to me, and one of the main causes of our inability to begin, as early as I would have otherwise wished, the aggressive movement which was being prepared against the enemy at Pittsburg Landing.

I officially assumed command on March 5 of the military district assigned to me. One of the first steps taken by me, in view of the evacuation of Columbus and of the concentration of our troops at or near Corinth, was to cause sufficient supplies of grain and provisions to be gathered at Union City, Humboldt, Jackson, and Henderson, in western Tennessee, and at Corinth, Grand Junction, and Iuka, in Mississippi. My principal supplying depots were Columbus, Mississippi, and Grenada.

On March 13, five Federal divisions, reinforced a few days later by 5,000 men under [Major] General C. F. Smith, arrived at Savannah, twelve miles below Pittsburg Landing, on the opposite side of the Tennessee River. They aggregated some 43,000 men of all arms. [Brigadier General William T.] Sherman's division, without effecting a landing at Savannah, had been sent up the river, with a view, it was said, to destroy the Memphis and Charleston Railroad at a short distance from Eastport. It was kept in check and deterred from even attempting to accomplish its purpose by two companies of infantry, acting as artillery, and belonging to General Chalmers's command—some 2,500 men—stationed near Iuka, five or six miles from the river. It attempted immediately afterward—but with no better success—to burn some railroad shops near Burnsville, eight miles west of Iuka, and finally dropped down to Pittsburg Landing on the night of March 14, having made a useless demonstration, but one which confirmed me in the opinion that Corinth would be the final objective point of the Federal movement. About that time, a small bridge, twenty-four miles north of Corinth, near Bethel Station, was burned by a raiding party from [Major General John] McClernand's division, which had been detached to destroy the Mobile and Ohio Railroad between Corinth and Jackson, but utterly failed to do so. There was hesitancy, then, on the part of the enemy. He was feeling his way, and with more than ordinary caution. General Grant had not yet assumed command, and, as he states, was "virtually in arrest, on board a steamer," near Fort Henry.[4] He only arrived, and officially relieved General Smith on or about March 17.

---

4. Beauregard here quotes from Ulysses S. Grant, "The Battle of Shiloh," *The Century Magazine*, February 1885, 594.

On the other hand, General Pope had appeared before New Madrid on March 3. He had with him some 25,000 men. He really and seriously began his attack on the twelfth, and reduced the works, after no great effort on his part, on the night of the fourteenth. He was thus, consciously or not, cooperating with the movements of the Federals on the Tennessee River. [Brigadier General John P.] McCown saved his men, however, and had them transferred to the other side of the river. Most of them were sent to support the batteries at Island Number Ten. General McCown was subsequently relieved of his duties, and General Mackall, General Johnston's able chief of staff, took command in his place. On March 16, Commodore [Andrew H.] Foote's fleet of gunboats and mortar boats began the regular bombardment of Island Number Ten. More endurance was exhibited there than at New Madrid. In fact, the garrison behaved creditably to itself and its commanders. But the easy fall of New Madrid led, almost inevitably, to the fall of Island Number Ten.

When, in my opinion, the enemy had sufficiently shown what his purpose was, I hurried the concentration of all the forces I could dispose of in western Tennessee and northern Mississippi. By the middle of March I had successfully collected and gathered, within short and easy marching from Corinth, about 23,000 men of all arms, exclusive of the forces originally under General Polk— some 14,000 men—which raised my aggregate to 44,000 men, more or less, of all arms. The greatest number of them were very indifferently armed and equipped. Some even—the cavalry especially—had no arms at all. They were mostly raw troops, unhabituated to camp life, undisciplined, and hardly drilled. But they were composed of the best element of the South, and had answered the call of their respective governors, and my own, with the determination of doing their whole duty toward the cause they had espoused.

General Johnston had been advised of all the dispositions I had taken for the troops thus being sent to me. He had invariably approved of all I had done; though, in his opinion, as appears by the following telegram—not generally known, and which I here append—Corinth was too near the Tennessee River to be considered the best point of concentration for our forces. The telegram read thus:

Decatur, March 15, 1862

To General G. T. Beauregard:
   Have you had the south bank of the Hatchie examined, near Bolivar? I recommend it to your attention. It has, besides the other advantages, that of being further from the enemy's line.

I could not agree with General Johnston in that regard, and although ready to admit, under ordinary circumstances, a good defensive line might have been established near Bolivar at the spot designated in the foregoing telegram, it was not, by far, the best one to be selected just then, in order to carry out the aggressive movement I was preparing, and for which I had even suggested Monterey, instead of Corinth, because of its greater proximity to Pittsburg Landing.

The whole Federal force destined for operations on the Tennessee River, under General Grant, were now assembled at Pittsburg Landing, with the exception of [Major General] Lew Wallace's division—about 7,000 men—which had been stationed at Crump's Landing, some five miles below Pittsburg, by General Smith, and left there by General Grant, who considered the position so well chosen that no orders were given to change it until the Confederate attack at Shiloh. In fact, General Grant, even as late as April 5, as he admitted himself, "felt by no means certain that Crump's Landing might not be the point of attack."[5]

General Buell, with seven divisions, aggregating an effective force of over 73,000 men, had quietly remained at Nashville after the fall of that place and had not materially interfered with General Johnston's retreat, first to Murfreesboro, afterward to Fayetteville, Huntsville, Decatur, and finally to Corinth. He was last ordered (March 15) by General Halleck to form a junction with the forces operating under General Grant on the Tennessee. He only had five divisions with him at that time, or some 40,000 men of all arms. The other two divisions, namely, the Seventh, under [Brigadier] General G. W. Morgan, and the Third, under [Brigadier] General O. M. Mitchel, had been detached from his main army for some special purpose; partly, it was said, for the destruction of the Memphis and Charleston Railroad, and partly for a raiding incursion in East Tennessee. General Buell's destination was first Savannah, and then Pittsburg Landing; though it seems he was not personally informed of the change, for during his march, which only averaged some eleven miles a day, he had determined to move to Hamburg, six miles above Pittsburg, and there to await further instructions.

The great point for us, and the essential feature of the campaign, was to strike a blow upon the enemy in our front before General Buell's junction with General Grant. My efforts tended to nothing else. But I knew that, with the forces under me, gathered as they had been and under such difficulties, no chance of success existed were I to attempt an aggressive movement upon the combined forces under Generals Grant and Buell, which would have aggregated from eighty to eighty-five thousand effectives of all arms. I informed General Johnston of the fact, urging him again to hurry on with his army, and I also renewed my call upon the War Department for the field officers I had so often—but thus far uselessly—asked for.

General Johnston arrived at Corinth late on March 22. His army came in after him but followed closely, the last files of his columns reaching their place of rendezvous on the twenty-seventh. One of his corps, under General Hardee, was stationed in the near vicinity of Corinth. It consisted of about 8,000 men. The

---

5. Grant, "Battle of Shiloh," 594.

other corps—some 5,000 more, exclusive of cavalry—commanded by [Major General George B.] Crittenden, took position at Burnsville and Iuka, on the Memphis and Charleston Railroad.

I had scarcely explained to General Johnston the situation around us, the position of the enemy in our front, and the most important details of the organization of the forces under me, in view of the plans he had already been advised of, when, to my surprise, he gravely and impressively declared, with visible emotion, that with my consent he would turn over to me the direct command of all the troops now collected at Corinth, including his own, and confine himself exclusively to the duties of department commander, establishing for the purpose his headquarters at Memphis or Holly Springs. He said that, in his opinion, the adoption of such a course would instill renewed confidence in the people, and even in the army, and eventually benefit the success of our cause. I thoroughly appreciated the motives actuating him, and admired and esteemed him all the more for it. I refused, nonetheless, to acquiesce in his proposal, and did so in terms befitting the occasion. There was no possibility for misinterpretation on my part as to the spirit and intention of General Johnston's offer to me. It was plain and significant, and I understood it.

It was then agreed that, together—he, as first in command, I as second—we would undertake the task laid out before us, and do our best to achieve success. With his authorization, and in fact at his request, I drew up the plan reorganizing the Army of the Mississippi, as it was then called, which was approved of and signed by him, as commander in chief, and subsequently published to our united forces, on March 29, as a general order.

The army, as it now stood, was divided into three corps: the First, under Major General Polk, consisted of the grand division, as originally organized in his former military district, except as to the artillery and cavalry otherwise disposed of, and excepting also the troops in garrison at Fort Pillow, Island Number Ten, and the other works on the Mississippi River. The Second, under Major General Bragg, was called the Second Grand Division of the Army of the Mississippi, with the same limitations as to artillery, cavalry, and the reserves. The Third Corps was under Major General Hardee. It consisted of the Army of Kentucky; that is to say, of the troops which had followed General Johnston from Bowling Green and Nashville, subject to the same restrictions with regard to artillery, cavalry, and the reserves. The infantry reserves, withdrawn from the three corps, as indicated above, formed a division of at least two brigades. They were placed at first under General Crittenden, and very soon subsequently under Brigadier General Breckinridge.

As Colonel Mackall, General Johnston's former adjutant, had been recently promoted and sent in command of one of the river defenses, Colonel Thomas Jordan, my chief of staff, was announced, in general orders, as adjutant general of the united forces of the Army of the Mississippi.

My hope had been that our onward movement could begin on April 1. I knew

General Braxton Bragg
(*Century*)

that General Buell was, at that time, at or near Franklin, and that several bridges—
and among them an important one on Duck River—had been destroyed on the
route he was following, and I counted upon these and similar hindrances to delay
and otherwise embarrass his march. Our deficiencies were such, however, and
so great was the inexperience of some of our subordinate commanders, so complete also our lack of engineers, inspectors, and other field officers that, to my
extreme disappointment our forces were not ready and did not make the projected advance as early as I had wished and striven to have it done.

A crisis was now unexpectedly brought upon us by the fact of a telegram
sent by [Major General Benjamin F.] Cheatham to General Polk, his corps commander, stating that late on the evening of April 2, at or near Bethel Station,
twenty-four miles north of Corinth, where was stationed a large body of the
enemy, which he took to be General Lew Wallace's division, had suddenly appeared in his front, with an apparent purpose of attack. General Polk forwarded the dispatch to Colonel Jordan, the adjutant general, who immediately sent
it to my quarters. I read it, thought over it a moment, and believing from its
context that the enemy had divided his forces to carry out his reported incursion against Bethel—for nothing showed General Cheatham's surmise as to Lew
Wallace's division to be correct—I ordered the telegram carried to General
Johnston, after writing the following words on the back of it: "Now is the moment to advance and strike the enemy at Pittsburg Landing."

Late as it was (nearly 11:00 P.M.) Colonel Jordan repaired to General Johnston's headquarters, and handed him the dispatch with my endorsement. He went with it to General Bragg's quarters, nearly opposite my own, and asked him to take cognizance of it. General Bragg did so and declared himself in favor of the suggestion. General Johnston was at first of a different opinion, which he urged with his usual earnestness. He thought our forces were not in a condition at that moment for such an onset, and that it would not be possible to collect our reserves in time. Colonel Jordan reassured him on that point, and added that, by hurrying the advance as suggested, my conviction was that we would take the enemy by surprise, and thus deal him a much heavier blow than by further delaying our projected plan; that we were as ready now as we could expect to be a few days later, when General Buell, in all likelihood, would have already effected his junction with General Grant. General Johnston thereupon yielded his assent, and instructed Colonel Jordan to prepare the necessary orders in view of the movement. This is in contrast with what was lately written about General Johnston's plan of campaign and his eagerness, at that time, for "immediate and decisive action"; while, on the other hand, it is stated General Bragg and myself were endeavoring to retard the attack for the purpose of "thorough reorganization."[6]

The substance of the orders thus prepared by Colonel Jordan, without leaving General Bragg's room, was that Generals Bragg, Polk, and Hardee should hold their several corps in condition to move at a moment's notice, having forty rounds of ammunition in their cartridge boxes and three days' cooked rations in their haversacks; also, sixty rounds of ammunition and uncooked rations in wagons for three days, etc.

Couriers were sent that very night with copies of said orders to Generals Polk and Hardee. General Breckinridge was notified by telegraphic dispatch. General Bragg needed no copy of the circular order, as he was present while it was being written at his own quarters.

PART 2

Early the next morning I sent for Colonel Jordan, and gave him the notes I had prepared in the night, as to the order of march from Corinth to Pittsburg Landing, and as to the manner in which our attack should be made. These notes served as the basis of the general order of march and battle, issued on April 3 as Special Orders Number Eight. General Johnston signed the same, as is certified to by Colonel Jordan, "without modification in a single particular." The fact is, it was agreed between General Johnston and myself, the day after his arrival at Corinth, that all orders relative to preparations for the intended movement against the enemy, as well as for all details of organization, should be left en-

---

6. William P. Johnston, "Albert Sidney Johnston at Shiloh," 619.

tirely to me. And it was to facilitate the carrying out of this agreement that Colonel Jordan, my chief of staff, became, upon my own recommendation, the adjutant general of our united forces.

To dwell upon the contents of the elaborate order of march and battle referred to above, and upon the preliminary steps taken in compliance with it, would consume more space than I can command in the pages of this review. Should more minute information on the subject be desired, it can be obtained by examining the original papers prepared at that time, and which are given in full in *The War of the Rebellion: A Compilation of the Official Records of the Union and Confederate Armies,* series one, volume ten, part one, page 392; and also in *The Military Operations of General Beauregard,* volume one, chapter nineteen.

At the request of General Johnston, and before Special Orders Number Eight were published and copies thereof forwarded to the corps commanders and to General Breckinridge, I explained verbally to Generals Bragg, Polk, and Hardee, in the presence of General Johnston, at my own headquarters, the general plan of operations, as suggested by me, and the details of the whole forward movement to be executed in accordance therewith. It was well understood then, that the troops would be marched from Corinth at the hour appointed—12:00 P.M.—before reception by the corps commanders of Special Orders Number Eight, and that copies of the same would be distributed to them on their way to the front.

It may "seem evident" to a few friends of General Johnston that he also had prepared a plan for the projected battle against the Federals at Pittsburg Landing, and that his purpose was that the Confederate assault should be "done by columns of corps"—not, as was the case, by "an array in three parallel lines of battle."[7] If such a plan was ever devised by General Johnston, he expressed it to no one; gave no instructions to carry it out; and has left no document—not a written line—to prove that such a thought had ever occurred to him. What purports to be "his plan" of battle, as "summed up" in a telegram forwarded by him to President Davis, on April 3, 1862, is but a synopsis of the strength of General Buell's army, of the position of the three Confederate corps in their line of march to the front, and of the names of their commanders. It is clearly no plan at all. The plan that eventually became his, is the plan contained in Special Orders Number Eight, and in the circular entitled "Memorandum for Officers," which bore the same date, namely, April 3, 1862. I suggested both of them, and caused both to be written. General Johnston merely adopted them, as commander in chief of our united armies. It is evident that, though suggested by me, neither of them would have issued from department headquarters, had General Johnston not given them his sanction. To that extent, therefore, General Johnston did have a plan of battle, namely, the plan of battle conceived by his second in command, and adopted and endorsed by him.

---

7. Ibid., 620.

Our forces should have been ready to move on April 3, at 12:00 P.M. at the latest. Such, however, was not the case. Orders had been misconstrued, owing to which delays had occurred that caused the rear columns of the First Corps to file out of Corinth at nearly dark on that day. Fully six hours had thus been lost. The march, on the fourth, was unsteady, irregular, and slow; and when the troops bivouacked that evening, they were not more than ten miles from their starting point. True, the roads followed were extremely narrow, and traversed a very thickly wooded country; and it had rained abundantly, which materially increased the difficulties on the way. There was another rainfall on the morning of the fifth; and most of the men, unused to marching, even on good roads, were all the more retarded by it. Added to those drawbacks, so serious under the circumstances, it had also happened, on the fourth, that part of the cavalry attached to General Bragg's corps had made a reconnaissance, without authority, it was said, from its immediate commanders—with none, assuredly, from the commanding general—which assumed such proportions, and created such a disturbance on the way, as to render it next to impossible that the enemy should not have been apprised of the advance of our army.

The formation of our lines of battle was not completed until late on the afternoon of April 5. It had actually taken us upwards of two days to go over a distance of less than eighteen miles.

As soon as it became certain that no engagement on our part could begin that evening, General Johnston invited his corps commanders, and the commander of the reserves, as well as myself, to an informal conference near his headquarters, which were, at that moment, less than two miles from the enemy's line of encampments. There it was ascertained that most of our men were already without rations and that the transportation wagons, with the extra rations and extra ammunition, were still far in the rear, with no certainty of their soon coming up with the troops.

When I understood the true condition of affairs, which, it will be admitted, was far from promising, I told General Johnston and the other officers present that, anxious as I was to carry out the aggressive movement I had, with their cooperations, striven so hard to bring about, I was not certain but that the delays we had met with on our march, and the lack of food threatening the army, and, added to these, the boisterous and regretful conduct of some of our cavalry the day before, had not already frustrated the object we had in view upon marching our forces from Corinth, namely, to reach our present position, take the enemy by surprise, and especially and above all, give him battle before General Buell's junction with General Grant. I plainly stated that, in my opinion, it was hardly possible to believe the enemy ignorant of our presence so near his lines. That vigilance on our part should be taken as proof of vigilance on his. That such being the case, we would likely find the enemy entrenched and ready to meet, with troops flushed with recent victories, the gallant but as yet undisciplined forces we had marched against him. That none could be more sorely disappointed than I was at seeing the great purpose we were about to execute probably lost to us through accident and mismanagement. But that prudence and a due regard to the safety of the army for future operations compelled me to say that I no longer favored an attack, but no preferred inviting one from the enemy, and thus change our offensive movement into a reconnaissance in force; the result of which might bring him nearer to our base and, therefore, farther from his own, and give us, eventually, the chance of retrieving the present lost opportunity.

My remarks were listened to with much attention both by the corps commanders and by General Johnston. He admitted the correctness of my views, but said that he still hoped the enemy would be unprepared to meet our onset, and that we could accomplish our end before the arrival of General Buell's army. That our troops were in line of battle at last, and it were better "to make the venture." The order was therefore given to begin the attack at dawn, the next day, according to the plan already agreed upon.

In adopting this course, General Johnston did what he had the unquestioned right to do. I will only say that he thereby assumed a responsibility which, under the circumstances, I would not have assumed.

It has been stated, in an article published in *The Century Magazine* of February [1885], to which I have already had occasion to recur in these pages, that, upon leaving the conference just spoken of, General Johnston, turning to one of his staff officers, said: "I would fight them if they were a million." It is also stated, in the same article, that my proposition, then "suddenly" given, was "that the army should be withdrawn and retreat to Corinth; that General Johnston seemed to be much surprised at the suggestion; that Polk and Bragg differed with Beauregard (me), and a warm discussion ensued between him (meaning me) and Polk, in which General Johnston took little part," etc.[8] These statements I pronounce entirely erroneous. First, General Johnston was too wise a man and too good a soldier to make the foolhardy remark attributed to him. On the other hand, his whole conduct prior to his arrival at Corinth, and his reason for yielding to my suggestion of an immediate advance on Pittsburg Landing, namely, to take advantage of General Buell's absence at the time, showed most unmistakably that the fact of attacking one army alone, or two armies combined was by no means, immaterial to him. Next, what I said during the conference led to no discussion among the officers there assembled, and to no surprise. The eventualities of war are too great and to numerous to give rise to any such feelings among educated soldiers. Nor was I acting without precedent; somewhat similar strategy had been resorted to by Wellington in 1810, when, advancing to attack Massena at Santarem, he unexpectedly found that able officer on his guard, ready for battle, on ground of his own choosing and much stronger than he had anticipated. After making some demonstration in front of his wily ad-

---

8. Ibid., 622.

versary, to draw him away from his stronghold, Wellington did not hesitate to retire without giving battle.

And it must be borne in mind that my proposition never was "to withdraw and retreat to Corinth"; but to convert the movement I had myself inaugurated and so strenuously supported up to this moment into a reconnaissance in force, so as to bring on an attack upon us from the enemy, instead of attacking him as projected, and thus to endeavor, by appropriate maneuvers, to draw him from his base, as already stated, and produce, or try to produce, some compensating result. It was clear that I only proposed this alternative because I deemed my first plan unsafe at this particular juncture, too much time having been lost by us to justify a fair hope of success. To assert that General Johnston had prepared a plan of battle, the main feature of which was to put his army "face to face with the enemy, knowing that the *chief strategy* of the battle was in the decision to fight,"[9] and that the plan I had formed was merely to appear before the enemy and then retreat to Corinth, is, when set up against existing documentary evidence, a palpable subversion of facts, scarcely deserving more than a passing rebuke.

On the evening of April 5, the Confederate forces, at a distance of less than two miles from the small log structure known as the Shiloh Meeting House, occupied three distinct lines of battle. General Hardee's corps formed the first line, extending, somewhat obliquely, over a space of nearly three miles, from Owl Creek, on the left, to Lick Creek, on the right, but without actually reaching either. It had been necessary, in order to cover the whole front, to place [Brigadier General A. H.] Gladden's brigade, of General Bragg's corps, at the extreme right of this line. The artillery attached to the corps occupied a position in its immediate rear, with cavalry protecting both flanks. Nine thousand and twenty-four men, infantry and artillery, constituted its effective strength. The second line, under General Bragg, was some 500 yards in rear of the first, arranged in similar order. It strength was 10,731 men, including artillery, but to the exclusion of cavalry. General Polk's corps, of 9,136 men, exclusive of cavalry, held the third line, and was deployed in columns of brigade, on the left of the Pittsburg road, its front being about 800 yards rearward of General Bragg's left wing. Each brigade had its own battery; and there was cavalry protecting the extreme left of this line. General Breckinridge's command, in rear of General Bragg's right wing, occupied a position somewhat similar to that of General Polk's corps behind General Bragg's left wing, between the Pittsburg road and Lick Creek, with cavalry supporting his right flank. It consisted of 7,062 men, not including cavalry. General Polk's and Breckinridge's commands constituted the reserve, and were to be thrown forward, as exigencies required, in support of the two front lines of battle.

This gave a total of 35,953, infantry and artillery; to which should be added

---

9. Ibid., 620.

4,382 cavalry; making an aggregate, of all arms, of 40,335 men. The cavalry, it must be said, notwithstanding the good element it was made of, could only be used for such outpost duty as involved no skirmishing.

We had pickets far in advance of our first line of battle, but nowhere could those of the enemy be seen; as if his lines were not guarded by outposts of any kind. Such, however, was not the case, as we discovered next morning.

As encamped, so near our forces, the Federals on that day occupied a position forming a continuous line from Lick Creek, on the left, to Owl Creek, a branch of Snake Creek, on the right, facing nearly south and possibly a little west. Their first line was held by General Sherman's and [Brigadier General Benjamin M.] Prentiss's divisions, extending from the bridge on Owl Creek to the Lick Creek Ford. General Sherman's first brigade formed the extreme right; his fourth was west of the Shiloh Meeting House and rested on it; his third brigade was east of the meeting house and also rested on it. Then began the line of General Prentiss's division; and afterwards, at a long interval, was posted General Sherman's second brigade, in close proximity to Lick Creek. Some half a mile from this line, in its rear, was [Major General John A.] McClernand's division, between Sherman and Prentiss. Then came [Brigadier General W. H. L.] Wallace's division, two miles in the rear and toward the Tennessee river. On its left [lay Brigadier General Stephen A.] Hurlbut's division, on the road leading to Hamburg, a mile and a half behind Sherman's second brigade, under [Colonel David] Stuart.

Darkness disappeared at last before the early brightness of the morning of April 6. A little before 5:00 A.M. on that eventful Sabbath, where the purest heaven I had seen for months was soon to witness perhaps the bloodiest and hardest fought battle of the war, General Hardee's pickets came against those of the enemy and, driving them in, met the main body of the advanced guard of Prentiss's division, which immediately began a scattering fire between the two outposts.

General Hardee thereupon ordered forward his entire line; and General Prentiss, hurriedly informing Wallace and Hurlbut of the attack made upon him, threw forth first a few regiments, and then his whole force, to resist this unexpected onslaught upon his lines. He had to give way, however, so impetuous was the shock he received, and our line, still advancing, next struck against General Sherman's pickets, which immediately fell back toward their encampment. General Sherman now called Generals McClernand, Prentiss, and Hurlbut to his assistance; and [Colonel James C.] Veatch's brigade, of Hurlbut's division, was rapidly sent out to protect General Sherman's left. Presently the firing increased on both sides, and continued very brisk for fully half an hour, when it gradually slackened and, before 7:00 A.M., had almost entirely died out. But our assailing line was still moving onward, and the enemy still losing ground before it.

It is singular that notwithstanding the evidence furnished by all Confederate and many Federal authorities, some Northern writers and Northern generals persevere in the idle assertion—idle because it has been proven groundless—that the Federal forces were not taken by surprise at Shiloh on April 6, 1862. I, myself, for reasons already referred to in this paper, had deemed a surprise improbable; but that it was effected is, nevertheless, a fact. I will merely say this:

On the evening of April 5, our army, amounting to some 40,000 men, was within a mile and a half of the Federal encampments. We had formed our lines of battle in the woods fronting these encampments. We had remained there a whole night, using but few precautionary measures to conceal our presence. We had moved on the next morning within easy sight of the enemy, without encountering any obstacle worthy of notice. When the first encampments were taken, many Federal officers and soldiers were yet lying in bed. Bread was being baked and was taken hot from the ovens by our men. Sutlers's stores were left wide open. Whole companies ran from their quarters, without having time to take their muskets or rifles with them. Our first columns of attack entered the first Federal lines as freely and as unimpeded as if by invitation. This alone is sufficient to prove a surprise in the fullest sense of the word. But this is not all. In [Thomas B.] Van Horne's *History of the Army of the Cumberland* [volume 1, page 102], the following passage occurs: A variety of facts support the assumption that neither General Halleck, General Grant, nor the division commanders on the field beyond Pittsburg Landing, had the remotest expectation that the enemy would advance in offense from Corinth with full strength. General Halleck proposed to command the united armies in their advance at Corinth, and yet was not to leave his headquarters at St. Louis, Missouri, until the seventh."

On April 5 General Sherman sent this telegram to General Grant at Savannah: "I do not apprehend anything like an attack upon our position."

General Grant on the same day telegraphs General Halleck as follows: "I have scarcely the faintest idea of an attack (general) being made upon us, but will be prepared should such a thing take place. . . . It is my present intention to send them (meaning Buell's three foremost divisions) to Hamburg, some few miles above Pittsburg, when they all get here."

And on the same evening (April 5) General Grant, being then at Savannah, and addressing Colonel [Jacob] Ammen, who commanded a brigade of [Brigadier General William] Nelson's division, Buell's army, said: "You cannot march through the swamps; make the troops comfortable; I will send boats for you Monday or Tuesday (the seventh or eighth), or some time next week. There will be no fight at Pittsburg Landing; we will have to go to Corinth, where the rebels are fortified. If they come to attack us, we can whip them, as I have more than twice as many troops as I had at Fort Donelson."

Further evidence to the same effect can be found in *Military Operations of General Beauregard,* volume one, chapter twenty-two.

At dawn of day I had ridden to General Johnston's headquarters to advise with him about our respective action in the impending battle. It was agreed between us that he would lead the attack on our right, and that I would supervise the movements of the field and direct the reserves. When the firing became heavier he mounted his horse and rode forward. This was our last meeting.

By that time the battle had fairly opened. To study its progress and follow its phases, I took the position which General Johnston had requested me to take, and which, as first in command, he should have occupied himself, near the center and in rear of our line; and, from the spot he had just left—which was called by me Headquarters Number One—I sent instructions and orders to various portions of the field as, in my opinion, the exigencies required. Thus, at 7:30 A.M., I ordered Generals Polk and Breckinridge to deploy in columns of brigades, the former on the left, the latter on the right, and to be ready to move at a moment's notice to assist either General Hardee's or General Bragg's line, or both, if it became necessary. And I freely availed myself of the services of every member of my personal and general staff all through the day to convey messages and orders to corps commanders and others, and to keep me well informed of the precise conditions of affairs in our front. Adjutant General Jordan I sent forward with instructions to inspect our lines of battle, secure the massing of the troops for unity of attack and prompt reinforcements to weakened points; also with impressive directions to the corps commanders to mass their batteries in action, and fight them twelve guns on a point.

To fill the space between Lick Creek and the right of General Hardee's line, Chalmers's brigade was ordered from the second line of battle and, with a battery, brought on the right of General Gladden, as prescribed by the order of march and battle. A very hot contest followed, during which General Gladden was mortally wounded, and died on the same day. His services had been invaluable; his conduct on the field worthy of the highest praise. Colonel [D. W.] Adams succeeded him, and, with General Chalmers, made so gallant a charge on the right that Prentiss's whole line broke and retired in confusion. Just then came up, through a previous order of mine, [Brigadier General Bushrod R.] Johnson's brigade, of Polk's corps, as an additional reinforcement to General Hardee's right. This being done, at about 9:30 A.M., I moved to another position, near the Pittsburg road, about a quarter of a mile in advance of the Shiloh Meeting House, which was called Headquarters Number Two.

The pillaging of the enemy's abandoned camps, and, therefore, the straggling of our men, had already begun. Upon being informed of the fact, I ordered members of my staff, aided by Captain Dreux, of my escort, to clear the camps thus invaded, collect the stragglers found in them, and send them on to their respective commands in front. There was much difficulty in executing these orders. This alarming feature was a source of great trouble to me, and brought back to my mind the remarks I had made at our conference the evening previous: "Nature has claims that cannot be disregarded. The best disciplined troops do not fight well on empty stomachs. And this is all the more true of raw troops, unaccustomed to the hardships of war."

General Ruggles's command, composed of [Colonel Randall L.] Gibson's,

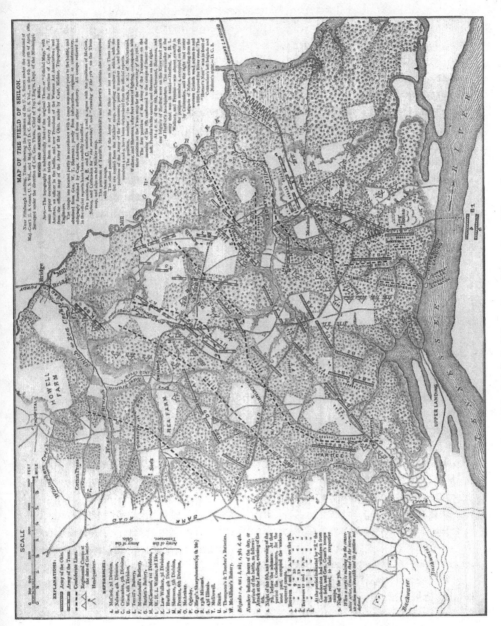

The Field of Shiloh (*Magazine of American History*)

[Brigadier General Patton] Anderson's, and Colonel Preston] Pond's brigades, had formed on General Hardee's left, to contend with General Sherman, who had not yet been dislodged from his position at Shiloh, and who was striving hard to maintain it, aided by McClernand's entire division, and a regiment belonging to one of Wallace's brigades. An interval had occurred between Gibson's brigade and the two others, which was filled by the opportune arrival of one of General Polk's brigades—[Colonel R. M.] Russell's—ordered forward by me some short time previous. He supported [Brigadier General Thomas C.] Hindman's assault upon McClernand and Veatch; and greatly contributed, with [Captain W. Irving] Hodgson's battery, and later on, with two sections of [Captain William H.] Ketchum's, to force General Sherman to fall back to the Purdy and Hamburg roads, and, by 10:00 A.M., to abandon the entire line of his camps.

The battle now raged with renewed fury on W. H. L. Wallace's and Hurlbut's front. Colonel Adams, with Gladden's brigade, had been sent to feel the enemy's strength. At this moment, and while Adams, for want of ammunition, was unable to move forward, Breckinridge's division was led into position by Colonel [Numa] Augustin, of my staff; and Cheatham's division, which I had ordered to the same quarter, came up also, and took a stand on the left. Both engaged the enemy at the same time and with equal impetus. But the forces under Wallace and Hurlbut showed much stubborn resistance, and did not, just then, lose their ground. They were well handled and behaved in a manner highly creditable to themselves and to their commanders.

All the opposing forces were now engaged. Our front line had been extended, right and left, and the troops of our second line, and those composing the reserve, occupied it at different intervening points. General Johnston, changing his position in rear of [Brigadier General Jones M.] Withers's division, came over, at about 11:00 A.M., to the rear of Breckinridge's division. A little before this, by agreement between Generals Bragg and Polk, the former took his stand near the right center of our line, the latter near the left center, and General Hardee remained near the extreme left. I continued to occupy a medial position on the line, towards the rear, in order to follow the general movements of our troops, in accordance with General Johnston's desire.

Learning, at about 1:00 P.M., that the forces under Sherman and McClernand showed signs of weakness and were about to give way, I ordered General Hardee to push on the cavalry against their retreating regiments, and to endeavor to cut them off from their line of encampment. This was done with great dash, and Captain [John Hunt] Morgan gave proof on that occasion, of what could be expected of him in the future. By my order, another vigorous assault was made by General Hardee upon Sherman's and McClernand's commands, which were rapidly driven back, the larger portion of them toward Snake Creek, and the other in the direction of Wallace's camps. My headquarters had again been advanced by this time, and were now beyond General Wallace's captured camps.

The Confederate left was next engaged with General Wallace's division, now

become the advanced Federal right, which had resolutely held its own and repulsed all assaults made upon it. General Bragg had spent more than three hours
in a stubborn yet powerless endeavor to force it to give way. There was Gibson's
brigade repulsed, after making four unavailing assaults, insisted upon by General Bragg, who now passed further to the right, leaving the responsibility of this
portion of the field to a staff officer, with authority to act in his name. General
Johnston had been, for nearly three-quarters of an hour, in rear of General
Breckinridge's division, which was, at that time, the advanced right of the main
Confederate line. The firing was unusually heavy in that quarter, and General
Johnston was astonished at the resolute resistance encountered there. After causing General Breckinridge to appeal to the soldiers, and after doing so himself,
he ordered a charge, which he led in person with his well-known valor, and
during which he was wounded in the leg, without at first realizing the extent of
his injury. The Federal line thus charged had slowly and reluctantly given way,
retiring to the next ridge beyond; but the temporary advantage we had gained
was dearly bought by the death of the general in chief, a gallant soldier and noble
citizen, whose life, had it been spared, would have been of inestimable value to
his country. General Johnston died in the arms of Governor [Isham] Harris of
Tennessee, one of his volunteer aides, at about 2:30 P.M.

Immediately after General Johnston had been wounded, and before being
apprised of it, Adjutant General Jordan, who had just arrive in that quarter of
the field and had found General Breckinridge's division not in action, ordered
it, in General Johnston's name, to charge the Federal forces in its front, which
were screened by a fence at the entrance of a wood. The movement was successfully effected after a hard struggle on both sides, and the enemy at last fell back,
abandoning the position he had held.

Meanwhile, my attention being turned to that portion of our line near the
center where General Bragg had vainly endeavored to dislodge the enemy about
an hour before, I ordered General Hardee to gather what force he could dispose
of for another advance in that quarter. I was not yet aware of the death of General Johnston. General Hardee obeyed and sent forward the remnants of Anderson's and Gibson's brigades, with two batteries of artillery, and several battalions organized as such by members of my staff, who had collected them from
stragglers and commands which had lost their proper positions in line. Colonel [Marshall J.] Smith's Crescent Regiment of New Orleans was added to these
troops, and, as it passed me to join in the movement, was urged on by me with
the following words: "Go forward, men, and drive them into the Tennessee!"

A serious and well-disputed contest ensued. The enemy finally yielded, losing ground more and more. But Prentiss and Hurlbut, further to the right, were
still successful in their resistance to the forces under Breckinridge and Cheatham.
[Brigadier General John K.] Jackson's and Chalmers's commands were called,
and came to their assistance under a raking fire from [Brigadier General Jacob
G.] Lauman's brigade. I was at that time in advance of McClernand's camps,

directing operations at that point. There it was that, shortly after 3:00 P.M., Governor Harris came up and informed me of General Johnston's death. (Colonel [Nathaniel] Wickliffe, of General Johnston's staff, brought the same news. I cannot now say whether he came before or after Governor Harris.) However deeply grieved I was at this distressing news, the struggle just then was too hot and the result as yet too undecided to allow me either time or opportunity to express all my regret. Messengers were hurriedly sent by me to the corps commanders, to inform them of what had occurred and to urge upon them the necessity of concealing the fact from the troops; and, feeling all the more the weighty responsibility resting upon me, I gave orders that the attack be continued and pushed forward with the utmost vigor.

It is but true to state here, that never from the opening of the battle up to the hour of his death had General Johnston occupied on the field the position which was properly his own as commander in chief of our forces. From the place he had himself selected on our line, and where he remained to the last, he was but acting the part of a corps or division commander, and as such, uselessly exposing his person. From where he was, he could not—nor in fact did he ever attempt to—direct the general movements of our forces. That most important trust devolved upon me, the second in command, and I performed it throughout the whole day, before, as well as after, the death of General Johnston.

What troops remained of Hindman's and Gladden's brigades, with the forces under Breckinridge and Cheatham, were now pressing Wallace's left. General Bragg was hotly assailing Prentiss's and Hurlbut's commands. Jackson and Chalmers were engaged with Hurlbut's front and left flank. Hurlbut now fell back, and the course he followed allowed Jackson and Chalmers to strike in flank the line held by Prentiss and Wallace. The space occupied by the two latter was being narrowed, more and more, around them. At that time, General Hardee, on the left, was confronting the remnants of McClernand's and Sherman's commands. Here also, and in spite of the resistance shown, the enemy was gradually falling back in conformity with the retreating movements of the other Federal forces. Wallace was now mortally wounded. He died that day. The Federals lost in him one of their ablest and most gallant commanders. Prentiss alone, it appears, did not follow in time the rearward movement of Wallace's division. He was not warned in season and clung to his position until, surrounded from all sides, he was compelled to surrender, with all that was left of his command, an aggregate of some 2,500 men, and among them General Prentiss himself. This took place at 5:30 P.M., about three hours after General Johnston's death.

The continuous fighting, marching, countermarching, and maneuvering of the troops all day long—and that mostly without food—finally produced the most telling effect upon them. Almost every position of the enemy was carried. His lines of encampments were taken. The Tennessee River was in sight, on several points of our line. We had captured small arms, guns, flag, and upwards of 3,000 prisoners; but the victory, nonetheless, was not wholly ours. It was far from being gained when General Johnston fell; it was not completely gained in spite of all that was accomplished after his death. Straggling among the men, which had begun before noon, had now assumed fearful proportions. And worse even than straggling was the fact that the men in front, who had never been out of action, were absolutely outdone by the need of food and by fatigue. To deny this is either to confess utter ignorance of what took place on the battlefield of Shiloh, or to show wanton intent to subvert the truth.

Notwithstanding this state of things, I determined to again deploy our forces into line for a concerted onslaught before it were too late, and did my utmost, with the assistance of the corps commanders, to successfully carry it out. The attack was made; but it was desultory, without spirit or ardor, and failed in effect.

There was an additional reason for our failure in this last advance upon the enemy; it was the massing of Colonel [J. D.] Webster's reserve artillery, consisting of some sixty guns (among them several 24-pounder siege guns), which had been placed along a ridge overlooking Pittsburg Landing, and were powerfully assisted by the two gunboats *Tyler* and *Lexington.* Supported by the remnants of Wallace's, McClernand's, and Hurlbut's divisions, and by Colonel Ammen's brigade of Nelson's division (Buell's army), which had arrived on the field a little after 5:00 P.M., these guns and gunboats enfiladed the limited stretch of broken and thickly wooded ground over which our troops had to pass in their assault, and did much to impair the success of their efforts.

The Final Stand of Grant's Army on April 6, 1862 (*Campfire and Battlefield*)

It was 6:00 P.M., just before sunset, when I ordered the cessation of hostilities, so that our forces could be withdrawn for rest, and thus avoid confusion in their rearward march. But, before that order was received by the corps commanders—and in many cases before it was issued—the contest had already virtually ceased on the greater portion of the field. It is absolutely erroneous to state that some of the subordinate commanders were preparing another concerted movement, and that it was prevented by my order to stop the fight. No one on the hard-fought field of Shiloh had the hope of victory more at heart than I had. The entire conception of the campaign had been mine, and I had directed the general movements of the troops throughout the day. But human endurance has its limits; and to quote the language of General Bragg, not as found in his report, written more than three months after the Battle of Shiloh, but as used by him while leaving the front on April 6 with his exhausted men: "They had done all that they would do and had better be withdrawn."

It was dusk when the troops began to leave the front to bivouac for the night. Many of them left after darkness had set in, and, on that account, got separated from their commands. General Chalmers, in his official report, says: "Our men . . . continued to fight until night closed the hostilities on both sides. . . . They were too much exhausted to storm the batteries on the hill."

Lieutenant Colonel [David] Urquhart, one of the members of General Bragg's personal staff, in a letter to General Jordan on this point, says: "When . . . this order was given, the plain truth must be told, that our troops at the front were a thin line of exhausted men, who were making no further headway, and were glad to receive orders to fall back."

A mass of evidence, collected with care from Federal and Confederate reports, could be accumulated here to sustain what I have just stated. I refrain from lack of space.

Later in the evening, some of the corps and division commanders visited my headquarters, established in what had been one of General Sherman's tents, near the Shiloh Meeting House. General Bragg was among them. They showed and expressed much satisfaction over the triumph of the day. No one intimated, directly or indirectly, within my hearing or that of my staff, that the order to cease firing and fall back to the captured camps of the enemy had been given too soon, or that it should not have been given at all. They were well aware that, though masters of the field, our victory had been incomplete; but acknowledged that the troops had done all that could be expected of them. The hope was entertained by all present that, upon resuming the offensive the next day, we would complete our work, and accomplish the end we were striving for. I handed to General Bragg and to the other officers there a dispatch I had just received, to the effect that some of the divisions of Buell's army were marching toward Florence and not to Pittsburg Landing. Unfortunately this news proved to be false. The troops referred to were of Mitchel's division, not then with Buell's army.

Having now instructed the corps commanders present, and sent orders to the others, to look to the comfort of their jaded troops and reorganize them for the next day's events, we separated for the night, and I retired to my temporary quarters to seek some rest, of which I was greatly in need.

· · ·

I do not propose to give more than a cursory description of the second day's fight at Shiloh. "Monday," it has been said, "was General Beauregard's battle."[10] It was, unquestionably; but not more than the battle of Sunday, for the reason that I directed the general movements of the army on both days.

Skirmishing began early on the morning of April 7. Gathering the forces that were at hand, Generals Hardee, Bragg, and Breckinridge hurried to the front to meet the enemy's onset. On the extreme right of our line was General Hardee, with Chalmers's and Jackson's brigades of Bragg's corps. General Bragg was at the left, with the remainder of his command, and [Brigadier General Charles] Clark's division of Polk's corps, and, shortly afterwards, [Colonel Robert P.] Trabue's Kentucky brigade. General Breckinridge was on the left of General Hardee. Between the former and General Bragg was a vacant space, assigned to General Polk, who had not yet made his appearance on the field. He arrived later in the morning, to my great relief, and promptly falling into line, led his men under fire with his wonted coolness and gallantry.

On the other hand, Nelson's division, next to the river, formed left of the enemy's front line. On his right came [Brigadier General Thomas L.] Crittenden; then [Brigadier General Alexander M.] McCook, whose division was the extreme right of General Buell's command. General Lew Wallace, with his fresh troops which had arrived late the evening before, was on the extreme right, near Snake Creek. The other Federal forces, gathered from the broken commands of the first day's battle—namely Sherman's, McClernand's, and Hurlbut's—were on the center.

The first Confederate pickets that came in contact with the enemy that morning were from [Colonel Nathan B.] Forrest's cavalry. They retired in good order toward General Hardee's line and sought, and found, shelter behind it. Nelson's advancing columns were soon confronted by Chalmers's brigade, with Colonel [John C.] Moore's regiment and a mixed command made up of troops from Jackson's and Gladden's brigades; added to which were the Crescent Regiment of New Orleans and the Twenty-sixth Alabama, with batteries to support them. Nelson's forces were compelled to fall back, but, at about 8:00 A.M., advanced a second time, being now reinforced by [Colonel William B.] Hazen's brigade. Our troops began to give way and, while doing so, lost one of their batteries. They soon rallied, however, and at 9:00 A.M., again took the offensive with the assistance of other batteries, and of reinforcements opportunely sent

---

10. Ibid., 628.

by me. Their first position was finally recovered, and the lost battery was theirs once more. Hazen's brigade suffered considerably in that encounter, and came very near falling into our hands. Ammen's brigade was also closely pressed, and would have been turned on its left, had it not been for the timely arrival of [Captain William R.] Terrill's battery, of McCook's division.

After Nelson's, Crittenden's division was engaged with General Hardee's forces and a part of General Breckinridge's. A hot contest ensued, in which, at about 10:00 A.M., some of General Grant's forces under McClernand and Hurlbut took an active part. This whole Federal force was kept at bay for several hours, and until two brigades of McCook's division was sent to reinforce it. It then began to gain ground, our troops slowly giving way—not, however, before I had resolved to retire from the field, and thus put an end to a useless loss of life and material.

It was evident that General Buell's arrival, with three divisions of his army, was an accomplished fact; and that my depleted forces were now confronting some 20,000 fresh troops, exclusive of Lew Wallace's division, aggregating about 7,000 men, and exclusive also of what remained of General Grant's troops of the day before, which amounted to not less than 20,000 men—though it is doubtful whether much more than half that number actively participated in the battle of Monday. Deducting our losses of the previous day, and the stragglers, amounting to thousands, I never had, ready for duty and with musket in hand, on April 7 more than 20,000 men—and at 1:00 P.M., not even 16,000, exclusive of cavalry; which, owing to the nature of the ground, and as General Grant himself admitted, "could not be used in front."[11]

Our left had been seriously threatened at about 1:00 P.M. General Bragg's forces at that point, weakened by the withdrawal of three brigades to reinforce our right and center, were closely pressed and unable any longer to hold their ground. He called on me for aid. I ordered the Eighteenth Louisiana and the Orleans Guard Battalion—now blended into one command—and remnants of an Alabama and a Tennessee regiment to be immediately sent to him, and, going on with them as they passed, led them myself in the charge. General Bragg thereupon resumed the offensive, and the enemy fell back some distance beyond the Shiloh Meeting House. I had established my headquarters, early in the morning, at that central point of our lines, where I remained, undisturbed, until nearly 2:30 P.M.

All the Confederate troops confronting, on April 7, the 40,000 Federals arrayed against them—about 27,000 of whom were composed of fresh troops—had fought hard, from early dawn to late in the evening of Sunday. Exhausted as they were, they fought again on the seventh with such spirit and endurance as to justify me in saying of them in my preliminary report to the War Depart-

---

11. Grant, "Battle of Shiloh," 600.

Saving His Master
(*Century*)

ment: "From the outset our troops, notwithstanding our fatigue and losses from the battle of the day before, exhibited the most cheering, veteran-like steadiness."

There was now but one course to pursue. It was, while inducing the enemy to believe in a determination on my part to continue the contest, to quietly prepare for a timely and honorable retreat. I acted with much caution and abstained from communicating my intention to the corps commanders and even, at first, to my chief of staff. Since 9:00 A.M., however, I had sent messengers to Corinth to inquire as to the arrival of General Van Dorn. I knew it was problematical, but was loathe to begin any retrograde movement before that last hope of relief had failed me. Meanwhile I caused reinforcements, made up of stragglers and disjointed commands gathered from the rear, to be hastened to the front as fast as they could be found; and, strange though it may seem, these became the only *reserves* I could dispose of to strengthen my thinned ranks, and with which the unequal contest then going on was prolonged for more than four hours with no sign of decisive advantage on the part of the enemy.

When at last the news was brought back that Van Dorn and his forces had not arrived, and that not even his whereabouts could be ascertained, I began seriously the difficult work before me; difficult, because it had to be done without weakness or hesitancy, so as neither to make it appear a defeat in the eye of the enemy, nor a cause of discouragement to our overwrought troops. I dispatched an aide to the rear, with a squadron of cavalry, for the purpose of clearing and preparing the roads for the passage of the army. I also instructed Adjutant General Jordan to select, at once, a convenient spot across the first ravine, toward the rear, and there to station infantry and artillery to protect our line of march, as the troops would be leaving the field. The corps commanders were then made aware of my plan; and, while taking the necessary measures to carry it out, were ordered to resume the offensive on diverse parts of the line, with a view to keep our adversary in ignorance of the true motive of our movement. They very ably executed the orders given them, and the retreat was begun by 2:30 P.M. and effected leisurely, quietly, and with much regularity.

General Breckinridge's command was the first to retire, the troops right and left of his position closing up the space it had just occupied. It was marched to the rear of the force collected by Colonel Jordan and there halted, as agreed upon, to act as a rear guard. General Polk's corps came next, then General Hardee's, and.lastly, General Bragg's. There was no flurry, no useless haste among men or officers, and even the stragglers dropped into line and rejoined their commands as they passed. No pursuit whatsoever was attempted by the enemy. In fact, the Federal troops that had fought the day before were as much outdone as our own. Generals Grant and Sherman acknowledge it in their reports. The former even stated, later on, and caused it to be published, that, though desirous of pursuing the retreating army, he "had not the heart to order it to men who had fought desperately for two days, lying in mud and rain, whenever not fighting."[12] Such was not the case, however, with the three divisions of General Buell's army. These were made up of fresh troops, though it is well to state that they had done most, if not all, of the fighting on Monday. But no order to pursue was given to General Buell. General Grant seems to have been diffident about it, and had not yet acquired the habit of giving orders to General Buell.

General Breckinridge, in command of the rear guard, bivouacked on the night of the seventh at a distance of not more than a mile and a half from the battlefield. No hostile force of any kind, not the crack of a rifle, nor the sound of a bugle, disturbed his rest. On the morning of April 8 he moved his force three miles further to the rear, and remained in that position for several days without being attacked or even annoyed in any manner whatever.

General Sherman, however, on the lower Corinth road, and [Brigadier General Thomas J.] Wood (of Buell's army), on the upper road, with two brigades each, did venture on a reconnaissance on the morning of the eighth, which was far from being a success. They came across our cavalry pickets, posted where General Breckinridge had bivouacked the previous night, and, being in such

---

12. Ibid., 605.

The Confederate Retreat from Shiloh (*Life of Sherman*)

number, easily drove them back, sending two regiments, one of infantry and one of cavalry, to press them further rearward and capture them, if possible. It so happened that the pursuers struck against Colonel Forrest, with a fraction of his own cavalry and a few companies under Captain Morgan, in all, 350 men. The Federal raiders fell back in the greatest hurry, leaving on the ground some fifteen men killed and twenty-five wounded. But Colonel Forrest followed them too far, and finally met the four reconnoitering brigades which barred his way and forced him to fall back. Colonel Forrest was very seriously wounded on that occasion, and had to leave the service for more than two months.

Our loss on both days was heavy; but it must be borne in mind that we were the assailants during the whole of Sunday, and also, very frequently on Monday. The list of casualties stood as follows: Killed, 1,728; wounded 8,012; missing 959; in all, 10,699, or an average of twenty-four and one-third per cent of those present on the field.

We carried back with us some twenty-six stands of colors, and about thirty pieces of artillery, leaving behind many more for lack of horses to remove them to the rear. We took, besides, a large number of small arms and, as before stated, more than 3,000 prisoners.

Our forces, with the exception of Breckinridge's and Chalmers's commands, resumed the positions they occupied at Corinth on April 3. The work of recruitment and reorganization was immediately begun. I applied to the War Department for two major generals, four brigadier generals, and a chief of artillery. I also recommended General Bragg for promotion.

During the comparative lull that followed, I was desirous of preparing a correct, final report of the Battle of Shiloh, and of substituting it to the hastily written—and in many respects imperfect—preliminary report I had forwarded to Richmond. This, however, I was debarred from doing, as none of the corps commanders were ready with their own reports. These, in fact, were only prepared months after the events they described; General Polk's not until nearly one year after; General Bragg's, though apparently written on April 30, was not completed before July 25; that is, more than three months after the battle. (I have never been able to procure that of General Breckinridge.) Contrary to all military usage, these reports were sent direct to the War Department, instead of being forwarded through me. Hence the errors, discrepancies, and misinterpretations to be found in certain portions of them. They are not sustained by actual facts, nor by what was stated in the official reports of brigade and regimental commanders, upon which they purported to have been based.

On April 11 General Van Dorn's forces arrived at Memphis. I sent [Brigadier General Albert] Rust's brigade to Fort Pillow, and [Brigadier General Henry] Little's to Rienzi, some twelve miles from Corinth, for the purpose of reconnoitering, and also of selecting a good defensive position for a retrograde movement, in case of need.

Shortly after the Battle of Shiloh, General Halleck took command of the Federal forces at Pittsburg Landing. They soon began to increase by the arrival of reinforcements and, later on, of General Pope's army, estimated at 25,000 men. General Halleck must have had then, under him, at least 125,000 men of all arms. Whereas the Confederate forces under me, including Van Dorn's 17,000 men, numbered not more than 50,000; daily decreasing on account of sickness, and with no hope of being reinforced.

When General Van Dorn reached Corinth, he was assigned to a position on the south side of the Memphis and Charleston Railroad, on the right and in rear of our defensive lines. These extended some three miles in advance of the town, on high grounds in rear of a creek, and had been established by General Bragg, while I was still at Jackson. They were defective, especially toward the left. I corrected them afterward, but not to the extent I would have wished.

General Hardee's corps extended along and from the Memphis and Charleston Railroad, in front of General Van Dorn's position, to the left, where it rested on the right of General Bragg, whose left in turn rested on the right of General Polk's corps, stretching across the Mobile and Ohio Railroad. The left of this command occupied some woods protected by abatis and rifle pits, each corps holding a few brigades in reserve.

Directly behind Corinth was General Breckinridge's command, which now, as before the Battle of Shiloh, constituted the reserve.

Sickness among the troops began to be so prevalent that the eventuality of a change of strategic position, to insure the health and safety of the army, soon forced itself upon me. Such a position was not easy to find; for, while from it the enemy had to be held in check, and the country in his rear protected, including Fort Pillow, a salubrious locality and a supply of good water, so much needed at Corinth, had also to be taken into serious consideration. Grand Junction, on that account, had been discarded. But the fear of losing Fort Pillow, which was still so essential to the safety of Vicksburg, around which, by my orders, defensive works were already in process of construction, caused me, for the time being, to waive all thought of a change, until compelled to revert to it anew, by the mode of approach of the enemy in my front.

It was hard to say just when my position would be seriously threatened by the advance of General Halleck upon it. That he was closing in upon Corinth, more and more every day, was an undoubted fact; but so extremely cautious were all his movements, that one less acquainted with our respective strength might have supposed he commanded my force of 50,000 men, and I his large army of 125,000. Nevertheless, I dispatched several officers of trust with special instructions to look for and report upon a good defensive position, healthy in every respect, and where an abundance of water could be readily be procured. Tupelo was the place finally designated and recommended.

On May 8, General Pope, whose line of encampments was near Hamburg, on the Tennessee, advanced with his entire force on Farmington, a small village four miles from Corinth. He had undertaken this aggressive movement, it was believed, without consultation with General Halleck. Between him and General Buell ran Seven Miles Creek, now filled by recent rains, and which completely separated him from his base. Seizing upon this opportunity, and desirous of cutting off his line of retreat, I ordered a concerted attack in full force upon his position. It was only partially successful, and failed through the inefficiency of General Van Dorn's guide, and the tardiness of one of his division commanders. As it was, however, two of General Pope's brigades barely escaped falling into our hands. Their casualties, in killed and wounded, were heavy. They also lost a large number of small arms and accouterments.

I prepared, a few days later, another concerted movement somewhat similar to the one just mentioned, and for the same purpose; but a series of rain storms baffled the attempt, and the troops were ordered back to their former positions. This was on May 18. General Halleck was still advancing upon us, slowly but safely, and the effectiveness of our troops were daily decreasing owing to the prevalence of disease among them.

It was now clear to me that the withdrawal of the army from Corinth should no longer be delayed. That by so doing we would lose a strategic point of greatest value, none appreciated more than I did; but there could be no hesitation between the holding of Corinth and the safety of our forces. I called the corps commanders together and, after fully expressing my views to them, asked that each should give his individual opinion upon the important question under advisement. The conclusion arrived at was unanimous: the evacuation of Corinth was a military necessity.

Orders were immediately given for the removal to Baldwyn, Tupelo, and other localities in the rear, of the heavy guns, ammunition, camp equipage, and also of the sick. Very minute instructions were given by me to the corps commanders. They were enjoined not to speak of the projected movement, but to spread the rumor that we were preparing for a general engagement.

The evacuation began on May 30, at 1:00 A.M. The main obstacles in the way had been removed; all the wagon trains and all the rearmost troops were sent on ahead.

In order to impress the enemy with the belief that we were about to take the offensive and were receiving reinforcements, I caused empty trains to be run at stated times during the night, and ordered the troops stationed near them to cheer vociferously as they arrived. The effect desired was produced, as is shown by the following telegram of General Pope to General Halleck: "The enemy are

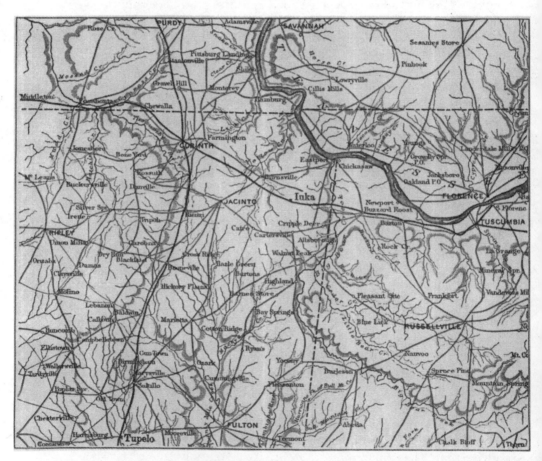

Northern Mississippi (*Century*)

The Evacuation of Corinth (*Life of Sherman*)

reinforcing in my front and left. The cars are running constantly, and the cheering is immense every time they unload in front of me. I have no doubt, from all appearances, that I shall be attacked in heavy force at daylight."

It is an undisputed fact that our last files were quietly marching out of Corinth when the above was forwarded. A thin line of skirmishers and some few cavalry had been left to keep up appearances.

It was only in the morning of the thirtieth, long after dawn, that the enemy, who had made vast preparations to meet the anticipated attack, at last discovered the entire withdrawal of the Confederate army from Corinth.

The retreat was orderly in every respect, and was effected as it had been planned. An army of 50,000 men disappeared from the immediate front of an army of 125,000, and brought away with it its munitions of war, its stores, its sick; and suffered no material loss of any kind. No pursuit was attempted by General Halleck. It is even doubtful whether he was aware of the direction taken by our forces on their line of retreat. That line was from Corinth to Rienzi, Booneville, Baldwyn, and, finally, to Tupelo (fifty miles south), which latter place was reached June 9. I had caused several halts to be made on the march; the first, six miles from Corinth, behind the Tuscumbia River; the second, at Rienzi, and the third at Baldwyn, to be ready to meet the enemy had he shown any willingness to follow; but he did not.

The evacuation of Corinth, if not an absolute Confederate victory, was unquestionably a barren triumph for the Federals. Such was, at the time, the conclusion reached by all unbiased minds. Such is the verdict of history today. It saved the army from incalculable disasters. It foiled the plans and preparations of the enemy, and prolonged the contest in the southwest for more than a year.

21

The Great Locomotive Chase

Private Jacob Parrott

"SPECIAL AND hazardous duty within the enemy's lines"—it was to be that, my captain said. Every soldier knows what that may mean, hanging perhaps as a spy! But it also meant excitement, and that was the view I took on April 7, 1862, when I was selected for such duty. My company was K, Thirty-third Ohio Volunteers, a part of [Brigadier General Orsmby M.] Mitchel's division of the western Union army, stationed near Murfreesboro, Tennessee. I was seventeen years old.

From Richmond to Memphis stretched a single line of railroad, marking, roughly, the whole Confederate front. It was the means of communication between all the Confederate armies scattered along it, whose safety depended on keeping it open. Roads branched from this east and west line at various points, piercing the Confederacy to the south, and by them the armies were fed and reinforced. Chattanooga lay almost at the center of the main line—then called the Memphis and Charleston Railroad—and south from it to Atlanta ran the Georgia State Railroad. Chattanooga, therefore, was the most vital point on the northern border of the Confederacy. The capture of it by the Union army would be a menace to all the forces scattered along the hundreds of miles to east and west. And the capture of Chattanooga depended upon possession of the Atlanta line.

I was told to doff my uniform and to report that night in citizen's clothes to Captain James J. Andrews, who was within our lines somewhere east of Shelbyville on the Wartron road.

As soon as it was dark I walked in that direction. I didn't know Andrews, but I had heard of him—everyone had. His fame as a scout went everywhere before him. When I had gone about a mile I saw other men approaching out of the darkness, and we converged in silence. At last a very tall, bearded man, who stooped a little, appeared among us. It was Andrews. He hesitated, with glances about. At last he said in low, distinct tones:

"Let us go a little from the road, boys."

We gathered about him in a thicket of dead trees. A thunderstorm was rising; the wind moaned through their naked branches, and the lightning revealed white eager faces, not one of which I knew. At each peal of thunder Andrews paused and then went quietly on.

"Orders," he said, "have been sent to the colonels of the three regiments of [Colonel Joshua W.] Sills's brigade to select a man from each company for dangerous service. When I have explained what it is, any of you will be at liberty to return without having your patriotism or your courage questioned. General Mitchel will advance at once toward the Memphis and Charleston Railroad, striking it near Huntsville, Alabama. His objective point will be Chattanooga, the key to all the South. The only hope the Confederates can have of help after it is captured is from the army now organizing near Atlanta. To destroy this line of reinforcements is our duty.

"Our expedition is composed of locomotive engineers and soldiers," he went on. "We are bound for Marietta, Georgia, on the railroad leading north from Atlanta to Chattanooga. You are to be at Marietta next Friday morning. There we will all board the early train bound for Chattanooga, and at Big Shanty, where there is no telegraph station, and the train stops twenty minutes for breakfast, we will steal the engine and run through to Chattanooga where we shall find General Mitchel's army. We are to destroy the telegraph line, tear up the track, and burn bridges, preventing Confederate reinforcements from being rushed to the front from the south."

Suppressed discussion and questioning followed this. After a time every man declared that he would undertake the work.

"Then," said Andrews, "we will break up at once into squads of two or three, travel east through the Cumberland Mountains, and south to the Tennessee River, and cross it somewhere west of Chattanooga not later than Thursday afternoon. From Chattanooga, take the afternoon train leaving at five o'clock for Marietta. I will meet you there at night. You have a long and difficult road to travel in only three days and nights. Under no circumstances recognize me unless you know we are alone."

"What account shall we give of ourselves, if we are challenged?" asked one of us.

"Tell them you are Kentuckians escaping from the Yankees and on your way south to join the Confederate army. If pressed"—he hesitated—"tell them that you are from Fleming County. There are no soldiers in the Southern army from there."

"But suppose," asked another, "they will not believe our stories—what then?"

"Enlist of course; do not hesitate. Have no fear of being suspected of desertion if found in the enemy's ranks. You will have no difficulty in getting into the Southern army; it will be hard to keep out of it. But let us meet at Marietta and stay together, or die together. We are undertaking a hazardous thing. I want you to realize that. If we succeed, all Eastern Tennessee will fall into the hands of the Union army. I repeat, we are to run through the heart of the Confederacy on one of its own trains, destroying bridges, cutting off all reinforcements!"

During all this a dog barked dismally out across the valley, and now the rain fell in torrents. Falling in with Samuel Robinson, Company G, I began the perilous journey. That night we stumbled ten miles in the darkness, knee-deep in mud, and soaked to the skin. We slept in a shed, breakfasted at a farm-house, and striking the mountains the next night, crossed the Confederate lines. The following day a squad of Confederate soldiers halted us, but they believed our story, as we were on the natural route south from Kentucky. At last we came to a ferry on the Tennessee River below Chattanooga. A rumor had reached here that the Yankees were coming, and as orders had been issued to allow no one to cross for three days, we trudged up-stream to Chattanooga to take chances at the ferry there.

It was on this walk that we fell in with members of the party who said that they had seen Andrews, and that he had given orders to assemble at Marietta on Saturday instead of Friday. The rains, he had said, would delay Mitchel's advance and give us a day to spare.

On our way we met a man whom we had seen at the ferry.

"Hello, Yanks," he said.

Were we recognized, suspected, shadowed? But it was a lonely spot, so Robinson said—loud enough for him to hear. "He's a Yankee spy. He takes us for Yankees," and we turned on him with drawn revolvers, making him throw up his hands. "We've come a long way to fight such fellows as you," we said. And then we searched him, found that he was a citizen of Chattanooga, and he came along with us.

At the river more of our party were waiting to cross. The ferryman said that the wind and waves were too high. That was well enough, but it was now Friday noon and strangers kept gathering about. I remember that we talked of the Battle of Shiloh, just fought; of the *Merrimac* and *Monitor*. The Southern army, said the Confederates, had achieved a great victory and were marching resistlessly on to lay waste the North; the *Merrimac* had towed the disabled *Monitor* to Norfolk with grappling irons, and was off to bombard New York and Boston.

It was nearly five o'clock, and we were getting desperate, when the man we had held up on the road, who knew the ferryman, said to him: "These fellows are all right—Kentucky boys sick of the Yanks, who've got to get down and join our army tonight." The ferryman believed him and we started.

The rough water was nothing; it was the guard on the other side we feared, but, strange to say, we stepped ashore unchallenged in Chattanooga. The train for Marietta had not left, and our Chattanooga friend even helped us to buy our tickets.

Headed for Atlanta, we all sat in the cars, thinking. How would it be on the up trip tomorrow? Should we dash back over these bridges seeing them behind through smoke, or were we doomed? The sun sank to rest among the hills of

Georgia. The station gong roused us at Dalton for supper, the last regular meal I had for eight months. I climbed back into my seat and we steamed on. The car was full of Confederate soldiers discussing the Federal advance. I dozed off. The call: "Marietta! Marietta!" woke me near midnight, and we piled out into the darkness. Other members of the party were here. Andrews among them, but I did not see him. Most of us went to bed in the station hotel, and the rest were housed around ready for the morrow.

The next morning—the memorable Saturday, April 12—we met in Andrews's room at daybreak for final instructions. Some of the men wanted to abandon the enterprise, urging that Mitchel must have moved on Chattanooga in spite of the rain, and that trains would be escaping south, crowding the railroad, and rendering our task impossible.

Andrews, almost in whisper, but with fire in his words, disposed of these objections. "Boys," he said, "I was on a raid before, and that failed. This time I succeed, or leave my bones in Dixie." Never was there such a leader; we would have trusted him to the ends of the earth.

"Listen," he concluded as quietly (Andrews never exhorted): "When we stop at Big Shanty, [W. W.] Brown, [Alfred] Wilson, and [William] Knight, our engineers, will go with me to the engine. Keep your seats, the rest of you, till I tell you to move. Then get off the train on the side away from the station, go forward, pass where the cars will have been uncoupled, and get aboard again. Keep your eye on me for directions in case anything happens. Shoot any one who interferes with you, but only if you must."

The train from Atlanta to Chattanooga was nearly due. Andrews grasped our hands and we hurried to the platform, where we bought tickets for different places to avoid suspicion. When the train drew in we noticed that three boxcars were coupled just behind the engine—the *General*. We all sat in the same coach, and a genial young man, almost a boy—a man after Andrews's own heart, as, to our sorrow we were soon to learn—took up our tickets. His name was [William A.] Fuller. He did not suspect us either. We whirled on past Kenesaw Mountain where [Major General William T.] Sherman and [General Joseph E.] Johnston fought afterwards so bloodily. At last came the call: "Big Shanty— twenty minutes for breakfast!" That cooled our nerves. Here was the moment for action, and all but the day's delay had fallen out as planned.

We stopped between the shed and the white tents of a big Confederate camp on our left, where we could see the guards patrolling. Andrews and Knight crowded out of the cars with the passengers, but we stayed in our seats. They got off by the left steps, instead of the right, by which the passengers rushed in to breakfast. What they did then took less time than to tell it, and all the while soldiers were lying on the ground a few yards from them, and a staring sentry stood twenty feet from the locomotive.

Andrews strolled on ahead of the engine to see if the track was clear. To us, waiting in that motionless car, he seemed to be gone an age: the tension was frightful. Then he walked back with Knight and, pointing between the last of the boxcars and the baggage car, said: "Uncouple here." We could see them from the windows walking about, talking leisurely. The he stepped to the door of our car and said in his matter-of-fact way: "Well, boys, I guess it's time to go."

We filed out on the camp side. There was Knight on the engine, and Wilson and Brown climbing into it. Andrews walked forward to the caboose, stopped a moment, turned, and, motioning to us with his hand, said lightly: "Get on, get on." We didn't stop to think of what would become of us if we didn't. Knight pulled the throttle as Andrews nodded to him and swung aboard.

Would that engine never start? It snorted, ground ahead, and then—stopped in its tracks with a great hiss of steam, and the wheels kept on buzzing around. That would alarm the trainmen. We wondered if they'd seen us. Not a sound came from the station, strange to say. It was a bad moment for us, penned up blind in the boxcars, for we did not know that Knight, in his excitement, had put the lever straight over to the full-speed notch, and the wheels had started too quickly and failed to bite on the rails.

At last we shot off at high speed. Even were they following now, we were safe, for there was no telegraph at Big Shanty. But in a moment the train slowed down and our hearts tightened up again. We were almost in sight of camp. But Knight found the trouble, opened the dampers, which had been closed for the stop at Big Shanty, so that the fire was nearly out, and in a moment we in the boxcars heard the roar of the oil-soaked waste they threw into the fire.

We were off. The thing had been done. This big detail of men had crossed the enemy's ranks without the least alarm, had stolen a train on a line that his very being depended upon, stolen it from one of his own camps, in the middle of his country. There, in the half-darkness of the car, we soldiers simply stared at each other.

In a moment our leader came in to us, laughing. We knew he had studied the situation and provided for every contingency. He knew what trains we had to meet and pass. He knew all the stations, switches, and engines on the line. Our confidence in him was implicit. We were certain of success.

The first station was Moon—simply a shed—where trackmen were at work. Brown stopped the train, got off, and asked for their crowbar as if he owned the road, and got it. We ran on at schedule speed, knowing that we had to pass the local down freight. Our bobtail train rumbled past little stations, and we could hear the engineers chuckling at the chapfallen faces of persons waiting for the train; and we laughed too. After each station we stopped and [John] Scott, who was agile as a cat, ran up the pole, knocked off the wire, swung down on it, and severed it with a saw found in the car. When we had a few lifted rails aboard our sense of security was exultant. And so we passed Altoona and came to Etowa, where there was a big bridge over a stream and a branch road led off east five miles to the Etowa Iron Works.

On that branch track stood an engine—the *Yonah*—and smoke was coming from its stack. "We'd better destroy that and the bridge," we heard Knight say to Andrews. "They're only five men there and we're twenty-two." Andrews hesitated. "No," he said, and paused again, "it makes no difference—no." Then they discussed it. "We mustn't alarm them too far from Chattanooga," said our captain quickly. "It'll be enough to burn the Oostenaula Bridge." So, he had known nothing of the *Yonah?* Now we passed Cartersville and came to Cass Station, seven miles from Kingston. From Kingston a branch road led west to Rome, and a train from there would be awaiting us. It was beginning to rain.

At Cass, where we stopped for wood, we heard the station-tender talking excitedly to Andrews; and Andrews answer: "Why, this is a special emergency train, under government orders, with ammunition for General [Pierre G. T.] Beauregard. He's hard pressed after Shiloh." After some talk the man answered: "Sir, I would send my shirt to Beauregard if he needed it." And he gave Andrews a timecard.

Then Kingston. Here we were to pass the local freight, the card said, and then—plain sailing. We were ahead of time and the freight had not arrived. We ran past the station and backed on the side track next to the Rome train.

Some one stepped over to our locomotive and we heard an oath. "Here's their engine with none of their men aboard," said the voice. We held our breath till we heard Andrews calmly repeating the Beauregard story. The nerve of the man! Next, he walked over to the telegraph office and demanded why the local freight was not here. He was shown a dispatch addressed to Fuller, ordering him to wait.

And it seemed we waited for hours. Penned up in the darkness, forced to silence in the boxcar, we—Beauregard's ammunition—could not understand the delay. The tension of mysterious danger was indescribable. How gladly we would have thrown open the doors and fought our way out! Low murmurs came from outside, the tread of feet, and Andrews now and then quietly answering questions.

At last we heard a whistle from the north. It was the freight. The suspense was broken. Now Andrews was talking to the freight conductor—telling the powder story, of course. We heard him raise his voice. "I tell you Beauregard must have it at once, and now you're signalling, there's another train behind you," he said. So there was a red flag on the rear of that freight, was there, and another train coming? Yes. And we heard that, after all, Mitchel had moved to Chattanooga, captured Huntsville, and that hundreds of cars were being run south.

"Mitchel is no such fool," protested Andrews. "I don't believe it. But run down the track there and let us out. I have my orders."

The freight rumbled away and the agony of waiting began again. We remembered the *Yonah*. Almost an hour had passed.

Then another whistle from the north. Now we could hear Andrews talking quite distinctly. And on this train also was a red flag!

It was too much to bear. Had we only risked making the next station and smashing into the thing! And soon we heard a voice whispering carelessly through the car wall—Knight's voice. "Be ready to jump out and fight," he said. "The folks about here are getting uneasy." That cheered us—the chance of fighting. But still came the voices and the tramp of feet. What were they all saying?

Now Andrews was talking a lot: they were talking at him. He was telling even of his life in Beauregard's camp. Why hadn't they heard from Atlanta of this powder train, they said? Andrews grew angry over the management of the road.

One hour and five minutes had passed—three hours from Big Shanty—when the third whistle came from the north. And it was the last. The freight went on south without stopping. We, too, moved; and stopped. Andrews was arguing with some one and the man was angry. We heard him demand by what authority Andrews ordered about the whole road, and in a moment the familiar voice laughed, "I've no time to waste with you, old fellow," and we heard the chink of keys as the angry switchman took them from their hook and unlocked the switch. We pulled out, the fellow's threats sounding sweet and loud as our car passed him, and the suspense in which we had grown old ended.

But for all this we should have been at Dalton, forty miles on, with the Oostenaula Bridge burned and the raid a glorious success. Had we only known how close *Fuller* was behind us! Four minutes's more delay and we should have been lost then and there.

The next stop was Adairsville, ten miles away, and it would never do to make the run without tearing up track. "Push her, boys; push her," said Andrews; and they did, but before long down came the brakes. We piled out, tore up track, cut the wire, and loaded on ties, for the old *General* was a woodburner. Soon the town moved into sight through the drizzle and there, to our joy, was the freight train we had to pass.

But while Andrews was repeating the Beauregard story in the usual storm of questions, we heard that a down passenger train, now half an hour late—the whole road was in a panic it seemed after Mitchel's move—ought to meet the freight here also. The engineer of the latter said: "Of course, you'll wait for it here. Tell them to overhaul me at Kingston."

Quick as a shot Andrews answered: "I'll do nothing of the kind. Suppose the Yankees attack Beauregard. He hasn't powder for three hours' fight."

A fear that we were pursued now seemed to overtake us. We had got over the joy of being released from Kingston. We had been terribly delayed. What might be happening down the road all this time? Why was every one getting so suspicious? We ran to Calhoun, nine miles away, at a frightful rate. Oil was poured on the wood. "Make her show her best," said Andrews, and for us, whose fire had been pent up all day, this dash was worth ten times the risk. All chances were that we should meet the passenger train head on, and to stop us would be to stop a cannonball. But we could not think of danger. We rose and fell wildly on the crooked track, we were jerked and pummeled about in the car; fire steamed from under the wheels; all Georgia rushed past, and now and then we had the dizzy illusion of shooting from the rails. "Give her more wood!" shouted Knight. "Give her more wood!" Well, didn't we prefer death in a smash-up to capture?

As the shriek of the whistle died away near Calhoun, we saw the passenger train backing to the station. They had seen us just in time. We had made nine miles in seven and a half minutes, but had we been a minute longer! The switch was opened and we backed on the side track.

On the side track, yes, and in front of them. They would not move and we could not get out. Andrews said they had plenty of time to reach Adairsville before Fuller's train—ours being a special, of course. But they grew suspicious; they demanded an explanation. He retold the powder story, but he did not tell it so well. Something seemed to have unnerved him—our escape from a smash-up perhaps. On this run we had pulled up no track, cut no wires, and a message might be going through at any minute. At last we heard him say, "I tell you, pull out your engine and let me ahead," and at this direct order they did so. Had they not we should have fired.

So now we were on the main track with no more trains to meet. An open road at last, with miles and miles of obstructions behind! It was our triumph. Only a few miles and the Resaca, beyond the Oostenaula Bridge. The bridge would be burned, and on clear rails, stopping no more, we should be running into Mitchel's arms at Chattanooga. But once more we had to stop to cut wires

"Once More We Had to Stop" (*McClure's*)

and take up tracks. We worked cheerfully. Scott was more agile than ever on the poles. We loaded ties like lightning. We drove and drove at the spikes; one after another they came out, but oh, how slowly! That iron bar was useless for such work. We would have given our lives for a crowfoot. Some of us were using a green wood lever to tear up a rail. Looking up, we saw Andrews for the first time showing impatience. He had thrown off his cape and high hat, and now wore a small black cap. But he, too, was thrilled somehow. Suddenly he seized the crowbar and, uttering an oath, was raining terrific blows upon a rail spike, when loud and clear from around a curve to the south came the whistle of a locomotive.

We left the bent end of the loosened rails turned up and jumped aboard. The train behind us was running at lightning speed. We could hear the clamor along the rails before Brown and Knight got the valve wide open, and we were thrown from our feet as the old *General* bounded on. They came into sight. We could see that they were armed with rifles. Would they never reach that upturned rail? Now they were at the pile of ties by the track; now they passed over the break—uninjured. At every turn luck was with them. Never would they have pressed us so daringly had they known our numbers.

And now, the Oostenaula Bridge. It all depended on that. Had we time to burn it? Everything was soaking wet and beyond lay Resaca full of soldiers.

First we drew away from them, then they caught up. Over and over again this happened. We kept catching glimpses of them. They had many men. Gradually it was becoming clear that we could not burn the bridge without a fight. We were almost at it and had to act quickly. Andrews gave the order—how we would have preferred an out and out fight to this strategy!—to reverse; and we hurled back a car at them. But they saw it coming, reversed also, and picked it up. The bridge was at hand and we began dropping out ties. When we reached the trestle we dropped another car. They were following us end for end. They had better fuel or a better engine. What engine? How did they get it?

It was long before we knew how back at Big Shanty, Conductor Fuller, Engineer Cain, and Anthony Murphy, master mechanic of the road, hearing the steam escaping from the locomotive as they sat at breakfast, rushed outside and saw their train disappearing around the curve. Believing it to be in the hands of escaped conscripts they had run on foot to Moon. There they seized a handcar, which they drove to Etowa, where they boarded that fatal *Yonah,* which would have left in another minute for the iron works. In it they reached Kingston exactly four minutes after our disastrous wait. Here they learned who we were and Fuller, rising to the emergency, as only he or Andrews could, seized the engine of the Rome train and followed us till stopped by our track wrecking. They ran on foot to Adairsville, met the approaching freight near the town, stopped it, ran back into the station, threw off the cars, and were hot after us with a fresh engine. . . .

Now they had caught the car we dropped on the trestle. We ran through Resaca slowly. Was all the road alarmed? A grim determination was fixed in our faces. Our hope now was to disable them. We stopped and placed a bent rail

"They Came into Sight"
(*McClure's*)

across the track. But they did not even slow up near it, and we saw them jounced a foot in air as they ran over it safely. What a race!

Fuel and ties were low, but Andrews began to give his orders more and more coolly. Ahead lay Green's Wood station and we hacked the walls of the car for fuel to reach it. They whistled to alarm the keeper, but we piled out at the place and threw on ties frantically. We were only half supplied when they hove in sight. They came so near that they had to reverse to prevent collision.

Then we were off again, dropping ties. Now and then they slowed up to clear the track, and we could see them working with our own fury. We had wood, a great head of steam now, and we might make it yet. We drew out of sight. We passed through Tilton and pulled up at the water tank. We needed water. Andrews told the old powder story and we could hardly keep straight faces in our wrecked car.

And before the tank was full they were in sight, and we were off again for Dalton. Dalton was the biggest town since Marietta. Before we reached it we halted on a curve, cut wires, and pulled up rails. In the town we stopped at the station switch and Andrews ran forward to see if the track was clear. He had no time for the powder story now. "I am running this train through to Chattanooga," he said, "and I have no time to spare." Then came the whistle of their locomotive. There was nothing to be gained by care now. He nodded to Knight,

Knight put on full steam, and we rushed at the depot which was built over the track, and pitched bewildered through a second's darkness right out upon a curve, where it seemed we were sliding off the rails. What the people there knew of us—what they thought of our battered car—what mattered anything now?

Once more we must cut the wires, for there was a telegraph at Dalton. It would be the last time, for beyond lay the Chickamauga bridges, and them we must burn if it cost us a fight or worse. But there came their whistle again. We did not know it then, but Scott swung down from the pole upon the wire too late—too late by a single minute, for the message Fuller sent from Dalton did get through, and even had we reached Chattanooga we should have been lost.

The tunnel was ahead now—an ideal place for an ambush, but Andrews gave no order to halt and fight. He was not a soldier and had never been in battle. We pitched on through the darkness. Fuller plunged in behind while our smoke still filled the holes. He did not quail at the chance of running into a trap or crashing into us. Fuller knew of the Chickamauga bridges.

Andrews gave orders to fire our last car. It was our only chance and he knew it. But car and fuel were drenched. We tore at the walls, poured oil on the wood, and nursed the flame. Before the covered bridge we slowed up, drew out the coupling, and all jumped aboard the engine. The blazing car stopped in the middle of the bridge. We came to rest beyond and watched it. This was the crisis. Everything depended on how soon the fire caught the structure. We had only a handful of wood left. Would the flames never lick up into the rafters? The car was burning fast, but the timbers above were too wet. There was their whistle now, the rumble of the foe along the track, and we could see their guns glint through the flames. The race was almost run.

We moved on slowly. They caught up the burning car and shoved it on. We ran slowly through the Ringgold, where they shunted it off. They followed on, always in sight. We threw on our last wood. They could have overtaken us easily—but why? They knew they were running us to destruction.

We threw our papers into the furnace and Andrews even burned his saddlebag.

How did we feel at this moment, knowing all was lost? No worse, I think, than on the eve of battle. We could still turn and attack them; we did not fear that. It had been talked of continually on the run. Here, five miles north of Ringgold, nineteen south of Chattanooga, in a rough woody country cut by the swollen branches of Chickamauga Creek, we huddled in the woodbox of the tender and looked to our leader for such an order. And he who saw the most cherished plans of his life fail at the brink of success, gave the fatal command: "Scatter in small parties and escape the best way you can."

We swung off one by one as the engine slowed down. Brown reversed the lever, and I saw him drop to the ground with Knight and Andrews as the old *General* which had behaved so splendidly rumbled slowly backwards. Fuller stopped his engine, received our exhausted one gently, and one of his men leaped over the tender and closed the valve. The railroad race was over.

When I had gathered my wits Robinson was at my side, and we dove off through the brush and over the ditch into the woods. Fast and blindly we traveled, not knowing where we were or what direction we took. As dawn appeared we climbed a ridge and hid by a log under some brush. Several times during the day we could hear searching parties, and at night, when we started down to the valley, ran into a squad of Confederates. We told the Flemingsburg, Kentucky story, and they nodded at each other wisely. I kept protesting my innocence, but at Tunnel Hill, where they took us, I was tied over a stone and given a hundred lashes. I bear the marks today.

What became of us all? We were all captured, scattered over miles and miles of that wild country, taken within three days. All told the Flemingsburg story and that came to stamp each of us, when challenged, as one of the raiders who had set the whole section wild in pursuit. And in that story lay a great irony, for, years before, Andrews had come from some unknown quarter to Flemingsburg, a ruined man, determined to begin life anew; from Flemingsburg he had first set out as a spy; at Flemingsburg lived a woman whom in six months he was pledged to wed.

How seven of us were hung from one scaffold eleven days after; how the rest of us suffered, chained in underground prisons; how we broke jail; how finally five of us were captured and exchanged, and, last of all, how Congress awarded the first medals of honor ever given to the service of private soldiers to the families of those who perished—all this is not the least part of the raid's history.

But Andrews left his bones in Dixie. He was tried by court-martial at Chattanooga and executed June 7, 1862. Quite unmoved and without the least tone of bravado, he said as he walked to the scaffold: "Boys, I have often thought I would like to see what lies on the other side of Jordan."

22

The Attack on Corinth

Clinton H. Parkhurst, Captain,
Sixteenth Iowa Volunteer Infantry

IT WAS THE evening of the second day of October, 1862, and the Iowa Brigade was "tenting on the old camp ground" near Corinth, Mississippi, after a brief but victorious campaign at Iuka. There was not a Confederate force within fifty miles of us, and probably not a Confederate soldier. So the wise folks told us, and so we fondly believed. In our regiment at least—the Sixteenth Iowa—there were to be no duties on the morrow, save a few absolutely necessary ones. Everybody was to rest and be happy. "Soldier rest!" was the watchword. With pleasant hallucinations we fell asleep.

"Get up! the long roll's beating" was the startling alarm at daylight next morning.

We had heard the long roll at Shiloh, without knowing what it meant, but we found out its meaning on that bloody field. It was beating again.

"Fall in, men! Fall in! Fall in quick!" shouted officers everywhere, and the drums beat the assembly on the color line.

Everyone jumped up, dressed in haste, belted on his cartridge box, grabbed his gun, and hastened to form line on the company parade ground. We then, with equal zeal, marched out and formed a regimental line. It was not many minutes before the entire brigade was in line of battle, and stood ready for orders. In the distance, and far to the right, heavy skirmishing began. A courier dashed up with orders, and we promptly moved at quick time in the direction of the firing. The morning air was stimulating, and tinged with the breath of southern autumn. Bugles sounded near Corinth, which lay much to the rear of us, and before we had gone half a mile we heard the roar of artillery ahead— not steadily, but at intervals. All around us pealed the opening notes of a general engagement. There was to be fighting, without a doubt, and with the coolness of veterans we marched out to bear our part.

In the preceding April, when we left Pittsburg Landing for the field of combat a few miles away, we cheered at the slightest provocation, sang war songs, and generally made an uproar. Now we marched in silence. Not a sound was heard save our steady tramp and the clink of bayonets. We had been at the front many months and knew that fighting was not a picnic. No schoolboy bravado was indulged in. In its place was the businesslike readiness for battle characteristic of trained soldiers. Our course lay through a heavily timbered region destitute of undergrowth; and the trees were in gorgeous autumn regalia. When we had gone about two miles, firing ceased. As we saw no other troops, nor any signs of an enemy, an impression prevailed that only a band of guerrillas had collided with the picket line and been repulsed. We reached an earth fort that contained no guns or garrison. It was part of [Major General Henry W.] Halleck's deserted, unused, and useless line of circumvallation that would have needed 100,000 men to hold—at least, to occupy.

Here we stacked arms and awaited an explanation of so serious a morning alarm. Our regiment formed immediately behind the fort. The other three regiments aligned a little to the rear of us. An artillery company soon joined us with four field pieces. One gun was wheeled into the fort and its muzzle pushed through an embrasure. Owing to the woods and hills we could see no troops in any direction, either friend or foe. We decided finally that we had been victimized by one of those sudden alarms that are common in war. All regiments stacked arms, and word was sent back to camp for the cooks to boil coffee and bring it out to us. After a long wait they arrived, their capacious kettles swung on poles in Chinese fashion. We had just filled our cups and commenced to quaff the amber beverage when a crash of musketry a mile or so to the front convinced us that we had come on no idle mission. Soon afterwards a cavalryman rode rapidly, with dispatches for headquarters, and hastily told us the news. A very large Confederate army was in motion—larger than [General] Albert Sidney Johnston had had at Shiloh—and hot work could be expected. A Wisconsin battalion of 600 men had been attacked the previous evening at a railroad station called Chewalla, and was then fighting in the woods, but before long would be driven over the intervening country toward us.

"Fall in! Take arms! Load at will—Load!" were commands quickly given, and we drove down minie balls for the advancing host.

Nevertheless we stacked arms again, drank our coffee, and made as good a breakfast as we could. Charley Harl, our company cook, swore that he boiled coffee only in times of peace. He carried his kettles back to camp, returned with a musket, and before evening received a mortal wound. After listening to the firing awhile we had orders to change position. We left the fort and drew up on the brow of a heavily timbered hill, more directly in the path of the incoming enemy. No works of any kind gave shelter and we built none. The Fifteenth and Sixteenth Iowa formed side by side, and afterwards fought the Confederates in that order. Commanding the Fifteenth that day was [Lieutenant Colonel William W.] Belknap, afterwards a brigadier general, and still afterwards secretary of war under President [Ulysses S.] Grant. The Sixteenth was commanded by Lieutenant Colonel Addison H. Sanders, afterwards colonel and brigadier, who was severely wounded in this battle. Extra ammunition was dealt out to us, each man having sixty rounds in all.

The Eleventh and Thirteenth Iowa formed in line about fifty yards to the rear of us. The battery was ordered to Corinth, and started at once. In front of the right wing of our regiment was a complete camp—tents, baggage, and all—but the troops it belonged to were gone. They had been moved out somewhere to meet the enemy. Not even a guard was left behind. It must have been 10:00 A.M. when deadly fighting commenced directly in front of us—over in the timber. The greater part of the firing we had heard up to this time had been by heavy skirmish lines, but now two lines of battle joined issue, and the terrible roar of musketry pealed through the woods. Till we heard it we had thought our brigade was the only considerable body of troops in that immediate environ, and that only pickets and skirmishers were scattered along our front. Some other regiment was trying to hold the Chewalla Road—probably the one whose deserted camp we saw—and was being roughly handled by the enemy.

We were close enough to hear the combat well, but not close enough to see it. Ridges and woods obstructed the view. We could see smoke floating in the timber, and in partial lulls of the firing could hear the excited commands of officers. The Union troops fought hard, but being greatly outnumbered, fought in vain. It seemed nonsense to have them there at all. A few heavy explosions of musketry broke on the air, in quick succession. Then followed victorious cheers that rang on the morning air with wonderful clearness. The Union troops fled in confusion toward us, the pickets and skirmishers nearby joining in the stampede. The enemy followed a short distance, firing and yelling like Indians.

All this time we could see nothing for the ridges and timber, but we could hear so distinctly that we needed no information. The fugitives poured into view like scattered sheep, and reaching our line rushed on to the rear, scores of them being bloody from wounds. Ambulances hurried by, filled and crowded with wounded men, whose cries of suffering and groans of agony it was distressing to hear. Beyond, at intervals, rose the clear, wild cheers of the Southerners.

Then a deathlike silence ensued. Not a skirmish line was now between us and the enemy. We knew that preparations must be going on to attack us, and to stand idly there awaiting the onset was a trying ordeal—a test of manhood keener than fighting. If I had been richer than Croesus, I would have given a liberal part of my wealth had it not been my duty to be there. While we waited with intense interest and much anxiety the next move in what was to us a momentous drama, an appalling burst of martial thunder came from a locality a mile or so to the right of us. Musketry and artillery mingled in one awful and prolonged peal. It was not an affair of a regiment or two, but seemed like the collision of two heavy lines of battle, and the roar was incessant as long as I was conscious of listening to it. Our thoughts, however, were almost immediately concentrated on events in front of us. We were watching the opposite hillside. Bullets began to cut the air from the rifles of unseen marksmen. A little later a long line of rebel skirmishers came into view, and without haste, and yet without hesitation, marched silently toward us.

"Don't fire on those men—they're not rebels," someone shouted. (Many of them wore portions of our uniform.)

Before this could be contradicted a Confederate brigade appeared, moving in splendid order. At this delicate juncture word came for our brigade to march to Corinth. It was too late for all to go, without danger of disaster, and the two rear regiments marched from the field, and the Fifteenth and Sixteenth remained to check the enemy. While the Confederate line was moving down the opposite hillside in "Battle's magnificently stern array," another hostile brigade appeared, considerably to the rear of the first one. Both marched at common time, in perfect silence, preserving faultless lines. In spite of the great excitement I was under, I admired the soldierly conduct of these troops. It would be impossible for infantry to march to battle in finer order or with firmer mien. On reaching the base of the hill, they marched up the slope toward us. The skirmishers in front of them entered the regimental camp I have spoken of, and began throwing down the Sibley tents that the line of battle might march over the ground without being disarranged.

We might have killed many of these skirmishers, for the tents nearest to us were not more than thirty yards distant, but as we desired the tents down also, we allowed the work to proceed undisturbed, and permitted the skirmishers to retire when the task was finished. When the tents were all flat on the ground, however, and the enemy was boldly moving in plain sight straight at us, and each moment was getting nearer, officers had extreme difficulty in keeping the men from opening fire. We had been ordered not to fire till the lieutenant colonel gave the word, and it seemed that the word would never be given. Captains and lieutenants walked up and down the front of their companies, sword in hand, striking up muskets that were being brought to a level by nervously impatient soldiers.

At length the front Confederate line was within fifty or sixty paces of us, and with perfect distinctness we saw the men of that line cock their muskets to fire. Ours were already cocked. We took deliberate aim, and with a crash we fired. That volley told with effect on the enemy. It was scarcely a moment before an answering volley hurled bullets among us. The Fifteenth Iowa fired at about the same time, and the battle opened with fury; but it was less trying to fight than to stand like statues waiting for the fray to begin. In a moment a wall of dust and smoke arose in front of us, and hid the enemy from view.

In our first battle we had sought shelter, as far as possible, behind trees and obstacles. On this occasion the result of incessant drilling we had gone through was apparent. A few men fought on one knee, but not a man lay down, and the great majority stood erect on the color line, and loaded and fired in drill-ground fashion. Habit is second nature. Men hit while fighting erect are less liable to have fatal wounds, than if struck while fighting on one knee. Once, while standing erect, I turned my left side to the enemy, to drive down a musket ball. The next instant a big bullet passed through my left pantaloons pocket, where I carried a package of ten rounds of ammunition. It tore the paper cartridges to pieces, but I was unhurt. Had I been facing squarely to the front I would have had a mortal wound.

After we had been fighting awhile a gust of air partly blew the smoke aside, and we saw that the enemy's line was not in perfect order, but the second line came up and more than restored the tide of battle. As we fought at remarkably short range, many of us rammed down two minie balls with each load of powder. There was little chance of taking exact aim, beyond calculating what would probably be too high or too low to hit a man, and under the circumstances two bullets were better than one. The direct attack of the enemy had been really checked, but flank firing opened on us, and indications appeared that an attempt would be made to capture us. Both regiments receded in slight disorder, falling back fifty or sixty yards or so. We couldn't whip the whole of [Major General Sterling] Price's army.

The command was then given to cease firing, and a new and perfect line was formed. The enemy ceased firing also, and with arms at a shoulder we again silently tendered battle. For some reason the mute challenge was not accepted, no advance toward us was attempted, nor did the skirmishers even annoy us with desultory shots. The fray being apparently over, for a time at least, and the sound of fighting elsewhere having almost ceased, we again had orders to march to Corinth. We moved off the field at common time, in perfect order, and so far as we could see, no one pursued us. Our dead we left, and a very few of our wounded were captured, but fell into our hands two days afterward. The other two regiments had marched out of sight. We saw no soldiers anywhere, friend or foe.

Retreating to town displeased us, for we knew nothing of the military situation. We had wondered greatly that half the brigade, and the battery, should be ordered away just before the action commenced. Reinforcements, we thought, should rather have reached us. We knew that fighting had ceased everywhere; we had fears of disaster, and many believed our forces were hastily deserting Corinth. Utter disgust was expressed, and even rage, and I heard several officers prophesy that we would be on the road to Pittsburg Landing before nightfall. We had no definite ideas concerning the number of Union troops in Corinth and around it, nor did we even know what general was in chief command. Most of us thought Grant was. Concerning everything important we seemed to be in the dark completely. The army was falling back unnecessarily, we thought, and without a proper struggle. A catastrophe somewhere else in the country was the general explanation.

"[Major General Don Carlos] Buell's been cleaned out of Kentucky," our second lieutenant said. Gloomy apprehensions prevailed.

For several miles we marched in silence through the woods, the occasional roar of artillery indicating that resistance to the enemy had not wholly ceased. Suddenly, as we came to the verge of a timbered ridge, a thrilling spectacle burst into view. From that point to town the trees had been freshly cut away, and were lying as they fell, the long boughs being lopped off and strewn on the ground. On a hill crest opposite us was a newly built earth fort, and high over its ramparts a large and beautiful garrison flag waved—Old Glory in richest attire, tossing its folds in defiance of the foe. We burst into cheers, hailing the scene as evidence that the battle had not been lost but had only begun.

The sight awoke enthusiasm. As we came nearer town we saw that a semicircle of earth forts had been hastily reared, and mounted with heavy siege guns that commanded all approaches. The gleam of arms could be seen in every direction as troops poured into the fortified semicircle and aligned at their designated stations. Instead of consternation and retreat we beheld order, and formidable preparations for the foe. [Major General William Starke] Rosecrans rode up to meet us, and we greeted him with tumultuous cheers. In a brief address he promised us victory on the morrow, a promise that was gloriously fulfilled.

Our regiment was immediately assigned to support the Fifth Ohio Battery, on the extreme left wing of the army. Without halting a moment we marched to our place. Supporting a battery is not always child's play. On the field of Shiloh we saw a captured Confederate battery where every cannoneer was killed and every horse killed or wounded. At Iuka the Sixteenth Iowa supported the Eleventh Ohio Battery. [Major General Earl] Van Dorn's Texan legion took its guns twice, and made a third attempt to take them, but failed. Without assistance from other troops the Sixteenth took them back each time, and held them at last, winning the highest honors of the battle. Three guns were spike by the enemy, and two were dragged some distance away, but were dragged back again. All the battery horses were killed or wounded, and of an artillery company of eighty men, only eight men escaped wounds or death.

The dangers of a mounted officer exceed those of a soldier. In two battles inside of fifteen days, every field officer of our regiment had been killed or wounded. [Lieutenant George M.] Lawrence, our splendid young adjutant, had been killed, and our colonel, lieutenant colonel, and major wounded. The colonel had been sent north, Lieutenant Colonel Sanders was in a hospital, and Major William Purcell (of Muscatine), despite a troublesome wound (his second of the war), assumed command of the regiment.

While we had been fighting on the Chewalla Road, our tents, baggage, and equipment had been hauled to town, and at nightfall the enemy's troops slept on our old campground—the fortunes of war.

. . .

Early in the morning of the second day [October 4, 1862] the rush of Confederate shells and their explosions awoke us. It was barely daylight. History says it was 3:00 A.M. A field battery in the edge of the woods, about 200 yards to the front of Robinett, opened a cannonade, and one of the forts replied. The Southern guns were hastily dragged into the woods, and one was captured. Drums rolled and bugles sounded. We belted and got into line. In the woods opposite us a cloud of Confederate sharpshooters deployed. Crouching behind logs, stumps, and trees, they began blazing away at everything and everybody. Similar operations ensued no doubt all along the front of the army. We should have made rifle pits the previous evening, but did not do so. Our line of battle stretched from one fort to the other, without defenses. A remarkable circumstance of this battle was that the Union troops faced to the north and the Confederate troops to the south.

At the extreme left of the Union line was Fort Phillips. Our regiment was on a low hill immediately to the left of it, supporting the Fifth Ohio Battery. The next fort to the right of Phillips was Robinett, which played a memorable part that day. It was not more than 500 yards from us, and we could look across and see everything that took place inside of it, and could also see a part of the ground in front of it. This gave us opportunity, in due time, to view a more thrilling combat than ever took place in the gladiatorial arena of Rome.

The Confederate sharpshooters gave us much trouble. The Ohio battery opened on them finally, but they treated the cannonade with contempt, wound-

An Encounter at Close Quarters (*McClure's*)

ed a few cannoneers, and dismounted the captain by killing his splendid war steed. A heavy detail was promptly made, and a considerable number of men scattered in the fallen timber at the front and opened on the sharpshooters. I happened to be one of this party. We improved matters considerably, and a Confederate battery tried to drive us out with grape and canister. Fort Phillips intervened with twenty-pound shells and drove the battery into the woods. Thus hot skirmishing went on in different fashions all day long. At most localities it was not very far from one line to the other.

On battle days, where one excitement follows another in swift succession, time moves with rapid pace. On the extreme right of the Union army, movements of importance began. The Union forts and batteries in that quarter opened with fury. We had seldom heard such a cannonade, and knew that something startling was in progress. Clouds of smoke rose thickly above the firing, and ere long a frightful crash of musketry denoted that infantry had engaged. Our whole line in that quarter had fired a volley, which was immediately followed by the smooth roar of steady fighting. The enemy's troops had come out of the woods in a huge column shaped like a wedge. Under a fearful artillery fire they advanced in the most intrepid manner. Missiles tore through the ranks with hideous effect. Grape, canister, musketry—nothing stopped the storming column.

At the first shock eight or ten Union regiments broke and fled; Fort Richardson was taken, and Confederate soldiers entered the very tent of Rosecrans—but he was not there. At the head of his staff he had galloped among the fugitives, and brought them to a halt. At this critical moment the Fifty-sixth Illinois Infantry charged the enemy, fired a deadly volley at close quarters, and then used the bayonet till Fort Richardson was retaken and had opened its guns on the foe. Led by Rosecrans, the rallied regiments hurried to the line, and then the whole Union right wing charged with thrilling cheers, driving the enemy, in panic and confusion, into the woods.

The enemy's plan had been for Van Dorn to assault Robinett at the same time that Price delivered his tremendous blow at our right wing. For some reason Van Dorn was not ready, and Price was hurled back with slaughter. Soon afterwards a storming column of four or five thousand men moved on Robinett. Colonel [William P.] Rogers of Texas had the perilous honor of leading. From our station on the skirmish line we saw the charge—one of the most heroic affairs of the Civil War. With defiant yells the Confederates came out of the woods on the double-quick. Mounted on a powerful steed Rogers rode at their head, waving the Lone Star flag of Texas. Fallen timber everywhere rendered perfect lines impossible, and the column was soon somewhat disordered, but this proved immaterial. Rogers rode rapidly along a highway that led to the fort, and his men followed closely, some in the road and others leaping over fallen trees and rubbish, intent on victory at any cost. The sharpshooters of the enemy quit firing and stood on stumps and logs to watch the charge, and we on the skirmish line did likewise.

The moment the column came into full view, it was swept with terrible effect by the heavy guns of Robinett. Fort Phillips also opened, and each moment some additional fort or battery tried to train guns on the stormers. Smoke, dust, and the explosion of shells more or less concealed the column from view, but we could see that the storm of death was disregarded. The ground was strewn with dead and dying, but Rogers rode undaunted, and not one of the stormers faltered. Death or victory was their evident intention. We could see every move in and around the fort. Not a man left his post. The cannoneers loaded and fired to the last moment, then snatched up muskets and fought as infantry. Rogers reached the ditch of the fort, tossed his banner to a soldier, who planted it on the work. It waved there a moment and fell. Rogers fell also. The last cannon fired killed him and blew his horse to pieces.

On either side of the fort Union infantry fought fiercely, and one regiment half-wheeled and enfiladed the front of the fort. The Confederates recoiled and crouched to the ground, but supporting troops came yelling to the rescue, brandishing arms and rushing to the charge. Blue and gray closed in a death struggle, and the fighting was brutal. The Sixty-third Ohio stood next to the fort, on the right, and lost half its men in a few moments, but never gave up an inch of ground. The Confederates staggered back, stood irresolute, and then turned to fly. The cannoneers sprang to their guns, and, double-loading them, filled the air with missiles. The ditch of the fort was piled level with dead, and fugitives, throwing themselves among fallen timber, waved their hats for quarter. Firing ceased, and many prisoners were taken. Of the entire storming column, not 500 got back to the woods. The rest were killed, wounded, or captured. Most were killed or wounded. A down east historian says that "more than 200 Confederates fell in this frightful assault." Not less than 1,000 were killed in front of Robinett.[1] The body of Colonel Rogers was given separate and honorable burial. A board was placed at his grave on which was inscribed his name and rank, and his fame filled both armies. No man ever led a forlorn hope with greater courage.

People who rave over the horrors of war, and view soldiers with aversion, will find in the ferocity of the fighting at Corinth an object lesson for their teachings. Let us bear in mind, however, that if the armies of the North had been beaten in the Civil War, human slavery would have spread over the great part of the Western Hemisphere, if not over the greater part of the world. This is to say nothing of the dissolution of the Union. To avert such calamities was worth all the blood it cost.

23

Losing a Division at Stones River
Richard W. Johnson, Brevet Major General, U.S.A.

THE UNSATISFACTORY termination of the Battle of Perryville decided the president on making a change in the commander of the Fourteenth Army Corps, and [Major General William Starke] Rosecrans, whose brilliant exploits in Mississippi and elsewhere had brought him prominently before the country as a great and successful commander, was selected to relieve [Major General Don Carlos] Buell.

---

1. Parkhurst badly exaggerates Confederate losses in front of Battery Robinett; the actual figure of killed and wounded probably rests in the mid-hundreds.

On assuming command, Rosecrans found [General Braxton] Bragg and his army in full retreat, which continued until he had reached Murfreesboro. It has always seemed to me that a great mistake was made by Bragg, as the line of the Cumberland River would have been much more easily defended than the position he took at Murfreesboro, which offered no natural defenses whatever. General Rosecrans occupied Nashville on November 7 [1862], and from that date to December 26 was untiring in his efforts to get the troops under him in readiness for an active, vigorous campaign. Every department of the staff was busily occupied, while Rosecrans, through a corps of faithful, energetic scouts, was informing himself in regard to the character and resources of the country, the position and strength of the enemy, and the avenues by which he could be reached.

General Bragg did not expect a winter campaign. He had established his army in winter quarters at Murfreesboro, and supposed that the Federal army would remain in Nashville all winter. In order that the cavalry could be more easily supplied with forage, and for the purpose of threatening the communications of Rosecrans, Bragg dispatched the greater part of that force under its skillful and able leaders to West Tennessee and Kentucky. The absence of these important forces was seized upon by Rosecrans as the opportune time to moved forward; so accordingly, the day following Christmas the Federal army, in "all the pomp and circumstances of glorious war," marched forth to meet the enemy.

It was positively known that the forces of [Lieutenant Generals Leonidas] Polk and [Edmund] Kirby Smith were at Murfreesboro, and that [Lieutenant General William J.] Hardee's corps was on the Shelbyville and Nolensville Turnpike, between Triune and Eaglesville. The Federal army moved in three columns, in accordance with the following instructions of General Rosecrans:

[Major General Alexander M.] McCook, with three divisions, to advance by the Nolensville Pike to Triune. [Major General George H.] Thomas, with two divisions, ([Brigadier General James S.] Negley's and [Major General Lovell H.] Rousseau's), to advance on his right, by the Franklin and Wilson pikes, threatening Hardee's right, and then to fall in by the crossroads to Nolensville. [Major General Thomas L.] Crittenden, with [Brigadier Generals Thomas J.] Wood's, [John M.] Palmer's, and [Horatio P.] Van Cleve's divisions, to advance by the Murfreesboro Turnpike to Lavergne.

With Thomas's two divisions at Nolensville, McCook was to attack Hardee at Triune, and if the enemy reinforced Hardee, Thomas was to support McCook.

If McCook defeated Hardee, or Hardee retreated, and the enemy met us at Stewart's Creek, five miles south of Lavergne, Crittenden was to attack him. Thomas was to come in on his left flank, and McCook, after detaching a division to pursue or observe Hardee, if retreating southward, was to move the remainder of his force in pursuit of him.

Here it will be well to understand that the Fourteenth Corps, for convenience, was subdivided into three parts—the right wing, the center, and the left wing. These subdivisions were commanded by McCook, Thomas, and

Brigadier General Richard
W. Johnson (Collection of
Peter Cozzens)

Crittenden, in the order named, and each was composed of three divisions. The second division, commanded by the writer, was composed of the following troops:

First Brigade: Brigadier General [August] Willich, commanding—Forty-ninth Ohio, Colonel W. H. Gibson; Fifteenth Ohio, Colonel [William] Wallace; Thirty-ninth Indiana, Lieutenant Colonel Fielding Jones; Thirty-second Indiana, Lieutenant Colonel [Frank] Erdelmeyer; Eighty-ninth Illinois, Lieutenant Colonel [Charles T.] Hotchkiss; [Captain Wilbur F.] Goodspeed's First Ohio Battery.

Second Brigade: Brigadier General E[dmund] N. Kirk—Thirty-eighth Indiana, Colonel J. B. Dodge; Twenty-ninth Indiana, Lieutenant Colonel [David M.] Dunn; Seventy-seventh Pennsylvania, Lieutenant Colonel [Peter B.] Housam; Seventy-ninth Illinois, Colonel [S. P.] Read; Thirty-fourth Illinois, Lieutenant Colonel [Hiram W.] Bristol; [Captain Warren] Edgarton's Battery, First Ohio Artillery.

Third Brigade: Colonel P[hilemon] P. Baldwin—Sixth Indiana, Lieutenant Colonel [Hagerman] Tripp; Fifth Kentucky (Louisville Legion), Lieutenant Colonel W. W. Berry; First Ohio, Major [Jacob] Stafford; Ninety-third Ohio, Colonel Charles Anderson; [Captain Peter] Simonson's Indiana Battery.

Major [Robert] Klein's Battalion, Third Indiana Cavalry, was on duty with the division.

I have been thus particular in giving the composition of my division, in order that the gallant men whom I had the honor to command at the Battle of Stones River may have justice done them even at this late day. I have always supposed that truth would ultimately vindicate itself, but in the evening of a life prolonged beyond the average, I am forced to say that error, when once well on its way, is very difficult to overtake and correct.

At 6:00 A.M. of December 26, [Brigadier General Jefferson C.] Davis's division moved out on the Edmonson Turnpike with orders to march to Prim's Blacksmith Shop, and thence by a country road to Nolensville. [Brigadier General Philip H.] Sheridan moved at the same hour on the direct road to Nolensville, followed by my division. Skirmishing was kept up all day by the advance, and the entire command of General McCook encamped on the hills beyond the town of Nolensville. It had rained almost incessantly the first day out, and the roads had become muddy and difficult of travel, but the enthusiasm of the men was very great at the prospect of meeting the enemy in an open combat.

At daylight on the twenty-seventh the command moved forward, [Brigadier General David S.] Stanley, with the cavalry, in advance, followed by my division. When about two miles out the advance became engaged with the enemy's cavalry, which was supported by artillery. The firing became quite brisk, the column pushed rapidly on until ascending a ridge, when it was opened on by shot and shell. A proper disposition of the troops was made, and the line moved cautiously, yet quickly, forward, overtaking the cavalry, which was steadily pushing the enemy back.

Soon the advance met the Confederates in force. While Edgarton's battery was playing upon the enemy, I directed Baldwin's brigade to take position on the right of the road. The First Ohio, Major Stafford, and the Sixth Indiana, Lieutenant Colonel Tripp, in deployed lines, supported by the Louisville Legion, Lieutenant Colonel Berry, and the Ninety-third Ohio, Colonel Anderson. Simonson's battery was posted on the road. My first brigade, General Willich, was held in reserve. Owing to the dense, heavy fog which settled down upon us, any movement we might make was hazardous, so it was deemed advisable to wait for it to rise, which it did about 8:00 A.M. or 9:00 A.M. We then moved forward for the balance of the day in the same order.

About 4:00 P.M. we ascended a high hill which overlooked the town of Triune. Here the enemy was in plain view in line of battle, with the center in the town, and the flanks extended to the right and left. Edgarton's and Simonson's batteries were brought into action and did good service, disabling one of the enemy's guns. The Sixth and Twenty-ninth Indiana, and Thirty-fourth Illinois charged upon the enemy's battery, but the artillerists did not stand to receive the bayonet. Just about this time it seemed that the floodgates of heaven were opened. The rain descended in blinding sheets, rendering pursuit out of the question. The storm continued about an hour, after which the pursuit was resumed until darkness closed in upon us. We encamped for the night about two miles south of the town of Triune, where we remained on the twenty-eighth awaiting developments.

Under instructions from General McCook, I sent Willich's brigade to determine whether the enemy had retired to Shelbyville or to Murfreesboro. This reconnaissance was extended seven miles to the front, and developed the fact that Hardee had retreated to Murfreesboro. This fact settled in our mind where the great battle was to be fought.

On the twenty-ninth McCook's command was again in motion on the Bole Jack Road. Baldwin's brigade of my division was ordered to remain at Triune as a corps of observation, taking a position on the north bank of Wilson's Creek. One company of Klein's cavalry and a section of Simonson's battery were left with this brigade. This position was only temporary, designed to protect the right flank of McCook's command. On the night of the twenty-ninth I encamped with Kirk's and Willich's brigades near the Salem Road, and within five miles of Murfreesboro and near Davis's division.

On December 30, McCook advanced his command, Sheridan's division covering the Wilkinson Pike and Davis in line on Sheridan's right. My division was held in reserve. McCook directed me to order Baldwin to join his proper division, which he did about dusk on the thirtieth.

The operations of the day had forced the enemy to develop his entire line of battle, and when night came we rested upon our arms in readiness for a heavy battle on the following morning. In the rear of McCook's main line was a large open cotton field. Sheridan and Davis were on the south side of this cotton field, while I was directed to go into camp in the timber on the north side, placing my command in the rear of the center of Davis's division, looking well to my right flank.

During the evening General McCook received a message from General Davis, in which he expressed some uneasiness in regard to the safety of his right flank, and requested that a brigade be sent from my division to take position on his right, and McCook so ordered. I directed Kirk's brigade to take position on Davis's right, and instructed him to refuse his right flank. Soon Kirk asked for troops to be placed on his right, and I sent Willich's brigade, instructing him to throw his right well to the rear. On the north side of the cotton field, and just in front of my reserve brigade, with which I was encamped, an ordinary country road was laid out, and upon this road Willich had his headquarters, distant from mine about a half mile. I mention this distance because it has been asserted by some camp followers that my headquarters were a mile and a half in rear of my line.

In the course of the evening General Rosecrans furnished General McCook with an order to the effect that a great battle was to be fought on the following day. "If our right was attacked, it was to fall back, slowly contesting the ground, and our left was to cross Stones River and move into Murfreesboro. If the enemy failed to attack, we were to do so at a signal to be given by General Rosecrans." McCook called his division commanders together and explained to each

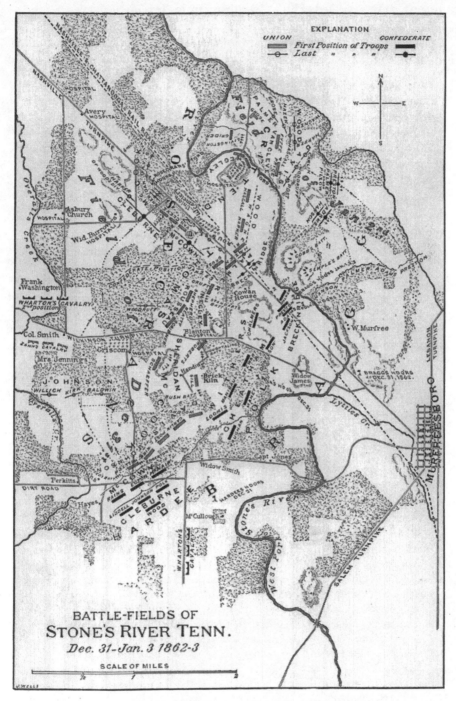

The Battle of Stones River (*Century*)

one what was expected of him. On retiring from General McCook's headquarters I called my brigade commanders around me and explained the order, and when they left each understood thoroughly what was required of his command.

The line of the entire army in its relative position was this: The right of Wood's division rested upon the Nashville Pike, and his left on Stones River; Palmer's was on Wood's right, Negley's on Palmer's right; Sheridan on Negley's right; Davis's on the right of Sheridan; and Kirk's and Willich's brigades of my division on the right and rear of Davis's division. The reserves of each division were in the rear of their respective divisions. General Rosecrans desired to create the impression that he was massing his forces heavily on our right. Accordingly he allowed no fires to be built by the troops in line, but had immense log fires made away off to our right, and Lieutenant Colonel [Bassett] Langdon, of the Second Ohio, who had an immensely heavy voice, was sent out to these fires to give commands locating imaginary divisions, brigades and regiments.

Now this plan would have succeeded with an unenterprising enemy, but Bragg knew as many of the tricks of war as Rosecrans. Feeling assured that where we professed to be strong we were really weak, Bragg during the night massed a force consisting of [Major Generals Patrick R.] Cleburne's and {John P.] Mc-Cown's divisions of infantry, flanked by [Brigadier General John A.] Wharton's cavalry, opposite to the right of our army. These divisions of the Confederate army were composed of four brigades each. Desiring to be entirely correct in regard to the troops opposed to me, I sent a copy of our official map of the battlefield to Major General [Benjamin Franklin] Cheatham, a distinguished officer of the Confederate army, and asked him to indicate thereon the position of the Confederate troops, which he kindly did, and returned to me with the following letter:

> Beech Grove, Coffee Co., Tenn.,
> October 18, 1885

> Dear General—I received your letter last evening, and, in reply, will say that Polk's corps was composed of two divisions, commanded by [Major General Jones M.] Withers and myself. Withers's, not having been in the Battle of Perryville, was stronger than mine, was placed in the front line, his right resting on the Nashville Pike, and extended a little north of west to the old road to Franklin. My division was formed in the rear of Withers's. Cleburne was on my left, and west of the Franklin Road. McCown was on the left of Cleburne, and Wharton's cavalry on McCown's left. McCown advanced first, and it was his troops that first struck Willich. By arrangement with General Withers, during the battle he commanded my two right brigades, and I commanded his two left brigades. You can rely upon the positions as given on the map as being correct. My headquarters were on the left of [Colonel J. G.] Coltart's brigade.
> Yours respectfully,
> B. F. Cheatham

Now we are able to determine just how the attack was made. [Brigadier Generals J. Patton] Anderson's and [James R.] Chalmers's brigades of Withers's division, supported by [Brigadier Generals Alexander P.] Stewart's and [Daniel S.] Donelson' brigades of Cheatham's division, attacked Sheridan.

Coltart's and [Brigadier General Arthur M.] Manigault's brigades of Withers's division, supported by [Colonel Alfred J.] Vaughan's and [Brigadier General George] Maney's brigades of Cheatham's division, attacked Davis.

Cleburne's four brigades attacked Kirk's brigade of my division, and Mc-Cown's four brigades attacked Willich's brigade, while Wharton's cavalry operated on Willich's flank.

The concentration of the force to attack my position was made during the night, and this movement on the part of the enemy was noticed by Lieutenant Colonel Fielding Jones, the officer in charge of my picket line, and he reported it to me. I reported to McCook, who at once made the fact known to General Rosecrans, who did not think it advisable to make any change in his program; at least none was made.

At 3:00 A.M. on December 31 I breakfasted, and had the transportation connected with my headquarters moved to the rear, a movement the teamsters did not stop until they had reached Nashville. The horses belonging to myself, staff, and orderlies were saddled and ready for immediate use.

About 6:00 A.M. General Willich rode up to my headquarters, and while talking with me a shot was fired. I looked at my watch, and it was just 6:22 A.M. At once Willich started at full speed to join his command, and in his haste ran through his line; his horse was killed, and he was captured by the enemy and his valuable services were lost to us.

Onward advanced the countless legions of the enemy. The color of their uniforms blending with the gray of the morning rendered their movements discernible only by the terrific fire of artillery and musketry, which mowed deep and broad furrows in our ranks. The muzzles of a hundred cannons belched forth fire, shot, and shell, and the earth and the air were tremulous with the terrific vibration. The atmosphere was heavy with sulphurous smoke from these countless engines of war. At times dense clouds would envelop the combatants, and then lift themselves up like feathery fringes and be carried away, revealing the advancing but depleted columns of the enemy.

McCook was everywhere urging the men to deeds of noble daring, while the ever-active Rosecrans, with the impetuosity of the winds, rushed from one command to another encouraging the men, and assuring them that "We would yet beat them," and so we did.

General Kirk was seriously wounded about the first fire, and had to leave the field. These two casualties necessitated the change of brigade commanders in the face of an outnumbering foe. Colonel Gibson succeeded Willich, and Colonel Dodge succeeded Kirk. Under these gallant commanders the brave men of these brigades were rallied, and did efficient service during the day. Now, anyone can see the utter absurdity of two brigades, outnumbered more than four to one, holding their ground against such odds. That they fell back in disorder was not to their discredit. No equal number of troops could have done better.

As soon as Willich started from my headquarters, I mounted and started down after him at full speed. Soon I heard a soldier say, "Don't go there, General, or you will be captured." Turning at once to the right, I joined Baldwin's reserve brigade, and had him deploy along a fence in front of which was an open field over which the enemy had to pass. While they were marching over that field the fire of this brigade told with fearful effect, but it, too, had to fall back. In a short time my division was reformed on the Nashville Pike, and assisted in checking the enemy in his victorious march.

The dead of both armies which were strewn on the field passed over by my command showed very conclusively that it did most excellent service. The first fire in the morning killed or crippled nearly all the horses in Edgarton's battery, and he, badly wounded, with his guns, fell into the hands of the enemy. It has been said many times that the reason this battery was lost was due to the fact that the horses had been taken away for water, and some have censured me for not having them harnessed and hitched. Now, is it not reasonably certain that if the horses had been taken away to water, they would have been taken to some pool or stream in the rear? If taken to the rear, would they have been captured? If the guns had been without horses, our loss would have been the guns only; but few, if any, of the horses were ever seen alive after that battle. If away to water, how can we account for the seventy-five dead horses around where the battery stood?

Admitting that they were taken to water, would it be expected that a division commander would have to tell a brigade commander to see that his artillery horses were harnessed and hitched, when he had already told him that a battle was to be fought on the following morning? I should think such a precaution as unnecessary as to instruct him to have his guns loaded when he went into battle, or to tell each man to press on the trigger of his gun when he wished to discharge it at an enemy.

But, unfortunately for those who raised that point, it was untrue. General Kirk was a gallant man, a good soldier, and a careful commander, who died from the wound received in this battle, thus sealing his devotion to his country with his life's blood. A braver man never went to battle than E. N. Kirk, and the members of his family have every reason to be proud of the splendid record, for courage and devotion to duty, which he has left them.

But this matter of sending the horses to water in the face of the enemy is one of the errors which times does not seem to correct.

The curtain of night fell upon the scene, and the tired and jaded soldiers lay down upon the battlefield to rest, in order to be prepared for a renewal of the contest on the following morning. Morning came, but the enemy had withdrawn during the night from our immediate front. On January 2 [1863], a large body of Confederates attacked with great fierceness General Crittenden's command on our left. One of my brigades, under Colonel Gibson, was sent to reinforce him. The enemy was severely punished, and fell back confused and demoralized. Murfreesboro was evacuated on the third, and our army took possession of the town. General Rosecrans, in his telegraphic report to the general in chief, stated, in substance, that the battle would have been a complete success on the first day had it not been for a "partial surprise" on our right. Time has not corrected this error. It was sent off hastily on the wings of lightning, penetrated every portion of the country, and today there are thousands who believe that our right was attacked while in bed. How absurd to suppose that the ever-vigilant McCook, always on the alert, should permit any troops under his command to be surprised! He belongs to a race of soldiers, and his courage has been tested in contests as fierce as ever shook the earth or crimsoned the battlefield.

How absurd to suppose that troops who had been up and breakfasted hours before the battle began could be taken by surprise! After the battle I rode over the field with General Rosecrans and others, and showed him my position and explained to him with what I had to contend, and he expressed himself as well satisfied with what I had done with my command, and said that no two brigades could stand up against such fearful odds. Yet the error first committed has passed into history, and will probably outlive all the participants in that terrific struggle.

After the war I was stationed in Murfreesboro, where I became acquainted with several returned Confederates of high rank who had participated in the battle at Stones River. By them I was assured that not less than 25,000 men attacked my position. When my line was repulsed, I suppose this force in part fell on Davis's line, and then on Sheridan's. The casualties in my division in this battle were killed, 260; wounded, 1,005; missing, 1,280. Of the missing it was subsequently ascertained that some had been killed, others wounded and captured, while some, becoming separated from their companies and regiments, did not find them for several days.

Our provision train having returned to Nashville, my command subsisted on parched corn until the evacuation of Murfreesboro, when supplies were brought forward.

Willich, Kirk, and Baldwin, my three original brigade commanders, are dead. Two were killed in battle, and one has died since the war. Braver officers or better commanders never drew swords nor commanded more gallant men than those composing my division at the Battle of Stones River.

PART 6

The Eastern Theatre in 1863

24

When the Rappahannock Ran Red

Brevet Brigadier General James R. O'Beirne, U.S.V.

TRAINED TO THE hour, fit in every way as an athlete, that incomparable organization, the Army of the Potomac, came to the Rappahannock late in April 1863, from its encampment on Falmouth Heights. Like a thorough engine of war it could be relied upon for anything expected of it. [Major] General Joseph Hooker, everywhere affectionately known as "Fighting Joe," was in command. Everyone knew what might be expected of him in strategic movement, hard persistent blows, and resourceful mastery of his forces. The attack on [General Robert E.] Lee was to be a brilliant, determined one, though not without great difficulties. A river of imposing width and depth, liable to be swollen by the gathering waters of latter April, was to be reckoned with at the outset. But what did General Hooker, with such an army, care for that? The sting of Fredericksburg's red slopes still rankled; but with it was the prime advantage of the trial upon the thews and muscles of an unconquerable army.

Straight to the river banks and the pontoons went this champion of war's finishing hand, though the opposite bank was lined with the enemy's sharpshooters and artillery, posted behind breastworks. The fire was unneeded, except to reply in kind. The work went bravely on, and the colors of such splendid corps as the Second, Third, Sixth, and others were swept forward with grim and stately tread, on and over the bridges toward Chancellorsville, where Hooker was resolved to clutch and struggle, which Hooker had chosen as the place where the Army of Northern Virginia was at last to be broken on the red wheel of war.

Up the heights and on to the plateau the commands stretch out gorgeously right and left, near to and beyond the Chancellor House. The bright, clear creek of the same name just beyond sparkles merrily in the sunlight. As it sings its song in echo to the birds that fly about the wilderness it seems to feel that its mission will be one of comfort and relief to the thirsty, wounded, and dying who will soon furnish a dirge in contrast to nature's joy.

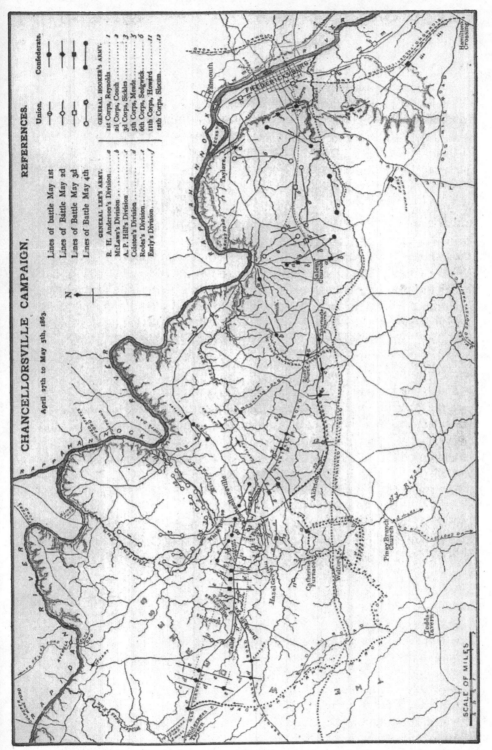

The Chancellorsville Campaign (*Atlas; Official Records*)

Remarkable marches and countermarches from right to left of our army continued throughout the day, and the first night found us wondering just where we of the Third Army Corps were to be engaged. Mud and water from the April rains were telling upon our clean uniforms and polished guns, while the brass Napoleons had lost their burnished brightness, in the splashes of what was humorously called by the men a "mud march."

The Irish Brigade, with other large bodies of troops, was held in reserve near the Chancellor House, destined to prove later a charnel house for our bright prospects and elated spirits.

Down the gently sloping Plank Road the Third Army Corps, the command which was to play a most important role, buoyantly marched in fine order, commanded by Major General [Daniel E.] Sickles. His ringing voice, as he passed the Irish Brigade at the Chancellor House, was heard in friendly benediction, greeting them as he drew in his splendid charger for a moment and said, "God bless the Irish Brigade!"

Occasional skirmishes, feeling the enemy with sharpshooters and light batteries, broke the monotony of marching and countermarching for position. The enemy had fallen back to the heavy woodlands beyond and taken up there well-selected and covered positions for offensive and defensive operations. In this their skill and judgment bore witness to their superior knowledge of the topography of the country. Undoubtedly the Union generals and engineer officers lacked the accuracy of information which the Southerners possessed. It often seemed that not until they reconnoitered, to place a battery or to deploy troops, was the full extent and direction of these hiding places made evident and available. Almost always, however, the Confederate armies sought and temporarily controlled these havens of vantage.

But the battle is on, in the low, densely wooded land about Chancellorsville, though higher ground might have been selected in the direction of Fredericksburg. The artillery found difficulty getting positions. The Third Corps moved out on the Plank Road by order, rapidly coming up behind the Second, Eleventh, Fifth, and Twelfth corps, making three columns in easy supporting distance—more than 50,000 men—driving all opposition before them. Soon, however, orders were sent to them to withdraw to the Chancellor House.

When Hooker was expostulated with by [Major General Darius] Couch he said: "It is all right, Couch. I have got Lee just where I want him. He must fight on my ground."

On the night of May 1 [1863] many changes were made in disposing the commands. Everything was like shifting scenes in a theater. The powerful corps of Sickles—in which was our regiment, the Thirty-seventh New York Volunteers, better known as the Irish Rifles, in [Colonel Samuel B.] Hayman's brigade, whose color company I commanded—was advanced on the Plank Road with the Eleventh Corps on the [right], its [right] flank unsupported. In the rear was an open space and in front a meadow stretching out for a quarter of a mile to heavy woods beyond it.

As soon as a halt was made with no prospect of camping, I gave the order to my company to throw up breastworks along their front, immediately passing the entrenching tools, when done with them, to the right and left, to continue the rough line of defense as far as practicable. I ordered our front to be masked with bushes and went some distance into the field, to see whether they concealed the rifle pits just scooped out, the army being stacked immediately behind them. Some of the men sat down to play cards, while others, more tired, lay down to smoke and rest.

Some time had elapsed when, on the afternoon of May 2, a picket on our [right] fired. Then came a volley of musketry. Shortly after a mass of men, in great agitation and confusion, came up the road to our [right], and with almost frenzied looks on their faces, pale with terror, rushed past us. We were almost overwhelmed as they cried, "Stonewall Jackson is coming!" This was the Eleventh Corps' stampede.

After some time spent in trying to calm them, and directing our men to form across the road, using their muskets horizontally as a guard and to press the fugitives back, the impact became so great that the men were swept aside, and a great rout appeared inevitable. Just then an army quartermaster's wagon came down the road in the other direction. Our men seized the mules and ran the wagon perpendicularly across the road, which enabled us to make a kind of barricade. But still some of the more active and terrified swarmed over the very canvas on top of it, with the agility of acrobats.

Finally a check was maintained, something like order was restored, and the Eleventh Corps stampeders went back quietly to their commands, their apprehensions having been overcome by the steady deportment of our men, who laughed them out of their fears. If this panic had not been arrested as it was, a most serious danger, if not catastrophe, to perhaps the entire army might have ensued then and there.

Later, [Lieutenant Justin E.] Dimick's battery was placed in position by [Major General Hiram G.] Berry's orders, and a destructive and effective fire opened upon the now slowly advancing enemy. The hurtling shells came in quick succession, like soap bubbles blown from an eager child's pipe. They came in a fixed direction, and left a scene of slaughter not to be imagined from mere description.

Everywhere maimed and dying, yet still uncomplaining, soldiers met us in accumulating groups, as we traversed back and forth over the same fighting ground. Guns and sabers were scattered here and there, amid haversacks, clothing, canteens, and side arms strewn broadcast, to lighten the burdens or given up with life itself as men quickly obeyed orders to rally on the colors, or faced the enemy's fire with unflinching celerity.

All this horrid debris, with abandoned accouterments and cartridge boxes, told of the repeated conflicts and charges that had taken place along the lines. An ocean storm, casting the wreckage of its violence upon the shores, violently tossing the fragments hither and thither in a relentless sowing of destruction, crashing and breaking the victims of its wrath with faces marbled and fierce from the grimaces of pain, could alone be comparable to the pitiless clash of men in deadly grapple for the mastery of that fated field of Virginia's wilderness.

General Sickles now ordered the whole artillery of his corps, composed of thirty field pieces, to open, supported by the Thirty-seventh New York Volunteers (Irish Rifles), Hayman's brigade, which helped to check Jackson's advance and plowed avenues through the ranks of gray. [Lieutenant George B.] Winslow's battery was an able second in delivering a destructive fire against the Confederate brigades of [Brigadier Generals George] Doles, [Stephen D.] Ramseur, and [E. F.] Paxton. These were finally driven out, though they had occupied for a time even our entrenchments.

Several times strategic points in the field were occupied alternately by Blue and Gray, and finally we ourselves returned to the ground over which we had fought and worsted the enemy a few hours before, to become again engaged there in the flanking movements that were taking place with an enemy as badly confused and crippled as we were in the now raging inferno of the burning woods. The artillery fire on both sides had been very destructive. An enormous concentration of the guns of the enemy on our angular formations was made easy, and our lines were swept with terrible effect, sometimes in flank, but oftener from enfilading points. [Captain George F.] Leppien's battery in the peach orchard had every officer in it killed or wounded. Lieutenant [Edmund] Kirby, of the First U.S. Artillery, took command of it by order of General Couch, and in a few minutes received mortal injuries. [Lieutenant Francis W. Seeley] was busy everywhere he could find a knoll. The guns of Dimick were belching flame wherever they could get near the enemy in the woods. Never were batteries kept more occupied. [Major General Alfred] Pleasanton with Sickles's reserve twenty guns opened with grape and canister at close range, an unusual and hazardous thing in handling artillery.

We had hardly passed over this retrospect of the day and the field of carnage, when, as somber evening fell, we were called from a bivouac rest in the open to prepare for the midnight attack decided upon by General Sickles to be made at the Plank Road, into the woods beyond, where we had been engaged supporting the artillery during the first onslaught of Stonewall Jackson's flanking column. This was in order to reestablish our connection on the right with the rest of the army, which it was reported had been broken by the resistless advance of Jackson's forces, now commanded by [Major General James Ewell Brown] Stuart, before he was repulsed so successfully by Sickles. This attack was a fitting sequel of the day and a fitting prelude to the conflict to follow on the morrow, for the clash of steel and the flame of musketry fire, which startled and worsted the Confederate left flank, was fierce and sanguinary.

Stonewall Jackson's troops, although jaded and worn, were found alert as Sickles's midnight charge with the bayonet steadily closed in. It was believed until it had been made that the Third Corps had been surrounded and cut off from the other corps on its right and left. Nothing like it! Sickles was on the *qui vive,* and everywhere active, determined to establish the line. This midnight charge was conceived, ordered, and carried out on his own initiative. As he loves still to claim, and rightly, it was his idea alone.

The artillery of the corps had been parked with care and covered in close order, out on the open plateau which we had gone over to and fro on May 1 and May 2. While the corps was executing its ghostly attack, wherein the silence of the approach was to be succeeded by the din and fury of a desperate onslaught and a determined defense, the guns were to be guarded by Pleasanton's cavalry. These guns had done much splendid execution on the previous day; they were entitled to a rest while the infantry went forward with just the cold steel. Not a cartridge was to be loaded in the rifles. The mute but irresistible bayonet was to do all the work necessary, held to the task by strong, eager, and steady hands.

This was the command given silently in the grim and noiseless hours of a dark night to the battalions, who were fascinated and buoyant under the tense effect of the novelty of the movement. It meant grisly work, no flinching, only direct, steady, and effective death-dealing thrusts. Man to man and breast to breast, when the contact should come, the desperate play was to be handled. Almost stealthily, like fierce and hungry panthers, thrusting their shoulders earnestly forward, moved the unswerving deadly line, waiting for the moment of charge, guard, and parry.

Guardedly the long line of battle groped through the woods. Steady were the steps and noiseless the onward tread. Not a word, even of command, was to be heard above a whisper. The enemy were believed, and proved to be, only a few hundred paces on our front, in rifle pits hastily thrown up. Glimpses only of the midnight moon flitted through the tall and closely sentineled forest trees and leafage and here and there gave a silver ghoul-like sheen to the battalions. The splendor of a spring night clothed the woodland with a shimmer of subdued light, softened by the leaves from which it danced to the soft moss carpeting the woods and muffling the sounds of the stealthy footfalls. Occasionally a soldier stumbled and pitched forward. Up! Forward again! No detention, no hesitation! How could he halt? The rear rank and others were striding on behind him at close distance.

In the awful hush, just as the front rank reached the Confederate position and developed it by forcible contact, a shot rang out, despite the orders against firing. In less time than it takes to tell it the Confederate ranks opened fire all along their line. Standing out in startling relief against the dark background of the night the musketry discharge, now at close range, took on an outline of a lurid, quivering, undulating sheet of flame. It was answered in steel by the fixed bayonets of the Third Corps.

Soon the conflict reached up and into the strong Confederate line. In one of the hottest centers the color company of the Thirty-seventh Irish Rifles, of Berry's division, which I commanded, moved, with one impulse of impatience, through the tangled woods, and suddenly brought up in the rebel rifle pits on their front. It seemed for the moment as if the doors of a blast furnace had opened upon us. But the bayonet was silently and effectively at work. It made no noise, but in desperate lunges scored a deadly reckoning. Yet it was soon evident that nothing human could remain in that fiery, undulating wave of sulphurous ignition and scorching blaze.

Struck by a ricocheted ball on the left of my forehead, I staggered and fell against a tree stump. I felt to find if there was a hole made by the shot; and, passing my hand hastily over the spot, I was seized with a spasm of delight, mingled with resentment, to discover I had not received a wound. I sprang up and forward, among the men, and in a moment was with them in the rifle pits of Stonewall Jackson's well-handled troops, who had flanked our army, surprised the Eleventh Corps, and afterward enveloped our [right]. I crouched sidewise, and rolled over the ridge of the breastwork, to avoid the fierce musketry fire, and with my men, having ordered them to fall back, landed in a safer position of defense if not of attack, on the other side of the fighting ditch.

Quickly new formations were made by us to take up another position. Our work was done. Jackson's movement around our army had been hazardous, though not so desperate as it looked. His hosts, accustomed to light punishment, while always inflicting more, and then getting away by a rapid flank movement (his favorite maneuver), had been thoroughly well hammered by the Third Corps under Sickles. They showed this now, by falling back and refusing to return our heavy fire of both infantry and artillery, which latter had opened on them in the midnight hours with telling effect. Their forced march, without rest, and the close clinches which they had had at the hands of this corps, put them in the condition of tired wrestlers, willing but weak. They would fain take a breathing spell, and, in truth, the beleaguered and roughly handled Third Corps was glad enough to do the same, after many hours of hard fighting.

The Union lines had now been straightened out. The Third Corps was not any longer cut off from the rest of the army, and its artillery had been saved after doing marvelous work in stopping Jackson and [Major General Ambrose Powell] Hill. Although we did not know it at the time, the former had been stricken unto death, and the latter sent from the field by wounds. Alas! poor Lieutenant Dimick, whose guns had made such a havoc from well-chosen points of the tangled battlefield, was swept away in death behind his belching guns before he could see how splendidly his arm of the service had come to the rescue. The constant fire of the artillery, with the bursting shells, had marked a road for Sickles to make his way back through the wilderness, after his gallant midnight attack had cleared the terrain to the Turnpike Road. His men must now get to their blankets for a bivouac of a few short hours, to be refreshed and ready for another death grapple at daybreak, for tomorrow, May 3, was to be another day of soul-racking combat. Its sunny dawn, the reawakening of nature, the opening of the woodland flowers, with accompaniment of bird song and balmy winds, were to be marred by war's rude alarms and the shocks of persistent battle. The night echoes were stirred with maneuvers for positions. The old Third Corps, accustomed to making a virtue of necessity, spread itself out decorously on the breast of Mother Earth behind stacked arms, under the blanketing wool and poncho, exhausted but buoyant, with no premonitions of aught but coming victory.

The sweet May morning of the third witnessed "the marshaling in arms of battle's magnificently stern array." Before the hastily brewed coffee of the camps had been cooled and swallowed the call "to arms" was sounded. Precipitately the men rushed to the stacked muskets. Companies were dressed, and wheeled into line of battle on the colors, which waved inspiringly along the regimental formations, as they answered the command "right dress—front forward—guide right!" Then they loaded as they moved forward to face the enemy in the woods, less than a half-mile distant, and quickly the firing began.

Just where the bivouac had been, now in our rear, remained a solitary apparent sleeper still wrapped in his blanket. I ordered him to be aroused by one of my lieutenants, James Boyle (now a Catholic priest in Massachusetts), who had been distinguished for gallantry and activity in several engagements of the Irish Rifles. He quickly returned from the blanketed form, and announced that the man, next to whom I had slept, crawling in gently so as not to disturb him while appropriating half of the covering, was not asleep but dead.

Quickly the edge of the woods in front of us became alive with Confederates in close column by division, who delivered at once a galling fire. The treetops had been populous with sharpshooters, instructed to pick off our officers wherever they could discern them. We charged with fixed bayonets to drive the cheering, confident force back as they surged toward us. This was subsequently repeated three times, when the attacking line on our front became so heavy and aggressive that we were forced to fall back. They had been massed to drive us before them with sheer force of numbers. The firing was terrific and well directed. After our third charge in the space of two hours our line officers and men became so decimated that it seemed useless to cope with the replenished ranks hurled against us, though we had cut them up considerably. As yet, our artillery could not be brought into position to open on them.

Reaching the right of the line after a rally, I directed the rear rank and file closers to close up, and maintain the line, still hard pressed by the swarming enemy. Some batteries opened viciously in oblique directions upon our right and left flank. The deadly fire kept up by the marksmen in the trees added to our discomfiture and loss. It looked as though nothing human could withstand it.

The officers were being picked off unerringly, and among them I received a minie rifle ball through the right lung. Staggering back from the right of the colors, I sank on one knee to investigate how much of a wound I had received. I wore white gloves, a red flannel shirt, and light blue trousers—the Union colors fancifully displayed in my personal attire. Passing my left gloved hand to my breast, my right having become paralyzed from the shock of the ball passing entirely through my body, I found that I was bleeding profusely, and growing weak. I rested my hip on the ground and steadied myself, in a half-sitting position, with the good arm. I concluded my best chance was to remain as quiet as possible. Lieutenant Boyle rushed to my side, and tenderly asked what was the extent of my injury. I told him I had been shot through the lung, and if there was any discretion to be used on my part, so as to pull through, it would be in keeping still. He said our line was being driven back, that the enemy still poured out of the woods in great numbers, and that if I remained where I was, I would surely be captured.

"So," he added, "you must make an effort and let us get you to the rear." There the surgeons and field hospital were located a half mile or so distant, near the Chancellor House.

Finally yielding to his entreaty, I got on my feet, and, my right arm hanging powerless, I tottered along with him. We had gone but a short distance when, the shelling and musketry fire having made the air murky and sulphurous, I saw what appeared to be a regiment lying on the ground on their arms and, as I supposed, held in reserve. I asked why they were not ordered into the fight, to support our line. Boyle looked at me in surprise as though I was deranged or jesting, and said: "Those men are all dead. They have been gathered by the hospital corps during the fighting, and placed there for burial as soon as possible."

I must confess that I experienced a sad consolation as I contrasted my condition with theirs. I stood a chance of recovery, or at least of being buried on the hillside at home. Glorious though it be to die on the field of battle, it is lonely to lie there, away from home and kindred, in the land of the stranger, and among the unknown, without burial service or the homage of respect and sorrow from the loved ones.

We reached the flowing creek near the Chancellor House. Its banks were some two and a half feet high, and a strip of sand ran for several feet in the middle. I was laid on this by Lieutenant Boyle so as to be out of range of the bullets which dug up the farther bank. Though sheltered for awhile, the fire again began to pour in our direction, and to our disadvantage, as the bullets were now coming downstream. [Brigadier General Amiel W.] Whipple's division, engaged near by, was driven back, and passed us in retreat. Colonel Hayman, of our regiment, rode up and spoke to me. He was now in command of the brigade (first of the Second Division). Shortly after the Irish Brigade followed, and Captain John Lynch, commanding his company, sympathetically spoke to me, shook hands with a tender good-bye, and walked off a few paces, when his head was taken off by a round shot. A man who had been called to come to help those carrying me in the blanket refused. A moment late he was struck by a shell fairly in the middle of the back and was thrown high in the air, his arms and legs spread out. I heard one of the men carrying me cry out, "Oh! boys, look at the rawhide."

In the going to and fro over the field, while engaged in the fighting of the first and second days, the ambulances and hospital supplies of our division were captured. At the Chancellor House we got a stretcher, upon which I was carried in reliefs by my men and taken to the field hospital of the Fifth Corps, some three miles distant. There a protected spot was selected and a shelter of brushwood and blankets made for me, when my men rejoined the regiment.

This comfort was not to be for long. Combined with all the horrors of the wounded men being obliged to remain in the open, laid down on the ground mostly, the work of the continued shelling made the place a very inferno. No such thing as sleep was possible through the terrible nights of the third and fourth. Three different times the dead leaves and moss which covered the ground in the woods were set on fire by the exploding shells, and the clothing of many of the more helpless greedily caught the flames. Many were painfully burned before their scant clothing could be torn from them. As they were led by, when the field hospital was moved, their pitiable appearance as they were supported or carried was heartrending.

Amputations were being made on all sides. One bright young lad next to me told the attending surgeon to wait till he took a chew of tobacco, when he would, as asked to do, hold the "flap" of his arm, after it was amputated above the elbow, until the supporting bandages could be adjusted temporarily on it. It was one of the finest exhibitions of real American grit I have ever had the good fortune to witness. No wonder such men never knew when they were whipped, and could laugh at the worst terrors of war.

Finally, after a third repetition of these blazes, the good and true men who were to carry me on the stretcher decided at my suggestion on a new line of conduct to escape any more of it. The army blanket, with bayonet fixed and hammer of the piece clamped on the bight of it, so as to give them handhold to lift my dead weight of more than 200 pounds, was replaced with a good new stretcher to carry me. At my suggestion they determined to carry me without stopping to the north side of the Rappahannock. We resolved to chance our luck there, until the army came over. I had been dosed with morphine, and none of us had had anything to eat for thirty hours. A pipe of tobacco and a pot of coffee were the only consolations to be had. The insensibility to pain and fatigue, through sleep, had been denied us. But the men were light hearted and philosophical.

When at last we had reached, near our old camp, a stopping place, the stretcher was carefully put down. In a drizzling rain, backed up to a campfire, they held a consultation about me. Between whiffs of his pipe, pressed by lips whose loud smack could be heard some distance, as he strongly pulled it, Patrick Feeney, the Sir Oracle of the company, who had been through the Crimean War with the British army, voiced the decision that my wounds would not prove fatal and that I would not die—not soon, at any rate. He was peremptorily questioned as to how he knew, and what reason he had for his opinion.

"Arrah!" says he, "did ye hear that rousing big oath he let out of him when we knocked agin a stump? If he was going to die, do you think he would swear that way?"

Their humor kept me in a cheerful condition until I got into the officers' hospital out of the rain. I was well soaked and chilled in the night air, which was very cold, because we had had no shelter in the log house where they put me, as it had no covering overhead.

What caused the drawn battle at Chancellorsville? Was it fate or misfortune? Perhaps. Incapacity of leaders or men? Conditions of the fighting machine? Never. What then? Artillery was never served with more accuracy and effect. The infantry firing was delivered with rare coolness and deadly direction, both at long and close ranges, wherever the enemy could be sighted. Defensive earth-works when necessary were thrown up with judgment and celerity, as well as engineering skill. Theoretically, and practically, no rout could happen. That of the Eleventh Corps only lasted a few hours, before it was stopped as with a break-water by the Second and Third corps. It did not great harm to the morale of the rest of the army. At no time, though sorely tried, was the rest of the army "out of hand." No power on earth could demoralize or stampede it.

Where, then, was the magic power to be produced, that would cause this splendid but deadly panorama of war to end differently? Was it generalship that fell short? No! a thousand times No! So far as capacity, fidelity, energy, and the best adaptability were concerned, the foremost leaders of the different corps and divisions were unsurpassed in military science and experience. Why, then, was not an undisputed victory achieved? General Sickles says the "ifs" did it. [Brig-adier General Andrew A.] Humphreys says: "The army was drawn in too close-ly in every direction. It had not the look of an army ready for battle. They were in no confusion, but they seemed to be unoccupied. The troops were in fine spirits, and we wanted to fight."

"We ought to have held our advanced positions," says [Major General Winfield S.] Hancock, "and still kept pushing on." [Brigadier General Gouv-erneur K.] Warren, chief of engineers, says the same. The judgment of these two men must be respected, for they were soldiers, every inch of them, and both of them went from the shattered hopes of Chancellorsville to Gettysburg and undying fame.

25

The Campaign and Battle of Gettysburg
Oliver Otis Howard, Major General, U.S.A.

AFTER THE Battle of Chancellorsville the Confederates were much en-couraged by the general condition of affairs. The Army of the Potomac kept losing men by expiration of enlistment, until we had less than 85,000 effectives, and these were badly organized, when General [Robert E.] Lee commenced his movement the last Of May 1863.

Our forces were distributed into eight army corps, necessarily of small size: the First under [Major General] John F. Reynolds; Second, [Major General Winfield S.] Hancock; Third, [Major General Daniel E.] Sickles; Fifth, [Major General George G.] Meade; Sixth, [Major General John] Sedgwick; Eleventh, [Major General Oliver O.] Howard; Twelfth, [Major General Henry W.] Slocum, and the cavalry under [Major General Alfred] Pleasanton, making an average for each corps of less than 11,000 men. The largest corps, Sedgwick's, was about 15,000 strong; the smallest, Reynolds's, numbered not more than 8,000 combatants.

General Lee seems to have actually commenced the northward movement June 3. It was always difficult for us to procure information of the movements of the enemy; more difficult than for him to gather corresponding information concerning us, because we were in the hostile country. I remember with what apparent ease and self-possession, during this northward march, farmers would be riding in pairs or threes, each with a bag of grain behind the saddle, appar-

Major General Oliver O. Howard (*Century*)

ently going to the neighboring mill; and how surprised beyond expression when their counterfeit character was revealed.

With few exceptions the Southern households, when opportunity rendered it possible, as at Chancellorsville, gave constant and full information to the enemy of our strength, position, and movements. However, in spite of difficulties, [Major General Joseph] Hooker had discovered and reported to Washington, as early as May 28, the collection of a large body of the enemy's cavalry at Culpeper and Jefferson. He justly concluded that a general movement was on foot, and presumed it would be the same substantially as that of the year before. Still, everything seemed to be conjecture till after the cavalry action of General Pleasanton, June 9, at Brandy Station.

This was, of course, merely a grand reconnaissance in force. It resulted in giving us this desired information: the corps of [Lieutenant Generals James] Longstreet and [Richard S.] Ewell, having turned our right flank, were already en route towards the north; and the enemy's cavalry surely, and his whole force probably, was destined for Maryland and Pennsylvania. From the information gathered from the prisoners and dispatches captured during this reconnaissance, and from scouts who had noted the time it took the enemy's column to pass a given point, it was plain to our commander that there was need of prompt action: either to cross the river and fall upon Lee's rear, or to follow up his movement upon the inner lines, ready to resist any flank movement he might make, or, if an opportunity should offer at some favorable moment, to strike him in flank. General Hooker seems to have meditated the first course, and to judge from his correspondence with Washington, he deemed it feasible. Doubtless, if he had had sufficient force, he might have cut off [Lieutenant General A. P.] Hill's corps, fallen upon and crushed it after the departure of Ewell and Longstreet, and afterwards, if Lee had not turned back, made as good time as Lee himself in reaching central Pennsylvania; but his general instructions to cover Washington, always a matter of vital importance, and the specific objection of the president made at the time in a letter to him, caused him to restrict himself to a reconnaissance by the Sixth Corps, while the other corps were marching parallel with Lee's column.

Each army in motion was covered in flank by its own cavalry. General Hooker kept steadily to his object, namely, to take positions of observation, protect the capital against sudden movements in that direction, and be ready to concentrate rapidly for any possible emergency.

I belonged to the right wing, temporarily constituted under the immediate charge of General Reynolds. It consisted of the First, Third, and Eleventh corps, and marched by the way of Bealeton, Manassas Junction (the old battlefield of Bull Run), Centreville, Gum Spring, and Goose Creek. Our three corps habitually encamped within five or six miles of each other, seldom following in precisely the same track except when forced to do so. The corps kept constant intercommunication. There were frequent cavalry contacts with [Major General

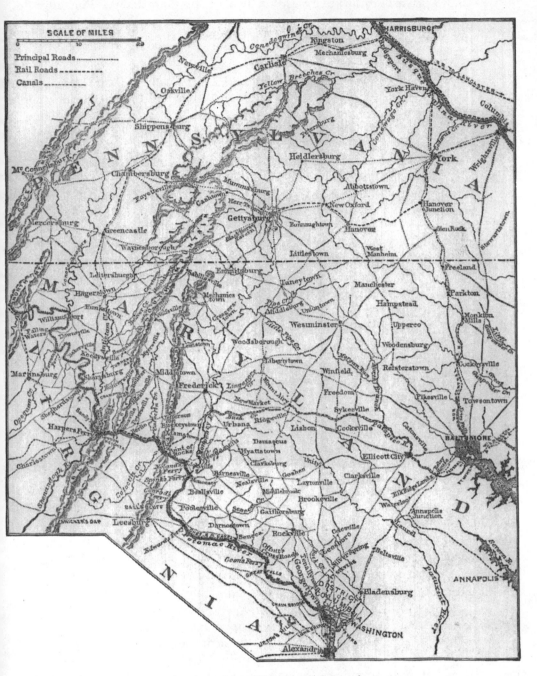

The Gettysburg Campaign (*Century*)

J. E. B.] Stuart's cavalry at the gaps in the Bull Run range and the Blue Ridge, but few that drew into action any considerable infantry force, though a regiment, a brigade, or sometimes a division was detached in support. [Major John S.] Mosby's cavalry, guerrillas, scouts, and spies penetrated our lines in spite of every precaution, picked off our aids and messengers on their swift journeying from corps to corps, and circulated every sort of false story that might be made use of to mislead us.

The major part of the Army of the Potomac was on June ?? not far from Edward's Ferry, the place selected for crossing the Potomac.

General Lee had rightly interpreted our movements, namely, the reconnaissance at Falmouth and at Beverly Ford, and the pressure of cavalry supported by infantry at the gap of the mountain ridges which run parallel with the Potomac, and he had scarcely been checked for an hour in the execution of *his* main purpose. He did encounter a force of about 7,000 men under [Major] General R. H. Milroy, at Winchester, Virginia, which force, in an isolated position, without support, could not afford to wait for Lee's arrival. But it was difficult for General Milroy, with his brave heart, to make up his mind to retreat till the enemy was actually upon him. He remained one day too long, and his retreat was cut off, and it is a wonderful fact that nearly half of his command escaped and succeeded in getting upon the other side of the Potomac, leaving the remainder of his men, twenty-nine guns, upwards of 200 wagons, and 400 horses and mules in the hands of the enemy.

This unfortunate affair, ending June 15, served to depress us and inspirit the enemy. He pressed on rapidly to Harper's Ferry, where doubtless he hoped to repeat the tactics of a former occasion, that is, of seizing the commanding points on the Virginia shore, and forcing a surrender. But this time we were fortunate in having in command there [Brigadier General Daniel] Tyler, an officer as quick of apprehension and as fertile in expedients as Lee's commanders. Tyler carefully withdrew to the almost impregnable position of Maryland Heights, a range of hills, on the eastern shore of the Potomac, which completely command the ground at Harper's Ferry; thus saving his command and taking an excellent position of observation.

General Hooker was entirely right when he asked for the control of this force. Had Milroy's and Tyler's troops been under his command, Milroy would have held merely an outpost for Tyler, and would doubtless have retired upon him on Lee's approach. In such emergencies independent wills work at cross-purposes. For war, you must get the best will you can, and trust it wholly.

I was ordered to cross the Potomac with my corps on June 24 at Edward's Ferry. The uncertainty of the enemy's movements, and correspondingly of our own, multiplied orders in an unusual manner. After my orders to cross the river and proceed to Sandy Hook, in the vicinity of Harper's Ferry, [Major General Daniel] Butterfield, the chief of Hooker's staff, signaled, "Have you received orders *not* to cross at Edward's Ferry till further orders, but to camp near the telegraph office there? You report from there to headquarters Army of Potomac." Another order was to cross and march to Harper's Ferry *via* Edward's. Then came a dispatch from Hooker himself, to put my corps in camp on the *south* side of the Potomac; next, one from [Brigadier General] Seth Williams, A.A.G., that I should guard the bridge and depots at Edward's Ferry on the *north* side of the Potomac at that place.

General Seth Williams writes, "General Tyler telegraphs from Maryland Heights, 'Longstreet's corps, which camped last night between Berryville and Charlestown, is today in motion, and before six o'clock this morning commenced crossing by the ford, one mile below Shepherdstown, to Sharpsburg. I have reports from reliable parties that at least 15,000 have crossed the ford this morning, mostly infantry and artillery. The troops are halted, and the wagon train at ten o'clock (this morning) was moving.'" General Hooker's letter of this same date, probably written early in the morning, to [Major General Henry] Halleck, explains that Ewell is already over the Potomac, and that if he can do so without observation he proposes to send to Harper's Ferry "a corps or two to sever Ewell from the balance of the rebel army, in case he should make a protracted sojourn with his Pennsylvania neighbors."

I presume that just as soon as General Hooker knew that Longstreet was also crossing the Potomac in force, he gave up the idea of the enemy's intention to make a single corps raid. Also he surrendered the hope of dividing Lee's army by way of Harper's Ferry. In keeping with this view, the next day, June 25, came new instructions to me: "The commanding general directs that you at once send a staff officer to report to General Reynolds, at or near the vicinity of Edward's Ferry, and that you move your own command in the direction of Middletown instead of Sandy Hook."

This movement was executed in conjunction with the First and Third corps; "with a view," General Hooker says, "to seize the passes of South Mountain . . . and confine him (Lee) to one line of invasion." These objects were fully accomplished. It was easy to concentrate at any one of the three points, Frederick, Middletown, or South Mountain, in a day. I do not wonder at General Hooker's disappointment that the left at Harper's Ferry should be absolutely anchored by keeping 10,000 men there to defend Maryland Heights. This was in effect the decision of General Halleck, general in chief, telegraphed from Washington June 27 to General Hooker, who in person had gone to Harper's Ferry to reconnoiter. General Hooker's prompt and well-known reply to Halleck's message was, "My original instructions were to cover Harper's Ferry and Washington. I have now imposed upon me, in addition, an enemy in my front of more than my numbers. I beg to be understood, respectfully but firmly, that I am unable to comply with these conditions with the means at my disposal; and I earnestly request that I may be at once relieved from the position I occupy."

On June 28, after his arrival at Frederick, General Hooker was relieved from command, and Meade was appointed to succeed him. I was not, at this time, familiar with the points of issue between Generals Halleck and Hooker, but I was somewhat acquainted with the feeling towards General Hooker among certain officers of rank in our army. President Lincoln wrote him on the subject in a letter dated June 14. He says, "I have some painful intimations that some of your corps and division commanders are not giving you their entire confidence." One of these officers, about June 18 or 19, quite fiercely assailed me for "constantly sustaining General Hooker," saying in substance that I was the only corps commander that spoke always in Hooker's defense. I replied that "I was always loyal to the officer the government saw fit to place over me."

Though I believed, and do so still, that my dispositions at Chancellorsville were as good as the position permitted, and that the defeat there was not due to any neglect on my part, willful or otherwise, but to other causes (as I could have explained, had I ever been called upon by the Committee on the Conduct of the War or by General Hooker), nevertheless I was made to feel soon after the battle that General Hooker blamed *me,* and was against me. This made me so much the more careful in what I said, particularly after [Major General Carl] Schurz wrote me to the same effect, with a view to prevail on me to withdraw from the corps. And whatever private grievance I might have, I trod it under

Major General George G. Meade (*Century*)

my feet, for I believed that General Hooker had grand qualities. He was cool and brave in action, clearheaded in council, and of a popular turn with the troops, and probably as able in matters purely military—in forming and executing plans of campaign embracing tactics and strategy—as General Lee. His great fault was that he was unmerciful in his criticism of senior and rival commanders. Judging of the army feeling as exhibited in private interviews, and in the usual canvassing of reputations around the campfires, I believe the change of commanders, ill-timed as it seemed, was acceptable to the officers.

After the telegrams between General Hooker and the government, Meade concentrated his army towards his right flank at Frederick, on the evening of the twenty-eighth, saying, "I propose to move this army tomorrow in the direction of York." After a little further consideration he set in execution, to be completed the evening of the thirtieth (really finished the twenty-ninth), a movement upon Emmitsburg and Westminster: First and Eleventh corps to Emmitsburg, Third and Twelfth to Taneytown, Second to Frizelburg, fifth to Union, and Sixth to New Windsor. He drew [Major General William H.] French (now properly under his command) from Harper's Ferry to Frederick, as a reserve and protection to his line of communications with Washington. He protected his flank with cavalry.

This dispersed the army considerably, grouping two corps at Emmitsburg, two at Taneytown, and three around Westminster, on a line from right to left of about twenty-five miles' frontage. General Meade's object, explained at the time, was, "If Lee is moving for Baltimore, I expect to get between his main army and that place. If he is crossing the Susquehanna, I shall rely upon [Major General Darius N.] Couch (at Harrisburg) holding him until I can fall upon his rear and give him battle."

A part of Stuart's cavalry had crossed the Potomac in our rear, and made a raid around us. Ewell was at this time believed to be in the vicinity of York and Harrisburg. So that with Lee's army apparently scattered from Hagerstown to Carlisle, Harrisburg, and York, Meade hoped, as he said, to fall upon some portion of it in detail. But on the evening of June 30, all our information showed that Lee was drawing in his divisions and brigades to locations between Chambersburg and Gettysburg.

The part my corps took in these grand movements of preparation was very simple. I marched on the afternoon of June 28 from the beautiful, fertile, loyal, hospitable valley of which Middletown is the center, to the north of Frederick. The next day, the twenty-ninth, my notes say, "The day was rainy, the roads heavy, and the march wearisome, yet the troops were in camp at Emmitsburg, having made about twenty miles, by 7:00 P.M."

Orders June 30 sent Reynolds with First Corps to Marsh Run, halfway from Emmitsburg to Gettysburg, about six miles on. I changed position from the right to the left of the town, and the Third Corps (Sickles's) encamped between Taneytown and my position. Slocum went to Littlestown. The cavalry kept in advance;

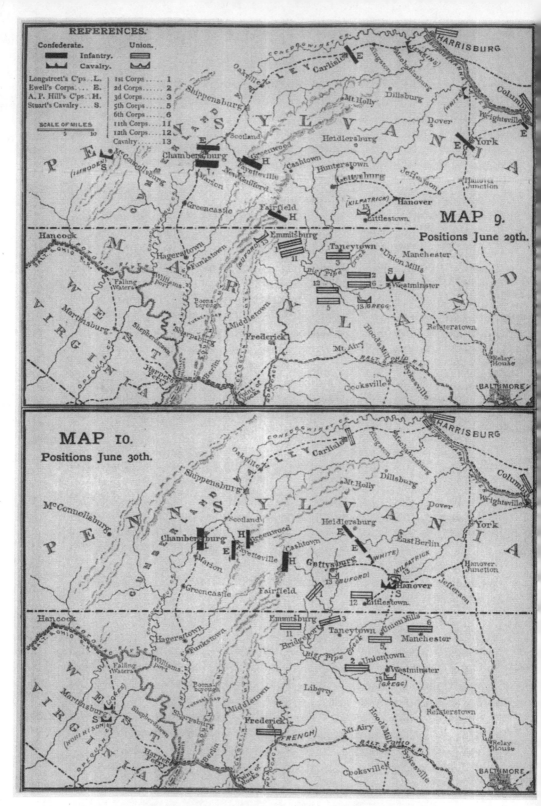

General Situation, June 29 and 30, 1863 (*Century*)

Major General John F.
Reynolds (*Century*)

Buford's division was already in Gettysburg. The rest of the army remained
substantially as on the day before. The Confederate corps of A. P. Hill, or a large
portion of it, was at Wingard's Farm, on the road from Funkstown to the Chambersburg Pike, the night before.

Just at night I received a note from General Reynolds requesting me to ride
up to Marsh Run and see him. He was stopping at a house on the right of the
road when I reached there, occupying a back room on the south side. He said
he was glad to see me, and immediately gave me General Meade's confidential
address, just issued, in which he required the officers in command fitly to address the troops, and appeal to every patriotic sentiment to stimulate his command on the approach of a great battle. He (Reynolds) showed me, in a bundle
of dispatches—the information brought to him during the day—evidence of
the nearness, position, and designs of the enemy. He sat down with me to study
the maps of the country, and we consulted upon these matters till eleven o'clock
at night, the last night of his life. He impressed me as unusually sad; perhaps

not more so than any clear-headed officer would be on the eve of an important battle. I took leave of him and rode rapidly back, six miles, to my command.

It seemed that I was hardly asleep before a messenger from army headquarters at Taneytown waked me with orders for General Reynolds as the wing commander. They were the orders of march for the day. I opened the dispatch and noted its contents (we read all dispatches, however directed, lest they should fall into the hands of the enemy and be lost), but did not attempt to execute the orders directed to another till sufficient time had been allowed him to give his own instructions based on them. But these orders of march, so soon known, enabled me to be in readiness. From them I quote the following:

"Orders. Headquarters at Taneytown. Third Corps to Emmitsburg; Second Corps to Taneytown; Fifth Corps to Hanover; Twelfth Corps to Two Taverns; First Corps to Gettysburg; Eleventh Corps to Gettysburg (in supporting distance); Sixth Corps to Manchester. Cavalry to front and flanks, well out in all directions, giving timely notice of positions and movements of the enemy."

After indicating the probable position of Longstreet and Hill between Chambersburg and Gettysburg, and Ewell at Carlisle and York, and expressing the opinion that movements favored a disposition on Lee's part to advance from Chambersburg to Gettysburg, General Meade concludes, "The general believes he has relieved Harrisburg and Philadelphia, and now desires to look to his own army and assume position for offensive or defensive, or for rest to the troops."

I will now ask the reader to narrow his view, and accompany me while I play the small part assigned to me, and note what I observed, remembering that if I write more fully of my own work it is no disparagement to others who distinguished themselves.

At 8:30 A.M., at Emmitsburg, I received the order of march from Reynolds, for the time my immediate commander, and at once set in motion two columns then in readiness. One, [Brigadier General Francis C.] Barlow's division, with a battery, was put upon the direct road from Emmitsburg to Gettysburg (eleven miles); the other two divisions, Schurz's and [Brigadier General Adolph von] Steinwehr's, with four batteries remaining, upon an indirect road (thirteen miles) by Horner's Mill, coming into Gettysburg by the Taneytown Road. An average of two and one half miles per hour on a hot July day, with the load of supplies each soldier had to carry, would be enough, and would bring Barlow's division into Gettysburg a little after 1:00 P.M. (His road was already cut up by Reynolds's wagons, and much obstructed all the way by trains and carriages. Schurz and Steinwehr, upon an unobstructed road, would do well to make an average of three miles per hour, and might come in about the same time with Barlow.)

As soon as the columns were in motion, accompanied by my staff I took the shortest route, riding rapidly by the side of the road; in the woods, in the fields, anywhere to get past the impediments and Reynolds's moving columns, and reached the vicinity of Gettysburg by 10:30 A.M. (All the time I give was by my own watch. I notice variations in the time from a half to three-quarters of an hour, as different officers have recorded the same event.) A staff officer met me from Reynolds as I came in sight of town, and said that [Brigadier General James S.] Wadsworth had come suddenly upon the enemy and was engaged beyond the seminary; and it was very evident from the sound and smoke that there was artillery firing and some musketry. Reynolds's column had left the road towards the west; one division seemed on the ground and another was skirting the Oak or Seminary Ridge, closing up.

My orders to keep within supporting distance, with a corps, would mean four or five miles back, if no combat was at hand. But Reynolds's word to me now by his aide was, "Come quite up to Gettysburg." And as I asked *where* he wished to place me, the aide said, in substance, "Encamp anywhere about here, according to your judgment at present." But circumstances change rapidly when an action has already begun. After his aide had gone and the firing seemed to increase, I became very anxious to see General Reynolds himself, that I might act with him to the best advantage. I sent an aide and orderlies to different places to look for him and report to me. Meanwhile, with the remainder of my staff I reconnoitered for the best position in which to locate my command. I went to the west of Sherfy's peach orchard, to a little rising ground there, then across the field, and ascended Cemetery Ridge. While there looking at the broad expanse of country over and beyond the little town at my feet, I distinctly remember turning to Colonel [T. A.] Meysenburg, the corps adjutant general, and saying, "This seems to be a *good position*, Colonel." He answered briefly, "It is the *only* position, General."

I now passed rapidly into the town and at first tried to get into the belfry of the court house, but found no ladder; someone recommended another place, across the street, through a store, up a stairway, through a lumber room, then up another flight of stairs, and out upon a balcony. It was probably the work of two minutes, when from what is now called Fahnestock's Observatory I had a fine post of observation. What could we see? The roads, now so familiar, from Bonnaughtown, York, Harrisburg, Carlisle, Shippensburg, Chambersburg, and Hagerstown; roads emerging from Gettysburg like the spokes from the hub of a wheel; roads which are exceedingly important for the soldier in command to have engraven on his memory. I saw [Brigadier General John] Buford's division of cavalry perhaps two miles off toward the northwest, seeming, in the distance and in the largeness of the field beyond the college, but a handful. I got glimpses of Wadsworth's division of infantry, fighting near the Oak Ridge railroad cut. Success was then attending him, and prisoners in gray were being conducted into the town. I saw [Major General Abner] Doubleday's division beyond the Lutheran Seminary, filing out of sight beyond the Oak Ridge to the south of west, a mile away.

As I stood there, and looked and heard and thought, of a sudden a young officer rode rapidly up the street from the west, touched his hat as he halted, and said, "General Reynolds is wounded, sir." I replied, "I am very sorry; I hope he will be able to keep the field." A few minutes after (about 11:30 A.M.), his aide-de-camp, Major [James C.] Biddle, brought me news of his death. His words were, "General Reynolds is dead, and you are the senior officer on the field."

Is it confessing weakness to say that when the responsibility of my position flashed upon me I was penetrated with an emotion never experienced before or since? I realized that we had close to us a large part of Lee's army, and that we ourselves had on the field *now* less than 10,000 men all told, and it seemed almost hopeless that Meade could gather his scattered forces in time for any considerable success to attend our arms. "But," I thought, "God helping us, we will stay here till the army comes." I assumed the command of the field, giving to General Schurz command of the Eleventh Corps. Doubleday succeeded to Reynolds, and Buford continued with his cavalry. I had sent an earnest call from Reynolds, received just before his death, back to the columns of Schurz and Barlow. It was his last order to me: "I am hardly pressed; have your troops move up at double quick." Immediately I sent the news to General Sickles, who must have been at Emmitsburg before that hour, urging him to come up as quickly as possible; and through him on to General Meade at or near Taneytown, back to Slocum along the Baltimore Pike to the vicinity of Two Taverns, where he was supposed to be; and again to the commanders of the Eleventh Corps on both roads of approach.

I then rode slowly to the position Meysenburg and I had agreed upon as a good one, near the Cemetery gate, where very soon I met General Carl Schurz in person, who had hastened on to see me; and I instructed him, as soon as the troops should arrive, to place his reserve batteries and Steinwehr's division in support on those heights, and to send his other two divisions, Barlow's and his own, now [Brigadier General Alexander] Schimmelfennig's, to the right of Doubleday's corps, as relief.

Several writers have criticized this disposition, one set asserting substantially that it was a lame attempt on my part to carry out the instructions of General Reynolds, which he himself would have modified had he lived; another, that I scattered my troops too much, and should have concentrated them at once; and another still, that the disposition was well enough, but that I should have entrenched or barricaded more than was done.

The first objection is simply not true. General Reynolds, as a true soldier and a military man of good capacity, met the enemy with his troops, which were but the advance of the main army, and attacked at once with boldness, as the wisest course to make the enemy more careful and slower in developing his forces; but he fell before he had informed me of any plan for a subsequent arrangement of troops.

The second objection would be of value provided there had been time to take and fortify prominent points in the enemy's front; but it was better to interpose a weak line to Ewell's corps than to let the flanking operation of Chancellorsville be repeated upon our exposed right flank. A well organized skirmish line is better than nothing. The alternative would have been to occupy, at once and fully, Cemetery Ridge and vicinity, and draw back the First Corps. But this could not be done safely so early in the morning. The repulse of the Oak Ridge line would surely have fallen upon the new line at the Cemetery, for the enemy's numbers present were at least two to our one. Possibly more barricading and entrenching might have been done, even in the presence of actual firing; I had it done in Georgia afterwards, under similar circumstances, but more was effected at Gettysburg than is usually believed. The batteries on the cemetery heights were many of them covered. The walls and fences were taken possession of, and the houses towards the north and west of the town, as I ordered and as I am informed, were prepared and used as barricades.

As soon as General Schurz had received his instructions near the cemetery gate, he met his column that appeared first on the Taneytown Road, and detached the brave Captain [Hubert] Dilger with his Battery [I, First Ohio Light] in advance, which passed through Gettysburg at a trot and went at once to a good position on the right of [Brigadier General John C.] Robinson's division. I insert a short extract from General Schurz's report to me. He says,

> The right of the First Corps seemed to extend across the Cashtown Road and the railroad northeast of it. It was difficult to see how far the ground was in our possession. Of the enemy we saw but little, and had no means of forming a just estimate of his strength. Either the enemy was before us in small force, and then we had to push him with all possible vigor, or he had the principal part of his army there, and then we had to establish ourselves in a position which would enable us to maintain ourselves until the arrival of reinforcements. Either of these cases being possible, provision was made for both.
>
> Accordingly you ordered me to take the Third and First divisions of the Eleventh Corps through the town, to endeavor to gain possession of the eastern prolongation of the ridge partly held by the First Corps, while you intended to establish the Second Division and the artillery (the reserve batteries, Major T. W. Osborne, commanding), except the batteries attached to the First and Third divisions, on the cemetery and the eminence east of it, as a reserve.
>
> The Third Division arrived at 12:45 P.M., at a double quick. The weather was sultry, and the troops, that had marched several hours without halting a single time, were much out of breath. I ordered General Schimmelfennig . . . to advance briskly through the town, and to deploy on the right of the First Corps in two lines. This order was executed with promptness and spirit. Shortly afterwards the First Division, under General Barlow, arrived by the Emmitsburg Road proper, advanced through the town, and was ordered by me to form on the right of the Third Division.

Meanwhile, as General Schurz was conducting his Third Division to battle, I left orders for Steinwehr and Osborne to halt and form upon Cemetery Ridge, and also directed my chief of staff to remain there with all that pertained to my headquarters, namely, clerks, orderlies, servants, horses, and the small cavalry detachment. I set forth with two or three officers for a personal reconnaissance of the troops engaged at the front. I was just in time to meet the head of Barlow's division, and accompanied it through the town along the street that is nearest the extension of the Emmitsburg Road. He detached [Lieutenant William] Wheeler's battery in advance. It moved with the utmost rapidity to join Captain Dilger. The infantry marched more slowly, that they might come fresher into battle. As the column passed along, the street and houses seemed almost deserted. But for the occasional firing beyond the seminary, echoing through the town, they were at this time as silent and undemonstrative as were the streets of Baltimore when we came through that city a few days after the riot in 1861 One beautiful exception greeted our eyes. A young lady, standing upon a piazza near a street corner upon our right, waved her handkerchief continuously as the men passed by. It gave them heart, reminding them of the true and loved ones for whom they were fighting. The soldiers answered with cheers, prolonged as the regiments came and went.

My senior aide de camp, Major C. H. Howard, was sent with orderlies to the position of General Buford to consult with him, reconnoiter, and bring me information. I then rode rapidly along our line from our right to the position of General Doubleday on the left. General Wadsworth in his testimony says: "General Howard had ridden over to see me about two o'clock, and told me to hold the position as long as I could and then to retire." Probably, as he was subordinate to General Doubleday, I told him those *would be* the instructions; my record of this visit is, "I found General Doubleday about a quarter of a mile beyond the seminary. His Third Division was drawn up with its front and left facing toward the northwest, making a large angle with the ridge; the artillery of this division was engaging the enemy at this time. His first division (Wadsworth's) was located a little to the right of the railroad (merely a railroad cut running from Gettysburg towards Chambersburg), and his second division (Robinson's) on Wadsworth's right." The left of Doubleday's line, resting on a small stream called Willoughby's Run, extended to an elevation north of the Chambersburg Road and was then refused. Then there was an interval, occupied after 1:00 P.M. by Wheeler's and Dilger's batteries belonging to the Eleventh Corps. From this place to Rock Creek, almost at right angles with the First Corps line, were the two divisions of the Eleventh Corps, Barlow's and Schimmelfennig's.

Such was the position of the troops. Now, with a view to relieve a constant pressure upon Doubleday's division, I directed General Schurz to move forward and seize a woody height in front of his left, on the prolongation of Oak Ridge. But before he had advanced many steps, the report of Ewell's corps advancing between the York and Harrisburg roads was brought in by Major Howard, and confirmed by reports from Generals Buford and Schurz. I saw at once that my right would be completely enveloped if I pressed on for the woody height referred to, so I ordered the line to be halted, and skirmishers to be sent to try to get upon and occupy that position. Before their arrival the enemy had it in force.

From this time, about 2:00 P.M., till 4:00 P.M., General Schurz with the advance division stood mainly on the defensive, constantly firing and receiving fire of artillery and infantry. General Barlow made one bold advance that for a few minutes broke the continuity of the line. The enemy's batteries could be distinctly seen on a prominent slope north of Gettysburg, between the Carlisle and Harrisburg roads. To these batteries we constantly replied from the three batteries at the front (Lieutenant [Bayard] Wilkeson's, of the Fourth [U.S.] Artillery, being with Barlow hotly engaged), and from [Captain J. Michael] Wiedrich's three-inch rifle guns on the cemetery heights near my headquarters. A sad complaint came from General Buford that our shots from the latter, Wiedrich's battery, fell short, and only reached his line. Fortunately nobody on our side was killed by this fire. The accident arose from the poorness of the ammunition, and not from want of skill in the artillery officers.

Not long after my return from Doubleday's, about 2:45 P.M., perceiving that a severe attack had actually been begun upon the Eleventh Corps and right of the First, I sent again to General Slocum, stating that my right flank was attacked and asking him if he was moving up to my relief. I stated that I was in danger of being turned and driven back. As to another message, owing to some difficulty in finding General Sickles's headquarters, my aide de camp, Captain [E. P.] Pearson, did not deliver it to him till 3:30 P.M., so that it was vain to expect help from that quarter short of two hours and a half.

The First Corps really did more fighting than the Eleventh. It began early, when Wadsworth's two brigades, [Brigadier General Lysander] Cutler's and [Brigadier General Solomon] Meredith's, came into position. Doubleday says, "General Reynolds took Cutler's brigade and [Captain James A.] Hall's battery to hold his part of the line, and directed the other brigade to be placed on a line with the first in a piece of woods which lay between the two roads (probably the Chambersburg and the next road to the south). These roads were already occupied by the enemy, who opened fire upon us, killing General Reynolds almost on the first volley."

The result of this first combat, thus begun, was to dislodge the enemy from the woods and take a large number of prisoners, his force being driven beyond Willoughby's Run. Here is where Colonel [Lucius] Fairchild so distinguished himself at the head of [the Sixth] Wisconsin regiment. Wadsworth's right being turned and a battery (Hall's) being nearly disabled, all the horses and men at one gun either killed or wounded, he fell back with a part of Cutler's brigade along the railroad cut towards town.

Doubleday now assumed the offensive with a reserve regiment and some others at hand, and attacked the enemy's advance in flank, enabling Wadsworth to catch in the railroad cut [Brigadier General James J.] Archer, of North Carolina, with part of his brigade and part of [Brigadier General Joseph R.] Davis's brigade, and made them prisoners. General Doubleday now extended his line with Robinson's division and supported his right with proper reserves.

This seems to have been the position of things when I went along his line. There was constant skirmishing and some artillery firing kept up all this time, but no vigorous attack again till it came along the whole line. My record is: "At 3:20 P.M. the enemy renewed his attack upon the First Corps, hotly pressing the First and Second divisions." This was simultaneous with Ewell's movement against Schurz on the right. Earnest requests came to me from both corps for reinforcements; Schurz must have another brigade on his right. My report says truly, "I had then only two small brigades of Steinwehr's in reserve, and had already placed three regiments from these ([Colonel Charles R.] Coster's brigade) in the north edge of the town, with a view to cover the Eleventh Corps should it be forced to retire." I feared the consequence of sparing another man from the cemetery. It was not a time to lose the nucleus for a new line that must soon be formed. I did, however, give General Schurz another battery from the reserve, and requested General Buford with his cavalry to retire from his advanced position, to support as well as he could the right of Doubleday's line.

At 3:45 P.M. Generals Doubleday and Wadsworth besought me again for reinforcements. I directed General Schurz if he could possibly spare a regiment to send one immediately to Wadsworth, for I deemed his front the ground which [Major] General George H. Thomas used to call "the hitch" (where the enemy is most obstinate). I have no record as to whether Schurz sent this regiment or not. In fact, fifteen minutes after this order left me, the musketry fire on the right and left became terrific, seemingly all along the line, and Doubleday was outflanked toward the left. I then sent an aide (I think it must have been Captain [Daniel] Hall) to General Doubleday with these words: "If you cannot hold out longer, you must fall back to the cemetery and take position on the left of the Baltimore Pike." The general, and I believe him a true man, does not give me credit for this order. It is possible the aide may have said, "We must hold on to the seminary as long as possible," in the excitement using *seminary* for *cemetery;* or he may have failed to reach him with the order.

A few minutes later, being satisfied I could hold the front no longer, at 4:10 P.M. I sent a positive order (General Schurz names this order in his report) to Generals Schurz and Doubleday to fall back gradually, disputing the ground obstinately, and to form near my position, the Eleventh Corps on the right and the First Corps on the left of the Baltimore Pike; and, as I knew our line would necessarily be short, and appear so to General Lee's observation, I asked General Buford to make all the show he could on our left, fronting the enemy's right. This he promptly did.

Now let it be remembered, when the staff officers left me with orders, our troops were already giving way. Soon the division of the Eleventh Corps nearest Doubleday was flying to the shelter of the town, widening the gap there; and the enemy line pressed rapidly through the interval. Of course Robinson and Wadsworth had to give way. General Doubleday says, "I think the retreat would have been a very successful one if it had not been unfortunately a case that a portion of the Eleventh Corps, which had held out very well on the extreme right, had been surrounded and had fallen back at the same time that my right flank fell back. These two bodies of men became entangled in the streets of the town, and quite a number were captured."

This was literally the case. The provisions made to cover the retirement of the troops, namely, the sending of Coster's brigade to the edge and front of the town, and the proper location and service of batteries by my chief of artillery, Major T. W. Osborne, checked the eager advance of the enemy, and broke and flung back a column of his in the act of turning the right flank of our new position. As the troops came up the Baltimore Pike, very much broken, Schimmelfennig, the commander of the leading division, lost his way, and to avoid falling into the enemy's hands hid himself among some piles of lumber, and did not succeed in joining his command until after the battle of the third day. Generals Schurz and Doubleday were in front of the town till the last minute, doing everything to inspirit their troops engaged, and save what they could of their broken columns.

I received the first regiment arriving and, leading the way with the corps flag, placed it in position on the right of Steinwehr's line. It colonel, [George] von Amsberg, seemed at the time utterly crestfallen and broken, but the German soldiers answered my action and followed my signal with a shout. [Brigadier] General Adelbert Ames, who succeeded General Barlow in command of his division after Barlow was badly wounded, came to me about this time and said, "I have no division: it is all cut to pieces." I replied, "Do what you can, Ames, to gather the fragments and extend the line to the right." He did so, and succeeded better than he had feared. The firing of the enemy now measurably subsided; only an occasional cannon shot and scattering musketry reached us.

At this moment, 4:30 P.M., according to the time I had gone by all day, General Hancock appeared. (He reports to the Committee on the Conduct of the War that he was at Cemetery Hill by 3:30 P.M.) General Doubleday states that his troops did not commence to give way till 3:45 P.M.; and surely it was half an hour later than this that he was leading his corps into position on Cemetery Ridge, where he and I first met Hancock. General Hancock greeted me in his usual frank and cordial manner, and used these words: "General Meade has sent me to represent him on the field." I replied, "All right, Hancock. This is no time for talking. You take the left of the pike and I will arrange these troops to the right." He said no more, and moved off in his peculiar gallant style to gather scattered brigades and put them into position. I noticed he sent Wadsworth's division, without consulting me, to the right of the Eleventh Corps, to Culp's Hill, but as it was just the thing to do, I made no objection—probably would not have made any in any event—but worked away, assisted by my officers, organizing and arranging batteries and infantry along the stone wall and fences toward Gettysburg, and along the northern crest of the ridge. It did not strike me then that Hancock, without troops, was doing more than directing matters as a temporary chief of staff for Meade.

But just before night, when the order from General Meade came to me, superseding me in command of the field by a junior in rank, I was of course deeply mortified, and immediately sought General Hancock and appealed to his magnanimity to represent to General Meade how I had performed my duty on that memorable day, which I think he then did. I know that afterward General Hancock said in substance to Vice President [Hannibal] Hamlin, concerning this battle, "The country will never know how much it owes to your Maine general, Howard."

At 7:00 P.M. I turned over the command to General Slocum, whom I saw in company with Hancock for the first time. He had placed his two divisions as I had requested, one at the extreme right, and the other at the left, some time before I saw him. Slocum answered me roughly that evening, and feeling that for some unaccountable reason I was blamed where I ought to be commended, I sat down and wrote a letter to General Meade:

> HEADQUARTERS Eleventh CORPS,
> July 1, 1863
>
> MAJOR GENERAL MEADE, commanding
> Army of the Potomac:
>
> GENERAL—General Hancock's order to assume command reached here in writing at 7:00 P.M. At that time, General Slocum being present, having just arrived at this point, I turned over the command to him. This evening I have read an order stating that if General Slocum was present he would assume command.
>
> I believe I have handled these two corps today from a little past eleven until four o'clock—when General Hancock assisted me in carrying out orders which I had already issued—as well as any of your corps commanders could have done. Had we received reinforcements a little sooner, the first position assumed by General Reynolds and held by General Doubleday till my corps came up might have been maintained; but the position was not a good one because both flanks were exposed, and a heavy force approaching from the north roads rendered it untenable, being already turned, so that I was forced to retire the command to the position now occupied, which I regard as a very strong one.
>
> The above has mortified and will disgrace me. Please inform me frankly if you disapprove my conduct today, that I may know what to do.
>
> I am, general, very respectfully, your obedient servant,
> O. O. HOWARD,
> Major General Commanding

General Sickles had meanwhile arrived with the Third Corps, and placed his command on our left, extending the line, heartily approving the position and distribution of the troops.

Thus ended the first day's battle, a rough, hard, bloody day. No sane man expected a victory over Lee's army to be gained with an advance guard, 22,000 infantry against 60,000 of the same blue-eyed Saxon race, in an open country, where there was no pass to be defended, no mountain or river to be used as an auxiliary obstacle. The First and Eleventh Corps and Buford's small division of cavalry did wonders; held the vast army of General Lee in check all day; took up a strong position; fought themselves into it, and kept it for the approaching Army of the Potomac to occupy with them, so as to meet the foe with better prospects of victory. General Lee saw our position, was deceived as to our numbers, and therefore waited for the remainder of his army before re-attacking. But the battle cost us many valuable lives.

Doubleday fixes his loss at upwards of five thousand. General Buford's and Schurz's would probably reach 4,000 killed, wounded, and prisoners; so that 22,000 effectives were reduced to within thirteen thousand.

Barlow with more than 1,000 other wounded men was left in the hands of the enemy. Mrs. Barlow generally kept near the field of battle where her husband was engaged, for he seldom escaped a shot. He was wounded in many battles. After Antietam he recovered with great difficulty and many drawbacks, under his wife's most careful nursing. I shall never forget Mrs. Barlow's coming up to the cemetery and saying she *must* go to her husband. She started at once down the Baltimore Pike into the town, but the skirmishers would not cease firing to enable her pass that way; then she returned and took another course, going west across the fields, where everybody could see her to be a noncombatant. This time she passed through both lines unharmed, and reached her husband.

General Slocum, with whom I had been acquainted at West Point, and with whom I had become better acquainted during our service together in the Army of the Potomac, sometimes serving under his temporary command, to my astonishment declined to come up to Gettysburg to participate in the action, and only sent his troops late in the afternoon at my request. He explained the course he took by showing that it was contrary to the plan and purpose of General Meade to bring on the battle at Gettysburg, he having arranged for another defensive position at Pipe Clay Creek. I think he did wrong to delay, and was hardly justified under the circumstances, even by the written orders of General Meade; still, in all his previous history and subsequent lengthy service by my side in the West and South he showed himself a patriot in spirit, a brave man, and an able commander. As the result proved, it is perhaps as well that he did not come earlier, for he and his troops were fresh for the very hardest fighting on subsequent days. I must speak of General Steinwehr. He came upon the field with a hearty spirit, ready to do his part. During the retreat he kept his men steadily in position on the Cemetery Ridge, as a nucleus on which the line of battle, probably the most important in the annals of our war, was formed.

Generals Slocum and Sickles and myself took up our quarters for the night near the cemetery gate. About 3:00 A.M. of July 2, General Meade and staff appeared at the cemetery. The first words he said to me were in substance that "he was very sorry to have seemed to cast any discredit upon me; he had no blame to affix."

General Butterfield, it seems (according to his own testimony), as soon as

Reynolds's death was known at Taneytown, had urged General Meade to go to Gettysburg himself, or send there his chief of staff. Meade not thinking this best, Butterfield said he ought to send some one on the field fully possessed of *his* views and intentions; adding, "I should entrust that duty to General Hancock." Meade assented, and Butterfield then drew the order accordingly, which did not take from me my corps, but placed me under the general command of an officer my senior in years and service in the old army, but my junior in the voluntary appointment.

From these statements it is now easy to understand General Meade's attitude toward me. He may have been prejudiced, but certainly, as I understood the matter at the time, General Meade really intended, and Hancock so implied in his conversation with me, that he (Hancock) was to represent Meade as Butterfield, the chief of staff, would have done on the field of battle. Of course it will make very little difference to posterity whether *I* served under Hancock unwittingly for two hours and a half or not. But it is of importance to me and to mine to explain the facts of the case.

General Meade then asked me concerning the position. I said, "I am confident we can hold this position." "I am glad to hear you say so," he replied, "for it is too late to leave it." General Sickles remarked, "It is a good place to fight from, General."

After a brief conversation concerning the location of the troops, as the dawn was just appearing in the east, we rode along the lines in rear of the sleeping soldiers, and the general saw for himself how much these lines needed strengthening and extension. The different corps, except the Sixth, were near at hand for this work. General Meade, stationed near where the soldiers' monument now is, took an officer's survey of the whole field, as the sun was rising at his back. The cannonade, which began and continued for an hour from a Confederate battery situated near Blocher's House beyond our right, and was replied to by our own guns, and the rattling of musketry along the picket lines, intensified every faculty of observation.

He could see Cemetery Ridge almost like a bastioned fort on his right, where it was broken by the valley of Rock Creek, with Culp's Hill fringed with trees for the flank, and the ridge thence to its crossing of the Baltimore Pike for its face. This ridge, turning near the town, passed in front of him, gradually diminishing in elevation, till, just beyond Zeigler's Grove, on his left, it is scarcely higher than the ground for a quarter of a mile in its front. He noticed then, a little farther to the south, what we called at the time Little Round Top, a small rocky spur rising abruptly, and beyond this a higher hill of the same nature, more wooded and more extended, called Big Round Top. Beginning at the crossing of Rock Creek, off to the right and rear of Meade's post of observation, near McAllister's Mill, and letting the eye sweep around westward by Culp's Hill to the highest point of Cemetery Hill, thence southward to the farthest end of Big Round Top, General Meade beheld the natural formation destined to be covered by his lines of infantry. It was shaped like a fishing hook (to which several writers have aptly compared it), the point resting at McAllister's Mill, the convex bend at the Cemetery Hill near Gettysburg, and the shank representing the remainder of the line.

The position of the enemy could be divined only by glimpses of batteries, location of skirmish lines, and general probabilities. Meade could see Oak or Seminary Ridge running north and south a mile to the westward, partially covered with trees. He caught the motion of a column of infantry far to the north, moving towards our right. He saw the several roads converging toward the town, the rolling interval to the northwest, the detached hills to the north beyond Rock Creek, which were in view, and evidently afforded excellent positions to the enemy for placing artillery on our front and flank, so as to bring a concentrated fire upon the cemetery.

The general stood here in this magnificent morning light with a panorama spread before him of hill and valley and mountain, of woodland and cultivated farms, of orchard and grassland, as beautiful as nature anywhere furnishes. But he saw not the beauty; he was planning for Lee and planning for himself; plan against plan, move against move. In a few minutes he turned away slowly and thoughtfully, rode back to the gate, and soon after, the army lines began to take form.

[Brigadier General John W.] Geary's division of Slocum's corps passed from the left, near Zeigler's Grove, to the east of Culp's Hill, and [Brigadier General Alpheus S.] Williams's division extended hence to McAllister's Mill; this located the Twelfth Corps line, partially entrenched or covered by rocks and trees, on the extreme right.

Wadsworth's division of the First Corps stayed and fortified Culp's Hill, where Hancock placed it the evening before. Ames's division of the Eleventh Corps carried on the line to the steep part of Cemetery Ridge, facing northwest. There were Schurz's and Steinwehr's divisions behind the famous stone wall and the apple orchard near town. Doubleday's and Robinson's divisions, First Corps, came next in order, strengthened by [Brigadier General George J.] Stannard's brigade of Vermont troops, newly arrived.

Hancock's Second Corps, which had marched up from Taneytown the night before, under [Brigadier General John] Gibbon, to within three miles of the battlefield, now filed into place, extending south of the lower land from and beyond Zeigler's Grove. Then Sickles's Third Corps was moved to the left and farther west than Hancock's, a part being in front of Little Round Top. About 8:00 A.M., the Fifth Corps, commanded by General Sykes coming in along the Hanover Road, marched through the fields to a position as a temporary reserve in rear of Little Round Top.

General Pleasanton's Cavalry Corps was disposed beyond Rock Creek to protect our flanks, [Brigadier General David M.] Gregg commanding a division operating on the extreme right, near the Bonnaughtown Road, and [Brigadier

General Judson] Kilpatrick's division, on the extreme left beyond Big Round Top, pushing towards the Emmitsburg Road. General Buford's division of cavalry, that had served so faithfully during the preliminary operations, was withdrawn from Sickles's left, where I had placed it, and sent on July 2 to guard our main trains at Westminster.

General Sedgwick, as soon as he received his orders on the night of the first, set his Sixth Corps in motion from Westminster about 9:00 P.M., and marched all night and the next day, with scarcely a halt, making thirty-four or thirty five miles in seventeen hours. At 2:00 P.M. I saw this corps move to the rear of the First and Second Corps, forming each brigade in line in rear of the preceding. As soon as a brigade reached its position the officers and men unslung their blankets and lay down, covering themselves for rest; they were soon sleeping soundly.

General Meade's headquarters were established at Mrs. [Lydia] Leister's house, situated on the Taneytown Road not far to the southeast of Zeigler's Grove, a point that proved to be more exposed to the enemy's artillery fire than any other within our lines, except the cemetery itself.

In rear of and near the middle of his own lines, where the Chambersburg Road crosses the Oak or Seminary Ridge, at the stone house of Mrs. Mary Marshall, General Robert E. Lee made his headquarters. They had an advantage over General Meade's, being less exposed to the fire and more commanding as a post of observation. His troops after getting into place were situated as follows: Ewell with three divisions opposite our right, [Major General Edward] Johnson's division having his left beyond Rock Creek at Benner's Hill, and [Major General Jubal A.] Early's division extending the line to near town, the two confronting Slocum, Wadsworth, and Ames. Then [Major General Robert E.] Rhodes's line, passing through Gettysburg along Middle Street, stretched out toward the Seminary Hill or Oak Ridge.

Hill's corps of three divisions faced the Eleventh Corps (my own), the First ([Major General John] Newton commanding), and the Second (Hancock's), extending from the Shippensburg Road to and a little beyond the Hagerstown Road; his divisions were commanded by [Major Generals Henry] Heth, [William D.] Pender, and [Richard H.] Anderson, in the order named.

Longstreet's corps continued the line along the Oak Ridge and across the fields to the Emmitsburg Road, [Major General John B.] Hood's division being located at the right of [Major General Lafayette] McLaws's, and [Major General George E.] Pickett's in reserve.

Lee's cavalry was not much used till near the close of the engagements at Gettysburg, being allowed to rest after its arduous service in the preliminary campaign and long raids around our right flank.

General Lee's artillery officers had placed their guns on every favorable position, as I have intimated, on front and flanks, having for use 275 guns. [Brigadier General Henry J.] Hunt, Meade's chief of artillery, saw to the posting of our batteries. Cemetery Ridge was covered with them, and batteries or parts of batteries were placed wherever there was an available point.

I took my headquarters in the cemetery at the highest point, where the ridge slopes to the eastward, very near the place where the monument now is. The officers and men were rested and encouraged by the usual influence of complete arrangements, confident movements, and large auxiliaries.

My record of the opening of this battle is as follows: "Very little occurred while the other corps were moving into position until about 4:00 P.M. Just before this, orders had been issued to the (my) divisions to make ready for battle, as the enemy was reported advancing on our left. Now the enemy opened fire from some dozen batteries (Hunt says 120 guns), to our right and front, bringing a concentrated fire upon our position." Osborne and [Colonel Charles S.] Wainwright replied with spirit. Projectiles filled the air; they went over us and set ambulances, spare wagons, and a host of army followers into rapid motion farther to the rear, for shelter. A part fell short and were harmless, or occasionally exploded, throwing out their fragments to trouble the artillery men and horses, or to rattle among the tombstones. Seldom did a shell explode on the crest where the infantry was lying; but now and then one more murderous than the rest would strike a regiment. One such shell, I remember, killed in a single regiment of ours twenty-seven men.

There was a battery directly in front of me that kept very actively at work during this cannonade. My attention was called to a young artilleryman who ran backward and forward from the gun to the limber, carrying ammunition. He was singing and whistling, and very active. As a shot or shell came near, the horses would spring to one side or pull back. He would then run to their heads and straighten the team, and return to his work, exhibiting no impatience. Just as I was remarking him for his heartiness and lively conduct, a solid shot struck him on his thigh; he gave one sharp cry, and was no more.

One who stood near me at this time writes, "Then came a storm of shot and shell; marble slabs were broken, iron fences shattered, horses disemboweled. The air was full of wild, hideous noises, the low buzz of round shot, the whizzing of elongated bolts, and the stunning explosion of shells overhead and all our around. . . . In three minutes (after our batteries opened) the earth shook with the tremendous concussion of 200 pieces of artillery."

Undoubtedly General Lee made up his mind from careful observation that the hills, Little and Big Round Top, afforded the key to our position. Could he get a lodgment on these heights, a single battery might be placed so as to paralyze our whole center and right. There would be an enfilading fire, sweeping the troops of Hancock, Newton, and myself, and a reverse fire—or fire from the rear—upon the rest of our line.

General Sickles, for the time constituting our left, had moved his corps forward to the slight ridge of land that runs obliquely from the cemetery southwest towards Oak Ridge, taking ground considerably in advance of Hancock's left. The position itself was doubtless intrinsically better for meeting an assault than the continuation of Hancock's line at that time, but it isolated the Third Corps and exposed its flank to be turned. While Longstreet made the main attack here, Ewell was to attack in his front, and Hill to threaten, each to work opposite his own place in the general line, that Meade might not reinforce.

In perhaps three quarters of an hour after the batteries began, there was for a few minutes a lull in the firing, when it again opened with redoubled violence on our left. Hood and McLaws in line moved to the attack. The division on Sickles's left, extending back from the Peach Orchard, rested its flank on Big Round Top. The brigades of [Brigadier General J. Hobart] Wood and [Colonel P. Regis] De Trobriand on that flank received the first onslaught, but, being posted as well as could be under the circumstances in that advanced position, returned the enemy's fire with vigor and effect. [Brigadier General Charles K.] Graham's brigade, making an angle just north of the orchard, and with little cover, met a fearfully destructive fire almost simultaneous with that on the left; it did not hold its ground long, though the contest at the Peach Orchard, and at Rose's house, a little to the south of it, was somewhat prolonged. Sickles's batteries here did wonderfully effective service; [Captain John] Bigelow's fired rapidly from a position near A. Trostle's barn, and when forced to retire, did so with the prolonge, keeping up the fire. The Confederates, pressing back the broken infantry line, came upon this battery with a rush. Bigelow is said to have blown them from the muzzles of his guns, but still they came on, and clambered over his limbers and shot his horses. Five of his noncommissioned officers and twenty-two of his men were killed or wounded, and he himself wounded in the side. Still he held on and fired till the corps chief of artillery, [Lieutenant Colonel Freeman] McGilvery, had brought up his reserve battery to the high ground in his rear. These brave men brought off only two guns, but they had done their part in delaying Longstreet's advance.

General Humphreys's division, being opposite A. P. Hill's men, was not hotly engaged till our troops on his left had been for some time in the fight, but by 6:00 P.M. the fierce battle rolled along to his front, and after making all possible resistance he retired slowly and in very good order to the position of Hancock.

During this fearful conflict between the round tops and the Emmitsburg Road, groves, orchards, trees, knolls, stone walls, large rocks, and every natural obstacle or cover had been taken advantage of by our men in retiring, and by the enemy in advancing, so that the necessary delay was effected to enable General Meade to do what it would of course have been wise to do before, namely, get the Fifth Corps upon the heights at the left. [Major General David B.] Birney had called for this corps as reinforcement before the action began. General Sykes is said to have replied "that he would be up in time, that his men were making coffee and were tired."

The coffee and the resting are often absolutely necessary to the soldier, to enable him to keep on his feet and bear his part. General Meade and not General Birney was Sykes's commander, and the later was clearly in position to reinforce Birney, in case of need, in a very few minutes. But to my mind there is a remarkable providence in the fact so much complained of, that "General Sickles had taken up an advanced position"; for thus he caused the delay of Longstreet, and enabled Meade to put Sykes into position to save his extreme left, which was the very high ground that Lee made his main attack to secure. General Sickles was severely wounded, losing his leg. He called upon Meade for reinforcements, and turned over his command to Birney.

While the Fifth Corps was moving into position, [Major General Gouverneur K.] Warren, Meade's chief engineer, kept the signal flags waving on Little Round Top, detached [Lieutenant Charles] Hazlett's battery and supported it by [Colonel Strong] Vincent's brigade of [Brigadier General James] Barnes's division, and undertook to secure this vital point. He was just in time, for Hood's men were upon them in five minutes; but they had our best troops to meet. They came with their fearful yell up the rough steeps, over the precipitous crags, only to be hurled back again.

"Never was there a wilder place for combat, and never was there a combat more fierce than was seen there on that hot July evening, with blazing musketry and hand-to-hand struggles, with clubbed firearms and jagged stones. For half an hour this conflict went on, when a charge from the Twentieth Maine, under Colonel [Joshua L.] Chamberlain hurled the Texans from the hill." Chamberlain occupied the left of our line, while Vincent's brigade and [Brigadier General Stephen H.] Weed's brigade of [Brigadier General Romeyn B.] Ayres's division and [Brigadier General Samuel W.] Crawford's division broke Hood's and McLaws's advance farther to the right.

General Hancock, after Sickles's wound, was given the care of the two corps, the Second and Third. He pressed forward reinforcements as they were needed. From my post of observation I could see brigades and divisions move out westward, with their flags flying and their bayonets gleaming in the sunlight; then the fearful rattling of the musketry would follow, and the brigades and even divisions would melt away. When Humphreys, on retiring, reached the open space at his rear, he thought for a moment the day was lost, and the enemy thought their victory sure. But in a few moments Meade had sent forward [Brigadier General Frank] Wheaton's division of the Sixth Corps, and the other fresh troops just named; the new line was complete; then, as soon as Humphreys's men were out of the way, a sheet of fire opened from Zeigler's Grove to Little Round Top, and the enemy were repulsed.

Histories, reports, testimonies, and letters are crowded with thrilling incidents in the battle I have outlined. General Weed fell at Hazlett's battery on Little Round Top. Lieutenant Hazlett saw his commander fall, and as he hastened to him to catch his last words, he was struck by a bullet and fell dead across the body of his general. Colonel Vincent, commanding the supporting brigade of Hazlett's battery, fell while standing in an elevated position where he could see and be seen, cheering on his men.

Colonel Edward E. Cross, in [Brigadier General John C.] Caldwell's division

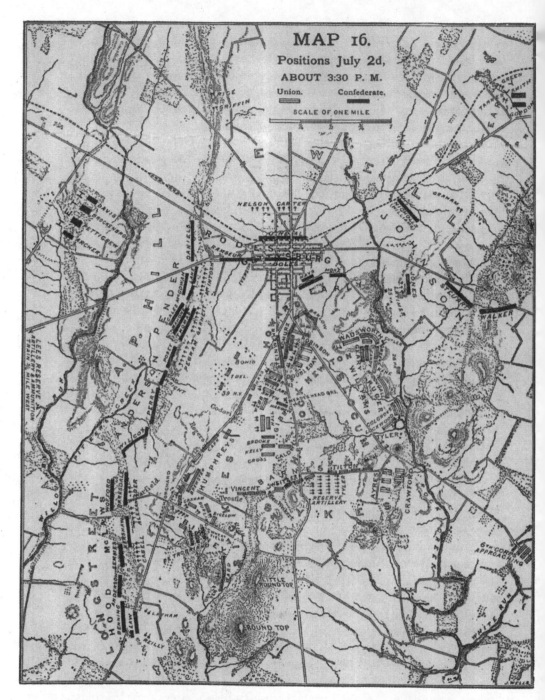

Positions, July 2, 1863, 3:30 P.M. (*Century*)

of Hancock's corps, commanded the brigade that I had led during McClellan's campaign. His regiment was the Fifth New Hampshire. He was tall, handsome, with a clear, black, restless eye, and a warm heart. Nothing seemed to please him better than the excitement of battle. He is said to have been wounded nine times in previous combats. He exclaimed, a few hours after the fatal shot had struck, "I did hope I would live to see peace and our country restored!"

[Brigadier General Samuel K.] Zook, of New York, in the same division, was another commander that I counted as a personal friend. He fell in Caldwell's advance. I remember distinctly his high character, pleasant face, and genial companionship, and can hardly realize that he is gone. My brother, who is a minister, having been sent by the Christian Commission, was moving around relieving the wounded, and found his own cousin, Major S. P. Lee, with his right arm shattered, and at first quite unconscious. He took charge of him and carefully nursed him till he became convalescent. After the struggle had closed, and when we supposed we should have a rest for the night, some troops in our front, said to be the Louisiana Tigers, sprang from their cover under the steep hill on the north end of Cemetery Ridge, broke through Ames's division, and in three minutes were upon our batteries, [Captain Michael] Wiedrich's and others, almost without firing a shot. General Schurz by my order sent a part of a brigade under Colonel [Wladimir] Krzyzanowski to the batteries' immediate relief; the artillerymen left their guns, and used sponge staffs, handspikes, or anything they could lay hold of, to beat back the enemy, and as soon as help came the batteries were cleared. Schurz also sent a brigade farther to the right to help [Brigadier General George S.] Greene, who requested reinforcements. I sent to Meade for more troops, as a part of Ames's division was forced back and a gap made. But Hancock, hearing the firing, had detached Colonel S. S. Carroll, with his spirited brigade, to my aid. His men formed at right angles to the general line, and swept swiftly over the highest ground northward, carrying everything before them.

Generals Steinwehr and Newton immediately filled any gaps made on my left by sudden withdrawals. This night engagement extended as far as Slocum had any troops. It was Ewell's effort on our right to assist Lee's main attack after Williams's and a part of Geary's divisions had been withdrawn and ordered off to reinforce the right. The enemy's troops took quiet possession of the points vacated, and really slept within our lines, but the ground was so rough, and the woods so thick, that their generals did not realize till morning what they had gained.

This then was the condition of things at the close of the second day. Lee held Sickles's advance position of the morning, and parts of our rifle pits or barricades between McAllister's Mill and Culp's Hill. Lee modestly says, "These partial successes determined me to continue the assault next day."

The detachments of the Twelfth Corps (Williams's division strengthened by [Brigadier General Henry H.] Lockwood's brigade) that had given efficient help on the left during July 2, and two brigades of Geary's division, which Meade says did not reach the scene of action from having mistaken the road, attempted after night to return to their breastworks on the extreme right of our line; but, as I have intimated, they found them already occupied by Johnson's Confederates. General Slocum was at this time in command of more troops than the Twelfth Corps, and General A. S. Williams had the latter. Williams made arrangements to attack the enemy at daylight and regain the position formerly occupied by the corps.

I slept with others inside of a family lot in the cemetery, beside an iron fence, with a grave mound for a pillow. Being very weary, for want of rest on previous nights, I was not awakened till 5:00 A.M., when I heard quick and sharp musketry firing, with an occasional sound of artillery. It began like the pattering of rain on a flat roof, only louder, and was at first intermittent. Then it would increase in volume till it attained a continuous roar.

Of course I sent at once to the right and to headquarters to ascertain what the firing meant. The reply came shortly, "The Twelfth Corps is regaining its lines." By 7:00 A.M. the battle was fully joined. The Confederates were determined to hold on, and disputed the ground with great obstinacy. But after a lively contest of five hours, Ewell was driven beyond Rock Creek, and the breastworks were reoccupied and held. I went over this ground five years after the battle, and marks of the struggle were still to be observed: the moss on the rocks was discolored in hundreds of places where the bullets had struck; the trees, as cut off, lopped down, or shivered, were still there; stumps and trees were perforated with holes where leaden balls had since been dug out, and remnants of the rough breastworks remained. I did not wonder that General Geary, who was in the thickest of the fight, thought the main battle of Gettysburg must have been fought there.

Stuart's cavalry made a demonstration at this time beyond Ewell. General Gregg's division, by Pleasanton's direction, engaged the enemy in an artillery duel near the Bonnaughtown Road, and checked his advance so as to prevent mischief from that quarter. About this time our bold, sanguine Kilpatrick moved his division of cavalry over beyond the enemy's right, near the Emmitsburg Road, where Pleasanton later in the day directed him "to pitch in with all his might on Longstreet's right." In these combats of Kilpatrick several valuable officers lost their lives; among them was [Brigadier General Elon J.] Farnsworth, in command of a brigade, near the time of Pickett's repulse. Pleasanton speaks of this work on the enemy's right as follows: "I have always been of the opinion that the demonstration of cavalry on our left materially checked the attack of the enemy on July 3; for General Hood, the rebel general, was attempting to turn our flank when he met these two brigades of cavalry, and the officers reported to me that at least two divisions of rebel infantry and a number of batteries were held back, expecting an attack from us on that flank."

The last bloody contest at Gettysburg opened about 1:00 P.M. by a cannonade. Lee's plan of attack was the same as that of the day before, except that Longstreet now had Pickett's division, and Lee added one division and two brigades of A. P. Hill to the attacking column. Also there was a different massing of the artillery. Longstreet is said to have brought together in his front, opposite the low ground north of Little Round Top, fifty-five long-range guns, and Hill massed some sixty more a little farther towards and opposite our center.

The signal gun was fired by the enemy, and from the southwest, west, north, and northeast, his batteries opened, hurling into the cemetery grounds missiles of every description. Shells burst in the air, on the ground, at our right and left and in front, killing men and horses, exploding caissons, overturning tombstones, and smashing fences. The troops hugged their cover, when they had any, as well as they could. One regiment of Steinwehr's was fearfully cut to pieces by a shell. Several officers passing a certain path within a stone's throw of my position were either killed or wounded. The German boy holding our horses under the cover of the Cemetery Hill, on the eastern slope, near a large rock, had his left arm clipped off with a fragment of a shell. Men fell while eating, or while the food was in their hands, and some with cigars in their mouths.

As there seemed to be actually no place of safety, my staff officers sat by me nearly in front of four twelve-pounder Parrott guns that played over our heads, almost every available space being covered with artillery. As the sabots (the pieces of wood that are placed between the cartridges and the elongated shot) would sometimes fly off and hit us when the guns fired, we made large piles of hardbread boxes, and sat in front of them, watching the operations of the enemy with our glasses; thus protected against our own guns, but exposed to the enemy's.

At 2:30 P.M. we ceased to reply. We had ammunition and were not silenced, but we knew that this cannonade preceded an attack, and we thought it possible the enemy would conclude that we had been stopped by their effective shots, and would proceed to the contemplated assault; then we should need batteries in readiness, and plenty of ammunition.

We were right. The firing of the enemy lulled, and I could see, better than the day before, their infantry in line; at least a quarter of a mile of it was exposed to my view, as it started from Oak Ridge, opposite our left. It was like an extensive parade; the flags were flying and the line steadily advancing. As I now know, these were Pickett's and [Brigadier General James J.] Pettigrew's divisions and part of Anderson's.

On, on they came. As soon as they were near enough Osborne, Wainwright, McGilvery, and other artillery chiefs started the fire of their batteries; first with solid shot, making hardly an impression, soon with shells exploding near and over and beyond the advancing line. Now gaps were plainly made, but quickly filled. When nearer, the canister was freely used, and the gaps in the enemy's line grew bigger and harder to close. Soon this array came within short musketry range of our full long line in their front, all concealed by temporary cover, breastworks, stone walls, and trenches.

As if by some simultaneous impulse, the whole line fired and continued to fire rapidly for perhaps five or ten minutes. As the smoke rose I saw no longer any enemy's line. There was running in every direction. Regiments of ours from Steinwehr's position to Round Top were moving into the valley with their flags flying and apparently without much order, taking flags, guns, and prisoners, and bringing them in. General Hancock commanded the majority of the troops on that front of attack, namely, the First, Second, and Third Corps; Newton having the First, Gibbon the Second, and Dirney the Third, during this day's combat. Hancock says:

> The shock of the assault fell on the Second and Third divisions of the Second Corps; and those were the troops, assisted by a small brigade of Vermont troops, together with the artillery of our line, which fired from Round Top to Cemetery Hill at the enemy, all the way as they advanced, whenever they had the opportunity. . . . No doubt there were other troops that fired a little, but these were the troops that really withstood the shock of the assault. . . . I was wounded at the close of the assault, and that ended my operations with the army for that campaign.

General Hancock mentions the fact that General Gibbon was also wounded during the assault and thinks that the absence of two commanders who knew thoroughly the circumstances at such a moment as this was a great detriment; otherwise, advantage would have been taken of the enemy's repulse by our making a decisive advance.

Longstreet's troops on the right of his attacking column attempted to turn our left, as I have previously stated, and such of them as were beyond our infantry were held in check by Kilpatrick's cavalry, while the remainder made nothing more than a demonstration against Big Round Top. But it is represented in the reports that as Ayres's regulars were disputing with the foe the possession of the ground near Little Round Top, General Meade himself made a visit to that point, accompanied by several general officers. He asked what command that was occupying the stone wall. When told it was Crawford's division of Sykes's corps, he directed Sykes to order Crawford to advance and clear the woods in his front.

General Crawford says: "I directed the command at once to advance. Hardly had the men unmasked from the hill before a battery of the enemy, stationed on a ridge beyond the Wheat Field, opened with grape and canister." Crawford's skirmishers pushed forward, and began to fire upon the cannoneers. The battery limbered up and fled. Crawford adjusted his line and charged across the Wheat Field and into the pieces of wood beyond, driving a brigade of Confederate troops, of Hood's division, before him, capturing 260 prisoners, a gun, caisson, 7,000 stand of arms, and all the wounded that had been there for some time uncared for. Crawford in this gallant charge, initiated by General Meade himself, retook the ground that had been lost the day before, and ended the battle.

Our entire loss is reported at 23,186, of whom 2,834 were killed, 13,709 wounded, and 6,643 missing. It is difficult to ascertain Lee's losses. We had in our hands upwards of 7,000 wounded Confederates, the most of whom were so severely injured that they could not accompany the retiring army. The hospital record gives the number 7,262. If we deduct this from the whole number of prisoners, which I believe is understated by General Meade at 13,621, it gives us 6,359 well prisoners. The most moderate estimate that I have seen of the enemy's loss in killed is 5,500. Now, if we place the number who were not so severely wounded as to be left behind, and those who escaped from the field and did not fall into our hands but were lost to the enemy, at 10,000 (probably the number was much greater), we have 29,121 for the aggregate of Lee's losses.

Another classmate of mine besides Weed was killed during this engagement, but on the other side, General Pender. He had a division in Hill's corps. The Richmond *Enquirer* blamed him for too strictly obeying his orders, and not pushing into action sooner. He was of rather small stature, full of quiet humor when a cadet, and quite popular. Our mathematical professor at West Point, Guy Peck, used to say to him, in his inimitable style, as he would ask some queer question during recitation: "Don't be facetious, Mr. Pender."

It was told me at this time that [Brigadier General Lewis A.] Armistead, one of Pickett's brigade commanders, started with his brigade, and moved straight forward till he reached our batteries. He had his hat on the point of his sword, pressing forward with his men diminishing in number till his surrender, when he had less than ten left. He was several times wounded, and died within our lines.

Nothing can ever give an adequate picture of that field of battle during the night of Friday and the two following days. There is an exhilaration in the preparation for conflict, there is spirited excitement during the storm of the heated engagement; but who can bear the sight of the blackened corpses, of the distorted faces of the dying, or of the pale, quiet sufferers who lie for hours and sometimes days for their turn to lose an arm or a leg at the hands of the overtasked surgeon?

I saw, just before leaving the cemetery on July 5, a large plat of ground covered with wounded Confederates, some of whom had been struck on the first and some on the second day's battle, not yet attended to. The army surgeons, and the physicians who now flocked to their aid by every incoming railroad train from the North, were doing their best, yet it took time and unremitting labor to go through the mass. The dirt and blood and pallor of this bruised mass of humanity I can never forget, pleading pathetically for peace and goodwill toward men.

A story is told by Hon. E. P. Smith of an army chaplain (William R. Eastman, Seventy-second New York Regiment), the son of the secretary of the American Tract Society. The incident probably occurred during Friday night. "His horse, plunging during the battle, struck him on the kneepan . . . the pain became almost unendurable. As he lay suffering and thinking, he heard a voice: 'Oh my God!' He thought, Can anybody be *swearing* in such a place a this! He listened again; a prayer began. He tried to draw up his stiffened limb, but he could not rise. He then thought, I can roll; and over and over he rolled, in pain and blood, and by dead bodies till he reached the dying man, and prayed with him. At length one of the line officers came up and said, 'Where's the chaplain? One of the staff officers is dying.' 'Here he is,' cried the sufferer. 'Can you come and see a dying officer?' 'I cannot move.' 'If I detail two men to carry you, can you go?' 'Yes.' They took him gently up and carried him, and that livelong night the two men bore him over the field and laid him beside bleeding, dying men, while he preached Christ, and prayed."

Would that every regiment at Gettysburg had had such a true hero for a chaplain, and that he had been desired and permitted thus to do his lawful work! The annals of the celebrated Christian Commission, of which the noble, indefatigable George H. Stuart was president, show the truly Christian work that was done through this channel at Gettysburg, in the alleviation of human suffering and the lifting up of human hearts into perennial joy. These facts relieve the gloom somewhat.

I have never been able satisfactorily to account for General Meade's apparent reluctance to push in his reserves promptly, after the repulse of the third day. He could have struck Lee's right flank vigorously with 20,000 fresh men before Lee could have recovered from the shock of his defeat, and before Ewell could with safety have brought reinforcements from his left. General Hancock testifies that Meade said, before the fight, that he intended to put the Fifth and Sixth Corps on the enemy's flank. He (Meade) said "he had ordered the movement, but the troops were slow in collecting, and moved so slowly that nothing was done before night," except what I have related of the division of General Crawford, who commanded the Pennsylvania Reserves.

I have thought that the fearful exposure of General Meade's headquarters, where so many of his general and staff officers were wounded, and where so much havoc was occasioned by the enemy's artillery, had so impressed General Meade that he did not at first realize the victory he had won. This he would have done from some other post of observation. Had he thus realized the situation, he would not at such a time have tolerated slowness on the part of any of his lieutenants. Still, it is well for our countrymen to remember that this was the end of three days of extraordinary anxiety and excitement. Officers and men were quite ready to be satisfied with the success which was apparent, for the sake of the much-needed rest, and were fearful of losing, by a too sudden advance, what had already been gained. And doubtless the greater sense of responsibility felt by the commanding general had the effect to increase his natural conservatism.

As soon as the news of Lee's defeat reached General French at Frederick, he reoccupied Harper's Ferry and destroyed Lee's bridge across the Potomac, so that it would seem that his defeated army was almost at our disposal. He withdrew from our front, during the night of July 4, by the way of Fairfield and Cashtown, and pushed on as rapidly as he could to Williamsport.

The circumstances of the retreat and our slow pursuit, the stand of Lee at the river, our council of war, where Wadsworth, Pleasanton, and myself urged an immediate attack, and our failure to attack, are familiar to all who were connected with the army.

When General Meade and his army received the thanks of Congress, Senator [James W.] Grimes, of Iowa, said on the floor of the Senate, "As I have read the history of the campaign, the man who selected the position where the Battle of Gettysburg was fought, and who, indeed, fought it on the first day, was General Howard; and to him the country is indebted as much for the credit of securing that victory as to any other person. I wish, therefore, as a recognition of his merits, to couple his name with that of General Meade in the vote of thanks."

It was so done. And surely I had a right to be glad and proud of this unsought and unexpected testimonial. But as it was intimated to me, after Lee's escape, that it was believed that I was ambitious for the command, for Meade's place, I wrote to Mr. Lincoln a letter which drew from him a characteristic answer. Since neither of these letters have ever been in print, I insert them both at length.

HEADQUARTERS, ELEVENTH CORPS,
ARMY OF THE POTOMAC, NEAR BERLIN
July 18, 1863

TO THE PRESIDENT OF THE UNITED STATES:

SIR—Having noticed in the newspapers certain statements bearing upon the Battle of Gettysburg and subsequent operations which I deem calculated to convey a wrong impression to your mind, I wish to submit a few statements. The successful issue of the Battle of Gettysburg was due mainly to the energetic operations of our present commanding general prior to the engagement, and to the manner in which he handled his troops on the field. The reserves have never before, during this war, been thrown in at just the right moment; in many cases when points were just being carried by the enemy, a regiment or brigade appeared, to stop his progress and hurl him back.

Moreover, I have never seen a more hearty cooperation on the part of the general officers than since General Meade took command. As to not attacking the enemy prior to leaving his stronghold beyond the Antietam, it is by no means certain that the repulse of Gettysburg might not have been turned upon us. At any rate, the commanding general was in favor of an immediate attack; but with the uncertainty of a success, and the strong conviction of our best military minds against the risks, I must say that I think the general acted wisely. As to my request to make a reconnaissance on the fourteenth, which the papers state was refused, the facts are that the general had required me to reconnoiter the evening before, and give my opinion as to the practicability of making a lodgment on the enemy's left; and his answer to my subsequent request was that the movements he had already ordered would subserve [sic] the same purpose. We have, if I may be allowed to say it, a commanding general in whom all the officers with whom I have come in contact express complete confidence.

I have said thus much because of the censure and of the misrepresentations which have grown out of the escape of Lee's army.

Very respectfully your obedient servant,

O. O. HOWARD,
Major General

EXECUTIVE MANSION, WASHINGTON
July 21, 1863

MY DEAR GENERAL HOWARD—

Your letter of the eighteenth is received. I was deeply mortified by the escape of Lee across the Potomac, because the substantial destruction of his army would have ended the war, and because I believed such destruction was perfectly easy; believed that General Meade and his noble army had expended all the skill and toil and blood up to the ripe harvest, and then let the crop go to waste. Perhaps my mortification was heightened because I had always believed—making my belief a hobby, possibly—that the main rebel army, going north of the Potomac, could never return if well attended to, and because I was so greatly flattered in this belief by the operations at Gettysburg. A few days having passed, I am now profoundly grateful for what *was* done, without criticism for what *was not* done. General Meade has my confidence as a brave and skillful officer and a true man.

Yours ever truly,

A. LINCOLN

The main hindrance to our concentrating at Gettysburg as rapidly as Lee was a strategic one. Meade threw forward the left flank of his general line, so that Lee was able to strike it. Had Gettysburg, and not Taneytown or Pipe Clay Creek, been Meade's objective point, his general line on June 30 would have been more nearly parallel to that of Lee. But a kind providence overruled even this mistake to our advantage, inducing as it did undue confidence on the part of General Lee.

For myself, I am content with the work accomplished at Gettysburg, and avoid aiming any bitter criticism whatever at those true-hearted officers and men, in any corps or division of our army, who there acted to the best of their ability.

26

Gettysburg: A Reply to General Howard
Winfield S. Hancock, Major General, U.S.A.

HAVING RECENTLY read the account of the "Campaign and Battle of Gettysburg," by [Major] General O. O. Howard, in the July number of the *Atlantic Monthly*, I feel called upon, in justice to myself as well as in the general interest of truthful history, to correct some of the errors in that article. My purpose is not to attempt a description of that famous battle, which covered three of the most anxious days of our struggle for national perpetuity, but simply to give, from personal knowledge and other evidence, a concise and correct account of those particular operations, on the first day of the engagement, which General Howard has seen fit to present in such a manner as to arrogate to himself services and honors which impartial history must assign to others.

When [Major General John F.] Reynolds fell, the command of our forces at the front devolved on General Howard as the senior officer. The Confederate army was advancing toward the town of Gettysburg. Our troops were sorely pressed, and at best were only adequate to the duty, important in itself, of retarding the enemy's hitherto triumphant progress until our army could be concentrated, on an advantageous line, for a general engagement. After Reynold's death, when [Brigadier General John] Buford said, "There seems to be no directing person," and "We need a controlling spirit," the commanding general of the army sent me forward to the scene of action with an order superseding General Howard. It is only natural that a soldier should feel chagrined at being thus relieved, by a junior, on the field. Acting under that feeling, General Howard wrote [Major General George G.] Meade a letter in which he said: "General Hancock's order to assume command . . . has mortified and will disgrace me." With these few words of explanation it will be easier to account for the special plea in the *Atlantic* article, to shield its author from the lack of confidence apparently implied in the order superseding him in command.

To give a clear understanding of the operations which General Howard has misstated, it is necessary that I should begin with the movements of my own command on the first day of the battle.

On the morning of July 1 [1863], in accordance with orders from General Meade, the Second Corps marched from Uniontown to Taneytown, where it arrived about 11:00 A.M. The troops were immediately massed, and I reported in person at headquarters of the Army of the Potomac, which were then at that point. While there, General Meade informed me of his plan for the coming battle. He stated, in general terms, that his intention was to fight on Pipe Creek; that he had not examined the ground, but, judging from his maps, it was the strongest position he could find; that the engineers were examining and mapping it, and that he had made an order for the movement to occupy that line. General Reynolds was in the advance in command of the left wing of the army, consisting of the First, Third, and Eleventh corps with General Buford's cavalry.

I returned to my corps headquarters, and shortly afterward General Meade received information that Reynolds, with the First and Eleventh corps (Howard's) and Buford's cavalry, was engaged with the enemy at Gettysburg. Subsequently, at about 1:00 P.M., he heard that Reynolds was either killed or mortally wounded. General Meade came immediately to my headquarters and told me to transfer the command of the Second Corps to [Brigadier General John] Gibbon, and proceed at once to the front, and in the event of the truth of the report of General Reynolds's death or disability, to assume command of the corps on that field—the First and Eleventh, and the Third which was at Em-

Major General Winfield S.
Hancock (*Century*)

mitsburg. I reminded him that [Brigadier General John C.] Caldwell, commanding the First Division of the Second Corps, was senior to General Gibbon, and
that General Howard was senior to myself as major general of volunteers. (The
commissions of Generals Howard and Sickles, as major generals of volunteers,
bore the same date as my own, but their commissions as brigadiers antedated
mine, and that determined our relative rank as major generals of volunteers.)

He replied that he had a communication from the secretary of war autho-
rizing him to make such changes as he saw fit in his commanders, and that any
changes made by him would be sustained by the secretary and the president.
Accordingly, written orders directing me to proceed to the front and assume
command of our forces on the field were furnished me on the spot, and read as
follows:

HEADQUARTERS ARMY OF THE POTOMAC
July 1, 1863—1:10 P.M.

Commanding Officer, Second Corps.
    The major general commanding has just been informed that General Reynolds
has been killed, or badly wounded. He directs that you turn over the command of
your corps to General Gibbon, that you proceed to the front, and by virtue of this
order, in case of the truth of General Reynolds's death, you assume command of
the corps there assembled, viz.: the Eleventh, First, and Third at Emmitsburg. If you

think the ground and position there a better one to fight a battle under existing circumstances, you will so advise the general, and he will order all the troops up. You know the general's view, and [Brigadier General Gouverneur K.] Warren, who is fully aware of them, has gone out to see General Reynolds.

LATER—1:15 P.M.

Reynolds has possession of Gettysburg and the enemy are reported as falling back from the front of Gettysburg. Hold your column ready to move.

Very respectfully, your obedient servant,

D. BUTTERFIELD,

Major General and Chief of Staff

It will be observed that, having been informed of General Meade's intentions to form his forces for the coming conflict on the line of Pipe Creek, these orders required me not only to assume command of the troops at the front, but also to examine the ground at Gettysburg, and if I thought the position there a better one to fight a battle under existing circumstances, I was so to advise him and he would order his whole army up.

The moment these instructions were given me I turned over the command of the Second Corps to General Gibbon, and then started with my personal staff at a very rapid pace for the battlefield, which was distant about thirteen miles. On the way we met an ambulance carrying the dead body of General Reynolds. Owing to the peculiar formation of the country, or the direction of the wind at the time, it was not until we had come within a few miles of the field that we heard the roar of the conflict then going on. I hurried to the front, and saw our troops retreating in disorder and confusion from the town, closely followed by the enemy. General Howard was on the crest of Cemetery Hill, apparently endeavoring to stop the retreat of the troops, many of whom were passing over the hill and down the Baltimore Pike. A portion of [Brigadier General Adolph von] Steinwehr's division of Howard's corps, which had been stationed on Cemetery Hill by order of General Reynolds, was still in position there, and had thus far taken no part in the battle.

As soon as I arrived on the field, at about 3:30 P.M., I rode directly to the crest of the hill where General Howard stood, and said to him that I had been sent by General Meade to take command of all the forces present; that I had written orders to that effect with me, and asked him if he wished to read them. He replied that he did not, but acquiesced in my assumption of command. As it was necessary at once to establish order to the confused mass of his troops on Cemetery Hill and the Baltimore Pike, I lost no time in conversation, but at once rode away and bent myself to the pressing task of making such dispositions as would prevent the enemy from seizing that vital point; and from that moment until evening, when I transferred the command to [Major General Henry W.] Slocum, I exercised positive and vigorous command over all the troops present, and General Howard, so far as my knowledge goes, gave no orders save to the troops of his own corps, the Eleventh.

This brings me to the first of the incorrect statements which I wish to notice in General Howard's article. He writes as follows:

> At this moment, 4:30 P.M., according to the time I had gone by all day, General Hancock appeared. (He reports to the Committee on the Conduct of the War that he was at Cemetery Hill by 3:30 P.M.) General Doubleday states that his troops did not commence to give way till 3:45 P.M.; and surely it was half an hour later than this that he was leading his corps into position on Cemetery Ridge, where he and I first met Hancock. General Hancock greeted me in his usual frank and cordial manner, and used these words: "General Meade has sent me to represent him on the field." I replied, "All right, Hancock. This is no time for talking. You take the left of the pike and I will arrange these troops to the right." He said no more, and moved off in his peculiar gallant style to gather scattered brigades and put them into position. I noticed that he sent [Brigadier General James S.] Wadsworth's division, without consulting me, to the right of the Eleventh Corps, to Culp's Hill; but as it was just the thing to do I made no objection—probably would not have made any in any event—but worked away, assisted by my officers, organizing and arranging batteries and infantry along the stone wall and fences toward Gettysburg, and along the northern crest of the ridge. It did not strike me then that Hancock, without troops, was doing more than directing matters as a temporary chief of staff for Meade.

In the next paragraph of his article General Howard states that the order superseding him came "just before night," and on the same page appears his letter of complaint, intercession, and excuse to General Meade, which reads thus:

HEADQUARTERS ELEVENTH CORPS,
JULY 1, 1863

Major General Meade, Commanding Army of the Potomac

GENERAL: General Hancock's order to assume command reached here in writing at 7:00 P.M. At that time, General Slocum being present, having just arrived at this point, I turned over the command to him. This evening I have read an order stating that if General Slocum was present, he would assume command.

I believe I have handled those two corps today from a little past eleven until four o'clock—when General Hancock assisted me in carrying out orders which I had already issued—as well as any of your corps commanders could have done. Had we received reinforcements a little sooner, the first position assumed by General Reynolds and held by General Doubleday till my corps came up might have been maintained; but the position was not a good one because both flanks were exposed, and a heavy force approaching from the north roads rendered it untenable, being already turned, so that I was forced to retire the command to the position now occupied, which I regard as a very strong one.

The above has mortified and will disgrace me. Please inform me frankly if you disapprove my conduct today, that I may know what to do. I am, General,

Very respectfully your obedient servant,

O. O. HOWARD,
Major General Commanding

The points at issue in the foregoing extract and letter are: the time of my arrival on the field, the time that General Howard relinquished command, and the meaning of the orders I bore from General Meade.

With reference to the first—the hour of my arrival—I do not know what time General Howard "had gone by all day," but the time of my arrival on the field was noted by my chief of staff and other staff officers, and I am well assured that I fixed it quite accurately in my testimony before the Committee on the Conduct of the War. As I have already stated, I left Taneytown shortly after receiving my instructions (1:15 P.M.) and rode toward Gettysburg at a very rapid gait.

I arrived at Cemetery Hill by 3:30 P.M., having had over two hours in which to travel thirteen miles—a distance very easily covered in that time. And, deeply impressed as I was with the importance of the duty entrusted to me, with Reynolds killed and the enemy pressing on, it is easy to understand that I wasted no time upon the road. My official report of the battle fixes the time of my arrival on the field at even an earlier hour—and I am certain that I met General Howard not later than 3:30 P.M. In his letter to General Meade, quoted above, General Howard himself admits that I was there making dispositions of troops at 4:00 P.M. There is abundance of direct and circumstantial evidence to show that I was on the field as early as 3:30 P.M. The exact moment of my arrival on the field, however, I do not consider of great importance—the essential matter is, the condition of affairs at the time of my arrival and assuming command, and what subsequently transpired.

With reference to the hour at which General Howard yielded his command, he says in that letter to General Meade, "General Hancock's order to assume command reached here in writing at 7:00 P.M." The apparent intention of that sentence is to convey the impression that he had no knowledge of the existence of that order until that time. But while it may be that 7:00 P.M. of that day was the time he received from the adjutant general of the army his copy of the written order, it was not the first time that day he had the opportunity to see that order, because, as I have stated, I offered to show him the original in writing when I first met him on the field and assumed command at about 3:30 P.M. He then said he did not desire to see it, and immediately yielded the command to me. And further, if he pretended to transfer the command to General Slocum at 7:00 P.M., when, he says, "General Hancock's order to assume command" reached him in writing, he was doing that which he had no authority to do. He knew that he was not vested with the command at that time; he knew that he had yielded it to me, without protest, when I arrived on the field and informed him that I had an order from General Meade to assume command of our forces; he knew that, by virtue of that order and his own relinquishment, I was formally vested with the command, and had actively exercised it from the moment of my arrival until the close of the day, "when," as I stated in my testimony before the Committee on the Conduct of the War, "General Slocum arrived, he being my senior and not included in this order to me, I turned the command over to him."

In fact General Meade instructed me verbally, through General Butterfield, chief of staff, before I left for the front, that I was to do so."

With reference to the meaning of the written order I received from General Meade to assume command of our forces on the field, I must say that in view of the fact that I stated its substance, and offered to hand the order itself to General Howard when I met him on Cemetery Hill, his acquiescence therein, and the fact that, to his personal knowledge, I assumed immediate command of those forces and exercised the same for some hours, it is incomprehensible to me how he can state, as he does in the extract already quoted, that it did not strike him then "that Hancock, without troops, was doing more than directing matters as a temporary chief of staff for Meade." Certainly that statement does not accord with the facts as they existed, and as I have related them. Recurring to this point, General Howard says: "As I understood the matter at the time, General Meade really intended, and Hancock so implied in his conversation with me, that he (Hancock) was to present Meade, as Butterfield, the chief of staff, would have done, on the field of battle."

In the first place, General Meade could not have so intended, for, in his conversation with me at Taneytown, and in his written order directing me to assume command of the forces on the field, it is clear as sunlight that he "really intended," and so directed, that General Howard should be superseded; and in the second place, knowing that General Meade had assigned me to that duty, having his written order in my pocket, it is impossible that I could have conveyed to General Howard the implication above quoted. My action and orders on the field show that I had no such idea of my duties as now occurs to General Howard. When I moved off, as he says, "to gather scattered brigades and put them into position," and when I sent Wadsworth's division to Culp's Hill, without consulting him, he knew I was exercising authority which no staff officer would have dared to personally exercise under any circumstances. At 6:00 P.M. General Meade telegraphed to General Halleck: "General Reynolds was killed this morning, early in the action. I immediately sent up General Hancock to assume command." But to be more explicit; I assert positively that I never implied in any conversation with General Howard that when I arrived at Gettysburg on that occasion I "was to represent Meade as Butterfield, the chief of staff would have done, on the field of battle."

General Howard claims that there was an understanding between us whereby I was to take charge of the troops on the left of the turnpike while he arranged those on the right. He does not disclose the fact that I exercised independent powers, but in his letter to General Meade, already quoted, says, "General Hancock assisted me in carrying out orders I had already issued."

Now, I had no such understanding with General Howard, and I did not so assist him in carrying out orders which he had already issued. The only pretext for his statement of such an understanding is, that as I was about riding away to the left I understood him to indicate to me that he would prefer the right, where his troops were then posted, for his own position, and he said that he would be found there personally; but there was no division of command between General Howard and myself. Indeed, one of the first orders I gave on assuming the command was for the troops of the Eleventh Corps (Howard's) to be pushed forward to the stone walls in the next field to give room for development, and to deter the enemy's advance. And about the same time I addressed a few words to his own troops on the left of the pike with a view to encourage them to hold the position while our lines were forming. I then rode on to place the First Corps further to the left, in order that we should cover the whole of Cemetery Hill, only a small portion of which was occupied when I arrived upon the field. General Doubleday, commanding the First Corps, after the fall of Reynolds, can give positive evidence that I assumed immediate command and directed the disposition of his troops as soon as he fell back to Cemetery Hill. General Buford was also directed by me to hold his command in the flat to the left and front of Cemetery Hill as long as possible in order to give me time to form our line of battle on the hill itself.

I took charge of all our forces on the field, as my orders directed me to do, and, seeing the importance of the point, immediately sent Wadsworth's division and a battery to occupy Culp's Hill. I had no idea of consulting General Howard as to the propriety of that movement, which he states he noticed, but to which he "made no objection." I ordered the movement because, as commander of the troops, and being responsible for what was done on the field, I considered it proper that it should be promptly made.

In regard to the service done by that division and the battery on the occasion referred to, I give the following extract from one of General [Robert E.] Lee's dispatches, as quoted in an article on Gettysburg, by the late Brigadier General C. H. Morgan: "With reference to [Lieutenant General Richard S.] Ewell's advance upon Culp's Hill, Lee's report says: 'General Ewell was therefore instructed to carry the hill occupied by the enemy if he found it practicable, but to avoid a general engagement until the arrival of the other divisions which were ordered to hasten forward. In the meantime the enemy occupied the point which General Ewell designed to seize (Culp's Hill).'"

Before proceeding further I shall quote a dispatch to Major General [Henry] Halleck, general in chief, from General Meade, a portion of the latter's testimony before the Committee on the Conduct of the War, a part of the testimony of General Warren, chief engineer of the Army of the Potomac, before the same committee, with my own verbal dispatch to General Meade, just after my arrival on the field, sent by my aide, all of which are given to show that his intentions and instructions to me, and my understanding of the same, were in perfect accord in regard to the fact that I was sent to Gettysburg to relieve General Howard of the command of all our forces there, and to determine and inform General Meade whether or not, in my opinion, Gettysburg was the place to fight the battle.

General Meade's dispatch to General Halleck is as follows:

HEADQUARTERS ARMY OF THE POTOMAC,
VIA FREDERICK, July 1, 1863—6 P.M.

General Halleck,

The First and Eleventh corps have been engaged all day in front of Gettysburg. The Twelfth, Third, and Fifth have been moving up, and all, I hope, by this time on the field. This leaves only the Sixth, which will move up tonight. General Reynolds was killed this morning early in the action. I immediately sent up General Hancock to assume command. A. P. Hill and Ewell are certainly concentrating, Longstreet's whereabouts I do not know. If he is not up tomorrow, I hope, with the forces I have concentrated, to defeat Hill and Ewell; at any rate I see no other course than to haz-ard a general battle. Circumstances during the night may alter this decision, of which I will try to advise you.

I have telegraphed [Major General Darius] Couch that if he can threaten Ewell's rear from Harrisburg, without endangering himself, to do so.

GEORGE G. MEADE, Major General

At the time the above telegram was written the Second Corps (whose posi-tion General Meade does not give) was on the march to and within a few miles of the battlefield.

General Meade, in his testimony before the Committee on the Conduct of the War, page 330, says:

On July 1, my headquarters being at Taneytown, and having directed the advance of two corps the previous day to Gettysburg, with the intention of occupying that place, about 1:00 P.M. or 2:00 P.M. that day, I should think, I received information that the advance of my army, under Major General Reynolds of the First Corps, on their reaching Gettysburg had encountered the enemy in force, and that the First and Eleventh corps were at that time engaged in a combat with such portions of the enemy as were there.

The moment I received this information I directed Major General Hancock, who was with me at the time, to proceed without delay to the scene of the contest, and having in view this preliminary order which I had issued him as well as to other corps commanders (the order referred to here was the one for the proposed occupation of the general line of Pipe Clay Creek), I directed him to make an examination of the ground in the neighborhood of Gettysburg, and to report to me, without loss of time, the facilities and advantages or disadvantages of that ground for receiving battle. I furthermore instructed him that in case, upon his arrival at Gettysburg—a place which I had never seen in my life, and had no more knowledge of than you have now—he should find the position unsuitable, and the advantages on the side of the enemy, he should examine the ground critically as he went out there, and report to me the nearest position in the immediate neighborhood of Gettysburg where a concentration of the army would be more advantageous than at Gettysburg.

Early in the evening of July 1, I should suppose about six or seven o'clock, I received a report from General Hancock, I think in person, giving me such an account of a position in the neighborhood of Gettysburg which could be occupied by my army, as caused me at once to determine to fight a battle at that point; having reasons to believe, from the account given me of the operations of July 1, that the enemy were concentrating there. Therefore, without any reference to, but entirely ignoring the preliminary order (the order for the general line at Pipe Clay Creek), which was a mere contingent one, and intended only to be executed under certain circumstances which had not occurred, and therefore the order fell to the ground, the army was ordered immediately to concentrate, and that night did concentrate on the field of Gettysburg, where the battle was eventually fought.

The report referred to by General Meade, in the foregoing extract, as having been received by him about 6:00 P.M. or 7:00 P.M., and which he thinks was from me in person, was a message sent by me from the field by my aide de camp, Major W. G. Mitchell. About 4:00 P.M. I sent that officer with a verbal message to General Meade, describing the state of affairs on the field at that time, and informing him that I could hold the position until nightfall, and that I thought that the place to fight our battle. Major Mitchell's report to me states that he arrived at General Meade's headquarters about 6:00 P.M., delivered my message to the general in person, and that General Meade replied, "I shall order up the troops." Other and later messages in writing were sent to General Meade.

General Meade, on page 348 of the report of the Committee on the Conduct of the War, continues:

> About 1:00 P.M. on July 1 I received the sad intelligence of the fall of General Reynolds, and the actual engagement of my troops at Gettysburg. Previous to receiving this intelligence I had had a long consultation with General Hancock, and explained to him fully my views as to my determination to fight in front, if practicable; if not, then to the rear or to the right or the left, as circumstances might require. Without any further reflection than the fact that General Reynolds was the officer upon whom I had relied under my instructions, and anxious to have someone in front who understood and who could carry out my views, I directed General Hancock to proceed to Gettysburg and take command of the troops there, and particularly to advise me of the condition of affairs there, and the practicability of fighting a battle there.

On page 349 he says: "I will call the attention of the committee to another dispatch received by me from General Buford, marked 'I,' and dated 3:20 P.M., and which must have been received by me after General Hancock had gone to the front. I read it to show that my sending General Hancock there was in a measure justified by the opinion of that distinguished officer, General Buford, now deceased."

The dispatch from General Buford, then at Gettysburg, mentioned by General Meade, reads thus:

HEADQUARTERS FIRST CAVALRY DIVISION
July 1, 1863—3:20 P.M.

General Pleasanton.

I am satisfied that Longstreet and Hill have made a junction. A tremendous battle has been raging since 9:30 A.M., with varying success. At the present moment the battle is raging on the road to Cashtown, and in short cannon range of this town; the enemy's line is a semicircle on the height from north to west. General Reynolds was killed early this morning. In my opinion there seems to be no directing person.

JOHN BUFORD,
Brigadier General of Volunteers

We need help now.

BUFORD

I have also in my possession a letter informing me that General Buford earlier in the day, directly after General Reynolds's death, wrote a dispatch to General Meade in the notebook of his signal officer, Lieutenant A. B. Jerome, which throws a still stronger light upon his views of how matters were going upon the field at that time, and the necessity for a "directing person" there. The letter is as follows:

NEW YORK, October 18, 1865

Major General Hancock.

GENERAL HANCOCK: A few moments after the death of Major General Reynolds the late General Buford wrote a short dispatch in my notebook to Major General Meade. If that message could be found, it would add still greater luster to your well-won reputation. The purport of that dispatch was this: "For God's sake, send up Hancock. Everything is going at odds, and we need a controlling spirit." Yet, General, in all the parade that has taken place since, of names and incidents, memories oratorical and poetical, from Edward Everett to General Howard, have you not noticed that your friend, the heroic Buford, has been nearly disregarded? I was a young lieutenant and staff officer, and loved the general, and I am sure you will pardon me if I call your attention to this injustice.

A squadron of the First Cavalry Division entered Gettysburg, driving the few pickets of the enemy before them. The general and staff took quarters in a hotel near the seminary. As signal officer I was sent to look out for a prominent position and watch the movements of the enemy.

As early as 7:00 A.M. I reported their advance, and took my station in the steeple of the Theological Seminary. General Buford came up and looked at them through my glass, and then formed his small cavalry force. The enemy pressed us in overwhelming numbers, and we would have been obliged to retreat, but looking in the direction of Emmitsburg, I called the attention of the general to an army corps advancing, some two miles distant, and shortly distinguished it as the First, on account of their corps flag.

The general held on with as stubborn a front as ever faced an enemy for half an hour unaided, against a whole corps of the rebels, when General Reynolds and a few of his staff rode up on a gallop, and hailed the general, who was with me in the steeple, our lines being but shortly advanced. In a familiar manner General Reynolds asked Buford how things were going, and received the characteristic answer, "Let's go and see."

In less than thirty minutes Reynolds was dead, his corps engaged against fearful odds, and Howard only in sight from my station, while the enemy were advancing on the right flank in numbers as large as our whole front. It was then the dispatch before alluded to was written. I carried a verbal message to General [Howard], asking him to double quick for life and death. When evening came the enemy had possession of the town, but many of the First Division rode round rather than retreat through it.

Excuse me, General, but it will be difficult to find a parallel in history to the resistance made by a small force of cavalry against such odds of infantrymen.

This letter has been suggested by a paragraph in the New York papers, stating that you had just returned from Gettysburg, and giving an account of your remarks, etc. Will you not, General, endeavor to bring General Buford's name more prominently forward.

Everyone knows that he in his day was first and foremost. I have the honor to enclose an extract from his report, which will show, I presume, that I speak from actual experience.

I have the honor to be, General,

Very respectfully, your obedient servant,

A. B. JEROME

As commander of our forces at Gettysburg, just after my arrival on the field, I sent [Brigadier General John W.] Geary's division of the Twelfth Corps, which had just arrived, to occupy the ground to the left, near Round Top, commanding the Gettysburg and Emmitsburg road, as well as the Gettysburg and Taneytown road to our rear. This was a part of General Slocum's corps; and although I had not been directed by General Meade to assume command of other than the First, Third, and Eleventh corps, I felt that in the urgency of the case (not having heard of General Slocum's arrival in person), and seeing that division approaching the field, my duty as commander required me to place it at the point where it would best protect our left and rear. In December 1865, more than two years after the battle, I received from General Geary the subjoined letter, relating to my disposition of his division on the occasion above described:

NEW CUMBERLAND, CUMBERLAND CO., PA.

December 5, 1865

Major General Hancock.

DEAR GENERAL: While in Washington I failed to obtain access to my report on the Battle of Gettysburg.

Upon my return I examined my retained copy, and I find that portion of it relating to the occupancy of the extreme left of the line under your orders is tolerably satisfactory. It is as follows:

"Not finding General Howard (to whom I was ordered to report), I reported to Major General Hancock, commanding Second Corps, who informed me the right could maintain itself, and the immediate need of a division on the left was imperative. By his direction, upon this threatening emergency, I took a position on the extreme left of the line of battle, as the enemy were reported to be attempting to flank it, and cavalry were already skirmishing in front of that position.

This line was held by the First and Third brigades. The Second Brigade, with two pieces of Battery K, Fifth U.S. Artillery, pursuant to orders from Major General Slocum, were detached during the march to take position in reserve on the immediate left of the turnpike, about two miles from Gettysburg.

No serious attack was made upon me at either point, the speedy formation of the line on the left frustrating the enemy's designs, which would, if successful, have proved so disastrous to the entire position. The command rested on their arms during the night."

Most respectfully submitted for your information.

Your devoted friend,

JNO. W. GEARY,

Brevet Major General

[Brigadier] General G. K. Warren, chief engineer of the Army of the Potomac, testified before the Committee on the Conduct of the War:

On the morning of July 1 we got information from General Buford that the enemy were moving down upon him at Gettysburg from the direction of Fairfield. I do not know how orders were issued; but I know that about that time General Reynolds moved forward to the support of General Buford, passing through the town of Gettysburg, and engaged the enemy there. This news came in very early in the morning. General Meade ordered me to go to Gettysburg to obtain information about it, and examine the ground. In consequence of mistaking my road, I went to Emmitsburg, a little out of the way. Almost the same time that I left news came down that General Reynolds had been killed. General Meade then sent up General Hancock, with discretionary orders, I think, to hold that place, if he thought it a good one, or, if not, then to fall back to the line of Pipe Creek, keeping General Meade informed.

General Hancock got there a little before I did. At that time General Reynolds's corps, the First Corps, had fallen back pretty badly damaged, and what there was of the Eleventh Corps (Howard's), that had gone out to help him, was coming back in great confusion. General Howard was then on Cemetery Ridge with one division. General Buford's cavalry was all in line of battle between our position there and the enemy. Our cavalry presented a very handsome front, and I think probably checked the advance of the enemy. General Hancock made a great deal of personal effort to get our troops into position; and I think his personal appearance did a great deal toward restoring order.

I went over the ground with General Hancock, and we came to the conclusion that if that position could be held until night, it would be the best place for the army to fight on if the army was attacked. General Hancock himself reported that to General Meade, who ordered all the army up to that position.

I have now given more than sufficient evidence, of a nature not to be questioned, to prove that I was sent to Gettysburg, when General Reynolds's death or fatal wounds became known to General Meade, to assume command of our forces there; that I did assume such command at once upon my arrival, and held the same, with all its great responsibilities, until nearly dark that evening, when I transferred it to General Slocum about 7:00 P.M.; and that General Howard was well aware of all the facts connected therewith; and I think also that I have fully shown the incorrectness and speciousness of his statement that it did not strike him "that Hancock, without troops, was doing more than directing matters as a temporary chief of staff for Meade."

The inaccuracies in the *Atlantic* article are glaring, and it is important in the interests of truthful history that they should be pointed out; but they are not so certain to convey unreliable information concerning the Battle of Gettysburg as similar errors embraced in his official report, which will be a public record for all time, and which I have seen since my attention was attracted to that article.

In his official report of his operations at Gettysburg to the adjutant general of the Army of the Potomac, dated August 31, 1863, which was made when he had all the facts fresh in his mind, and presumably the order to which he refers before his eyes, General Howard says: "General Hancock came to me about this time (4:30 P.M.), and said General Meade had sent him on learning the state of affairs; that he had given him his instructions while under the impression that he was my senior."

This proves that General Howard contradicts himself. In this report he admits that when I arrived upon the field he knew General Meade had sent me to supersede him, and in his article he says it did not strike him then "that Hancock, without troops, was doing more than directing matters as a temporary chief of staff for Meade." If he stands by his report, he falls by his article; if he stands by his article, he falls by his report. But the fact is that he falls by both, for both statements, as he makes them, are incorrect as well as contradictory. I have shown that his statement in his article that I implied that General Meade had sent me to represent him "as Butterfield, the chief of staff, would have done, on the field of battle," has no foundation in fact.

I now most emphatically assert that I made no such statement to General Howard as that contained in the foregoing extract from his report. General Meade was well aware that General Howard was my senior, as major general of volunteers, before I left Taneytown for the front, because, as I said in the beginning, I called his attention to the fact before I separated from him, and his answer to me was that the secretary of war had authorized him to make such changes as he saw fit in his commanders, and that any such changes made by him would be sustained by the secretary and the president.

Nor was this the only instance during the Gettysburg campaign in which General Meade superseded commanders by juniors in rank. On that very occasion when I was about setting out from Taneytown for Gettysburg, as I have already stated, he placed General Gibbon in command of the Second Corps, although [Brigadier General John C.] Caldwell, commanding the First Division, was senior to Gibbon, who commanded the Second Division of that corps. He also superseded General Doubleday, in command of the First Corps, on the battlefield, by [Major General John] Newton, his junior, as is well known, and as General Doubleday states in his testimony before the Committee on the Conduct of the War; and both Gibbon and Newton held the commands thus assigned them until the close of the battle.

General Howard is careful to forget that I assumed command of the left wing of our army at all on the first day. As bearing on the subject, I attach an extract giving a striking description of these occurrences at the time I took command of the left wing at Gettysburg, written by the late Brigadier General C. H. Morgan, United States Army, then my chief of staff, who accompanied me to the battlefield from Taneytown:

General Hancock on Cemetery Ridge, July 3, 1863 (*Magazine of American History*)

About 3:30 P.M. he (General Hancock) reached Cemetery Hill. Near the cemetery gate he met General Howard, and announced that he had been ordered to assume command. General Howard did not ask to see the order, but remarked that he was pleased that General Hancock had come. No time was spent in conversation, the pressing duty of the moment, it was evident, being to establish order in the confused mass on Cemetery Hill.

Buford's cavalry was holding the front in the most gallant manner; the horse holders in some instances voluntarily giving up their horses to retreating infantrymen and going themselves to the skirmish line. General Buford himself was on Cemetery Hill with General Warren, where General Hancock met them for a moment. Generals Howard, Buford, and Warren all assisted in forming the troops. By threats and persuasion the tide flowing along the Baltimore Turnpike was diverted, and lines of battle formed behind the stone walls on either side of the road. To show the disorder into which General Howard's troops had been thrown by the unequal conflict they had waged during the day, it is only necessary to mention that 1,500 fugitives were collected by the provost guard of the Twelfth Corps some miles in rear of the field.

Wadsworth's division and [Captain James A.] Hall's [Second] Maine Battery were at once sent to the western slope of Culp's Hill, which important position they held during the entire battle. The brave Wadsworth was by no means daunted or weakened by the day's work, but was still full of fight.

The lines having been so established as to deter the enemy from further advance, General Hancock dispatched his senior aide, Major Mitchell, with a verbal message to General Meade, "that General Hancock could hold Cemetery Hill until nightfall, and that he considered Gettysburg the place to fight the coming battle." Major Mitchell left Gettysburg about 4:00 P.M., and arrived at Taneytown before 6:00 P.M. Having delivered his message to General Meade, the latter replied, "I will send up the troops."

The following is the disposition of the troops as made by General Hancock: The First Corps—except Wadsworth's division, which was placed as above—was on the right and left of the Taneytown Road. The Eleventh Corps was on its right, on both sides of the Baltimore Turnpike.

Apparently to make his claim for honors at Gettysburg still stronger, General Howard says: "I know that afterward General Hancock said in substance to Vice President [Hannibal] Hamlin concerning this battle: 'The country will never know how much it owes to your Maine general, Howard.'"

In regard to this I have only to say that I have rarely lost an opportune occasion to speak in exalted terms of the *Maine troops* who served under me during the war; and in conversation with General Howard's friends, I have never felt called upon to dissent from their claims for faithful services rendered by him during the period of his connection with the Army of the Potomac, in which he held high command, and in whose battles he lost an arm, and often risked his life.

I recollect an accidental conversation with the distinguished citizen of Maine referred to, whom I met at St. Paul, Minnesota, and it is probable that the character and services of *Maine troops* were mentioned then, and those of General

Howard as well. I do not now recall the conversation in detail, but I am well satisfied that if the gentleman informed General Howard that I made the remarks concerning him which he quotes in his article in the *Atlantic Monthly*, he either misunderstood my meaning, and applied what I said of the Maine *men* to General Howard personally, or that he had forgotten the exact purport of what I did say.

In concluding this subject General Howard says: "Of course it will make very little difference to posterity whether I served under Hancock unwittingly for two hours and a half or not, but it is of importance to me and mine to explain the facts of the case." Whatever posterity may think of the matter, if it think anything at all, it might just as well have the facts of the case as they transpired. That General Howard served under Hancock unwittingly for two hours and a half on that occasion is certainly not a fact. On the contrary, that I assumed absolute command of our forces at Gettysburg immediately on my arrival, exercising the same for several hours, until I transferred it to General Slocum, and did so with the full knowledge of General Howard, are facts of the case which cannot be refuted.

Had Gettysburg gone against us instead of crowning our arms with a great success, few would come forward to claim the responsibilities and possible censures of those anxious hours. Now, however, a claimant for undue honors steps forward, and I have found it necessary to show in part what his claim is worth. I have heretofore avoided making any publication concerning the operations of my command during our Civil War, and any writings other than my official reports save when called upon to correct mistakes or verify facts for others. For myself I have been quite content to leave the historian of the future to say what was the value of the services I was enabled to render my country during the period of her great extremity. As the terrible contest at Gettysburg contributed in its results probably more than any other battle of the war to the maintenance of the Union in its integrity, so, far above private interests or individual reputations rises the great renown won on that field by the grand old Army of the Potomac.

27

Why Lee Lost at Gettysburg

Henry Heth, Major General, C.S.A.

IT HAS BEEN said that the morale of an army is to numbers as three to one. If this be correct the Army of Northern Virginia was never stronger than on entering Pennsylvania, and I am perfectly satisfied in my mind that this fact entered very largely in determining General [Robert E.] Lee to make the attack on July 3 at Gettysburg, for there was not an officer or soldier in the Army of Northern Virginia, from General Lee to the drummer boy, who did not believe, when we invaded Pennsylvania in 1863, that it was able to drive the Federal army into the Atlantic Ocean. Not that the fighting capacity of its great adversary was underestimated, but possibly the Army of Northern Virginia had an overweening opinion of its own powers.

Just here let us take a retrospective view and consider what the Army of Northern Virginia had in one year accomplished. In 1862, eighty thousand strong, it attacked the Federal army 100,000 strong, and after seven days' fighting drove that army to shelter under its gunboats. Following up this success, after a series of engagements, [Major General John] Pope was driven across the Potomac. Then followed the Battle of Sharpsburg (Antietam), when possibly the fighting capacity of the Army of Northern Virginia never shone brighter. Its numbers reduced by fighting, fatigue, and hard marching to less than 40,000 strong, it gained a drawn battle against an adversary who numbered nearly, if not quite, 100,000 men. Then came Fredericksburg, where, with its ranks recuperated to 78,000, it hurled across the Rappahannock River an adversary who had crossed with 110,000 men. Then follows that most daring and wonderful battle, Chancellorsville, where it again triumphed, 50,000 strong, against its adversary numbering 132,000, compelling him again to seek shelter behind the Rappahannock. After such a series of successes, with such disparity of numbers, is it wonderful that the Army of Northern Virginia and its great leader should have believed it capable of accomplishing anything in the power of an army to accomplish?

The Count of Paris [Louis Philippe Albert d'Orleans, Comte de Paris] says "it was a mistake to invade the Northern states at all," and then give very clearly and concisely his reasons for entertaining this opinion. Some of the reasons substantiating this view I shall answer hereafter. I think from the count's standpoint, and especially looking at the sequel of the invasion of Pennsylvania in 1863, he is correct, and I have no doubt that by far the greater number of historians who may follow him will entertain like opinions. It is, possibly, very natural for myself and other officers who served in the Army of Northern Virginia to permit our judgments to be biased by the opinions of one whom we loved, admired, and trusted in, as much as we did, in any opinion entertained by our greater commander.

I will state General Lee's views in regard to the invasion of Pennsylvania, as given by him to me and to another. A short time before [Lieutenant General Ulysses S.] Grant crossed the Rapidan, in the spring of 1864, General Lee said to me: "If I could do so—unfortunately I cannot—I would again cross the Potomac and invade Pennsylvania. I believe it to be our true policy, notwithstanding the failure of last year. An invasion of the enemy's country breaks up all of his preconceived plans, relieves our country of his presence, and we subsist while there on his resources. The question of food for this army gives me more trouble and uneasiness than anything else combined; the absence of the army from Virginia gives our people an opportunity to collect supplies ahead. The legitimate fruits of a victory, if gained in Pennsylvania, could be more readily reaped than on our own soil. We would have been in a few days' march of Philadelphia, and the occupation of that city would have given us peace."

It is difficult for anyone not connected with the Army of Northern Virginia to realize how straitened we were for supplies of all kinds, especially food. The ration of a general officer was double that of a private, and so meager was that double supply that frequently to appease my hunger I robbed my horse of a handful of corn, which, parched in the fire, served to allay the cravings of nature. What must have been the condition of the private?

After the Battle of Gettysburg the president of the Confederate States, desiring to communicate with General Lee, sent Major Seddon, a brother of the secretary of war, to General Lee's headquarters, when the following conversation took place. General Lee said, "Major Seddon, from what you have observed, are the people as much depressed at the Battle of Gettysburg as the newspapers appear to indicate?"

Upon Major Seddon's reply that he thought they were, General Lee continued:

> To show you how little value is to be attached to popular sentiment in such matters, I beg to call your attention to the popular feeling after the battles of Fredericksburg and Chancellorsville. At Fredericksburg we gained a battle, inflicting very severe loss on the enemy in men and material; our people were greatly elated—I was much depressed. We had really accomplished nothing. We had not gained a foot of ground, and I knew the enemy could easily replace the men he had lost and the loss of material was, if anything, rather beneficial to him, as it gave an opportunity to contractors to make money.
>
> At Chancellorsville we gained another victory; our people were wild with delight—I, on the contrary, was more depressed than after Fredericksburg; our loss was severe, and again we had gained not an inch of ground and the enemy could not be pursued.
>
> After the Battle of Chancellorsville matters stood thus: [Major General Joseph] Hooker in my front, with an army more than 100,000 strong; [Major General John G.] Foster preparing to advance in North Carolina; [Major General John A.] Dix preparing to advance on Richmond from Fortress Monroe; [Brigadier General Daniel] Tyler in the Kanawha Valley preparing to unite with [Brigadier General Robert H.] Milroy, who was in the Valley of Virginia, collecting men and material for an advance on Staunton. To oppose these movements I had 60,000 men. It would have been folly to have divided my army; the armies of the enemy were too far apart for me to attempt to fall upon them in detail. I considered the problem in every possible phase, and to my mind it resolved itself into the choice of one of two things—either to retire on Richmond and stand a siege, which must ultimately have ended in surrender, or to invade Pennsylvania. I chose the latter. Milroy was in my route; I crushed him, and as soon as the First Corps of my army crossed the Potomac orders were issued countermanding the advance of Foster and Dix. As soon as

my Second Corps crossed Hooker loosened his hold, and Old Virginia was freer of Federal troops than she had ever been since the commencement of the war. Had any cavalry been in place my plans would have been very different, and I think the result very different.

In speaking of the fight of July 3 at Gettysburg, General Lee said:

I shall ever believe if General Pender had remained on his horse half an hour longer we would have carried the enemy's position. After Pender died the command of his division devolved on an officer unknown to the division; hence the failure of [Major General George] Pickett's receiving the support of this division. Our loss was heavy at Gettysburg, but in my opinion no greater than it would have been from the series of battles I would have been compelled to fight, had I remained in Virginia.

"General Lee," says Major Seddon, "then rose from his seat, and with an emphatic gesture said, 'and, sir, we did whip them at Gettysburg, and it will be seen for the next six months that army will be as quiet as a sucking dove.'" The Army of the Potomac made no aggressive movement, saving the fiasco known as Mine Run, from July 3, 1863, until General Grant crossed the Rapidan in May 1864, precisely ten months afterward.

Whatever opinions may be entertained in regard to the details of the Battle of Gettysburg, whether if Stonewall Jackson had been in command of [Lieutenant General A. P.] Hill's corps on the first day—July 1—a different result would have been obtained; whether [Lieutenant General James] Longstreet unnecessarily delayed his attack on the second day; whether, as the Count of Paris expresses it, "the way in which the fights of the second day were directed does not show the same coordination which insured the success of the Southern arms at Gaines' Mill and Chancellorsville"; whether the fight on July 2 should have been made at all; whether the attack on the third, known as Pickett's Charge, should have been made, or, whether the failure of this attack was due to the fact that General Lee's orders were shamefully disobeyed, in its not being supported, thereby causing him to lose the battle—or, whether General Lee, seeing the great strength of the enemy's position should have turned it, are opinions upon which men will differ; but they sink into insignificance, in my judgment, when compared with the *great cause,* which brought about the failure of the Pennsylvania campaign of 1863.

The failure to crush the Federal army in Pennsylvania in 1863, in the opinion of almost all of the officers of the Army of Northern Virginia, can be expressed in five words—*the absence of our cavalry.*

Train a giant for an encounter and he can be whipped by a pygmy—if you put out his eyes. The eyes of an army are its cavalry. Before [Lieutenant General Richard S.] Ewell crossed the Potomac, General Lee wrote to [Major General James Ewell Brown] Stuart, commanding the cavalry, in substance, as follows: "Ewell will cross the Potomac on a certain day, at a certain point. Hill will follow Ewell, crossing on a given day at a given point; Longstreet will hold the gaps in the mountains and protect the crossing of these two corps; after Hill has crossed Longstreet will vacate the gaps, and follow Hill; on Longstreet vacating the gaps in the mountains, you will seize them and protect Longstreet's crossing; then follow Longstreet, throw yourself on the right flank of the army, watch the enemy, give me all the information you can gather of his movements, and collect supplies."

General Stuart, probably thinking he could carry out General Lee's orders, and at the same time make a brilliant dash toward and threatening Washington, worked by his right flank, separating himself from Longstreet, crossing the Potomac between the enemy and Washington city—making a swoop toward Washington, then turning west to join the Army of Northern Virginia, when he found the enemy had crossed the Potomac and were between him and that army. This necessitated his riding entirely around the Federal army, and brought him, whether from necessity or not I cannot say, to Carlisle, Pennsylvania. From this point he struck south and joined the Army of Northern Virginia, being late in the evening of July 2.

It is thus evident that so far as deriving any assistance from his cavalry from

Major General James Ewell
Brown Stuart (*Century*)

the [twenty-fourth] of June to the evening of July 2, it might as well have had no existence. Every officer who conversed with General Lee for several days previous to the Battle of Gettysburg, well remembers having heard such expressions as these: "Can you tell me where General Stuart is?" "Where on earth is my cavalry?" "Have you any news of the enemy's movements?" "What is the enemy going to do?" "If the enemy does not find us, we must try and find him, in the absence of our cavalry, as best we can!"

The eyes of the giant were out; he knew not where to strike; a movement in any direction might prove a disastrous blunder.

I have stated above that General Lee's purpose in invading Pennsylvania was to break up the enemy's combinations, to draw him from our own territory, and to subsist his army on that of the enemy's. While this is true, his intention was to strike his enemy the very first available opportunity that offered—believing he could, when such an opportunity offered, crush him. And I here beg leave to differ from the Count of Paris, when referring to the invasion of Pennsylvania, he says: "The proof is that as soon as the latter ([Major General George G.] Meade) began to move, Lee, who had undertaken nothing but a raid on too large a scale, found himself so much endangered that he was obliged to fight an offensive action on the ground where Meade chose to await him." This determination to strike his enemy was not from the position he found himself, consequent upon invasion, but from a leading characteristic of the man. General Lee, not excepting Jackson, was the most aggressive man in his army. This cannot and will not be contradicted, I am satisfied. General Lee, had he seen fit, could have assumed a defensive position, and popular opinion in the northern states would have forced the commander of the Federal army to attack him.

And further, to corroborate the fact that General Lee was not compelled to attack Meade "where Meade chose to wait for him," I will show, I am confident, that the Battle of Gettysburg was the result purely of an accident, for which I am probably, more than anyone else, accountable. Napoleon is said to have remarked that "a dog fight might determine the result of a great battle." Almost as trivial a circumstance determined the Battle of Gettysburg being fought at Gettysburg. It is well known that General Meade had chosen another point as his battlefield. On June 29, 1863, General Lee's army was disposed as follows: Longstreet's corps, at or near Chambersburg; Ewell's corps, which had been pushed east as far as York, had received orders to countermarch and concentrate on Hill's corps, which lay on and at the base of South Mountain; the leading division (Heth's) occupying Cashtown, at the base of the mountain; the cavalry not heard from, probably at or near Carlisle.

Hearing that a supply of shoes was to be obtained in Gettysburg, eight miles distant from Cashtown, and greatly needing shoes for my men, I directed [Brigadier General James J.] Pettigrew to go to Gettysburg and get these supplies.

On June 30, General Pettigrew with his brigade went near Gettysburg, but did not enter the town, returning the same evening to Cashtown, reporting that he had not carried out my orders, as Gettysburg was occupied by the enemy's cavalry, and that some of his officers reported hearing drums beating on the farther side of the town; that under these circumstances he did not deem it advisable to enter Gettysburg. About this time General Hill rode up, and this information was given him. He remarked, "The only force at Gettysburg is cavalry, probably a detachment of observation. I am just from General Lee, and the information he has from his scouts corroborates what I have received from mine—that is, the enemy are still at Middleburg, and have not yet struck their tents." I then said if there is no objection, I will take my division tomorrow and go to Gettysburg and get those shoes! Hill replied, "None in the world."

On July 1 I moved my division from Cashtown in the direction of Gettysburg, reaching the heights, a mile (more or less) from the town, about 9:00 A.M. No opposition had been made and no enemy discovered. While the division was coming up, I placed several batteries in position and shelled the woods to the right and left of the town. No reply was made. Two brigades were then deployed to the right and left of the railroad leading into Gettysburg, and with the railroad as a point of direction were ordered to advance and occupy Gettysburg. These brigades on moving forward soon struck the enemy, which proved to be [Major General John F.] Reynolds's corps of the Federal army, and were driven back with some loss. This was the first intimation that General Lee had that the enemy had moved from the point he supposed him to occupy, possibly thirty miles distant.

My division was then formed in a wooded ravine to the right of the railroad, the ground rising in front and in rear. The enemy was evidently in force in my front. [Brigadier General Robert E.] Rodes, commanding a division of Ewell's corps en route to Cashtown, was following a road running north of Gettysburg. Rodes, hearing the firing at Gettysburg, faced by the left flank and approached the town. He soon became heavily engaged, and seeing this, I sought for and found General Lee. Saying to the general: "Rodes is very heavily engaged, had I not better attack?" General Lee replied: "No; I am not prepared to bring on a general engagement today—Longstreet is not up."

Returning to my division, I soon discovered that the enemy were moving troops from my front and pushing them against Rodes. I reported this fact to General Lee and again requested to be permitted to attack. Permission was given. My division numbered some 7,000 muskets. I found in my front a heavy skirmish line and two lines of battle. My division swept over these without halting. My loss was severe. In twenty-five minutes I lost 270 men killed and wounded. The last I saw or remember of this day's fight was seeing the enemy in my front completely and utterly routed, and my division in hot pursuit. I was then shot and rendered insensible for some hours.

I mention this attack made by my division on July 1, and its result, to show, as far as my observation and opinion goes, that the Count of Paris is wrong in supposing that the Federal troops at Gettysburg fought "ten times better than

Close-Quarters Fighting on the First Day at Gettysburg (*Campfire and Battlefield*)

in Virginia." The Federal troops fought quite as well when we attacked them the second day at Chancellorsville, and better on May 5 in the Wilderness, and again at Spotsylvania Court House. I speak, of course, of my individual experience and observation in these several engagements.

The sentimental idea desired to be conveyed by the Count of Paris in saying that the Federal troops fought ten times better at Gettysburg than in Virginia, is based upon the supposition that troops are much more willing to die when fighting on their own soil and in its defense. Attacking a sentiment is not popular, I know. I am not singular, I am satisfied, in expressing the opinion that not one man in a thousand engaged in battle ever thinks what soil he is fighting on, but would rather be on any other soil than just that soil at that time. For different emotions fill the breasts of men at such times. I confess I am matter-of-fact enough to believe that Leonidas and his celebrated 300 would not have all died at Thermopylae, but for the fact that they were surrounded and could not get away. Human nature was pretty much the same 2,357 years ago as it is today. The part that the uninitiated would have sentiment play in warfare is very sure to be eradicated by actual participation in such a war as raged in this country from 1861 to 1865.

The fight at Gettysburg on July 1 was without order or system, the several divisions attacking the enemy in their front as they arrived on the field—nor do I see how there could have been a systematic plan of battle formed, as I have, I think, clearly shown that we accidentally stumbled into this fight.

Longstreet's attack on July 2 was, in my judgment, made entirely too late in the day. If it could not have been made earlier, it should not have been made at all. I was by General Lee's side when this attack was made, and the thought occurred to me then that if Longstreet was successful night would rob him of the legitimate fruits of a victory. The attack on July 3, known as Pickett's Charge, made by Pickett's division, numbering some 4,500 strong, and my own shattered division, under General Pettigrew, numbering about 4,300 muskets, unsupported, was, as was said of the famous charge of the 600 at Balaklava, "*très grande, mais c'est ne pas la queue.*"

In justice to General Lee it must be here stated that orders were given by him for other troops to attack at the same time, which orders were not obeyed. Who should shoulder this responsibility I know not. I think the fight of July 3 was a mistake; that General Lee should have so maneuvered as to have drawn Meade from his stronghold; and such I believe were General Lee's views after the fight, as he remarked to me, at Orange Court House, during the winter of 1863–1864, when, animadverting upon the criticisms made upon the Gettysburg fight, especially referring to the fight of July 3, "after it is all over, as stupid a fellow as I am can see the mistakes that were made," adding, "I notice, however, my mistakes are never told me until it is too late, and you, and all my officers know that I am always ready and anxious to have their suggestions." The fact is, General Lee believed the Army of Northern Virginia, as it then existed, could accomplish anything.

Had our cavalry been in position, General Lee would have known of Reynolds's approach in the direction of Gettysburg twenty-four hours before this corps reached Gettysburg. General Lee could and probably would, had he known the enemy were in motion, have occupied Gettysburg on June 29 or 30, and rendered his position impregnable.

Had our cavalry been in position, General Lee, if he saw proper, could have permitted Reynolds's corps to have occupied Gettysburg as it did—but instead of this corps being unmasked by two brigades of my division, it would have been attacked by Longstreet, Ewell, and Hill's corps. In that case the fate of this corps no one can doubt; and had the enemy thrown forward reinforcements as he did, they would have been crushed in detail.

Had our cavalry been in position, the chances are that the battle never would have been fought at Gettysburg; but whether there or elsewhere, the battle would have been planned and digested with that consummate skill and boldness which characterized the plans of the greatest of American soldiers in his seven days' fights around Richmond, his discomfiture of Pope, his Chancellorsville fight, and his series of battles in 1864, from the Wilderness to Cold Harbor.

28

Lincoln at Gettysburg
Isaac Wayne MacVeagh, Late Attorney General
of the United States

THE POLITICAL campaign of 1863 in Pennsylvania involving the reelection of Governor [Andrew G.] Curtin was of very great interest and importance to the national administration as well as to the whole country. The year before, by the election of Governor [Horatio] Seymour, New York had arrayed herself substantially against the vigorous prosecution of the war; and Mr. Lincoln, as well as the members of his cabinet and other leading Republicans throughout the country, thought it would be a very great disaster if Pennsylvania, in 1863, followed the example set by the Empire State in 1862, and also arrayed herself against the course the government was pursuing for the suppression of the rebellion.

As I happened to be charged with the conduct of the canvass as chairman of the Republican State Committee of Pennsylvania, I was necessarily thrown into close and constant intercourse with Mr. Lincoln and several members of his cabinet, especially Secretary [of the Treasury Salmon P.] Chase and Secretary [Edwin M.] Stanton, and was in frequent consultation with them in Washington.

One of the consequences of this intimacy with Mr. Lincoln was that he acquired the habit of talking to me with great freedom about the different problems with which he was confronted, and on more than one occasion even did me the honor to ask my advice on matters not relating to Pennsylvania. In this respect he was followed by Secretary Chase and Secretary Stanton. I have always thought that their regard for and confidence in me was probably increased by the fact that when some prominent politicians of Pennsylvania had strongly insisted that the reelection of Governor Curtin could be rendered more secure if, in making large contracts for army supplies, a margin of exceptional profits was allowed, which profits could be utilized in the approaching election, of course I had very promptly and very emphatically disapproved of the suggestion.

It happened that I was in Washington in consultation with Mr. Lincoln and Secretary Stanton a few days before the dedication ceremonies were to take place at Gettysburg, and, as I was leaving, Mr. Lincoln kindly asked me to come back at the appointed time and go with him as a guest on his special train. [Major General Darius] Couch, on whose staff I had been serving during the summer, had kindly offered to take me with him as his aide but Mr. Lincoln said he wished to talk with me about some matters, and could do it more conveniently on the way to Gettysburg and back than at any other time. Of course I at once accepted his invitation with great pleasure.

As I was then in the very active practice of my profession, I did most of my traveling at night, and I told Secretary Stanton, who then expected to go with us, that I would come down on the night train, meeting the party at the station in the morning. He kindly asked me to go from the station to his house, take breakfast with him, and then we could go to the train together. I accordingly went to his house, but at breakfast he told me that an unexpected emergency had arisen in the War Department which would keep him in Washington, but that he had obtained the consent of the president to send his (Stanton's) son with us, and asked me to look after him on the journey. He proved to be a most agreeable and promising young gentleman, and afterward became a very prominent lawyer at the Washington bar; but he died prematurely, to the extreme regret of all his associates and, indeed, of everybody who was privileged to know him.

At the station, in company with Mr. Lincoln, I found Mr. [William H.] Seward and several other members of the cabinet, the French minister, and one or two other diplomats, Mr. [John G.] Nicolay, Mr. [John] Hay, and, as I now remember, the daughter of Mr. [Edward] Everett, who was going to meet her father, who had then been several days in Gettysburg and was to deliver the oration on the occasion.

At Baltimore a baggage-car in which had been provided luncheon was attached to the train, and thither we were invited just as we were leaving Baltimore. As the train had entered a deep cut on the line of the railway, the baggage-car was even darker than usual, and, of course, the noise of the train was greater. Mr. Lincoln, at the head of the table, at once said that the situation reminded him of a friend of his in southern Illinois who, riding over a corduroy road where the logs were not sufficiently close together, was frightened by a thunder-storm. In the glimpses of light afforded by the lightning, his horse would endeavor to reach another log, but too frequently missed it, and fell with his rider. As a result of several such mishaps, the traveler, although not accustomed to prayer, thought that the time had come to address his Maker, and said: "Oh, Lord, if it would suit you equally well, it would suit me much better if I had a little more light and a little less noise." As Mr. Lincoln concluded his story, the train passed into the open, where there was much more light and much less noise. Most stories are old, and this may have been heard before, but I had never heard it, nor have I heard it since.

Whenever the train stopped, Mr. Lincoln was required to address from the rear platform some words to the few people who had gathered to pay their respects to him, but I remember nothing of importance said by him on any of these occasions.

At Gettysburg several of us, including Mr. Seward and Colonel [John W.] Forney, who was then publishing a daily newspaper both in Washington and Philadelphia, were serenaded, and were asked to address the very considerable assemblage that had gathered in front of the hotel. As we had been traveling most of the day through Maryland, it was not surprising that Mr. Seward began his remarks by stating that it was the first time that he had been honored by the request to address his fellow-citizens of a slave State. His mistake was promptly corrected, in excellent humor, by the crowd, and he then gave a very terse and comprehensive statement of the only possible basis on which free government could endure, which was that the minority should loyally accept the result of an election and devote their energies only to appeals to the reason of the voters to transform their party into a majority when the test at the polls was renewed. Colonel Forney utilized the opportunity to explain that while he had supported Senator [Stephen A.] Douglas instead of Mr. Lincoln for the Presidency in 1860, his action had really been of greater assistance to the election of Mr. Lincoln than if he had supported him; for he had induced more than twice as many voters to withhold their votes from Mr. [John C.] Breckenridge than he could possibly have induced to vote directly for Mr. Lincoln. When my turn came, I confined myself to some words of earnest praise of [Major General John F.] Reynolds, who had been killed in the first day's battle, with his back to his birthplace at Lancaster, and his face, as always, to the foe. He had been very kind to me the year before, when he was in command at Chambersburg and I had led a company of mounted men to assist in patrolling the Potomac, and I was glad of the occasion to bear my testimony to his admirable qualities.

Somewhat later there was a reception at the house of Mr. David Wills, where Mr. Lincoln was staying, and he greatly enjoyed my account of the speeches of Mr. Seward and Colonel Forney. Soon afterward he said to me that he was about to withdraw because he wished to consider further the few words he was expected to say the next day, and I recall nothing more until the next morning when we arrived at the platform from which Mr. Everett was to speak. Mr. Hay, who was sitting by my side, said, after the prayer had been made, that he regarded it as the finest invocation ever addressed to an American audience, which was the first of many delightful and illuminating witticisms that I was privileged to hear from him in our long and friendly intercourse, which was terminated only by his death. The address of Mr. Everett seemed to me then, as it has whenever I have read it since, perfectly adapted to the occasion, and exactly what such an oration ought to be. It was of necessity elaborate and long, because it involved a complete justification of the war then in progress and a graphic and detailed description of the battle which had been so recently fought where we were standing; but it was eminently scholarly, and eloquent; the classic product of a mind familiar with the masterpieces of all oratory, ancient and modern; and at its conclusion I think every intelligent person who heard it must have felt most favorably impressed with the manner in which the duty imposed upon Mr. Everett had been discharged.

At its close, as I remember, there was a short interval of music, and then Mr. Lincoln was presented, as only to accept, in a few formal words, the cemetery in behalf of the nation. As he came forward, he seemed to me, and I was sitting near to him, visibly to dominate the scene, and while over his plain and rugged countenance appeared to settle a great melancholy, it was somehow lightened as by a great hope. As he began to speak, I instinctively felt that the occasion was taking on a new grandeur, as of a great moment in history, and then there followed, in slow and very impressive and far-reaching utterance, the words with which the whole world has long been familiar. As each word was spoken, it appeared to me so clearly fraught with a message not only for us of his day, but for the untold generations of men, that before he concluded I found myself possessed by a reverential awe for its complete justification of the great war he was conducting, as if conducted, as in truth it was, in the interest of mankind. Surely at that moment he justified the inspired portraiture of [James Russell] Lowell.

> Great captains, with their guns and drums
> > Disturb our judgment for the hour,
> But at last silence comes;
> > These all are gone, and, standing like a tower,
> Our children shall behold his fame,
> > The kindly earnest, brave, foreseeing man,
> Sagacious, patient, dreading praise, not blame.
> > New birth of our new soil, the first American.

And now comes the only inexplicable part of this statement. I waited until the distinguished guests who wished to do so had spoken to him, and then I said to him with great earnestness, "You have made an immortal address."

To which he quickly replied: "Oh, you must not say that. You must not be extravagant about it."

Others came around him, and I did not see him again until on the train on our way home. He was suffering from a severe headache, and lying down in the drawing-room, with his forehead bathed in cold water. He had sent for me, as I knew, to renew our talk of the day before but I could not restrain myself from saying to him: "You did not like what I said this morning about your address, and I have thought it carefully over, and I can only say that the words you spoke will live with the land's language."

He answered: "You are more extravagant than ever, and you are the only person who has such a misconception of what I said; but I did not send for you to talk about my address, but about more important matters."

I had told him on the way from Washington that I should be obliged to leave him at Hanover Junction on the return journey to keep a professional engagement of importance; and it was probably that reason that he sent for me so soon after leaving Gettysburg. We then discussed at some length the matter he wished to talk over, and I shortly afterward left the train and returned to Philadelphia.

I looked at the next day's newspapers with some eagerness, and was greatly surprised to find no such adequate recognition as I thought due his address; and yet I could not persuade myself that I had really exaggerated its true character.

A few evenings afterward I was entertained at dinner at the Union League, and at the table were two very accomplished orators, Mr. Morton McMichael and Mr. Daniel Dougherty, whose charming gifts of speech old Philadelphians still remember. Mr. Dougherty asked me to tell about Mr. Lincoln at Gettysburg, and I then gave substantially the same account I have now written. I find it impossible to suppose that I am influenced in these recollections by the subsequent acclaim of the greatness of the address, for on many subsequent social occasions both Mr. McMichael and Mr. Dougherty asked me to gratify the gentlemen present by repeating the impression that Mr. Lincoln's address had made upon me.

Perhaps I should feel more unwilling to tell the story which seems to place me almost alone in a category of appreciation of those immortal words, but I was supported by Mr. Everett; for when on the platform I offered him my most sincere and hearty congratulations on his noble oration, he said: "You are very kind, but Mr. Lincoln perhaps said more to the purpose in his brief speech than I in my long one."

That, however, was the only expression that I heard from anybody at the time to indicate that the address had made any profound impression; and I feel that I owe the readers of *Century* the assurance that nothing but the continued entreaty of my good friend, its editor in chief, could have induced me to relate occurrences which seem to rebound to my credit and to that of Mr. Everett, as being comparatively alone in anticipating in this matter the consenting verdict of history.

PART 7

The Western Theatre in 1863

29

A Winter at Vicksburg

Dabney H. Maury, Major General, C.S.A.

A RECENTLY published article about Vicksburg revives some of my recollections of the defense of that place in the years 1862 and 1863. This article is to record my memories of those interesting experiences from the autumn of 1862 to the time of the passage of Admiral [David D.] Porter's fleet by the batteries, April 17, 1863. I fully comprehend it is necessary to review certain movements of the troops taking part in the campaign.

It will be remembered that [Major General Earl] Van Dorn, with the Army of the West, attacked [Major General William S.] Rosecrans in Corinth on October 3 and 4, 1862, and after flattering successes during the fighting on the third was repulsed on the fourth with very heavy losses. We had to fight again at Davis' Bridge over the Hatchie, on the fifth, to effect the safe retreat of our train and army. But with an unexplained inertness, our beaten and disorganized army was permitted to remain undisturbed in its encampment about Holly Springs for more than one month, during which time we were refitting and recruiting our forces, until they were brought up again to the point of efficiency which they were in when we had marched against the Federal army of [Major General Ulysses S.] Grant at Iuka six weeks before.

Van Dorn's defeat at Corinth caused great anxiety through the Confederacy, and especially in the state of Mississippi, which seemed to be threatened with immediate and permanent occupation by the enemy. The president of the Confederacy in response to it determined to relieve Van Dorn from the chief command of the Department of the Mississippi.

[Major] General John Pemberton was promoted to the rank of lieutenant general and superseded Van Dorn as department commander, but Van Dorn was kept in immediate command of the forces in the field. The Army of the West, under [Major] General Sterling Price, was encamped about Lampkin's Pond, near Holly Springs, when Pemberton arrived in October to review the troops.

Major General Dabney H.
Maury (*Century*)

By that time we had refitted and recruited our forces and repaired our morale
as well, so that General Pemberton was very much surprised to find the little
corps, so lately torn to pieces, again in fine array and excellent drill and discipline. He expressed this to General Price in very strong terms, saying: "General, I was prepared to find your command an armed mob; I assure you I have seen
no troops in the Army of [Northern] Virginia that can surpass those in soldierly bearing and precision of movements." The old man gracefully replied: "But
General, I am not entitled to any of the credit for it; my division commanders
have brought these troops to this condition."

And Pemberton was right as to those Missouri troops; I doubt if any infantry in the world could surpass them in any quality of soldiers. I have heard officers familiar with all of our armies say the same. When I first met them, nearly a
year before they, by the influence and exertions of [Brigadier] General Henry
Little, had been brought to a high degree of efficiency, and to the day of his death,
in the moment of victory at Iuka, his close interest and constant vigilance had
not been relaxed, so that the impression then made by him endured to the very
end of their glorious career. They were 8,000 strong at Elk Horn; 'twas there I
first saw them, and for three years after it was my good fortune to have those
troops by me in critical times. Their numbers dwindled continually through-

out the war by losses in battle. They were always in the front and bore the brunt of every battle, and no troops the enemy ever brought against them could stand before them in equal numbers.

In 1864 they came to me at Mobile, and I was very desirous to keep them there and spare them from further wreck and destruction in the desperate field encounters for which they seemed to be reserved. But after a fine review on Government Street, in which they marched 1,600 strong, I was ordered to send them again to the field. I did it most reluctantly on many accounts. About one year after they returned to me 450 strong, and under their favorite, Colonel [Elijah] Gates, they were captured at Blakely, April 9, 1865, at 5:00 P.M.

These Missourians were the last to surrender at Blakely, and they surrendered 450 survivors, and it is safe to say there was a scar for every man of them.

Soon after Pemberton's review of the army Grant moved against us, and we retired from Holly Springs to our position behind the Tallahatchie, which had been by Van Dorn's command made ready for defense. We lay there awaiting Grant's advance for nearly one month, when he came moving with his main army squarely upon us, while he sent a corps to turn our left and rear. Then we moved again and took position behind the Yallobusha at Grenada. During these movements we had several light affairs with the enemy. Our forces numbered about 16,000 men of all arms. Grant's army was reported at 60,000. His plan of operations was well conceived and well executed wherever he was in person. After forcing us down behind the Yallobusha he gave orders to [Major General William T.] Sherman to move from Memphis with a heavy force and carry Vicksburg by a *coup de main*. That place was then guarded by a very inadequate force; it was the barrier of the Mississippi River and held the access to the states west of it open, and so long as Port Hudson below it and Vicksburg could keep the Federal fleets from passing them, the Confederacy on both sides of that river was cooperative.

Grant's plan of operations was masterly. Sherman, having carried Vicksburg, would move at once to Jackson, in our rear, and compel us to make our way out of Mississippi into Alabama, if we could effect our escape. But Van Dorn defeated Grant's advance by a brilliant conception and its daring execution. A few days before Christmas 1862 he confided to me his purpose to take in person the command of 2,000 cavalry of the army, pass behind Grant's army, then close in our front, and destroy his stores at his main depot at Holly Springs. "This," he said, "will compel him to retreat and will save the state of Mississippi." The operation was most brilliantly executed and produced the results predicted. It is not too much to say that no use made of mounted troops during the war was equal in execution and effect to this.

Van Dorn destroyed all the provisions for the campaign. Grant at once had to fall back, and our army was set free to meet Sherman's at Vicksburg. Van Dorn had the capacities of a cavalry commander in an eminent degree—none in either any higher. He was full of resources; he was unconquerable. His courage

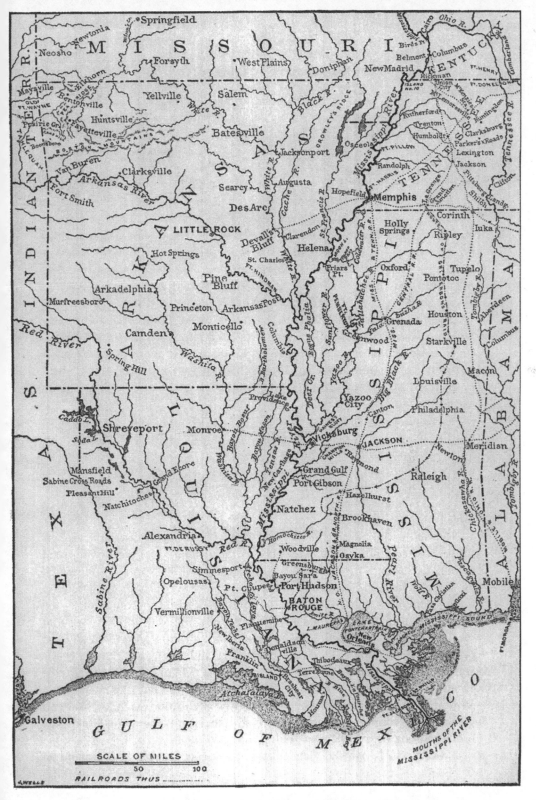

Campaigns of the Mississippi Valley (*Century*)

was of that high order that could not understand a coward. He had no personal animosities, but he had a great scorn for meanness or any unmanliness, and with all, he was as gentle and generous as a woman. Wherever his flag flew, "manly warfare reared his honest front." Any word or act of ungentleness to prisoners or other helpless victims of the cruelty of war was impossible to his manly nature. He was absolutely brave, truthful, honest, and generous.

On Christmas Eve 1862, news reached us at Grenada that Van Dorn had captured the garrison at Holly Spring and destroyed Grant's stores and Grant had, consequently, fallen back from our front. Christmas Day a magnificent citizen of Grenada gave a grand Christmas dinner in honor of General Price and the principal generals and staff officers. It was a sumptuous feast, and we were all attuned to the occasion, and had just begun to improve it when a dispatch was brought to General Price ordering me to move at once to Vicksburg to assist in resisting Sherman, who had made his appearance there with an immense fleet of gunboats and transports, convoying and transporting an army of over 30,000 troops to attempt the capture of the city.

The division moved by rail with three days' rations. I was ordered by Pemberton, strangely, to leave my wagon train. But my quartermaster marched his train across the country and joined us at Vicksburg. We got away from Grenada that night, but were delayed on the way till sundown on December 29, when, as the train rolled into Vicksburg, we heard the distant cannon shots which closed the battle of that day.

Sherman had been sent by Grant to get behind our left and rear and force us to break up our line on the Yallobusha, just as once before Grant had thrown a corps behind our left and rear and forced us to break our line on the Yallobusha. It was strategy always practicable in such a case of disparity of forces. Grant taught it to Sherman, and Sherman used it afterwards during his movements on General [Joseph E.] Johnston's army between Dalton and Atlanta, probably under Grant's directions.

Night closed in, dark and cold and rainy. The troops, however, had their supper cooked for them. We were only 400, the division 5,000 were on the road to join us. As soon as the men had eaten and rested awhile we took up our march for the battlefield on Chickasaw Bayou, about five or six miles above Vicksburg. I don't remember to have ever been out in so dark a night. I could not see my hand against the sky. But I had a guide who knew the road and said he could see it. I gave him the halter of my horse, and told him to lead, and on we went slowly and uncertainly through the driving rain and the thick darkness for several hours, when we found ourselves crossing the field of battle. On every side groans of the wounded and lanterns of the surgeons and hospital men made a weird and fearful picture of the night, suggestive of the morrow for us. Now and then a single cannon shot across the field warned the enemy on Chickasaw Bayou to cease their work upon their pontoon bridge.

I was met by [Brigadier] General Stephen D. Lee, who was in command on the field, and had all the troops of the Vicksburg garrison, excepting the heavy artillery manning the batteries and one regiment to support them in the city. I said: "Lee, here I am with only 400 of my men, the rest will be along in time; place me where you think best. I don't know where our lines are. I don't know where the enemy is. I don't know where I am. I rank you, but just do with me as you please; I will be responsible for all the failures if any occur, and you shall have all the glory. I know you are going to win." This common sense and frank statement seemed to please Lee and put us both at our ease at once, so far as we could be, at 2:00 A.M., with the rain falling cold and fast, and the darkness over the face of the earth and a critical battle impending as soon as there would be light enough to fight by.

Sherman says in his narrative he had 33,000 men when he attacked us at Chickasaw Bayou. Lee's force of infantry was just 2,300 men and eight guns (two batteries) when he repulsed Sherman. He was by that repulse finally and conclusively defeated. From that moment his whole movements were to secure a safe retreat for his army. His loss was 1,929 men: 191 killed, 982 wounded, and 750 missing (United States Surgeon General's Office). S. D. Lee's loss was 36 killed and 78 wounded. He captured on this field 332 prisoners and four stands of colors. Two hundred dead bodies were counted. S. D. Lee had permitted the infirmary corps of the enemy to carry off many of their wounded immediately

Brigadier General Stephen D. Lee (*Century*)

after the battle. He also ordered his infirmary corps to succor them, but they were fired upon while bearing off the Federal wounded. There was not a Federal armed soldier across the bayou when the infirmary corps was fired on. Many of the Federal wounded had to lie on the field till after dark, when eighty of their number were moved into and treated at our field hospitals.

The morning (December 30) broke chill and gloomy, and revealed to us Sherman's army formed as if for defense, beyond the bayou. As the field of battle was clearly in our possession, parties were sent out to bury the Federal dead, 200 of whom lay close to our lines. Sherman's pickets fired upon these parties, as they had done upon our infirmary corps bearing off his wounded, and the bodies lay swelling and festering in the rains and sun in sight of both armies.

All during the next day Sherman's line of battle stood inactive in the woods beyond the bayou, and my division was coming up as fast as our overtaxed railroad transportation could bear them. [Major General Carter L.] Stevenson too

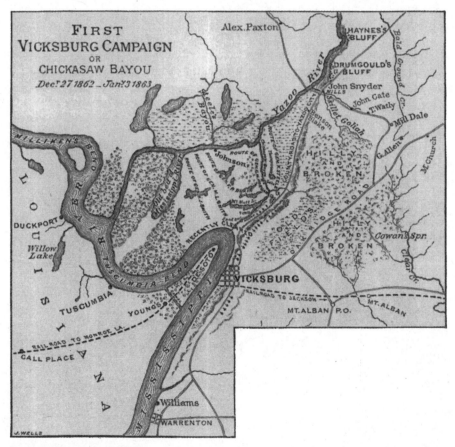

First Vicksburg Campaign (Chickasaw Bayou) (*Century*)

arrived, and his division, 10,000 strong, coming from Tennessee, began to rein-force us. And still Sherman made no sign till the third day. Towards midday a flag of truce came from his army asking permission to bury his dead. The letter was signed by [Brigadier] General George Morgan of Ohio, a very manly fel-low whom I had known at West Point. S. D. Lee was instructed to reply to him and to grant four hours' truce. By that time the rains and the heat had made the dead disgusting to sight and to scent. They lay unpleasantly close to us.

All of Stevenson's division being now up, we were prepared to assume the offensive with about 17,000 men. But during that night Sherman disappeared, reembarking his large army upon his transports, and when the fog lifted up in the morning there was no line of battle in our front and only the smoke of the retreating steamers could be seen above the tree tops as they were passing down the Yazoo. Lee was directed to take five or six regiments and push rapidly across the bayou. He soon drew up near the bank of the river, where the gunboats, with grape and canister from their heavy guns, acted as a rear guard, for none of Sherman's infantry were visible and all soon disappeared.

And thus were Grant's able combined movements defeated by the daring soldiership of Van Dorn, by the skill and cool generalship of Stephen D. Lee, aided by the steady rifles of his brave brigade, which on that occasion achieved the most signal victory of the war. Mississippi was free from invasion and the Confederate flags still waved along the great river.

No man ever had so fine an opportunity given him as Sherman had on this occasion, and his generalship is certainly open to criticism. He arrived with his fleet of transports in the Yazoo River on Christmas Day. The river had been for several days previously patrolled by Federal gunboats as high up as Haynes' Bluff. At this point was a battery of only three or four heavy guns. This was also the point at which the bluffs, or high hills, running from Vicksburg met the river. A dirt road ran along the foot of these hills to Vicksburg, thirteen miles distant, and from this road to the Yazoo River the average distance was only about two and one half miles. Chickasaw Bayou is half way between Vicksburg and Haynes' Bluff, running back from the road, perpendicularly to the Yazoo. From this bayou towards Vicksburg, Willow Bayou runs parallel to the dirt road to its in-tersection with the Mississippi River, near Vicksburg, and only from one-quar-ter to one-half mile from the road. Willow Bayou was dry at its intersection with Chickasaw Bayou, also at a point three miles from Vicksburg and near the Mis-sissippi River, and at no point was it more than thirty yards across. From Chick-asaw Bayou towards Haynes' Bluff, for about four miles, was a swamp. Two miles short of the bluff was good ground almost to the Yazoo River.

When Sherman arrived in the Yazoo, Christmas Day, Vicksburg was defend-ed by an infantry force of about 3,500 men and the artillery manning the heavy guns. There was at Haynes' Bluff a few heavy guns and about a regiment of in-fantry and several light batteries. The first reinforcements to arrive were brought by myself, excepting, perhaps, one regiment. General S. D. Lee, with less than

3,000 men, marched out of Vicksburg to defend the line from Vicksburg to Haynes' Bluff (thirteen miles), facing Sherman's fleet and army on the Yazoo, and with this force, necessarily weakened by pickets along that entire distance, he concentrated, and with less than 2,500 men fought and defeated Sherman in the only attempt he made from December 25, 1862, to January 3, 1863, to reach the bluffs from the lowlands adjacent to the river.

In the battle S. D. Lee's center was in front of the dry opening at the intersection of Chickasaw and Willow bayous, and through which it was evident Sherman was preparing to debouch to the attack. The line of battle was along the road at the foot of the hills, with the bluffs behind him, which would have been an insuperable barrier to his escape had disaster overtaken him. In his front was an open cotton field, from a quarter to three-quarters of a mile in width and terminating on Willow Bayou, which ran almost parallel to the dirt road, and hence perpendicularly to Chickasaw Bayou. His wings were better posted than his center and afforded some protection to his troops, whereas his center was only covered by irregularities in the road, amounting to but little shelter.

All the arrangements having been completed on both sides during the morning of December 29, the Federals opened the battle with a furious artillery fire for about an hour, when their columns—from six to ten thousand—about midday moved gallantly forward, crossing Willow and Chickasaw bayous, near their intersection, and as they arose the banks [sic] reformed their lines under the fire of eight guns and moved steadily toward the center of Lee's line of battle. The Confederate infantry reserved their fire until the columns were within easy range and it was then delivered with terrible effect. At the same time two regiments on the left of Lee's line moved forward to the right and fired a volley into the flanks of the Federals. The fire was such that no troops could live under it and they were driven back with great slaughter—many lying down to avoid the fire.

There was no victory during the war more complete than this, when we consider the results, the disparity of the numbers engaged on the two sides, and one where the disparity of losses was so great. Sherman had only to show a force on Chickasaw Bayou to hold Lee's little force there, while he should make his way to the hills between the bayou and Vicksburg, or pass up the Yazoo in his steamers, land his army near Haynes' Bluff, capture that place or avoid it and pass between the battery there and Lee's force (six miles off), marching around him and on the country roads into Vicksburg.

This he could have done almost unopposed. The railroads and the dirt roads were all at his service, and his entrance into that place would have been really unresisted because all of the moveable forces were in the vicinity of Chickasaw Bayou, six miles distant, and held unmovable there. For four or five days this plan was open to him. He failed to do anything until December 29, when he made the only attempt to reach the bluff, then he lost heart altogether and concentrated his whole efforts on effecting a safe retreat. [Brigadier General Francis P.] Blair [Jr.] conducted the assault, and Sherman was never seen in the front that we heard of.

The Attack on Haynes' Bluff (*Life of Sherman*)

Such was the end of this magnificent expedition. The grandeur and magnitude of the conception and equipment is in marked contrast to the impotent conclusion. The delay and hesitancy in making the attack and the one effort to reach the bluffs do not seem sufficient for the expenditure and occasion.

In marked contrast with the lack of enterprise and boldness on the part of Sherman was that of his antagonist, General S. D. Lee, who, like Sherman, was for the first time commanding on a field when all was committed to the hazard of battle. The odds against him were very great, nearly ten to one; still he displayed nerve and, instead of forming his line of battle on the bluffs, he put it at the base of the hills and staked his all to win and succeeded. Had he been attacked at any other point at the same time there would have been no troops to meet it.

After his defeat at Vicksburg Sherman passed up the river and took part in the capture of Arkansas Post by the fleet under Admiral Porter. He was there when Grant came in person to take Vicksburg, and brought Sherman and his army back with him. Meantime Vicksburg had become the object of chief interest to the Western armies. All the available troops of the departments were assembled there, vast lines of defenses were made, occupying all assailable points, from Haynes' Bluff, thirteen miles above Vicksburg, down to Warrenton, eight miles below Vicksburg. The whole line from Vicksburg to Haynes' Bluff was one right wing, garrisoned by about 20,000 infantry and many light batteries under my command. [Brigadier] General Seth Barton was placed in command of the lines from Vicksburg down to Warrenton—our left wing. [Major] General Carter L. Stevenson was in command of the whole army and defenses of Vicksburg, and a very able and devoted officer he was. General Pemberton made his own office and the supply offices at Jackson the headquarters of the department.

Grant assembled this great army over on the flat land in front of Vicksburg, where, with Porter's fleet, he held us for many months on the alert. We bivouacked in line of battle. We had no tents or shelter of any kind for the troops, who lay where they could find the driest or most sheltered spots in their allotted lines. The winter was unusually cold and wet. The victuals and clothing of the soldiers were quite insufficient. For many weeks they suffered more than our forefathers did at Valley Forge. There was no coffee, very little sugar. The ration was corn and fresh beef and some bacon. The cornmeal was furnished by contract with the chief commissary at Jackson and from one small mill in Vicksburg.

By contract all of the fresh beef for the troops was slaughtered in Vicksburg and distributed from there daily along the line of thirty miles. The contractor received the "fifth quarter" and $2.50 for every beef issued, and such beef was never offered to Christians before nor since. The contractor bought many of his cattle in the trans-Mississippi region. They were driven a long way through the scant pasturage of that season and swam across the river below Vicksburg. By the time they reached the shambles they were generally utterly unfit for food, and whole carcasses were for weeks to be found thrown out from the bivouacs because they could not be eaten. This condition of affairs was aggravated by the sight of the fat cattle grazing in the canebrakes about us.

These evils were borne by the men with a fortitude becoming their high character as Southern soldiers. Their field officers soon began to call attention in behalf of the troops to their suffering, saying, at the same time, if this is the best that can be done for us, the men wish you to understand they will continue to endure it, but, if there be any remedy, it is called for quickly.

General Stevenson applied the remedy. He ordered General Barton, General S. D. Lee, and myself to be a board of survey and to inquire into the complaints and their remedy. We met February 22 and made a very careful investigation, and recommended the immediate abrogation of this rascally contract and the supplying of the troops by their brigade commissaries, after which, until the siege began, there was no further cause for complaint. The region about Vicksburg, along the Yazoo and Sunflower and Deer Creek, abounded in all the meat and corn the army needed, and, by means of the steamboats (fourteen river steamers, I believe) which we had about Haynes' Bluff, and by means of the steam and horse mills on every plantation, there was unusual facility for victualing the troops and we never knew why the place was not victualed for a year's defense with good wholesome food.

During the usual flood of that season Sherman and Admiral Porter undertook to conduct a combined force of gunboats and troops (Sherman's corps) through Steele's Bayou into Deer Creek and hoped to get into the Sunflower

River and thence into Yazoo, above Vicksburg. I was ordered to take charge of the operations to defeat them. Colonel Sam Ferguson was in immediate command in that country—Deer Creek—and was a vigilant and able officer. I had reinforced him with [Major H. W.] Bridges's battalion and six guns, just before Porter came through Steele's Bayou from the Mississippi River. He had his gunboats ironclad, so far as rifle balls and small artillery were concerned. Ferguson met them on the Rolling Fork and stopped them and turned them back, and had I been able to give him more troops in time he would have captured the whole fleet. As it was they were happy to escape, which they did by backing down the bayou. It was too narrow to admit of their turning. Sherman came on behind the fleet; he too went back down the creek. I had sent S. D. Lee with a force from Haynes' Bluff to reconnoiter in his rear. His troops were to follow, if practicable, but his retreat was so precipitate we could not catch him. The Deer Creek expedition was Sherman's second failure in these operations.

Not very long after this, in April, I was ordered to go to Greenwood to reinforce [Major General William W.] Loring, who was then disputing the passage of a force stated at 10,000 men, under [Brigadier General Isaac F.] Quinby. They had come down through the Yazoo Pass during high water. They had gunboats. Loring stopped them at Fort Pemberton. He was short of ammunition, and after repulsing the gunboats found that he had only three rounds of cartridges for his best guns. His telegram for more was returned by the chief of ordnance with an admonition that he must make his requisitions according to ordnance regulations.

I was ordered to go to help him with 4,000 men. I found him as full of fight as usual, but more hostile to that intelligent ordnance officer than the enemy. I believe General Loring made some remarks to headquarters at Jackson about these ordnance regulations, and I think the air about Fort Pemberton was blue for awhile. But General Quinby returned soon and my command, after a week or so of good time with the bacon sides and shoulders and hams and good cornmeal in which that country abounded, returned to Vicksburg about the middle of April.

Next day I received orders to go to command the Department of East Tennessee. General Stevenson asked me to remain a day or two, because Grant was making a move. That night my pickets, soon after midnight, began firing. All of my staff were at a ball given by Colonel Watts and Major Carrill, commissioners for exchange of prisoners. All the fashion and beauty of the city were there, and all the officers who were so fortunate as to be invited and who enjoyed such an occasion. Since the "sound of cavalry by night" in Belgium's capital, no such startling call was made as Porter's fleet occasioned that night. All of the young officers (and some of the old) ran off to their commands. The girls fled in panic in their thin robes and slippers along the muddy road to their several nests. It was long past midnight when the thirteen vessels, including the transports, came swinging around the point. Our bonfires promptly lighted up the whole riverfront and every line and every rivet of every ship could be plainly seen as they moved bravely down under the fire of all our batteries. The others got safely by and joined [Admiral David G.] Farragut with the *Hartford* and the *Albatross*.

On April 18 I went to my command in East Tennessee, and have no personal knowledge of subsequent events about Vicksburg. But I have always understood that we lost 32,000 prisoners there, and that Loring carried out with him about 8,000 men during the fighting on Big Black, and I think there is not to be found a reasonable man of military perception who will justify the attempt to hold Vicksburg after the fleets occupied the river between Port Hudson and Vicksburg any more than one can find a soldier who can explain why Sherman, with 38,000 men, did not, while he was occupying S. D. Lee with 6,000 or 8,000, march around him with the other 30,000 and occupy Vicksburg.

Before leaving Grenada for Vicksburg I had met General Joe Johnston. He came with President Davis, who reviewed our army at Grenada and had then been at Vicksburg. He said there had been a great deal of entrenching done there—enough for a great army to occupy, and he thought it would be better, instead of having so many of our troops kept from active field operations, to strongly fortify one point at Vicksburg, garrisoned with 2,000 or 3,000 good troops, keep it well supplied for a siege and use all of the balance of the army in active field operations. I considered this opinion our great strategist amply justified by the result, and have in more recent visits to Vicksburg been much impressed by them. A strong fort might have been made just opposite the point around which Porter's fleet came that night, with an outwork over on the point which would have closed the river effectually and saved the 30,000 men.

That was a fearful summer for the Confederate cause. We lost at Vicksburg 32,000; Port Hudson, 7,000; Arkansas Post, 5,000 prisoners of war, with arms in their hands, besides the loss of 24,000 killed and wounded at Gettysburg, and with them we lost our separate nationality.

30

Defending Port Hudson

P. F. de Gournay, Colonel, C.S.A.

MANY VALUABLE papers have been published of late in the columns of the *Weekly Times* which throw light on incidents of the war of secession and correct errors that had appeared in previous reports. The usefulness of these publications is apparent. History cannot be written while heated passions influence the pen, and it must be left to another generation to furnish the historian who, with cool judgment and unbiased mind, will sift the vast amount of contemporary chaff and extract therefrom the sound grain which is to be handed down to posterity.

But since the Confederate flag was furled, thirteen years have sunk into the abyss of eternity, carrying down with them many of the participants in that eventful struggle; the fierce passions that armed brother against brother are at rest; peace reigns over the land, and testimony is acceptable which is now brought forward—not with a view to reopen old issues and fan the ashes of the burnt-out fires of hatred, but simply as a contribution to history. The only question is the importance of the testimony thus adduced. I do not know that the history of the little Louisiana village, perched upon the high bluffs of the Mississippi and with a handful of defenders, holding at bay, during sixty-one days, a formidable fleet and a powerful army, will throw much light on the causes of our disasters in that eventful year—1863; but I believe that acts of devotion, such as the most exalted patriotism alone can inspire, should be placed on record in order that history may do justice to them and hold them up to future generations as worthy of imitation.

The name of the late Major General [Franklin] Gardner should ever be remembered with admiration for his defense of Port Hudson. That defense was remarkable, not merely for the gallantry displayed—gallantry was too common to be remarkable—but for the spirit that inspired it; the spirit of self-sacrifice before which all minor considerations disappear—the loftiest conception of the word duty.

The relative strength of the two places considered, Port Hudson was looked upon as an outpost of Vicksburg; hence public attention was centered in the latter, whose stupendous fall gave such a shock that there was no interest left to be spent on minor calamities. Historians, after descanting at length upon the events of that memorable Fourth of July, on which date navigation of the Mississippi and the Red [rivers] was surrendered, together with an army of 30,000 men, remark: "Vicksburg having fallen, the surrender of its outpost—Port Hudson—necessarily followed." On the other hand, from the time Port Hudson was first occupied by Confederate troops to the day of the surrender, Federal reports systematically exaggerated the strength of its armament and garrison, thereby adding to the glory of their own arms while detracting from ours. Thus the little "outpost" was overrated by the one and underrated by the other. I cannot resist the temptation to give here an example of these misrepresentations as a preliminary to the history of the siege.

On September 7, 1862, Port Hudson had been occupied about one month by Confederate troops, and the work of fortifying it was progressing slowly. I had arrived a few days before from Richmond with four companies of my Heavy Artillery Battalion. I found two 42-pounders manned by a crew from the ram

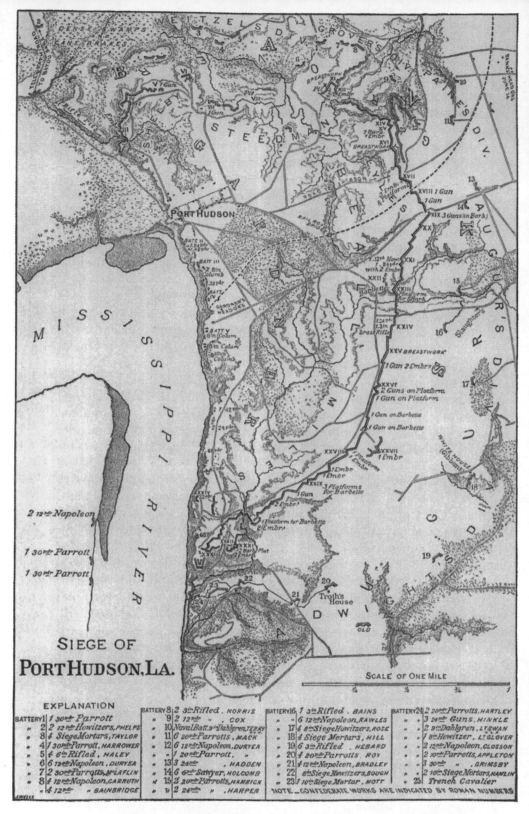

Siege of Port Hudson (*Century*)

Arkansas, which had been destroyed a short time before; one 20-pounder Parrott gun belonging to Miles' Legion and a few pieces of light artillery. There were not heavy guns for my command and we did not receive any until some weeks after this.

On that seventh of September, at 4 o'clock in the morning, the ironclad *Essex,* with the steamboat *Anglo-American* lashed on her starboard side, ran past Port Hudson. Our boys opened fire on her with the ordnance above-described, though it was scarcely probable her heavy plating could be injured by our light projectiles. She fired three or four running shots, killing a horse at his paddock at the upper end of the village.

The whole affair lasted but a few minutes, and half the men on duty in the batteries didn't tumble out of bed quick enough to see the boats. We were, therefore, much elated some time after, when we read in *Harper's Magazine* an article of eighteen columns, headed "The Gunboat *Essex,*" which, the editor said, "forms one of the most striking chapters in the history of our war in the Southwest," and in which our little brush was reported as follows:

Leaving Natchez the *Essex* continued her way down the river, clearing ship for action at 3:30 A.M. on September 7, on her approach to Port Hudson, where an attack from the enemy was expected. At 4:15 A.M. the *Essex,* then about fifteen hundred yards from town, came within range of the enemy's first or upper battery, the guns of which opened on the gallant vessel with tremendous vigor, sending their 10, 9 and 8-inch shot, some of which were from rifled cannon, with great precision. Hard and sharp the *Essex* returned the fire, advancing nearer and nearer to this first fort, when a second, and almost immediately after a third, battery opened on the devoted ship. Battery No. 3, or the central, as it may be termed, is situated in the extreme bend of the river, which there is scarcely in width five hundred yards across, and the channel running close to the bank compelled the *Essex* to run within thirty yards of the battery, at the same time having to receive the cross-fire from the two other batteries. Steadily, however, she went on, the shot crashing against her sides and shell exploding in every direction, and vigorously pouring on the Confederate forts the fire of her forward and aft guns, damaging at every shot, until the second battery was partially destroyed. The firing of the enemy was good—far better than at Vicksburg. A 10, and 9-inch, as also a 32-pounder, solid shot struck the *Essex* within a square of ten feet almost simultaneously, the concussion sending in the 24-inch woodwork as if it were of the most fragile character, shattering the iron and rubber, though no shot penetrated the ship's side. For an hour and twenty-five minutes the brave little craft continued this fight against from thirty-five to forty guns, until her ammunition, previously low, was exhausted. She then dropped down the river slowly out of range and continued under way to New Orleans.

The veracious writer goes on to describe our imposing bluffs and says: "Those bluffs are fortified, having 120-pounder, 68-pounder, and other siege guns in battery, while the plateau at the base and either approach to these heights have heavy batteries with siege guns of similar caliber."

He states further on that the *Essex* was severely damaged in the Port Hudson fight and heavy repairs were found necessary. So it was a very glorious affair for us after all.

We remained in undisturbed possession until the month of March 1863. Those six months were not idly spent, however, for we completed our line of defense. This line, as originally marked out and actually commenced, would have been eight miles in length, requiring, consequently, for its defense a force of at least 30,000 men, with an adequate supply of artillery. A more contracted line was subsequently decided upon, which, while it required a smaller force, possessed natural advantage of ground that made it more formidable. This new line was four-and-a-half-miles long, with a water front of two-and-a-half miles. It would have required 18,000 to 20,000 defenders. General Gardner subsequently held it for sixty-one days against a formidable fleet and an army five times stronger than his own.

When, about March 10, it became known that [Major General Nathaniel P.] Banks was preparing to move from Baton Rouge on Port Hudson, we were fully prepared to receive him. Major General Frank Gardner had assumed command in December, and early in January troops had commenced arriving in considerable numbers. We now had four brigades, commanded respectively by Brigadier Generals W. N. R. Beall, S. B. Maxey, John Gregg, and [Albert] Rust. The river defense, however, was not so strong as might be desired. It consisted of nineteen heavy guns—mostly old-fashioned ordinance—divided into eleven batteries and classified as follows: Two 10-inch Columbiads, one 8-inch Columbiad, one 8-inch howitzer, one rifled 32-pounder, five rifled 24-pounders, one 30-pounder Parrott, one 20-pounder Parrott, two smoothbore 42-pounders, two smoothbore 32-pounders, two smoothbore 24-pounders, and one 12-pounder rifled piece. I can certify to the correctness of this classification. Fifteen of these guns belonged to the left wing of the river defenses, which I commanded, and which necessarily became the point of the attack by the fleet. The other four formed the right wing and were in charge of four companies of the First Regiment Alabama Volunteers, Colonel W. G. Steadman. The total weight of metal that we could hurl upon an attacking fleet was 770 pounds— much less than a single broadside from some of the ships under Admiral [David G.] Farragut.

General Banks left Baton Rouge on the twelfth. On the evening of the fourteenth his vanguard came upon Rust's brigade, which had taken a position in the woods in advance of our line. Some skirmishing took place, and Rust tried to draw the enemy on toward our center, held by General Maxey, when Gregg and Beall would move out on the right and left and attack him on both flanks, as pre-concerted. But General Banks did but nibble at the bait—he would not be caught—and Rust's proposition to make his way around and attack the enemy's rear, driving him up, had to be rejected by General Gardner, for department orders limited his operations to the defense of his lines.

We had expected a vigorous attack and were at a loss to know why General

Banks, like the French king who, with an army of twenty thousand strong, "marched up the hill and marched down the hill again," had taken his whole force from Baton Rouge to our picket line in front of Port Hudson and marched back without even seeing our breastworks. Historians say he came to make a diversion while Farragut's fleet fought its way past the batteries, and returned when he judged that the admiral had accomplished this object. We fail to see what influence his presence in the neighborhood could have on the result of the naval attack, repulsed by the heavy artillery alone, and the only "diversion" we can conceive as resulting from this promenade militaire is that experienced by the Federal army when it thus became an unseen and unseeing audience—a deeply interested one, doubtless—to the demonical concert given on the river front of Port Hudson.

The fleet had come in sight during the afternoon and had taken a position five miles below Port Hudson, in full sight but out of range of our batteries. It presented a very formidable appearance. There were the *Hartford* (flagship), *Monongahela, Richmond, Kineo, Mississippi, Albatross,* and *Genessee,* carrying a total of 110 guns and supported by the ironclad *Essex.* At 10 o'clock that night they steamed quietly up from their anchorage. The darkness was intense, and they got quite near to our lower battery before they were discovered by our signalmen. The mortar boats, which had remained below with the *Essex,* now opened fire, while the rest, with the *Hartford* in the lead, pressed on, discharging broadside after broadside into our old batteries, of which they had obtained the plan through their spies.

They were not aware that we had quite recently moved our guns to much better positions—a very lucky move, for in the abandoned water battery, whose guns had been removed just beyond, our men next morning filled several buckets with the grape and canister poured into it during the first stage of the advance. But the sailors rectified their mistake as fast as our guns were discharged, the flash revealing their true position. Pretty soon the smoke increased the darkness to such a degree that we cold tell the position of the ships only when they fired.

A very different description of this engagement is given in the *History of the Civil War in the United States,* by Samuel M. Schmucker, L.L.D., revised and completed by Dr. L. P. Brockett, which, it is claimed, contains "full, impartial, and graphic" descriptions of the various engagements, etc. It says: "The moon and stars shone brightly in the heavens. The formidable batteries of Port Hudson were visible in the distance." This reads finely as an introduction, but the effect will be spoiled if the truth-seeker will consult the almanac for 1863. The moon, unfortunately, did not shine on the night of March 14. "As the fleet approached Port Hudson five Rebel gunboats were seen nearing the batteries from above, from which a body of troops were landed to strengthen the defenders of the fortifications." What became of these five gunboats? Did they interrupt the *Hartford* after it had passed the batteries, or did the *Hartford* capture them? We are left in the dark concerning their fate. They were doubtless phantom ships which vanished after landing their ghostly crews.

> As the Federals slowly approached the immense works of the Confederates, the latter employed a novel stratagem, which essentially aided their purpose. They kindled an immense bonfire immediately in front of the most formidable of their fortifications, the glaring light of which was refracted from the walls across the stream in such a manner as to expose each vessel clearly to view as it passed. It was this expedient more than any other which enabled the rebel engineers to direct their shot and shell with such destructive accuracy upon the Union vessels.

Bon trevalo! A novel stratagem indeed it must have been, this building a bonfire in front of a battery, thereby placing a wall of flame and smoke between the gunner and the object to be hit. The truth of the matter is that the fire-piles, carefully built at a point on the opposite shore, and which, as proved by experiment, should have illumined the head of the river, were not kindled, the officer in charge being absent from his post when the alarm was given. But for this dereliction of duty not a vessel would have passed Port Hudson.

After firing a few broadsides the *Hartford* and its consort, the *Albatross*, sped on silently in the darkness and passed. The *Mississippi* went as far as the center battery and, being disabled, got aground and was set on fire. The other vessels never reached the fourth battery, and when the burning *Mississippi* lighted up the river they had already drifted down stream and were soon out of range.

Our batteries, with one exception, were placed on high bluffs; the night was remarkably calm as well as dark, and it may be easily understood how the smoke formed a curtain between us and the enemy. While we peered into this dark abyss, striving to catch the dim outline of the black hulls, the crest of our parapets—all the guns were en barbette—lighted up by the burning matches we were compelled to use for want of good friction-primers, were marked out in bold relief, their great elevation being their only protection.

The whole affair, from the firing of the first gun to the firing of the last parting shot sent after the retreating fleet, lasted two hours and ten minutes. It was a bold attempt, gallantly made—it was not a victory. True, Admiral Farragut passed with two vessels, but this would have availed little if the upper fleet had not succeeded in passing the Vicksburg batteries. The advantage, if any, was at all events dearly bought. The fine ship *Mississippi* was entirely destroyed, and every one of the vessels engaged severely crippled. The reported loss was fifty killed, ninety wounded, and forty missing. (The latter, from the burning ship, were nearly all picked up by a detachment of our cavalry and sent over to Port Hudson.) On our side the casualties were two men wounded by fragments of exploding shells. Our guns and works were uninjured, though the ground around was plowed by shells.

During the remainder of the month of March and the whole of that of April, we were let severely alone. Occasionally a gunboat would show itself at the old

Passing the Batteries at Port Hudson (*History of 16th New Hampshire*)

anchorage below, as if to make sure we were still there and Farragut was not coming back, but it never came near enough to exchange a shot. A masterly inactivity prevailed with us while General Banks was operating against [Major General Richard] Taylor. A very effective diversion might have been made with the fine body of troops kept idle in Port Hudson, but General Gardner had no choice in the matter.

Meanwhile the success of the fleet at Vicksburg had made matters critical in the department. At last General Joseph E. Johnston was sent South to see if anything could be done, and soon thereafter the order came to evacuate Port Hudson and send its garrison to the assistance of Vicksburg and Jackson, Mississippi.

The troops commenced moving in obedience to this order, and on May 8 there only remained General Beall's brigade and the heavy artillery. On the seventh the mortar fleet had made its appearance at the old anchorage, and on the eighth it commenced the bombardment which was to be kept up night after night, with an occasional matinee performance, until June 18. On the ninth the commanding officer of the heavy artillery obtained permission to try and dislodge these boats, and four guns—one 24-pounder, one 20-pounder Parrott, one 12-pounder, and one 6-pounder rifled piece—were sent out in the night to attack the six mortar boats, the *Essex, Richmond,* and another gunboat.

The place selected, a high bluff about half way to Prophet's Island, was in good range, but during the day the mortar boats had slightly changed their position and were now found to be nearly concealed by the point of the island. The *Essex* and *Richmond,* however, were in full sight. The fight commenced at 4 o'clock and was kept up until half-past six, with what damage to the fleet we could not say. Our metal was too light to do much injury to the vessels named, and our object—the destruction of the mortar boats—failed, owing to the cause given above. We had one man killed.

The enemy had got wind of the removal of so great a part of our troops, and General Gardner, who had left on the eighth with his staff, had got as far as Clinton, La., when he learned that [Major General Christopher C.] Augur's division was marching from Baton Rouge upon Port Hudson, while General Banks, abandoning his Louisiana campaign, was approaching the Mississippi River by forced marches, with a view to crossing at Bayou Sara.

General Gardner instantly returned to Port Hudson. The object of this order, as before stated, had been the strengthening of the Vicksburg and Jackson garrisons, and to achieve this it might be worth it to give up Port Hudson. But now that Banks was crossing the Mississippi between Port Hudson and Vicksburg the situation was changed. Port Hudson evacuated, his rear was safe from attack and he could move his army where he chose—go to reinforce Grant or march upon Jackson. The question to be considered, then, was this: If we leave Port Hudson we must abandon our heavy guns and material, for which we have no means of transportation; we add about 5,000 men to the garrison of Vicksburg or that of Jackson, but the enemy's strength is similarly increased by the men under Banks, and the lower fleet will immediately steam up the river. On the other hand, if, with our small force, we can keep the fleet at bay and detain Banks's army around our works, will we not be doing a greater service to the cause? The answer could only be affirmative, and it was decided that we should defend Port Hudson at all hazards.

That the place, left to itself, must eventually fall, was a question that did not admit of doubt. General Johnston's whole efforts must tend to compel Grant to raise the siege of Vicksburg. There he had Pemberton's army to cooperate with him. He had ordered Port Hudson to be evacuated; he would probably approve of General Gardner's determination to hold it under the changed circumstances, but it was not likely that he had troops to spare to send to its relief. No officer, aware of the true condition of things in the department could doubt that, once entered on our self-assumed mission, we must rely on ourselves only. This mission was simply to neutralize Banks's army so long as we could. Voluntarily putting ourselves in the clutches of our enemy, we held him where we wanted him, and when the surrender came, after a sixty-one days' tussle, it was brought about by the only contingency we had failed to consider, i.e., the fall of Vicksburg.

The left wing of our river defenses and right wing of our works on the land line had been under continual fire of the fleet since May 8. On the twentieth General Augur's division arrived from Baton Rouge and the fighting commenced. On the twenty-second we were skirmishing with General Banks' advance from Bayou Sara, and on the twenty-fourth Port Hudson was closely invested on all sides. We were completely cut out from the outer world. From this time to July 8 the roar of artillery was incessant, fighting went on day and night on some point or other, and the garrison repulsed two grand attacks and twenty-four charges or attempts to storm our lines.

The swamp extending above Port Hudson and the heavy timber further back of the town, crossed by Sandy Creek, formed a natural defense, and as no attack was anticipated on that side, fortifications had not been erected. The enemy, however, having undertaken to overcome these obstacles by dint of much labor and skillful engineering, it became necessary to defend a new line in the woods from the left of our breastworks to the creek. This arduous task was entrusted to Colonel G. W. Steadman, of the First Alabama Regiment. The troops under his command—the left wing—were the Fifteenth Arkansas, Colonel Ben Johnson; the Tenth Arkansas, Lieutenant Colonel [E. L.] Vaughan; First Alabama, Lieutenant Colonel M. B. Locke; Eighteenth Arkansas, Lieutenant Colonel J. C. Parish; Thirty-ninth Mississippi, Colonel W. B. Shelby; [Lieutenant Colonel J. H.] Wingfield's cavalry [battalion], dismounted; [Captain A. J.] Herod's Battery [B, First Mississippi Light Artillery Regiment]; and a section apiece from [Captain J. L.] Bradford's and [the] Watson Battery from Mississippi.

The center was commanded by Brigadier General Beall, who had the following troops: Twelfth Arkansas, Colonel T. J. Reed; First Arkansas Battalion, Lieutenant Colonel [B.] Jones; Sixteenth Arkansas, Colonel [David] Provence; First

Mississippi, Lieutenant Colonel [A. S.] Hamilton; Twenty-third Arkansas, Colonel O. P. Lyles; and the Forty-ninth Alabama, Major [T. A.] Street, with [Captain George F.] Abbay's Battery [K, 1st Mississippi Light Artillery Regiment] and two sections of the Watson Battery and a section of Bradford's Battery.

The right wing was defended by Colonel [W. R.] Miles, with the following troops: Miles' Legion, Lieutenant Colonel F. B. Brand; Ninth Louisiana Battalion, Captain T. B. R. Chinn; a battalion formed of Texans, belonging to Maxey's brigade, organized under Captain S. A. Whiteside; a detachment from De Bournay's Heavy Artillery, acting as infantry, under command of Major Anderson Merchant; [Captain R. M.] Boone's Battery and two sections of [Captain Calvit] Roberts' Battery.

The left wing of the river defenses was under command of Lieutenant Colonel de Gournay, with his own battalion of heavy artillery, which, although originally from Louisiana, had one company of Virginians, organized in Richmond in 1862, and commanded by Captain W. N. Coffin, and the First Battalion of Tennessee Artillery, consisting of three companies, under the respective commands of Captain J. A. Fisher, Sparkman, and Waller.

The right wing consisted of four batteries in charge of Captain J. F. Whitfield, J. D. Meadows, R. H. Riley, of the First Alabama Infantry, and D. W. Ramsey. Lieutenant Colonel Marshall J. Smith, chief of heavy artillery, superintended the river defenses.

This small force, with its scant supply of ordinance, had to defend a line of works that should have had three times as many men, according to military rule. A single relief was kept at the heavy batteries, and every available man sent to the front. Even then the breastworks were but poorly lined, and had the enemy succeeded in making a general assault on every point simultaneously, it would not have been possible to meet them with successful resistance. But the nature of the ground around our works and the difficulty of bringing up large bodies of troops to time, militated in our favor, and the first attacking column was generally repulsed and routed ere the second could work itself to its point of attack. Our fellows then would double-quick to the right or left, as the case might be, and reinforce the point threatened.

Colonel Steadman, with no other protection than hastily thrown-up rifle pits, held his line in the woods against repeated attacks, fighting day and night and defeating every attempt at a surprise. Colonel Ben Johnson, with 295 officers and men, held a ridge jutting out from our line and which would have been a commanding position for the enemy. With superhuman activity and labor he built a regular parapet and extended a ditch three-quarters of a mile around the line.

Repeated attacks were made upon this stronghold, which had become known as Fort Desperate. The enemy assaulted it on both flanks and on two occasions succeeded so far as to get in the ditch; but the old smoothbore muskets in the hands of the Arkansas boys were as unerring as the best rifle, and they held the fort to the last, though they had 142 killed and wounded.

It was during the first land attack, on May 27, that the famous charge by Negro troops was made, about which so much has been said both in army orders and by the press at large. Two Negro regiments, under Colonel [C. J.] Paine, with a line of white troops behind them, came out of the willow swamp on the extreme left, close to the river, and which was separated by a clearing of six or seven hundred feet from a line of rifle pits we had dug in the bluffs, where two small mountain howitzers were also in position.

The Negroes came up in fine order, charging at a double-quick as soon as they reached clear ground. A party of skirmishers, concealed in a little copse on their flank, fired upon them, while they were saluted in front by a volley from the rifle pits and the simultaneous discharge of the howitzers. The head of the advancing column was shattered by this fire, and the poor fellows, seeing their comrades fall by the dozen, broke and ran to cover among the willows. We had the range of this willow swamp, and two heavy guns on the river side were immediately turned on it and shelled it for several hours, tearing the slender willows into splinters and causing much slaughter. Over 250 blacks were counted, dead or too badly wounded to crawl out of sight. The nearest to our rifle pits were about 20 yards. Foremost among them was a young mulatto named Pierre Caillon, a native of New Orleans, who was recognized by some of our boys who hailed from that city. He wore a captain's uniform, and his commission, signed by [Major General Benjamin F.] Butler, was found in his pocket.

This was the first and last we saw of the Negro troops during the Siege of Port Hudson. How many of the poor wretches perished in the fatal trap into which they had been so unwisely driven I cannot say. In conversation with Federal officers and men after the surrender I have heard the number estimated as high as six hundred.

During that day and that night we were to hear the groans of the wounded that had fallen among the willows, and the dead lay festering in the hot sun, creating a sickening stench. Unable to stand this, some of our boys started the next morning on a blackberrying expedition, as they styled it, with grim pleasantry. They found a wounded Negro among the dead, under the willows. He was suffering excruciating torture from several wounds. They gave the poor fellow some water, placed him on a blanket and carried him to the hospital. He recovered enough strength to whisper a few grateful words, but life was nearly extinct and he died two hours after being admitted into the hospital.

The battle of May 27 was a vigorous assault, made with much confidence. Our left and center were the points threatened. The left was first attacked, and when [Brigadier General Thomas W.] Sherman's brigade advanced, in most imposing order upon our center, it had few defenders, General Beall having just sent the greater part of his forces to reinforce Colonel Steadman. But Colonel Miles, from his post on the right wing, saw the emergency and started half his command at a double-quick to the center. The charge, though gallantly made, was repulsed.

The enemy after this commenced regular siege approaches. They built batteries and mounted heavy guns to command some of our works. Preponderance in the number of guns, weight of metal and character of projectiles, all was vastly in favor of the Federals. Early in the siege these advantages told fearfully against us, many of our guns being dismounted and their crews killed or wounded. At one exposed but important point, defended by a single Blakely gun of small caliber, the Tennessee battalion of artillery, which had been transferred from the river front to the land works, lost successively four officers, Captains Sparkman and Waller and Lieutenants Cook and Bledsoe, besides many men and non-commissioned officers. It was a fatal post. Lieutenants James Lahey and Oswald Tilghman were, I believe, the only officers in command of it who escaped unhurt.

There was not a day or night when fighting was not going on somewhere on the line. On the river front the heavy artillery was in that most trying position—remaining passive under a continual fire. It was seldom they had a chance to return the fire of the enemy's long-range guns. Sometimes, deceived by the prolonged silence of the batteries or by the artifice of using small charges of powder to make the range of our guns appear still shorter than it was, some of the vessels would creep up, but soon drop back, severely punished. But such occasions were rare, and the only military virtue our heavy artillerists could display during the long siege was endurance.

A bombardment may be very effective in a crowded city; it will soon make it a pile of ruins, and the moral effect on the inhabitants must be severe, but in an open place like Port Hudson it avails little. A few buildings were destroyed, the roads were torn up and straggling cattle stampeded more than once; yet, strange to relate, not a battery was injured by the fire of the fleet, and the loss of the heavy artillery by the explosion of shells during sixty-one days' bombardment was fifteen men killed and wounded, though all the batteries were en barbette and the men had not the protection of casemates or covered ways. They had got used to the deafening roar, and it did not hinder them from sleeping. When the signal for the nightly concert of the fleet was given they would say: "Hear those blasted fools! Will they never be tired of playing 'Much Ado about Nothing?'"

On June 10 a bombardment, unprecedented in its fury, was commenced early in the morning by the fleet and the land batteries and kept up without interruption for twenty-four hours. Early on the eleventh an attempt at an assault was made; another on the evening of the twelfth, and still another on the thirteenth, at noon. This last was of short duration, and immediately after General Banks sent a many-worded demand of surrender:

HEADQUARTERS UNITED STATES FORCES,
BEFORE PORT HUDSON, June 13, 1863

SIR: Respect for the usages of war and a desire to avoid unnecessary sacrifice of life impose on me the necessity of formally demanding the surrender of the garrison of Port Hudson.

I am not unconscious in making this demand that the garrison is capable of continuing a vigorous and gallant defense. The events that have transpired during the pending investment exhibit in the commander and the garrison the spirit of constancy and courage that, in a different cause, would be universally regarded as heroism, but I know the extremities to which they are reduced. I have many deserters and prisoners of war. I have captured the couriers of the garrison and have in my possession the secret dispatches of its commander. I have at my command a train of artillery seldom equaled in extent and efficiency, which no ordinarily fortress can successfully resist, and an infantry force of greatly superior numbers and most determined purpose that cannot fail to place Port Hudson in my possession at my will. To push the contest to extremities, however, may place the protection of life beyond the control of the commanders of the respective forces. I desire to avoid unnecessary slaughter and I therefore demand the immediate surrender of the garrison, subject to such conditions only as are imposed by the usages of civilized warfare.

I have the honor to be, sir, very respectfully, your obedient servant,

N. P. BANKS
Major General, Commanding.

Major General Frank Gardner, Confederate States Army,
Commanding at Port Hudson.

General Gardner did not undertake to discuss the good taste of his lengthy epistle. His reply was brief, and gave the one reason why he could not accommodate General Banks:

HEADQUARTERS PORT HUDSON,
June 13, 1863

SIR: Your note of this date has just been handed to me, and in reply I have to state that my duty requires me to defend this position, and therefore I decline to surrender.

I have the honor to be, sir, very respectfully, your obedient servant,

FRANK GARDNER,

Major General commanding C.S. forces
Major General N. P. Banks, commanding United States forces near Port Hudson.

That night the mortar boats kept up an incessant bombardment, and at daybreak, when they ceased, the ships and the land batteries took it up. Pending this terrific fire, which, it was hoped, would demoralize us, the enemy made their second and greatest assault on our lines.

It was a desperate effort. The Federals tried their best and in several instances got as far in as our ditch. Every part of the line was engaged, but, fortunately, the pressure on the three wings was not simultaneous, and the three commanders reinforced each other as circumstances required and repulsed seven distinct charges.

After four hours of desperate efforts to penetrate our lines the enemy gave up the attempt, but large numbers, after the failure of their charges, had taken some sheltered positions near the works, and there was sharp and incessant firing all along the dead-strewn field until night lowered its screen between besiegers and besieged. The loss of the Federals must have been fearful. They acknowledged 1,000 killed and wounded.

On the fifteenth, while his dead lay unburied in front of our lines, General Banks issued the following order to his troops:

> HEADQUARTERS, DEPARTMENT OF THE GULF,
> NINETEENTH ARMY CORPS
> BEFORE PORT HUDSON, June 15, 1863
>
> The commanding general congratulates the troops before Port Hudson upon the steady advance made upon the enemy's works, and is confident of an immediate and triumphant issue of the contest. We are at all points upon the threshold of his fortifications. One more advance and they are ours!
>
> For the last duty that victory imposes, the commanding general summons the bold men of the corps to the organization of a storming column of 1,000 men, to vindicate the flag of the Union and the memory of its defenders who have fallen! Let them come forward!
>
> Officers who lead the column of victory in this last assault may be assured of the just recognition of their services by promotion, and every officer and soldier who shares its perils and its glory shall receive a medal fit to commemorate the first grand success of the campaign of 1863 for the freedom of the Mississippi. His name will be placed in general orders upon the Roll of Honor.
>
> Division commanders will at once report the names of the officers and men who may volunteer for this service, in order that the organization of the column may be completed without delay.
>
> By command of Major General Banks.
>
> RICHARD B. IRWIN, A.A.G.

This eloquent appeal was responded to by the Sixth Michigan and Fourth Wisconsin. The charge was made on the seventeenth, but, checked at the onset, it did not lead to a general assault. The greater portion of the storming part were killed, wounded, or, taken prisoners. After this the spade superseded, but the cannonading did not cease. Should an enterprising speculator undertake to dig in and about Port Hudson he would, doubtless, make a little fortune in shells and balls—even counting them as so much old iron.

One little incident that broke the monotony of those days was the return, on the night of June 26, of Captain R. S. Pryme, of the Fourth Louisiana, bringing dispatches from General Johnston, to whom he had been sent at an earlier period of the siege. He was the only one of several messengers sent out by General Gardner who succeeded in evading the vigilance of the enemy. Going he had floated down the river, passing between the vessels at anchor. On his return he had made his way through a Federal force opposite Port Hudson, and crawling to the water had swam across.

If any hope of relief had existed in the breast of the defenders of Port Hudson that hope was now dispelled. The spirit of resistance, however, was only made stronger by the certainty that we must rely on ourselves only. We had suffered much, but it did not enter any man's mind to end these sufferings by a surrender. As a jolly major, whose foible was an inordinate love for the game of poker, exclaimed: "We have staked too heavily already not to see the game out."

Yet affairs were critical enough with us. Our ammunition had run down so low that we only fired sure shots; in the way of provisions we had an abundance of molasses and some unshelled corn; our mills had been destroyed, and though a temporary one was set up by one of the engineers, who turned to account an old railroad engine, it could barely grind meal enough for the hospital. Hereafter our daily ration must consist of four ears of corn, half a pound of mule meat and molasses ad libitum. Rats were active, and a bird of any kind commanded a premium, and the lucky soldier who caught a good-sized fish—shells exploding in the water sometimes made much havoc among the finny tribe—made a little fortune by retailing it cut up in slices. Coffee was made out of parched corn and burnt molasses, and every substitute for tobacco that could be imagined was tried. The worst feature was the want of medicine. Hardships, exposure and privations began to tell on our brave fellows, and our hospitals were getting full as our ranks grew thinner and thinner every day.

On July 7, about the middle of the day, we heard loud hurrahs in the Federal camp, and the artillery began to thunder in every direction. Every man ran to his post, thinking a general assault was preparing, but the wonder was still increased when it was noticed that these repeated discharges were not followed by the heavy whiz of the balls or the crash of exploding shells. "They are firing blank cartridges!" "It's a salute." "What can it mean?" were the eager questions. The answer came from some Federal soldiers at a point where there was a sort of tacit truce between the men on duty: "We have taken Vicksburg!"

The news was received with disdainful incredulity. Did they think they could discourage us with such bosh. Vicksburg fallen with its fine army and superior resources, while we held on to our little post? What a stupid lie! What Yankee trick was in preparation? A parley ensued between some officers at the point already mentioned, and a Federal colonel gave one of us a copy of the order, just read to his regiment, which announced the stupendous fact. This document was carried to General Gardner.

That night a council of war was held. We had defended Port Hudson at all hazard to help in the defense of Vicksburg; the main post having fallen, the duty of the holders of the outpost was ended. That duty had been discharged faithfully at the cost of much suffering; successfully by dint of superhuman efforts. What could be gained by a protracted defense? We were cut off from the rest of the world; the country around us was in the hands of the Federals. We had scanty rations for another week, and we could certainly hold out that much longer, but then the end would come. No Confederate army could march to our assistance, and our fate could have no influence on the fortune of the Confederacy. The honor of the flag was safe; nothing short of an impossible victory over the vastly superior forces of the enemy could add to the glory of our arms. Would the commanding general be justified in sacrificing more lives with no possible benefit to the cause? It was resolved that we should surrender if we obtained honorable terms.

Before daylight on the eighth General Gardner sent a flag of truce with a communication to General Banks, asking him for confirmation of the news of the fall of Vicksburg. This confirmation, substantiated by copies of the official dispatches, was immediately given, and at nine o'clock General Gardner sent three commissioners to treat of the surrender. The preliminaries occupied the whole day, and it was not until late in the afternoon that the commissioners returned.

An unconditional surrender had been insisted upon, but the terms verbally agreed upon were satisfactory. The enlisted men were to be paroled and set free; the officers would remain prisoners of war, but would be allowed to retain their arms and private property. The ceremony of surrender would take place at seven o'clock on the next morning.

There had been much discussion during the lengthy interview. Our commissioners asked a good deal and defended their pretensions inch by inch, claim-

The Confederates Grounding Arms at Port Hudson
(*History of 16th New Hampshire*)

ing that we could hold the place another month, if not indefinitely, and would hold it unless we got our own terms.

When, late in the afternoon, the terms agreed upon had been referred to General Banks and had received his sanction, Colonel Miles exclaimed: "That's not all! I have another demand to make!" "What!" retorted [Brigadier General Charles P.] Stone, "are you going to raise new difficulties after all the trouble we have had to come to an agreement? What can you want after we have granted you so much?" "Are we not virtually your prisoners, now that we have agreed on the terms?" asked Miles. "Assuredly." "Well, you are bound to feed your prisoners. We are tired of our half rations of mule meat and hard corn, and must have a square meal tonight." General Stone burst out laughing. "That's cool," said he. "Here you have been bragging of your ability to hold out as long as you please, and you confess now that you are out of provisions." "It was my duty to make a strong case, but now I am not pleading, the case is settled and the truth may as well come out," replied Colonel Miles, who was a lawyer and as well known for his hits at the bar as for his indomitable bravery in the field. "By the by, General," he resumed, "I may as well add that we are about as short of ammunition as of provisions." "We shan't send you ammunition," laughed Stone, "but provisions you shall have, and that speedily."

Abundant rations did come that evening, and what was more precious, medicine for the sick. A large number of Federals entered our lines at different points, seeking the particular commands against which they had been pitted, and fraternizing with the men. It is only the coward or the savage who will tram-

Raising the Stars and Stripes at Port Hudson (*History of 16th New Hampshire*)

ple upon the vanquished foe. The marks of respect and sympathy the defenders of Port Hudson received at the hands of Banks' victorious army was as a soothing balm that took away much of the bitterness of defeat.

On the morning of the ninth a little over 3,000 gaunt, weather-beaten men formed into line. The remainder of the devoted garrison were lying sick or wounded in the hospital. Two hundred fifty slept under the green sod of the Port Hudson hills.

General Gardner rode up to the right of the line and awaited the approach of [Brigadier General George L.] Andrews, the officer designated to receive the surrender, who, with his staff, preceded the Federal column. On his riding up General Gardner advanced, and presenting the hilt of his drawn sword to General Andrews, said: "Having thoroughly defended this position as long as I deemed it necessary, I now surrender to you my sword, and with it this post and its garrison."

General Andrews replied: "I return your sword with my compliment to the gallant commander of such gallant men and their conduct that would be heroic for another cause."

This last remark, stereotyped from General Banks' first demand of surrender, was properly rebuked by General Gardner's words, as he returned his sword to the scabbard with an emphatic clang: "This is neither the time nor place to discuss the cause."

31

From Tullahoma to Chattanooga
William S. Rosecrans, Major General, U.S.V.

As A DUTY to the living and to the dead, I avail myself of the opportunity here afforded to perpetuate testimony concerning the strategy and grand tactics of that wonderful campaign of Chattanooga in which the Battle of Chickamauga was an inevitable incident. In the performance of this peculiar duty, it is a relief to know that, thanks to Congress and to Colonel R. N. Scott, the publication of reports, correspondence, orders, and dispatches relating to these events will soon be made in a forthcoming volume of the *Records of Union and Confederate Armies* during the Rebellion, which will enable an interested public to verify the accuracy of what I shall state.

On October 30, 1862, at Bowling Green, Kentucky, I assumed command of the troops which had been under the able and conscientious Major General D. C. Buell. They consisted of the Fourteenth Army Corps and such reenforcements as had joined it previous to the Battle of Perryville, Kentucky, which drove the Confederates advancing under [General Braxton] Bragg, back into Tennessee. There were, in all, 10 divisions of infantry, about 34 batteries of artillery, and some 18 regiments of gallant but untrained cavalry.

The Army of the Cumberland was molded out of these by organizing the infantry and artillery into grand divisions: the right under Major General A[lexander] McD. McCook; the center under Major General Thomas L. Crittenden. The cavalry was under [Major] General D. S. Stanley, an experienced chief. There was a pioneer brigade, formed by details from the infantry, under the chief engineer, and inspector general and topographical staffs for corps, division, and brigade service, detailed from officers of the line. Through interchanges, the muskets of each brigade were reduced to a single caliber; and battleflags were prescribed to distinguish corps, divisions, and brigades on the

Major General William S. Rosecrans (*Century*)

battle-field and march. With this army, under instructions from Major General [Henry] Halleck, general in chief, I was to "go to East Tennessee, driving the rebels out of Middle Tennessee."

It was November [1862]. The autumn rains were near at hand. East Tennessee was 150 miles away, over the Cumberland Mountains. It had been stripped of army supplies by the Confederates. We had not wagons enough to haul supplies to subsist our troops fifty miles from their depots, as had just been demonstrated in their pursuit of Bragg after Perryville. Hence our route to East Tennessee must be by the Nashville and Chattanooga Railroad, or within less than fifty miles right or left of it. The shortest and best line lies through that gap in the mountains where all the drainage of East Tennessee breaks through and flows westward from Chattanooga, forty miles by river, into Middle Tennessee at Bridgeport.

In the first week of November the Army of the Cumberland, therefore, proceeded to Nashville, and as soon as it was prepared to do so, December 26, began its movement for Chattanooga, distant 151 miles. Meanwhile, the enemy under Bragg concentrated at Murfreesboro, thirty-two miles from Nashville. The opposing armies met on the bloody field of Stones River, December 30, and after a contest of four days, in which twenty per cent of its brave officers and men were killed and wounded, the Army of the Cumberland took Murfreesboro.

The Confederates retired to Duck River, thirty-two miles south, and established a formidable entrenched camp across the roads leading southward at Shelbyville. Another entrenched camp was constructed by Bragg eighteen miles south of Shelbyville at Tullahoma, where the McMinnville branch intersects the main Nashville and Chattanooga Railroad.

The winter rains made the country roads impassable for large military operations. Our adversary's cavalry outnumbered ours nearly three to one. It occupied the corn regions of Duck and Elk rivers. Ours had to live in regions exhausted of supplies, to watch and guard the line of the railroad which supplied us—thirty-two miles to Nashville, and the Louisville and Nashville Railway for 185 miles farther northward to Louisville. We lost many of our animals for want of long forage. Meanwhile we hardened our cavalry, drilled our infantry, fortified Nashville and Murfreesboro for secondary depots, and arranged our plans for the coming campaign upon the opening of the roads, which were expected to be good by May 1, 1863.

[Major General Ambrose] Burnside, commanding the Department of the Ohio, including Ohio, Indiana, and Kentucky (with headquarters at Cincinnati), sent his next in command, Major General George L. Hartsuff, to arrange for his forces to cooperate with ours for the relief of East Tennessee, which, though largely Union in sentiment, was now occupied by the enemy under [Lieutenant General Simon B.] Buckner.

I explained to Hartsuff my plan, the details of which I gave to no other. It was, briefly:

First. We must follow the line of the Nashville and Chattanooga Railway.

Second. We must surprise and manoeuvre Bragg out of his entrenched camps by moving our routes east of him to seize the line of the Nashville and Chattanooga Railway in his rear; beat him if he fights, and follow and damage him as best we can, until we see him across the Tennessee.

Third. We must deceive him as to the point of our crossing the Tennessee, and securely establish ourselves on the south side.

Fourth. We must then manoeuvre him out of Chattanooga, get between him and that point, and fight him, if possible, on ground of our own choosing, and if not, upon such ground as we can.

Fifth. Burnside must follow and guard the left flank of our movement, especially when we get into the mountains. His entrance into East Tennessee will lead Bragg's attention to Chattanooga and northward, while we cross below that point.

Sixth. Since our forces in rear of Vicksburg would be endangered by General Joseph E. Johnston, if he should have enough troops, we must not drive Bragg out of Middle Tennessee until it shall be too late for his command to reenforce Johnston's.

Bragg's army is now, apparently, holding this army in check. It is the most important service he can render to his cause. The Confederate authorities know it. They will not order, nor will Bragg venture to send away any substantial detachments. In fact, he is now holding us here by his nose, which he has inserted between our teeth for that purpose. We shall keep our teeth closed on his nose by our attitude, until we are assured that Vicksburg is within three weeks of its fall.

General Hartsuff reported this to Burnside, and advised me of their assent to the plan and to concurrent action.

The news that Vicksburg could not hold out over two or three weeks having reached us, we began our movements to dislodge Bragg from his entrenched camp on June 24, 1863. It rained for seventeen consecutive days. The roads were so bad that it required seventeen days for Crittenden's corps to march seventeen miles. Yet, on the Fourth of July, we had possession of both the enemy's entrenched camps, and by the 7th, Bragg's army was in full retreat over the Cumberland Mountains into Sequatchie Valley, whence he proceeded to Chattanooga, leaving us in full possession of Middle Tennessee and of the damaged Nashville and Chattanooga Railway, with my headquarters at Winchester, fifty miles from our starting-point, Murfreesboro. This movement was accomplished in fifteen days, and with a loss of only 586 killed and wounded.

From Winchester by railroad to Chattanooga is about sixty-nine miles. By wagon roads it is much greater. To pass over this distance, greater than from the Rappahannock to Richmond, Virginia, with intervening obstacles far more formidable, was our greatest work. In front of us were the Cumberland Mountains. Beyond them was the broad Tennessee River, from 400 to 900 yards wide. On the north side of it, beyond the Cumberland Mountains, lay Sequatchie Valley,

3 or 4 miles wide and 60 miles long. East of that, Walden's Ridge, the eastern half of the Southern Appalachian range, cut from the Cumberlands by the flows of the Tennessee above Chattanooga, from 400 to 600 yards wide. On the south of the Tennessee tower cliffs of Sand Mountain, 600 or 700 feet high. Beyond that broad, flat, wooded top is Trenton Valley, 40 or 50 miles long, ascending southerly to the top of the plateau; and east of it the long frowning cliffs of Lookout Mountain, a thousand feet above this valley, stretch northward to the gap at Chattanooga with not a single road of ascent for twenty-six miles, and not another until Valley Head, forty miles southward from Chattanooga.

The task before us was:

First. To convince General Bragg, a wary and experienced officer, that we would cross the Tennessee at some point far above Chattanooga. This required time and serious movements.

Second. Meanwhile, without attracting his attention, to repair the Nashville and Chattanooga Railway to Bridgeport on the Tennessee.

Third. To subsist our troops and accumulate twenty days' rations at Stevenson, without allowing him to get the faintest intimation of our intentions and doings.

Fourth. To construct a large pontoon bridge train, bring it and the Pioneer Brigade forward by rail to the vicinity of Stevenson, wholly concealed from the enemy's knowledge, and have the men trained to lay and take up bridging.

Fifth. Our movement must be delayed until the new corn is fit for horse feed; because when we cross the river and go into the mountains, our trains must carry twenty days' rations and ammunition enough for two great battles. We have not trains to carry anything beyond this, and hence feed for our animals must be obtained from the coming corn crop of the country into which we are going, or our campaign will be a failure.

Sixth. When we cross the Tennessee, we must so move as to endanger Bragg's

Chattanooga and Vicinity (*Century*)

communications by rail and oblige him, for their protection, to fall back far enough to give us time and space to concentrate between him and Chattanooga and, if possible, to choose our own battle-ground; for doubtless he will fight us with all the force he can assemble.

How all this was done we have not space to tell. Nor can we relate how it came to pass that the Army of the Cumberland had to proceed on its perilous mission alone, unaided, unassisted, either by our Army of the Tennessee, unemployed since the surrender of Vicksburg, or by the activity of the Army of the Potomac, which might have kept [General Robert E.] Lee from sending [Lieutenant General James] Longstreet to fight us; or by the Department of the Gulf, which, instead of threatening the enemy's Gulf coast to keep troops from going to Bragg, by a useless expedition to Texas had given bonds, so to speak, not to molest them; or by Burnside's command, which was so far away to the north of us that, in the hour of need, with forty thousand men of all arms, he could do nothing to help us.

I only repeat that we were ordered forward alone, regardless alike of the counsels of commanders, the clamors of the press, the principles of military art and science, and the interests of our country. Of all this the corps commanders of the Army of the Cumberland and myself were well aware. They knew that the secretary of war, without reason or justice, was implacably hostile to me. They knew more. They knew that those great loyal governors, [Andrew G.] Curtin of Pennsylvania, [John A.] Andrew of Massachusetts, and [Richard] Yates of Illinois, offered seven regiments of two-years' veterans, who were willing to reenlist on condition that they should go as mounted infantry to the Army of the Cumberland; that [Major] General Lovell H. Rousseau bore a letter to Secretary [of War Edwin M.] Stanton, explaining how very important would be the services of such a body of men in guarding the long and exposed line of our communications, soon to be lengthened by our advance to Chattanooga; that this line *must* be guarded; that every such mounted man in that move would give us three infantry men at the front. They knew that when the Secretary had read my letter, he rudely said to General Rousseau: "I would rather you would come to ask the command of the Army of the Cumberland than to ask reenforcements for General Rosecrans. He shall not have another damned man."

On August 4, General Halleck telegraphed me: "Your forces must move forward without further delay. You will daily report the movement of each corps till you cross the Tennessee."

On the sixth, after full consideration and consultation with my corps commanders, I replied:

> My arrangements for beginning a continuous movement will be completed, and the execution begun, by Monday next. . . . It is necessary to have our means of crossing the river completed and our supplies provided to cross sixty miles of mountain, and sustain ourselves during the operations of crossing and fighting, before we move.

To obey your order literally would be to put our troops at once into the mountains on narrow and difficult roads destitute of pasture and forage and short of water, where they would not be able to manoeuvre as exigencies may demand, and would certainly cause ultimate delay and probably disaster. If, therefore, the movement which I propose cannot be regarded as obedience to your order, I respectfully request a modification of it, or to be relieved from the command.

The War Department did not think it prudent to relieve me, and therefore gave consent in terms sufficient to convict it of reckless ignorance, or worse.

But we were soldiers. We moved to our work with every energy bent on ensuring its success. On August 10 our movement began. On the fourteenth all our corps were crossing the Cumberlands. It required six or seven days. The movement appeared as if directed toward Knoxville, but it was really to concentrate near Bridgeport and Stevenson. Crittenden crossed the Cumberlands into Sequatchie Valley and made a bivouac many miles long; sent [Brigadier General Horatio] Van Cleve's division with our left wing cavalry to Pikeville; ordered two infantry brigades to cross Walden's Ridge by roads some miles apart, and to bivouac in long lines on its eastern edge, in sight of observers from the opposite side of the river, who would take them for strong advances of heavy columns of troops of all arms. This appearance was confirmed by the boldness of our cavalry and mounted infantry, which descended into the valley of the Tennessee and drove everything across to the enemy's side of the river. The other corps were concealed in the forests north and west of Stevenson.

The pontoon bridge train came down from Nashville by rail on August 24, and the pioneers took it away out of observation, practiced laying and taking up pontoon bridges until the 29th, when they laid a bridge across the Tennessee at Caperton's, ten miles below Bridgeport, in four and a half hours. It was 1,254 feet long, and the work was done at the rate of 4.6 feet per minute.

Meanwhile, to prepare for sustaining our army at Chattanooga, I contracted with great railway bridge-building firms to rebuild the railway bridge at Bridgeport, over 2,700 feet long, in four weeks, and the Running Water Bridge, three spans, 171 feet each, to be done within two weeks thereafter; and ordered Captain [Arthur] Edwards, assistant quartermaster, to have constructed, with all dispatch, five flat-bottomed stern-wheel steamboats of light draft, to run on the Tennessee between Bridgeport and Chattanooga.

Our first bridge was ready, August 29, and the Twentieth Corps was ordered across it to Valley Head, the south end of Trenton Valley, forty miles south of Chattanooga. Thence a road leads down the eastern slopes of Lookout, by Alpine, into Broomtown Valley, whence there are roads toward the Northern Georgia railway line and to Rome. This heavy corps of all arms, so far south of Bragg's position at Chattanooga, made him uneasy. But when [Major General George H.] Thomas, after crossing, moved with his corps up Trenton Valley in the same direction, with all his train, Bragg became still more anxious. Then came Crittenden following Thomas with merely an unostentatious column in observation on the direct road to Chattanooga. This movement portended mischief and it was strong enough to do plenty of it. As a prudent commander, Bragg could not afford to leave us forty miles south of his position, to get quietly down and concentrate between him and Atlanta.

Bragg was reluctant to leave his stronghold Chattanooga, and yet he yielded to his apprehensions. On the eighth he slowly retired southward, giving out rumors that he would go back to Rome or to Atlanta. On September 9 Crittenden's leading division entered Chattanooga. On the afternoon of the same day our cavalry and infantry, from the north side of the river, crossed over into town. The cavalry moved out to see if the enemy had gone. He was beyond Rossville and behind Missionary Ridge, but not far away. To keep up Bragg's apprehensions, McCook was ordered, without exposing his command, to appear advancing. On the twelfth Thomas crossed over Lookout, up Johnson's Pass and down Cooper's, putting his command in snug defensive position at its foot. Crittenden had moved his whole corps into Chattanooga over the road at the north end of Lookout, but was ordered not to push out into danger. On the tenth the story of Bragg's retreat to Atlanta was found to be false, and, behind our cavalry and mounted infantry, Crittenden's infantry moved cautiously out.

By September 12, I found that the enemy was concentrating behind Pigeon Mountain near Lafayette. When Crittenden's reconnaissance in force, of the twelfth and thirteenth, showed the rear of Bragg's retiring columns near the Chickamauga, I instantly ordered him to move westward within supporting distance of Thomas as speedily and secretly as possible. At the same time orders were dispatched to McCook to join Thomas at the foot of Cooper's Gap with the utmost celerity.

Our fate now depended, first upon prompt concentration, and next, on our choosing our own battleground, where our flanks would be protected and where we could have full use of our artillery. Everything indicated that the enemy must soon attack us. Bragg issued his order for it, dated September 16, 1863, in which he says to his command, "You have been amply reenforced." Yes! The Confederate authorities had wisely given Bragg every man they thought it possible to spare, from Virginia, Florida, Georgia, Alabama, and Mississippi. Even the prisoners paroled at Vicksburg contributed to strengthen him.

Our command received none from our authorities, who had abundant force at their disposition. About September 10, aroused by fear of consequences, General Halleck began telegraphing orders for reenforcements, but we were involved in the mountains and beyond reach, and it was entirely too late for any useful results; but it was a confession that support ought to have been ordered at the proper time, and might serve for ulterior operations after our fate was decided.

At last, on September 18, McCook's corps came within reach of the enemy, who was then moving through the gaps in the Pigeon Mountain to attack us. Over the treetops we saw clouds of dust moving toward our left. Bragg wanted to get between us and Chattanooga. We had no time to lose.

The whole Twentieth Corps came down the mountain, and Thomas, with three of his divisions, was ordered to move north-eastward through the forests by lines of fires, until his command was placed across the Reed's Bridge road and the more westwardly roads leading to Chattanooga *via* Rossville. Crittenden and McCook were to follow when the enemy's plan developed.

Eight o'clock on the morning of September 19 found Thomas and his wearied men in position. Before 9:00 A.M. the fighting began. Crittenden, with [Major General John M.] Palmer and Van Cleve, moved on the Lafayette road toward Thomas's right. The enemy soon abandoned his attempts on our left, and concentrated toward our center. [Brigadier General Richard] Johnson's division was ordered from McCook to Thomas; Van Cleve was driven, and [Brigadier General Jefferson C.] Davis's division gave ground. [Major General James S.] Negley was sent to Van Cleve's position at 5:00 P.M., and [Major General Philip H.] Sheridan earlier to help Davis. The fight raged. The enemy went back and the day closed.

The corps commanders came to my headquarters. They said they had fought superior numbers. The were cool, experienced commanders; they had been in many bloody battles; their opinions had great weight. I saw that the morrow was likely to be more bloody and decisive than that day. I determined the new line, so that there should be the least possible moving of the tired troops, and that it should be short enough to give us seven brigades in reserve. All but one had been in action that day. Thomas must hold the left to the last extremity. If beaten, he must retire on Rossville and Chattanooga. He must send his trains there at once. He had the four divisions of his own corps (the Fourteenth), Johnson's from the Twentieth and Palmer's from the Twenty-first Corps. [Major General Gordon] Granger, with three brigades of the Reserve Corps, was in rear of his left at Rossville. This was all of our whole army on the field, save ten brigades. But the defense of our left was the defense of our army and of Chattanooga.

On September 20, shortly after daylight, I examined Thomas's whole line, and at 6:00 A.M. he wrote that he would like to have his right division (Negley's) to place on his extreme left. I ordered General Crittenden to send [Major General Thomas J.] Wood to replace Negley in the line. At 9:00 A.M. I found Wood in line of battle half a mile in rear of Negley. He said that he had understood that his order was to *support* Negley, not to *relieve* him, and proceeded to do what should have been done at least half hour before. Meanwhile the battle had begun on Thomas's left. It moved toward the right. Heavier and heavier rolled the musketry and thundered the cannon. Captain [J. P.] Willard came from Thomas and asked for Negley. He had been waiting to be relieved, but now, at last, he went filing out of the woods by his left. Van Cleve was ordered farther to the north-east; McCook had had the most repeated and emphatic orders to keep his troops closing to the left.

At 11:00 A.M., Major [Sanford C.] Kellogg came from Thomas, who wished to know if he could have [Brigadier General John M.] Brannan. I replied: "Yes;

tell him to dispose of Brannan, who has only one brigade in line, and to hold his position, and we will reenforce him, if need be, with all the right"; and said to Major [Frank S.] Bond, of my staff, "If Brannan goes out, Wood must fill his place. Write him that the commanding general directs him to close to the left on [Major General Joseph] Reynolds and support him."

Major Kellogg went to Brannan and gave him the order to move his command toward the left.

Brannan's skirmishers being driven in at this time, he consulted Reynolds, who said: "Under the circumstances, stay and send General Thomas word you are being attacked, and ask him if, under such circumstances, you shall leave." To this message General Thomas replied: "No, by no means."

When an orderly handed Wood his order "to close on Reynolds and support him," his skirmishers, on Opdycke's front, were being driven. Without seeking explanations from Brannan or Reynolds, and without notifying me (I was in the open field not 600 yards from him), he drew his command out of the line. Jefferson C. Davis, under orders to keep closed to the left, moved in to fill Wood's place, and his two brigades were struck by Longstreet, who, with a column "brigade front" and five lines deep, assaulted that part of the line and drove it out of place. Sheridan's three brigades were ordered to the break, but had only force enough to break a line or two, and were obliged to withdraw.

Watching the unavailing effort of Sheridan to stem the tide, I observed the long line of Longstreet's wing coming from the south-east in line of battle, outreaching our right by at least a half mile. I ordered Davis and Sheridan to fall back northward and rally on the Dry Valley road at the first good point for defense, leaving most of my staff to aid in rallying these troops; and with my chief of staff, senior aide, and a few orderlies proceeded over toward the rear of our center, directing such of Van Cleve's broken rear of column as I met to join Sheridan on the Dry Valley road.

In view of all the interests at stake, I decided what must be done. Halting at a road coming from the west and leading eastward toward the rear of our left, I said to [Brigadier General James A.] Garfield and Major Bond:

> By the sound of the battle over to the southeast, we hold our ground. Our greatest danger is, that Longstreet will follow us up on the Dry Valley road over yonder to the west of us. [Colonel Philip Sidney] Post, with all of our commissary stores, except those of the Twenty-first Corps, is over that ridge, not more than two or three miles from the Dry Valley road. If Longstreet advances and finds that out, he may capture them. This would be fatal to us. If he comes this way he will turn the rear of our left, seize the gap at Rossville, and disperse us. To provide against what may happen:
>
> *First.* Sheridan and Davis must have renewed orders to resist the enemy's advance on the Dry Valley road;
>
> *Second.* Post must be ordered to push all our commissary trains into Chattanooga and securely park them there;
>
> *Third.* Orders must go to [Brigadier General Robert] Mitchell to extend his

cavalry line obliquely across the ridge, connect with the right of Sheridan's position on this valley, and cover Post's trains from the enemy until they are out of danger.

Fourth. Orders must go to [Brigadier General James] Spears's brigade, now arrived near there, to take possession of the Rolling-mill bridge across Chattanooga Creek, put it in good order, hold it until Post arrives with his trains, then turn the bridge over to him, and march out on the Rossville road and await orders;

Fifth. [Brigadier General George D.] Wagner in Chattanooga must have orders to park our reserve artillery defensively, guard our pontoon bridge across the Tennessee, north of the town, and have his men under arms ready to move as may be required;

Sixth. General Thomas must be seen as to the condition of the battle and be informed of these dispositions.

"General Garfield, can you not give these orders?" I asked. Garfield answered: "General, there are so many of them, I fear I might make some mistake; but I can go to General Thomas for you, see how things are, tell him what you will do, and report to you." "Very well. I will take Major Bond and give the orders myself. I will be in Chattanooga as soon as possible. The telegraph line reaches Rossville, and we have an officer there. Go by Sheridan and Davis and tell them what I wish, then go to Thomas and telegraph me the situation."

I dispatched my orders, by messenger, to Mitchell and Post, gave them in person to Spears and Wagner, and awaited Garfield's report, which, dated 3:45 P.M. from the battlefield, reached me at 5:00 P.M., saying: "We are intact after terrific fighting, getting short of ammunition, and the enemy is going to assault our lines once more. Our troops are in good spirits and fighting splendidly."

I ordered Garfield by dispatch to tell Thomas to use his discretion at the close of the fight whether to stop on the ground he occupied or to retire on Rossville, and said that I would send ammunition and troops accordingly. Thomas used that discretion and retired to Rossville, where our troops halted, and, in spite of their condition, wearied with three days and a night of marching and fighting, were by 11 o'clock in fair defensive position. I ordered up ammunition and rations. On the next morning, Monday, September 21, our lines at Rossville were rectified, and advantageous positions were taken to receive the enemy if he desired to attack us.

After reconnoitering a few points, he found us there and desisted from further efforts. We were now concentrated between the enemy and Chattanooga, with ammunition to fight another battle. During the day I selected the defensive lines our command would occupy around Chattanooga, directed the manner of retiring from Rossville and of taking position on these lines, to which the heads of columns were guided by staff and engineer officers. The troops began quietly to withdraw at 10:00 P.M., and on Tuesday morning, September 22, they were entrenching the lines for holding permanent possession of the objective point of our campaign.

Rosecrans and His Staff at Chickamauga, September 20, 1863
(*Campfire and Battlefield*)

It will be remembered that we started for Chattanooga from Murfreesboro, on June 24, 1863. The direct distance by rail is 119 miles. To the battle-ground of Chickamauga is twenty miles farther, or 139 miles. We dislodged our adversary from two strongly fortified camps; crossed the Cumberland Mountains, the Tennessee River, Sand Mountains and Lookout Mountain; fought the battle of Chickamauga; and on September 22, just ninety-two days from starting, we held Chattanooga, for the possession of which at any time within the previous two years we would willingly have paid all that it had cost.

In a note to Halleck, dated from the Executive Mansion, September 21, 1863, President [Abraham] Lincoln, speaking of this possession, says:

> If held, with Cleveland inclusive, it keeps all Tennessee clear of the enemy and breaks one of his most important railroad lines. To prevent these consequences, so vital to his cause that he cannot give up the effort to dislodge us from the position thus bringing him to us, and saving us the labor, expense, and hazard of going further to find him, and giving us the advantage of choosing our own ground and preparing it to fight him upon. The details must, of course, be left to General Rosecrans, while we furnish him the means to the utmost of our ability. . . . If he can only maintain the position, without more, the rebellion can only eke out a short and feeble existence, as an animal may sometimes with a thorn in his vitals.

In presence of the facts I have just stated, and in view of all their marching, combats, and bloody battles to get possession of Chattanooga, can the reader be made to believe that the Army of the Cumberland and its commander were likely to abandon or fail to hold it?

32

Chickamauga

Benjamin F. Sawyer, Colonel,
Twenty-fourth Alabama Infantry

THE TIRESOME but uneventful retreat of [General Braxton] Bragg from Shelbyville and Tullahoma in June 1863 was followed by the Confederate army going into camp around Chattanooga, where the early summer was spent in monotonous idleness, an idleness really more demoralizing than the retreat had been. It was only when the cautious but steady advance of the Federals and [Major General William Starke] Rosecrans was unmistakably known that our lazy repose was broken and the busy work of fortifying the place commenced. Then, like an ant hill disturbed by an intrusive alarm, our camp became alive with active life, and the hills and knolls which dotted the valley around the city swarmed with men armed with axes, picks, and spades, and soon, almost like magic, a cordon of earthworks, forts, and redoubts encircled the town.

We had scarcely completed these works, pronouncing them impregnable and ensuring the more timid of our conscript recruits that one man could hold his place against any ten that could come against it, when we were called to abandon them, without a shot, to the enemy. The crossing of the Tennessee River by [Major General Alexander M.] McCook below and by [Major General Thomas L.] Crittenden above, the one pushing through to the Chattanooga Valley on our left and the other marching against Dalton on our right, indicated the Federal purpose to flank our position and necessitated a corresponding movement on our part to meet them in the mountain passes, or to strike the isolated columns in detail. Then, abandoning our works, began what the boys termed the grand chase, swinging from McFarland's Springs to Harrison's Landing and back again to Rossville, then back to Harrison's Landing and back again to Rossville, and from Rossville to Crawfish Springs—and from Crawfish Springs across into McClemore's Cove, to meet McCook.

Chattanooga from the North Side of the Tennessee River (*Century*)

There in McLemore's Cove were fired the first guns of the Chickamauga campaign. [Major General James S. Negley's] division had crossed Lookout Mountain through a narrow and difficult pass and his eager troops filled the little cove. [Major General Thomas L.] Hindman's division, of [Lieutenant General Leonidas] Polk's corps, to which I belonged, was dispatched to attack and capture him before he could recross the mountain or assistance could come. Hindman advanced in gallant style, his troops eager for the fight. It was a golden opportunity, but he let it slip. We found the enemy unprepared and slightly demoralized by our unexpected appearance. A vigorous onset would have completed their discomfiture, and we ought to have captured the entire division. But instead of attacking at once, as he should have done, Hindman spent the whole afternoon in flourishing his trumpets and beating his drums.

The next morning [September 12, Negley] was gone. He succeeded that night in recrossing that toilsome mountain gap without the loss of a gun or a wagon. The plan of Bragg's campaign, that of striking the scattered Federal columns in detail, was developed to Rosecrans and the whole order of things was changed.

Poor Hindman, he was a pleasant gentleman, genial and kind, a nice ladies' man, but utterly unfit to command a division of fighting men. He is dead now, God rest his soul, but had an abler man commanded that division that day [Negley] would not have recrossed that mountain without paying dearly for the temerity that led him into its danger. We loitered the next day upon the field of our "might have been glory" until late in the afternoon, when leaving a picket to guard the gap we moved back to rejoin the main army, which was concentrating at Lafayette, the sleepy little town of Walker County, Georgia. Here we rested for a day or two and then were aroused up one night to march back to Rock Springs to attack Crittenden, who, with his corps, had been recalled from his advance and was hurrying back to rejoin Rosecrans, who since the fiasco at McClemore's Cove was reconcentrating his army at Rossville.

We reached Rock Springs the next day, only in time to see the dust of Crittenden's wagon train, by that time far away towards Chattanooga. Then we gathered apples, for the orchards were laden with the golden fruit. Later we marched back to our camps at Lafayette. But our rest was short. The next Thursday night [September 17] we were again aroused, this time for serious work. Rosecrans, with [Major General George H.] Thomas and Crittenden, had advanced to the Chickamauga valley and, with headquarters at Crawfish Springs, was perfecting his plan for an advance. The arrival of [Lieutenant General James] Longstreet, with [Major General John Bell] Hood's division of his admirable corps from the Army of Virginia, determined Bragg to advance and meet him where he stood.

It was early Friday morning [September 18] when we started for the battlefield. It was a glorious autumn morning. The troops were in the finest spirits. I chanced to be division officer for the day of our division (Hindman's), and during the march of fifteen miles from Lafayette to the battlefield, I did not see one straggler. All were well up in ranks and each man seemed eager for the fight. It was noon before we came in sound of the enemy. Rosecrans, not at all unwilling to meet Bragg, had advanced his lines and took position upon the north and west bank of Chickamauga Creek, reaching from Lee and Gordon's mills on our left for miles and miles down the stream. Hindman's division had been for the occasion detached from Polk's and assigned to Longstreet's corps. Polk commanded the right wing of the Confederates and Longstreet the left. This threw our division, my immediate command, upon the extreme Confederate left. Having deployed and advanced a line of skirmishers, our brigade was advanced through the open field. Soon the Federal pickets were developed on the opposite bank of the stream and our line was halted in the field, where the afternoon was spent in listening to the desultory popping of the skirmishers and waiting for the battle.

The line being now halted was ordered to lie down. Now a line laying flat upon the ground presents a difficult mark for an artillerist a mile away, but the hawk eye of the gunner caught it and the next shot came plowing through, killing two men in the Nineteenth South Carolina as they lay prone upon their faces. This was a shell which also ricocheted and, bursting in the rear, killed an ambulance mule. The next came, scarce ten paces on my right, striking the knapsack that was strapped to the back of Private Kimbrell of the Twenty-fourth Alabama, stripping it from his shoulders as he, too, lay flat on his belly and knocking it high in the air, but doing no hurt to the man save a terrible fright. It was laughable to see the bewildered look of the poor fellow as he bounced up, feeling a moment with his hands for the back of his head and then turning and running away as fast as his long limber legs could carry him. Fortunately for us [Captain D. D. Waters's] Alabama Battery came in now at a gallop, and quickly unlimbering on a little hill to our right engaged the troublesome gun, relieving us from its fateful attentions. At sundown we moved by the right flank a short distance, where we slept for the night.

It was noon the next day, Saturday, September 19, before the battle opened in earnest and then it was far down the creek to our right.

We listened to it—I speak for my comrades more than for myself—with hopeful enthusiasm. First the indescribable pop, pop, popping of the musketry and then the glorious roar and thunder of the artillery. It was evident from the direction of the firing that the battle was to be fought far down the creek, and distant several miles from our present position. Soon a brigade of cavalry relieved us of our watch at the mills, and we were ordered to move by the right flank. Keeping our ranks well closed up we moved through the woods and, crossing the creek three miles below, wading the stream up to our waists, were fronted and advanced to relieve Hood's division, which had been hotly engaged all the afternoon. Gallantly the advance was made, and just as the sun was setting we were brought in the fire, striking the enemy's right center which, already weakened by the fierce assaults of Hood, wavered, and in the confusion of the early twilight fell back. The darkness prevented our following, and throwing out a strong line of pickets we bivouacked on the ground surrounded by the Federal wounded, dying, and dead. At first we suffered a painful discomfort from the chill of our wet clothing, being afraid to kindle lights for fear of attracting the enemy's fire, but the cold becoming too severe to be endured with patience, at first here and there, and then larger ones more frequent, until at last a line of cheery fires blazed all along the line, giving warmth to our limbs and casting a weird glamour over the scene.

It would seem strange, almost incredible, that one could sleep amid such surroundings and under such tragic circumstances, but sleep we did, soundly and refreshingly, only waking up occasionally to replenish the dying fires. But no so our enemies. While we were asleep they were busy rectifying and reestablishing their broken and disordered lines, felling trees, throwing up breastworks and strengthening their position for the morrow's battle. All through the night the sound of their busy work could be heard almost a mile in our front. It was a strange contrast presented by the two armies that night, the one sleeping in careless security as unmindful of thought for the morrow as if on a couch at home, the other busy with anxious care and preparation.

And aptly does the contrast illustrate the characteristics of the two people. The one reckless, free, off-handed, improvident even of their own lives, relying upon dash and vim and headlong daring; the other cool, calculating, provident, careful even of contingencies, depending upon skill and method and science, as well as upon personal courage for success. I thought of it that night as I watched my sleeping comrades and listened to the falling of trees, the rumbling of wagons, and anxious shouts of command that came from the lines of our enemy.

As before stated we bivouacked upon the ground from which we had driven the enemy just at sundown and slept in the midst of the Federal dead and wounded. It was sad to see them writhing in their pain and pitiful to listen to their appeals for help we could not give.

The great dread with many seemed the danger that would come to them from the battle of tomorrow. The pain of their present suffering seemed to be forgotten in this great dread. "Please have me moved from here. I don't want to be killed tomorrow and by my own people!" was the cry from many a pale lip that night. Of course we could not help them, but we assured them the best we could that there would be no danger to them from the morrow. "The fighting will be over yonder!" we said, "Where you hear that racket."

It was poor comfort, but was all we could give. One brave fellow, Lieutenant David Baker of the Eighth Kansas Volunteers, was desperately wounded in the thigh and asked to be sent back to a place of safety. As this could not be done he bravely resigned himself to his fate, believing that he would either die there that night or else be killed the next day as he lay. It was a sad fate to face, but he faced it like a man, entrusting me with his effects, $100, to be sent, if possible, with his dying message to his wife. I am sorry to say that the poor lady received neither the money nor the message, but happy to know that the gallant lieutenant lived to present to her in person a more grateful one, and to thank me for the little kindness it was in my power to render him in his hour of sore distress.

The next morning—Sunday [September 20]—we woke up at daybreak. A hasty breakfast, munched with avidity, and then a rigid inspection of arms and we were ready for action. We were on the left of Hindman's division, almost on the extreme left of our line, and after rectifying the line stood ready for the command. But the movement was slow to begin. We had expected to advance at sunrise, General Polk, on the right, having orders to attack at daybreak. From some cause never satisfactorily explained he failed to do so, and it was nearly 10 o'clock before the movement commenced. A dense fog, mingled with the smoke of the battle the day before, threw a curtain almost as dark as night over the field. This darkness, it's said, delayed Polk, but it did not impede [Major] General Gordon Granger, who, Blucher-like, was hurrying forward. At length the movement began, and "Forward, guide, right, march!" was sung out. Forward we stepped, glad at last to be relieved from the dread and suspense of waiting. We had not moved twenty paces before, from away down the creek far to the right, came the din and rush and roar of battle, drawing fatefully near as each line successively swung into action. Like the enormous jaws of some heroic monster the two lines of battle closed inexorable and merciless.

A half mile, struggling through a tangle of scrubby brushwood, brought us to a field where, rising to the crest of a little ridge, we saw the Federal lines on the opposite edge, strongly posted behind its hastily improvised but efficient breastworks. We had scarcely gotten in range before they opened upon us with a continuous sheet of fire. We had no time to pause for thought of dread or danger. We were in the very jaws of the monster. We could not retreat. The danger would be greater than to press forward, and onward we pressed, realizing safety only in breaking that line. It was a fearful alternative and fearfully it cost us. One-fourth of my regiment was cut down. Never before had I, nor since have I, seen such terrible execution in so short a time. It was more than mortal nerve could bear, and to avoid the point-blank fire the men instinctively and without command moved by the right flank into a skirt of woods, thus doubling upon [Brigadier General J. Patton] Anderson's brigade of Mississippians, which, under cover of the woods, had escape the terrible cyclone of minie balls, grape-shot and shell which so sadly decimated our own ranks. And now we were to have our revenge. With Anderson we pressed forward in an impetuous, irresistible charge, mounting the works of loose stone, fence rails and brushwood and delivering a well-deserved volley in the very faces of our enemies. Then the Federal line was broken, doubling back on its left, where Thomas stood like an iron wall grimly defying the assault of Polk.

Like chaff we pressed them back across the road, through the woods, over little hills and through little valleys, firing as we went, giving them no time to rally or to reform their broken ranks, until rising to the crest of a mighty hill we struck the freshly-arrived corps of Granger, who came up just in time to save the army from utter rout.

A Confederate Line of Battle (*Life of Sherman*)

I remember our track that day. It stands before me a black, clear-cut silhouette upon the pages of memory. It was strewn with our own as well as with Federal dead. The gallant Confederate [Brigadier] General Preston H. Smith, of [Major General Benjamin Franklin] Cheatham's division, lay in its path cold in death. Upon its bloody maize lay the chivalrous [Captain D. E.] Huger, of [Brigadier General Arthur M.] Manigault's staff, as brave a man and courtly gentleman as ever gave his life to his country. The equally brave and knightly Federal [Brigadier General William H.] Lytle, the poet-soldier and cultured gentleman, lay there, too, with his back to the field and his face to the foe. I stopped a moment to wonder who he was, as my attention was called to the leaf on his collar. I thought it no cowardice to breathe a prayer for his soul, as I lifted my hat and rode on. The carnage was fearful; the ground was strewn with human dead. Artillery horses were piled pell-mell in great heaps. Gun carriages, exploded caissons, broken wheels encumbered the ground. Great trees were shattered and cut down like straws. Fences, houses, everything in the track of that battle storm were battered into fragments.

It was there, in the midst of this carnival of death, this saturnalia of human wrath and diabolical fury, we saw a sight that strongly touched us. In the very heat of the battle, only a few paces in the Federal rear, stood a squatter's log hut, a miserable den chinked with poles and daubed with mud. Underneath the loose board floor was a hole, dug out for the purpose of getting mud with which to daub the chimney. Into this little pit scarcely eighteen inches deep and less than five feet in diameter were crowded a mother and three little children.

During all the fierce onslaught of battle they were there huddled like so many scared rabbits. A thousand bullets seemed to have been embedded in the logs of the hut, its roof was knocked into splinters by shells and hardly a stick of its chimney was left, and yet, strange to say, not a hair of their heads was hurt. I remember their little bright eyes peering half curiously, half terrified, from their hiding place as the Federal line was broken and we passed in yelling pursuit. It would have been a hard heart, indeed, not to have opened to bless their helpless, innocent heads and to thank the God of battles for holding them safely in the hollow of His hand. More than one powder-begrimed soldier hushed a moment to bless them as we passed.

But our victory was not yet won. Thomas still stood on our right firm as the overlooking cliffs of Lookout Mountain themselves. His right had crumbled and was scurrying back to Chattanooga in disorder. Only Gordon Granger stood to protect his rear, and there on that rugged spur of the mountain we fought, surging backward and forward. At last we got [Captain D. D. Waters's] battery on the hill and then with one more mighty surge we forced them back, just as the sun went down; and Thomas, seeing the day's work done, broke too, and made his escape back to Chattanooga to find a haven of safety in the very works we had been at so much care to build.

To him, the gallant Thomas, and to his bulldog courage and desperate resolution, is due the escape of Rosecrans's magnificent army. Had he yielded one inch, disaster, irretrievable as well as defeat, would have overwhelmed that army. But he stood. All honor to his pluck. The army was saved. Under cover of darkness it made its way in disorderly retreat to the Tennessee, while we, too tired to follow, slept on the field so desperately won.

33

Holding Burnside in Check in East Tennessee[1]
Major General Samuel Jones, C.S.A.

IN A RECENT narrative [Major General William S.] Rosecrans tells the story of his Chickamauga campaign concisely and clearly, and with the frankness of the true gentleman and soldier.[2] In the course of his narrative, referring to the failure of [Major General Ambrose] Burnside to give him the aid and support he confidently expected, he says: "On September 19, the first day of the battle, Halleck telegraphed me that he had no direct communication with Burnside or [Major General Stephen A.] Hurlbut. It was too late then. Burnside was hunting, with 22,000 men at his back, for General Sam Jones, who, with less than 6,000 men, was pulling him off up into West Virginia." The services of a small body of troops that had the effect of occupying the attention of so large a force of the enemy during an important campaign and keeping it from participating in the great Battle of Chickamauga, where its presence was so much needed, deserve a more extended notice than the terse allusion General Rosecrans has given them.

The writer knew General Burnside well, appreciated the many admirable qualities that so endeared him to his friends, and has no desire or intention to criticize his operations in East Tennessee in the autumn of 1863. His course apparently was dictated more by political or civil than military considerations. General Jones had himself commanded the Department of East Tennessee just

---

1. Jones supplemented his text with numerous, lengthy extracts from official correspondence and reports. As they are readily available in the *Official Records,* I have deleted those that did not add materially to the narrative.

2. Jones here refers to Rosecrans's "The Chattanooga Campaign," which appeared in the March 6, 1882, issue of the *National Tribune,* and which formed the basis of his later *Century* article, "The Campaign for Chattanooga," reprinted in this volume as "From Tullahoma to Chattanooga."

Major General Ambrose E. Burnside (*Century*)

a year previously, and could well appreciate the influence such considerations exercised over General Burnside. There was a strong Union element in that section of the country, and it was Burnside's policy to strengthen and protect it and to organize, arm, and equip a large military force of native East Tennesseans, and he went supplied with arms for that purpose. To secure possession of that country was an object very near the heart of Mr. [Abraham] Lincoln, and Burnside desired to accomplish it and doubtless thought it the best service his large force, two army corps, could accomplish. It is believed, however, that that important end would have been more surely and speedily attained by leaving a good division of cavalry to hold in check any force coming from the east and carrying the main body of his army to cooperate with General Rosecrans at Chickamauga, and, in the battle that was impending, crush and scatter, if possible, General [Braxton] Bragg's army, when East Tennessee might have been quietly occupied and reconstructed.

At the time referred to, General Jones commanded the Trans-Allegheny or Western Department of Virginia. Its boundaries, from the nature of things, were not clearly defined, but varied with the exigencies of the times. In the summer of 1863 he had been obliged to send a portion of his troops to the Valley of Virginia. On September 1 his command extended from the vicinity of Staunton, in the Valley, to Saltville, in Southwest Virginia, a distance, as the crow flies, of about 200 miles, and by the traveled routes of nearly 300. The southwestern counties of the state, bordering on Kentucky and Tennessee, formed, from their geographical position, a part of the Department of East Tennessee, then commanded by Major General S. B. Buckner. General Jones' total effective force was less than 6,000 men. It was wholly inadequate for the defense of so extensive and important a country, from which a large part of the supplies for General [Robert E.] Lee's army was drawn, and a line of railroad of nearly 200 miles in length, the only line of transportation from East Tennessee through to eastern Virginia.

Confronting him on the north was Brigadier General B. F. Kelly on the Union side, commanding the Department of West Virginia, extending from Harper's Ferry to the Kanawha Valley, with an army, as his return for September shows, of 26,879 men, of which 23,269 were present for duty. Of this force, Brigadier General W. W. Averill, who was very active and aggressive, commanded about 4,000, at and near Beverly. Brigadier General [Eliakim P.] Scammon had about 5,000 in the Kanawha Valley. On the west, General Burnside had something more than 3,000 men of his army on the Big Sandy and the southeastern borders of Kentucky, in dangerous proximity to the Virginia salt works, the chief source of supply for that indispensable article to the Confederates.

General Jones's headquarters were at Dublin, on the Virginia and East Tennessee Railroad, halfway between Lynchburg and Bristol, on the Tennessee line, about 100 miles from each, but the nature of his duties required him to be frequently in distant parts of the department.

On September 1 or 2, when about eighty miles from Dublin, a courier brought him the following telegram:

Loudon, Tenn., August 31, 1863

Major General S. Jones,
    Brigadier General A. E. Jackson, of this command, is ordered with his troops to Bristol, and is instructed to report to you and obey your orders and those of [Brigadier General John S.] Williams. You can telegraph him at Jonesboro. Take charge of southwestern Virginia for me.
    S. B. Buckner, Major General

The same courier brought to General Jones a dispatch from General A. E. Jackson, telling him he had fallen back to Bristol and desiring to know if he should burn the bridges over the Holston and Watauga. A little later Jones received another dispatch, telling him of the invasion of East Tennessee by General Burnside, and that Buckner had gone with all of his effective force to join General Bragg at Chattanooga. Jones replied to Buckner that he would do what he could for southwestern Virginia, and directed General Jackson not to burn any bridges, adding that he would be with him in a few days.

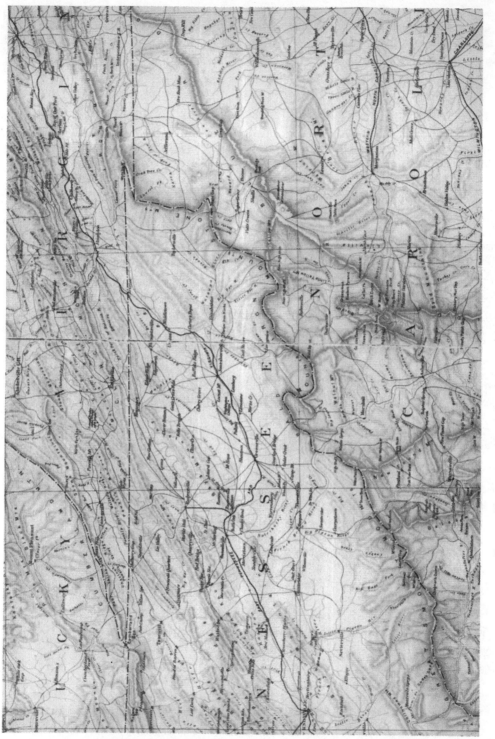

Eastern Tennessee and Southwestern Virginia (*Atlas; Official Records*)

It happened that a few days before, on August 26 and 27, Jones, with one of his brigades, had encountered General Averill and his command near the Virginia White Sulphur Springs, and after a sharp and well-contested fight, lasting through the twenty-sixth, and until about 11:00 A.M. on the twenty-seventh, Averill was repulsed and retreated hurriedly to his base near Beverly, pursued by the Confederate cavalry, and so crippled, it was believed, as to relieve any apprehension of danger from him for a month or two.

This enabled General Jones to send a part of his troops to the defense of southwestern Virginia. [Brigadier General Gabriel C.] Wharton's brigade, composed of the Forty-fifth and Fifty-first regiments and Thirteenth Battalion Virginia Infantry and the Otey battery of artillery (the Forty-fifth had borne a conspicuous part in the fight on August 26 and 27), was ordered to the vicinity of the salt works near Abingdon, and General Jones went to the latter place on September 6. General Buckner had left General A. E. Jackson with a brigade, so-called, east of Knoxville, composed of fractional parts of regiments, battalions, and companies, depot and bridge guards, and the like, reported to be about 1,300 men, scattered from the borders of North Carolina to the East Tennessee and Virginia Railroad. Brigadier General J. B. Frazer was left in command at Cumberland Gap, with something more than 2,000 men. Brigadier General John S. Williams was at Saltville endeavoring to recruit and organize a brigade. He had the Tenth Kentucky Battalion of cavalry, Major [Bernard P.] Chenoweth.

General Burnside's army was composed of the Ninth and Twenty-third army corps. The Twenty-third Corps had entered Tennessee at points west of Cumberland Gap. On August 30 he was at Montgomery. There was nothing in his front to oppose his further advance, and his troops occupied Knoxville, Kingston, Loudon, and, indeed, overran the country generally, and advanced to within a few miles of Bristol on the Virginia line, driving the little detachments, quartermasters' and commissaries' guards, into southwestern Virginia.

Immediately on General Jones's arrival at Abingdon he telegraphed General Jackson at Bristol: "Our reinforcements are on the way. It is very important that the enemy should not be permitted to advance further in this direction. Hold Watauga Bridge (Carter's Station) as long as possible and Zollicoffer at all hazards. Watch closely the roads to your right and left and keep me fully advised."

General John S. Williams was ordered to take his little force from Saltville into East Tennessee, join Jackson, and go on to Jonesboro, the enemy having fallen back west of that place. It was important to know something of the condition of Cumberland Gap and what was transpiring there. A few hours after arriving at Abingdon, General Jones addressed the following letter to General Frazer and dispatched it by a trusty and intelligent courier:

Hdqrs. Department W. Va. and E. Tenn.
Abingdon, September 6, 1863

Brigadier General J. W. Frazer, Commanding etc.,
    Cumberland Gap,

General: Agreeably to the request of Major General Buckner, and under instructions from the War Department, I have assumed command, temporarily, of that part of Southwest Virginia embraced in the Department of East Tennessee, and all the troops of that department east of Knoxville. I am not informed as to the number or description of the troops under your immediate command or the state of your commissary and quartermaster's supplies, and am anxious to be fully informed on those points. It may be imprudent, however, to send me such information in writing unless you have and can use the cipher and keyword used by Buckner. If you have, inform me in cipher as fully as possible of your condition, sending to me at this place a thoroughly trustworthy courier. If you have not the cipher send an intelligent officer who can inform me fully. Reinforcements are now on the way to Northeast Tennessee, and in sufficient force, it is believed, to drive the enemy from that section of the country. In that view of the case it is of great importance that you should hold Cumberland Gap as long as you can possibly do so. Do not abandon it without the most determined resistance of which you are capable.

If you have any cavalry or mounted infantry which you do not need or cannot forage, send it to Zollicoffer promptly, to report to Brigadier General John S. Williams. The officer in command of the cavalry should sent forward reliable scouts in advance to obtain information to avoid falling into the hands of the enemy. He should also notify me of the movement.

Very respectfully, etc.,
Sam Jones, Major General

The courier bearing this letter to General Frazer had been but four or five hours on the road when Jones received a dispatch from General Buckner, dated Chattanooga, September 6, saying: "Send an order to General Frazer at Cumberland Gap to evacuate the gap, destroying all stores which he cannot bring away. His line of retreat should be directed upon Abingdon. That is Bragg's order."

General Jones immediately telegraphed Buckner's dispatch to the secretary of war, adding that before receiving it he had sent exactly contrary orders to General Frazer, ordering him to hold the gap as long as possible, giving the secretary some of his reasons for so doing, and asking instructions on that particular point. In reply he was informed that President Davis ordered Cumberland Gap to be held at all hazards.

General Jones's reason for particularly desiring to hold Cumberland Gap at that time was this: He believed that General Burnside would attempt to capture it before carrying or sending any considerable part of his army to General Rosecrans, and the position being naturally very strong and fortified, he would send against it three or four times the force Frazer had there, which was estimated from the best information that could be obtained at about 2,500 men. That force, it was believed, could hold out against three or four times their number as long as their supply of food and ammunition would last, and that Frazer and his men could render no better service than by giving employment to some eight or ten thousand men, keeping them away from General Rosecrans's support and from participation in the impending battle near Chattanooga.

About September 5 a small party of Union troops, advancing along the line of the railroad, came as far east as Carter's Station (Watauga Bridge), when they found a bridge guard, commanded by Captain [H. L. W.] McClung, who declined to give up his post when summoned to do so and the party fell back west of Jonesboro. General Jones had sent General Jackson to this town, and on the ninth, ascertaining that [Lieutenant Colonel Edwin L.] Hayes, with the One Hundredth Ohio Infantry was a few miles west of him, he attacked and drove him back to Limestone Station where, after a sharp fight, he captured the whole party.

This little affair was most creditable to the officers and men engaged, especially to General Jackson, Colonel [H. L.] Giltner of the Fourth Kentucky Cavalry, Lieutenant Colonel [W. C.] Walker of the Thomas Legion, and [Lieutenant Colonel Milton L.] Haynes, of the artillery. It was especially welcomed, as it served to encourage and inspirit the men after the panic that had been created by Burnside overrunning the country with little or no opposition.

In the meantime, Cumberland Gap had been invested, but, so far as General Jones knew, with a surprisingly little force, so small as to suggest the practicability of driving it off, and possibly with the cooperation of the garrison, capturing or dispersing it before the other part of the investing force could come up. Before night [September 11] General Jones received information which dashed his hopes in that quarter. General Frazer had surrendered Cumberland Gap on the ninth.

While the Confederate courier was hastening to the gap with General Jones's order to Frazer to hold out as long as possible the enemy was gathering around it. On September 7 [Brigadier General [James M.] Shackelford, with about 4,000 men, arrived from the south on the Tennessee side and summoned General Frazer to surrender, which he declined. The next day Shackelford renewed his summons and Colonel [John F.] De Courcy, from the Kentucky side, also sent in a summons, both of which Frazer promptly declined. On September 9 General Burnside arrived at Shackelford's headquarters with two regiments of infantry and two of cavalry, about 1,500 men, and summoned Frazer to surrender. Some negotiations ensued and at about 3:00 P.M. Frazer surrendered unconditionally the post, a little over 2,000 men and fourteen pieces of artillery. On arriving in the vicinity of the gap Jones's courier found it surrounded by the enemy. With much difficulty and delay he succeed in eluding the pickets and made his way by mountain paths to Frazer's headquarters on the afternoon of September 9 and delivered Jones's letter.

The courier was closely questioned by General Frazer, but all the information he could obtain from him was not such as to change, but rather to confirm, his conviction that the loss of the pass was inevitable, and that immediate surrender was the most prudent and best course to pursue. It is not a little singular that this noted pass through the Cumberland Mountains, which was regarded by both belligerents as a most important strategic point, was three times surrendered during the war without firing a shot—once by the Union and twice by the Confederate forces. General Frazer was severely censured by President Davis in his subsequent message to Congress. He, Frazer, was a prisoner and could not promptly vindicate himself, but his report and accompanying papers, rendered more than a year later, fully exonerated him from all blame and Mr. Davis acknowledges it in his recently published history.

This surrender greatly embarrassed General Jones, who had hoped to detain Burnside at the gap some weeks. His troops were now available for such service as General Burnside might choose to assign them. The prospect before General Jones was anything but encouraging. The left wing of Rosecrans's army had occupied Chattanooga on September 9. East Tennessee was wide open to Burnside, and he commanded an army of two army corps, the Ninth and Twenty-third, numbering about 26,000 men present for duty equipped. His return for September 20 showed 21,792 present for duty equipped. The Twenty-third Army Corps was already in the heart of East Tennessee and occupied the most important points. The Ninth Army Corps was on the march and arrived on September 21. A division of about 6,000 men of the Twenty-third Corps, left in Kentucky, was ordered to the front, which would swell his force to about 28,000 men.

There was absolutely no force in the Department of East Tennessee, which included southwestern Virginia and the important salt works near Abingdon, save about 4,000 men near the Virginia and East Tennessee line. There was little to prevent Burnside from carrying out any policy he might think proper to adopt. General Jones supposed he would either carry his army to the support of General Rosecrans, near Chattanooga, to take part in the approaching battle, leaving one division to hold Jones's force in check, or that he would move with his whole command into southwestern Virginia to take possession of and destroy the salt works, a result which would have been almost, if not quite, as disastrous to the Confederacy as the loss of the Battle of Chickamauga. Indeed, this second movement, if vigorously made, was capable of leading to most important results. At that time Rosecrans and Bragg were confronting each other near Chattanooga. [Major General Ulysses S.] Grant, having captured Vicksburg on the Fourth of July, a large part of the Army of the Tennessee was available to reinforce the Army of the Cumberland, as it did a little later. General Lee's army on the Rapidan was greatly outnumbered by the Army of the Potomac under [Major General George G.] Meade.

There was no organized military force between General Burnside and Lynchburg save the force that General Jones had in northeastern Tennessee and southwestern Virginia. If General Burnside had moved with his whole force to the salt works near Abingdon, it was General Jones's purpose and expectation to have accepted battle at all hazards, if offered, at that point, so important to the Confederacy. In the event of a Confederate defeat the road to Lynchburg would have been open and General Burnside could have moved steadily on towards that place, subsisting on the country, from which a great part of General Lee's supplies were drawn. This movement seems to have been in contemplation, for in a dispatch dated Washington, September 11, 1863, [Major General Henry] Halleck says to General Burnside: "General Rosecrans will occupy Delhi or some point on the railroad, to close all access from Atlanta, and also the mountain passes on the west. This being done, it will be determined whether the moveable force shall advance into Georgia and Alabama or into the Valley of Virginia and North Carolina."

General Halleck was in Washington commanding all the Union armies, with telegraphic instruments at his fingers's ends communicating with the various commanders. It would have seemed not difficult so to have timed the various movements as to ensure every reasonable prospect of success. If General Burnside had made that movement successfully it would have deranged General Lee's plans and placed his whole army in a most precarious position. It is probable that there would have been no necessity for [Major General William T.] Sherman's march to the sea or General Grant's to the James and to Appomattox. But that was not to be. The end was not yet.

To return. On hearing of Frazer's surrender General Jones countermanded the order he had a few hours before sent to General Williams to move on Cumberland Gap, but reiterated the order "to fell the enemy in your front and, if possible, drive him back. No time should be lost." He had immediately on going into southwestern Virginia given orders for strengthening the defensive works at Saltville. There was hardly a man or woman in that section of country who did not appreciate the importance of the source from which they drew their supplies of salt, and he appealed to prominent gentlemen to exert themselves to the utmost to organize home guards for their defense, and they responded promptly to the appeal. He urged upon the secretary of war and General Lee the necessity of sending reinforcements to that section of the country.

General Lee could ill afford to send reinforcements from his army. He had already sent [Lieutenant General James] Longstreet's corps to General Bragg, some 900 miles off. His army was reduced to 48,064 aggregate effectives present for duty, and he was confronted on the Rapidan by the Army of the Potomac, of about double as many men present for duty, under General Meade. But with a comprehensive view that took in the whole field of military operations and that magnanimity and forgetfulness of self that characterized and prompted him to extend a helping hand to anyone who needed it, he sent one of his Virginia infantry brigades, [Brigadier General Montgomery D.] Corse's.

In view of all the circumstances it seemed to General Jones that the best service he could render with the small force under his command would be to protect the chief source of supply of salt and if possible give employment to General Burnside and detain him and his army in that part of the country until Generals Bragg and Rosecrans had tried conclusions in the vicinity of Chattanooga, and that purpose controlled his subsequent actions.

Reports reached him that the force at Cumberland Gap was moving directly towards Abingdon, and as he was in constant apprehension that it would be joined by another force penetrating by way of Pound Gap, Wharton's brigade was, therefore, left near Saltville. The cavalry and some infantry and artillery were at Jonesboro. Burnside did not move the troops from Cumberland Gap through Virginia toward the salt works, but sent them to Greenville, and between that point and Jonesboro he concentrated his whole force, with the exception of a mounted brigade at or near Athens. With the force between Greenville and Jonesboro he proposed, as he tells General Halleck, "to capture or drive out a large force of the enemy under General Sam Jones, stationed on the road from Bristol to Jonesboro. . . . The force under Jones at Zollicoffer is over 6,000."

It was about this time that General Burnside began to be embarrassed in carrying out his plans by instructions from General Halleck. Information of a disturbing nature had reached Washington from Chattanooga. General Halleck dispatched to General Burnside in quick succession the following telegrams:

September 13—It is important that all the available forces of your command be pushed forward into East Tennessee. All your scattered forces should be concentrated there. So long as we hold Tennessee, Kentucky is perfectly safe. Move down your infantry as rapidly as possible towards Chattanooga, to connect with Rosecrans. Bragg may merely hold the passes in the mountains to cover Atlanta and move his main army through Alabama to reach the Tennessee River and turn Rosecrans's right and cut off his supplies. In that case he will turn Chattanooga over to you and move to intercept Bragg.

September 14, 3:00 P.M.—There are reasons why you should reinforce General Rosecrans with all possible dispatch. It is believed that the enemy will concentrate to give him battle. You must be there to help him.

September 14, 4:30 P.M.—From information received here today it is very probable that three divisions of Lee's army have been sent to reinforce Bragg. It is important that all the troops in your department be brought to the front with all possible dispatch, so as to help General Rosecrans.

It was true that reinforcements had gone from the Army of Northern Virginia to General Bragg. General Lee, after the serious reverse at Gettysburg, had retired into Virginia followed by the triumphant Union army, which greatly exceeded in numbers the Army of Northern Virginia. It was most reasonable to suppose that General Meade would very soon resume vigorous offensive operations. To make any large detachments from Lee's army at that time was most hazardous. But Lee, with great magnanimity, accepted the hazard and sent nearly one-third of his effective force 900 miles to the succor of General Bragg's army. The movement was made with great secrecy—so secret that for many days it was not known to General Meade, who was in the immediate front, and even General Bragg's corps commanders did not know the reinforcements were coming from Virginia until the head of General Longstreet's column appeared in their midst.

General Burnside did not receive General Halleck's dispatches of September 13 and 14 until the sixteenth and seventeenth. He immediately ordered a few of his troops near Knoxville to turn back and go towards Chattanooga. But the main body of the Twenty-third Corps was well up the valley and in the vicinity of the Confederates, so near that he did not think it safe to attempt to withdraw them. "It does not seem possible," he telegraphed General Halleck, "for me to successfully withdraw my forces from the presence of Jones until he should be beaten back or captured," and very naturally desired to free himself of the enemy on his left before going to General Rosecrans's support. He, therefore, made his dispositions to accomplish that purpose, and moved his main body of the Twenty-third Army Corps steadily on towards Jonesboro. On September 15 Jones telegraphed from Jonesboro to President Davis, in reply to a dispatch from him: "I shall withdraw the troops from this to the line of the Watauga and Holston to await the reinforcements (Corse's brigade) and be in better position to meet an advance on Saltville. No reliable information of the movements of the enemy from Cumberland Gap. Pickets skirmishing in front every day. Our pickets behaving well." On the sixteenth he telegraphed Mr. Davis:

> The indications in front of Jonesboro yesterday are such that I did not think it necessary to withdraw to the line of the Watauga and Holston, being reluctant to yield any more ground. I cannot withdraw any more troops from Lewisburg or Princeton, Virginia, without exposing too much of the Virginia and East Tennessee Railroad. I left [Brigadier General A. G.] Jenkins's cavalry brigade on the Staunton and Parkersburg Turnpike, near Monterey. Can I withdraw it with safety to Staunton?

Later in the day the indications near Jonesboro warned Jones to retire. The country about that place was not well adapted to the purpose proposed to be carried out, namely, to check and detain a greatly superior numerical force until after the impending battle at Chickamauga had been fought. The cavalry had been skirmishing for several days and was greatly exhausted. There were two important railroad bridges in our immediate rear, over the Watauga and Holtson, which the enemy could destroy with his large cavalry force. We had little or no field transportation, the troops having been brought together hastily from distant points, and we were therefore dependent mainly on the railroad for supplies. Brigadier General Williams, commanding the troops near Jonesboro, was therefore directed to fall back to Carter's Station in the night of September 16, which he did successfully and without opposition. Brigadier General Corse, who was then bringing a brigade to East Tennessee by rail, was directed to halt at Zollicoffer, nine miles east of Carter's Depot.

Rebuilding a Railroad Bridge (*Life of Sherman*)

We left Jonesboro none to soon. The enemy in greatly superior force was close at hand and occupied the place on the morning of September 17, and moved steadily on toward Carter's Depot. General Burnside had sent a brigade of cavalry, the Second Brigade, Fourth Division, [Colonel John W.] Foster commanding, to pass to our rear by way of Kingsport. On the eighteenth Foster drove the First Tennessee Cavalry (Colonel J. E. Carter) from Kingsport and pursued it beyond Bristol. He damaged the railroad some distance on both sides of Bristol, destroying some stores, and returned to Blountville, six miles northwest of Zollicoffer, on the evening of September 19. Corse's brigade having arrived the day before it was determined to endeavor to strike Foster at daylight on the twentieth, and some troops were ordered up from Carter's Depot to join Corse in the attack. As they did not arrive in time, Colonel C. H. Tyler, who happened to be at headquarters, was instructed to take the Sixteenth Georgia Battalion of cavalry and two companies of the First Tennessee Cavalry, which had been cut off from their regiment at Kingsport, and feel the enemy at Blountville early in the morning and endeavor to draw them on to attack us near Zollicoffer. Corse's brigade, with a field battery, took a strong position to receive them.

Colonel Tyler and his men performed the duty assigned them handsomely and drew the enemy on. They felt Corse cautiously, and finding him strongly posted endeavored to turn his left. But General Williams had brought the Forty-fifth Regiment Virginia Infantry and [Colonel William E.] Peters's dismounted battalion from Carter's Depot and taken position on Corse's left. The skirmishing continued several hours, when the enemy fell back to Blountville and moved off towards Carter's Depot.

In the meantime General Burnside had concentrated his forces to capture or drive out the enemy in his front between Bristol and Carter's Station, which he estimated to amount to at least 6,000 men. He overestimated the force in his front, which was less than 4,000 men between the points mentioned in East Tennessee. Early on the morning of September 23 General Burnside's proposed movement eastward along the line of the railroad began. His advance troops formed and moved forward to attack the Confederates at Carter's Station, but it was too late. The position had been abandoned in the night.

Burnside's movements for four or five days were evidently for the purpose of ascertaining the positions and numbers of the enemy in his immediate front and to cut his railroad communications in the rear. Having accomplished these purposes to his satisfaction he proposed to engage General Jones's attention at Zollicoffer with his cavalry until he could with superior force surround and capture the troops at Carter's Station. Our force was altogether too small to enable us to hold both Carter's Station and Zollicoffer. General Williams was, therefore, ordered to abandon the latter place and fall back towards the former in the night of the twenty-second, which he did successfully and without opposition, bringing with him all stores and property of value, and then General Burnside's proposed advance eastward was arrested and turned back by events which had occurred at Chickamauga. In the night of September 22 General Jones received a dispatch from President Davis telling him of the Battle of Chickamauga and expressing his congratulations and thanks for the services rendered by the troops under his command.

On September 21, General Halleck telegraphed General Burnside that General Rosecrans had been driven back to near Chattanooga, and added: "General Rosecrans will require all the assistance you can give him to hold Chattanooga." And again on the twenty-second he says: "Yours of yesterday is received. I must again urge you to move immediately to Rosecrans's relief. I hear your delay has already permitted Bragg to prevent your junction."

These telegrams, no doubt, arrested the advance eastward and turned General Burnside back towards Knoxville. He indicated his relinquishment, for the present, of any advance towards Virginia by destroying the bridge over the Watauga at Carter's Station, and that point was immediately reoccupied by the Confederates.

On August 30 General Burnside [had] arrived with the Twenty-third Corps of his army at Montgomery, Tennessee, moved directly on to Kingston and Knoxville and occupied those places, and by September 5 [had] occupied the principal points in the heart of East Tennessee. On the ninth he occupied the pass of Cumberland Gap, and immediately concentrated his main force at and near Greenville, fifty-seven miles by railroad from the Virginia line, for the purpose of capturing or driving off all opposing force in that part of the state. On September 22 he prepared to attack the enemy in his immediate front at Carter's Station, which, however, eluded him by retiring a few miles in the night. On September 23, in obedience to urgent instructions from General Halleck to go to the assistance of General Rosecrans, instructions repeated almost daily from the thirteenth to the twenty-second, he arrested his movement eastward and turned back towards Chattanooga. But for any service his troops might have rendered in the Battle of Chickamauga, he was, as General Rosecrans says, "too late then."

. . .

When the first news of the Battle of September 19 and 20, 1863, at Chickamauga was flashed over the wires, it was very generally believed throughout the country, North and South, that the Confederates had gained a great victory and that the Army of the Cumberland had suffered a crushing defeat. But in truth the battle was indecisive. Both armies had suffered greatly in killed and wounded. In strict military parlance the Confederates gained a victory, but it was comparatively barren. They occupied the field of battle and the Union army fell back some twenty miles. But General Rosecrans had succeeded in seizing Chattanooga, the most important strategic position in that section of the country, and the objective point of his campaign, and was preparing, even before the close of the battle, to hold it with a tenacious grasp.

The important question was, could he continue to hold it? And that question was one of anxious consideration and apprehension for the Federal government. Another battle was necessary to decide it. The bloody work must be gone over again. The belligerents were busily engaged in binding up their wounds, repairing damages and preparing for another great trial of arms.

As the details of the battle reached Washington, they seem to have greatly increased the solicitude felt for the safety of Chattanooga and all of East Tennessee. Not only were Generals Grant and Burnside urged to move their forces rapidly to that section of country, but having at last discovered beyond any doubt that General Lee had sent a large part of his army to General Bragg's support, the Eleventh and Twelfth Corps, from fourteen to fifteen thousand men, were drawn from the Army of the Potomac and sent to the vicinity of Chattanooga. General Halleck's instructions to General Burnside to go to General Rosecrans's support became more than ever urgent and peremptory. "General Rosecrans," he telegraphed to Burnside, "will require all the assistance you can give him to hold Chattanooga. Sam Jones is not likely to move far down the valley without reinforcements. If the enemy should cross the Tennessee above Chattanooga you will be hopelessly separated from Rosecrans, who may not be able to hold out on the south side." General Burnside, in his official report, referring to the telegrams that passed between General Halleck and himself at that time, says: "Some misunderstanding occurred in regard to the purpose of these dispatches."[3]

---

3. See *The War of the Rebellion: A Compilation of the Official Records of the Union and Confederate Armies* (Washington, D.C., 1888–1901), series 1, vol. 30, part 3, pages 904–6, for the complete text of two telegrams passing between Burnside and Halleck on September 27, 1863, to which Burnside here refers, and to which Jones refers in the next paragraph.

It resulted from these instructions that General Burnside did not follow either of the two lines of action that the Confederate commander in that quarter supposed he would adopt. He neither carried the main body of his army, or, indeed, any part of it, to General Rosecrans's assistance, nor moved it eastward with a determined and sustained effort to defeat and drive the Confederates from Northeast Tennessee and carry the war into southwestern Virginia. On September 30 he informed General Halleck that his army was then concentrated and in readiness to move in accordance with either of three plans that he suggested. One of these plans was substantially the same that General Sherman carried out the next year, namely:

> To move on the south side of the Tennessee through Athens, Columbus, and Benton, pass the right flank of the enemy, sending a body of cavalry along the railroad, or on its west side, to threaten the enemy's flank and cover the movements of the main body, which, consisting of 7,000 infantry and 5,000 cavalry, will move rapidly down the line of the East Tennessee and Georgia Railroad to Dalton, destroying the enemy's communications; sending a cavalry force to Rome to destroy the machinery, works, and powder mills at that place, the main body moving rapidly on the direct road to Atlanta, the railroad center, thus entirely destroying the enemy's communications, and breaking up his depots at once, thence moving to such point on the coast where cover can be obtained as shall be agreed upon with you.

But while General Burnside was ready to undertake the foregoing enterprise or any other of the plans suggested, he evidently preferred and thought it the best policy to continue to hold East Tennessee and do the enemy material harm by operating in the direction of the salt works and Lynchburg.

None of the plans suggested by General Burnside was adopted and carried out in detail. He was permitted to carry out the spirit of the instructions, as he understood them; and if success be the proper criterion by which to judge military operations, General Burnside's course was judicious. He succeeded in holding East Tennessee, and the Union army held Chattanooga, but without his assistance. General Burnside had said to General Halleck that it did not "seem possible" for him to withdraw his troops from the presence of General Jones until the latter had been driven back or captured. Jones's force had not been captured, or driven out of Tennessee, or in any way crippled. When, therefore, the Union commander yielded to the urgent instructions of General Halleck, with evident reluctance, because against his judgement and turned his troops back toward Chattanooga, he covered the movement with a strong rear guard of cavalry and artillery, which presented a bold front. Two brigades of Confederate infantry advanced to Jonesboro, but the Union rear guard, being mounted, could not be successfully pursued by the Confederate infantry. The cavalry, however, under General John S. Williams, pursued, skirmishing with the rear guard, and pressed it down the railroad through Greenville to Bull's Gap.

The difficulty of withdrawing his troops from the presence of the Confederates had not been by any means as great as General Burnside had anticipated. At no time after the Union army entered East Tennessee had the Confederate force been strong enough to take the offensive vigorously. With the aid of very small reinforcements from General Lee's army it had maintained a hold on East Tennessee and given occupation to a great part of General Burnside's army. But no sooner was it known in Richmond and to Lee that General Burnside had arrested his eastward movement and turned back towards Chattanooga than Jones was called on to return Corse's brigade to Lee, and asked, if possible, to send reinforcements into eastern Virginia.

There were other difficulties in the way of a further advance into Tennessee. From the time of his arrival in that part of the country reports had continuously reached the Confederate commander of threatened advances of the Union troops from the Kanawha Valley and from about Beverly to the Virginia and East Tennessee Railroad, the great artery of supplies from that region. That section of the country was unquestionably greatly exposed, and it was very natural that the people should feel anxious and dissatisfied whilst so large a part of the force that was regarded as necessary for their protection was so far away.

After the Battle of Chickamauga these reports of raids on the railroad assumed more positive and definite form. On September 22 General Halleck telegraphed General Kelly, commanding the Department of West Virginia: "General Burnside reports Sam Jones with 6,000 men at Zollicoffer, between Bristol and Jonesboro, East Tennessee. If so the country between there and Lynchburg must be undefended. Cannot your cavalry make a raid and cut the road? An attempt will, at least, draw Jones out of East Tennessee." He had before that informed General Kelly, who already had about 25,000 men, that he could get reinforcements from [Brigadier General William T. H.] Brooks at Pittsburgh, Pennsylvania, if he desired them.

On October 4 General Kelly, having, as he informed General Halleck, satisfactory and reliable information that a part of the Confederate force in Greenbrier and Pocahontas had been withdrawn and had either been sent to Lee or had joined Jones on the Virginia and Tennessee Railroad, proposed, with Halleck's approval, to send Generals Averill and Scammon from Beverly and the Kanawha to "drive the Confederates from Greenbrier, Pocahontas, and Monroe, with orders, if the information obtained at Lewisburg will warrant such a movement, to push on to Dublin Station or Christianburg, on the Virginia and East Tennessee Railroad, and destroy the bridges in that neighborhood."

Of course these dispatches passing between Generals Halleck and Kelly were not known to the Confederate commander, but the preparations and movements resulting from them, such as the concentration of a large cavalry force under a general officer in the Kanawha Valley, gave rise to reports that necessarily influenced the course of the Confederate commander. General Halleck was quite right. The Virginia and East Tennessee Railroad was at that time wide open to raids, and a bold and sustained move towards it would unquestionably have withdrawn Jones's forces from East Tennessee.

With the uneasy feeling ever present with him that the long and important line of railroad in his rear and the adjacent country, with its indispensable stores of army supplies, were in jeopardy every hour, General Jones did not think it prudent to press forward further into East Tennessee in pursuit of a force that could elude or turn upon him with four times his number, whenever so disposed. Even if he had felt secure as to his rear, a further advance into Tennessee would have been rash, seeing that the Union cavalry and artillery alone greatly outnumbered his force of all arms combined—so rash that nothing but the most unlooked for success would excuse it. He therefore halted his infantry in front of Jonesboro and pushed his cavalry, under General Williams, with a small infantry support, beyond Grenville to the vicinity of Bull's Gap, which Burnside held in force. From Carter's Station, at 5:00 P.M., on September 28, Jones wrote to General Williams:

> I am strongly of the opinion that the force in your front is small and composed of cavalry and mounted infantry and disloyal East Tennesseans, organized for the Federal service. If I am correct in this opinion we cannot force them to fight us. They can elude us whenever they please and my infantry cannot overtake them. It is of great importance that I should have correct information on this point. I can only get it from my cavalry. You will therefore press the enemy this evening, ascertain if he is retreating; if so, whether in haste or in good order, and whether he has infantry and artillery. Let me have this information by 10:00 P.M. tonight, as it is of the first importance.

The records of the Department of West Virginia were burned near the close of the war and no copies of the dispatches received by Jones during the operations in the autumn of 1863 have been found. His dispatches to Mr. Davis indicate what agrees strictly with his distinct recollection, that so far from getting the reinforcements he so much needed, the few that had been sent to him were recalled and he was urged, if possible, to send reinforcements to Lee.

General Burnside, on the contrary, was receiving reinforcements. By September 30 the whole of the Ninth Army Corps had reached him, and on October 5 [Brigadier] General O. B. Willcox arrived with a division of reinforcements from Camp Nelson, Kentucky, consisting of the One Hundred Fifteenth, One Hundred Sixteenth, One Hundred Seventeenth, and One Hundred Eighteenth Indiana Volunteers, Twelfth Michigan, Twenty-first Ohio, and Twenty-third Indiana batteries of field artillery. On October 8 he was at Bull's Gap, and the next morning, on the march to Blue Springs, was joined by [Colonel William A.] Hoskins's brigade of the Twenty-third Army Corps and two companies of the Third Indiana Cavalry. General Burnside had determined to turn eastward again and move against the Confederates, who were giving him some trouble in that quarter.

The Ninth Army Corps, under Brigadier General R. B. Potter (6,000 men), together with all the cavalry except [Colonel Robert K.] Byrd's and [Colonel

Frank] Wolford's brigades, under General Shackelford (3,500), General Wilcox's division, and Colonel Hoskins's brigade attached (3,500) of the Twenty-third Army Corps, in all about 13,000 men present for duty, were concentrated at Bull's Gap on October 8. [Brigadier General Milo S.] Hascall's division (3,500) of the Twenty-third Army Corps was at Morristown, about fifteen miles west of Bull's Gap. General Burnside went in person, overtook his troops at Bull's Gap on the ninth, [and] prepared to advance upon the Confederates the next morning.

Major General Robert Ransom, having reported to General Jones for duty, was assigned by him, about October 1, to the immediate command of the troops in Northeast Tennessee; General Williams commanded the Confederate cavalry, about 1,600 men, with a field battery and one section at Blue Springs, about halfway between Greenville and Bull's Gap. Brigadier General A. E. Jackson, with about 400 infantry and home guards, was at Greenville.

On the morning of October 10, General Burnside advanced towards Greenville. Let us quote:

> At Blue Springs, midway between Bull's Gap and Greenville the enemy were found posted in heavy force and in a strong position between the wagon road and the railroad to Greenville. Our cavalry occupied him with skirmishing until late in the afternoon. Colonel J. W. Foster's brigade was sent around to the rear of the enemy, with instructions to establish himself on the line over which he would be obliged to retreat, at a point near Rheatown. It was not desirable to press the enemy until Colonel Foster had time to reach this point. I directed Captain [Orlando M.] Poe, my chief engineer, to make a reconnaissance of the enemy's position with a view to making the attack at the proper time.
>
> The ground was selected upon which the attacking force was to be formed, and at 3:30 P.M., believing sufficient time had been given to Colonel Foster to reach the desired point, I ordered General Potter to move up his command and endeavor to break through the center of the enemy's line. By 5:00 P.M. he had formed [[Brigadier General Edward] Ferrero's division for the attack. When the order to advance was given, this division moved forward in the most dashing manner, driving the enemy from the first fire. During the night he retreated, and we pursued early in the morning, driving him again beyond the Watauga River, beyond which point our cavalry was directed to hold him. Colonel Foster's brigade, which had been sent to cut off his retreat, met with serious difficulties in the way of rough roads, so that he did not reach the point on the enemy's line of retreat in time to make the necessary preparations to check him until the pursuing force could come up.

That is General Burnside's description of the affair, given in his official report.

The enemy that General Burnside found at Blue Springs, "posted in heavy force and in a strong position," was the brigade of cavalry, with six or eight pieces of field artillery, in all about 1,600 men, under General Williams. Both commanders had begun their military careers in the war with Mexico, and very recently served together as members of the United States Senate. They saw the affair from different points of view and not exactly in the same light.

At 10:00 A.M. Saturday, October 10, says General Williams in his official report to General Jones,

> the enemy, in force, moved upon my encampment, driving in my videttes and pickets. The action soon became general, our men stubbornly resisting the attack—the right wing under command of Colonel Carter, of the First Tennessee Cavalry, and the left under Colonel Giltner, Fourth Kentucky Cavalry, both of whom displayed the greatest gallantry and skill in the management of their commands.
>
> During the day the enemy received reinforcements and continued to extend his lines, to meet which I was compelled to lengthen my own, until my front was more than two miles long, and became nothing but a line of skirmishers. Our four pieces of artillery were well posted and supported by two companies. At about 8:00 P.M. the enemy, discovering the weakness of our lines, made a furious assault on the center, composed of a battalion under Lieutenant Colonel [Edwin] Trimble, numbering between seventy-five and one hundred men, against which were precipitated two regiments and a battalion of infantry and a battery of six pieces of artillery. Our center was compelled to give way, but withdrew handsomely upon the right and left wings and the enemy pressed straight towards our batteries, which did not open until they approached within 250 yards; then our four heavier pieces of Lieutenant [James J.] Schoolfield's battery of Williams's guns opened upon them with grape and canister, mowing them down.
>
> The enemy broke and attempted to escape under cover of a ravine and woodlands toward our left, when Giltner's rifles dealt destruction to their discomfited ranks. With heavy loss they fled to their original positions and darkness covered the field.
>
> During the night reliable information reached me that a brigade of Indiana infantry, passing through Cumberland Gap, Tazewell, and Morristown, had arrived at Blue Springs and was being placed in position to engage us next morning. I also had positive information that a heavy force of cavalry had passed through Rogersville on the road to Jonesboro.

Early in the night Williams telegraphed to Jones the condition of affairs, informing him that the enemy in his immediate front was at least 5,000 strong, with reinforcements coming up, and was instructed to retire with his cavalry on the road to Blountville, and Jackson's four or five hundred infantry by railroad towards Zollicoffer.

Williams's position was most critical. Finding himself in the immediate presence of overwhelming numbers, he could not withdraw by daylight without discovering to the enemy the weakness of his command. The enemy in his front, ready to attack in the morning, outnumbered him by about six or seven to one, and a cavalry and artillery force as large as his own had passed to his rear and was established on his line of retreat. He retreated rapidly during the night, was joined by General Jackson, with four or five hundred infantry and home guards at Greenville, and continued the retreat.

At daybreak on Sunday, October 11, says Williams, "we came upon the brigade of the enemy, commanded by Colonel Foster, 2,200 strong, and six pieces of artillery, posted. I ordered General Jackson to charge the enemy on the right with his 300 infantry, and Colonel Carter, with the First Tennessee Cavalry and the commands of Lieutenant Colonel Trimble and Major [S. P.] Halsey to charge on our left, which was done in handsome style and the enemy completely routed. We passed on without the loss of a wagon or a single head of beef cattle."

General Burnside, reporting the same affair, says: "The intercepting force met them at Henderson's, but owing to some misunderstanding withdrew and allowed them to pass with only a slight check." The Union commander states his loss at about 100 killed and wounded; that those of the Confederates, he says, was much greater, and that about 150 Confederates were captured. Williams's loss is not reported. He had gallantly and successfully extricated his command from a most perilous position. He was overtaken about two miles east of Rheatown, where he was obliged to face about and defend himself in a sharp combat.

On October 13 the Confederate cavalry was again struck near Blountville and driven back to Zollicoffer, where it met Wharton's brigade of infantry. Finding that the enemy in large force was turning their right and moving on Bristol, the Confederates fell back to that place and continued the retreat, followed by the enemy to within about six miles of Abingdon.

It seemed that General Burnside had at last decided to carry the war into Virginia—one of the plans that it had been supposed from the beginning he would adopt. But he had not. On the contrary, it appears from his dispatches that his moved eastward had been designed, in view of the emergency that might at any time require him to go to General Rosecrans's assistance, only to clear his left flank of the Confederate force that threatened it, to bring his "army about the Virginia line, showing him (the enemy) that we were ready to meet any force that he might send against us in that direction, and possibly creating a diversion in favor of Meade's army and so destroy the railroad as to prevent the movement of any large force from Virginia."

It was soon manifest that Burnside had no intention of invading Virginia. Having followed the Confederates a few miles beyond the Tennessee line, to the surprise of the Confederate commander his troops turned back, destroyed the railroad bridge, burning the long and important bridge at Zollicoffer and five other bridges, and all of the locomotives and cars they found in their progress, and took position at Jonesboro and Rogersville, with advance guards posted near Carter's Station, scouting on the line of the Holston.

The Confederates were in no condition to take immediate advantage of this retrograde movement and enter again on offensive operations. The cavalry had been continuously and actively engaged for six or seven weeks. Men and horses were without shoes and greatly exhausted; Wharton's infantry brigade had been marching almost continuously, from Staunton to Winchester, Virginia, thence by Orange Court House and Warm Springs, Virginia, to Jonesboro, Tennessee, and back to Abingdon. His men were badly clad; scarcely one-third of them were shod. Corse's brigade, which had returned to that part of the country, was but little, if at all, better provided for and had no field transportation, now become indispensable because of the destruction of the railroad bridges.

Some delay near Abingdon was, therefore, unavoidable. In the meantime Jones tried again to obtain reinforcements, but so far from succeeding he was called upon to send a part of his troops to Lee.

Failing to procure reinforcements from eastern Virginia or elsewhere outside of his own department, Jones ordered a regiment of infantry to the salt works and a regiment and two battalions of cavalry. The regiment and battalions of cavalry, together with other fractional cavalry organizations, were united to form a brigade and the command was given to Brigadier General William E. Jones.

As soon as the Confederate troops about Abingdon were in condition to take the field again they were moved into East Tennessee and by November 1 occupied very much the same position that they had occupied early in September. The force was much too small to undertake active offensive operations, but there were other considerations that made it proper to push them as far into Tennessee as prudence would permit. The necessity of procuring food not only for the troops in that section of country, but for Lee's army, was most pressing, and it was the best time of the year for collecting beef cattle and hogs. Hence it was important to occupy as large an extent of country as possible from which such supplies could be procured.

When the Confederates entered Tennessee General Shackelford, commanding all of the Union cavalry in that part of the country, drew in his outposts from Kingsport, Blountville, and Carter's Station and fell back to Rheatown; the road from Kingsport to Rogersville was thus left unguarded. At the latter place was a Union brigade, composed of the Seventh Ohio Cavalry, Second East Tennessee Mounted Infantry, and a field battery (M, Second Illinois Light Artillery, Captain [John C.] Phillips), commanded by Colonel Israel Garrard, Seventh Ohio Cavalry. General Robert Ransom, commanding the Confederates in that district, thought the brigade could be surprised and probably captured.

On November 3 he instructed General W. E. Jones and Colonel Giltner, temporarily commanding Williams's brigade of cavalry, to move rapidly and as secretly as possible and attack the enemy at Rogersville early in the morning of the sixth. To surprise the enemy the march to Rogersville was to be made in the night. W. E. Jones and Giltner were directed to attack from different points, but to communicate with each other and attack simultaneously. The night was dark, the roads to be followed and the fords crossed difficult, which prevented the attacks from being made simultaneously. But they were both gallantly and successfully made.

Generals Burnside and Willcox both report that Colonel Garrard's brigade was "completely routed." About 850 prisoners, 1,000 horses and mules, four pieces of artillery, sixty wagons, and a quantity of quartermaster, subsistence, ordnance, and medical stores, camp equipage, flags, and official records were captured. The loss in killed and wounded was small. Colonel Garrard fled with the remnant of his shattered brigade to Morristown, where General Burnside concentrated that part of his army east of Knoxville. This retrograde movement of the Union troops left the Confederates, after two months of active operations, in possession of a large and productive part of East Tennessee, none of which did they occupy when the campaign commenced.

The time had now passed when General Burnside could carry the war into Virginia or turn again upon the Confederate troops. He was himself on the defensive. He was forced by the operations of General Longstreet's corps from the south to concentrate the great part of his army at Knoxville on the night of November 16. His telegraphic communication was cut and the greater part of his army besieged in Knoxville.

34

Charging with Sheridan up Missionary Ridge
Michael V. Sheridan, Brigadier General, U.S.A.

THIS IS THE story of one of the most spectacular, sensational battles of the war—Chattanooga. It is not a general-officer's story—the why and the wherefore, the strategy of the battle; it is not the story of a line officer nor of a private—concerned with the how, the tactics, of the fighting; it is the story of an eyewitness who participated—a fine-drawn distinction this, and unusual. The direct results of Chattanooga have been done and done by historians; the indirect, but far-reaching results have been dwelt upon but lightly, and so I stop the story to put them in: It was Chattanooga that did much to place General [Ulysses S.] Grant in the saddle of the Lieutenant-General of the armies of the United States—the first to occupy it since General George Washington; also, the battle resulted in the appointment of General Philip H. Sheridan to the command of the Cavalry Corps of the Army of the Potomac, and later to that of commander of the Army of the Shenandoah.

My brother, the General (it is customary in the army to address one's relatives by their rank rather than by their given names, and so in speaking of or to my brother he was always "the General," and to me he is "the General" even to this day) shortly before Chickamauga appointed me to his staff as aide-de-camp, a greatly to be desired position. Until then I had been a second lieutenant of the

Brigadier General Michael
V. Sheridan, Late in Life
(U.S. Army Military Histo-
ry Institute)

Second Missouri. There were four of us aides on the General's staff, Captain
H. C. Ransom, Lieutenants T. W. C. Moore, Frank H. Allen and myself. I mention my rank for I wish to show what exceptional opportunities an aide enjoys
for observing a large part of the battle in which he is engaged. During a battle
an aide, whose chief duty is to carry messages and dispatches, often verbal orders of the greatest importance, is here, there, everywhere; now out on the front
line where men are dropping all about him, now to this flank, now to that, and
now, awaiting orders, sitting his horse quietly near his general with the whole
battle spread out before him. Thus comparatively few men saw the Battle of Missionary Ridge—that is, that part of the battle fought by the Army of the Cumberland—as I had opportunity to see it.

 After our defeat at Chickamauga, the Army of the Cumberland returned to
Chattanooga and entrenched; and our victors, [General Braxton] Bragg's army,
followed and occupied and fortified Lookout Mountain and Missionary Ridge.
Now this was the picturesque setting of the stage for that spectacular and melo-

dramatic series of battles which made up the three days' Battle of Chattanooga. The Army of the Cumberland lay in and about the little town of Chattanooga at the valley's mouth on the south side of Tennessee River. We gazed to the left, the east, over our strong entrenchments at a wall of mountain and of men—grim old Missionary Ridge, fortified at its base and midway up its steep side and, heavily, for miles along its crest. We looked, close at hand, to the west—a wall of rock and of men, Lookout Mountain; its 2,200 feet towered straight up from the river and seemed to hang over our heads. We looked before us up the valley; from wall to wall and but two and a half miles away stood a manmade barrier of strong entrenchments filled with powerful enemies fresh from victory over us. Grim and rugged enough before we came were those old hills and mountains, covered, for the most part, with woods and thickets, studded with huge boulders, and gashed with countless narrow ravines. Now that we had come they were seamed, too, with interminable lines of entrenchments—raw yellow ocher seams, ugly as a wound. As the almost ceaseless autumnal rains dashed the brown leaves from bush and tree, the lines, against the bluegray of the mountainsides, stood out clearer and clearer day by day. There we lay besieged in Chattanooga, between the horns of our enemy with the Tennessee River at our back. And there we lay for nine dreary weeks until we fought again.

My brother's division took up its position on the morning of September 22, 1863, on the west outskirts of the town, close by the gloomy, dismantled old ironworks, and in the very shadow of Lookout Mountain. Above us on the mountain's tip was a battery of Whitworth guns—rifled cannon of tremendous power, brought in from England by blockade-runners. All the time that we lay there we were under shellfire from those guns, yet in all that time the only casualty received by us—that ever I knew of—for we were well protected by casemates and bombproofs, came in a very roundabout way. These shells kept dropping down upon us at any hour of the day or night but chiefly they came at night and broke our rest mightily, not so much by the tremendous bang of their bursting as by their hellish screeching in mid-air, a screech which sounded, the General used to say, as though they were yelling: "Where are you? Where are you?" Such of the twenty-pounder, octagonal shells as failed to explode—and more than a few did fail—were a great curiosity to our men, what with their strange shape and the cluster of percussion-caps set in the shell's point. One day a shell fell quite near where I was standing, and it did not burst. Presently three privates came along and one of them carried the shell over in front of a tree and laid it down, and he himself got behind the tree, reached around it, and, before I knew what he was about, he brought down a hatchet—smash—upon the percussion caps. Of course, the shell exploded. It tore off the arm of the man behind the tree and instantly killed his two comrades. That man doubtless tells today how he lost his arm while storming Missionary Ridge.

Our headquarters tents were pitched on Mr. William Crutchfield's grounds, and a fine old gentleman we found him to be, loyal Unionist to the backbone, and of great help to the General as a guide the night of the battle, after he had made the charge with us. But I am getting on too fast, for that was not to be for many and many a day. And with each day until General Grant came there was less and less likelihood of the Army of the Cumberland making a charge across level fields let alone up Missionary Ridge out there, or up the towering rocky walls of Lookout Mountain. Starvation—that was why the Army of the Cumberland was growing each day less able to attack, less able to stay in Chattanooga, less able even to retreat north of the Tennessee. And there was not ammunition enough for one day's fighting. Not that any man starved to death, or even came down to horseflesh (that I know of); but when four hardtack biscuits and a quarter of a pound of bacon make rations for *three days*, it is close enough to starvation to be called that; and, further, on the morning of October 30 there were left just four boxes of hardtack in the commissary warehouses in Chattanooga.

In Bridgeport, our base of supplies, were food and clothing, plenty and to spare, and Bridgeport was but twenty-six miles away, by rail; but the railroad was in the hands of the enemy as were all the more direct roads, so that Bridgeport was really, by wagon road, sixty miles away, and range upon range of mountains in between. Very shortly after we entrenched, the rain came and with each day the mud grew stickier and deeper and the mountain roads to Bridgeport became sixty morasslike miles in which no wagon, even an empty one, was hardly ever less than hub-under. There was no chance whatever to transport

Thomas's Army Starving in Chattanooga (*Life of Sherman*)

fodder for our wretched animals. Ten thousand mules and horses starved to death there in Chattanooga and on that terrible road to Bridgeport. For a time, pyres, on which were burning these animals that had died in the town, blazed by night and by day; those that died on the road were dragged aside among the broken and abandoned wagons. Then fuel on our side of the river gave out; what we had was carried on the shoulders of the men to their campfires, for there were no animals to drag out. Jefferson Davis came from Richmond and looked complacently down into our camps and agreed with General Braxton Bragg that we were held at his mercy and that our destruction was only a matter of time.

As for the starving I can write of it only as an eyewitness, and the way of that was this—worth the telling since there was nothing else like it in the Army of the Cumberland: After Chickamauga, Captain Lowell H. Thickston's company of the Second Kentucky Cavalry had attached itself, without authority, to the general's headquarters and had remained there undisturbed because of the coming reorganization of the army. This company the general dispatched into the Sequatchie Valley, and there they hid themselves in a little cove whence they sent us a goodly supply of provisions for officers and men, and considerable fodder (so that we saved some of our horses), and often we had poultry and eggs enough to divide with officers' messes less fortunate than ours. Not an hour but that Captain Thickston and his brave little band were in danger of death or capture at the hands of [Major General Joseph] Wheeler's cavalry, but there they stayed until after the battle; and very great service they did us.

Then General Grant came—[Major General George H.] Thomas having already relieved our greatly beloved [Major General William S.] Rosecrans of his command—and completed the plans, already under way, for the relief of our starving army. Within a week the Tennessee opened and the so-called "Cracker Line"—a little stern-wheel steamer built for the purpose in Bridgeport—was bringing bargeload after bargeload of provisions and fodder, ammunition, clothing, and shoes. [Major General Joseph] Hooker with the Eleventh and Twelfth Corps of the Army of the Potomac advanced from Bridgeport; and from Memphis, more than 300 miles away, [Major General William T.] Sherman's Army of the Tennessee was coming, by forced marches, each day nearer and nearer.

The Army of the Cumberland, once so weak and listless (but uncomplaining), which for so long had sullenly awaited retreat or capture, now looked with a gleam in its eyes at the yellow lines of earthworks across the valley and along the ridges—earthworks over which it now felt sure it would one day go storming. The Army of the Cumberland had been reorganized so that now General Sheridan commanded the Second Division of the Fourth Corps—twenty-five regiments of about 6,000 men. We had been moved out beyond Chattanooga's eastern side to face Missionary Ridge instead of Lookout Mountain. Then at last came Sherman and the Army of the Tennessee, and the Battle of Chattanooga began.

On the morning of November 23 the Federal army confronted its enemy in the rough form of a letter *S* lying on its back from southwest to northeast. Hooker's command faced the tip of Lookout Mountain; our Army of the Cumberland under Thomas fronted the ridge about whose blunt nose was hooked Sherman's Army of the Tennessee. Here, thus, for the first and only time during the war, stood Grant and Sherman, Sheridan and Thomas and Hooker, together on the same battlefield.

At noon came orders for the divisions of Generals Sheridan and [Thomas J.] Wood to drive in the enemy's pickets, and occupy and hold Orchard Knob. The knob was a rough, steep hill about one hundred feet high that rose abruptly out of Chattanooga Valley midway between our outposts and the Confederate entrenchments at the base of Missionary Ridge. On our Fort Wood's parapet stood a great group of general officers, Grant and Thomas, [Major General Gordon] Granger our corps commander, and [Major General Oliver O.] Howard and Hooker and many and many more, all come to watch this spectacle. The Confederates, idly looking down from the ridge, believed that they were looking upon a mere review. Our companies and regiments marched and counter-marched and wheeled into line unmolested, and the bands played and the flags snapped and fluttered, and the bright sun shone upon 10,000 glittering bayonets and musket barrels. We must have been of a very handsome and martial aspect.

Suddenly the bands of music dropped to the rear, and the regimental bugles shrilled, and the company snare-drums rolled into the "Charge!" The long line swept out onto the level field and swung into the double, and that part of the Battle of Chattanooga was won. Thus our division (together with that of General Wood) struck its first blow; also it was to be that—more than sixty hours later—we were to strike the last.

Compared with what was to follow, this assault on Orchard Knob was nothing at all. Of course, a very heavy fire was poured down upon us from the ridge, and the moment we entered the enemy's rifle pits on the knob and for half a mile to right and left of it—from which the Confederates had scampered without much ado—every man worked desperately to "turn" the pits, that is, to throw the parapet to the other side of the trench so as to be between us and the rain of bullets and shells from the ridge.

And there (Wood's division on the knob and ours to the south of it), right there in those cold, muddy trenches, officers and men together, we huddled for forty-eight wretched, anxious, interminable hours. Not an hour of those forty-eight that we did not expect the order to charge. No conceivable suspense surpasses that of lying under arms hour after hour waiting in cold blood to go into action; dreading the battle, yet longing for it to begin in order the sooner to get it over with. I have read, and I have been told, of men who enjoyed battles and who gloried in fighting, and men have told me the same about themselves (when there was no war). Personally, I have never known such a man. With me a battle was what I was there for, and it had to be gone through with. But at the

Seizing Orchard Knob (*Life of Sherman*)

moment of going under fire my heart and lungs and stomach never felt right (though I have been in forty-eight battles and skirmishes), and it is my belief that that is so of every man. Once the battle begins, the hurry and noise, the confusion and excitement, are so tremendous that a man becomes, mentally and physically, abnormal and hence gets through with it. But as for *enjoying* a battle—don't believe it.

And so, all that Monday afternoon we waited on mental tiptoes in the captured trenches and impatiently watched the slow hours lag by. With darkness came the certainty of bivouacking there where we lay, and many were the regretful thoughts of our tents—palaces of comfort contrasted with the bleak discomfort of the cold, hard ground. There was but little sleep. Morning brought with it a drizzling rain, the coldest, most penetrating that ever I felt; but for us no order to advance, or, indeed, to do anything. Behind us the valley was veiled in mist and rain, and Lookout Mountain was completely blotted out. The rain soon ceased, and the mist lifted from the valley only to make the gray wall between us and the mountain all the more impenetrable. Then, very early in the morning, from out of this mist arose the roar of battle. [Major General Joseph] Hooker was sending his men, foot by foot, up the mountainside! There under our very noses was being fought a fierce battle that was as invisible to us—save for yellow flashes and red glares in the fog—as though it were being fought in another continent. Ever the roar grew. Now it came muffled by the fog, a great, dull rumbling that shook the heavy air and rose and ebbed; then suddenly it would swell out for an instant, through some displacement of the mist, into the sharp crackle of musketry and the crash of bursting shells—great waves and torrents of sound.

Hour after hour we lay there, literally lay, for, from the ridge above us, from dawn to dark, there came a rain of shells which caused great discomfort of mind to us all and loss of life to more than a few. So we lay, watching the spurting flames amid the eddying gray clouds and the red sheets that flashed from cannon mouth and exploding shell. Once, for the space of a minute or two, there came a rift in the curtain, and the glorious sight of a straggling gray line falling back across a clearing pressed sharply by a charging line of blue. Then the fog swept down again. From thirty thousand throats went up such a storm of cheers and huzzahs that the thunder of musketry and artillery—even that of the sullen guns firing down upon us from the ridge—was overborne by that shout of triumph.

Soon after noon the rumble of battle doubled in volume: [Major General William T.] Sherman's Army of the Tennessee on our left was attacking the north end of the ridge. To us of the Army of the Cumberland the tension became almost unsupportable; the very next instant there would surely come our order to charge across the fields and through the wood and go storming up the steep, rocky, entrenchment-line side of grim old Missionary. But no order came. We could see the spurting belt of fire rising higher and higher through the fog upon

Lookout Mountain; we could hear the roar of the Army of the Tennessee slowly rolling toward us; it seemed to us that our vengeance for Chickamauga was being withheld from the Army of the Cumberland and given to those who had nothing to avenge. About 2:00 P.M. the firing on Lookout dwindled to a scattered popping of skirmishers; later we learned that it had grown so dark there in the clouds, and Hooker's men were so nearly out of ammunition, that they had been halted a little short of the summit. The Battle of Lookout Mountain was at an end.

To the present generation Lookout Mountain is one of the best known battles of the Civil War, not because of unusually fierce fighting or important results, but chiefly because of its sobriquet "The Battle above the Clouds." Had Missionary Ridge been called Missionary Mountain or had the battle been fought in clouds or fog so that it might have received that popular and descriptive sobriquet, then the Battle of Missionary Ridge would rise to be among those few battles that the present generation can call to mind when asked to name a dozen battle of the war. It is enough to say of the two battles, in comparison, that in our division alone we lost several hundred more men in forty-five minutes (one regiment, the Fifteenth Indiana, losing 202 out of 337) than General Hooker lost in the entire Battle of Lookout Mountain, and only several hundred less than the Army of the Tennessee lost in their fight of two days.

For several hours after the close of the Battle above the Clouds the storm of shot and shell continued at the north end of Missionary. From man to man along our lines the news was passed that Sherman was sweeping on victoriously, and our excitement became more and more intense. Not until next day did we learn that the Army of the Tennessee had been sharply checked and was held on the farther side of the valley that separated the foothills from the north end of Missionary Ridge proper. But that Tuesday afternoon there was nothing for us to do but speculate on the progress of Sherman's battle, and querulously ask each other if we were never to be "sent in." Of us all, the General was the most impatient and fidgety. It was always that way with him during inaction before battle; let the moment of action come and few others had nerves and brain in such supreme control. But now in this prolonged period of suspense his nervous tension was tremendous. I remember that half a dozen newspapers which we young officers had in some manner got hold of, were read and reread those three days—advertisements and all—until they were all but in tatters.

For me the interminable wait was broken by the welcome order from the General directing me to report to our corps commander, [Major General] Gordon Granger, over in Fort Wood, and offer him my services—a mere commonplace of military courtesy. I found General Granger enjoying himself hugely. He always had the idea that he had a wonderful eye for artillery, so now I found him going from gun to gun of Fort Wood's great siege ordnance, sighting each at the ridge, and watching with much satisfaction the results of the shots. Just as I reached him, General Grant and General Thomas approached, and, after watching for a moment, General Thomas very testily ordered: "Pay more attention to your corps, sir!" So General Granger, considerably chagrined, returned to his corps, and I went back to my place in the trenches.

Toward dusk there burst out from Lookout Mountain a terrific cannonading; half a hundred pieces of artillery seemed to be in furious action. The General sent Lieutenant Moore over at a hard gallop to see if assistance were needed. Very soon Lieutenant Moore returned laughing at what might be called the "Battle of Echoes." All this great noise of a general engagement was being magnified by existing atmospheric conditions and by rocky cliff and jutting spur, from a perfunctory little rear-guard fight between only two sections of field artillery!

Darkness fell; the mist entirely cleared away, and in the crisp, still air the campfires spangled the valley and the sides and crests of Lookout and Missionary in seemingly countless thousands. Hour after hour artillery continued its loud roaring, but slowly, sullenly; pickets sniped each other by starlight; little by little the firing fell away; the campfire embers died; midnight brought silence and, for the exhausted men upon Lookout and upon the north slope of Missionary, sleep; but for the highly wrought men of the Army of the Cumberland there was only the most fitful slumber. For there, in front of and above us, lay the unshaken enemy; Sherman's attack had thus far failed; Hooker's capture of Lookout had had no effect upon the issue; on Missionary Ridge the enemy held like granite. Every man in the Army of the Cumberland knew that, as inevitable as sunrise, we, on the morrow, would be called upon to charge up Missionary Ridge.

Yet dawn came—snappy-cold and clear as crystal—and then sunrise, and still no orders. Long before the sun rose from behind Missionary every eye had turned toward Lookout Mountain. While the valley still was in dusky shadow the first rays of sunlight struck across the dark gulf, touched Lookout's summit, and shone full upon the Stars and Stripes! During the night the enemy had retreated, and ere earliest dawn Hooker's men had raised our flag on Lookout Point.

From the left arose the roar of the Army of the Tennessee's renewed battle. And still inactive we lay in our trenches waiting in a torment of suspense and impatience. Generals Grant and Thomas, Granger and others took up position on Orchard Knob, from which the entire field could be seen. Their presence made the coming charge seem yet more imminent. In front of us the crest of the ridge stood out sharply against the bright sky, and now along this crest there marched the two divisions that so lately had been on Lookout. All night long they had marched and now they were going into action against Sherman. I am not sure now that we then knew what troops they were, but I dare say we surmised. On the ridge directly in front of our division stood the Thurman House, now General Bragg's headquarters. What a coming and going of furious-riding aides! With our glasses we could see them dash up, fling themselves from their horses and rush into the house, only to reappear a moment later and go furiously galloping away again. As the battle with the Army of the Tennessee grew fiercer and fiercer, column after column of the enemy wheeled into line and went hurrying along the ridge crest—an almost endless procession of brightly shining muskets and tossing, bright-hued battle-flags. In momentary lulls we caught the rumble and clatter of batteries galloping northward to bear upon the assaulting Army of the Tennessee.

Noon came. One o'clock; two o'clock; three o'clock; the sun of the short November day was low over Lookout Mountain; the day was almost done. And still no sign of Hooker; every ear was straining for the sound of his guns at Rossville at the farther end of the ridge. When his attack should draw off troops from in front of Sherman and from the center (that is, in our front) then the Army of the Cumberland would charge. (Hooker, we were to learn, had been blocked four hours by Chattanooga Creek, whose bridge had been burned by those Confederates retreating from Lookout Mountain). Since sunrise assault after assault by the Army of the Tennessee had failed; their fire was dwindling; Hooker's attack could no longer be awaited, for the pressure upon the Army of the Tennessee must be relieved. The battle of Chattanooga had reached its crisis. General Grant peremptorily ordered the Army of the Cumberland to strike.

At a signal of six guns from Orchard Knob we were to charge. The order was to re-form after taking the first line of rifle-pits. Already, at the earliest sign of our preparation for the coming assault, the Confederates began rushing troops from their left—the south end of the ridge, where Hooker should have been attacking—into their entrenchments in front of us. We watched them coming along the crest at the double, their colors flying—every moment, more of them. It was curious to be watching so passively the men whom we were so soon to be fighting, probably hand to hand. The General sent Captain Ransom at a mad gallop to General Granger for confirmation of the order. To *stop* in the first trenches in such a fire as that which would be poured upon us. It could not be. Scarcely had Ransom left when—Boom, boom—boom, boom, boom—boom; the signal. Twenty thousand men rose from their places and swept forward to take and hold an untenable position.

To the civilian a line of battle is a row, or perhaps a double row, of shoulder-touching soldiers. Now this is the manner in which that great battle-line moved: Our division's right, for example (though in the other brigades the number of regiments varied), was Colonel Francis T. Sherman's brigade of nine regiments; it moved with a front of three regiments, between each regiment a small gap; in each regiment were ten companies, separated from each other by lesser gaps; each company moved in front and rear ranks. Behind the first three regiments a wide space, then behind them, three regiments; a wide space, then three regiments more. Thus Colonel Sherman's brigade moved in six parallel lines (three pairs) of thirty groups each. Our division's center was the brigade of Colonel Charles G. Harker; our left that of Brigadier-General George D. Wagner. Our one division of three brigades covered a front of more than half a mile. Three other divisions were in the charge besides ours. On our right, a

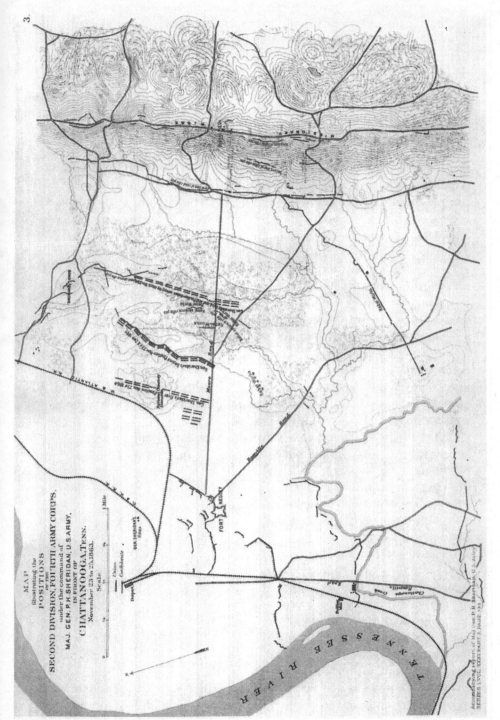

Positions of Sheridan's Division at Chattanooga (*Atlas; Official Records*)

wide interval, then [Brigadier-General Richard W.] Johnson's division; on our left, a wide interval, then Wood's; to the left of Wood's, an interval, then the division of [Brigadier-General Absalom] Baird. In front of all, of course, was a double line of skirmishers. Yet the effect, seemingly so broken up, from end to end of this battle-line of four divisions, was that of long, regular lines of surf sweeping in upon a cliff. Would they surge over it, or would they be hurled back? The Army of the Cumberland charged.

Looked down upon from the ridge it must have been a sight to inspire terror, awe. Looked at from my position it was magnificent; a sight to live as long as memory lasts. Far out in front, the thin, swift-moving double line of skirmishers; then a wide, empty space in which moved only two men—General Sheridan and an orderly; the General on his great, black horse, Rienzi, a proud, stately horse moving at a swift walk without curvettings and prancings and giving no hint of excitement except the switching of its tail. In our division General Sheridan and his orderly were the only men on horseback. On either hand as far as eye could see swept forward, faster and faster, twenty thousand glittering bayonets—surf-like lines of silver against bright blue, topped by more than four-score regimental battle-flags that whipped out straight from their staffs in the sharp breeze. There was not a cheer, not a sound except the loud jangle of accouterments and the deep rumble of forty thousand feet rhythmically falling upon frozen ground. Then from Missionary Ridge rose such a roar as no man may describe in a way that will be understood by those who, themselves, have not heard. The ground trembled. Even in the midst of that terrific roaring could be heard as an undercurrent the hiss and buzz of thousands upon thousands of invisible missiles.

What a man tells of a charge is that which an inner consciousness has retained and later gives back to him. The brain is a succession of photographic plates, automatically exposed, but which must be developed afterward. After the first clutch at the heart lessens there is no time to think, no instant when the confusion does not all but overwhelm.

Since the General would not permit to ride with him a large target of mounted officers to draw the especial fire of the enemy, Lieutenants Moore and Allen and I and a group of orderlies dismounted by the General's orders and followed at the rear of Colonel Harker's brigade. Our orders were to rejoin the General at the first line of Confederate entrenchments; we had only to lead—or drag—our horses, keep our footing over the rough ground, and keep up with the charge. In front of a great part of General Baird's, and the whole of General Wood's, divisions was an almost unbroken growth of young timber up to the crest of the ridge, but in front of us there was only a narrow belt of open woods beyond which was a shelterless plain. In front of the first line of the enemy's rifle-pits was a broad abattis—trees felled with the branches toward us; above, the ridge, almost bare of trees, rose rough and steep, four or five hundred feet high. The moment our line burst out of the thin belt of timber the inferno seemed to double and treble in volume; from behind us rolled the deep bass roar of our own siege-guns in Chattanooga firing over our heads at the ridge. So terrible was the din, so deafening, that men must shriek their words to be understood by those whose elbows touched them. The ridge seemed to have disintegrated and to be rising in whirling clouds of smoke, but from our ranks not a shot was fired. Nor was there any dust. We ran in clear air and brilliant, sparkling sunshine.

The crossing of that plain was a matter of minutes; it was only two-thirds of a mile. Even veterans will duck and dodge now and again, in entrenchments, when a shell (sometimes even a bullet) seems to be coming straight for them; there was no ducking or dodging here. If you were to be hit you would be hit; you had good luck or you had bad luck; whichever way it went it was the will of God, and there was no getting around it. So every man just ran as fast as he could (and still preserve the alignment), for the quicker we got there the sooner it would be over with, and each of us would have done anything to get out of that missile-swept plain. The time did not seem long; it did not seem short; time ceased to exist; we just ran and ran, and presently those of us who were alive and unhurt were there.

The first line of entrenchments was carried by just nothing at all but the weight and momentum of thousands of human bodies. So swift was the charge that the Confederate skirmishers and our own skirmish line were rolled upon and over by the first rank of our battle-line, and together they all swept over the entrenchments while the second and third ranks and we aides were still out in the plain. Some few of the Confederates had scampered for dear life up the face of the ridge for the second line of entrenchments, but the most of them had flung down their weapons and raised their hands in surrender before those thousands of bayonets could reach them. I remember these would-be Confederate prisoners. The "prisoners," having been ordered to the rear, came tearing toward us; there was not a sign of a guard with them. By some oversight no provost-guard had been detailed, and so, prisoners being the business of nobody in particular, nobody gave a thought to them, or of anything else except to get himself out of that murderous fire. The nearer you got to the enemy the safer you were, for the Confederates on the ridge-crest were firing a little high to avoid hitting their own men in the midway entrenchments. Thus the prisoners seeking our rear were every instant in greater danger of being shot in the back by their own men; the further out from the captured lines they got the greater was their danger and the faster they ran. A large group of them, seeing that we were officers, made for us aides. As they neared us they yelled, without slackening speed, "Where shall we go? Where shall we go?" And we, not knowing or caring where they were to go, so only that they did not detain us an instant longer out in that fire, gestured with our thumbs toward Chattanooga, and yelled: "Go that way. Go that way." Without the loss of a stride we passed each other in mid-plain, every man of us running as fast as the Lord let him.

Still another incident I remember of that charge across the shelterless plain. I remember seeing—though at the time I was but vaguely conscious that I saw— no less than six, and I think it was seven, battleflags pitch forward only to be caught up by brave hands that we could not see, ere they could touch the ground.

The charge was by no means over yet. We hugged the captured entrenchments and the face of the ridge itself as closely as we could hug them, but on all sides men were being killed by dozens.

I do not know how long this lasted—not more than a very few minutes— before one of the strangest things took place that ever occurred in any battle in any war. The *men* began to charge. No one ordered them up the face of Missionary. There was a sudden stirring, then a surge, then in a moment every man was scrambling up the hill. It was just that they felt that, inactive, they could not stay there and endure such a fire; they would not retreat; and, besides, just above them were the very men who had defeated them at Chickamauga. The private soldiers of the Army of the Cumberland again charged.

[Lieutenant Colonel Joseph] Fullerton, our corps commander's chief of staff, who was on Orchard Knob, writes of what took place on the Knob:

> As soon as this movement was seen from Orchard Knob, Grant quickly turned to Thomas, who stood by his side, and I heard him say, angrily, "Thomas, who ordered those men up the ridge?" Thomas replied in his usual slow, quiet manner: "I don't know; I did not." Then, addressing General Granger, he said, "Did you order them up, Granger?" "No," said Granger; "they started up without orders. When those fellows get started all hell can't stop them." General Grant said something to the effect that somebody would suffer if it did not turn out well, and then, turning, stoically watched the ridge. He gave no further orders.
>
> As soon as Granger had replied to Thomas, he turned to me, his chief-of-staff, and said, "Ride at once to Wood, and then to Sheridan, and ask them if they ordered their men up the ridge, and tell them, if they can take it, to push ahead." As I was mounting, Granger added: "It is hot over there and you may not get through. I shall send Captain Avery to Sheridan, and other officers after both of you." As fast as my horse could carry me, I rode first to General Wood, and delivered the message. "I didn't order them up," said Wood; "they started up on their own account and they are going up, too. Tell Granger, if we are supported, we will take and hold the ridge." As soon as I reached General Wood, Captain Avery got to Sheridan, and delivered his message. "I didn't order them up," said Sheridan; "but we are going to take the ridge."

The Army of the Cumberland took the ridge. Captain Ransom had returned from Orchard Knob with the order that we were to take only the rifle pits at the base, but by then the troops were already halfway up the hill. The whole battle-line was for the most part a series of regiments each in wedge shape—at each apex a battleflag. It seemed a race of the flags up the ridge. In half a dozen places the men simultaneously broke the Confederate line.

We leaped our horses over the parapet of the captured entrenchments into the midst of the wildest exultation that ever I have seen upon a field of battle. Caps flung high in air; blankets whirled about heads; a din of bayonets tink-tinkling against canteens; everywhere men were smiting each other upon the back with great buffets of rough soldier joy; everywhere were men sobbing and laughing with excitement, and essaying to cheer—rasped throats and lungs producing only hoarse yells and howlings. To be alive and unhurt, victorious, to have made such a charge—it was enough to fill any man's soul with mad rejoicing and triumph.

I glanced at my watch; it was twenty-five minutes past four. Only forty-five minutes had passed—less time that it takes to eat lunch—since we had heard the signal to charge. Almost thirty men a minute had fallen in our division alone during that three-quarters of an hour: 123 officers and 1,181 men.

But there was little time given us by General Sheridan for rejoicing. Our division reformed and pressed after the retreating Confederates. At the range of hills a mile and a half away came a sudden cooling to our hot pursuit: eight

Scaling Missionary Ridge (*Life of Sherman*)

Confederate guns had been posted there with such supports as had been rallied. It was quite dark now. Only flashes of cannon and musketry showed the positions of pursuer and pursued. The Confederate line held. Our flanking columns to right and left disappeared into the darkness to surround the hilltop. The moon rose from behind the hill—a seemingly huge moon, blood-red in the haze of powder smoke. To us who watched there suddenly appeared one of our swiftly marching columns along the hill crest—every man and musket and battleflag silhouetted against the slowly rising, blood-red moon. The enemy, almost surrounded, dashed into his last retreat. More guns, more prisoners, more of his wagon train fell into our hands.

35

The Forgotten Fight on Tunnel Hill
Green B. Raum, Brigadier General, U.S.V.

ON THE MORNING of November 25, 1863, the forces of [Major Generals George H.] Thomas, [William T.] Sherman, and [Joseph] Hooker were in close communication; their lines did not actually connect, but their objective was the same, namely, [General Braxton] Bragg's army on Missionary Ridge. The morning was cold and raw; during the early hours clouds and mists hung low and obscured objects in the valley and on the high ground.

General [Ulysses S.] Grant's plan for the battle of November 25 was for General Sherman to attack Bragg's right flank, threaten his rear, and make the greatest possible demonstration of strength to induce General Bragg to withdraw forces from his center; for General Hooker to move against General Bragg's left flank upon Missionary Ridge at Rossville Gap and force the fighting there, and for General Thomas, with the Army of the Cumberland, to attack and carry Bragg's center at the opportune moment. At midnight on November 24, he instructed General Sherman to attack the enemy at dawn, giving the information that Thomas would also attack at an early hour.

The Army of the Tennessee was ready for the conflict before the dawn of day. General Sherman and his staff examined the entire line from left to right. He had seized, fortified, and now held the north end of Missionary Ridge. His position threatened the right wing of Bragg's army and Chickamauga Station, the base of supplies for the Confederate forces.

General Sherman's position was one of great natural strength, and it had

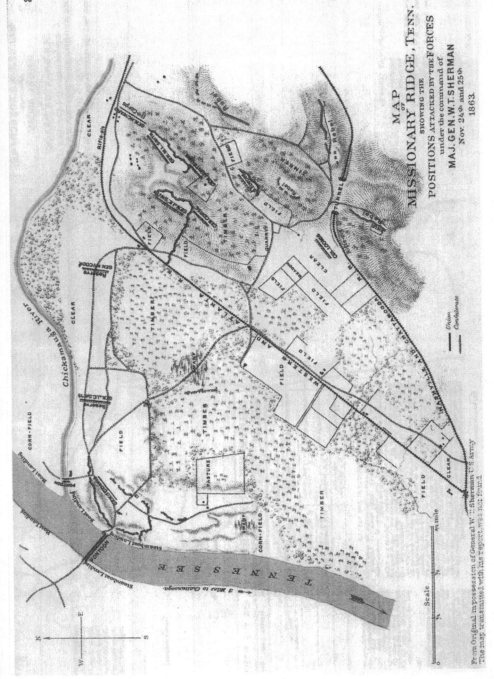

MAP
of
MISSIONARY RIDGE, TENN.
SHOWING THE
POSITIONS ATTACKED BY THE FORCES
under the command of
MAJ. GEN. W. T. SHERMAN
Nov. 24th and 25th
1863

Union
Confederate

Scale
¼ mile

From Original in possession of General W.T. Sherman U.S Army.
The map transmitted with his report, was not found.

Missionary Ridge and Tunnel Hill (*Atlas; Official Records*) been well fortified during the night, but his right wing was on a spur of high ground detached from the main ridge. This spur sloped off gradually into the valley before reaching a point opposite the tunnel. There was a deep valley between this spur and the main ridge, through which the tunnel passed.

In studying all the maps, General Sherman had concluded that Missionary Ridge was a continuous hill; but he found himself separated by a deep gorge from the main ridge over the tunnel, which was his chief objective point. The ground he had gained was so important, however, that he could leave nothing to chance, and he fortified the position during the night. This spur is almost 1,200 yards north of the tunnel and about 600 yards west of the main ridge, with very steep slopes to the east and west. It is a position of great natural strength, both for offensive and defensive operations.

When the fight for Tunnel Hill began three divisions of the Confederate army were in position in the immediate neighborhood of the tunnel, Lieutenant General William J. Hardee in command. [Major General Patrick R.] Cleburne commanded the defenses of Tunnel Hill. His division was composed of the following troops: Brigadier General St. John R. Liddell's brigade [temporarily commanded by Colonel Daniel Govan]; Brigadier General J. A. Smith's brigade; Brigadier General Lucius E. Polk's brigade; [and] Brigadier General W. P. Lowrey's brigade. One of these brigades, however, was detached to another part of the field, under the direct orders of General Bragg.

The division of Brigadier General William H. T. Walker was assigned to a position on Missionary Ridge a short distance south of the tunnel.

Major General Carter L. Stevenson, with his division, had withdrawn from Lookout Mountain during the night and reported to General Hardee for the defense of Tunnel Hill.

Strong works had been erected by the Confederates upon high ground, both north of south of the tunnel; the most skillful preparations had been made to resist every attack. Batteries of artillery had been posted at every available point, including a battery immediately over the tunnel.

Generals Hardee and Cleburne laid out the works, assigned the troops to their positions, and posted the artillery. The Confederate forces stood upon the defensive. They awaited an attack by General Sherman's troops.

The left flank of General Sherman's army held an entrenched position at the extreme north end of Missionary Ridge, occupying two spurs of the ridge. The entire Second Division, Fifteenth Corps, commanded by Brigadier General Morgan L. Smith, held this part of the line.

[Brigadier General Joseph A.] Lightburn was assigned the duty of holding the north end of the entrenched line, leaving [Brigadier] General Giles A. Smith's brigade free to operate with the assaulting column if required.

Colonel [Jesse I.] Alexander carried his position on the ridge on the afternoon of the twenty-fourth by an enthusiastic rush of his brigade up the hill. He strongly entrenched his position during the night.

Hauling up Artillery (*Life of Sherman*)

[Brigadier General John M.] Corse, with his brigade, had seized a position on the ridge to the right of Alexander, and had fortified it during the night of November 24.

Colonel Joseph R. Cockerill occupied the ridge south of General Corse with his Third Brigade, Fourth Division, Fifteenth Army Corps. This brigade had gallantly seized the southern extremity of the detached spur which overlooks the tunnel, had dragged two pieces of artillery to the crest, and had constructed a strong work along their front of the ridge, and extending down the hill to the valley. This work completed the defenses of the high ground.

[Brigadier] General Hugh Ewing, commander of the Fourth Division, superintended the laying out of Cockerill's works and took a part in making the preparations for the attack upon the enemy. He held the right of the Fifteenth Corps. To General Lightburn, Colonel Alexander, and Colonel Cockerill, with their brigades, was assigned the duty of occupying and holding the entrenched position on these ridges, while other portions of the army operated directly against the enemy. The First Brigade of General Ewing's division, commanded by Colonel John M. Loomis, occupied a position in the valley some distance to the right of Cockerill's works. The Second Brigade of General Ewing's division, commanded by Brigadier General John M. Corse, was assigned the duty of assaulting the enemy at Tunnel Hill. The Second and Third brigades of General [Brigadier] General John E. Smith's Third Division, Seventeenth Corps, were held in reserve in the valley near the base of the ridge. I commanded the Second Brigade. The Third Brigade [was] commanded by Brigadier General Charles L. Matthies.

As the morning dawned on November 25, 1863, the Army of the Tennessee was astir and was soon ready for action. All night long large working parties had been engaged in the erection of earthworks on the ridges occupied by our advanced troops.

General Sherman's headquarters were on the isolated ridge at the south end of his line, nearly opposite the tunnel, now known as Sherman Heights. The general was in the saddle at an early hour. He and his staff rode along the line examining the works. When the sun rose the day soon became bright and clear; the temperature of the air was pleasant; in fact, it was an ideal November morning.

It could now be clearly seen that the enemy had not been idle during the night. Extensive works had been thrown up on Missionary Ridge. The elevated piece of ground about 250 yards north of the gorge through which the tunnel passes, and now known as Tunnel Hill, was fortified with logs and fresh earth. It was clearly visible from General Sherman's point of view. This work, somewhat in the shape of a letter "V" with the point to the northwest, was full of men. At and near the angle eight pieces of artillery were posted. This work was our objective point. It was the most northern defensive structure for the right wing of the Confederate army.

The Fortieth Illinois, supported by the Forty-sixth Ohio on our right center, with the Thirteenth Ohio, moved down the face of the hill, known as Sherman Heights, and up that held by the enemy, known as Tunnel Hill. This line was led by General Corse in person and advanced to within about eighty yards of the Confederate entrenchments, where they found a secondary crest, which they gained and held. General Corse ordered up the reserves to this point, and asked for reinforcements, which were sent him.

General Morgan L. Smith gained ground on the left spur on Missionary Ridge, and Colonel Loomis advanced until he reached a point abreast of the tunnel and the railroad embankment. He drew upon his command a heavy fire from the battery over the tunnel and from the Confederate rifle pits. Our artillery kept up their fire, observing every precaution to avoid endangering our own men. General Corse led an assault upon the enemy's works, but failed to carry them; but he held on to his first position, and from this he could not be driven. While the fight was raging furiously about 10:00 P.M., General Corse received a severe wound in the leg and was brought off the field.

The command of the brigade devolved upon Colonel C. C. Walcutt, of the Forty-sixth Ohio, who performed the duties with ability and courage. He held the position that had been gained and kept up the contest with great spirit. He had no rifle pit for the protection of his brigade and no entrenching tools; his men took such cover as the brow of the hill afforded. For more than two hours they kept up a constant fire upon the enemy, at times silencing their artillery.

Colonel Loomis encountered heavy opposition in the valley and did not attempt to relieve Walcutt by a direct movement, but drew as much of the Confederate strength as possible against himself.

My brigade was drawn up at the base of Sherman Heights, just out of range of the enemy's artillery, but in full view from Missionary Ridge.

I rode out well to the front, from a point from which I could observe every movement on both sides. It is an interesting and exciting spectacle to witness the movements of the troops in a great battle and see the struggle for mastery—the roar of artillery, the rattling of musketry, the impetuous charge, the shouts of the men, the sturdy resistance of the assailed. All this I saw and heard, knowing full well that in a short time my own command would be in the midst of the fray.

• • •

The unequal contest on Tunnel Hill between Corse's and Loomis's brigades on the one hand and the entire Confederate forces defending that position [under Major General Patrick R. Cleburne] on the other had been going on for over five hours. No body of men could have displayed greater courage and fortitude than the National troops, but it became obvious to those who were closely observing the battle that Ewing's division had not sufficient strength to capture the ridge. The enemy had a considerable force near the foot of the ridge, both north and south of the tunnel; they held Glass's house and all the outbuildings and had four pieces of artillery in position over the tunnel which raked Loomis's line.

The enemy had from the early morning been constantly receiving reinforcements for the defense of Tunnel Hill. It was perfectly clear that the assembling upon the right flank of General Bragg's army of six divisions of troops composed of sixteen brigades, all under the command of General Sherman, had caused General Bragg and his leading subordinates serious apprehension, and they had determined to leave nothing undone to maintain their hold upon the railroad system leading south.

A remarkable feature of this battle was that the movements of the troops of each army to reinforce positions, or to prepare for an attack, were seen by the officers and men of their antagonists. Particularly was this so with the Confederates on Missionary Ridge. Their elevation was so great that they had a complete view of the valley in which General Grant's army was operating. He could perform no secret, strategic movements, and so, on our side, the movement of troops by Bragg to strengthen his right flank was as well known by General Grant and the rank and file of our army as by General Bragg himself.

About 12:30 P.M., General Sherman directed that Colonel Loomis advance and place the left of his brigade on the Tunnel Hill wagon road and hold the ground. This advance was promptly made, and the position was taken under heavy fire and with severe loss.

Loomis's skirmishers carried the railroad. The enemy was driven from Glass's house and the outbuildings. These were set on fire by the enemy as they retired.

The Confederate commander sent additional troops down the face of the ridge north of the tunnel, and also a strong detachment down the wagon road from the gorge over the tunnel. Colonel Loomis extended his left flank with the Twenty-seventh and Seventy-third Pennsylvania regiments. These troops crossed the valley under a heavy fire, attacked, and drove the enemy up the hill.

Loomis having called for reinforcements, [Brigadier General John E.] Smith ordered Matthies to report with his brigade to General Ewing, who at once directed Matthies to cooperate in meeting this advance of the enemy down from the ridge. Matthies threw his brigade into the fight with great spirit, and soon put the enemy to flight. They retreated up the hill, fighting as they went. Matthies and [Major Peter A.] McAloon's command rushed up the hill to join in the assault upon the enemy's works.

In the meantime, General Ewing called for additional reinforcements, and General Smith directed me to report with my brigade to General Ewing, which I did without a moment's delay.

General Smith had kept these two reserve brigades in readiness to move at a moment's notice.

General Ewing wished to extend the right wing of Loomis's line with my brigade. Loomis's troops were occupying a rifle pit. In compliance with General Ewing's orders I posted two regiments about twenty paces in front of his rifle pit, and extended the line to [the] right with the balance of the brigade. While General Ewing's troops were under cover, my brigade was in the open. General Smith came upon the ground in a few moments, and immediately observed the situation. He protested vigorously against such a use of his command, but no change was then made in the formation.

More serious work was in store for my brigade, and it was but a short time until it was called upon to perform it.

Major McAloon with the veteran Pennsylvanians and General Matthies with his heroic brigade had ascended the hill. They were upon the right of Corse's brigade. They reached the brow of the ridge, 400 feet above the plain. They were within 100 feet of the enemy's entrenchment. Those works were filled with determined men. Eight pieces of artillery were placed in these works, four bearing due north and four at the salient angle. As these devoted troops reached the brow of the ridge a tremendous volley of musketry and artillery welcomed them.

The men were ordered to lie down. They took shelter as best they could, and opened fire. McAloon had fought at Gettysburg. Matthies had fought from Island Number Ten to Vicksburg. Their men were veterans. They were there to fight, and to die, if need be, for their country. An incessant fire was kept up on both sides. This tragic scene continued for an hour and a half.

My brigade had been withdrawn from its anomalous position, and was held in readiness at the southern slope of Sherman's ridge. I had been standing at the southern base of the ridge for more than an hour, watching the progress of events.

Loomis's line was intact, his right still resting upon the railroad. He still held the log house at Glass's place, but he had been unable to make any impression upon the enemy in his front.

The Pennsylvania troops, led by McAloon, Matthies's brigade, and Corse's brigade, now commanded by Colonel Walcutt, still held their position, and kept up a destructive fire upon the enemy. The batteries on Sherman's hill and Lieutenant [Henry B.] Plant's battery, near the base of the ridge, kept up as effectual a fire as was possible without destroying our own men. But the fire of the enemy had been terribly destructive. They were protected by well-constructed works, had been largely reinforced, and were now able to bring more men to bear upon a given point on the ridge than the two and a half brigades could do which were now in their front.

At 2:00 P.M. General John E. Smith and General Hugh Ewing rode down from General Sherman's headquarters on the hill to where I was standing with my staff. They stated that General Sherman had directed that I should reinforce Matthies with my brigade. I replied that I had felt for some time that Matthies needed help. I asked for instructions as to the movement. Both General Smith and General Ewing requested my views upon the subject. I proposed to form the brigade in two lines, left in front, and march diagonally across the valley to the left to a point in the rear of Matthies, the front line to march up the hill to the rear of Matthies's brigade, and the rear line to form in a road which ran north up the valley at the base of Missionary Ridge. The plan was approved, and I immediately gave orders for its execution. The Eightieth Ohio, [Lieutenant] Colonel Pren Metham, and Seventeenth Iowa, Colonel Clark R. Wever to form the front line, and the Tenth Missouri, Colonel F. C. Deimling, and Fifty-sixth Illinois, Major Pinckney J. Welsh, to form the rear line; the lines to be formed parallel with each other; all field officers to dismount and march on foot.

As the formation was being made I called the commanders of the regiments together and pointed out to them the line of march and the position the lines were to take when they reached the field. I also called attention to a four-gun battery on the ridge, which would no doubt open upon us as soon as we were in range. I stated that the column would move in quick-time until the battery began firing, then I would give the order to double-quick and would gallop forward with my staff.

The lines were formed with alacrity, about fifteen paces apart, the order to advance was given, and these veteran soldiers, who had heard the sound of battle many times before, marched forward with a firm step as though they were on parade.

I kept an eye out for the battery on the hill. We had not advanced more than 200 yards when I saw the smoke of the guns. Instantly I gave the order to double-quick and galloped forward, followed closely by the troops, who maintained their lines intact. The shells flew thick and fast, and many exploded, but fortunately the guns were trained too high; not a man was killed, and only two or three slightly injured. When we reached the proper point the troops were faced to the right and moved to the front, adjusting their lines as they went. I dismounted at the foot of the ridge, paused a moment to see that the reserve line took its place, and was glad to find that the wagon road in which the formation was made was cut into the hillside, thus affording almost as much protection to the men as a rifle pit.

I immediately pushed up the hill, and in a few moments met General Matthies coming down. He had received a painful wound in the head, and was quite bloody, but able to walk. We conversed a moment. He stated that his brigade was almost out of ammunition; that their losses had been very heavy, including Colonel [Holden] Putnam, of the Ninety-third Illinois. I hurried up the hill, and soon came upon the Seventeenth Iowa. I met Colonel Wever, and informed him that we must push forward until we came up to the Third Brigade, and pass over them, through their line, and take their places at the front. Colonel Wever ordered his regiment to advance. The men went forward rapidly, the Eightieth Ohio on the left, moving in unison. We reached the rear of the Third Brigade, when the unlooked for happened.

A strong force which had been assembled by General Cleburne in the gorge over the tunnel sallied forth, charged around the hill, and made a determined attack upon the right flank of our line. At the same time troops from the Confederate breastworks came out and made a front[al] attack. The Pennsylvania troops fought with great distinction, as did the right of Matthies's brigade, which extended a considerable distance to the right of the Seventeenth Iowa.

I was right up with the advance, and saw the Confederate troops both upon our front and flank. This front[al] attack could, and no doubt would, have been resisted, as others had been earlier in the day; but the movement upon our right flank was so sudden, and pushed with such energy and determination, that there was no time to make a change of front to meet it.

Our right flank was practically in the air; it was not refused so as to offer serious resistance to a flank movement. The Twenty-seventh Pennsylvania, the Ninety-third Illinois, and the Fifth Iowa were on the right of our line, and were the first to receive the shock of the Confederate charge upon our flank.

These heroic men fought gallantly against a greatly superior force, holding their ground until 112 of their number were surrounded and captured. I saw the first break in our line on the right. It crumbled away rapidly, yielding to the pressure of the Confederate charge.

I was in the midst of the Third Brigade and Seventeenth Iowa troops, and by word and act sought to keep up the fight; but the advantage of numbers and position were against us, and these veteran soldiers retired from the hill. I was the last man of the Third Division to withdraw.

I must confess I did not stand upon the order of my going. The question was whether I should be killed, captured, or escape. I went at once, followed by an eager line of the enemy, who were not content to remain on the crest of the hill in a place then of comparative safety, but were anxious, now that their blood was up, to have it out with us. I ran down Missionary Ridge as fast as my legs would carry me. I passed a number of killed and wounded on my way, but I had no time to stop and make inquiries.

The ground was rough and rocky. I fell twice, but hurriedly scrambled to my feet and rushed on to keep out of the way of the determined men who were close upon my heels. I could not see my reserve line, but I knew that the Fifty-sixth Illinois and Tenth Missouri were in the road at the foot of the hill, and would be there when I arrived.

The officers saw me coming down the hill. They saw the Confederates also, and were waiting for them. Not a shot was fired by my men until I reached the line. I knew they were ready and, as I jumped down into the road, with a loud voice I shouted, "Fire!"

The advance of the Confederates were within thirty yards of our line, but the withering volley delivered by the two regiments brought them to a sudden halt. Four or five volleys were exchanged with deadly effect, when the Confederate troops retired precipitately up the hill.

The Eightieth Ohio, being on the extreme left of our assaulting column,

"I Ran down Missionary Ridge" (*National Tribune*)

received less of the shock of the Confederate charge. Colonel Metham withdrew his men to the north, rallied his regiment when about halfway down the hill, and materially aided in repulsing the forces that charged down the ridge.

Thus three of my regiments kept the field and were ready to renew the attack. The Seventeenth Iowa rallied in the rear of our fortified ridge. Colonel Wever reported his whereabouts to me and also to General Smith.

At our extreme right the Confederates also charged down the hill, attacked the Seventy-third Pennsylvania, [and] were met with great spirit. Lieutenant Colonel Joseph B. Taft was mortally wounded at the head of the regiment, and eighty-five men were surrounded or captured.

Corse's brigade, on the left of our line, was able to hold their ground. Loomis's brigade, at the foot of the ridge, near the tunnel, and Smith's brigade, then under command of Colonel Nathan W. Tupper, at the foot of the ridge on the east, held their positions.

The fortified line on the ridge occupied by [Colonel Joseph R.] Cockerill, [Colonel Jesse I.] Alexander, and [Brigadier General Joseph A. J.] Lightburn, with the Eleventh Corps, and [Brigadier] General Jefferson C. Davis's division, in easy supporting distance, were prepared for either offensive or defensive operations.

The regiments which were overwhelmed and forced from the ridge were at once reorganized and ready for action. It was an interesting fact that as the men fell in for a roll call they had their guns.

This great body of veteran troops on the evening of November 25, although baffled in their first attempt to capture Tunnel Hill, were in no sense of the word disheartened. They knew that they were in a position which threatened Bragg's right and rear, and they were ready to undertake any new enterprise against the enemy upon which they might be ordered.

Every brigade commander who led his troops up that acclivity was wounded. I received a gunshot wound through the left thigh, but was able to remain on the field until the enemy was repulsed, and driven back up the hill. I sent for Colonel F. C. Deimling, colonel of the Tenth Missouri, and turned the command of the brigade over to him, and was borne from the field at 3:30 P.M.

Assistant Surgeon C. C. Biser, of the Seventeenth Iowa, had charge of the ambulance corps, and he performed his duty well. It was my fortune to fall into the doctor's hands. I was in splendid health, and really sustained no shock whatever by the wound; in fact, during the excitement of the conflict I did not realize that I was wounded until I observed that my left boot was filling with blood. I at once took from my pocket a bandage and, removing a piece from the roll, tied it firmly around the leg above the wound; this partially stopped the flow of blood. It was not a great while, however, until the leg refused to perform its duty.

When I reached Dr. Biser he looked me over a little, tightened the bandage, placed me in an ambulance with two soldiers who were wounded, quite as severely as I, and we were driven to the field hospital.

Arriving there, I was met my Dr. Buell, my brigade surgeon, who expressed great joy at seeing me. He said that news had reached him that I was killed, but upon the contrary, he found me strong and vigorous. He at once stripped the leg and made an examination. His first remark was: "Well, Colonel, you have a beautiful wound; the bone has not been injured."

I told him that his report was very satisfactory, and for him to leave me quiet for a time until others who were worse hurt received attention. In a short time Major Pinckney J. Welsh, who commanded the Fifty-sixth Illinois, was brought to the hospital. The major had been shot through the left arm and through the body near the left hip. He was suffering considerable pain, but bore up manfully.

Night was coming on, every surgeon was busy, and the number of wounded was constantly increasing. I made inquiry for some able-bodied men of my brigade, and soon a soldier reported to me. I gave him instructions to go at once to our camp and bring over my headquarters tent, my personal baggage, bedding, etc., and my mess chest, provisions, and colored cook, and also to bring Major Welsh's baggage.

Upon inquiry I found that the arrangements of the hospital were very limited for cooking and serving food to the great crowd of men who had so suddenly been thrown together, and my aim was to try to relieve the embarrassment.

While lying quietly waiting events, a gentleman in citizen's clothing came to me, notebook in hand. He was a newspaper correspondent from St. Louis; his mission was to make up the list of killed and wounded. In a brief conversation with him I requested him to be careful to put me down in the list of slightly wounded, and not to make the mistake of entering my name in the list of killed, in accordance with the rumor afloat after the battle. He assured me that my wishes should be complied with, that he recognized the fact that I really was alive, and he would not kill me off in his dispatches. I have no doubt he made a correct report, but it happened that, on the morning of November 26, one of the great morning papers of St. Louis had my name in the list of killed. My people at home were terribly shocked at this report; but as other papers placed me in the list of wounded, they took hope and were soon informed as to the truth of the matter.

In good time my headquarters wagon drove into the hospital camp, bringing my belongings. Betsy, the colored cook, and two colored men came along. Every old soldier will remember how soon we could set up a tent and go to housekeeping. It required only a few minutes for my tent to be pitched and everything put in order, two cots set up, and Major Welsh and myself established for the night. Betsy selected a place for her kitchen, the men built a fire, brought water, and generally lent a hand.

I informed Betsy that we would keep an open house, and that the doctors would have the liberty to eat with us at their pleasure. Betsy was a most competent and efficient person, tireless in her efforts to contribute to the comfort of all around her. She won golden opinions of everyone who observed her work.

Major Welsh, poor fellow, suffered very severely for some time; his sleep was troubled, and he rested but little for several nights. As for myself, while I had a hole through my thigh about eight inches long, which, of course, totally disabled the leg, I was otherwise well and strong, and felt very much disgusted at the idea that I would be compelled to lie still for a couple of months until nature could do its work of repair.

I remained in the field hospital eight days. I obtained a pair of crutches and visited patients in the hospital. One night, while sitting by my campfire, I observed some persons riding across the bridge, and in a few moments [Major General John A.] Logan rode up and dismounted. He came to pay me a visit.

I was very glad to see him; his words of sympathy and good cheer were very gratifying. We had been warm friends for years, and each took an earnest interest in the welfare of the other. The general had just been assigned to the command of the Fifteenth Corps, [Major General Francis P.] Blair [Jr.] being transferred to the command of the Seventeenth Corps.

On December 2 [1863], I was sent to Chattanooga and admitted to Officers' General Hospital, Major Welsh accompanying me. On December 4, with many others, I was given a leave of absence by General Grant. General Matthies and Major Welsh were also given leaves of absence. We then arranged that we would go North together.

On the afternoon of December 4 we left Chattanooga in an ambulance, it being necessary to drive down the river around the rapids to Kelly's Ferry to take a steamboat to Bridgeport, to which point the railroad from Nashville then ran. The wagon road was very rough. We had to cross a spur of a mountain where rocks were plentiful in the road. Here, for the first time, because of the severe jolting, I experience serious discomforts. While making the ascent of this spur our ambulance broke down and could go no farther. While we were considering plans for continuing our journey, a citizen with an empty wagon came up from the ferry. It required some earnest arguments to have him turn back, but a small amount of force and sufficient amount of pay brought him to terms. We reached the ferry at dark, and were informed that the steamer would be ready to start at 6:00 A.M. the next morning. We passed the night in a small house occupied by a citizen.

The next morning the road down to the landing was filled with men on their way to the boat. Some were hauled in ambulances, but most of the men were able to make the trip without assistance. I used crutches. As we approached the boat I observed a man who was very busy in attention to the soldiers. When I came near him I saw that he gave a loaf of bread and a tin cup full of hot coffee to each man as he passed.

I at once became interested in this work. It was entirely out of the line of the Quartermaster Department. I stopped and talked with this good Samaritan and learned that he represented the Christian Commission. There he was, with bread and coffee and tin cups. These were freely and graciously given to every man taking passage on the boat. I must confess that I was deeply moved by this exhibition of loving care that the people at home were anxious to bestow upon the soldiers of the Union.

The steam packet that plied between Kelly's Ferry and Bridgeport was a flatboat without a roof, with an engine and a stern wheel. This vessel had been improvised by [Major] General W. F. Smith, chief engineer upon General Grant's staff. It was not a palace; it had no staterooms; it had no kitchen for the preparation of sumptuous meals; but it could navigate the Tennessee River, and carried us in safety to our place of destination.

On reaching Bridgeport we were taken charge of by the officers of the General Field Hospital, Army of the Cumberland, and given quarters. We remained there one night. On the morning of December 6 a train of hospital cars was made up, and we took passage on this. The cars were plainly but comfortably fitted up with bunks, and each passenger had his sleeping apartment. We made the passage to Nashville in due time in charge of the Medical Department, and all received the kindest and best of treatment.

Upon reaching Nashville, General Matthies, Welsh, and myself parted company with the surgeons, and took passage on a steamer for the Ohio River. We boarded the steamer in the afternoon. The captain informed us that he would leave the city about midnight.

After remaining aboard a short time General Matthies decided to look over the city a little. It will be remembered that Matthies had receive a scalp wound, which, although an ugly affair, did not interfere with locomotion. So the general went to town and remained there until supper time, when he again made his appearance aboard of the boat.

When at supper he remarked: "Well, we are going to have some fun tonight." I inquired: "How is that, General?" He replied: "We are all going to the theater." I expostulated that it was quite out of the question for me to venture out on such an expedition, but he said: "I have the tickets and have engaged a carriage, and the captain will hold the boat until we return, and so you must get ready and go." And go we did.

Matthies had his head covered with a plaster, Welsh had his arm in a sling and his side tied up, and I hobbled on crutches. When we reached the theater Matthies led the way. The place was full of soldiers. Our appearance there was a great surprise to those who met us. A number of officers and soldiers called at our seats to pay their respects and to express their sympathy and good wishes. We enjoyed the play, and returned to the boat without accident.

A trip from Nashville down the Cumberland River is always a pleasant episode. The river winds through a beautiful country, has a great deal of fine scenery, and a number of pleasant towns upon its banks. Although it was December 7 the weather was pleasant. Winter was not yet set in. We enjoyed the trip. We reached Smithland, Kentucky, at the mouth of the Cumberland, just as night set in. Our steamer was bound for St. Louis, and would carry General Matthies to that point on his journey home to Iowa, but Major Welsh and I were bound up the Ohio, he to Shawneetown and I to Golconda. Fortunately for us an up-river steamer was lying at the wharfboat when our boat rounded to, so we encountered no delay.

From Smithland to Golconda is but eighteen miles. Before bedtime the whistle was blown for the landing. I stood out on the guard of the boat; the night was cloudy and dark. I could see lanterns flickering along Front Street and down toward the wharfboat. In those days of war the interest and anxiety was so great that the landing of a steamboat at a town drew a great crowd. They wanted to hear the latest news. Such was the case on this occasion.

As the steamer approached the wharfboat I could see a crowd of people. My steamer towed a barge on the side next [to] the wharfboat. This made the landing slow. Finally a line was thrown and made fast to the wharfboat. Stage planks were pushed across the open barge, and on these I began the passage to the wharfboat. I was compelled to use my crutches. The people saw me coming; they raised their lanterns; the light fell upon my form and face; those men, all of whom knew me, many of them from boyhood, recognized me. Joel W. McCoy, an old merchant, was the first to speak. "My God, there is Green B. Raum," were his pathetic words. Some of the men mounted to the staging, and assisted me to descend the wharfboat. McCoy at once said: "Go for his mother and a carriage."

My mother and father soon arrived, and I was driven to the old homestead. The news of my arrival spread throughout the town, and many of my old friends looked in to see me. Men, women, and children came. They were wrought up to a high pitch of sympathetic excitement—not in respect to one soldier, but in respect to the great army of men who had gone out to fight the battles of their country.

I remained at my father's house but one night. It was still thirty miles to my own home, the town of Harrisburg, where my wife and four children were anxiously awaiting my return.

On the morning of December 8, my mother accompanied me, and we drove over the hills from Golconda to Harrisburg. I knew every resident along that road. I met the same sympathetic reception everywhere as at Golconda. I brought messages from the army to some of the families. Late in the afternoon we reached my home. I will leave to the imagination of the reader the scene with wife and children and friends that occurred on that occasion.

PART 8

The Eastern Theatre in 1864

36

Grant's Conduct of the Wilderness and Spotsylvania Campaigns

Edward Porter Alexander, Brigadier General, C.S.A.

THE SUBJECT assigned me for this evening's discussion is the Wilderness campaign, or so much of it as time will permit. I will assume a general familiarity with the principal armies and their forces by all of my hearers. At the opening of the campaign, in which [Lieutenant General Ulysses S.] Grant took the aggressive, he lay north of the Rapidan in command of two armies: the Army of the Potomac, under [Major General George G.] Meade, comprising the Second, Fifth, and Sixth Corps; and the Ninth Corps, under [Major General Ambrose] Burnside, which was organized as a separate army, taking its orders direct from Grant, as also did the Army of the Potomac under General Meade. This was a distinctly bad arrangement. There are few axioms of war better established than those which condemn divided commands and in this case experience again pronounced against it. It is never an economical arrangement and adds much to the duties of staff officers.

It was apparently solely for reasons of this sort that a change was finally made, when on May 24 [1864], the Ninth Corps was formally taken into the Army of the Potomac. Already the awkwardness of having so much to look after had so hampered Grant in his plans that he had allowed them to consume several unnecessary hours which, had they been spent in marching, might have carried him beyond the fields both of the Wilderness and Spotsylvania. Or, if the Sixth Corps had been assigned to the duty of guarding the trains of the army, they might have been concentrated and cared for on such duty during the passage of the Rapidan and Wilderness, and delivered to their respective corps as they emerged into the open country beyond. Had Grant done this there would have been no battles of the Wilderness and Spotsylvania, but probably a battle on a line behind the North Anna.

The question arises whether [General Robert E.] Lee could have himself saved time and arrived earlier. He could have done so had he brought [Lieutenant General James] Longstreet's corps, on its way up from Bristol, to the vicinity of Louisa Court House and encamped it there, behind our right flank instead of behind our left, instead of stopping it where he did, southwest of Gordonsville. Had he done this he might have met Grant's army face to face in the Wilderness. But we must assume that he practically did this, for Longstreet's corps did arrive in time.

It was Lee's policy to fight his battles under cover of the Wilderness, and he practically won a victory by bringing Longstreet into the action just in the nick of time; and perhaps we must say that Grant lost the battle by his faulty organization of having two separate armies under independent commanders operating in the same field.

It is a little surprising to find that Grant, having the initiative and the greater force of artillery, did not make a greater effort to get himself clear of the Wilderness before he encountered Lee's army. Evidently, however, he considered himself abundantly able to meet Lee on any ground, and, finding him in the Wilderness, he at once took the aggressive with such vigor that, had he had sufficient daylight, he would have made Lee regret his mistake in locating his supporting infantry under Longstreet behind his left flank; for he fully expected Grant's attack upon his right, as it actually occurred.

The Wilderness country was very fertile in tricks and surprises, as it had already shown itself. It was now about to repeat upon each of the combatants some of its famous tricks of the year before. In 1863 [Lieutenant General Thomas J.] Jackson had hidden his army in the woods and marched completely around [Major General Joseph] Hooker, and then surprised him by a flank attack. Longstreet was now about to repeat Jackson's maneuver, and like Jackson, was to fall by the fire of his own men just at the moment of victory.

The battle of the previous day, May 5, had ended after dark with the advantages decidedly in favor of the Federals, but the arrival of Longstreet's two divisions had now restored the equilibrium. This was accomplished and the roar of the battle (which had already impressed General Grant as fiercer than he had ever listened to before) began to slacken, when word was brought to Longstreet that an old unfinished railroad track, passing our flank on the right, presented a fine opportunity to attack the enemy. He at once formed a scratch division, bringing together [Brigadier General Joseph R.] Davis's brigade of [[Major General Henry] Heth's division, [Brigadier General William] Mahone's brigade of [Major General Richard H.] Anderson's division, [Brigadier General William T.] Wooford's of [Brigadier General Joseph B.] Kershaw's division, and Brigadier General] G. T. Anderson's of [Major General Charles W.] Field's division, and placed them under the command of a particularly gallant officer who had heretofore been on his personal staff as adjutant, Colonel G. Moxley Sorrel.

This command was rapidly gotten together, though all of different divisions,

The Wilderness (*Century*)

and they were as rapidly pushed through the Wilderness and thrown upon the enemy's flank. The usual result happened. The first two brigades, [Colonel Paul] Frank's and [Colonel Robert] McAllister's, were practically overrun, and the confusion quickly extended to the adjoining troops who retreated rapidly. Even the personal bearing and influence of [Major Generals Winfield S.] Hancock and [David B.] Birney were unable to rally the fugitives until they were finally reformed in two lines on the Brock Road, over a mile distant, whence they had advanced before daylight.

They were not pursued more than about half this distance; for the attack was not kept up. It paused. A volley had been fired by our own men, the Twelfth Virginia of Mahone's brigade, which volley shot Longstreet through the throat and killed [Brigadier General Micah] Jenkins and two of his staff officers. Just before it was fired Jenkins had congratulated Longstreet on the success they were making and said that they would put Grant across the Rapidan before night. A detachment of Mahone's brigade in the forest had seen Longstreet with his staff and officers passing where they had very recently been firing at fugitives from [Brigadier General James S.] Wadsworth's division. Jenkins's brigade leveled to return the fire, but Kershaw shouted "F-r-i-e-n-d-s" and arms were recovered and the men lay down. Lee was sent for and after several hours' delay continued the attack.

Meanwhile the enemy, recovering from their panic and having reoccupied and fortified their lines, were able to repulse our attack. [Major] General A. A. Humphreys writes of this attack: "Could it have been made early in the day, and followed up, it would have had important consequences." This is very likely; for beside Jenkins's large brigade with Anderson's and Field's divisions, [Major General Lafayette] McLaws's division would have overwhelmed the already disorganized masses to which Wadsworth's and Birney's divisions had now been reduced. Prisoners whom we captured on this occasion said that they had been in the fourth line of battle which was put to flight. It was really too late in the evening when the renewed attack was made to undertake an affair of such magnitude; but nevertheless Jenkins's brigade carried the entrenchments of [Brigadier General J. H. H.] Ward's brigade and a portion of [Brigadier General Gresham] Mott's. Hancock compliments both the attack and the defense.

Still later, too, another surprise was sprung upon Grant. Early in the day [Brigadier General John B.] Gordon's brigade had found itself where by a short march it could surprise two brigades of the enemy by an attack on their flank and rear. He reported the situation to both [Major General Jubal A.] Early and [Lieutenant General Richard S.] Ewell, but both of these officers thought that Grant had Burnside's Ninth Corps in support of the Sixth near the Federal position. In vain Gordon urged that the Ninth Corps was not there. In vain he begged Early to come and see; and in vain he appealed to Ewell.

The whole day was allowed to pass until late in the evening, when General Lee arrived on the ground, and asked if nothing could be done upon that flank.

Gordon's proposal was mentioned, which Early at once combated. Lee listened to his excuses for non-action in grim silence, and at once gave the orders for the attack. A third brigade was added and the attack was as immediately and as brilliantly successful as Longstreet's had been, capturing two brigadiers and several hundred prisoners. Although the *War Records* have shown that the Ninth Corps was never in support of the Sixth, Early never would admit that he had been mistaken.

On the morning of May 7 Grant did not renew his attack, but instead inaugurated a foot race for the possession of Spotsylvania Court House. Lee saw the movement of Grant's trains about 3:00 P.M., and ordered Anderson, commanding Longstreet's corps, to march at 8:30 P.M. for the blockhouse, a controlling position about 12 miles distant. [Major General] Fitzhugh Lee's cavalry held a position in front of it, and [Major General Wade] Hampton defended Corbin's Bridge across the Po, by which it could be approached. Both Fitz Lee and Hampton had cut down trees and defended their positions so well that during the hours of darkness they could not be moved.

After daylight [Major General Gouverneur K.] Warren's division was advanced and told to use the bayonet in clearing the road. They made a gallant charge, but now found that Fitz Lee's brigades of cavalry had just been replaced by [Brigadier General Benjamin G.] Humphreys's and Kershaw's infantry and they were driven back with a severe loss. [Major General John] Sedgwick's corps soon reinforced Warren's, and the entire day was consumed in the battle which ensued.

Late in the afternoon Ewell's corps arrived and extended our line to the right, and on the next day, the ninth, the whole of both armies were occupied in taking position opposite each other and entrenching themselves. General Sedgwick was killed by one of our sharpshooters. [Major General Philip H.] Sheridan was ordered to concentrate his cavalry and move upon our communications as far as the James River, there renew his supplies, and then return to the army. During these movements of the troops, a part of Burnside's corps encountered on May 9 some dismounted cavalrymen, whom they mistook for Longstreet's men moving toward Fredericksburg. This was reported to Grant, and led to his ordering Hancock to cross the Po River and turn our left flank.

Hancock at once put three divisions to cross at different points. The farthest upstream met a stout resistance from dismounted cavalry, but it was soon driven off by troops crossing below, where a second division met but feeble resistance and a third division none. Pontoon bridges were thrown at each point and troops pushed downstream toward the Shady Grove Bridge. Darkness, however, soon forced a halt and the river was not fordable. At dawn Hancock reconnoitered, but found Mahone's brigade too strongly posted opposite to be attacked. About 10:00 A.M. Hancock was ordered to return two divisions of his three to the north side of the Po, to take part in an assault at 5:00 A.M. Birney's and [Brigadier General John] Gibbon's divisions returned, leaving [Brigadier General Francis

C.] Barlow's below. Meanwhile, when Hancock had crossed the Po the day before, Lee had sent Heth to cross the Po below our left flank, turn to his right, and find Hancock's flank and attack it.

Heth's division was composed of only three small brigades; Barlow's the only one of Hancock's divisions left, had four large brigades. Fortunately for Heth he did not find Hancock's flank until Birney's and Gibbon's divisions had been withdrawn, which left him only Barlow's to deal with. But he found it. He made two spirited charges upon all four of Barlow's brigades, drawn up behind the crest of a ridge; two brigades supported by two in the rear. Both charges were repulsed with severe loss and [Brigadier General James A.] Walker was badly wounded. Meanwhile a fire broke out in Barlow's rear and Meade ordered him withdrawn. One gun was lost by becoming wedged between trees in the withdrawal, and our artillery across the Po also fired heavily upon Barlow's retreat. At night Heth's division was returned to the north side of the Po.

During the day of May 10 heavy shelling had been kept up along all our lines, and during the afternoon three unsuccessful Federal assaults were made at different points. One carefully planned assault had been fixed upon for 5:00 P.M., but at 3:30 Warren thought the moment so favorable that he made it without further delay, wearing his full uniform to inspire his men, who were of [Brigadier General Lysander] Cutler's and [Brigadier General Samuel W.] Crawford's divisions and [Brigadier General Alexander S.] Webb's and [Colonel Samuel S.] Carroll's brigades. Their advance was through dense thickets which concealed their approach until quite near. Then our artillery opened on them through the thickets whence they emerged in bad order and were soon driven back with heavy loss, which included [Brigadier General James C.] Rice mortally wounded. Not satisfied with this effort Hancock tried a second one at 7:00 P.M., but it was also repulsed with a heavy loss.

The enemy had found a place, however, where they might approach our entrenchments within 200 yards without being seen. Here a special assault was ordered on the evening of the tenth under the direction of Colonel [Emory] Upton, who was a distinguished tactician and leader of troops. His troops were in twelve regiments formed in four lines. No commands were given while moving into position. Muskets were loaded and bayonets fixed, but only the front line of men had their pieces capped. Upon reaching our works the first line would divide, half sweeping to the right and half to the left. During the advance each officer would continue to repeat the shout "Forward."

This attack fell upon [Brigadier General George] Doles's Georgia brigade, of [Major General Robert E.] Rodes's division, and Upton thus describes how the charge was met:

> Here occurred a deadly hand-to-hand conflict. The enemy, sitting in their pits with pieces upright, loaded, and with bayonets fixed, ready to impale the first who should leap over, absolutely refused to yield the ground. The first of our men who tried to

surmount the works fell pierced through the head by musket balls. Others, seeing the fate of their comrades, held their pieces at arms length and fired downwards, while others, poising their pieces vertically, hurled them down upon their enemy, pinning them to the ground. . . . Numbers prevailed and like a resistless wave the column passed over the works quickly, putting hors de combat those who resisted, and sending to the rear those who surrendered.

Mott's division was to have supported Upton on the left, but it did not appear. When it attempted to advance it found itself the target of a severe artillery fire under which it broke. Meanwhile the Confederate brigades on the right and left had attacked Upton on both flanks, and [Brigadier General Cullen A.] Battle's brigade, brought up from the rear, had attacked him in front. He brought up his fourth line in vain in a hard fight, but was finally driven back with loss, which he states at about 1,000 in killed, wounded, and prisoners, probably about twenty per cent of his command.

On the next day, May 11, Grant planned a much more powerful attack to be made by the whole of the Second and Ninth corps, in preparation for which the corps commanders were ordered to ascertain the least force which could hold their lines, leaving the remainder available for service elsewhere. They were also directed to press their skirmishers forward, so as to allow the closest possible reconnaissance of our works. Later he decided upon the salient angle, which has ever since been known as the Bloody Angle, as the point of his attack and gave all the necessary orders for carrying it into effect.

On May 8 Ewell's corps, to occupy some commanding ground in his front, had gone nearly a mile north, and had then returned making a right-angled salient and coming back near to the position of Doles's brigade, before resuming an eastern course. There resulted the great salient, which was a piece of bad engineering, certain to invite an attack as soon as the enemy understood it. This it only required a little while to do in spite of the sharpshooters. The fire of the sharpshooters coming over the parapets in front had begun to injure men on opposite sides of the opposing parapets, and these men protected themselves by building inclined parapets inside of their lines which were easily modified afterwards into rows of pens, in which the men soon sheltered themselves closely.

On the eleventh [Colonel Nelson A.] Miles was sent to reconnoiter across the Po, but some movement was entirely misunderstood by Lee, who seemed to anticipate that night an attack upon his right flank, for all of our guns were ordered withdrawn at sundown so that if ordered for any movement to the flank during the night it could be done quietly. Orders were sent to each chief of artillery to this effect, but on the line of Longstreet's corps I ventured to accomplish the same result, and still retain all my guns in position. I had visited every battery and had its chests mounted, and roads improved in the rear that the guns could be handled without noise. Hill's chief of artillery, [Colonel R. Lindsay] Walker, and Ewell's chief, [Brigadier General Armistead L.] Long, withdrew during the night twenty-two guns of [Major Richard C. M.] Page's and [Major

Hail to the Chief! Grant in the Wilderness (*Harper's New Monthly Magazine*)

W. E.] Cutshaw's battalions from the very lines which Grant was preparing to assault in the morning. The withdrawal of these guns was the one fatal Confederate blunder of this whole campaign.

What the particular movement of what particular division or what particular brigade of any division which first suggested or inspired the issuance of this fatal order by General Lee could have been, the most careful study of Humphreys's narrative does not permit me to suggest.[1] The orders were issued about three or four o'clock in the afternoon. Both Page's and Cutshaw's battalions of artillery were withdrawn during the night, but being called for by the infantry they attempted to return, and all of them except the two rear guns were captured on their way back.

Meanwhile the enemy, having taken Major General [Edward] Johnson, Brigadier General [George H.] Steuart, and about 4,000 prisoners, attempted to pursue their advantage, but were met by the brigades of Gordon from the right and of [Brigadier Generals Junius] Daniel and [Stephen D.] Ramseur from the left, who all attacked with great spirit. The enemy soon became so crowded and disorganized that no progress could be made and soon the fire from men in rear, who occupied positions on the outer slopes of the parapets, swept all the available space inside with a terrible fire. As an illustration of its intensity there is yet exhibited in Washington an oak tree twenty-two inches in diameter which was cut down by musketry fire alone, a fire that killed the whole forest in its front and even whipped the logs into basket stuff. Many of the Federal infantry, being liberally supplied with ammunition, fired over 300 rounds. The defense made by [Brigadier Generals John] Gregg's and [Nathaniel H.] Harris's brigades was heroic; [Brigadier General Abner] Perrin was killed and General Gregg severely wounded. The trenches ran with blood, and it became necessary, more than once, to clear them of dead bodies. This furious fighting lasted throughout the livelong day, and when night approached Federal brigades were designated to keep up the fire during the night. These brigades kept at it up at least until after 3:00 A.M. One feature of the occasion which added much to its discomfort and suffering was the rain which fell almost incessantly for two nights and a day.

We may pause here in our narrative to draw an obvious conclusion from it. It is that there is a maximum limit to the force which can be judiciously employed in an attack. An excessive force may paralyze its own efforts, and this was the practical outcome of this day's battle.

We may now pass to the left to Longstreet's front, which lay opposite Warren's corps, the Fifth, and which had a very strange experience still unexplained. Warren had opened artillery all along his line and pressed forward his skirmishers, hoping soon to see us sending forces to our right to meet Hancock's victori-

---

1. In speaking of Humphreys's narrative, Alexander here, and elsewhere, refers to Humphreys's book, *The Virginia Campaign of '64 and '65: The Army of the Potomac and the Army of the James* (New York, 1883).

ous advance. But, as we have already seen, Hancock had overdone his effort, and his advance was but brief. All of our guns were behind their parapets and opened fire as vigorously in reply to the Federal guns as they had done the day before. Warren saw no encouragement to attempt an attack, so he waited. At 9:15 A.M. he received an order from Meade "to attack at once at all hazards and with his whole force if necessary." About 10:15 A.M. we saw his men advancing across the open field, where they had made their first assault on the morning of May 8.

By common consent both our artillery and infantry reserved their fire and let them approach until they were within fifty yards. Then both opened fire and the line was driven back with heavy loss to them, but little or none to ourselves. In falling back they inclined to the left and disappeared down a considerable hollow making up from the direction of the Po River. We followed their disappearance with a random fire of artillery as long as we could see them. I can still remember the morning very distinctly, and can recall that there was a severe musketry fire heard, out of our sight down in the direction in which they had retreated, which was kept up for a long time. Personally my recollection cannot fix the duration of this noise of conflict, but I can distinctly recall it and conversing with [Brigadier General John] Bratton about it, and he tells the following story about it in his official report of the battle:

> It seemed a heavy battle, and we had nothing to do with it. Skirmishers from the First and Fifth (South Carolina) regiments were ordered up to the crest to discover what it meant. They found them lying behind the crest firing at what did not clearly appear, but they, the skirmishers, with great gallantry, charged them with a yell, routed and put the whole mass to flight, most precipitate and headlong, capturing some forty prisoners. In their haste and panic a multitude of them ran across an open space and gave our battery and my line of battle on the right a shot at them—the skirmishers, too. We kept up a most effective fire on them, and that field also was thickly dotted with their dead and wounded.

No Federal report is to be found of a single officer of a single regiment of either [Brigadier General Charles] Griffin's or of Cutler's divisions, though all were on the ground, and engaged and presumably made reports, none of which reports seem to have been preserved or ever afterwards heard of. Griffin reported for the brigades of [Brigadier General Romeyn B.] Ayres, [Colonel Jacob B.] Sweitzer, and [Brigadier General Joseph J.] Bartlett; and Cutler for those of Cutler [and] Rice. Griffin says his force was engaged for three hours on the morning of the twelfth, Cutler estimates the time he was engaged as four hours. Warren's account of the action gives suspiciously few details, not even noting the divisions engaged. Here is the whole of Warren's account: "I also again assailed the enemy's entrenchments, suffering heavy loss but failing to get in."

Can it be that these two Federal divisions, partly masked by intervening woods, exchanged fire with each other for some hours that morning and that all reference to the incident has been suppressed in the official reports of the day? It would seem so. For the official diary of Longstreet's corps describes the action only as "two violent assaults," between 9:00 A.M. and 10:00 A.M., "on a part of Field's line." What, then, can have prolonged the engagements of Griffin and Cutler between three and four hours?

Having enjoyed the pleasure of a very free and frank correspondence with Colonel H. H. Humphreys, a son of General Andrew A. Humphreys, who was Grant's chief of staff during this campaign, I addressed him on the subject of the incident, and have a letter from him, from which I quote an additional portion of General Bratton's same report and also Humphreys's conclusion of the whole matter:

> I find on page 1,066 of Serial No. 67, *Official Records of the Union and Confederate Armies,* that the official report of General Bratton does mention such an occurrence, in the following language, to wit: "Unfortunately the commander of the battery informed me (Bratton) that his orders were to save ammunition, and to fire only when he was certain of doing execution. I could not be certain of this, and fearing that ammunition might be scarce, ordered him to cease firing, and thus saved the lives of many Yankees. They kept up an active fusillade—indeed, a terrific roar of musketry—all the while. Our men were quietly awaiting their appearance over the crest. This continued so long (for some hours) that we began to suspect that by some happy mistake they were fighting themselves. It seemed a heavy battle and we had nothing to do with it."

My own recollection of this occasion is very clear, a messenger coming from Captain [William W.] Parker's battery, begging permission to keep up the fire the battery was maintaining without being able to see the effect of their shot, but feeling sure that it was effective. General Humphreys's book throws no light on this subject beyond this foot note: "I was overlooking the right of the army, and gave the order for the assaults there to cease as soon as I was satisfied they could not succeed, and directed the transfer of the troops to the center for the attack there."

Colonel Humphreys's letter explains that "had such an affair taken place, Meade would certainly have brought the officers concerned before a court of inquiry, for it would have been a reflection upon the discipline of the corps." Those two divisions of the Fifth Corps were subsequently sent to the aid of the Sixth Corps, which was attacking the west front of the Bloody Angle, Crawford holding his own front, as well as the front of the other two divisions of the corps, and Humphreys thus sums up his conclusion of the matter in the following verdict: "It is possible General Bratton's description may have been regarding their firing there aiding the Sixth Corps. But nevertheless, his language is emphatic. I cannot explain it, and am of the belief it will remain one of those cases in which one side says it did and the other says it did not. Something like a Scotch verdict 'not proven.'"

37

Lee's Response to Grant's Overland Campaign of 1864

William R. Livermore, Colonel, U.S.A.

THE FACTS of this campaign and the general features of the military operations are so well known, especially after the interesting account by [Brigadier General Edward Porter] Alexander, that it would not be courteous in me to occupy your attention with a detailed description of them, except so far as they have a direct bearing upon General [Robert E.] Lee's conduct.

At the opening of the campaign the general situation was as follows: Vicksburg and Port Hudson and Chattanooga had fallen and the great anaconda had wrapped its huge form around the Confederacy. Great Britain was not willing to go to war for the sake of cotton. Supplies could no longer come from abroad or from the west of the Mississippi as in the early years of the war. The movements of the Federal army were no longer directed by the politicians in Washington. [Lieutenant General Ulysses S.] Grant's policy was that of the administration and the administration in its turn supported him as it had never supported the commander of the Army of the Potomac before.

Richmond was the capital of Virginia and of the Confederacy, and the factories there were one of the main sources of supply for its war material. If Richmond should fall, Grant could knock away the defenses of the Atlantic seaports from the north as [Major General William T.] Sherman did in the following year from the south. With the sea and the navy as a base of operations, the Federal armies could advance to the interior. The only hope of the Confederacy lay in foreign intervention or in the political success of the peace party in the North. The fall of Richmond would soon have ended the war. The fall of Washington would probably have influenced the Europeans. The immediate effect would have been favorable to the hopes of the Confederacy. Both cities were strongly defended by earthworks and neither could be carried by assault if properly garrisoned. At all events Lee's problem was to defend Richmond and, if strong enough, to attack Washington.

For about two years Lee had defended the line of the Rappahannock. In placing himself between Grant and Richmond, he was also separating Grant on the Rapidan from [Major General Benjamin F.] Butler, who soon appeared on the James. Grant's army has been estimated at 115,000 men, Lee's at 70,000, and Butler's at 30,000. If Lee chose to fall back at once behind the fortifications of Richmond, Grant could not possibly prevent him; but Lee did not wish to abandon a large part of Virginia and allow Grant to unite his own army with that of Butler and to reinforce it with perhaps 30,000 men from the garrison of Washington.

On the Rapidan, Lee's numerical strength was about sixty per cent of Grant's. His troops were veterans of several hard campaigns in this region, and the best proof of their efficiency is found in the law of natural selection or survival of the fittest. On the other hand, the hardships that they had endured were a severe strain on the constitutions of even the strongest. They were poorly clad and seldom fed. The Northern troops were, on the whole, not as well seasoned and not as experienced in warfare of the Wilderness. Perhaps two-thirds were well-seasoned soldiers and one-third raw recruits who had been induced to join the ranks by requirements of the draft or the allurement of a large bounty. On the other hand, in the rank and file of the Northern army many were skilled in trades or educated in sciences that found some application in war. The Northern army was perhaps as well fed and clothed as any army in the world, and taking this into consideration it would be safe to consider the two armies equal, man for man, and the Northern upon the whole superior to the Southern in the ratio of one hundred to sixty.

It has been said that Lee had the advantage of the defensive, because he was fighting behind breastworks, where one man was equal to more than four of the attacking force. This would be perfectly true in a narrow pass where neither flank could be turned, but it would not otherwise be a fair measure of relative strength. Where the attack is twice as strong as the defense, it should be able to choose its own ground. The advantage of the initiative may be equal to that which the defense derives from its fortifications. In the Wilderness campaign the numerical strength appears to be a fair measure of the relative advantages of the opposing parties on land; but on sea Grant had the navy and the sea for a base on which he could fall back and from which he could draw his supplies. I think it will appear from this paper that it was due to Lee's skill that he fought behind breastworks, and his skill can perhaps be better understood by considering the dangers to which he was exposed.

Grant, as we all remember, crossed on May 4 [1864]. Lee at once gave orders for a march by the right flank. General Alexander suggested that [Lieutenant General James] Longstreet's corps should have been moved up to the north of Louisa Court House. I think it should have been moved much farther, and that [Lieutenant Generals Richard S.] Ewell and [Ambrose Powell] Hill should [not] have halted until all were in supporting distance.

The Wilderness had been the home of Lee's army for many months, and if his troops should be scattered they could find a rallying point at every opening. He thought that if he were to meet the enemy it should be there, and not in the open ground, where the Federal troops could maneuver and use their powerful artillery. Just a year ago, in this very Wilderness, Lee had played havoc with [Major General Joseph] Hooker's army and had moved the pieces on both sides of the chessboard, and it is not surprising that he was tempted to make the same experiment with the same army, though under a different leader. If Grant should cross the Rapidan it was right for Lee to attack him, provided he could throw a large part of his army upon a small part of Grant's before Grant could concentrate to oppose him, or if he could get possession of Grant's trains without exposing his own army to destruction. It will be remembered that when Hooker spoke of crossing the Rappahannock again after Chancellorsville, President Lincoln cautioned him not to be rash and get his army like an ox jumped half over a fence, where he can neither gore the dogs in front nor kick those behind him. There is no better way to destroy an army than to catch it in such a position, but in this case the ox jumped over the fence at one bound.

On the evening of May 5, a gap of about a mile separated the two wings of

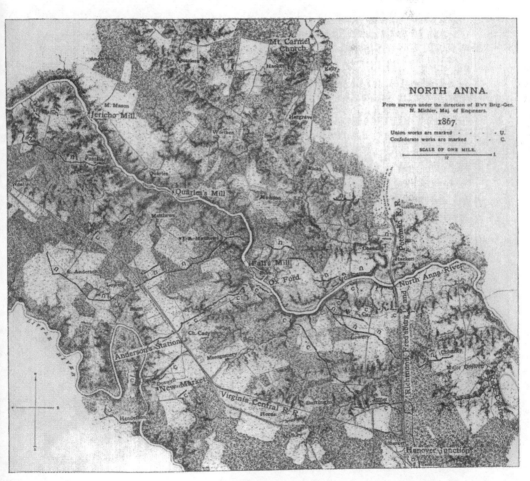

North Anna (*Century*)

Lee's army. Longstreet had not joined Lee and [Major General Ambrose] Burnside had not joined Grant. Lee was in great danger. [Major General Philip H.] Sheridan's cavalry held the Brock Road, on [Major General Winfield S.] Hancock's left, and if Grant should extend Hancock farther around Hill's right and send [Major General Gouverneur K.] Warren and Burnside through the gap on Hill's left and rear, Hill's two divisions might be routed, and if Longstreet should come up he might share Hill's fate. Probably Lee realized the danger, but believed that in such a maneuver his enemy would be entangled in the Wilderness.

On the sixth, on Lee's left, [Major General John] Sedgwick and Warren attacked Ewell's breastworks in vain. One Lee's right, Hancock advanced along the [Orange] Plank Road, outflanked Hill, and drove his men in confusion for more than a mile down the road. Then Longstreet came up. General Lee tried to lead the attack, but his men shouted: "Lee to the rear! Turn back, Marse Robert!" and seized his horse by the bridle. Longstreet relieved Hill, and after hard fighting drove Hancock back in disorder, but I think it extremely doubtful whether all of Grant's right wing would have been routed even if Longstreet had not been wounded. The fight and the march through the thicket had disorganized the attack as well as the defense. It is true that Longstreet had fresh brigades in reserve and that Hancock's first line was rolled up and broken into fragments, but north of the [Orange] Plank Road his regiments were generally entire. South of the road many were broken into companies or squads, but he had two lines of breastworks, his artillery, and five fresh brigades on the Brock Road. The advance which Lee made after Longstreet was wounded was not pushed so far as to involve the rout of his own army if it failed. It showed that Grant was strong on that wing and probably weak on the other, and Lee's object was to find a weak spot and concentrate his forces upon it.

Just before dark the extreme right of the Federal line was surprised and some prisoners captured, when darkness put an end to the fight. Like Joshua at Jericho and Stonewall Jackson at Chancellorsville, Lee would have been glad to have more time to fight. He had a chance to turn Grant's right. It is not certain that he would have succeeded, for here as elsewhere the assailants were disorganized in the woods and suffered from the fire of their own men. Grant was in greater force than Lee on this wing and had at least two brigades in reserve. The fact, however, that Lee had a fair chance of success on each flank fully justified these experiments.

Although Lee was the aggressor in this battle, the fights were so conducted that his men fought much of the time on the defensive. Grant's attacks were more persistent; Lee felt his way more skillfully, but still I think a little too boldly. The Federals were more disorganized in marching through the woods and more frequently outflanked and dispersed. This time Lee's opponent was not Hooker, nor yet was he Napoleon. Lee did not drive the Army of the Potomac across the Rapidan, but he escaped with his own army from the danger to which it was exposed.

Grant had said to [Major General George G.] Meade, "Lee's army will be your objective point. Wherever Lee goes, there you will go also." And as long as Grant fought it out on this line, wherever Meade went there Lee sat down before him and behind a parapet. At Spotsylvania, at North Anna, and at Cold Harbor friend and foe united in praise of Lee's skill in meeting all Grant's efforts to turn his flank. This fact cannot be dismissed by saying that the defender could always entrench before the aggressor appeared. With such disparity of force it would have been impossible, if his adversaries had made the very best use of their forces in every instant.

This paper is not concerned with the division of responsibility between Grant and his subordinates, nor with the question whether upon the whole he did not do as well as could have been expected against so skillful an adversary. Lee's conduct of the campaign was brilliant, but, of course, not perfect. Unless he were favored by fortune or by his own superior skill, his problem was impossible. He could not hope to keep Grant from taking Richmond or shutting him up in its fortifications. With Grant's superiority in infantry and cavalry, he might have cut off at least a large part of Lee's army at one of the halts between the Rapidan and Richmond.

On May 7, as both sides were entrenched, neither Grant nor Lee had any desire to attack. As Lee thought that Grant's next move would be by his left flank, he gave orders to have a road cut leading from his own right flank to Spotsylvania. In the afternoon [Major General James Ewell Brown] Stuart's cavalry reported that Grant's trains were moving off and Lee gave orders for intercepting him. At night [Major General Fitzhugh] Lee's cavalry felled trees in the road over which Grant's leading corps was to march, and [Major General Richard H.] Anderson with Longstreet's corps was the first to reach Spotsylvania. There he entrenched on the morning of the eighth and in the afternoon Ewell, who followed him, entrenched on the right, but extended his flank so far to the front that he had to bend it back again at what was afterwards known as the Salient or the Bloody Angle. When Lee saw the line, he said he did not see how it could be held. It was here shaped like an acorn or a huge irregular bastion and each face was exposed to enfilade and reverse fire from an enemy attacking the other. That Lee did not at once draw back his line to the gorge of the Salient is one of the very few points in the conduct of this battle for which he can be criticized.

Two motives may have influenced his conduct in holding this line which Ewell had taken up. Fitzhugh Lee says of his uncle, "Lee to the strong courage of the man united the loving heart of the woman. He had a reluctance to oppose the wishes of others or to order anything that would be disagreeable or to which they would not consent." Another motive, I think, was his natural combativeness, and the delight which a strong intellect derives from overcoming great obstacles. He knew the Salient would be assaulted and probably by heavy columns and, as General Alexander has explained, he so posted his artillery as to strike these heavy masses where one shot would do the work of twenty.

In the Battle of Spotsylvania Grant tried repeatedly to turn Lee's flanks, but in every case he found them defended, and he repeatedly dashed his troops against Lee's breastworks with heavy loss to the assailants. In the attacks on the Salient he captured several thousand prisoners before he fell back. On May 13, Lee drew in his line to the gorge of the Salient.

On the nineteenth, suspecting that Grant was beginning a flanking movement toward his left, Lee sent Ewell forward to feel his right. After a fight of several hours, Ewell found that the Federal army had not left and retired with considerable loss. Lee was doubtless right in ordering this reconnaissance, but such a maneuver should be tentative, and in this instance Ewell pushed it too far.

At Spotsylvania, Lee fought behind breastworks, except in his counterattack to recover the Salient. There his men were exposed to fire from the front, flank, and rear as they would not have been if the line had been properly laid out. Lee's losses at the Salient were about equal to Grant's. Elsewhere they were very slight, while Grant's were terrific.

After Lee's line had been broken at the Salient it might possibly have been cut in two and rolled up by the assailants pouring in through the gap supported by a frontal attack on their right and left, but this is doubtful. The assailants would be exposed to a front and flank fire from Lee's supports, and he generally had a second line of defense to fall back upon. In any event, Lee's defensive tactics did not hang on so slender a thread as to break down whenever his line was pierced.

If while Grant was assaulting the Salient he wanted to distract the rest of Lee's forces, I think it would have been better to extend one of his wings, leaving thin lines to keep up the demonstrations, instead of heavy lines to make desperate assaults against the breastworks.

On May 9 Sheridan's cavalry rode off to Richmond. It was superior to Stuart's in numbers and equipment, and if Grant had kept it with him he could have detached as much infantry as might be required to support it. If it had been present to watch Lee's movements, to block them as Fitzhugh Lee had blocked Grant's, and to intercept spies who brought Lee information of his movements, the result might have been different. Grant might, perhaps, have turned Lee's flank and routed his army. Lee very wisely retained about half of Stuart's cavalry with the army and sent off the rest to follow Sheridan. If Grant's cavalry had held the ground on Lee's flanks, Lee would have had to fall back, and in falling back he would have been exposed to attack in the open unless he could entrench as fast as cavalry could gallop.

It is apparent that Lee was not attempting a passive defense, but was waiting for an opportunity to take Grant at a disadvantage by throwing the main force of his own army upon a small portion of Grant's, and that Grant's object was now either to outflank Lee or compel him to leave his entrenchments and fight in the open on an equal footing. It occurred to Grant that if he should detach a portion of his army Lee would probably attack it and place himself at a disadvantage. Hancock's corps, which was to serve as a bait for Lee, moved far down on a circuitous road toward Richmond and entrenched.

Very early on the morning of May 21 Lee, having learned of the movement through his cavalry, brought Ewell to his right and posted him across the direct road to Richmond. The movement of Grant's other corps could not be concealed. The bait was perhaps at the wrong end of the fish line. Lee did not attack the three corps that were left behind, nor did he go in pursuit of the detached corps, knowing, as he did, that the rest of the army was following, but, taking the direct route which Grant had failed to seize, he moved to the south side of the North Anna and took up a strong position across Grant's path. There he was joined by reinforcements of 8,000 or 9,000 men. Grant arrived on the twenty-third, and Warren crossed the river above Lee's position. Lee was indignant that Hill, who was guarding his left, allowed Warren to cross.

On May 24 Hancock crossed on Lee's right and Burnside tried in vain to force a passage in the center. Both sides were entrenched. Lee's front rested on the North Anna and each wing, thrown obliquely to the rear, rested on Little River. Here, thought Lee, was a chance to throw all his forces on one flank of Grant's army, while the other flank would have to cross the river twice in order to come to its rescue, but Lee was sick and confined to his tent. He cried out in impatience: "We must strike them. We must never let them pass us again." But the success of such a movement would have been very doubtful, as the Federal positions were strong, and Lee's officers advised against it. On the twenty-fourth Sheridan's cavalry returned and on the night of May 26 Grant withdrew from Lee's front for another flank march on the east side of the Pamunky River. Lee learned of the movement on the morning of the twenty-seventh and moved at once by a shorter road to intercept him or to cover Richmond.

On the twenty-eighth Grant recrossed to the south bank, only to find Lee again drawn up to oppose him along the Totopotomy. The efforts to drive him from his position, which extended from time to time, gave rise to the Battle of Cold Harbor, where the maneuvers of Spotsylvania were repeated, excepting that here there was no salient in Lee's line to invite an attack. On the other hand, Lee was far from contenting himself with a passive defense, but seized upon every opportunity to strike at a weak point whenever it was, or appeared to be, presented. Lee's sickness continued, but he kept at the front each day. He sent to [General Pierre G. T.] Beauregard for reinforcements.

On May 30 Grant's army came up and drove back Lee's skirmishers. On his left Sheridan drove Fitz Lee back to Cold Harbor. Lee thought that Grant would make another flank movement to the south and in the afternoon sent [Major General Jubal A.] Early forward from his right to intercept it by attacking Grant's left before it could fortify. After a partial success Early was driven back.

On May 31 Sheridan drove Fitz Lee from Cold Harbor, entrenched and occupied it with his dismounted cavalry armed with breechloading carbines, and held it against a counterattack by Fitz Lee reinforced late in the day by [Major

General Richard F.] Hoke's division of infantry which had come up from Beauregard. No infantry had yet appeared to extend Grant's left, but Lee was now satisfied that he would continue his flanking march, and during the night Anderson was withdrawn from his center to fill the gap between Hoke and Early. Lee's plan was for Anderson and Hoke to drive Sheridan from Cold Harbor and turn Grant's left and sweep along his line from the flank while Hill and Ewell attacked from the front. General Lee was far from well and was not with the right flank. Anderson and Hoke did not fully comprehend what was expected. The two brigades on Anderson's right attacked the dismounted cavalry, but were driven back and all the line entrenched.

When we consider that Sheridan with part of his cavalry had held Cold Harbor so long against the attacks of infantry, we can perhaps realize the danger to which Lee would have been exposed if this cavalry had been thrown across his path when Grant was trying to outflank him on the marches and battlefields from the Rapidan to Cold Harbor.

At 6:00 P.M. [May 31, Major Generals Horatio G.] Wright and [William F.] Smith formed at Cold Harbor, attacked Anderson and Hoke in their entrenchments, carried the advanced line, and penetrated an undefended gap between them, but were surrounded and driven back from the main line. Meanwhile Lee made a demonstration from his left to relieve the pressure on his right, but nothing was accomplished there.

On the morning of June 2 Lee learned that Hancock's corps had gone from the right of Grant's army. He moved [Major General John C.] Breckinridge and Hill from his own left to his right. Having a shorter march they arrived before Hancock and extended Lee's line to the Chickahominy. In the afternoon Lee told Early, then on his left, to cross the lines which had been deserted by Hancock and sweep down to the right. Burnside was driven back in confusion, uncovering Warren's right. Warren changed front and after a hard fight Early was forced back, but held an advanced position across Grant's right flank.

The details of the bloody assault on Lee's entrenchments on June 3 need not be repeated. Lee's position was made strong throughout by entrenchments. There were few supports, but the line was so strong that if it should be penetrated men could be spared from the right and left to surround the intruders and drive them back. Lee's right rested on the Chickahominy and his left on the wooded swamps at the head of the Totopotomy and of the Matadequin. Grant attacked all along the line, but in greatest force on Lee's left center, with the result that is too well known as the climax of the hammering tactics. On Lee's left Early was attacked by infantry in front and flank and by cavalry in his rear. He lost some ground, but the attack was withdrawn after the repulse of the main attack on his right. If on the night of the second Grant had concentrated a heavy force of infantry and cavalry on his right, Lee would have been in great danger. This chance he was willing to take. A passive defense was distasteful to him. These bold thrusts that he was always making restricted Grant's movements, and by

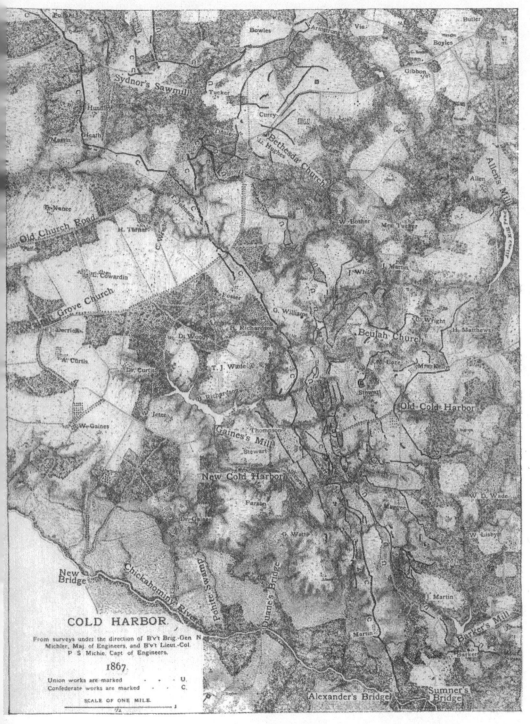

Cold Harbor (*Century*)

keeping the Federal troops in constant alarm wore out their activity, their health, and their endurance. There was always a chance of finding a weak point to strike a blow which if successful could be followed up in greater force. Such maneuvers made with a delicate touch are essential to an active defense.

After the Battle of Cold Harbor the army under Lee became involved in operations in other fields than those of the Wilderness from the Rapidan to Richmond, and it would be hard to do justice to all the military and political problems that arose without exceeding the time allotted to this paper.

Lee returned Hoke's division to Beauregard and sent Early and Breckinridge to defend the valley of the Shenandoah. On June 11 Grant's forces began to withdraw from Cold Harbor, but this time to the rear and not by the flank. Lee had but two corps left and did not think it wise to move far enough from his base to follow. Grant by a skillful maneuver crossed the James and attacked Petersburg. Beauregard repeatedly asked for aid, but did not convince Lee that it was required. [Brevet Brigadier General Adam] Badeau, who was Grant's friend and biographer, says that a withdrawal to the south side of the James would have weakened Grant's hold on the nation, and that this among other considerations influenced him in ordering the assault at Cold Harbor. Several times before, Beauregard had failed to convince Lee of the accuracy of his judgment, and strong evidence was required to satisfy him that Grant would give up the determination to fight out the campaign on the line from the Rapidan to Richmond if it took all summer.

Grant's hammering tactics had proved more damaging to his own army than to Lee's. Of the army that crossed the Rapidan only about sixty per cent reached the James, and the loss fell heaviest on the best and the bravest, and a large part of the officers who literally led their men were killed or wounded. Lee's loss is not accurately known. It was surely much less. Some of those who defend the hammering tactics say that it was as great or greater in proportion to his strength, but less in number because he fought behind breastworks. If Grant had been as fortunate and had conducted the campaign with the same skill as Lee, the loss that he inflicted would have been proportionate to his own numbers, and not to those of his adversary. It would have been five-thirds and not three-fifths of that which he suffered. In other words, it would have been two or three times as great as it actually was.

There are few campaigns that furnish as rich a field for military study as that of the Wilderness, and it is now more than ever engaging the careful attention of the officers of European armies. Lee saved Richmond and a large part of Virginia and conducted the campaign in a manner that won for him the esteem and respect of both friend and foe, and this campaign alone would entitle him to the high place he so justly holds among the great commanders of the world.

38

Grant and Sheridan in 1864:
A Study in Contrasts

Rutherford B. Hayes, President of the United States, and
Brevet Major General, U.S.V.

ELSEWHERE THIS WEEK we publish a very interesting paper read by
[Brevet Major General Rutherford B.] Hayes before the National Command-
ery of the Loyal Legion and repeated by request before the Ohio Commandery.
The general prefaced it by the two characteristic anecdotes given below.

"I met," said General Hayes, "at an army dinner, sometime ago, [Lieuten-
ant Colonel Theodore S.] Bowers, a favorite aide of [Lieutenant General Ulysses S.] Grant's, and asked him, during the evening, 'What was the most striking exhibition of fear, anxiety, or a sense of responsibility that you ever noticed
in General Grant?'"

Replied Bowers, "Well, if there was one instance above all others where he
seemed to be affected by the stress of care it was during the five days' fight down
in the Wilderness. On one of the days, I think the fourth, the fighting commenced
early in the morning, and continued all through the day. At the end of the day
there had been great slaughter on both sides, and we had not carried a point; we
had been repulsed on every side. There was not an absolute defeat, but we all felt
that our army had been badly shaken, and that possibly a severe, determined
return attack by [General Robert E.] Lee's army might be disastrous.

"Just at dark that night, we were all gathered about a log fire that was built
on the greensward at Grant's quarters. All Grant's staff were about the fire, and
as the flickering flames lighted up their faces it could be seen that they were all
oppressed with the greatness of the losses of the day and the preceding days.
Nothing was said. The log crackled and sputtered in the fire. Grant stood by,
looking at the bright flames, his hands behind his back, a cigar in his mouth,
saying nothing. Suddenly there broke out on the night air a mile or two off, a
heavy firing. It was evidently a determined attack on our lines. The firing grew
as it came nearer. We all jumped up from our places about the glowing fire and
listened eagerly.

"Grant stood and listened intently to the firing. He said to an officer, after a
moment or two: 'Ride forward; see what it is and come back to me.' The officer
leaped into his saddle and galloped rapidly out into the darkness beyond the
circle of light made by the campfire. Gradually the firing ceased and soon naught

To the Front: Sheridan and His Staff (*Harper's New Monthly Magazine*)

was to be heard save here and there the sharp report of a musket. Grant straightened up, yawned, and said: 'I haven't slept for some time, and I think I'll go to bed.' He then tossed away the stump of his cigar and entered his tent."

Said General Hayes: "Grant hadn't slept for three or four nights. He had been in the saddle every night, examining the lines and looking after the men. Grant was in his tent. Through the fly, which was open, could be seen the yellow glimmer of a flickering candle. Grant always kept a candle burning in his tent at night when he slept. Bowers, with the rest of the officers who remained up, after awhile heard the thud of a horse's hoofs galloping rapidly toward headquarters, and soon the officer who had been sent out to see what the firing meant dashed into camp and dismounted. Bowers got the news from the officer, and went in to awaken Grant, for he had gone to sleep. The news wasn't important, for the firing was simply the enemy straightening its lines, or something like that, and not serious. Bowers went to Grant's tent, and looked in. He supposed the general was asleep, and he didn't think the news of importance enough to awaken him. Grant was lying on his face and hands, and when Bowers looked into the tent, he said, 'Well, Bowers, what is it?' Grant had evidently not gone to sleep at all, tired as he was."

"That query of Grant's," said Mr. Bowers, "was the most striking exhibition of care, anxiety, sensation, call it what you will, that I ever knew Grant to exhibit."

"On the other hand," said General Hayes, "Sheridan was all enthusiasm, and showed his mind by his manner," and proceeded to illustrate the point by this anecdote: At one of the battles about Winchester, when the enemy in the immediate front of his division had been routed, Hayes was ordered to move rapidly forward with a battery. Riding in advance of the battery, and coming over a hill he saw an officer to the right riding across a field toward the road he was on as rapidly as he could urge his horse, followed at a distance by several aides or orderlies struggling to keep up.

When he could distinguish the uniform he wondered who that could be riding out in front of the army, and what could be his business. As he came closer it was seen it was Sheridan. Hayes did not then know how the battle had gone on the right, and rode forward to inquire. "Glorious! glorious!" said Sheridan, reining up his horse and clapping his hands with the enthusiasm of a schoolboy. "We have just smashed them. And now if I just had a battery I could capture the whole thing. I know a splendid place to put one!"

"I have a battery right here," said Hayes.

"Where? Where?" said Sheridan, "I don't see any battery."

"It will be here in less than a minute," was the reply; "it is just over the hill."

Just then it came in sight, and Sheridan took charge of it and moved it rapidly forward to a point where the road made a square angle to the right. About a mile further on it made a square turn to the left. The road between the first and second angles for a distance of half a mile was crowded with guns, caissons, wagons, and ambulances, not one or two abreast, but literally packed full, and all struggling forward to the second turn in the road.

The battery was placed in position and the gunner directed to fire at the turn in the road, near which was the head of the struggling mass. Sheridan cautioned him to aim carefully. The shell overshot the mark, and Sheridan manifested great impatience. "Lower! Lower!" he said.

The next shell exploded just in the angle of the road. "That's the place! That's the place!" said Sheridan, and at the same time the drivers began to cut loose their horses and mules, mount, and break for the rear, across the fields, abandoning their guns and wagons. Sheridan clapped his hands and fairly danced for joy, showing his feelings without any attempt at restraint.

The two stories were listened to with breathless attention, Grant's being received in silence, and Sheridan's with an outburst of enthusiasm, the auditors seeming to catch the spirit of the men and the incidents.

39

A Tough Tussle with Sheridan
Lieutenant Colonel Jacob Weddle

As it seems to be the thing just at this time to find in print many incidents and anecdotes personally connected with that great leader and military chieftain, [Major General Philip H.] Sheridan, I thought I could do no less than many others and relate a little bout I had with Sheridan while serving in his army in the Shenandoah Valley in the year 1864, the first and only time that I ever had the honor of talking to Sheridan.

The Battle of Winchester, September 19 [1864] had been fought; then Fisher's Hill, after which the enemy was pursued, being routed and many captured, to beyond Staunton. The army settled itself down in and around Harrisburg and for some time lay there, foraging off the country all there was at that time to forage. Finally marching orders were given, and then we started to fall back nearer our old base. This was the time that Sheridan laid waste the valley by fire. This order to march was in three columns, infantry on the left, cavalry on the right, the artillery and wagons in the road.

Ours was the Second Division of [Brevet Major General George] Crook's corps, with my colonel, [Joseph] Thorn, in command of the division. Colonel [William B.] Curtis of the Twelfth West Virginia was our brigade commander, a most excellent and efficient officer. Colonel Curtis, at the time of which I write, was away on account of an attack of typhoid fever. This left no higher rank in our brigade than a lieutenant colonel. Lieutenant Colonel [Robert S.] Northcott of the Twelfth West Virginia was the ranking officer and of course took command of the brigade.

Now, Colonel Northcott was an editor of a newspaper at home, of fine education and as fine an old gentleman as you would wish to meet. But so far as the military was concerned he did not know the first principle, and it seemed as though he would not or could not learn anything pertaining thereto. I remember when he desired to change direction to right or left he would not give a command but say, "Well, gentlemen, turn off to the right there,"—or left—as the case might be.

Our first day's march, and part of the night I might say, was made to the foot of Rude's Hill. Here the road crosses considerable of a stream of water, a branch of the Shenandoah River. Our corps camped on the south side of the stream, and our division on the lower side of the road. The bridge across this stream was a military one, and only admitted one wagon, so far as width was concerned. There were positive orders that the progress of the wagon train and artillery should in no way be interfered with.

The troops were ready and received orders to march at 6:00 A.M. next morning. The wagon train and artillery were moving at daylight. The train was well closed up, and Colonel Northcott was in a dilemma as was the whole division. There we were on the right of the road when we should have been on the left, and then the water below the bridge would swim a horse while above it was not over ankle deep, there being a riffle above. We had to get on the other side of that wagon train. But how to do it and not interfere with that artillery and the wagons.

At this time Colonel Northcott called out to me, "Colonel Weddle, get across the river the best way you can." I looked about me, not knowing what to do, when all at once I heard Colonel [Thomas M.] Harris, of the [Third] Brigade, give the command, throwing his brigade into column by companies. After the movement was completed he gave the command, "Forward, double-quick, march!" And he went through that wagon train with his five regiments like a thunderbolt. The consequence was it made an interval in the train of from two to five hundred yards.

I was not slow to take advantage. I gave the command forward and over the bridge I marched my boys, dry shod, and I did not encroach on the existing orders either, for not a wagon was near my rear when I marched off the bridge. Not another regiment followed me over the ridge, but they all took advantage of the gap, and crossed the pike to the upper side.

Now on the west or north side of the bridge and to the left of the pike was quite a raise or knoll, and on this was Sheridan with his staff. Sheridan himself was dismounted. He was looking at the troops crossing. There was a large group

of officers around him—[Brevet Major General William H.] Emory of the Nineteenth Corps, [Major General Horatio G.] Wright of the Sixth Corps, Crook,
and I think [Major General George A.] Custer was there, all with their staffs.
Our division commander was there also, Colonel Thoburn, standing close to
Crook.

Now Sheridan did not notice the gap in the train until he saw me come
marching my regiment across the bridge. It set him in a passion in a moment.
He rushed down the embankment right for me, and blurted out, "God damn
you, what the hell are you doing on that bridge?"

I replied, "God damn *you!* I am marching my regiment across."

He said, "Get off of it, damn quick!"

I turned in my saddle and yelled out, "Get off that bridge, damn quick, boys;
double-quick, march."

Sheridan yelled out, "Common time, damn it; you will shake the bridge
down!"

I yelled out the same as he had. He walked up the bank, and as I filed off to
the left I heard him say to Crook, "Crook, who is that officer?"

Crook knew me and replied, "I believe that is Colonel Weddle, of the First
West Virginia Infantry," and turning to Thoburn said, "Is it not, Thoburn?"

Thoburn replied, "Yes; that is my old regiment."

Sheridan said, "No matter who he is, I order him in arrest."

It was not long until I saw a division aide coming at a gallop. I knew his
message before he delivered it. He rode up and saluted me and said, "Colonel
Weddle, by General Sheridan's orders you are in arrest." I asked him if there were
any restrictions in the order. He said, "No, sir," and I handed him my sword.
He rode off and I told my major to take command as I was in arrest.

It was not long until a company of the First New York Cavalry came by going out scouting. Being acquainted with the officer in command I asked him if
he wanted company. He said, "Yes, come on." I joined him and we had a grand
time that day. We did not get in that night until about 9:00 P.M., and found the
army camped at the foot of Fisher's Hill and vicinity. I was very tired. I at once
got something to eat and turned in, knowing my horse was well attended to.

Next morning about 10:00 A.M. I was sitting on a log by the edge of a little
brook that ran close by the camp. I was smoking, when I observe my old colonel approaching. We bade each other the time of day, etc. He had my sword in
his hand and began questioning me how the matter of yesterday came about. I
told him all about it, which he already knew, for he had talked with the major
and other officers of the regiment in regard to it. I told him I did not feel the
least alarmed about the situation, and I would do the same thing over under
the same circumstances. He said, "Well, here is your sword; I released you from
arrest, and I want you to take command of the brigade until Colonel Curtis
returns." He said, "I will go and issue the order at once."

I said, "Hold, Colonel; I shall not take the command of the brigade so long as Colonel Northcott is in the brigade for duty. I will not assume to command my superior officer, and Colonel Northcott is my superior by five days in date of commission."

He said, "I don't care; Colonel Northcott is not capable, and I order you to take charge of the brigade."

I said, "Well, you will have to detach Northcott or get him out of the brigade before I will do it."

He looked at me for a moment, and then said, "I wish to God that all the officers had one-tenth of the mule nature in them that you have."

I said, "Thank you."

I don't know what might have come out of this, but that afternoon Colonel Curtis returned, and that settled that difficulty. Along about 11:30 A.M., as I was standing near my headquarters I saw an orderly approaching with a large envelope fastened in his sword belt. He rode up to me and saluted, and inquired for Lieutenant Colonel Weddle. I told him I was the person he was looking for. He hand me the official envelope he carried in his belt. I opened it and read its contents, which was: "Lieutenant Colonel Weddle, commanding First West Virginia Infantry, will please call at these headquarters at his earliest convenience. P. H. Sheridan, Major General."

I wrote my name on the back of the envelope, and handed it to the orderly and said, "No answer, Orderly." He saluted and rode off. Then I looked over that request again, and tried to think what in the name of sense he could want with me personally. However, I had nothing to do but go and find out. So I told my man to have the horses ready and looking nice by 1:30 P.M. in the afternoon. Then I had my boots blackened and my sword hilt and scabbard polished up. I had a nice clean uniform in my valise and a pair of long milk-white gauntlets that somebody had presented me. At the proper time I got into my harness. At 1:30 P.M. that afternoon if you had seen me you would have thought I had just been lifted out of a bandbox. My horse was ready, I mounted, and off I and an orderly started for Sheridan's headquarters.

When I rode up in front of the general's quarters, some staff officers were lounging around outside. I dismounted and out with the request I had received from Sheridan in the forenoon, and handed it to one of the staff. He excused himself and went inside. I heard him saying something, but could not distinguish what it was. But I heard Sheridan say, "Yes, show him in." The officer came out and said, "General Sheridan desires you to come in."

I followed the officer in, who presented me to Sheridan. The general arose and held out his hand, saying, "You are Colonel Weddle."

"Yes, sir," I said, "and I have both the pleasure and honor of talking with General Sheridan."

"Well, I am glad to see you," he said, "I wanted to see you and talk to you. I want to know a man that had and has enough vim in him to cuss me back when I cuss him."

"Well, General," said I, "you have found your man. I will not permit anyone on earth to curse me. I would curse Abe Lincoln if he cursed me first. No man has any right to curse another."

He said, "Certainly not." He had seated me, and we talked over the affair of the day before satisfactorily. I sat perhaps a half hour, excused myself, and bade him good day. He invited me to call again, but of course I never did, and never spoke to Sheridan again, as opportunity did not offer.

40

Boys in Battle at New Market
John S. Wise, Cadet, Virginia Military Institute

LEXINGTON, VIRGINIA, is a somewhat historic spot now, being the burial place of Robert E. Lee and of "Stonewall" Jackson; and it is by no means inaccessible, having no fewer than three railroads. When I first knew it, nearly twenty-five years ago, it not only had little pretense to fame, but was one of the most out-of-the-way spots in the state.

In the year 1839 the state of Virginia, having an arsenal at Lexington, established there a military school and placed her property in charge of the officers and cadets of the Virginia Military Institute. Under the control of its superintendent, Colonel Francis H. Smith, a West Point graduate, the Virginia Military Institute prospered up to the period of the war of 1861.

With the outbreak of the war came, of course, a new impetus to everything pertaining to military knowledge; and the Virginia Institute, being the largest and the best-equipped establishment of its kind in the South, at once became prominent as a training school. At a later period of the war it had, I believe, the exceptional honor of having sent its corps of cadets, as a body, into battle. It is to chronicle that episode that I write; for the single martial exploit of that young band of boys was as brave as the archery of the boy-marksman of the Iliad who launched forth death to the foe from behind the shield of Ajax Telamon.

In the summer of 1862 the writer, then a lad under the regulation age of sixteen, but admitted as a special favor, reported as a cadet to the superintendent of the institute. It was almost the only school then open in the state. Men had been killed in battle upon the campus of old William and Mary College at Williamsburg. Her lecture rooms were filled with sick and wounded. Grass was growing upon the pavements of the Virginia university; the colonnades of

Washington College were deserted. Teachers and scholars had marched away from all these to the great passion play. But never, in her whole history, had the Virginia Military Institute been so crowded to overflowing, or so aglow with life. Almost entirely depleted at the outbreak of hostilities by the draft of a splendid body of young officers from the corps, she had been replenished by the youngsters whom President [Jefferson] Davis afterwards called "the seed corn of the Confederacy," and scarcely a historic family in the South was without its youthful representative there, preparing himself in the military art.

The times were stirring. The boy who sought military education then did so, not with the vague idea that at some future day it *might* prove useful, but almost in hearing of the thunder of the guns. And at the period of my entering the institute the impatience of boyhood had been taught that there was little danger the war would end before we had our chance. Big Bethel and Manassas had been fought; the *Merrimac* and the *Monitor* had met; our armies had passed a winter in camp; the disasters of Roanoke Island, Forts Henry and Donelson, and bloody Shiloh; the Seven Days' fighting around Richmond—all these had tempered the arrogance and subdued the confidence of men. Predictions of peace in ninety days had ceased, and too many hearts were already bleeding to make the hideous death grapple longer the subject of empty boast or trivial jest.

Virginia Military Institute Cadet in Marching Outfit (*Century*)

Both North and South were settling down grimly to that agony of war which God grant that you who have never known it may always be spared.

The ante-bellum equipment of the Virginia cadet corps had been very complete and striking. It was fully as handsome as the West Point outfit and very much the same. Several years before I had seen those wonderful coats with their forty-four buttons of shining brass, those marvelous cross belts, and the patent-leather hats with nodding plume or pompon; and since peace has come again they have bloomed afresh, in all their pristine glory. On my journey visions of all this finery had filled my youthful imagination; but when I arrived I found that the blockade and the growing scarcity of everything like luxury and adornment had wrought great changes in the dapper appearance of the corps.

In May 1862 the cadets had been marched to [Stonewall] Jackson's aid at McDowell in the Shenandoah Valley. They had arrived too late to take part in the battle, but the effect of the march had been to wear out the last vestige of the peace uniforms. Then we had resort to coarse sheep's-gray jacket and trousers, with seven buttons and a plain black tape stripe. The cadet of today appears with felt chapeau and a ten-inch cock plume that never knew how to strut until, plucked from a rooster's tail, it was stuck on the top of a cadet's head. We were content with a simple forage cap, blue or gray, as we could procure it. The cadet of today disports himself in white cross-belts, shining plates, and patent leather accouterments. Then, we had a plain leather cartridge box, and waist belt with a harness buckle. The cadet of today handles a bronzed-barreled breech-loading rifle, of the latest Springfield pattern. Then, we went into the Battle of New Market with muzzle-loading Belgian rifles as clumsy as pickaxes.

As the war progressed, our uniforms ceased to be uniform; for as the difficulty of procuring cloth increased we were permitted to supply ourselves with whatever our parents could procure, and in time we appeared in every shade from Melton gray to Georgia butternut.

Cadet fare in those days was also very simple—so very simple, indeed, that I doubt whether any body of boys were ever so healthy as we were. What we did get was nutritious and palatable, save an ever-to-be-remembered lot of Nassau bacon that appeared to have been saturated with tar on its blockade-running cruise, and one apparently inexhaustible supply of pickled beef so old and tough that it glittered with prismatic splendor in the light.

The course of studies was faithfully pursued. The full professors were nearly all too old for active service. General Smith, Colonel [William] Gilham, Colonel [Thomas H.] Williamson, and Colonel [J. T. L.] Preston, after valuable services rendered at the outbreak in organizing forces, had returned to the institute. Colonel [Stapleton] Crutchfield returned once, wounded, and then went back to die most gloriously. Stonewall Jackson, who had been a professor, never, if I remember rightly, saw his classroom again; and after he went into the service never entered the building until, borne upon the shoulders of eight weeping boys, his pale face looked up from the casket on the spot where he had taught, and his voiceless lips filled his old precinct with a silent eloquence which made soldiers and heroes at a single lesson.

The institute was an asylum for its wounded alumni, and many such, banished from home by invasion or distance, occupied the period of convalescence in teaching. One day [Major W. E.] Cutshaw, one of Lee's best artillerists, shot all to pieces at the front and sent home to die, would teach us mathematics until he could wear his wooden leg back to his battery; another day [Captain Frank] Preston with his empty sleeve would show us that none of his Latin was lost with his arm. At another time [Major M. B.] "Tige" Hardin, pale and broken, would come to teach until he could fight again, or Colonel Marshall McDonald, now famous as [United States] fish commissioner, would hobble in to point with crutch at problems on the blackboard until strong enough once more to point with sword toward the "looming bastion fringed with fire."

From such as these we learned with zest and zeal. They had our hearts to back their efforts. Their very appearance taught us lessons every hour which have been dropped from the curriculum in these tame days of peace.

The *esprit de corps* of the institute was superb. When the command marched forth for any purpose it moved as one man. The drill was perfect. Obedience was instant and implicit. As the war wore on, the stirring events following each other so rapidly and so near at hand bred a restlessness and discontent in every high-strung boy among us. Each battle seemed to infuse fresh impatience in the cadets, who would assemble at the sally port for discussion; the mails were crowded with letters begging parents and guardians for permission to resign and go to the war. Good boys became bad ones to secure dismissal, and as the result of these conspiracies regular hegiras would occur. Many a night have I paced the sentry-beat, thinking now of the last gay party that had scrambled to the top of the departing stage, commissioned for active service; now envying the careless gaiety of the veterans assembled in their officers' quarters, as from time to time their joyous laughter over campaigning yarns burst from the window of some tower room; then hoping against hope, as it seemed, for the day when, like them, I would be a soldier indeed.

The combat deepened. Sharpsburg, Fredericksburg, Chancellorsville, Gettysburg, Vicksburg, Chickamauga, Missionary Ridge, and a hundred lesser battles were taking place around us. One day we buried poor [Brigadier General Elisha F.] Paxton; soon after [Major William L.] Davidson was borne home to us; and a little later Stonewall Jackson, in the zenith of his brilliant career, was brought back by his comrades to his home. Who shall tell with what yearning our eyes followed those brave officers as they hurried back to battle from his grave? They left us there, as if we had been babes.

But our hour was to come at last. Gettysburg is often referred to as the turning point in the war. It was, indeed, in many ways. Not only was it so in the fact that it baffled and disheartened the almost invincible army of Lee, but also in this, that for the first time it aroused the North to the dangers, the horrors, and the possibilities of fighting upon its own soil, and to the necessity of unprecedented effort if the recurrence of invasion was to be prevented. To such an extent were the Federal armies recruited that from the surplus troops a system of raids and incursions was begun by bodies operating independently of the grand armies; and while our diminishing forces were grappling with [Lieutenant General Ulysses S.] Grant and [Major General William T.] Sherman, raiding parties commanded by [Major General Philip H.] Sheridan, [Major General George] Stoneman, [Brigadier General James H.] Wilson, [Colonel August V.] Kautz, [Brigadier General William W.] Averell, [Major General David] Hunter, [Brigadier General Stephen G.] Burbridge, and others rode on their flanks or in their rear with torch and sword.

This policy was begun late in the summer of 1863. Averell, appearing in the neighborhood of Covington, gave the cadet corps a long and fruitless march. The winter of 1863–64 was gloomy enough in the Confederacy. Our soldiers no longer returned from the front exuberant with the joys of camp life and of victory. They were worn and ragged, and, if not actually dispirited, were at least sobered and reflective. The thoughtful, the wise, shook their heads sadly at the prospects of the opening spring campaign. But in one spot of the Confederacy, at least, the martial spirit still burned high, and the hope of battle flamed fresh as on the morning of Manassas. One little nest of fledglings yet remained who, all untried, too young to reason, too buoyant to doubt, were longing to try their wings.

On May 10, 1864, the cadet corps was the very pink of drill and discipline, and mustered 350 strong. The plebes of the last fall had passed through squad and company drill, and the battalion was now proficient in the most intricate maneuver. The broad parade ground lay spread out like a green carpet. The far-off ranges of the Blue Ridge seemed nearer in the clear light of spring. The old guard tree, once more luxuriantly green, sheltered its watching groups of admiring girls and prattling children.

The battalion wheeled, charged, and counter-marched in mimicry of war, until at sunset we formed in line for dress parade. The band played up and down the line. The last rays faded upon the neighboring peak of House Mountain. The evening gun boomed out upon the stillness. The colors of the institute dropped lazily from their staff. Never in all her history seemed Lexington and her surroundings more gently beautiful, more calmly peaceful.

Such was the sunset hour of that lovely day on which we sought our cots, almost forgetful of the troubled world elsewhere. At midnight, save in the guard room at the sally port, every light had disappeared. Suddenly the barracks reverberated with the throbbing of drums; we awoke and recognized the long roll. Lights were up; the stoops resounded with the rush of footsteps seeking place in the ranks; the adjutant, by lantern-light, read our orders amid breathless silence. They told us that the enemy was in the Valley, that [Major General John C.] Breckinridge needed help, and that we were ordered to march for Staunton at daybreak—a battalion of infantry and a section of artillery—with three days' rations. Not a sound was uttered, not a man moved from the military posture of "parade rest." Our beating hearts told us that our hour had come at last.

"Parade's dismissed," piped the adjutant. Then came a wild halloo, as company after company broke ranks. Again in fancy I see the excited rush of that gay throng, eager as greyhounds in the leash, hurrying back and forth, preparing for the start, forgetful that it would be six hours before they should march.

Daybreak found us on the Staunton pike after a sleepless night and a breakfast by candlelight. We had jeered the little boys who were left behind. We had tramped heavily upon the covered bridge that spans the river, until it rocked and swayed beneath our tread. Exuberant with the joyousness of boyhood, we had cheered the fading turrets of the institute as they sank beneath the hills. And now, fairly started upon our journey, we were plodding on right merrily, our gallant little battery rumbling behind.

At midday on May 12 we marched into Staunton to the tune of "The Girl I Left Behind Me." We were not quite as fresh or as neat as at the outset, but still game and saucy. I fear it was not the girls we left behind us that occupied our thoughts just then. Staunton, then as now, was filled with girls' schools, and we were very much occupied with the fair faces around us. Our preparation had been simple. Being muddy to the knees, we had waded a creek until our shoes and trousers were cleansed, and then, picking our way daintily upon the rocks until we reached the pavements, adjusted our locks in a fence corner by the aid of pocket comb and glass, and hurried forward to society. The cadets were the favorites. Perhaps there was something of resentment for this that prompted a veteran regiment to sing "Rock-a-bye, Baby," when we marched past them in the streets.

There was little time, however, for gaiety. Breckinridge's army, which had hurried up from southwestern Virginia to meet [Major General Franz] Sigel, soon filled the town and suburbs. Now and then a bespattered trooper came up wearily from Woodstock or Harrisonburg to report the steady advance of Sigel with an army thrice the size of our own. Ever and anon the serious shook their heads and predicted hot work in store for us. Even in the hour of levity the shadow of impending bloodshed hung over all but the cadet. At evening parade the command came to move down the Valley.

Morning found us promptly on the march. A few lame ducks had succumbed and were left behind, but the body of the corps were still elated and eager, although rain had overtaken us. The first day's march brought us to Harrisonburg; the second to Lacy's Springs, within ten miles of New Market. On this day evidences of the enemy's approach thickened on every hand. At short intervals upon the pike, the great artery of travel in the Valley, carriages and vehicles of all sorts filled the way, laden with people and their household effects, fleeing from the hostile advance. Now and then a haggard trooper, dispirited by long skirmishing against overwhelming force, would gloomily suggest the power and numbers of the enemy. Towards nightfall, in a little grove by a church, we came upon a squad of Federal prisoners, the first that many of us had ever seen. It was a stolid lot of Germans, who eyed us with curious inquiry as we passed. Laughter and badinage had somewhat subsided when we pitched camp that night in sight of our picket-fires twinkling in the gloaming but a few miles below us down the Valley. We learned, beyond doubt, that Franz Sigel and his army were sleeping within ten miles of the spot on which we rested.

For a while the woodland resounded with the axe-stroke, or the cheery halloo of the men from campfire to campfire; for a while the firelight danced, and the air was savory with the odor of cooking viands; for a while the boys grouped around the campfire for warmth and to dry their wet clothing. But soon the silence was broken only now and then by the fall of a passing shower, or the champing of the colonel's horse upon his provender.

I was corporal of the guard. A single sentinel stood post, while the guard and drummers lay stretched before the watch-fire in deep, refreshing sleep. It was an hour past midnight when I caught the sound of hoofs upon the pike advancing at a trot, and a moment later the call of the sentry brought me to him, where I found an aide bearing orders from the commanding general. On being aroused our commandant rubbed his eyes, muttered, "Move forward at once," and ordered me to rouse the camp. The rolls were rattled off; the short, crisp commands went forth, and soon the battalion debouched upon the pike, heading in the darkness and the mud for New Market.

Before we left our camp something occurred that even now may be a solace to those boys who died so gloriously on that day. In the gloom of the night, Captain Preston, neither afraid nor ashamed to pray, sent up an appeal to God for protection of our little band. It was a humble, earnest appeal that sunk into the heart of every hearer. Few were the dry eyes, little the frivolity, in the command, when he had ceased to speak of home, of father, of mother, of country, of victory and defeat, of life, of death, of eternity. Those who, but a few hours later, heard him commanding "B" Company in the thickest of the fight, his already empty sleeve showing that he was no stranger to the perilous edge of battle, realized as few can how the same voice can at one time plead reverently and tenderly and at another pipe higher than the roar of battle.

The day, breaking gray and gloomy, found us plodding onward in the mud. The exceedingly sober cast of our reflections was relieved by the light-heartedness of the veterans. [Brigadier General Gabriel C.] Wharton's brigade, with smiling "Old Gabe" at their head, cheered us heartily as we came up to the spot where they were cooking breakfast by the roadside. Many were the good-natured gibes with which they restored our confidence. The old soldiers were as merry, nonchalant, and indifferent to the coming fight as if it was a daily occupation.

One fellow came round with a pair of scissors and a package of cards, offering to cut off love locks to be sent home after we were dead. They inquired if we wanted rosewood coffins, satin-lined, with name and age on plate. In a word, they made us ashamed of the solemnity of our last six miles of marching, and renewed within our breasts the true daredevil spirit of soldiery.

The mile posts on the pike scored four miles, three miles, two miles, one mile to New Market. Then the mounted skirmishers crowded past us, hurrying to the front. Cheering began in our rear and was caught up by the troops along the line of march. We learned its import as Breckinridge and his staff approached, and we joined in the huzzah as that soldierly man, mounted magnificently, dashed past us, uncovered, bowing, and riding like the Cid. Along the crest of the elevation in our front we beheld our line of mounted pickets and the smoldering fires of their night's bivouac. We halted with the realization that one turn in the road would bring us in full view of the enemy's position. [Brigadier General John] Echols's and Wharton's brigades hurried past us. There was not much banter then. "Forward!" was the word once more, and New Market appeared in sight.

The turn of the road displayed the whole position. A bold range of hills parallel with the mountains divides the Shenandoah Valley into two smaller valleys, and in the eastern most of these lies New Market.

The Valley pike, on which we had advanced, passes through the town parallel with the Massanutten range on our right, and Smith's Creek running along its base. The range of hills on our left breaks as it nears the town and slopes down to it from the south and west, swelling up again beyond it to the north and west. On the right of the pike, looking towards New Market, and running over the creek, a beautiful stretch of meadowland spreads out down to and beyond the town. Orchards skirt the village in these meadows between our position and the town, and they are filled with the enemy's skirmishers. A heavy stone fence and a deep lane run westward from the town and parallel with our line of battle. Here the enemy's infantry was posted to receive our left flank, and behind it his artillery was posted on a slope, the ground rising gradually until, a short distance beyond the town, to the left of the pike, its spreads out in an elevated plateau. The hillsides from this plateau to the pike are gradual and broken by several gullies heavily wooded by scrub cedar.

It was Sunday morning, and 11:00 A.M. In a picturesque little churchyard, right under the shadow of the village spire and among the white tombstones, a six-gun battery was posted in rear of the infantry line of the enemy. The moment we debouched, it opened upon us.

Away off to the right, in the Luray Gap of the Massanutten range, our signal corps was telegraphing the position and numbers of the enemy. Our cavalry was moving at a gallop to the cover of the creek to attempt to flank the town. Echols's brigade was moving from the pike at a double-quick by the right flank and went into line of battle across the meadow, its left resting on the pike. Simultaneously his skirmishers were thrown forward at a run and engaged the enemy. Out of the orchards and out on the meadows arose puff after puff of blue smoke as our sharpshooters advanced, the "*pop, pop*" of their rifles ringing forth excitingly.

Thundering down the pike came [Major William] McLaughlin with his artillery, and wheeling out into the meadows he swung into battery action left, and let fly with all his guns. The cadet section of artillery pressing a little farther forward wheeled to the left, toiled up the slope, and with a plunging fire replied to the Federal battery in the graveyard. At the first discharge of our guns a beautiful wreath of smoke shot upward and hovered over them.

The little town, which a moment before had seemed to sleep so peacefully upon that Sabbath morn, was now wreathed in battle smoke and swarming with troops hurrying to their positions. We had their range beautifully, and every shell, striking some obstruction, exploded in the streets. Every man of our army was in sight. Every position of the enemy was plainly visible. His numbers were but too well known to us, for notwithstanding that his line of battle, already formed, was equal to our own, the reports still came that the pike was filled with his infantry.

Our left wing consisted of Wharton's brigade; the center of the Sixty-second Virginia Infantry and the cadets; and our right of Echols's brigade and the cavalry.

Up to this time I was still corporal of the guard, in charge of the baggage wagon, with a detail of three men, [Washington F.] Redwood, [Jacqueline B.] Stanard, and [Pierre W.] Woodlief [Jr.]. We had not been relieved, in the general bustle and confusion. My orders were to remain with the wagons at the bend in the pike, unless our forces were driven back; in which case we were to retire to a point of safety.

When it became evident that a battle was imminent, a single thought took possession of me, and that was, that I would never be able to look my father [Brigadier General Henry A. Wise] in the face again if I sat on a baggage wagon while my command was in its first, perhaps its only, engagement. He was a grim old fighter, at that moment commanding at Petersburg, and a month later fighting at odds against [Major General William F.] "Baldy" Smith until Lee could come up. He had a tongue of satire and ridicule like a lash of scorpions. I had nearly worried him out of his life with applications to leave the institute and enter the army. If, now that I had the opportunity, I should fail to take part in the fight I knew what was in store for me.

Napoleon in Egypt pointed to the Pyramids and told his soldiers that from their heights forty centuries looked down upon them. My oration, delivered from the baggage wagon, was not so elevated in tone, but equally emphatic. It ran about this wise: "Boys, the enemy is in our front. Our command is about to go into action. I like fighting no better than anyone else. But I have an enemy in my rear as dreadful as any before us. If I return home and tell my father that I was on the baggage guard when my comrades were fighting I know my fate. He will kill me with worse than bullets—ridicule. I shall join the command forthwith. Anyone who chooses to remain may do so." All the guard followed. The wagon was left in charge of the Black driver. Of the four who thus went, one was killed and two were wounded.

We rejoined the battalion as it marched by the left flank from the pike. Moving at double-quick we were in an instant in line of battle, our right near the turnpike. Rising ground in our immediate front concealed us from the enemy. The command was given to strip for action. Knapsacks, blankets, everything but guns, canteens, and cartridge boxes, were thrown down upon the ground. Our boys were silent then. Every lip was tightly drawn, every cheek was pale; but not with fear. With a peculiar nervous jerk we pulled our cartridge boxes round to the front and tightened our belts. Whistling rifled-shell screamed over us as, tipping the hill crest in our own front, they bounded over our heads. Across the pike to our right [Colonel George S.] Patton's brigade was lying down, abreast of us.

"At-ten-tion-n-n! Battalion Forward! Guide—Center-r-rr!" shouted [Colonel Scott] Ship, and off we started. At that moment, from the left of the line, sprang Sergeant Major [Jonathan] Woodbridge, and posted himself forty paces in front of the colors as directing guide. Brave [Oliver] Evans, standing over six feet-two, unfurled our colors that for days had hung limp and bedraggled about the staff, and every cadet in the institute leaped forward, dressing to the ensign, elated and thrilling with the consciousness that "*This is war!*" We reached the hill crest in our front, where we were abreast of our smoking battery and in full sight and range of the enemy. We were pressing towards him at "arms port" with the light tripping gait of the French infantry. The enemy had obtained our range, and began to drop his shell under our noses along the slope. Echols's brigade rose up and were charging on our right with the Rebel Yell.

Woodbridge, who was holding his position as directing sergeant, was ordered to resume his place in line.

Down the green slope we went, answering the wild cry of our comrades as their musketry rattled out its opening volleys. In another moment we should expect a pelting rain of lead from the blue line crouching behind the stone wall at the lane. Then came a sound more stunning than thunder, that burst directly in my face; lightning leaped; fire flashed; the earth rocked; the sky whirled round, and I stumbled. My gun pitched forward, and I fell upon my knees. [Cadet] Sergeant [William] Cabell looked back at me sternly, pityingly, and called out "Close up, men," as he passed on.

I knew no more. When consciousness returned it was raining in torrents. I was lying on the ground, which all about was torn and plowed with shell which were still screeching in the air and bounding on the earth.

Poor little Captain [Govan] Hill of "C" Company was lying near, bathed in blood, with a fearful gash over the temple, and was gasping like a dying fish. [Cadet Private Charles] Read, [Cadet James L.] Merritt, and another [Cadet Pierre W. Woodlief], also badly shot, were near at hand.

The battalion was 300 yards away clouded in smoke and hotly engaged. They had crossed the lane the enemy held, and the Federal battery in the graveyard had fallen back to the high ground beyond. "How came they there?" I thought,

The Cadets in the Wheatfield (*Century*)

and, "Why am I here?" Then I saw that I was bleeding from a deep and ugly gash in my head. That villainous rifled shell that burst in our faces brought five of us to the ground. "Hurrah!" I thought, "youth's dream is realized at last. *I've got a wound and am not dead yet!*" And so, realizing the savory truth, another moment found me on my feet trudging along to the hospital, almost whistling with delight at the thought that the next mail would bear the glorious news to the old folks at home, with a rather taunting suggestion that after all their trouble they had not been able to keep me from having my share in the fun.

From this time forth I may speak of the gallant behavior of the cadets without imputation of vanity, for I was no longer a participant in their glory. The fighting around the town was fierce and bloody on our left wing. Patton's movements on our right were rapid and effective. He had pressed forward and gained the village, and our line was now concave with an angle just beyond the town.

The Federal infantry had fallen back to their second line, and our left had now before it the task of ascending the slope, on the crest of which they were posted. Pausing under the cover of the deep lane to breathe awhile and correct the alignment, our troops once more advanced, clambering up the bank and over the stone fence, and at once delivering and receiving a withering fire. At a point below the town where the turnpike curved the enemy's reserves were massed; in what numbers we could not yet descry. A momentary confusion on our right, as our troops pressed through the streets of New Market, gave invitation for a charge of the enemy's cavalry, who were unable to see McLaughlin's battery which had been moved up, unlimbered in the streets, and double-shotted with grape and canister. The cavalry dashed forward, squadron front, in full career. Our infantry scrambled over the fences, cleared the pike, and gave the artillery a fair opportunity to rake them. They saw the trap too late. They drew up and sought to wheel about. Heavens! What a blizzard McLaughlin gave them. They reeled, staggered, wheeled, and fled. The road was filled with fallen men and horses. A few riderless steeds galloped towards our lines, neighed, circled, and rejoined their comrades. One gallant fellow, whose horse became unmanageable, rode through the battery, and, at full speed, passed beyond, behind, and around our line, safely rejoining his comrades and cheered for his daring by his enemies. This was the end of the cavalry in that fight.

Our left had meanwhile performed its allotted task. Up the slope, right up to the second line of infantry, it went; and a second time the Federal infantry was forced to retire. The veteran troops had secured two guns of the battery, and the remaining four had galloped back to a new position in a farmyard on the plateau at the head of the cedar-skirted gully. Our boys had captured over a hundred prisoners. Charley Faulkner, now a grave senator from West Virginia, came back radiant, in charge of twenty-three Germans large enough to swallow him, and insisted that he captured every man of them himself. Bloody work had been done. The space between the enemy's old and new positions was dotted with their dead and wounded—shot as they fled across the open field. But this same exposed ground now lay before, and must be crossed by our own men, under a galling fire from a strong and protected position. The distance was not 300 yards, but the ground to be traversed was a level green field of young wheat.

Again the advance was ordered. Our men responded with a cheer. Poor fellows! They had already been put upon their mettle in two assaults. Exhausted, wet to the skin, muddied to their eyebrows with the stiff clay through which they had pulled—some of them actually shoeless after their struggle across the plowed ground—they nevertheless advanced with great grit and eagerness; for the shouting on their right meant victory.

But the foe in our front was far from conquered. As our fellows came on with a dash the enemy stood his ground most courageously. That battery, now charged with canister and shrapnel, opened upon the cadets with a murderous hail the moment they uncovered. The infantry, lying behind fence-rails piled upon the ground, poured in a steady, deadly fire. At one discharge, poor Cabell, our first sergeant, by whose side I had marched so long, fell dead, and by his side [Cadet Privates Charles] Crockett and [Henry] Jones. A blanket would have covered the three. They were awfully mangled with the canister. A few steps beyond, [Cadet Private William H.] McDowell, a mere child, sunk to his knees with a bullet through his heart. [Cadet Corporal Samuel F.] Atwill, [Cadet Privates Thomas G.] Jefferson, and [Joseph] Wheelwright, fell upon the green sward and expired; [Samuel S.] Shriver's sword arm dropped helpless to his side, and "C" Company thereby lost her cadet as well as her professor-captain. The men were falling right and left. The veterans on the right of the cadets seemed to waver. Ship, our commandant, fell wounded. For the first time the cadets seemed irresolute. Some one cried out, "Lie down," and all obeyed, firing from the knee—all but [Oliver] Evans, the ensign, who standing bolt upright. Poor Stanard's limbs were torn asunder, and he lay there bleeding to death. Some one cried out, "Fall back, and rally on [Colonel George M.] Edgar's battalion." Several boys moved as if to obey; but [Andrew] Pizzini [Jr.], orderly of "B" Company, with his Italian blood at the boiling point, cocked his gun and swore he would shoot the first man who ran. Preston, brave and inspiring, with a smile lay down upon his only arm, remarking that he would at least save that. [Benjamin] Colonna, captain of "D," was speaking words of encouragement and bidding the boys shoot close. The boys were being decimated; manifestly they must charge or retire; and charge it was. For at that moment, Henry A. Wise, our first captain, beloved of every boy in the command, sprung to his feet, shouted the charge, and led the cadet corps forward to the guns.

The guns of the battery were served superbly; the musketry fairly rolled. The cadets reached the firm green sward of the farmyard in which the battery was planted. The Federal infantry began to break and run behind the buildings. Before the order to "Limber up" could be obeyed our boys disabled the trails and were close upon the guns; the gunners dropped their sponges and sought safety in flight. [Cadet] Lieutenant [John F.] Hanna hammered a burly gunner over the head with his cadet sword. Winder Garrett outran another and attacked him with his bayonet. The boys leaped on the guns, and the battery was theirs; while Evans was wildly waving the cadet colors from the top of a caisson.

A straggling fire of infantry was still kept up from the gully, now on our right flank, although the cadets could see the masses of blue retiring in confusion down the hill. Then came the command to reform the battalion, to mark time, and to half-wheel to the right, when it advanced again, firing as it went, and did not pause until it gained the pike. The broken columns of the enemy hurried on towards Mount Jackson, hotly pressed by our infantry and cavalry. Our artillery advanced to Rude's Hill, and shelled their confused ranks, until they passed beyond the burning bridge that spanned the Shenandoah at Mount Jackson.

We had won a victory—not a Manassas or an Appomattox, but, for all that, a right comforting bit of news went up the pike that night to General Lee; for from where he lay, locked in the death grapple with Grant in the Wilderness, his thoughts were, doubtless, ever turning wearily and anxiously towards this flank movement in the Valley.

The pursuit down the pike was more like a foot-race than a march. Our boys straggled badly, for all realized that the fight was over, and many were too exhausted to go farther. As evening fell the clouds burst away; the sun came forth; and, when night closed in, no sound of battle broke the Sabbath calm, save a solitary Napoleon gun, pounding away at the smoldering ruins of the bridge across the river. The picket-fires of the cadets were lit at beautiful Mount Airy, while the main body bivouacked upon the pike a mile below New Market.

Of a corps of 225 men we had lost fifty-six in killed and wounded.

Shortly before sundown, having had my head sewed up and bandaged, and

Professor-Captain Henry
A. Wise Jr. (*Century*)

having rendered such service as I could to wounded comrades, I sallied forth
to procure a blanket. We had left our trappings unguarded when we stripped
for action. Nobody would consent to be detailed. The result was that the camp-
followers had made away with nearly all our haversacks and blankets. I entered
the town and found it filled with soldiers laughing and carousing as light heart-
edly as if it were a feast or holiday. A great throng of Federal prisoners was corralled in a side street, under guard. They were nearly all Germans. Every type
of prisoner was there. Some affable, some defiant, some light-hearted and careless, some gloomy and dejected. One fellow in particular afforded great merriment in his quaint recital of the manner of his capture. Said he, "Dem leetle tevils
mit der vhite vlag vas doo mutch fur us. Dey shoost smash mine head, ven I vos
cry 'Zurrender' all der dime." A loud peal of laughter went up from the bystanders, among whom I recognized several cadets. His allusion to the white flag was
to our colors. We had a handsome flag with a white and gilt ground and a picture of Washington. It puzzled our adversaries not a little. Several whom I have
met since then tell me they could not make us out at all. Our strange colors, our
diminutive size, and our unusual precision of movement made them think we
were some foreign mercenary regulars.

The jeers and banter of the veterans had now ceased. We had fairly won our
spurs. We could mingle with them fraternally and discuss the battle on equal

terms, and we did so. Glorious fellows those veterans were. To them was due ninety-nine hundredths of the glory of the victory; yet they seemed to delight in giving all praise to "dem leetle tevils mit der vhite flag." The ladies of the town also overwhelmed us with tenderness, and as for ourselves we drank in greedily the praise which made us the lions of the hour.

Leaving the village I sought the plateau where most of our losses had occurred. A little above the town, in the fatal wheatfield, I came upon the dead bodies of three cadets. One wore the chevrons of an orderly sergeant. Lying upon his face, stiff and stark, with outstretched arms, his hands had clutched and torn great tufts of soil and grass; his lips retracted; his teeth tightly locked; his face as hard as flint, with staring, bloodshot eyes. It was hard, indeed, to recognize all that remained of Cabell, who, but a few hours before, had stood first in his class as a scholar, second as a soldier, and the peer of any boy that ever lived in every trait of physical and moral manliness.

A little removed from the spot where Cabell fell, and nearer to the position of the enemy, lay McDowell. It was a sight to wring one's heart. That little boy was lying there asleep, more fit, indeed, for the cradle than the grave. He was barely sixteen, I judge, and by no means robust for his age. He was a North Carolinian. He had torn open his jacket and shirt, and, even in death, lay clutching them back, exposing a fair breast with its red wound. I had come too late. Stanard had breathed his last but a few moments before I reached the old farmhouse where the battery had stood, now converted into a hospital. His body was still warm and his last messages had been words of love. Poor Jack! Playmate, roommate, friend—farewell.

Standing there, my mind sped back to the old scenes at Lexington when we were shooting together in the "Grassy Hills"; to our games and sports; to that day, one week ago, when he had knelt at the chapel and was confirmed; to the previous night at the guard fire when he confessed a presentiment that he would be killed; to his wistful, earnest farewell when we parted at the baggage wagon, and my heart half reproached me for ordering him into the fight. The warm tears of youthful friendship came welling up for one I had learned to love as a brother; and now, twenty-four years later, I thank God that life's buffetings and the cold heartedness of later struggles have not dammed the pure fountains of boyhood's friendship. A truer-hearted, braver, better fellow never died than Jacqueline B. Stanard.

A few of us brought up a limber chest, threw our poor boys across it, and bore their remains to a deserted storehouse in the village. The next day we buried them with the honors of war, bowed down with grief at a victory so dearly bought.

We started up the Valley crestfallen and dejected. Our victory was almost forgotten in our distress for our friends and comrades dead and maimed. We were still young in this ghastly sport. But we proved apt scholars. As we moved up the Valley we were not hailed as sorrowing friends, but greeted as heroes and victors. At Harrisonburg, at Staunton, at Charlottesville, everywhere, an ovation awaited us such as we did not dream of, and such as has seldom greeted any troops. The dead, and the poor fellows who were still tossing on cots of fever and delirium, were almost forgotten by the selfish comrades whose fame their blood had bought.

We were ordered to Richmond. All our sadness disappeared. A week later the cadet corps, garlanded, cheered by ten thousand throats, intoxicated with praise unstinted, wheeled proudly beneath the shadow of the Washington Monument at Richmond to receive a stand of colors from the governor, the band playing lustily—

> Oh! There's not a trade that's going
> Worth showing, or knowing,
> Like that from glory growing
> For the bold soldier boy.

The boys who formed the corps of the West Point of the Confederacy are no longer boys. Many are dead. Many fill high stations in mature manhood. Many are already gray with care. The Virginia Military Institute still survives the wreck of war. But it is not the hotbed of war that it was in those days.

41

Fighting for Petersburg
Thomas T. Roche, Company K,
Sixteenth Mississippi Regiment

FROM JUNE until the latter part of November, 1864, [Brigadier General William] Mahone's Division defended that part of the Confederate line extending from some distance to the right of Fort Mahone, better known as "Fort Damnation," to within less than half a mile of the "Crater." Although protecting a long stretch of the line in front of Petersburg, Mahone would frequently be twenty miles away operating with a large portion of his command. His division consisted of five brigades. Often four of those would be withdrawn at one time while the fifth would be stretched to cover the space made vacant; the pickets of the brigades withdrawn invariably remained till the return of their respective commands. I have known men to perform this duty for eight days without relief. I have also known part of a company to maintain a picket line in front of Petersburg and another part of the same company would be performing like service on the north side of the James River, twenty-two miles away, while the main body would be operating at some other point.

I remember reading in the Richmond *Examiner,* in the autumn of 1864, what purported to be a review of the operations of Mahone's Division for the months of June, July and August, giving the number of prisoners, cannons, small arms and stands of colors captured. I forget the exact figures, except that the number of prisoners more than doubled the strength of the whole division, while the artillery and small arms taken were sufficient to equip over twenty thousand men. In the third week of June, near the Weldon Railroad, Mahone took three thousand prisoners and seven pieces of artillery. About a week later, at Ream's Station, in conjunction with Fitzhugh Lee's cavalry, twelve pieces of artillery and twelve hundred prisoners were taken. On July 20 three of his brigades, consisting of [Colonel David A.] Weisiger's Virginia (Mahone's old brigade), [Brigadier General Victor J. B.] Girardey's Georgia and [Brigadier General John C. C.] Sanders' Alabama brigades—all as true as tempered steel—drove the enemy from the Crater and reestablished our lines, capturing many prisoners and a large number of small arms. These, with the numerous engagements and skirmishes along the Weldon Railroad and on the north side of the James river during the months of June and August, greatly swelled the number.

About the middle of August [Lieutenant General Ulysses S.] Grant moved a large force under [Major General Winfield S.] Hancock to the north side of the James, his real object being to conceal a formidable movement against the Weldon Railroad. Sanders' Alabama, Girardey's Georgia and [Brigadier General Nathaniel H.] Harris's Mississippi brigades, of Mahone's Division, were

Interior of Fort Mahone (*Century*)

dispatched to oppose him. Taking position at Deep Bottom, they were vigorously attacked by Hancock's forces. The first assault was repulsed with heavy
loss, but the second, which was fiercer and more determined, forced back in
disorder the right and center of the Georgia brigade. Pressing through the gaps
they had made, Hancock's men endeavored to widen it by a pressure on the flank
of the Alabamians, who were to the right of the Georgians, and also the portion of the latter, which was still intact. Sanders, seeing the disaster to his left,
swung that portion of his brigade around in a square with his original position,
but not before his extreme left company had been captured. Sanders's men met
the enemy with dogged persistence, repelling every attack made on their two
fronts. General Girardey in the meantime was fighting the remnant of his brigade with unflinching firmness until his fall. The situation, immediately after,
looked critical in the extreme, as the Federals were now pouring rapidly through
the gap; but in another instant a fine, large brigade (unknown to the writer)
came sweeping forward at a double-quick, and fell upon the new triumphant
foe. Their fury bore down all resistance as they swept the enemy back over the
breastworks.

On August 19 the Sixteenth Mississippi was sent forward to reconnoiter and
feel the strength of the enemy in our front. As we crossed the Bottom we advanced up a steep hill, covered with pine timber, and driving in their pickets we
soon found that we were in front of their works. We were made sensible of the
fact in a way that we did not at all appreciate. In passing forward our main object was to capture some prisoners who could give us information, but we were
met by a determined foe, who poured volley after volley into our small force,
causing us to reel and falter and finally to retire down that hill, making better
time than we had done in going up. We lost many of our best men in this little
affair as well as several officers, and nothing was accomplished.

When we arrived at the base of the hill we found that our colors were missing. The bearer had been shot down and another who took his place had met
with the same fate. Our men determined not to give up our flag without a struggle to regain it, and we were about to advance over the same ground, when a
dozen men stepped forward and volunteered to recover it. Six were chosen, three
with their muskets and three without; they advanced up the hill until within
sight of the enemy; they were ordered to "come in, Johnny, and surrender!" Their
answer was: "All right"; so keeping on their course till they reached the colors
where they had fallen, they snatched them quickly and rushed down the hill.
The Federals gave them a parting salute, which hurried them on, but all escaped
without a scratch.

The same day Grant unfolded his plans by throwing the bulk of his army
against the Weldon Railroad. [Lieutenant] General A. P. Hill endeavored to recover the lost ground, but was repulsed with heavy loss. Early on the morning of
August 20 it was discovered that the Federals had disappeared from our front, and
Mahone's three brigades were ordered back to Petersburg, where they arrived the

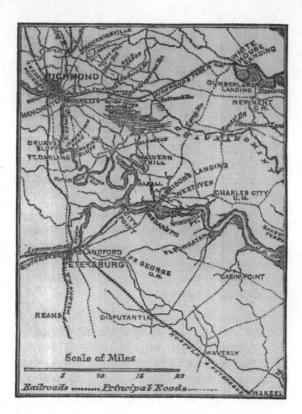

Region between Cold Harbor and Petersburg (*Century*)

same evening, having marched twenty-five miles under the rays of an August sun and over the dustiest road I ever saw. The morning breeze on the twenty-first brought to our ears the sound of artillery from down the Weldon Railroad. Our brigade was quickly put in motion and double-quicked to the Yellow House, some three miles down the railroad, which was near the scene of the disaster of the nineteenth, the rest of the division having marched during the night.

After having formed we moved forward under the guidance of an ex-general, who was at that time acting as an independent scout. It was said that he knew every foot of ground in the vicinity, and also the position occupied by the enemy. The object was to strike the enemy on the flank and rear, but instead of this he led us into the very jaws of death. Passing through a piece of woods we met Brigadier General [Joseph] Finegan's brigade coming back in a panic, their gallant commander trying to rally and reform them. As we emerged from the woods we entered a cornfield, about 300 yards wide, on the opposite side of which were the enemy's formidable works, fairly bristling with artillery. Instantly a sheet of flame leaped from the works, as if suddenly controlled by electricity. It was an explosion in its suddenness, but the metallic peal of the solid shot, the sharp clap and the flat crash of the shell that rose from side to side with rapid-

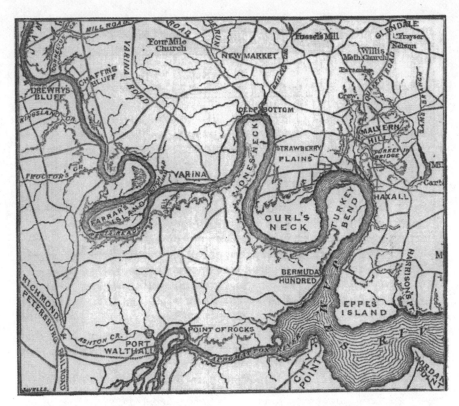

Deep Bottom and Bermuda Hundred (*Century*)

ity cannot be described in one word. This, with the long roll of the musketry, mingled with the yells and cheers of the infantry, was deafening.

The Mississippians rushed forward in the face of a perfect blizzard of lead and iron hail, having long since learned from experience that the quicker such work is accomplished the lighter would be the losses. Before we had covered half the distance they opened a cross fire on us. They were now not only mowing us down from the front, but also pouring a murderous enfilade down both flanks, which caused us to redouble our speed and press on. But we were fast melting away and more than half our number had already fallen. Still we pressed on, almost up to their works, with our ranks shattered and torn. To go forward now with our small handful was to be captured; to retire was almost certain death. So dropping into a shallow ditch some twenty-five yards in front of the works we opened on the enemy a general fusillade, hoping by accurate fire to keep their heads down behind the works until fresh troops could reach us. The hiss of the canister and minies, with the whir of the grape, as it all went tearing, slashing, and cutting through the cornfield, carrying death and agony in its path made it a perfect hell spot.

Many of the men now attempted to crawl back, but in doing so a great number of them lost their lives. Several of my best friends were wounded five or six times before reaching the timber and died before they could be brought to the rear. In addition to our killed and wounded we lost over 100 prisoners. The Alabamians and Georgians who went in further to our left and, who like ourselves supposed they were striking the enemy in the rear, met with a severe repulse. The Alabamians lost their gallant commander, General Sanders, who was killed. Some of our men who were taken prisoners in the cornfield told me afterward that the Federals had three lines of battle in our front and they numbered at least five to our one.

General Grant now held possession of the Weldon Railroad, Lee's main artery to the south, by which was brought the bulk of the forage and supplies for the army. That night, when our report was made out, we found that out of the 900 men that morning we had but 300 left. The next morning we were joined by 100 men, whom we had left on picket on the north side of the James.

During the day we resumed our old position in the trenches, in front of which we still had 150 men, who had remained on duty on the picket line since their comrades had been sent to the north side a week previous. Harris's brigade now had 550 muskets, whereas three years before it had numbered more than 4,000 men. In the Battle of the Yellow House, as it was called by some, the Sixteenth Mississippi lost every commissioned officer engaged, from the colonel down. Our commander, Colonel [E. C.] Councell, was mortally wounded and died when he reached Washington. The Sixteenth, now reduced to 100 men (having formerly numbered about 1,400), was consolidated into five companies. Lieutenant [Abram M.] Feltus, of Company K, who was left in command of the pickets in front of Petersburg, was the only commissioned officer in the regiment. General Harris placed Lieutenant Colonel J. H. Duncan, of the Nineteenth, in command. He was as tender in his feelings as a woman, and true and calm as he was brave. Poor fellow, he only survived the war a short time.

On October 27, the Federals moved a heavy force against the Southside Railroad, consisting of Hancock's and [Major General Gouverneur K.] Warren's corps and a portion of another corps, with a strong force of cavalry. They came prepared to stay, as they had six days's rations. Crossing the Roawanty Creek they were met by [Major] General Wade Hampton, who contested every inch of ground. He fell back from one position only to take another. Thus he struggled to gain time till the infantry should come up. Four brigades of Mahone's division were withdrawn from the trenches and sent to the relief of the cavalry.

A little more than three hours later found us at Burgess's Mill, between seven and eight miles west of Petersburg. Hancock held the bridge below the mill, thus cutting off Hampton from all assistance. Mahone took in the situation at a glance. Placing Harris's brigade at the bridge he crossed the other three, Sanders's (now [Colonel William H.] Forney's), Girardey's (now [Brigadier General G. Moxley] Sorrel's), and Weisiger's lower down, suddenly throwing them on the flank [and] rear of the enemy. The three brigades captured six pieces of artillery and 500 prisoners. The Federals now concentrated all their available force to crush this little wasp. General Lee said of this attack: "Mahone met it with that dash and stubbornness now proverbial in the army, and hurling his three brigades against the advancing column broke through three lines of battle and drove them back."

At the same time Harris crossed at the bridge and attacked vigorously and steadily and pressed the enemy back. During the night the Federals retreated. On the next day, after burying the enemy's dead, we returned to Petersburg and resumed our position in the trenches.

As the winter advanced the suffering became more severe, the army being only half-clad and half-fed. Many were barefooted, treading the frozen ground, while our blankets were so threadbare that they afforded little protection against the winds of winter. Even fuel was scarce. It was doled out, and the half-frozen veterans made a harrowing picture as they huddled around fires scarcely enough to warm the tips of their fingers. With all these difficulties to contend against there was no rest, for the sound of musketry and artillery seemed never to cease. The mortar shells were the most dreaded of all, for the breastworks were no protection against them as they described their curves by day and flaming arches by night, bursting and raining missiles of death, killing one and wounding another. Thus it was that Lee's strength was being reduced day after day, month after month. And this was the way the long, dark winter was passed in the trenches.

During the later part of November, Mahone's division was permanently withdrawn from the trenches and went into winter quarters on the north side of the Boydtown Plank Road, two miles west of Petersburg. While there the division maintained an entrenched picket line about two miles in extent and running a mile south of our quarters. About one-fourth of the command was required for this duty. Half way between the picket line and our camps was our main line of works. Under such perfect discipline did Mahone have his men that had we been suddenly attacked he could have placed us almost instantly in position without confusion. Fortunately, during our stay of over three months everything was quiet on that part of the line, the enemy in our front being peaceable, gentlemanly, and obliging.

To show their kindly feeling there are a few incidents worthy of mention that occurred between the pickets. The ground which separated the pickets was covered with heavy timber. Strict orders had been issued against our men entering the neutral ground, as some of them had used it as a cover to desert to the enemy.

The winter was very cold and wood was scarce, and the little we could procure for the picket line had to be carried a mile on our shoulders. This seemed a hardship when there was so much wood just in front of us. One bitter cold day we concluded to disobey orders by cutting wood in front if our friends on the other side did not object. Not a shot had been exchanged since our advent,

Scene among the Rifle Pits
before Petersburg
(*Century*)

a month previous; in fact, we had not even had a glimpse of the "boys in blue," who, no doubt, were as anxious for some of the wood as we were.

After pounding away for some time with our worn-out Confederate axes, an unarmed squad of Federals appeared, who greeted us with "Hello, Johnnies, are you after wood?" In a few minutes Yanks and Rebs were on the best of terms. Strange sight, but nevertheless true. The Federals tendered us the use of their sharp axes, which was readily accepted. Some of the Federals were so anxious to show their kind feelings for us that they actually helped us cut our wood! This neighborly feeling existed as long as we remained there.

Once some of the Federals invited me to accompany them to their picket line and dine with them. I expressed grave doubts about getting back, but they assured me on their honor as soldiers that if I went they would see me returned safely. With this assurance I went and remained for more than an hour. They vied with each other in hospitality. But with all their assurances I felt ill at ease, for I did not know what might prevent my return, as in such an event I would be classed a deserter. But, true to their promise, I was safely returned. These facts may seem strange and improbable to the reader who did not participate in the late unpleasantness, but there are thousands today who cherish the remembrance of many such incidents.

But we must not forget our quarters. They were to the north of the Plank

Road, about 300 yards further north of which, between our quarters and Petersburg, were two unfinished redoubts. These redoubts had been begun in the early part of the siege, but work had long since ceased, as it was thought they would be of no service. The redoubts were between 250 and 300 yards apart. The one on the right was known as Fort Gregg, and stood 200 yards east of our quarters. The other, on the left, was called Fort Whitworth. Half a mile to the left of Whitworth there was a small stream which crossed the Boydtown Plank Road with a formidable dam, which had been built for the purpose of backing its waters up its bed, thus forming an artificial water barrier. General Lee had to depend greatly on the science of engineering as a substitute for his deficiency in men. The ground, stretching to our breastworks, was almost level and clear. It had been stripped of fences and trees for firewood, even the roots having been dug up for that purpose.

To the north of the Plank Road the ground was slightly rolling. About 300 yards to the rear of our quarters, on a hill, stood a stately brick mansion, the property of a Mr. Whitworth, on the grounds of which were General Mahone's headquarters. About 300 yards north of the Whitworth house ran the Cox Road, and between the two at this point flowed a small stream, which crossed the road a short distance above. Between the Cox road and the Appomattox River was the headquarters of General Lee, while 500 yards northeast of the Whitworth house were the old defenses that encircled Petersburg. It was here that Grant pierced the Confederate line in April 1865, of which more anon.

During our stay of four months at this camp, Mahone's division was not idle, but was constantly engaged in arduous service. Mahone was a restless spirit, who was nervous and dissatisfied unless actively engaged. We had company drill in the morning and battalion drill in the afternoon, while every other day we would be marched two miles at quick time and back again at a double-quick, without halting. In this way the command was always very efficient.

Mahone was noted as an epicure, and it was said that his larder was supplied with the best that the Confederacy could afford. While in camp he kept a cow in order to have cream for his coffee. About the middle of January he had a nice lot of turkeys. One day a ragged and hungry Georgian thought that he would like a turkey. So with a baited fishing hook and line he strolled leisurely in the direction of Mahone's quarters. A hundred yards distant strutted a large gobbler. Mahone, with some of his staff, was sitting in front of his tent engaged in pleasant conversation. The Georgian apparently sauntered carelessly by, and in doing so dropped the bait, which the turkey seized. The soldier continued his walk now in an opposite direction. The turkey, as a natural consequence, followed. The general's attention was attracted. The man now broke into a brisk trot with the turkey at his heels.

General Mahone was one of the most accomplished swearers in the Confederacy. One this occasion he broke out in his peculiar sharp, screeching voice: "Boys, look at that damned coward running from my turkey!" The Georgian, by this time, was in full run, forcing the turkey to flop and jump spasmodically as he sped on after his captor. Mahone shouted: "Just look at my turkey running after that cowardly lout! Look at him, boys; just look at him! Come, let us follow them and see the fun!"

Just then the man and turkey disappeared over the hill and escaped. Next day written notices were posted offering a reward of twenty dollars for the apprehension of the man that stole Mahone's turkey. A few weeks after a similar search was made in every quarter in the camps for Mahone's cow, but not a vestige of hair or hide could ever be seen. I believe the horns were found, but never the wicked thief.

During the winter Lee's cavalry force became greatly diminished, and finally Wade Hampton's division went south to get fresh horses and fill up the shattered ranks. In the Confederate service cavalry horses were private property, and when a cavalryman became dismounted or lost his horse he was forced to join the infantry or artillery service. The enemy, taking advantage of our small force of poorly equipped and half-starved cavalry, were constantly raiding on our lines of communication with their superbly mounted horsemen. One time they would sweep in the direction of the Richmond and Danville or Southside Railroad; again it would be Hicksford, forty-five miles south of Petersburg. At another time they would cross the Nottoway into Brunswick, Dinwiddie, or Sus-

Daybreak in the Woods at Hatcher's Run (*St. Nicholas*)

sex. Our small cavalry force not being able to cope with such raiders, Mahone's "web foot" cavalry were called on. The rapidity of the movements which marked the operations of this division gave Mahone's men the name of foot cavalry. I have known them to march more than thirty-five miles a day and feel comparatively fresh. Thus the long winter months of 1864 and 1865 dragged along.

On February 5 [1865] General Grant made a general movement against our right, his object being to turn Lee's flank and seize the Southside Railroad. Crossing Hatcher's Run he was met by [Major General John B.] Gordon's corps and a portion of [Major General William H.] Fitzhugh Lee's cavalry. Both sides fought with much spirit. The prompt arrival of Mahone's division saved the day for Lee.

This arrival occurred at about 3:30 P.M. After a forced march of ten miles, the last three at a double-quick, Harris's brigade being the last to arrive, was the first to break the enemy's lines. Rapidly forming on the left of the division, with our left resting on the Vaughan Road, everything on our front looked critical, as Gordon's men were coming back in droves, reporting the enemy in overwhelming force and their commands all cut to pieces.

General Harris had barely aligned the brigade when the division advanced. Harris, with flaming eyes and sword drawn, and in his clear, ringing voice, which was heard distinctly above the roll of musketry, shouted: "On first battalion, by direction; forward, guide center!" Just as the brigade swept forward the troops that were fighting in our front came rushing back in a panic, being closely followed by a triumphant foe. With a yell the Mississippians charged up the wooded slope, with the Virginians and Alabamians on their right. The enemy, who were above us, poured a volley over us, not a shot taking effect. The Federals, being elated at their temporary success, made a gallant stand, holding their ground until we had almost crossed bayonets with them. But the onslaught was so sudden and determined that they could not resist it, so they fled, leaving many of their comrades prisoners in our hands.

Up to this time we had not fired a shot. To our right the line had not yet been broken, but stood like a firm wall, apparently not intending to give a foot of ground to Weisiger and Forney, who were pressing forward against it. But our right poured a volley down the flank and rear of the enemy, which had the effect of throwing them into confusion. At the same instant a fresh line appeared in our front. Pouring a volley into it and charging at the same time the Federals became demoralized and broke in confusion. All opposition having ceased, the rout became a chase, as we forced them back for nearly a mile, when the division was halted near a creek. About dark we were withdrawn to near the point whence the Federals had been driven, and made ready to renew the struggle on the next morning.

But the elements were hostile, for in the night a heavy sleet had fallen, and continued for three days, making military movements impossible, so the two great opponents looked at each other with lines drawn up. It was the coldest weather I ever experienced, and although we had an abundance of great log fires during those three memorable days the army was enclosed in a solid coat of ice, the clothing being frozen stiff. While one side would be thawed out by getting close to the fire, the other side would be freezing. The suffering of the pickets was terrible. They had to be relieved every twenty-five minutes, and to keep their blood in circulation they kept up a constant skirmish. At one time the Federals would drive the Confederates, only to be driven back, and vice versa. On the fourth day hostilities ceased and we returned to camp.

About March 12 our brigade, under cover of darkness, was moved rapidly to Richmond, as at that time all movements we wished concealed from the enemy had to be made at night, as he had a clear view of the surrounding country from his tall wooden towers in his rear.

Arriving in Richmond at daylight the next morning we moved out on the Brooke Road some two miles from the city and awaited the coming of [Major General Philip H.] Sheridan, who was on his last great raid. The men were highly elated at the prospect, for if there was any kind of fighting that they did enjoy it was an encounter with the cavalry. We were disappointed, as Sheridan did not attack Richmond, but passed to the north. Rounding the left of our army he crossed the Pamunky and joined the right wing of the Federal Army.

Harris's brigade had now been in service nearly four years and during that long period the men had been engaged in arduous service at the front. But now, finding themselves so near the gay capital of the Confederacy, they were bent on fun and frolic. Few passes were allowed, and unless a soldier was armed with one he could not expect to gain admission to the precincts of the city. Even if he were fortunate enough to pass the cordons of guards, he was almost certain to be arrested by the provost guards, who were stationed at nearly every corner, and landed in the Crow's Nest.

But we were old soldiers and equal to any emergency, so we wrote our own passes. One who wrote a pass would sign his company commander's name. Number two would approve it and countersign it as colonel, while number three would affix General Harris's autograph. Shortly after dark one night the writer and four comrades ran the blockade into Richmond, thinking we would be the only representatives of Harris's brigade at the theater. But we were surprised to find about fifty already there waiting for the doors to be opened. Still they came and kept coming, each one bringing gun and accouterments. General Harris, finding his brigade melting away, ordered out guards on all avenues leading into the city, with instructions to arrest every man found away from the line, but the guards also had theater on the brain. When the curtain rose more than half the audience were composed of ragged Mississippians. The play, "Lady Audley's Secret," was in keeping with everything in the Confederacy at that time. The scenery, furniture, and lights and general paraphernalia were rusty and torn. While the acting would be no credit to a fourth-rate amateur troupe, it was a change to us and we enjoyed it.

The next day we were again placed in the trenches, this time relieving a portion of [Major General George E.] Pickett's division at Bermuda Hundred, just in front of the batteries erected by [Major General Benjamin F.] Butler at Dutch Gap. These works were different from anything we had been accustomed to. They were simply immense. The heavy ordnance that was placed along the line was so large that the cannons of our acquaintance were but popguns in comparison. The ground in front and rear of our works was plowed, rooted, and fissured by thousands of tons of iron hurled from the heavy Federal rifle and mortar batteries at Dutch Gap. I asked one of Pickett's men, whom I interviewed, if their losses had been heavy at this point, and was surprised when he told me that during six months' stay there one man had been wounded and one dog killed.

A few days later we were joined by all of our division, relieving the rest of Pickett's men, who were sent to Petersburg. Harris's brigade was now moved near to Swift Run Creek, which was on the right of the division. It was a delightful place, the works extending through tall pine timber. Comfortable cabins stretched along the rear of the works. About 300 yards in front was our entrenched picket line. In front of each was a formidable abatis. We felt that we could repulse any attack that the enemy might make, although we were stretched out ten feet apart.

Both sides were on good terms. One great discomfort here were short rations, for we seldom had the pleasure of a good meal, thanks to the energy of General Sheridan for cutting the canal and railroad, which in a great measure cut off our supplies. During the last days a soldier's rations was a quarter of a pound of rancid bacon and three quarters of a pound of corn meal, with a little salt thrown in. It was not uncommon for us to be all day without food, and sometimes two days elapsed without rations being issued, which was rarely ever made up. I have often seen, in those dark days, men draw two days' rations and eat the whole at one meal and then go without until they would draw again. To give the reader of today an idea of what provisions were worth during the last days, I will say that in the middle of March I paid 150 dollars for a gallon of molasses. I have forgotten the price of a barrel of flour, but I think it was 1,000 dollars.

With all this, we enjoyed the rest. As April approached the weather became more charming. The birds sung as though all were peace and quietness, while nature lay before us, robed in smiles and sunshine. We had no work, no drill, only one day's picket duty out of every five; we basked in the sunshine, slept, and dreamed of the good things of life. Nearly all the men were happy in the belief that we would be allowed to remain here through the summer and recruit our shattered ranks, while others said it was too pleasant to last, and, sure enough, the latter were right, for on the morning of April 1, 1865, Harris's brigade drew its last ration from the Confederate government.

About the last of March General Grant sent Sheridan, assisted by Warren, to act against the Southside Railroad and turn the right flank of the Confederate army. To meet it Lee had to again weaken his lines by drawing out Pickett's and [Major General] Bushrod Johnson's divisions. On the next day, April 1, Sheridan furiously attacked the Confederates at Five Forks, completely routing the divisions of Pickett and Johnson and capturing more than half of their commands. Here fell, mortally wounded, [Colonel William J.] Pegram, the young artillerist, while serving his guns until the enemy were at the muzzles. The army recognized in him on the bravest of the brave.

The withdrawal of the divisions of Pickett and Johnson had so weakened the Confederate lines before Petersburg that the least pressure must snap it. On that night [Lieutenant General James] Longstreet, who was defending Richmond on the north side of the James, was ordered by his chief to join him at Petersburg. After daylight on the morning of April 2, and before Longstreet had time to obey Lee's order, Grant discovered from his tall wooden towers the weakest point of the confederate line. He immediately threw [Major General John] Gibbon's corps against that portion which had been held by Mahone's division during the winter, but now manned by [Major General Cadmus M.] Wilcox's division, of [Lieutenant General Ambrose P.] Hill's corps. The Federals swept forward with slight resistance, as there were but few to oppose them, piercing our lines and bulging inward. Here our brilliant and successful corps commander, General A. P. Hill, fell while attempting to rally Wilcox's division.

General Mahone says: "About midnight General Lee telegraphed, 'Can you spare me a brigade of your division?' My answer was, 'Harris's Mississippi brigade is under orders and on its way to you.'" About 1:00 A.M. or 2:00 A.M. of the morning of April 2 we were awakened and ordered to fall into the breastworks as expeditiously and quietly as possible, and not take anything except guns and accouterments. Not having heard of the disaster at Five Forks the day previous, we could not imagine the cause of alarm, as everything was perfectly quiet on our front.

In less than five minutes we were moving away, and when we were out of earshot of the enemy we broke into double-quick and we were soon at the railroad, where we were quickly packed into boxcars in waiting and rolled rapidly to Petersburg. About daylight we arrived near Pocahontas, a small village on the north bank of the Appomattox, opposite Petersburg. One of General Lee's staff officers was waiting to hurry us forward. Sweeping rapidly up the road at a run, the sound of artillery and roll of musketry plainly told in words of thunder that there was warm work ahead.

Crossing at the upper pontoon bridge, two miles above, we now hastened on in the direction of General Lee's headquarters. The brigade stretched out for nearly half a mile, only those who were long-winded being well up. General Lee was mounted on his iron gray, his favorite war horse. Just as General Harris reported, a staff officer rode up and said that General Gordon did not require any help. General Lee then directed Harris to report to General Wilcox near the Boydtown [Plank] Road. On gaining the hill on which the Whitworth house stood a surprising sight met our gaze, as we had not heard of the disaster of the morning. Away to the right and to the left were the oncoming long blue lines of infantry, their gun barrels shining like silver in the sun as they carried them at a right shoulder shift.

Our breastworks were now some distance in their rear. Their long ordnance trains moved down the Church Road, which debouched into the Plank Road, the black tops of the wagons giving it the appearance of a huge black serpent. To the right, as far as I could see, there was nothing to oppose the enemy; while to our left, the nearest infantry I saw were at the dam, a half mile away. In front of Fort Gregg, and near the Plank Road, was a portion of one company of the battalion of Washington Artillery of New Orleans. This organization had become distinguished for its service, having been often tried and always found as true as tempered steel. They were the only Confederates I saw for the distance of more than two miles.

All this I took in at a glance as we moved rapidly in the direction of the Plank Road. We passed General Wilcox between Fort Gregg and our old winter quarters. He was dismounted and inclined to be a little profane that morning, for just as we were passing I heard him say, "Boys, we'll drive them back yet; one of you are equal to 100 of those damned cowardly fellows!" Crossing the Plank

Fighting against Fate (*Harper's New Monthly Magazine*)

Roadto the west of the Newman house, which had been the headquarters of General Harris the previous winter, we were formed in line of one rank with an interval of one yard apart. At a right angle with the road the writer's company, which was on the right of the brigade, rested on the road. Two men from each company were advanced as skirmishers. In this order we moved forward for some distance, the two guns of the Washington artillery accompanying us.

The Federals were moving in three columns, two of which, more than half a mile away, were going in the direction of the Plank Road, while the third was moving in line from our breastworks. One of the columns, on reaching the Plank Road, halted and came to a front. They seemed to be in no hurry, but very deliberately dressed their line and then moved forward.

It was a grand but awful sight, the Federals moving with the same precision as though on parade. No obstacles were in their path, the ground being level and clear. The Mississippians were crouched low on one knee, awaiting the living flood, which came in their direction and threatened all with destruction. I never saw our men as determined as they were that morning. All understood the situation and could not hope to turn back such a force, but were determined to make a sacrifice, just to gain time, as Longstreet was momentarily expected. It reminded me at the time of the fierce little terrier waiting his opportunity to spring at the throat of a large mastiff.

In a short time our skirmishers came rushing in, while the enemy continued to advance at the same steady gait, as though he held our slim line in utter contempt and intended to engulf us. When within a few hundred yards Harris' men raised their guns and fired, and apparently every shot had its effect. At the same time the Southerners sprang to their feet with a yell and started to charge, but were ordered to stand fast. The shock was so sudden to the enemy that they broke in disorder. Our skirmishers were again advanced and our line dressed.

On looking round I saw General Lee in the road talking to General Wilcox. As he rode off he directed General Harris to send a company to occupy the quarters on the right of the road to prevent the enemy from using them as a cover. Companies K and C, which had been consolidated under Lieutenant Feltus, and numbered twenty-five men, were ordered there. On our arrival General Lee rode up and instructed us to set fire to the quarters, beginning next [to] the road; that we must "by no means allow those people to occupy them." In many of them the fire was yet burning in the large mud chimneys, over which the frugal breakfast had been placed to cook, while the soldiers' scanty wardrobes were scattered round in disorder, showing the haste in which the recent occupants had been called forth. In the meantime the rest of the brigade retired to Forts Gregg and Whitworth.

The enemy advanced their infantry columns well up to the Plank Road, massed their artillery, with which they opened a heavy fire on Gregg. The two guns of the Washington Artillery, which had been placed in position in the work, replied with great accuracy until both were disabled. Shortly after their artillery ceased firing, their infantry advanced.

The left of their column, which was in our front, on reaching the road halted and lay down, they finding it impossible to advance through a wall of fire. But the portion of it that advanced against Gregg charged gallantly up the parapet in the face of a perfect hail of minie balls. As they seemed to be badly led, however, after a faint attempt to enter the fort, they appeared to lose courage, dropped down and huddled together in the ditch.

As we were farther advanced than Gregg, we rapidly continued to fire the quarters, so as to bring us on a line with the fort, as we feared that the enemy, should he fall back from Gregg, would rush for the cover of the cabins and cut us off. The work was quickly accomplished, as the cabins were built of combustible material. Another column was sent against Gregg, but met with the same success as the first, receiving a terrible punishment,

With the large force now in the ditch it would have been short work to overpower the Confederates, had they passed around the rear, as the work was open at that point—in fact, it was not necessary to have sacrificed the life of a single man in taking those works. If General Gibbon had advanced a force to our right he could have passed around in the rear of Batteries Gregg and Whitworth and could have taken possession of the inner line of works. Another and another and still another column rolled up against Gregg. In every charge the men moved steadily until they reached the Plank Road and then rushed forward at a double-quick, their guns at a trail, their bodies bent forward and heads bowed down, as though they were beating against a hail storm. Each attacking column seemed determined to carry everything before it, but on nearing the fort they must have been appalled by the sight that met their eyes, for they, too, fell flat on the ground. For 100 yards in front of the work the ground was completely covered with one trembling mass of human beings. During the hours that Gregg was besieged, many an anxious glance was cast to the rear in hopes of seeing the column of the "Old Warhorse." Suddenly, the Federals jumped to their feet, and with a mighty cheer scrambled up onto the parapet. But the Mississippians and artillery had not yielded, for they were seen to jump on the work, and with muskets clubbed, to endeavor to beat off the exultant foe. Then it was that our men were soon overborne and compelled to yield. The old battle flag, in shreds from the effects of bullets and blackened by the smoke of battle, and which had been proudly borne along the fair fields of the Shenandoah, over the plains of Manassas, Sharpsburg, Fredericksburg, Chancellorsville, along the mountains of Pennsylvania and through the thickets of the Wilderness and Spotsylvania, and in more than fifty other battles, was torn down and folded forever! (This flag was concealed on the person of B. F. Chisholm, color bearer of the Sixteenth Mississippi.)

From my position I could not see Whitworth, as Gregg was between us and that point. Immediately after the fall of Gregg we saw General Harris and his two regiments making good time in the direction of the inner line of works, which suggested to us the propriety of availing ourselves of the same privilege. Sometime before the fall of Gregg, General Gibbon advanced a column of infantry and a battery of artillery around to our right and rear, the battery taking position on the hill 300 yards southwest of the Whitworth house, but did not fire any till after the fall of Gregg.

The situation of our small force was critical in the extreme, as the troops on our right were pushing toward the Whitworth house, our only point of exit, while those to our left, who had possession of Gregg, sent a force to look after us. To reach the house we had about 300 yards to go, a long distance of it, however, under cover of the cabins.

I think there was no better time made during the war than we did in getting over that space. On reaching the open field it seemed to rain bullets, as the thousands at Gregg gave us their parting compliments. Strange to say no one was hurt. As we were passing the Whitworth house its owner came rushing out. He was about seventy years of age, erect in stature, with long, gray hair falling over his shoulders. He was dressed in a suit of black broadcloth, which at that time was a rare thing to see. His whole appearance denoted that stately old Virginian. With hands uplifted he accosted us with: "Men, what are you running for? You are all cowards! You are a disgrace to your country; stop and help drive them back!" As I was passing him, I hurriedly remarked: "My friend, we haven't time, and you don't know what you are talking about! Go into the house quick

A Dead Confederate at Fort Mahone (*Century*)

or you will be hurt!" The last I saw of him he stood heaping anathemas upon our cowardly heads.

As we emerged to the west side of the house we saw that we had beaten the Federal column that was pushing from the right about 100 yards. They seeing that we had slipped through their fingers gave a parting salute; as we rushed down the lane leading to the Cox Road the sound of the bullets on the fence rails was like peas falling on a rawhide.

My recollection is that Gregg was attacked about 8:00 A.M. and fell between 9:00 A.M. and 10:00 A.M. I have always understood that when Gregg fell, General Lee sent the memorable telegram to President Davis in church announcing to him that the last day of resistance of Petersburg and Richmond had at length arrived.

On reaching the branch we met the head of Longstreet's column, consisting of [Brigadier General Henry L.] Benning's Georgia brigade of [Major General Charles W.] Field's division, which was quickly placed in line. Benning's brigade met the on-pouring flood and checked it long enough to enable the rest of the division to hurry up and form a fresh line in the inner works. The delay, purchased by the obstinate defense of Gregg and the masterly handling of Field's division by General Longstreet, saved Petersburg until preparations for its evacuation could be made, and about 8:00 P.M. that evening the army began its retreat to Appomattox.

PART 9

The Western Theatre in 1864

A Terrible Day:
The Battle of Atlanta, July 22, 1864
John W. Fuller, Brevet Major General, U.S.V.

THE BATTLE of July 22, 1864, commonly called the Battle of Atlanta, was fought to the east and southeast of the city. On our side the fighting was confined to [Major General James B.] McPherson's command—the Army of the Tennessee. McPherson's front, which faced three cardinal points of the compass, extended altogether nearly three miles.

The Fifteenth Corps faced to the west, confronting Atlanta. The line of the Seventeenth swerved to the east, so that this corps faced substantially to the south. The Sixteenth Corps, most of which had just marched over from the north of the railroad, was halted about a miles behind the Fifteenth, and when the battle opened faced to the east. Between the Fifteenth and Sixteenth corps, who stood back to back, were parked the large supply trains of McPherson's command.

[Lieutenant General William J.] Hardee's corps, during the night of July 21, marched from Atlanta in a southeasterly direction until they passed entirely beyond our lines, and then turned to the north, so as to bring the Army of the Tennessee between them and Atlanta. Then facing to the west, they began their part of the program by marching in line of battle for our rear.

[General John Bell] Hood's old corps was massed behind the entrenchments near the city, all ready to assail in front so soon as they should hear the sound of Hardee's guns in rear of our army.

Hood hoped this simultaneous attack upon front and rear would crush such portion of [Major General William T.] Sherman's army as might stand between. But for the accidental position of the Sixteenth Corps, which Hardee encountered a mile before he expected to fight, it seems probable the enemy would have gotten possession of our trains. What more he might have won is another question.

It is not my purpose to write a history of the battle, but only to recall the scenes which came under my observation during the day.

The day before the battle we received orders to march to a position in rear of the Seventeenth Corps. I was in command of the Fourth Division, Sixteenth Corps. Just as we were ready to start an order came to send a brigade back to Decatur, to watch there, and to protect some supply trains coming up from the river. Colonel J. W. Sprague, commanding the Second Brigade, was accordingly sent back. This left with me only the First Brigade (Colonel John Morrill), two batteries, and a small battalion of pioneers, for the Third Brigade had not yet come up from the Tennessee [River].

When we reached the Seventeenth Corps, either [Major General Francis P.] Blair [Jr.] or [Brigadier General Mortimer D.] Leggett directed us to bivouac in the woods in rear of Leggett's left. There was a newly-cut road through the woods which led from the open fields where the trains of the Army of the Tennessee were parked to the fortified line of the Seventeenth Corps. On either side of this road our infantry bivouacked. The only battery then with us was Company F, Second United States Artillery, and this was ordered away from us by General Blair to take position in the line of his corps (the Seventeenth). During the evening of July 21, or before daylight of the twenty-second, our pioneer corps covered it well with an earthwork. My own tents were pitched in the open fields, perhaps fifty rods in rear of the infantry, and not far from the large trains of the Army of the Tennessee.

On the morning of July 22 rumors were rife that the enemy was abandoning Atlanta; but these were soon followed by the statement that he had merely fallen back to a new and stronger line. Several of the enemy's regiments, however, were seen moving to the southeast, and this strengthened the belief that "he soon *would* evacuate, anyhow."

[Major General Grenville M.] Dodge, the commander of our corps, rode over to my headquarters before noon, and told us that as soon as the Seventeenth Corps had advanced and established itself in its new position, our corps (the Sixteenth) would move up and form the extreme left flank of the army. While I was talking with General Dodge, Lieutenant [Seth M.] Laird reported with his battery (the Fourteenth Ohio), having marched over with the Second Division. I directed him to park his guns on a little elevation not far from our headquarters tents. He asked if there "would be time to unhitch and water his horses in the brook nearby."

"Oh yes," was the reply. "We may stay here half the afternoon."

Dinner was announced, and General Dodge sat down with us. While we were eating, skirmishing was heard in an easterly direction, almost opposite to that of Atlanta. We dropped knives and forks to listen. The noise grew louder, and General Dodge remarked, "There must be some rebel cavalry raiding in our rear," and then said: "You had better post one of your regiments so as to cover our trains." Captain [Daniel] Weber, of my staff, rode into the woods for a regiment, and General Dodge, mounting his horse, rode over to the Second Division, which had halted nearby. As the firing rapidly increased, almost directly after General Dodge left us another staff officer was sent to order out all the regiments on the double-quick, and to say I would show them where to form when they arrived.

Riding immediately a few rods to the eastward, I crossed a little rivulet, and was soon on quite high ground. It was an open field, from whence could be seen the Second Division forming line facing to the east. As the field seemed such a commanding position, I at once decided to form a line on its westerly side, and especially since it was substantially a prolongation of the line of the Second Division.

As this field was the scene of bloody strife, let me describe it. It was nearly square, though rather longer from east to west than from north to south. There was not a tree nor shrub, not even a stump, in the field to obscure the view or to afford any shelter; its westerly side was flanked by the little stream I had just crossed, the banks of which were fringed with bushes not much higher than a man's head. The rivulet, after washing the westerly edge of the field, made a sharp bend to the east, following a deep ravine which skirts the field on the north. On the west and south sides stood the forest. To the south we knew the forest was held by [Brigadier General] Giles A. Smith's division of the Seventeenth Corps—half a mile away. What was there to the east?

As the regiments came out of the woods the line was formed near, and parallel to the little rivulet on the western edge of the field, near enough the crest to overlook the field and yet have the men partially covered. Kneeling, they would be fully hidden. The Thirty-ninth Ohio came first, and at the northeast corner formed the left of our line. The Twenty-seventh Ohio arrive next, and was formed on the right of the Thirty-ninth. The sixty-fourth Illinois was formed on the opposite side of the rivulet, slightly in rear, but substantially a continuation of the line to the right. This regiment stretched to the edge of the forest. The Eighteenth Missouri was in reserve behind the Thirty-ninth Ohio.

Captain [O. W.] Pollock, of my staff, rode over to order the Fourteenth Ohio Battery to get ready for action just where they stood; but we could see Laird putting his guns in battery before Pollock reached him. Just behind the battery was posted the Eighty-first Ohio.

We were now in position, with our back toward Atlanta, facing to the east. As the situation is commanding and the outlook fine, let us note it for just a moment. To our left stretches the Second Division of our corps, which is seen entire. Between their right and us is our battery (the Fourteenth Ohio), not far off, but separated from us by the ravine. As our ground is higher, we can see every man and every horse. If we face about and look to our rear, we can see the large trains of the Army of the Tennessee pulling out on a trot to the northwest to escape the stray bullets which pass over our heads; while still farther off, perhaps a mile away, we can see "Bald Hill," the right of Leggett's division, and to

The Battle of Atlanta, the Sixteenth Corps Engaged (*Campfire and Battlefield*)

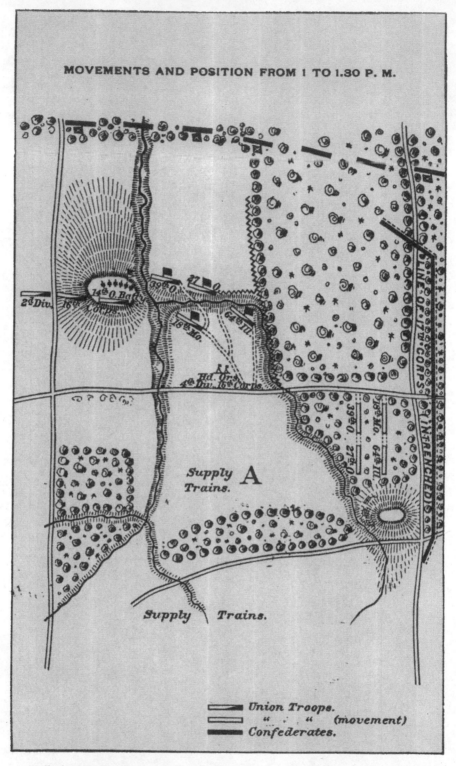

Fuller's Division in the Battle of Atlanta, July 22, 1864, 1:00 P.M.–1:30 P.M.
(*Official Records*)

the right of that, the Fifteenth Corps—all, of course, with their backs toward us, for they are facing Atlanta.

We cannot look long, for the skirmishers sent forward to cover our front are coming rapidly back upon us. Orders were now given to keep down until the enemy's line of battle should be near us, and at the signal to rise, firing a volley, and charge. Soon the enemy appeared, and before he was in good musket range our battery opened fire. This seemed a surprise; for he halted, then retired into the woods to reform his line. Very soon, however, he marched out from the forest, and in good order moved toward us. He had come not more than a quarter of the way across the field when the Eighty-first Ohio, across the ravine to our left, and in plain sight, charged against a rebel regiment which was threatening our battery. The cheer of this regiment and their gallant charge was so contagious that the men of the Thirty-ninth Ohio rose to their feet, fired a volley, and went for the Johnnies on the double-quick. The Twenty-seventh, next on the right, seeing the Thirty-ninth charging the enemy, arose also and joined the race. It was too soon; for our boys had too far to run, and the rebels were still so near the woods they could quickly reach shelter. The Thirty-ninth, however, were in time to capture the colonel, adjutant, a captain, and all who did not run of the Sixty-sixth Georgia, a regiment of [Major General William B.] Bate's division.

But that part of the rebel line which was not struck by the two Ohio regiments continued their march toward the west, and the extraordinary spectacle presented itself of our men rushing across the field in one direction, while the rebels on their right were marching steadily the opposite way. It is true the enemy kept pretty closely to the line of woods to the south, but as they approached the western side they began to widen out into the field. Directly the Sixty-fourth Illinois, partly hidden by a piece of fence and by the bushes which lined the rivulet, opened fire at close range. This regiment was armed with the Henry Repeating Rifle, and could fire fourteen volleys without stopping to reload. They demoralized the rebel line in short order, so that it began to waver and break.

Just then a fine-looking officer brought another regiment out of the woods. He rode forward, hat in hand, to rally his men; but by this time Colonel [Charles S.] Sheldon had moved up the Eighteenth Missouri so as to get a flank fire on the rebels, and this proved more than they could stand. The officer who was so conspicuous was immediately shot down, and the whole mass swayed back into the forest. As the last of them were retiring voices were heard shouting "Bring off the general." Some prisoners told us that the general was [Major General William H. T.] Walker, the commander of their division.

This combat, though brief, was very sharp. Colonel Sheldon, whose regiment buried the rebel dead next day, told me he found thirteen dead rebels in one fence corner.

But the charge of the two Ohio regiments had taken them some distance away from the others, and I went over to see how things looked, intending to order them back. I had scarcely reached them when we saw some rebel regiments

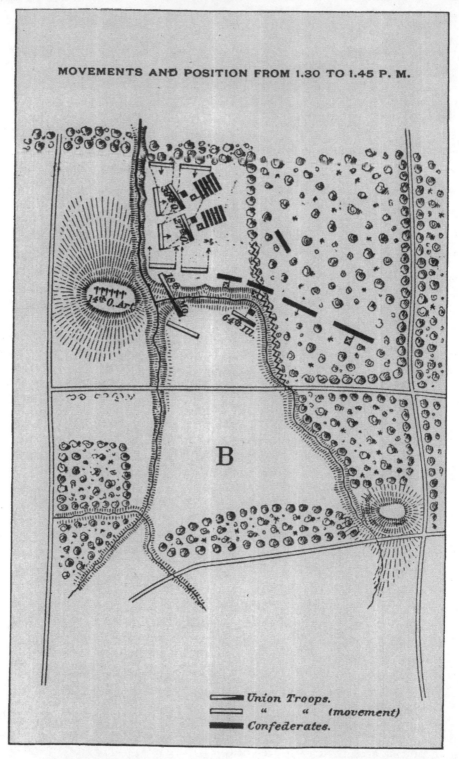

Fuller's Division in the Battle of Atlanta, July 22, 1864, 1:30 P.M.–1:45 P.M.
(*Official Records*)

formed in column coming out of the woods at the south side of the field. If they pushed on they would come between us and our other regiments. If they deployed to fire they would take us in flank and enfilade our line while we were not in shape to reply. There was not a moment to lose. We must "change front to the rear on our left"; i.e., face about and swing around to the north side of the field. The movement was double-quick for the Twenty-seventh, for they formed the outside of the wheel, and were also nearest the enemy.

A heavy fire opened as soon as the movement began, and the men of the Twenty-seventh, with their backs to the enemy, seemed to think that there was some mistake. They kept stopping and turning about to fire. This broke their formation, and they were coming around in a mass.

I had been colonel of that regiment and knew the men would try to do anything called for, if they understood what was wanted. I hurried across to meet them at the point where they should halt and face about. There was no time to explain anything, for the rebels were coming on in fine style, not more than 100 yards away. Grabbing the colors, I ran a few paces toward the enemy, then turning around stuck the flagstaff in the ground, and with my sword showed where

General Fuller Plants the Colors of the Twenty-seventh Ohio (*Century*)

to reform the line. With a great shout the men came forward and instantly formed. Bayonets were brought down for a charge. [Lieutenant Colonel Mendal] Churchill shouted "Forward!," [Lieutenant Colonel Henry T.] McDowell gave the same command to the Thirty-ninth, which had faced about and was all ready, and away they went for the Johnnies.

As the two regiments rushed on, their line was as fine as if on parade. Instantly the enemy came to a right-about and ran back for the woods. Seeing the enemy would not stand, our line was halted, and the men brought up their muskets and sent a volley into the retreating column. They were so close that the effect seemed terrible, and when the rebels had disappeared in the forest the southeast corner of that field was well carpeted with butternut.

While the combats just described were raging General McPherson sat watching us from high ground in our rear, and when the enemy had been driven the second time from the field he expressed his satisfaction at the result and said: "Well, the Sixteenth Corps is all right; now I'll ride over and see how Giles Smith is getting on."

Putting spurs to his horse he galloped past our right flank, entering the woods by the new road, where our men had bivouacked, and over which they marched hardly an hour before. None of us then knew that the enemy had passed our flank, for the dense foliage had hidden everything from view. But almost as soon as McPherson passed out of sight he rode into the rebel line of skirmishers. He was ordered to halt, but, lifting his hat to salute his enemies, he reined his horse to the right and endeavored to escape. A volley was fired. One bullet struck him in the back and passed through very near his heart.

His orderly, close behind, reined also to the right, and just as McPherson was falling the orderly's head struck the limb of a tree, and he fell senseless from his horse. When he recovered, some rebels were holding him, and were ordering him off, a prisoner. They halted briefly, however, where McPherson lay, and the orderly tells us, "For a moment a tremor ran over his whole body, and then he was still, and I think he was dead." This orderly (A. J. Thompson, of Brown County, Ohio) was held a prisoner. Another story has been told by a soldier who claimed to have given the general water from his canteen. But the nature of McPherson's wound, as ascertained by our surgeons, seems to forbid this, and the statement of Thompson seems truthful beyond doubt.

A few minutes after McPherson passed us the rebels returned to the edge of the forest, and from the south side of our field opened a heavy fire on us. Captain [George] Robinson was sent across the ravine in our rear to the Fourteenth Ohio Battery, which by our change of front was now directly behind us, with directions to throw shells over our heads into the edge of the wood, and about the same time Colonel Morrill was ordered to move the Sixty-fourth Illinois to the right (now west) until he reached the new road, then to march into the woods a few rods, and thence move upon the flank of the enemy who was making it so hot for us.

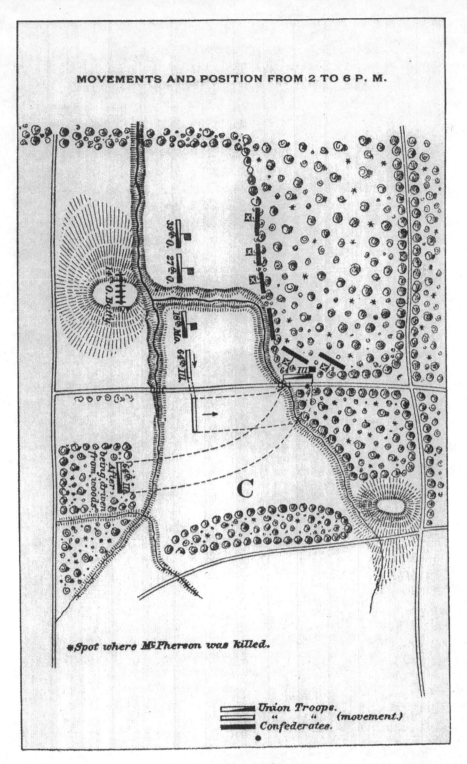

MOVEMENTS AND POSITION FROM 2 TO 6 P. M.

Spot where McPherson was killed.

Union Troops.
"   "   (movement.)
Confederates.

Fuller's Division in the Battle of Atlanta, July 22, 1864, 2:00 P.M.–6:00 P.M.
(*Official Records*)

Major General James B.
McPherson (*Century*)

Lieutenant Laird soon began to drop shells beautifully into the edge of the forest, but Morrill struck a regiment of [Major General Patrick R.] Cleburne's division almost as soon as he began to move into the woods on the new road. The repeating rifles of Morrill's men again blazed away so rapidly that the rebel regiment was very soon routed. They captured forty of Cleburne's men and a stand of colors, and sent the prisoners and colors to the rear under guard. They did more, for this advance drove back the rebels who had possession of McPherson's body, and cleared the way for Colonel [William E.] Strong and others to run in and recover all that was left of our [be]loved commander.

When the forty prisoners captured by the Sixty-fourth Illinois were searched, in the knapsack of one was found McPherson's field glass. Another had his gauntlets. But the most important thing found was a note written by Sherman to McPherson only that morning, explaining what he intended to do. That note could have been seen by nobody but the soldier who took it from McPherson's pocket, and even he could scarcely have read it. I was glad to give assurance of this to my commander when sending the note to him that evening.

But Cleburne's men were not to be driven far by a single regiment, and back they came very soon, with reinforcements. They concentrated a heavy fire on the Sixty-fourth, until seven officers and seventy-nine men had fallen, and what was also of great importance, the colonel of the Sixty-fourth had been severely wounded and sent to the rear. There was no officer who could make up for the loss of Colonel Morrill, and when attacked by these fresh troops, the regiment was driven out of the woods pell-mell, and did not stop until they reached a clump of pines a quarter of a mile to the rear.

From this time on the rebels frequently returned to the south edge of our field, where they made a slight breastwork of rails, from behind which they did some wicked firing. Our boys, lying flat as they could, would rise enough to respond, and our battery dropped shells over our heads among the Johnnies so effectively that they never after came far into our field, and before night retired from our front.

Toward night we also withdrew from the field. It was fresh and verdant and beautiful under the noonday sun. The storm of battle had swept over it, and evening found only desolation and ruin. Every third man of the Twenty-seventh Ohio who stood in the ranks at noon, and every fourth man of the Thirty-ninth Ohio, was now either killed or wounded. A wide strip of rebel dead bordered the side near the forest. Opposite, numerous patches of blue showed where our boys had fallen.

Some incidents of the battle may, perhaps, be of interest. Soon after the second charge described, and while the firing was heavy, Colonel Churchill of the Twenty-seventh Ohio was wounded. He came backward from the line with coat and vest unbuttoned, and in a sad voice, said to me, "I am sorry to retire, General, but I am wounded." "Where is your wound, Colonel?" I asked. He replied, in one word, "Abdomen." We had often discussed the subject of wounds, and it was understood that a wound in the abdomen was generally fatal. As he passed back into the ravine, I thought a good soldier and a fast friend was gone. I went forward to see that the major (Frank Lynch) was in command, and I found him, though slightly wounded, so full of pluck and active in his duty that I took heart again. Five minutes after, back from the ravine came Churchill. His face, which had been a yard long, was now lit up by a smile of at least 500-candle power. "It was a flank shot," said he; "the bullet only scooped out a little flesh and did not enter my bread basket. I am going back to command my regiment." He was back none too soon, for Lynch got a second and frightful wound, and was carried off the field.

Quite late in the afternoon [Lieutenant Colonel J. J.] Phillips, of General Dodge's staff, came over and said the general desired us to fall back and form on the right of the Second Division. This division, on our left when the battle opened, was, after our change of front, directly in our rear. Now it had also changed front, and was in line parallel with us, perhaps 300 yards behind us. We had a good many wounded who had not been removed, and who, together with our dead, might fall into the hands of the enemy if we should then retire.

So I asked permission to stay where we were until we could get them off. Permission was given; but I soon learned of McPherson's death, and of the loss of our battery, which was with the Seventeenth Corps. I was also told that General Giles Smith had been driven from his entrenched line and some of his regiments had been captured.

These statements impressed me; for, though we had beaten all the Johnnies who had tried to get a footing in our field, these stories seemed to indicated disaster. If Giles Smith, whom we supposed was fighting on the other side of the woods, half a mile away, was gone, we formed an outpost and were in a dangerous place.

We hastened to remove the wounded, and then, deploying one regiment as skirmishers to hold the field if they could, we made preparations to withdraw.

The left regiment was retired and moved behind the line until it reached the right, where it was halted. The next then passed in the same manner till it formed the right, and thus we kept gaining ground to the right until we uncovered the front of the Second Division, and then all retired in line to the position assigned us. Our skirmishers left on the field were not attacked. After dark there was a tacit truce between the skirmishers of both armies. The rebels removed most of their dead, and ours were brought back and buried in long trenches near some clumps of pine.

One incident of the afternoon led me to watch with special interest the work of those detailed to bury the dead. When running over from the left of the line to reach the place where the Twenty-seventh Ohio would come when changing front—the most critical time of the battle—I saw, rushing back from the ranks of the Thirty-ninth Ohio, a soldier whom I thought demoralized. He was making for the ravine on the north side (rear) of the field. I was hastening to the right, and our paths crossed as we came together. I had shouted to him one or twice "Go back, sir; go back to your regiment!" but as he paid no attention, I struck at him with the flat of my sword. We were both running fast, and I hit harder than I intended. He spun around and faced me with an astonished look, when I recognized a trusty soldier who, more than once, had served as corporal of our headquarters guard.

In an instant he tore open his coat and showed me a bloody wound in his breast. Neither of us spoke, but his face said, as plainly as if he had uttered the words: "You see, you were mistaken. I am no coward." I suppose my face must have answered back some profound apology, for his countenance lighted up with a kindly, beaming smile, and then he dropped at my feet.

I could not stop to see whether he had fainted, or whether he was dying; but when the dead were brought in at night I looked on with undefined and mournful interest. An old soldier of the Thirty-ninth Ohio had a lantern. Nobody knows where he found it, but I told him I wanted to see whom we had lost. Without telling him why, I asked him to show to me those who belonged to his regiment. The lantern showed us the features of one after another, until at last the face of my young corporal, wearing the very same smile he had given me that afternoon, lay before us.

The old soldier with the lantern seemed to wonder why I wanted to assist in laying the corporal in his last resting place. I did not explain, but when we had carefully covered him up, merely said: "He was the corporal of my head-quarters guard." If the old soldier is still living, and shall read these lines, he will understand.

43

The March to the Sea, an Armed Picnic
William P. Carlin, Brevet Major General, U.S.V.

IT WAS, I believe, on November 15 [1864] that [Major General William T.] Sherman promulgated to his army in general orders his intention of cutting loose from his depots and lines of communication and striking out for some point on the seacoast. The order is in all the histories, and is worth reading. I only wish to allude to it here. I remember only two general injunctions the army was required to observe: First, to "forage liberally on the country, and, second-ly, not to encumber the trains and troops with refugees," referring especially to colored people who might be expected to join the armies with the expectation of getting subsistence and transportation to what some of them were pleased to call "God's Country."

Of course the men might have been made useful as laborers and even as soldiers, but women and children, as well as all old people, could only be a bur-den to us. The order, in this last respect, was wise and far-sighted, and better it would have been for the army and for many of those ignorant people if it had been rigidly enforced. Instead of that several thousand of these useless creatures were allowed to follow the different corps of the army, encumbering the trains and devouring the subsistence along the line of march so much needed for the soldiers.

On the night of November 15, as I was sitting in my tent, an officer came and called my attention to the extraordinary illumination of the heavens in the di-rection of the town. It was very evident that Atlanta was on fire.

To me it was not a pleasant sight. It was not from any sort of sympathy with the owners of the property thus destroyed, but it seemed to me to be a destruc-tion of wealth that belonged, or would soon belong, to the whole country.

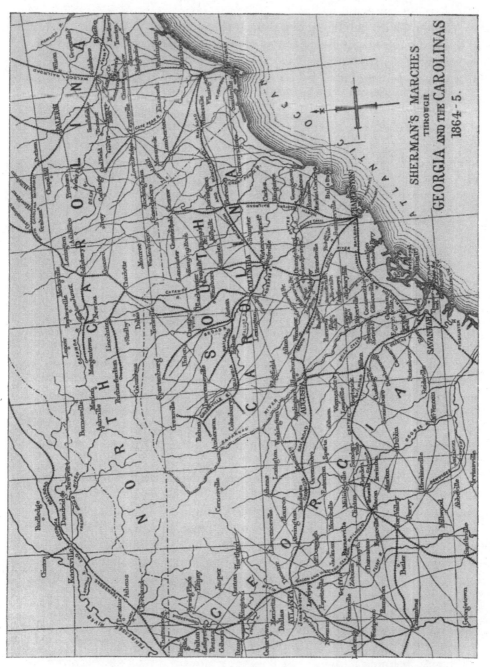

Sherman's March through Georgia and the Carolinas (*Magazine of American History*)

Sherman's order marked out in the clear and perspicuous language for which all his writings are so remarkable the exact line of march for each army, corps, and division. It fell to me to march out on the morning of November 16, 1864, to Decatur and Stone Mountain, on the road leading eastward toward Augusta, Georgia, and Charleston, South Carolina, and along the railroad leading from Atlanta to those two cities.

To us the war had assumed a different aspect. There was no armed enemy to confront us or to harass us in any manner. It was easy and comfortable marching through an old and well-cultivated country, where everybody seemed to produce on their farms enough to eat and to wear. At many plantations we found sorghum syrup in process of manufacture; at all, great quantities of fine sweet potatoes were found—and, in fact, the sweet potatoes had much to do with carrying Sherman's army through Georgia. There was also a large quantity of most excellent bacon produced in that country. Our soldiers liked it very much, and they had ways of finding it that seemed almost miraculous.

Much has been written about the witch hazel and the divining rod, but from my observation the ramrod of a Union musket was the most infallible divining rod in all cases where bacon was the subterranean object sought for, of which I have any knowledge. I have seen soldiers going around among trees and in fields,

Leaving Atlanta (*Life of Sherman*)

with a ramrod in hand, which they would ever and anon drive into the ground till they seemed sure they had struck a mine of bacon, or, perhaps, something also more valuable to those who were not hungry. Whether the soldiers had hints from the Negro slaves before beginning their experiments with ramrods or not, I am unable to say; but I was then under the impression that the slaves did not betray the secrets of their masters and mistresses, unless they wanted these provisions and valuables for themselves, to which event they very coolly helped themselves when the "Yankee" army was near at hand.

Before coming to this point in my narrative it should have been stated that as a preliminary step towards the daring and dangerous operations of transferring his army to the seacoast and depending on the enemy's country for supplies, Sherman had made a new organization of his armies and corps. The Fifteenth and Seventeenth Corps were to constitute the Army of the Tennessee, and this was to be commanded by Major General O. O. Howard, U.S. Volunteers. The Fourteenth and Twentieth Corps constituted the Army of Georgia, which was commanded by Major General H. W. Slocum, U.S. Volunteers. Major General Frank P. Blair commanded the Seventeenth Corps. The Fourteenth Corps was commanded by [Brigadier] General Jefferson C. Davis from Atlanta to Savannah. Major General John A. Logan was the permanent commander of the Fifteenth Corps, but did not accompany it on this march. Major General Alpheus J. Williams commanded the Twentieth Corps.

The Fourth Corps, under [Major General David S.] Stanley, and the Twenty-third Corps, under [Major General Jacob D.] Cox, had become, under command of Major General J. M. Schofield, the principal nucleus of [Major General George H.] Thomas's army in Tennessee, and this army was already in front of [General John Bell] Hood and was advancing to delay his advance toward Nashville till Thomas could prepare a suitable reception for him.

The Army of Georgia was the left wing of Sherman's grand army; the Army of the Tennessee was its right wing. The latter, under command of Major General O. O. Howard, struck southeasterly towards McDonough, Jonesboro, and Macon, in order to reach the Georgia Central Railroad and other roads passing through Macon. From Stone Mountain and Decatur the white wagon covers of Howard's trains and the glistening muskets of his troops could be seen shimmering in the sun off to the south towards McDonough.

When at Decatur we seemed to be at a great elevation above the country lying southward. This was a time when all from the generals to the last private felt free and exuberant. We didn't know where we were going, but we felt certain that [we] were doing a work that would prove decisive of the great conflict; that with its interior railroads destroyed and the productions of the country devoured by our armies, the Confederacy must soon succumb. Besides, there was a delightful relief in the minds of all, that for some weeks at least we would have some exemption from the carnage of battle. It was wearing on soul and body to have every step of our way marked with the blood of the fallen, and their graves dotting the landscape wherever the eye was cast. This march to the sea assumed, therefore, something of the character of an armed picnic on a grand scale, minus the bright eyes and enchanting smiles of woman.

The art of destroying railroads had by this time become thoroughly understood by every officer and man in the army. As General Sherman has in his memoirs given a graphic description of the various processes by which this branch of war may be conducted, those who are interested are respectfully referred to the aforementioned work.

There was often merry singing among the young men in the rank and file, and the bands of such regiments as were blessed with bands played with unwonted sweetness in the camp, on the march when starting out for the day, and especially in passing through the towns and villages. We followed along the railroad leading from Atlanta to Augusta, destroying the road as we went along. The Twentieth Corps pursued this route as far east as Madison. The Fourteenth Corps turned southeastwardly from Covington, Georgia, a fine old town.

The first night out from Atlanta we camped near Stone Mountain. General Sherman and his staff accompanied the left wing of his army till it arrived at Milledgeville. Shortly after leaving Covington we passed through a little village called Shady Dale, which, in consequence of its poetical name, as well as the signs of comfort, wealth, and elegance about it, I have distinctly remembered ever since. It was not a large town, but a mere crossroads hamlet, where several wealthy planters seemed to have joined together and built their residences near each other, in order to enjoy the pleasures of society, church, schools, and good neighborhood. There was neatly trimmed shrubbery about the houses, and these were tastefully planned and well built. But the most notable feature of the place

Wrecking the Railway (*St. Nicholas*)

was in its Negro population. I saw no white people. The owners of the places and the slaves had probably, in the language of a "poor white" miss, who was asked where all her wealthy neighbors had gone, "gone a refugeein' of it."

The column was halted a short time in this village and the band of one of the regiments struck up "John Brown's body lies moldering in his grave, but his soul goes marching on." To us there was nothing new in this, but what was new and striking was that a large number of young Negro girls—probably a dozen—came out from the several mansions in the vicinity, formed into a ring around the band at the head of the column, and with a weird, plaintive wail danced in a circle in a most solemn, dignified, and impressive manner. There was not a man in this dance, nor was there a word spoken, according to my recollection, between any of these girls and the officers or men of my command. What their meaning was I did not know then, nor do I now, but I, of course, interpreted it as expressive of goodwill to our cause. The modest and serious deportment of those girls in this peculiar dance produced a favorable impression on me, and doubtless on others who witnessed it. This occurred on the public highway, where the road was very sandy, and where dancing was not altogether an amusement, but somewhat of a labor.

We had already entered a land, if not flowing with milk and honey, at least abounding in ham of [the] sweetest bacon, sorghum, sweet potatoes, poultry of all kinds, and forage for horses. In obedience to the orders of the general to forage liberally on the country, a party was organized in each brigade, consisting of a commissioned officer and a suitable number of noncommissioned officers and privates of each regiment. These foraging parties always started out from camp before the main body left camp. Many of them were mounted. They would diverge from the line of march and visit the plantations and farms that promised the best yield of the necessaries of life, and would generally reach the campground for the day as soon as the command to which they belonged. Sometimes they would get back to the road before reaching the campground. The supplies gathered would then, at camp, be turned over to the brigade commissaries and divided out among the regimental commissaries, who would issue them to their regiments. In this way all wanton destruction of subsistence was prevented and a fair division was made.

I would not mock the unfortunate or laugh at the humiliation of any defeated people, for I never ceased to remember that this same humiliation might have befallen my own people in the more fortunate state of Illinois. But if all the horrors of civil war were faithfully depicted in history, it cannot be doubted that it would aid in educating the people on a subject which is really of the utmost importance to them now, and ever will be to their posterity. I refer to the subject of civil war. When political questions have been debated with such fierce zeal as to inflame the passions of the different sections of the country against each other, it is time to call a halt, and to call in new leaders and new representatives.

Foraging Liberally on the Country (*Life of Sherman*)

This matter of foraging on the country, though not necessarily destructive of life and property, is really one of the most humiliating operations of war. The noncombatant enemy is not asked to sell his products. He is not asked his price. He is not consulted at all about the disposal of his corn, his meat, his rice, or anything that he has which an army can use. It is simply seized before his eyes, if he stays to see it taken. But in the majority of cases the owner in Georgia had departed before the troops arrived. But the arrival of a foraging party at camp would make a fine subject for a picture by an expert animal painter. On one occasion I remember seeing an old family carriage, drawn by a yoke of oxen. In the carriage were geese, chickens, turkeys, hams, bacon, and cornmeal. On another occasion I was reliably informed that at a certain white frame house in the heart of Georgia a piano was broken up in order to procure fuel to cook a breakfast for two or three "bummers."

One or two days' march beyond Shady Dale a cold wind, accompanied by snow, came on and lasted nearly all day and night. The cold seemed piercing, as if I had been far north of the Ohio River.

About Eatonton the Twentieth Corps formed a junction with the Fourteenth, and the two continued on to Milledgeville together, arriving there about one week after leaving Atlanta. Sherman's object in moving towards both Augusta and Macon was to deceive the Confederate military authorities and prevent any great concentration of forces in his front. At Macon and thereabouts there was considerable resistance by the Georgia military under [Major Generals] G. W.

A Foraging Party at Work (*St. Nicholas*)

Smith, Howell Cobb, and [Brigadier General Alfred] Iverson [Jr.]. The left wing under Slocum met no resistance on the march to Milledgeville. The right under Howard did not reach Milledgeville, but was near enough to communicate with Sherman. The cavalry, under Kilpatrick, kept open communications between the two wings up to this point.

Georgia has had the good sense since the war to remove her seat of government to Atlanta, an energetic and enterprising city. Milledgeville seemed to be a sleepy and quiet old place. Governor [Joseph E.] Brown took a hasty departure from his capital on the approach of Sherman, and took everything that was movable and edible. Sherman says he took the cabbages and other vegetables from his cellars, and left the muskets and ammunition and public archives behind. I remember that the servants of Governor Brown and Negroes of Milledgeville spoke of him as "a mighty good man."

Although his loyalty to the Confederacy was questioned by some eminent Confederate leaders, this same Governor Brown seemed to have the only efficient sate militia in the entire Confederacy. His militia was well organized, and made itself felt even against Sherman. It captured [Major General George] Stoneman and a large body of cavalry that Sherman had sent on a raid against the railroads about Macon. And, again, when Atlanta had fallen, and the main Confederate army, under Hood, had left Georgia and entered Tennessee, this same militia opposed small commands, notably [Brigadier General Charles C.] Walcutt's brigade, near Macon, and in other localities. Again, at Savannah, when Sherman's entire army had invested that city, its breastworks were manned and held for some days, chiefly by state militia. This militia, however, did not intend to leave their state and fight against the Federals, but by a trick of Robert Toombs they were sent over a railroad into South Carolina, where they were compelled again to fight the Federals at Pocataligo. But to return from this digression to Milledgeville and renew my narrative.

During the brief stay at Milledgeville some of the officers assembled in the legislative hall of the capitol and organized a mock legislature. Some very humorous legislation was done by this transient body of lawmakers. It is regretted that no authentic record of the bills introduced and of the speeches made on this occasion are known to exist either among the archives of Georgia or the records of the rebellion. The ordnance of secession was, however, formally repealed, but it is not probable that this act of legislation had as much influence on the restoration of Georgia to the Union as the other operations of Sherman's army against railroads and supplies of all kinds for the Confederate armies.

On the next day, November 24, I believe it was, my division set out for Sandersville via Louisville and Davisborough. We crossed the Oconee River about a mile from town, on an old wooden bridge. I remember that a woman on horseback crossed at the same time with a pass from General Sherman, from which circumstance it was understood that she was a spy for him. When we came to the town of Louisville, on the Georgia Central Railroad, there was a somewhat melancholy illustration of the uncertainty of human promises and the instability of riches when invested in human chattels. There was an accomplished young lady who had by a series of misfortunes been left entirely alone at her residence, excepting such protection and companionship as her Negro slaves afforded. These professed the utmost devotion and loyalty to their young mistress, and declared they would stay with her and, if need be, defend her to the last drop of their precious blood against the Yankees. Relying on these professions the young lady remained at home till the Yankees came. Then she observed that her beds and bedding began to disappear, also her tableware and kitchen furniture. Finally her women servants boldly appeared in her own dresses and carried away what they did not require on their persons. What became of the lady I never heard; but unfortunately the colored people followed Sherman's army, and a considerable number of them met with a sad end at Ebenezer Creek, as I will relate further on.

A few days after leaving Milledgeville we began again to hear of [Major General Joseph] Wheeler's cavalry. The last time we heard of this general and his famous raiders he was up in Tennessee with numerous bodies of Federal infantry and cavalry after him. Now, towards the close of November, he was down in Georgia, between Milledgeville and Augusta, and was watching the left wing of Sherman's army. [Major General Judson] Kilpatrick had fallen in with him, and had called for help from General Davis, commanding the Fourteenth Corps. A brigade of [Brigadier General Absalom] Baird's division had been sent to support him.

When the affair was over I was ordered, with my division, to open communications with General Sherman and the right wing, then on the Georgia Central Railroad, and near the Ogeechee River. Marching across the country along country roads and lanes, I found General Sherman sitting on the track of the road and wearing an old blue greatcoat. When I left the main column of Slocum's wing I understood that Wheeler had driven Kilpatrick back near the infantry, and that Kilpatrick had called for a brigade of infantry to support him. General Sherman asked me the news as soon as I reported to him, and I told him the above-mentioned fact. Sherman seemed surprised, and said: "Why, ——, the fellow has just reported to me that he was whipped Wheeler, ——!"

That is a way some commanders had throughout the war. It is a valuable lesson to learn, perhaps, in the art of war. But whipping Wheeler's cavalry nev-

Marching through Georgia (*St. Nicholas*)

er seemed to disturb them much. They always came around again. I do not mean to say they were fierce fighters by any means, but they were active light cavalry, and always fought well enough to find out what our troops were doing, where they were going, and about how many there were of them. They sometimes, too, captured trains and did immense damage in that way—as in Sequatchie Valley during the siege of Chattanooga, for instance. The Southern people, at their homes, dreaded a visit from Wheeler's cavalry rather more than the Union troops did.

It was somewhere in the vicinity of Sandersville that a sad and provoking incident occurred, involving the death, apparently a cold-blooded murder, of one of the men in my division. It was reported to me that the man was found dead at the farmhouse of a widow woman. A citizen, or a man in civilian's dress, was arrested and brought into camp on suspicion of the murder. No witnesses could be found, but the civilian had blood on his clothes. To account for this he said he had been killing a hog for the woman at the house. We were on the march. There was no way of trying the man there and then, and, therefore, I did not feel justified in keeping him in custody. It was true, however, that the soldier had been killed at the house or near it, but by whom I never learned; but after reflection I became convinced that the citizen arrested and released was guilty of the murder.

The Fourteenth Corps was ordered to Lumpkin Station, on a railroad leading from Augusta to Millen, and about ten miles from the latter place. At that time a large number of Union men were confined there (at Millen), and General Sheridan had ordered Kilpatrick to make a raid on Millen and release our prisoners. He reached Millen, but found that the prisoners had been removed farther south.

At Lumpkin Station we were in what was there called Lester's District—a country of yellow pine, stiff wire grass, and almost white, sandy soil. From that point the character of the country deteriorated as an agricultural region. It became more difficult to procure forage and provisions.

We were now approaching the Savannah River, and the space between that and the Ogeechee was rapidly narrowing. The right wing was following the general direction of the Ogeechee and the Georgia Central Railroad, on both sides of that river. We were now able, without direct information from the general commanding, to infer that we were bound for Savannah. We might still have kept straight on eastward, crossing the Savannah and striking for Port Royal, or even up to Charleston; or, if we had been beaten or seriously opposed, we might have turned southwestwardly to Pensacola. But, from the fact that the right wing was hugging the Ogeechee and the left was keeping within communicating distance of the right, and both were gradually approaching each other in the narrow space between these two rivers, all doubt as to our destination was solved by the time the left wing struck the Savannah River, which it did at or about Ebenezer Church, some thirty miles, more or less, from Savannah.

We had now left the agricultural region of Georgia, except so far as rice may be considered an agricultural product. It seems to be more aquatic than agricultural. The country had ceased to respond to the foragers' efforts, because they did not consider rice worth the risk and labor of getting.

Running into the Savannah on the west are several deep creeks, with steep, muddy banks. The country along this stream is anything but beautiful or valuable. It looks as if it had not been long enough above water to be called land, and as if it might again be submerged any night, without any great convulsion of nature. One fancies that alligators, serpents, and noxious reptiles make their homes in these creeks. The cypress and live oak give a gloomy aspect to the landscape. The air seems laden with chills and fevers. The moss hanging from the branches of the live oak forms the only pleasing feature of the woods. The few people we found had a haggard and debilitated appearance.

At a little village on the Savannah, near Ebenezer Creek (the name of which I now forget), I met an intelligent lady, who talked as if she were somewhat free from Southern prejudices, without professing to be a Union woman. She had heard that Sherman's army burned everything that it didn't carry along with it—at least, all houses, fences, barns, cotton, etc. She spoke of it as our "policy," and asked why it had not been adopted at an earlier day in the war. As I did not understand it to be our policy or practice either, I could not answer her question satisfactorily. She then most positively declared that it was the only policy that could succeed, and that "the north," or "United States," had made a mistake in not adopting that policy sooner. She was very positive in declaring her convictions that if the Union armies should persevere in destroying everything by fire and sword, that peace would soon be restored. Yet this lady seemed to be a Southerner by birth and residence.

I had seen the smoke of several houses and other buildings ascending into the air as we marched through Georgia, and, of course, the smoke of burning railroad ties was familiar to every member of Sherman's army; but I can solemnly declare that I never knew any officer or man belonging to my command (First Division, Fourteenth Corps) to participate in setting fire to any residence or other buildings of any description (except railroads and buildings appertaining to them) on the march of Sherman's army through Georgia or the Carolinas.

In the winter of 1864, after Sherman's army had swept through Georgia and destroyed its system of railway transportation, I do not believe any additional burning was needed to bring the rebellion to an end. The last destruction of property by fire that I witnessed was that of a large body of cotton stored away in sheds on a plantation not far from Lumpkin Station.

I was approached by a very sensible Negro man, who was a slave on the plantation. He asked me some very discreet questions in regard to the policy of the United States towards the colored people after the war. He was very anxious to know if it was really the intention of the United States to give freedom to the slaves. I told him that I thought freedom would be a necessary consequence of our success and asked him why it was that colored men did not move to help the Union army, when they (the Negroes) were to profit by its sufferings, trials, and successes? He answered that they dared not move in that direction; that it would be death to them and their families. He asked what the colored people could do, if they were disposed to do anything, for the Union cause? I replied that they could have helped us very much by destroying telegraph lines, railroad bridges, etc. His only reply was that we (the Union soldiers) did not know the danger there was in these things.

During the conversation I observed that a light-blue flame was creeping over the cotton in the shed, and in a few minutes the entire lot and all the sheds were in flames. Cotton at that time was worth nearly a dollar a pound. Perhaps this is too high, but it was enormously high in price. The entire lot at that time must have been worth nearly a quarter of a million dollars. There were the crops for at least two years. The owner was in Europe. His name was Conner. Who was the incendiary I never learned, though the fire broke out before my eyes.

When we arrived at Ebenezer Creek it was necessary to throw a pontoon bridge over it. Colonel George P. Buell, Forty-ninth Indiana, commanded a brigade in my division, and had charge of the pontoon train. He laid the bridge. It will be remembered that Sherman's order governing the conduct of his army toward Negroes on the march from Atlanta to the sea discouraged the collection of all such persons in the camps and trains of the army, but encouraged the formation of working parties of men only.

Notwithstanding these judicious warnings of General Sherman hundreds of Negro women and children and many men left the homes of their masters and followed Sherman's army. When approaching Savannah, forage and food became an object of great importance. As stated before, the country yielded little to the forager, and that little was rice. While preparing to cross Ebenezer Creek, an order was issued by General Davis, commanding the Fourteenth Corps, directing the officer in charge of the provost guard to prevent the crossing of all Negro refugees who had joined the army in Georgia. A detachment of the guard was stationed at the ferry to execute this order, and it was faithfully executed. Thus were left a large number of women, children, and some men on the north side of the creek, which was a very deep and broad stream; or, perhaps, it might be called more properly a bayou or arm of the Savannah.

Following closely behind us was the Confederate cavalry under Wheeler. The rear guard of the Fourteenth Corps had no sooner crossed the creek than Wheeler's cavalry charged into the crowd of refugees. Many women leaped into the water, some with children in their arms. Some were drowned; some were reported to have been killed by the Confederate cavalry. The remainder were held as prisoners and sent back to their former masters.

We continued to advance towards Savannah and reach out toward the Ogeechee to communicate with the right wing. About fifteen miles from Savannah strong earthworks had been thrown up and were occupied by [Major General Lafayette] McClaws's division of the Confederate army. McClaws did not wait for Sherman's advance, but fell back into the defensive line around Savannah. We continued to close up towards the defenses of Savannah, and on December 9 and 10, 1864, the entire army of General Sherman confronted the rebel troops behind their breastworks. The Twentieth Corps was next the Savannah River; on its right was the Fourteenth Corps; then came the Nineteenth, and on the extreme right the Fifteenth.

A Federal fleet under [Rear Admiral John A.] Dahlgren had previously as sembled in Ossabaw Sound, to be on hand when Sherman should arrive at or near Savannah. But its communication with the army was prevented by the guns of Fort McAllister on the Ogeechee River. General Howard had previously sent scouts down the Ogeechee in a boat to find the fleet. Among these scouts was Myron J. Amick, the man who at the Battle of Stones River had insisted on my taking his horse after mine had been crippled and captured. These scouts, Captain C. C. Duncan being in charge, reached the fleet. But it was necessary to capture Fort McAllister before any supplies could be procured for the army, and accordingly General Sherman addressed himself to that object first. [Major] General W. B. Hazen was ordered to assault the post with his division. This was done late on the afternoon of December 13, and the fort was captured very handsomely. Then supplies began to be shipped up the Ogeechee to the army.

It was understood that the troops holding the defenses in my front were Georgia militia and residents of Savannah. I caused the artillery to throw shells into their camps occasionally, and on one occasion, having observed that many men (Confederates) were in the habit of entering a frame building just inside their works, and that the brick chimney to this house was on the outside, fronting our line, I directed Captain [Mark H.] Prescott, of an Illinois battery, to take that chimney as a target and fire a few shots into it. The first shot went directly through the center of the chimney. The house was vacated as rapidly as men could get out.

Having reconnoitered and studied the position of the enemy in my front, and being anxious that the First Division, Fourteenth Corps, should be the first to enter Savannah, I asked General Jefferson C. Davis for permission to assault the works of the enemy, with the view of taking them and entering the city. General Davis and General Slocum visited the ground over which I proposed to move my command. After examining it, and, perhaps, having consulted General Sherman, I was informed that my application [was] not favorably considered.

General Sherman had some hope of a surrender of the city and troops defending it by [Lieutenant] General W. J. Hardee, the Confederate commander, and sent him a letter suggesting such a course, and giving some reasons in support of the step. General Hardee was evidently not convinced by General Sherman's letter, and replied in a way that showed it. As I look over these letters now it seems to me that General Sherman's letter was not well conceived, considering the purpose in view. There was still a good opening for Hardee to escape with all his army, perhaps 15,000 men.

By throwing a bridge of boats across the Savannah he was in easy communication with South Carolina and the Confederate forces at Pocataligo. In fact, all South Carolina was open to him. Sherman saw the weak point, and desired to have this avenue of escape closed; but instead of sending part of his army, he started by water to see [Major] General J. G. Foster, the Federal commander at Port Royal, with the view of having him send a command to hold the plank road that led from Savannah through the swamps into South Carolina. While General Sherman was gone on this mission, Hardee laid the bridge across the Savannah and marched his army over it and escaped without losing a man. He left, of course, all the heavy guns that were mounted in and around Savannah. A vast quantity of cotton was also left in the city, which was a fair capture by the army. If the navy had captured Savannah the cotton would have been a prize of war, and the officers and seamen would have been enriched, for the cotton then at Savannah was estimated at many millions of dollars' worth —there were at least 30,000 bales.

Those who were now vigilant in detecting the absence of rebel pickets on the morning of December 21 were those who had the honor of first entering the city of Savannah, and [Major] General John W. Geary, commanding a division in the Twentieth Corps, was the man. His division was the first to enter the abandoned city. I was disappointed in this, as I had endeavored to have this distinction for my division by attacking the entrenchments. But we marched in early that day, and found Savannah a deserted, dull place; deserted by the armed enemy and men generally, but not by the women.

Capture of Fort McAllister (*Life of Sherman*)

We marched down Bull Street, which had been a beautiful avenue, with a fine square planted in shrubbery at every alternate street crossing. The paving stones had all been taken up and used in blockading the Savannah River, leaving the street a very sandy and unlovely passageway.

Thus in twenty-four days we had marched from Atlanta to Savannah. We had besieged the place for eleven days, and entered it after its evacuation. A little rest was a grateful thing, and while General Sherman and General Grant were considering what next that army should do, we had a few weeks of rest in Savannah.

44

The Red River Expedition
William S. Burns, Captain, U.S.V.

IN *Camp, Court, and Siege,* by [Wickham] Hoffman,[1] a work highly spoken of by the press, and justly so in many respects, occurs the following in reference to the Red River expedition, after writing of the Battle of Pleasant Hill:

> [Major General Nathaniel P.] Banks now wanted to continue his onward march to Shreveport, but [Brigadier] General A. J. Smith opposed it. He said that he belonged to [Major General William T.] Sherman's command and had been lent to Banks for a season only; that he was under orders to return to Sherman by a certain day; that much time had been lost; and that if he undertook the march to Shreveport he could not return by the date appointed. Our supplies, too, were rather short—the cavalry having lost their wagon train. We fell back, therefore, upon Grand Ecore, where we rejoined the fleet. Here a serious incident occurred. An officer in high position came to [Major General William B.] Franklin and said that the army was in a very critical situation; that it required generalship to extricate it; that under Banks it would probably be captured or destroyed, and proposed to put Banks on board of a steamer and send him to New Orleans; and that Franklin should take command, "and my men, General," he said, "will stand by you to the last man." Of course, Franklin treated it as a joke and laughed it off. But there can be no doubt that the officer was in earnest.

---

1. Wickham Hoffman, *Camp, Court, and Siege: A Narrative of Personal Adventure and Observation during Two Wars: 1861–1865, 1870–1871* (New York, 1877).

There is error as well as truth in the above extract. Error in the statement that "General A. J. Smith opposed the onward march to Shreveport," and truth that "an officer in high position" requested General Franklin to arrest General Banks. If Major Hoffman had mentioned who the "officer in high position" was, and the correct reason why he desired the arrest of General Banks, he would have refuted his statement that General Smith opposed the onward march; but he may not have known the true reason, as he locates the incident at Grand Ecore.

I realize fully the difficulty of presenting all the facts of our late war to the public in such shape that they will be incorporated in the true history of the war yet to be written. In reading the above extract, an experience which has been lying (comparatively) dormant for fifteen years has been revived, and I have been led to write out for the "Annals of the War" the part taken in the Red River expedition by the command of General A. J. Smith, and introducing the facts of the incidents referred to by Major Hoffman in their chronological order, giving not only my own testimony to the actual facts drawn from memory, journal notes, and letters written by me at the time when they were fresh in my mind, but also adding the testimony of others who were there, which may bring out some facts never in print, and which should be told in the interest of history before they shall have passed from living men.

Take the events, the results, as they are grouped together, and they are probably to a degree clear in the recollection of many, but the particular details that preceded them have, to a certain extent, become obscured, even if they were ever known outside of the army lines. It will not be my intent to give minute descriptions of the battles fought from a military point of view, as those can be best obtained from official reports (although I shall, in one or two instances, quote from such reports), but shall endeavor to write a journalistic account of the campaign as jotted down at the time when all the circumstances were taking place.

On March 4, 1864, the troops under command of General W. T. Sherman (one division of which was commanded by General A. J. Smith) arrived at Vicksburg upon their return from the Meridian raid—one of the most successful raids yet made into the heart of Dixie; not only driving the Reverend [Lieutenant] General Leonidas Polk's command from the vicinity of Vicksburg to the eastern line of the state of Mississippi, but also most thoroughly destroying the Mobile and Ohio Railroad for miles in every direction from Meridian. Not since the campaign through Arkansas in 1862, following the Battle of Pea Ridge, had I looked upon such crowds of slaves following our army as came with us toward Vicksburg. It was a strange, a suggestive sight. As there were thousands of these contrabands accompanied our troops into Helena in 1862, so there were thousands now on our return to Vicksburg.

On March 6, General Smith received a letter from General Sherman, of which the following extracts are the pith:

By an order this day issued you are to command a strong, well-appointed detachment of the Army of the Tennessee, sent to reinforce a movement up the Red River, but more especially against the fortified position at Shreveport. You will embark your command as soon as possible. . . . Proceed to the mouth of the Red River and confer with Admiral [David D.] Porter; consult with him, and in all the expedition rely on him implicitly, as he is the approved friend of the Army of the Tennessee. . . .

I have undertaken, with General Banks, that you will be at Alexandria, Louisiana, on or before March 17. General Banks will start by land from Franklin, in the Teche country, either the fifth or seventh, and will march via Opelousas to Alexandria. You will meet him there, report to him, and act under his orders. . . .

My understanding with General Banks is that he will not need the cooperation of your force beyond thirty days from the date you reach Red River. As soon as he has taken Shreveport, or as soon as he can spare you, return to Vicksburg with all dispatch. . . .

Having faith in your sound judgment and experience, I confide this important and delicate command to you, with certainty that you will harmonize perfectly with Admiral Porter and General Banks, with whom you are to act, and thereby insure success.

In conformity with the above instructions, 7,500 men of the Sixteenth Army Corps, under command of Brigadier General Joseph A. Mower, and 2,500 men of the Seventeenth Army Corps, under command of Brigadier General Thomas Kilby Smith—all commanded by Brigadier General A. J. Smith—took part in the Red River expedition.

On the afternoon of March 10 the signal gun was fired and our fleet of nineteen boats swung into the Mississippi at Vicksburg and started on the journey southward. Soon after daylight next morning we touched at "Natchez under the Hill," and at noon anchored at the mouth of Red River, where we found Admiral D. D. Porter, with a fleet of twenty-one gunboats, also [Brigadier General Alfred W.] Ellett, with a part of his Marine Brigade, ready to ascend the river with us. At noon the next day (March 12) we left our anchorage and four hours afterward, we arrived at Simmsport, in the Atchafalaya River, at which point we came in sight of rebel pickets—there being a small fork, three miles away, on the Yellow Bayou, said to be garrisoned by 2,500 men under [Brigadier General William R.] Scurry.

On the morning of the thirteenth we marched to this fort, but found it abandoned. Our next destination was Fort De Russy, on the Red River, thirty-five miles across the country from Simmsport. At midnight on the thirteenth we bivouacked nine miles on our way, and at daylight of the fourteenth moved again.

Upon our arrival at Bayou De Glais, [we] found the bridge destroyed and the enemy on the opposite bank prepared to dispute our advance, but a few rounds of shell from the Third Indiana Battery scattered them. Infantry were ferried over in an old scow and drove the enemy some distance and held them while repairs were underway. In an hour or two a new bridge was built and we resumed the march. Soon after crossing this bayou and driving the enemy through a piece of woods the country opened into a beautiful prairie (Avoyelle Prairie), and as we passed through four small villages we were told by the citizens that we should find a force of several thousand at Fort De Russy. Nearly all the citizens were French, and at almost every house the French flag was flying to protect them, which annoyed many of us, considering the French performances then being enacted in Mexico.

Soon after passing through Marksville, and when within one mile and a half of the fort, we came to a woods, at the edge of which were several horsemen watching our approach. Seven of us, who were riding in the advance with General Smith, having obtained his consent, started for them.

After we had ridden about three-quarters of a mile through the woods, we came to a bend in the road and in sight of the fort, but still kept on at full speed; a few shots at the running horsemen and they disappeared behind the fort. About 500 yards from the fort, we came to some outside barracks on fire; here we captured a prisoner, who told us that the fort was full of men, though, as yet, we could not see a man.

As we stood there in plain view, wondering why the enemy didn't show himself, all at once the whole front was lined with heads and shoulders. Having with me a Wesson breech-loading rifle I fired three shots into the fort before we saw any signs indicating that we were to receive attention from the enemy, and then we turned, put spurs to our horses and started back to the column, which had just made its appearance at the bend of the road.

As we reached it the Third Indiana Battery was taking position, the enemy having opened upon them the moment they were visible, and [Brigadier General Joseph A.] Mower was placing his men in line for the attack. The first line was under the immediate command of Colonel W. T. Shaw, Fourteenth Iowa Infantry, commanding Second Brigade, Third Division, Sixteenth Army Corps, composed of the Fourteenth and Thirty-second Iowa, Twenty-fourth Missouri, and Third Indiana Battery (the Twenty-seventh Iowa belonged to this brigade, but at this time was at the rear, closing up). The space intervening between this point and the fort on the right of the main road was an old chopping, with tree trunks scattered over the field; on the left of the road was woods.

It was now 4:00 P.M. Part of the Fourteenth Iowa were sent out as skirmishers and soon crossed the old chopping to within about 350 yards of the fort, where were some earthworks or rifle pits, into which they went, and during the progress of the fight did good execution as sharpshooters. In the meantime the Fifty-eighth Illinois, Eighth Wisconsin (the "Eagle Regiment," so called because of its ownership of the war eagle "Old Abe") and Twenty-seventh Iowa (which had come up from the rear) were advancing with the troops above-mentioned. In fact, all the troops were advancing, but the above-mentioned were in the immediate front.

During this time the fire from the fort was very severe, but did not do much execution. For two hours shell, solid shot, shrapnel, and bullets passed between the two parties. We expected every moment to hear the heavy guns from the gunboats, but not a sound, and it was well; as in all probability, unless every shot could have been planted in the fort our troops would have suffered more from them than the enemy would, and fear of this prevented Admiral Porter from firing.

At the expiration of two hours from the commencement of the attack, our troops having advanced until sufficiently near the fort for the assault, the order was given and the charge was made. What a roll of musketry—what cheering. Into the moat they went; up again over the walls, and our flag floated on the fort. The garrison, consisting of twenty-four officers and about 275 private soldiers immediately surrendered. The main portion of the enemy, said to be about 4,500, under command of [Major General John G.] Walker, left the fort before our arrival. Aside from the garrison we captured ten guns, small arms, and stores.

I was told by one of the captured officers that one man was wounded by one of my shots; that at first they mistook it for some of their own vedettes, but soon saw their mistake, and their sharpshooters were preparing to fire upon us when we left.

Our transports arrived at the fort on time, and on March 15 the navy (except two boats) and a part of the army under General Mower, on the transports, proceeded toward Alexandria. General Smith, with a few troops, remained at the fort to blow up and dismantle it, which was done most effectually on the sixteenth, when we had two grand exhibitions. The first was a trial of an 100-pounder Parrott gun (on a gunboat) against a casemated water battery, which fell into our hands with the fort. It was a quarter of a mile from the fort, and connected with it by a deep, well-protected trench, through which the men could pass in perfect safety from one to the other. This battery was made of heavy oak timbers, three or four feet in thickness, covered with double tiers of railroad iron (T rail), one layer spiked on the timber, another turned over and pushed between, fitting in the grooves. Five shots were fired and they broke through the iron and penetrated the timber two or three feet, splitting the timbers on the inside.

In the evening was the grandest display—the simultaneous blowing up of three powder magazines (in other words, Fort De Russy). Three thousand pounds of powder were used. We stood on the upper deck of our steamer (which was half a mile away). First came the bright, triple flash, and we saw distinctly the timbers, earth, etc., flying through the air. Then followed the report and the quivering of the steamer and the roll of reverberations, and the ruin was complete, leaving only three immense excavations, broken timbers, scraps of iron, etc., where stood, the day before, one of the most formidable forts in the Southern Confederacy.

General Smith arrived at Alexandria on March 18. His advance of 5,000 men, under General Mower, arrived on the sixteenth, accompanied by the navy, and upon their arrival [Major] General Dick Taylor, with 15,000 men (so reported), left the city with such haste that he forgot three pieces of artillery. We had arrived at Alexandria on time, but General Banks did not, and here commenced that series of delays which eventuated finally in such great disaster and such deep humiliation, and has left the Red River expedition a term of reproach, synonymous with failure and disgrace.

One week (until March 25) we waited impatiently for the arrival of General Banks's infantry (his cavalry having arrived on the nineteenth). In the meantime our troops occupied about ten miles of the country south of the river, and a beautiful country it was—the roads level and lined with most extensive sugar plantations and fine residences, luxuriant hedges growing, and a great deal of palmetto, among which flitted the beautiful red birds. Colonel Shaw, with his friends, made the plantation of ex-Governor [Thomas] Moore (who was the prime mover in having Louisiana secede, and who lived nine miles from Alexandria) his camp during our occupation of this limited territory.

There was but one military episode during our enforced residence at Alexandria. One dark and rainy night General Mower, with a small force, marched out into the unknown country, made a wide detour and came in the rear of the camp of the Second Louisiana Cavalry, captured a courier with dispatches to General Taylor (who was in camp eight or ten miles still further to the rear), passed himself off as General Taylor seeking the camp of the Second Louisiana Cavalry, accused the courier of being a Yankee spy, which was of course denied by him, and to prove his Southern loyalty led the supposed Confederate general directly into the camp, which, with all its contents, except the lieutenant colonel, who escaped, was at once captured. The booty taken consisted of twenty-two officers, 260 privates, four pieces of artillery, 120 horses, and small arms and ammunition in corresponding ratio.

A day or two after this exploit I rode out to see Colonel Shaw, and when I arrived the colonel and Mrs. Moore were sitting on the front piazza, and as I related General Mower's achievement, Mrs. Moore said: "You say the lieutenant colonel was not captured? How did he escape?" I answered: "As we have heard, he hid in a hen house." Her reply came quick and sharp: "Well, I should have supposed that would be the first spot where your soldiers would have found anything."

The Marine Brigade of General Ellett left us at Alexandria and returned to Vicksburg, having been called for by [Major General James B.] McPherson. On March 25, General Banks's infantry, led by General Franklin, arrived at Alexandria, and next day General Smith's command moved forward and arrived at Bayou Rapids on the twenty-seventh, where we encamped, waiting again for General Banks. His command passed our camps on the thirtieth, and on April 2 we received orders to advance, when we embarked on our boats and arrived at Grand Ecore on the third, disembarked, and went into camp. I here saw for the first time [Brigadier General Charles P.] Stone (now in the Egyptian army), and looked at him with much interest as I thought of his past experience. He impressed me as a man under a cloud—very quiet and unassuming. I was pleased with him and wondered if he deserved the harsh judgment entertained against him since Ball's Bluff.

On April 6, General Banks's troops, composed of part of the Thirteenth and Nineteenth corps and a cavalry division under [Brigadier] General A. L. Lee, marched from Grand Ecore or Natchitoches (four miles distant). General A. J. Smith, with his command, left on the seventh, except the division of the Seventeenth Corps of 2,500 men, under [Brigadier] General T. Kilby Smith, who had been sent with Admiral Porter and the navy as an escort to the transports conveying supplies, ordnance stores, etc., and were to meet us at Springfield Landing with rations, etc., on April 10.

Our line of march was through rain and a forsaken-looking country; a rough and narrow road winding through an almost continuous pine forest, with a few mud-thatched, miserable log houses scattered sparsely along its length. On the afternoon of the eighth we heard the roar of artillery far ahead of us. At dark, [we] arrived at or near Pleasant Hill, thirty-five miles from Grand Ecore, where we encamped. During the evening we heard rumors of disaster, and about 11:00 P.M. Colonel [John S.] Clark, a member of General Banks's staff, arrived at our camp with information that "the cavalry and Thirteenth Corps had been fighting sixteen miles ahead, at Sabine Cross Roads, had been whipped and were falling back; that the enemy had captured 150 wagons and twenty-two pieces of artillery, and had killed, disabled, and captured about 2,000 men."

It does not come within the scope of this article to speak of that disaster or the cause of it, as General Smith's troops were not engaged in it, but a reference to it may not be amiss. In the first excitement it was attributed entirely to the presence of the cavalry wagon train, which was between the infantry and cavalry; but a calmer, more dispassionate judgment will, I think, throw the blame upon General Banks, who neglected to put in practice that good war maxim: "Choose your own ground and make the enemy attack you." The cavalry, instead of holding its ground and calling for infantry, should have fallen back upon its infantry support, as General Franklin desired. General Franklin did his best to prevent the separation of the troops, but without avail, as General Banks would listen to no suggestion, but ordered the infantry forward by brigades and divisions, so that they were whipped in detail. General Franklin had arranged to have his troops wait for the arrival of General Smith's command at a point eight miles in front of Pleasant Hill (to the west) and, could he have had his own way, the Sabine Cross Roads fight would have probably taken place twenty-four or forty-eight hours later than it did and there would have been several thousand more infantry engaged, which would, without doubt, have given us the victory and taken us to Shreveport.

On the morning of April 9 preparations were made for the attack of the enemy, which we felt confident would come after their success on the eighth. During the forenoon, as General Banks's forces arrived on the ground, on their retrograde movement, he sent the cavalry (except about 500 men), Thirteenth

Corps (whose commander, Brigadier General T. E. G. Ransom, had been severely wounded the day previous), a great part of the artillery and the baggage train (what there was left of it) to the rear—the advance of a shameful retreat, and so hurried was this retreat that the medical supply train of the Nineteenth Corps was sent also, to the surprise and annoyance of the medical director, Doctor [Eugene F.] Sanger, who, before night, had such pressing need for its contents—thus leaving General Smith, with his command, and the Nineteenth Corps, under General Franklin, to stand the coming shock, and at 4:00 P.M. it came.

Our preparations were completed for the reception of the enemy by 10:00 A.M. The position was fine one; the small hamlet, Pleasant Hill (a few old houses, a store or two, one building of some pretensions, an academy, which General Banks occupied as his headquarters and which was also used as a hospital), was situated on a slight eminence, the ground sloping down in all directions and rising again to the west, forming another eminence about three-quarters of a mile from the village; the country was thickly timbered, but with open fields to the west. On and about the crest of this latter eminence, among trees, behind fences, etc., was our battle line, while our reserves were in waiting, joining the village on the left.

The road leading toward Shreveport passed through our battle line about the center, which battle line was formed as follows: The First Division of the Nineteenth Corps, consisting of three brigades (First, Brigadier General William Dwight; Second, Brigadier General James W. McMillan; Third, Colonel Lewis Benedict), under command of [Brigadier General William H.] Emory, was the main line. Colonel Shaw's brigade (1,700 men) of General Smith's command was ordered to report for duty to General Emory and replaced General McMillan's brigade, which was withdrawn and kept as a reserve. The above-mentioned troops were placed as follows: General Dwight's brigade on the right, Colonel Shaw's in the center, and Colonel Benedict's on the left; but through some misconception of orders, or neglect to give them, there was a gap left between the two last-mentioned brigades, into which, during the battle, the enemy poured his troops—the result of which was the cause of much loss of life and almost irreparable disaster.

General Smith's command (with the exception of the above-mentioned brigade of Colonel Shaw, and also excepting the division of the Seventeenth Corps, which, as already stated, was with Admiral Porter), now reduced in consequence of the above "absentees" to about 5,800 men, formed the reserve, or second line, and were stationed to the left and rear of Colonel Benedict's brigade as follows: The Third Brigade, Third Division, Sixteenth Corps, under command of Colonel R. M. Moore (One Hundred Seventeenth and Forty-ninth Illinois, and One Hundred Seventy-eighth New York) was placed on the right, its right resting on the houses of Pleasant Hill, among which was stationed a battery. Colonel Moore's own regiment (One Hundred Seventeenth Illinois) was not under his command during the battle, having been detached early in the morning under Lieutenant Colonel [Jonathan] Merriam and stationed upon the extreme left, with orders to hold three roads which converged from the south-west, and this regiment was not actively engaged during the day.

On the left of Colonel Moore's brigade was the First Brigade, Third Division (Fifty-eighth and One Hundred Nineteenth Illinois, Eighty-ninth Indiana, and Ninth Indiana Battery), under command of Colonel [William F.] Lynch (afterward a prominent Fenian general).

In the rear of these was stationed the Second Brigade, First Division (Thirty-fifth Iowa, Thirty-third Missouri, eighth Wisconsin, Fifth Minnesota, and Forty-seventh Illinois), under command of Colonel [Sylvester G.] Hill. With these reserves were the Third Indiana and First Vermont batteries. The reserves were under the immediate command of General Mower.

General Smith's troops were fresh, not having met the enemy since the capture of Fort De Russy, while General Emory's command had fought and, in fact, had held back the enemy the day before, after it had beaten back the cavalry and Thirteenth Army Corps.

There was an occasional shot during the day between our outposts and the enemy's cavalry, sufficient to show that they were advancing. At 4:00 P.M., as we were sitting at our mess table, eating a late dinner, with General Franklin as our guest, and wrapped in our overcoats, as the day was cold, we heard the opening gun. Others followed in quick succession. We hurriedly mounted our horses, rode to the front, and found the battle had begun.

It was a general attack along the whole line, but Colonel Shaw's brigade, being somewhat in advance and on both sides of the Shreveport road, received the first blow. In front of the Fourteenth Iowa and Twenty-fourth Missouri was an open field, on the opposite side of which was a dense woods, from which the enemy opened fire upon the colonel with artillery, which was replied to by the Twenty-fifth New York Battery, belonging to the Nineteenth Corps, on his right.

Very soon thereafter the enemy's cavalry was forming for a charge at the edge of the woods. They moved forward at a rapid pace, sweeping across the field in one of the most perfect cavalry charges the late war produced, and its reception was as fatal as ever befell a charging column—that is, for the number engaged. Colonel Shaw ordered his men to reserve their fire until the horsemen approached sufficiently near to receive the full benefit of a close and steady volley. Fully one-half of both men and horses were disabled at the first fire, but the rest were not checked—they still came forward, falling rapidly. As the men thus advanced, and falling as they advanced, an officer (riding a magnificent horse) at full speed, holding a revolver in his hand, pitched from his horse and fell dead among our men near where Colonel Shaw was. Lieutenant [G. H.] Logan (Fourteenth Iowa) handed the pistol to his colonel, and the name of Colonel [Arthur P.] Bagby was engraved on it. The remaining few straggled back to the cover of the woods. I doubt if there was ever a more complete annihilation of a cavalry regiment.

I have stated that Colonel Shaw's brigade was somewhat in advance. It was caused as follows: When he relieved General McMillan's brigade he found to his right and about 100 yards in front, four guns of the Twenty-fifth New York Battery on a ridge completely covering the road upon which the enemy was likely to advance, and he moved forward and occupied this most advantageous position. This caused the gap I have referred to on his left, and also left General Dwight to his rear, on the right. This change of position made it necessary for Colonel Shaw to communicate with General Dwight. At his headquarters he found his assistant adjutant general, who informed him that the general was away, and Colonel Shaw reports: "His assistant adjutant general said he would send me word as soon as he returned. After waiting some time I again went to his headquarters, but was unable to learn where he could be found. About 3:00 P.M. I again went in search of him, and this time found him, and he promised to send the necessary support. This he failed to do."

General Stone examined the line during the afternoon, and as Colonel Shaw explained to him his changed position he said: "Your position is well chosen. It is admirable. It could not be better. I will see that your flanks are properly supported, for this position must be held at all hazards." But as the battle opened almost immediately upon this promise, no supports made their appearance.

Immediately after the crushing defeat of the above-mentioned cavalry charge, the rebel infantry, in perfect order, in double battle line, emerged from the woods and advanced through the same open field, but so extended as to overlap Colonel Shaw's brigade, who reports:

> They advanced steadily, but in good order across the open field in my front till they got within easy range, when my whole line opened upon them, stopping their advance, but not preventing them from replying vigorously to my fire, causing heavy loss. My men held their ground, keeping up a steady and well-directed fire, which soon compelled their first line to fall back in disorder. In the meantime fighting had commenced on my left, and the line to my left had fallen back so as to enable the enemy to pass in its rear. They had also passed around my right, and were firing on my flank when their second line advanced, and I was again engaged along my whole front.

It was now that the two brigades of Colonels Shaw and Benedict were outflanked; the enemy filing past both flanks of the former and, consequently, the right of the latter, into the treacherous gap. Here we suffered the greatest loss of the battle, not only losing Colonel Benedict, who was killed, but Colonel Shaw lost in killed, wounded, and missing about 500 men. Looking upon this part of the battlefield as the pivot upon which the whole struggle revolved, I give more time and prominence to it than to any other portion, and will give an extract from the official report of Colonel Scott (Thirty-second Iowa), whose regiment was the extreme left of Colonel Shaw's brigade:

The fire of my command was reserved until the enemy was within easy range, and when opened was so destructive that he faltered, passed to my left through the open space, and to my rear, losing heavily by the fire of my left wing as he passed, but threatening to cut off my command from our main forces. I at once sent information to my superior, and to the commander of the troops on my immediate right, of this peril to the whole line; but, without orders to abandon my position, though very critical, I could do nothing but change the front of my extreme left to face the new danger and protect my flank and rear, if possible. This was done, and a well-directed fire kept up to the front and left, which kept the enemy at bay.

Meantime he was steadily pouring his columns past my left and working across the rear of my position, so that in a short time the battle was in full force in my rear. In this state of affairs I discovered that all the troops on my right had been withdrawn, taking with them a portion of my right wing. . . . The timber and undergrowth were such that I could not observe my whole line from any one point. . . . My line now faced in three directions. I was completely enveloped, without orders, and virtually in the hands of the enemy had he dared to close in and overwhelm us with his masses now around us.

Colonel Scott remained in this position until the final charge of our troops drove the enemy from the field, when he joined them in the pursuit as they came from his rear. I will quote again from Colonel Shaw's report, in direct continuation of the extract already given:

At this time I received an order from General Smith to fall back, as the enemy were getting in my rear. My staff officers having all been dispatched to different officers for support, and being myself on the right of my brigade, I had to ride to the left in rear of my brigade to give the order to withdraw. The brush and timber were so thick that I could scarcely see ten paces. As I passed down the line, I sent the order to Colonel [James I.] Gilbert, Twenty-seventh Iowa, to fall back as soon as the regiments on his right should commence retreating. I then pushed on to give the necessary orders to Colonel Scott, when I met the enemy's forces entirely in his rear, preventing me from communicating with him. I was, therefore, compelled to leave him to act without orders. Hurrying back to the right, I found the Twenty-fourth Missouri had been compelled to change its front to receive the attack from the right, and that the enemy was pressing my front with overwhelming numbers. . . . I therefore considered it necessary to give the order to fall back to the three regiments with which I could communicate, leaving Colonel Scott to extricate himself as best he could.

It is appropriate to add an extract from General Emory's report:

The enemy emerged from the woods in all directions, and in heavy columns, completely outflanking and overpowering my left wing, composed of the Third Brigade and a brigade of General Smith's command, which broke in some confusion. . . .

My right stood firm and repulsed the enemy handsomely, and the left, I think, would have done so, but for the great interval which was left between it and the troops to the left, leaving that flank entirely exposed.

It will be seen by the foregoing that General Emory attributes a defeat to Colonel Shaw, which in reality did not occur, as the enemy, instead of driving him, were passing to his rear, which General Emory, in all probability, did not see, but which General Smith did, and who, under the circumstances, took the responsibility of ordering Colonel Shaw to retire.

Toward the close of the foregoing-described struggle a portion of both Colonels Lynch and Moore's brigades, although reserve forces, were brought into active service and fought gallantly. Our troops being hard pressed, slowly fell back upon the reserves, part of whom were quietly awaiting the order necessary to bring them into action.

The decisive moment had arrived, and the final struggle commenced which resulted in so overwhelming a defeat to the enemy. When the order was given, our troops rose to their feet and poured upon the advancing foe a most murderous volley, and then with General Mower at their head sprung forward in a grand charge. Even at this late day, when so many war experiences appear more like a dream than a reality, my blood warms with excitement as I remember this charge, having personally participated in it, riding at the head of one of the charging regiments with its commanding officer. It was the most exhilarating period of my war life.

This new and fresh line of troops, added to those already fighting, thus hurled upon the enemy, was undoubtedly a surprise to them, and after the first effort to continue the struggle, they became convinced that the advance was irresistible, and in resigning themselves to the fate so inevitable, they, as if actuated by one common consent, turned and fled in the utmost panic, many of them throwing away their arms. Our victorious troops followed, capturing prisoners, small arms, several pieces of artillery and drove them for two or three miles, until darkness precluded any further advance. We now missed our cavalry which, if within reach, could have captured a large percentage of the rebel army.

I would here record an incident I witnessed when the battle was nearly over. General Smith and staff met General Banks on the field. General Banks took off his hat, shook hands with General Smith, and said: "You are doing your work nobly, General; may God bless you for it."

In the above description of the Battle of Pleasant Hill I have only given a portraiture of the part taken in it by General Smith's troops. I have endeavored to make it plain and at the same time concise, and have copied from the official reports of Colonels Shaw and Scott because I have never seen them in print, except the copy I have, for which I sent to Iowa.[2] Although General Franklin had been wounded at Sabine Cross Roads he kept his saddle during the whole of Pleasant Hill, overlooking the disposition of his men, etc. And I would here state that my prejudice against General Stone, entertained ever since the Battle of

2. The reports of Colonels Shaw and Scott do appear in the *Official Records*.

Ball's Bluff, entirely disappeared on the battlefield of Pleasant Hill, as I witnessed his ceaseless, tireless activity in the performance of his duties as General Banks's chief of staff, and when almost immediately after this battle he was relieved from his position and General Dwight appointed in his place, we felt one more scapegoat, and as he left active service there and then he certainly took with him the sympathy of all in the Sixteenth Army Corps and also of many in the Nineteenth.

Our victory being so complete, General Banks had ordered the retreating train to be halted, turned about, and everything prepared for an early advance next morning, and about midnight I fell asleep amidst the groans of the wounded, but at 9:00 A.M. was awakened to hear that we were ordered to retreat.

Imagine our feelings! General Smith, upon receipt of the order, had gone to General Banks and urged an advance; but when he found the order to retreat was imperative, he begged the privilege of remaining on the field to bury the dead and take care of the wounded; but even this was not allowed.

Disgraceful! Criminal! Inhuman! At this late day, when time has mitigated the intensity of the keen feeling then experienced by us who fled, my notes and letters seems overdrawn, and I hesitate to quote literally, but they are a true history, not only of my own personal sense of bitter humiliation—then in my mind—but are a true index of the inner consciousness of nine-tenths of the army; and, although "military discipline" kept it under, yet so the soldiers thought, talked, and some of them wrote, and even now, when fifteen years have passed away, it is difficult to review these events and write with any degree of calmness or patience of our retreat.

. . .

General Smith could not make up his mind—even at the command of his superior officer—to abandon all the fruits of a dearly bought victory; to leave his dead and dying in the hands of the enemy and to desert his fleet and 2,500 of his men to the risk of capture (for he "felt in his bones" that the enemy, when they found our army were retreating, would naturally attempt the capture and destruction of the fleet, etc., and his surmise was correct), and he went to General Franklin and proposed the arrest of General Banks; that Franklin should take command; that they should bury their dead; care for their wounded; push across the Springfield Landing, on the river, to the assistance of Admiral Porter and General T. Kilby Smith, and then, if practicable, march upon Shreveport.

But General Franklin would not consent, and General Smith was obliged to submit to the unavoidable and turn his back upon a retreating, demoralized enemy. General Banks did, however, give us the post of honor—to cover the retreat when no enemy followed. Colonel [Thomas J.] Lucas, of the cavalry division, was with us in the rear, with about 500 men.

Our rear guard did not leave Pleasant Hill until just as day was breaking. During the forenoon, while our surgeons (who were left on the battlefield) were trying to make comfortable the wounded, they were surprised at the appearance of a party from the camp of the enemy—under a flag of truce—asking permission to bury their dead. Words can hardly express their astonishment when they learned our army was retreating. After so complete a victory, followed by so shameful an abandonment of everything, I am not surprised that Colonel Scott should write: "This was a defeat, but a defeat only to our foe. The stake fought for by him was the Trans-Mississippi empire; by our commanding general the safe retreat of his army. We won both. Abandoned the former to the enemy after he had retreated, and gave to a brilliant victory all the moral results of a defeat. Finally, the Thirty-second Iowa blushes to place upon its banner the name of a field where its dead and wounded were cruelly abandoned to an enemy who, many hours afterward, humbly asked leave to care for his own."

It will be seen by the foregoing that my evidence differs from Major Hoffman's, and I will now produce evidence from others. The correspondent of the Missouri *Republican,* in writing from Grand Ecore, April 13, says: "General A. J. Smith protested against the retreat from Pleasant Hill. He wanted to pursue the rebels on Sunday on his own hook, instead of falling back, but General Banks was firm, and ordered all the forces to return."

Doctor Sanger, medical director of the Nineteenth Army Corps, says: "General A. J. Smith was strongly in favor of advancing, and insisted upon it, that he would not retire. I met him as I left Pleasant Hill, and he insisted we should have gone on; that our victory was complete."

In reply to letters from me, I give the following extracts. General Franklin writes: "Major Hoffman is certainly wrong in his statement that General Smith opposed a forward movement from Pleasant Hill. For my part the only question that came to me was, shall we stay at Pleasant Hill or go to Grand Ecore— not shall we advance. The idea of an advance after what I had just experienced of Banks's generalship was odious to me, and the scattered condition of the troops made the junction a matter of several days."

Doctor [George M.] Staples (at that time surgeon on the staff of Colonel Shaw, but subsequently medical director on the staff of General Smith) writes:

> At about 10:00 P.M. of the day of the battle an orderly came to the hospital and informed me that we would resume our march for Shreveport next day and it would be necessary for me to make arrangements accordingly. At 1:00 A.M. the orderly returned and brought orders for me to make the best disposition I could of my wounded, for peremptory orders had been received to commence falling back on Grand Ecore at 3:00 A.M.
> Subsequently I learned from General Smith's own lips that about midnight, when he was resting in the full expectation of resuming the advance in the morning, as General Banks had assured him in the early evening, an orderly came with orders to fall back at 3:00 A.M. Astounded at the order, he immediately visited General Banks to know what it meant. General Banks pleaded its necessity on the ground of the general discouragement of the officers of the Nineteenth Corps, the scarcity of com-

missary stores, the great losses sustained, etc. He then requested permission to advance with his own command alone, then to be allowed to remain a day upon the field to bury his dead, and finally to stay until 9:00 A.M., all of which was refused. It was then, as I understood from him, that, with grief and indignation, he sought General Franklin's headquarters and urged him to assume command by the arrest of Banks and he (Smith) would sustain him. But, meeting with no favor, he was compelled to reluctantly turn away and submit to the disgraceful retreat.

Colonel Shaw writes:

My recollection of the matter you refer to is that about 11:00 P.M., after the battle, General Smith told me General Banks had ordered a retreat to commence immediately, and that his teams and ambulances were already on their way, leaving the dead unburied, adding in his usual style, that it was an outrage, and that General Banks ought to be arrested. That our retreat would expose our transports with General T. Kilby Smith's command and our sick and supplies to destruction and capture. I replied to him that, as I had been ordered to report to General Emory the morning before the battle, and as I had received no orders from him to retreat, I would see Banks and his whole army in hell before I would leave, till I had taken care of my wounded. General Smith said he would see General Franklin, and started to find him.

After some time he came back in a very bad humor, but what occurred between him and General Franklin I either did not hear or have forgotten. We, however, stayed till morning, provided the best we could for our wounded, and left after sunrise.

As to the threat of General Smith to have Banks arrested at Grand Ecore, as well as I can recollect, the circumstances were these: Our transports had been stopped above Grand Ecore by rebel batteries. I applied to General Smith for permission to go to their relief. He replied that he was not in command, and could do nothing without General Banks's orders, that the whole army would be sacrificed through his incompetency, and that the only way to save the army was to have him arrested and put some other officer in command. Thus you may perceive that you may be correct as to the circumstance at Pleasant Hill, and also the statement that the request for his arrest at Grand Ecore was also correct.

Captain John Hough, assistant adjutant general on the staff of General Smith, writes:

As to General Smith's request to General Franklin to put General Banks under arrest, it was made after we got the order "to withdraw our troops silently from Pleasant Hill, and take the rear of the column back to Grand Ecore," and before we left Pleasant Hill.

You will remember we got the order about 11:30 P.M., the night of the battle, and did not go until after daylight. During this interim the incident you speak of occurred. After receiving the order General Smith first went to Banks and begged leave to be allowed to stay until noon the next day, in order to bury his dead and take care of the wounded, as the battle continued until dark and many were scattered where they could not be found till daylight. Banks refused. General Smith then asked to be allowed to stay until daylight, so that the wounded could be properly cared for, stating that the details from his command were but gathering them up as fast as possible and he did not want to leave any uncared for, but Banks's reply was that the order must be obeyed. Then General Smith went to General Franklin and told him that the Thirteenth Corps had formerly been under his (Smith's) command, and the divisions of the Sixteenth and Seventeenth corps, that were now under his command, would sustain Franklin, every officer and man of them, if he would put Banks under arrest, assume the command, and go on with the expedition. Franklin did not care to assume the responsibility and replied: "Smith, that is mutiny," and there the matter dropped.

Lieutenant John B. Pannes, ordnance officer on General Smith's staff, writes:

We had our headquarters under a tree near the battlefield. I had been sent by General Smith to follow Banks's retreating army to get ammunition. Having detained five wagons loaded with cartridges, I brought them back, and having corralled them, joined headquarters at about midnight. About two hours afterward someone shook me and said: "General, you must prepare to retreat." I told the shaker I was not the general, but that he was asleep on the other side of the tree. Well, the general was awakened, and a conversation followed, which I but imperfectly understood. It was General Franklin who had awakened the general. Smith begged Franklin not to retreat, saying: "We have beaten them like hell." However, I at once received my orders to have my train hitched up, and went ahead about my business. I understood from Hough that General Smith told him to go with him to Franklin's headquarters; that Smith asked Franklin to assume command and to go ahead. Franklin was taking a cup of coffee. He stirred it slowly, and finally said: "Smith, don't you know this is mutiny?"

I saw General Smith last November in St. Louis, and we talked over this whole affair pretty thoroughly, and he fully confirmed the above statements, that his request was made at Pleasant Hill the night of the battle, and that he had no recollection of having made the request the second time at Grand Ecore. But General Franklin sustains Major Hoffman. In answer to a letter from me he writes:

Major Hoffman is right as to the place of the interview in question. I was confined to my bed at the time with a wound in the leg, received at Sabine Cross Roads, and only learned what was going on from those who visited me, and when General Smith made the proposition to me to assume the command I did not entertain it for a moment, for, confined as I was, my mind was cool, while he, on the contrary, saw how badly things went from day to day and was excited and troubled. My reply to him was: "Will you guarantee that I will not be hanged after the campaign is over if I do?" I know that General Smith had made what, if taken seriously, was a mutinous proposition, and I at once saw that the matter must not be discussed between us at all. However wise the proposition was, we would have been trifling with our lives if I had accepted it. My answer to General Smith's proposition was made in the most friendly spirit toward him. He was certainly serious in the proposition. At the time I was suffering great pain from my wound, and I remember that the interview suddenly took the pain out of my leg, and I forgot it until after Smith left my tent.

Upon receipt of [the] above letters from Captain Hough and Lieutenant Pannes, I sent a copy of each to General Franklin, and he replied as follows:

> Captain Hough's evidence is very direct and would stagger me, except that I remember the circumstance of finding General Smith at his headquarters after all the troops except his had started to Grand Ecore, and impressing upon him the fact that he was left alone there with his troops. When I went to Smith's headquarters, at the time Lieutenant Pannes specifies, it was to let him know that the remainder of the army was in motion.
>
> It seems to me that if the proposition had been made to me at Pleasant Hill it would have impressed itself upon my memory as much as it did when made at Grand Ecore, yet I may have wished to banish it from my memory and may have succeeded in so doing. I do not remember that I saw General Smith between the time of the fight and the time when I awoke him, as described by Lieutenant Pannes. If I had seen him, perhaps things might have taken a different turn. Now, the night in question was the third in succession that I had passed without sleep, and I was also suffering great pain from my wound. It may be that under these circumstances I may forget what happened during a part of the night, but I do not think I do.
>
> This discussion shows the extreme difficulty of getting at the truth in such matters. Until I received your first letter I did not dream that there could be any question as to the matter. Now it appears that there is good evidence against mine, and although I still think I am not mistaken as to the time and place, yet as there are other persons (General Smith particularly) who believe that it occurred the night after the Pleasant Hill battle, it is proper to so state.

There may have been two occasions when General Smith made this request, and the second one may have been after our return to Grand Ecore, as I know he was impatient there under restraint and inactivity. It may be immaterial where it was in proving the fact that such a request actually occurred, for this incident is so curious in the annals of war that the reading public are inclined to doubt it.

At a late dinner party in Philadelphia, a gentleman said he had lately read Hoffman's *Camp, Court, and Siege,* which contained a curious statement, the truth of which he doubted. He then related the incident. Fortunately, there was present a gentleman who was subsequently to the Red River campaign an officer on General Smith's staff (Mr. Hunn Hanson, a resident of Philadelphia), who said the statement was true; that he had heard it from the general himself in his tent at Eastport after the Battle of Nashville, and never before nor since had he heard the general mention it, nor had he ever seen him so moved as he was then, while relating it.

It is not strange that it should be doubted, even if related by so good an authority as Major Hoffman (who, I have forgotten to state, was adjutant general on General Franklin's staff), as it was unusual, to say the least, but the circumstances were unusual—a victorious army running away from a defeated foe. If General Smith had been next in rank to General Banks I have no doubt he would have arrested him, but as General Franklin ranked him he was applied to. It is not to be wondered at that General Franklin declined to accede to his request, for it was a responsible move to make. Had it been done and the onward movement been a success, in all probability it would have been condoned at Washington. But had the result been disastrous it is but reasonable to presume that both Generals Franklin and Smith would have been held to a strict accountability. Major Hoffman says: "Of course, General Franklin treated it as a joke and laughed it off. But there can be no doubt that the officer was in earnest." No one who belonged to the military family of General Smith at that time, and saw him in the privacy of his headquarters that night and for days afterward, can ever forget his quivering lip and tear-dimmed eye when the subject was mentioned, nor could doubt his earnestness, and when he made that proposition there could have been nothing in his demeanor to indicate a joke. He felt too keenly the humiliation and disgrace of the whole situation, and as General Franklin states in the above letter, "he was certainly serious in the proposition."

That our troops gained a most decisive victory at Pleasant Hill is, I believe, universally admitted, although General Dick Taylor, in his address to his army, says: "In spite of the strength of the enemy's position, held by fresh troops of the Sixteenth Corps, your valor and devotion triumphed over all. Darkness closed one of the hottest fights of the war. The morning of the tenth dawned upon a flying foe with our cavalry in pursuit, capturing prisoners at every step."

It was too true, we were "a flying foe"—more shame to General Banks than credit to our enemy—but we were not a defeated foe. General Taylor knew that the foregoing, "with our cavalry in pursuit, capturing prisoners at every step," was imaginary, unless he meant by prisoners our dead and wounded left upon the battlefield. Not only my own notes (already quoted) say "when no enemy followed," but the correspondent of the Missouri *Republican* writes: "In our retreat to Grand Ecore we were not molested in the least." The correspondent of the *Chicago Tribune* writes: "On Sunday and Monday the entire Union army retreated in good order to Grand Ecore without any molestation, the rebels being evidently unable to follow us after their defeat at Pleasant Hill." Here is also evidence drawn from the enemy; it is from a captured letter: "That it was impossible for us to pursue Banks immediately after Pleasant Hill (under four or five days), cannot be gainsaid. It was impossible, because we did not have transportation for supplies, and impossible because we had been beaten, demoralized, paralyzed in the fight of the ninth." Then, after describing the battle, he continues: "Neither our cavalry nor that of the enemy did anything in this fight. The next morning after sunrise, very much to our surprise, we learned the enemy had retreated during the night. Cavalry was immediately sent in pursuit while the infantry was taken back to Mansfield for organization, rest, and supply," and he naively adds, "The enemy evidently considered himself whipped. He ought to know." The only exception I take to the above is that "neither our cavalry nor that of the enemy did anything in the fight." For the almost total annihilation of one of their cavalry regiments, as already described by me, is a fact, witnessed by too many to admit of contradiction. And as to their "cavalry was immediately sent in pursuit," I cannot deny; but the fact remains, they did not overtake us, "capturing prisoners at every step."

Having whipped our enemy and driven him miles from the battlefield, then to be ordered to run! We could see no reason for it then and cannot yet, although it may be true, as General Banks says in his official report: "The occupation of Shreveport could not have been maintained."

But it is not the object of this article to enter into the merits or otherwise of General Banks's decision to retreat, for, of course, there are two sides to every question, but I do censure him for leaving the dead unburied and the wounded (i.e., the greater part of them) to fall into the hands of the enemy. If he had to retreat, why such haste? Why not wait at least one day and care for the dead and dying?

General Banks is hardly fair toward General Smith in his official report. He says: "General Smith never declined cooperation with me, nor did he receive orders from me." It may seem to the prejudice of order and military discipline for me, a subordinate, to question the veracity of a commanding general, but when he says, "nor did he receive orders from me," I do call his veracity into question. As I have shown, Colonel Shaw, of General Smith's command, reported to General Emory for duty at Pleasant Hill. As no one stood between Generals Banks and Smith—that is, with any authority to command General Smith—who, but General Banks could have ordered this? And in Colonel Shaw's official report he says: "I was ordered to report with my brigade to General Banks. By him I was ordered to proceed to the front and report to General Emory." I could give many other instances where General Smith did receive orders from General Banks. From the moment he reported to him at Alexandria he was under his orders and received them and obeyed them every day while under his command. To even imagine any other state of affairs would be ridiculous and not tenable. When I reach the cotton chapter of the expedition I will give one instance where he questioned one of Banks's orders; but that the circumstances fully justified him in this, will be, I think, the verdict of all honest men.

I now resume from my journal. We arrived at Grand Ecore on April 11 and found that the gunboats and transports had not returned from up the river. Next day we heard the heavy guns of the former fighting their way back (for, of course, when the rebels sent in a flag of truce and found us gone, they immediately went to the river to catch our boats). On the thirteenth the firing was continued, and as we listened to the sounds of fighting between our forces and the enemy, and wondered why we were not ordered to their assistance, our anxiety and impatience at our inactivity was hard to endure.

Colonel Shaw came to our headquarters in the afternoon and asked permission to go to the rescue. General Smith told him he had no authority to send him and could get no orders to go himself, and used strong, emphatic language as to General Banks's lack of military ability. The colonel then said he would like to go without orders, and, as he received no positive orders to the contrary, he took about 1,000 of his men and started. As he was crossing the river he met General Banks, who asked him where he was going. He replied: "To the rescue of our transports, troops, [and] supplies with General Kilby Smith." General Banks then sent an order to General A. J. Smith to follow with about 1,000 men, which he did.

Upon our arrival at Campti (twelve or fifteen miles) we found our boats, with the enemy on both banks; the latter left at once. The boats had had a tough time and presented a mixed appearance. Sacks of oats, bales of hay, boxes of hardtack, and every imaginable or get-at-able article piled up for breastworks.

We remained at Campti all night and returned to Grand Ecore the next day. The fleet had a hazardous gauntlet to run in coming down the river, having been attacked by [Brigadier Generals St. John R.] Liddell and [Thomas] Green with several thousand men. Green and about 450 men were left dead on the banks of the river. The loss on the fleet was about fifty in killed and wounded.

We remained at Grand Ecore eight days, being detained by the navy. While there, Doctor N. R. Darby, medical director on General Smith's staff, was sent down the river to Alexandria with our sick and to get medical supplies. The boat was fired upon and the doctor was struck by a bullet. For days his life was despaired of, and he was never able to resume his position. We were not much annoyed by the enemy during our stay at Grand Ecore. That they were about us and watching our movements we knew, and one day rather a serious attempt to pry into our camp having been made, and our cavalry being somewhat pressed—strange as it may appear—the cavalry were, by order of General Banks, ordered inside our lines of defense or stockade.

General Banks says in his official report of General Smith: "When his thirty days were up he claimed the right at Grand Ecore to return to Vicksburg, irrespective of the condition of the army or the fleet, and did not consider himself at all responsible for the inevitable consequences of his withdrawal to the army and navy, nor for that detention which their preservation demanded. That responsibility I was called upon to assume in written orders."

It is true, as above stated, that General Smith and his command were loaned for thirty days, and that time expired on April 10; and it is true that he was restless and anxious under the then state of affairs, but General Smith was too good a soldier to withdraw his command and abandon the rest of the army and navy to their destruction, when "their preservation demanded" his presence and support. Even if Major Hoffman's statement as to the time and place when General Smith asked for the arrest of General Banks is true, it was not that the forces of General Banks should be abandoned, but that they should be extricated. And when I reach Alexandria I will show that it was General Banks who meditated the abandonment of the fleet and General Smith who assured Admiral Porter that he would never abandon him.

On April 20 General Smith's command marched out of Natchitoches (about four miles) and encamped in line of battle. The object of this movement was to hold the enemy back while General Banks, with his army (or rather General Franklin, who had now been placed in command by General Banks) should move down the river road toward Alexandria, and as soon as the road should be clear General Smith was to move and bring up the rear of the retreating army. We remained in battle line nearly all day of the twenty-first, while the Thirteenth and Nineteenth corps were moving down the bank of the river.

During this day an officer arrived at our headquarters and reported himself as a signal officer, with orders to report to General Smith for duty. General Smith's reply was a characteristic one: "Well, lieutenant, I am glad to see you; make yourself at home; we have a pleasant family at headquarters and I think you will enjoy yourself with us; but, really, I don't think there will be any occasion for your signals. My signal will be my artillery, and that sound can be heard easier than your flags can be seen." The lieutenant looked at him as if he had found a curiosity; but, of course, he remained with us in the rear, and waved his flags as [the] occasion demanded.

About dark (April 21) we drew in our forces and followed the army. We had with us a brigade of cavalry, under command of either Colonel Lucas, or Colonel [Nathan A. M.] Dudley. After a six days' march and almost constant fighting, we re-arrived at Alexandria on the twenty-sixth. On April 22, 23, and 24 the enemy pressed us so closely that we had to form a regular line of battle and fight them. Each fight lasted an hour or two and were quite brisk affairs, the enemy being repulsed every time.

The brunt of this fighting fell to the lot of the Seventeenth Corps, under General T. Kilby Smith. On the twenty-fourth the rebels opened upon us with artillery at 3:00 A.M., some of their shells bursting in our open-air camp. About sunrise they made a furious attack, which was handsomely repelled, and was the last real stroke they made, as they were well punished for disturbing us at so early an hour. On the twenty-third General Franklin had a more serious affair in the advance than any one we had in the rear, as the rebels contested his crossing the Cane River. The enemy followed us all the way to Alexandria and demonstrated just enough to keep our artillery and the cavalry in active service, but we had no battle after April 24.

Upon our arrival at Alexandria, as General Smith rode to the front, after having kept in the rear for six days and fighting one-half of them, he was greeted with waving of hats, cheers, and such shouts of welcome and admiration as must have been most gratifying. It was a perfect ovation, not only from his own men, but from the men of the Thirteenth and Nineteenth corps, right up to the tent of General Banks. And his staff, although of minor importance, as we galloped with him down that long line of cheering men, were proud to belong to him, and that we had endured the hardships and dangers of the last few weeks with him. How refreshing it was that night, when we retired to our tents and took off our clothes, something we had not done for six nights.

Owing to the low stage of the water in the river it was very evident that the gunboats could not pass over the falls at Alexandria, and between Admiral Porter and General Banks it was decided that the only way to save the fleet was to build a dam and thereby raise the water on the falls, which skillful feat of engineering was given to Lieutenant Colonel [Joseph] Bailey (Fourth Wisconsin) to accomplish. Endeavoring to limit this article to a narration of the part taken by General Smith's troops in this campaign, it is not for me to give a history of this grand achievement. It is well told in Admiral Porter's official report. While referring to it, I would state that the face of the immediate neighborhood underwent a rapid transformation as the work progressed. As if by magic, brick sugar-mills and all available stone and brick buildings and standing trees disappeared, and regiments of soldiers and mules drew material of every description to the river bank, where other regiments of soldiers soon disposed of it, under the masterly superintendency of Lieutenant Colonel Bailey.

During our encampment at Alexandria the division of the Seventeenth Corps crossed the river and encamped for a few days on the grounds of the University of Louisiana, of which institution General Sherman was president at the breaking out of the rebellion. General Franklin left us at Alexandria and General Banks again took command of the army. The enemy were now all about us and our troops were camping and sleeping in line of battle; the river was blockaded below and the enemy were capturing and destroying steamers. Admiral Porter also lost three of his gunboats—one, the *Eastport*, he was obliged to blow up, as he could not get it down to Alexandria.

On May 4, General Smith's command advanced out to ex-Governor Moore's plantation, where they had a skirmish with the enemy, and driving him two or three miles we again made our camp on the ex-governor's plantation, where we had daily skirmishing during our stay. General Smith and staff were out there every day, sometimes remaining overnight and sometimes riding in to Alexandria in the evening, sleeping on our headquarters steamer, and then [riding] out again early in the morning.

What a sad picture was now to be seen, where all was beauty and luxury when we first saw it in March. Governor Moore was with his friends further south, and while fighting over his plantation one day, his wife was advised to leave, and as she left her house the tears came to her eyes as she said: "Goodbye, once happy home." Who made it an unhappy one? We all concluded that it was her husband, as the natural result of treason. Living far in the interior of Dixie as he did, he undoubtedly thought the war's desolation would never reach his happy home. Three years had passed away, and he was an exile—his family leaving their home; the flag he insulted and defied waving over the ruins of his "once happy home." Was it not a just retribution?

We were now entirely cut off from the outside world, the blockade of the river being most effectual. A large mail for us was captured and destroyed on one of the transports. General Banks would not let us go out in force and give the enemy battle, having issued positive orders not to bring on a general engagement, which order caused a good deal of animated (but private) discussion. It is appropriate at this point to quote again from the letter of the Southern soldier already quoted from:

> The enemy showed less enterprise than I have ever known them to evince. Banks is clearly no commander. Once or twice while he was at Alexandria, the posture of our forces was such that by a sure and comparatively safe movement of 10,000 men he might have ensured, beyond peradventure, the capture of [Brigadier General Camille J.] Polignac's division. He must have been in the main aware of the position and strength of our forces. Along with the hope of accomplishing his main purposed he seems to have given up all desire to acquit himself with any credit.

The above view is a fair reflection of our own. We, too, felt that General Banks had "given up all desire to acquit himself with any credit," and showed an unaccountable lack of enterprise. Of course, we knew nothing as to the certain result above predicted, of the "sure and comparatively safe movement of 10,000 men." But having about that number General Smith, having his hands tied by the order not to bring on a general engagement, and being obliged in conformity with it (another instance of receipt of orders from General Banks) to sit down quietly on Governor Moore's plantation, and simply sweep away the enemy when too closely reconnoitering our position, might be excused for giving vent to his feelings in unmistakable language, at such (to him, a West Pointer) a new phase of military life.

I have stated that when I reached Alexandria I would show that it was General Banks, not General Smith, who meditated the abandonment of the fleet. Doctor Staples (who, owing to the wound of Doctor Derby, already spoken of, was now acting medical director on General Smith's staff) writes me as follows:

> One day, when the wing dams were about half completed, General Smith asked me to accompany him to General Emory's quarters. They were soon engaged in earnest conversation, and I heard Emory say there was a bad outlook; that General Banks had just informed him it would take a week longer to get the fleet over the falls, and Banks was very uneasy and seriously contemplated abandoning the fleet to its fate and marching away. General Smith replied, with some Anglo-Saxon more forcible than polite, that he wouldn't leave Admiral Porter until that locality, from which we all hoped to escape, had frozen over. We went from General Emory's to Admiral Porter's boat, and General Smith told the admiral what he had just heard, and assured him that, orders or no orders, his command should not leave the fleet until they saw it safe through to the Mississippi River. Admiral Porter replied that he was not surprised to hear such news, as he had been anticipating as much. He expressed much gratitude for General Smith's proffers of aid, and declared that if the expedition had been under his [Smith's] command it would not have failed.

I have now come to a subject which requires delicate handling, but even a historical sketch of the Red River campaign cannot well be written without a reference to it. As the expedition had been a decided failure in a military point of view, so it was a great success as a cotton speculation. It was difficult for us to believe that which our eyes saw, but it was the expressed and indignant belief of many in the army that something was wrong in the manipulation of cotton now being enacted before our eyes. We all saw an immense amount of bagging and roping among the steamer *Black Hawk* (General Banks's headquarters boat) when it arrived at Alexandria, and it was then said it was for cotton. And during our occupancy of Alexandria on our retreat, I myself saw steamers loaded with cotton and sent down the river under the protection of the hospital flag, and Lieutenant Pannes (ordnance officer on General Smith's staff) sends me the following extract from his diary: "April 29, 1864—Cotton is being loaded on the boats by General Banks's order. Even the hospital boat *Superior* is used for that purpose; went out with Captain Burns to convince myself of that fact. May 1— The three cotton boats returned, having been fired into."

In a letter written by Colonel Shaw, who was at this time with his brigade at Governor Moore's plantation, he says:

> The ostensible purpose of occupying the position was the securing of forage, but as scarcely any was procured and several thousand bushels of corn were carelessly burned, it was thought a somewhat suspicious circumstance that a large ginning establishment, which was covered by our lines, was turning out some fifteen or twenty bales of cotton per day. But whether well founded or not, the impression was well nigh universal that army movements were controlled to a considerable extent by the cotton interest. Such a state of affairs was most demoralizing and disheartening.

From our first entrance into the Red River country we had been daily hearing reports which seemed too preposterous for belief; reports that an understanding existed between somebody and somebody else that there was to be no fighting on this campaign, but that the Southern army was to fall back gradually as our army advanced and gathered up the cotton, for which, in some way not explained, the Southerners were to be paid. Also that Generals A. J. Smith and Dick Taylor, not having been informed of this secret, and both being fighting men, had entered the campaign to fight when it became necessary, and General Smith's capture of Fort De Russy and Dick Taylor's forcing the fight at Sabine Cross Roads had upset the calculations of different somebodies. This report of a secret understanding was reiterated day after day until it was believed by many to be true, but many more of us were incredulous until we witnessed this strange shipment of cotton under the *hospital flag,* which was either a gross deception under the sacredness of a hospital flag or the carrying out of a bargain.

In all this, General Smith's character stood out clear and incorruptible; he was the thorough soldier and would have nothing to do with anything except a soldier's duty, not even permitting cotton to be placed on his transports when they descended the river. It was in this connection that the feeling of antagonism between Generals Banks and Smith had about reached its culminating point, and an irreconcilable explosion would have taken place between them if

General Banks had insisted upon the enforcement of his order, which order was, according to my recollection, that General Smith should turn over to him (Banks) his fleet of transports for the purpose of transporting cotton down the river. This order General Smith would not obey. Lieutenant Pannes agrees with me. He writes:

> My recollection of the order of General Banks to General Smith, at Alexandria, on our retreat, to turn over his transports to Banks for the purpose of loading up with cotton, is that the matter was talked over a good deal; that Smith was very indignant and emphatic in his expressions about it. General T. Kilby Smith reports: General Smith gave orders that no cotton should be placed upon his boats for any purpose whatever; and, if my memory serves me right (I have no written memoranda in regard to it), he refused most positively to obey an order in that behalf, with the remark that while he controlled transports they should not be used for the transportation of cotton.

Colonel Shaw has a different version. He writes me:

> My recollection of the order is that Banks sent an order to Smith to receive on board of his boats the supplies belonging to Banks's army (or that part of it not including Smith's command); that General Smith returned the order with the endorsement that he was ready to receive any government supplies on his boats as soon as the boats under Banks's orders discharged their loads of cotton, held on private account, and then, if he (Banks) could not take all his supplies, he would do what he could to assist him.

The report of this "disobedience of orders" reached our troops at Governor Moore's plantation, with this addition, that General Banks had put General Smith under arrest, and next morning, as we rode out there and came to the troops, exchanging shots with the enemy, we noticed the men looked at us with much scrutiny and spoke to each other in angry and excited tones. It was so marked that we were puzzled. Evidently something had happened of which we were ignorant. It seemed to portend a mutiny—more attention was paid to us than to the enemy. We soon learned the cause: it was this rumor of General Smith's arrest, and that morning when he made his appearance he (as often happened before, but with no such rumor to excite the men and cause them to notice its absence) did not wear his sabre, which, to the soldiers, was proof positive that the report was true. They were soon informed that there was no truth in it, and the cheers that then went up were ample proof to the general of the love his men had for him.

General T. Kilby Smith reports that when he was ordered to proceed to Springfield Landing with the transports he applied to one of the quartermasters of the Department of the Gulf for permission to place some of his troops on one of his boats, but was refused because the room was needed for cotton. To show General A. J. Smith's utter detestation of this cotton mania, I will relate an incident: I reported to him one day that there was a cotton mill inside our lines filled with cotton belonging to a man who was a cavalry officer in the Southern army, and who, during General Banks's occupancy of the country a year or two before, had claimed to be a Union man and, as such, had received protection. He told me to go to Captain Hough (his adjutant general) and tell him to issue me an order to burn it. I did so, and the captain handed me a box of matches without saying a word, but with a significant twinkle in his eye. I returned to the general and, showing him the matches, told him that was my order. He looked at me and said: "Go and execute your order," which I did. I do not mean to say that no cotton was taken except by the army, for the navy took possession of a large quantity.

The dam being finished, on the morning of May 13 a sight was witnessed in Alexandria which can never be forgotten by those who stood on the banks of Red River. A sight, novel and exciting—the passage of the gunboats over the falls. As they passed one by one through the narrow gap between the two wings of the dam, where the water was rushing and seething, and plunged down over the falls, each one as it reached a place of safety below, being cheered by thousands of soldiers who lined the banks, was a grand sight, and was not only appreciated by us for its novelty, but also because it set us free, and we could now shake off the feeling of depression, humiliation, and wasting of time under which we were living. During this day the advance of General Banks's army left Alexandria by the river road. As they were leaving a fire broke out in the city which destroyed a large part of it, although every effort was made to extinguish it by the officers, soldiers, and citizens. General Smith and staff remained in Alexandria until late in the afternoon, then rode out to Governor Moore's, where his troops were still spread out like a fan, keeping the enemy at bay. We remained there in camp that night and early next morning took up our line of march so as to fall in the rear of General Banks's column. As we marched down the bank of the river—side by side with the boats—we were fired at occasionally from the opposite bank, but not much harm ensued.

On May 15 the whole column came to a halt—the enemy had appeared in front in force, and the prospect of a fight was good—and orders came back from General Banks to General Smith to bring his command to the front. As the Thirteenth and Nineteenth corps drew off on the left of the road we passed to the front, and while do so many jokes were passed between the soldiers of the different corps at this "change of base."

When we reached the front we found the cavalry skirmishing with and driving the enemy. As it was now about dark, we went into camp half way between Fort De Russy and Marksville. Captain Hough and I rode down to the ruins of the fort and there found a gunboat from the Mississippi River (our own fleet not having arrived). We were gladly welcomed on board and spent a very pleasant hour with the officers, giving them the news from the interior and receiving news from the outside world.

Next morning, as we entered upon the beautiful open prairie (Avoyelle), the cavalry drove the enemy's pickets through Marksville, and we found the enemy posted in the edge of the woods bordering the prairie, from which they opened upon us with twelve or fifteen pieces of artillery. Our whole force (from 20,000 to 25,000 men, having been increased by the garrison of Alexandria and reinforcements) were brought out in battle line on the prairie—General Emory on the left and General Smith on the right. Our artillery replied, and for two or three hours there was as lively an artillery duel as one would wish to see. We were about one mile apart and, although shot and shell flew unpleasantly near, yet very few persons were killed or wounded.

As our forces slowly advanced and changed position from time to time—all in plain view—it was the grandest battle scene, without its horrors, I ever saw. As we neared the woods and sent out skirmishers, among them were some Indians from a Minnesota or Wisconsin regiment, who were unerring shots with the rifle. Whether it was the result of their skill or the artillery practice I don't know, but the enemy fled and swung around to our rear and our army resumed its march, General Smith falling in in his old place—the rear. We had no further annoyance from our foe that day. Next day (May 17), however, they made their appearance, and once they pressed us so hard that General Smith halted his men, formed a battle line and received them with his artillery, but after a few shots they passed out of sight. That afternoon we arrived and encamped at the fort on Yellow Bayou, within three miles of Simmsport, on the Atchafalaya River, and as we were going into camp we heard of the removal of General Banks from his command, having been superseded by [Major General E. R. S.] Canby—since so treacherously murdered by the Modoc Indians.

The advance, under General Banks, having arrived at Simmsport, and there being no bridge over the Atchafalaya, Lieutenant Colonel Bailey (who built the dam at Alexandria) at once proceeded to improvise a bridge from the transports which had also arrived there. The river at that point is about one-third of a mile in width. Transports sufficient in number to span the river were placed side by side and fastened together by ropes, and across their decks the army marched.

In the meantime (on the eighteenth), General Smith's command was in battle line at Yellow Bayou, and during that afternoon the enemy, under Prince Polignac, made the most impetuous, spirited attack upon us that had bee made during the whole campaign. It seemed to be, and was, their last dying effort; but for dash and spirit it equalled any attack of [Lieutenant General Nathan B.] Forrest, who was well known for his impetuosity.

The "prince general" undoubtedly thought we were in a trap, and a bold fight on his part would furnish them with prisoners and material of war enough to well repay the Confederate army for their long rear chase, but most woefully were they disappointed.

General Smith was at Simmsport, and not in the fight. General Mower was in command of our troops and the Battle of Yellow Bayou was his fight, and well did he sustain his reputation as a fighting general. I cannot speak of this battle from personal experience, as I was with General Smith at Simmsport, witnessing the building of the bridge of boats. Word did not reach us that there was fighting until nearly dark, the sound of artillery having been deadened by the noise of bridge building, although once or twice we thought we heard artillery firing. We then road out to the bayou, but the fight was over, and the battlefield was lighted up by about one-half acre of tall dead pine trees on fire from the bursting of one of our caissons, which had been exploded by one of the enemy's shells. We had about 250 men in killed and wounded and had taken 220 prisoners. Among our wounded was Colonel Lynch, Fifty-eighth Illinois, commanding brigade, whom we passed on our way to the bayou, coming in in an ambulance with one leg crushed by a ball. The number of our killed and wounded in the short space of an hour or two is good evidence of the fierceness of the attack and the desperate reception they met, ending in the repulse of the enemy, who were driven from the field with a loss of about 450 killed and wounded, in addition to the prisoners captured.

General Smith's troops remained at Yellow Bayou during the nineteenth, while the Army of the Gulf crossed the Atchafalaya, and on May 20 the Army of the Tennessee crossed over, after which the bridge dissolved into boats again, and started for the Mississippi River to meet us. As we reached the east bank of the Atchafalaya I saw for the first time General Canby, our new commander, and also heard the good news that General Smith had been commissioned a major general.

On May 21 we marched over the strip of land between the Atchafalaya and Mississippi rivers, where we met our boats, and on the twenty-second were on our way to Vicksburg, where we arrived on May 24—the Thirteenth and Nineteenth corps in the meantime going to New Orleans.

45

A Question of Command at Franklin

Generals David S. Stanley and Jacob D. Cox, and Colonel Henry Stone

A NOTE FROM GENERAL STANLEY

There appears in *The Century Magazine* for August 1887 [reprinted in *Battles and Leaders,* volume four], an article by Colonel Henry Stone on [General John Bell] Hood's campaign in Tennessee in general, and the Battle of Franklin in particular, in which there are two errors to which I deem it proper to call attention.

On page 603 of the magazine Colonel Stone states: "Beyond Ruger, reaching from the ravine to the river below, was [Brigadier General Nathan] Kimball's division of the Fourth Corps—all veterans—consisting of three brigades, commanded by [Brigadier] Generals William Grose and Walter C. Whitaker and Colonel [Isaac M.] Kirby. *All the troops in the works were ordered to report to [Major General Jacob D.] Cox, to whom was assigned the command of the defenses.*" The italics are mine.

Colonel Stone did not view these statements from the standpoint of an officer well informed as to the rights of command. Had he done so he would have seen that General Cox was in reality only the commander of a division of the Twenty-third (Major General John M. Schofield's) Corps, that for the time being he was in command of that corps, that "all the troops in the works" could not have been ordered to report to him without removing me from the command of the Fourth Corps, and that no one will claim that the latter idea was ever thought of by any one.

Colonel Stone personally knew very little about the matter he described, and perhaps is excusable to some extent, as he easily could have been led into making this misstatement by General Cox himself; for the latter, in the book written by him entitled *The March to the Sea: Franklin and Nashville*, on page 86 complacently styles himself "commandant upon the line."

Headquarters Army of the Ohio,
Franklin, Tenn., Nov. 30, 1864.

General Kimball: The Commanding General directs that you report with your command to Brigadier General J. D. Cox for position on the line today. Very respectfully,
J. A. Campbell,
Major and A.A.G.

This so-called order was as informal as a written order well could be, and was simply a direction to General Kimball as to where he could find information as to the place to which he had been assigned.

General Schofield, in a letter to me of September 5, 1887, says in reference to the order: "*My recollection is, and I infer the same from their language, that the orders had reference solely to the posting of the troops on the designated line.*"

If General Schofield had directed General Kimball to report with his command to one of General Schofield's aides de camp for position on the line, that aide de camp could have asserted that he was "the commandant upon the line" with as much propriety as General Cox has now done.

The order, on its face, clearly indicates to a military person, even though he were ignorant of the facts, that the direction was given only for the temporary purpose therein stated.

An orderly or a guide might have been sent to show General Kimball where he was to go, but it is usual to transmit important orders by an officer, and

General Cox was the one selected by General Schofield; and in order that there might be no mistake that it was by his order, General Schofield sent the memorandum order to General Kimball.

The Twenty-third (Schofield's) Corps consisted of Cox's and two brigades of [Brigadier General Thomas H.] Ruger's division, and was the first corps to arrive on the field, about daylight, and was followed in about three hours by the Fourth (Stanley's) Corps, composed of Kimball's, [Brigadier General George D.] Wagner's, and [Brigadier General Thomas J.] Wood's divisions. General Kimball's division was the lading division of the Fourth Corps, and it was quite natural that General Schofield should direct General Cox—who had been on the ground since daylight—to show General Kimball his position in line, and having done this, his authority ceased; and this brief authority, little as it was, only lasted a few minutes, and had entirely ceased long before the battle was commenced, and could not warrant the statement that General Cox was "commandant upon the line" even for a minute.

So far as I know and believe, General Cox gave no orders to the Fourth Corps after showing General Kimball where he was to go. It should have made very little difference if he had attempted to assume the authority to give orders, as my division commanders, knowing he could not have had authority to give orders, would have paid no attention to them.

The following is a copy of a letter from General Schofield, which was written in reply to one I wrote to him concerning the misleading statement of Colonel Stone's:

Headquarters, Division of the Atlantic
Governor's Island, New York City,
September 5, 1887

General D. S. Stanley, Department of Texas,
San Antonio, Texas

Dear General: Your letter of August 29 was received here September 3. From my best recollection and from examination of my records, I have no doubt General Cox quotes in the appendix to his *Franklin and Nashville* the only orders given by me at Franklin which could be construed as placing any part of your corps, the Fourth, under his command. Those orders directed General Kimball, commanding your lead division, and Captain [Lyman] Bridges, with four batteries of artillery, to report to General Cox "for position on the line."

Those orders were given in the morning, when you were understood to be with your rear guard retarding the advance of the enemy, and hence not at the head of your column. My recollection is, and I infer the same from their language, that the orders had reference solely to the position of the troops on the designated line, as they arrived at Franklin, under the direction of General Cox, who was the senior officer then present at that point. How those orders were construed by General Cox I do not know, though I observe that he refers to himself as "the commandant upon the line," by which I suppose he may mean simply the senior officer actually present there at the moment.

Of course it was not intended by me to deprive you at any time of the command of any portion of your corps which might be within reach of your orders. But you will doubtless recall the fact that the movement of the enemy which we had most reason to guard against was not a direct attack in front at Franklin, but one to strike our flank and rear by crossing the Harpeth above that point, and it was necessary to be prepared for either or both of those attacks. Hence it could not have been known in the morning, when those orders were issued, whether you would be in the afternoon on the line south of Franklin with Cox, or on the north side of the river and several miles from Franklin with [Major General James H.] Wilson, resisting Hood's attempt to cross the river; nor what portion of your corps would, in the latter case, be with you, and what portion would have to remain with Cox. Therefore the orders given relative to the temporary posting of your troops in the morning could have had nothing to do with the question of your command of any of them in any battle which did occur, or might have occurred, in the afternoon. The latter question would have been determined in either case by the One Hundred Twenty-second Article of War, which is applicable in all such cases.

As the enemy chose the direct attack in front at Franklin, you of course remained in command, except perhaps for a moment, of all your troops engaged in resisting that attack, while I assumed *immediate* command, during the battle, of Wood's division of your corps, which had been stationed on the north bank of the river in readiness to support Wilson, and hence was beyond the reach of your orders while you were engaged in the battle on the south side of the river. I observe that Cox says, "The commandants of the two corps (you and he) met on the turnpike just as [Colonel Emerson] Opdycke and his men were rushing to the front." Assuming this to be exact, there must have been a moment of time before that meeting when Cox had the authority, and it was his duty, to order your reserve brigade (Opdycke's) into action; not by reason of any order I had given, but under the authority and duty imposed upon him by the One Hundred Twenty-second Article of War. In respect to your being with me on the north side of the river before the battle, I say most emphatically that was your proper place. The usual preparations for battle on the south side of the river had long since been made. The vital question remaining was to meet in line any attempt of the enemy in force to cross the river above. The moment such attempt was known it would have been your duty to lead Wood's division, followed by Kimball's, and in turn by such other troops as I should judge necessary and expedient, as rapidly as possible in support of Wilson. To do this without delay it was necessary for you to be where you were. And as soon as it became known that Hood had decided to make the attack in front, you rode to that point as rapidly as possible. What more could a corps commander do?

Thoughtless critics seem to assume that all the corps commanders of an army ought to be together at the point where the enemy chooses to make an attack. But I do not think any intelligent reader of military history will question the propriety of your conduct at Franklin.

It has not seemed to me that General Cox intended to do you any injustice. Yet he evidently wrote his account of the events which actually happened without giving so much thought, as you must necessarily have done, to those other probable events which did not happen, and in which, if they had, you would have been called upon to act by far the most important part. All the soldiers of an army can't act the same part in the same battle, nor any soldier the same part in any two consecutive battles.

That Cox happened to form the curtain of the main line at Franklin was because you had done the most vital service all the previous day and night. You acted nobly the part assigned you, so did also Cox. The honor gained was enough for both. I hope there will be no difference between you.

Inclosed you will find an extract from a letter on this subject written by me to General Cox from Rome, Italy, December 5, 1881.

Yours very truly,

J. M. Schofield

Again, Colonel Stone states in his article in *The Century,* on page 605, "Meantime, General Schofield had retired to the fort, on a high bluff on the other side of the river, some two miles away, by the road, and had taken General Stanley with him."

This statement is erroneous. The facts are that General Schofield's headquarters were not over three-quarters of a mile from the nearest point of our main line.

Before it was certainly known that there was to be an attack, I was with him and went to the front as soon as the firing commenced. When it began General Schofield, who was not far away, came forward to Fort Granger on the bluff, within a quarter of a mile of the nearest line, where he could see the whole field, which was the proper place for him to be.

The following letter from General Kimball fully corroborates the foregoing, as does also my report of the battle which will be published in a future volume of the War Records:

Ogden, Utah, May 22, 1888

General D. S. Stanley,
U.S. Army, San Antonio, Texas

Dear General: I am in receipt of your letter of the twelfth instant, with the printed correspondence. Referring to the battle at Franklin, Tennessee, on November 30, 1864, I have to say that I did not receive any order or other command from General Cox on that day or during the battle, excepting the direction given me as to the position my division was to occupy in the line of battle. I was directed in orders from General Schofield, commanding the army, to "report to General Cox for position on the line today." My division was in the lead of our corps from Spring Hill, and the first to arrive at Franklin inside the line already formed by the troops of General Cox's command (Cox's and Ruger's divisions, Twenty-third Corps). While waiting your arrival with the other divisions of your command, and your orders as to our positions in line of battle, General Cox requested me to form on his right; but not knowing what might be your orders in relation to positions to be occupied by your divisions I was somewhat slow in complying with his request, but soon afterwards, and before your arrival, I received the orders from General Schofield above alluded to. Complying, I immediately formed my division on the line indicated by General Cox, my left forming his right near the locust grove and west of Carter's house, my line extending westward until my right rested near the river below the town, and in this position you found me upon your arrival; and when I informed you of General Cox's request and of General Schofield's order, and my action in the matter, you approved, and directed me to remain in line as formed and to hold it, which I did during the battle and until our withdrawal after midnight by order of General Schofield.

I then understood that General Schofield had command of and directed the movements of our forces from Pulaski to and during the battle at Franklin, and thence to Nashville, and that you had command of the Fourth Corps, and Cox of the troops comprising the Twenty-third Corps. I received no orders from General Cox other than the direction as to my position in line heretofore mentioned; after that, none. I did not know that he was, or that he assumed to be, in command of our forces in line during that battle. I *know* that he did not command nor give me *any* directions during that battle. I had no orders from any officer until I received the order from General Schofield directing the withdrawal from Franklin and the retirement to Brentwood and Nashville. . . .

Very respectfully yours,
Nathan Kimball

D. S. Stanley,
Brigadier General, U.S. Army

REPLY BY GENERAL COX

I have hitherto believed that General Stanley and myself were in entire accord as to the facts of the Battle of Franklin. The reasons are as follows: In August 1881, when I was preparing to write the volume in the Scribner war series of histories entitled *The March to the Sea: Franklin and Nashville*, General Stanley opened a correspondence with me, kindly offering to assist me by the loan of papers, etc. In a letter dated Cincinnati, August 24, 1881, thankfully accepting the offer, I took the opportunity to compare our recollections of the principal facts. I wrote:

Let me state a few consecutive points within my own memory and ask you to compare it with yours, premising that I have not yet begun the systematic review of the documents in my possession.

1. Two divisions of the Twenty-third Corps were present and acting under my command, Ruger's on the right of the Columbia Pike and my own (Brigadier General James A. Reilly commanding) on the left.

2. Schofield had only intended to cover the crossing of trains, and had not meant to fight south of the Harpeth. He had therefore ordered me to send my own artillery and wagons over the river early, and had arranged that Major [Wilbur F.] Goodspeed, your chief of artillery, should detail some batteries as your troops came in, and they reported to me.

3. After putting my own command in position, I reported to General Schofield that my troops were not sufficient to reach the river on the right, and that flank was consequently exposed. Kimball's division reported to me and was assigned that place.

4. I received a written dispatch from General Schofield saying that two brigades of Wagner's were out as rear guard, and one (Opdycke's) would report within the lines to act as my reserve; that Wagner was ordered to bring the other two brigades in whenever Hood showed a purpose of serious attack. I showed this note to Wagner and found he had such orders.

5. When Hood formed and advanced, Wagner did not order in the two brigades, but ordered them to fight. One of my staff, still living, heard him send the order from the Carter house. In his excitement he had forgotten his orders apparently, and did not change, though reminded of them.

6. Being at the left of the line on the parapet, watching the enemy's advance, I was amazed to see Wagner's two brigades open fire. They were quickly run over by the enemy and came back in confusion.

7. I immediately sent an aide to Opdycke to warn him to be ready to advance in case of a break at the center, and to order the commandants of brigades to withhold their fire till Wagner's men should get in. The two aides who were with me are both dead, one being killed while performing part of the above duty. Opdycke afterward told me that he got no order and acted on his own judgment, and I have accepted that as the fact.

8. I almost immediately followed my order and rode to the pike. There I met Opdycke advancing, and met you also. We all went forward together. When Opdycke reached the parapet you and I were trying to rally the fugitives immediately in rear of the line. While thus employed you were wounded, and your horse was also hit. You asked me to look at the hurt, and I urged you to go and have surgical attention to it. I dismounted Captain [Edward E.] Tracy, one of my aides, and gave you my horse, which he was riding. To say anything *here* of the impression your conduct made on me would violate the old maxim about "praise to face."

9. Opdycke and the artillery continued to act under my orders till we left the lines at midnight. Orders to the rest of Wagner's division and to Kimball went from your headquarters, you continuing in command of the Fourth Corps till we got back to Nashville, notwithstanding your hurt.

As I have already said, I have not yet begun the collation of documents; but I have taken advantage of your kind letter to give the above outline, and to ask for any illustration, correction, or addition which may occur to you, so that I may give careful attention to any point on which my memory should differ from yours.

To this General Stanley replied from Fort Clark, Texas, under date of October 17, 1881, saying, among other things: "The nine points submitted in your letter are, to the best of my memory, exactly correct. I think it may be true that Opdycke did not receive your order. When I arrived at the left of his brigade the men were just getting to their feet, as they had been lying down, I presume to avoid the enemy's bullets."

This outline, thus explicitly agreed upon, is that which I followed in the volume referred to. The use of the designation "commandant upon the line" means, of course, as the context shows, the line south of the Harpeth River, upon which Hood made his principal attack. I may say, with the utmost sincerity, that my personal relation to that line is so clearly shown in the "nine points" that I did not regard the use of the designation as making any claim, but only as a periphrase to avoid repetition of the author's own name in a narrative written in the third person. I should be quite content to have the reader substitute the proper name for the phrase.

I should be equally indifferent to the conclusion that the command I exercised was by virtue of an Article of War instead of by the orders of General Schofield, if it were not that, both from clear memory and many circumstances, I have always felt personally sure that my mode of statement was the true one. The order to the batteries to supply the place of mine, already sent over the river, was identical in form to that to General Kimball. If it put these under my command, it had the same effect in the other case. It had been one of the liveliest surprises of my life to learn that anybody took a different view of the matter.

General Stanley came to the center of the Twenty-third Corps line, on the Columbia Turnpike, when Wagner's two brigades of the Fourth Corps came through it in their retreat. In rallying those brigades he was wounded, and went back to his quarters north of the river. With the exception of those few minutes, there is complete agreement that I was the senior officer on that line from daylight in the morning till midnight, and the agreed "nine points" show whether this was merely nominal.

The same "points" had settled the fact that I sent no orders to Kimball's division during the actual engagement; but it may be proper now to add that no one else did, the original directions to hold the re-curved extension of our right proving to be all that were necessary.

If any statement of mine could fairly be interpreted to derogate from the full personal command of General Schofield over the whole army, I should indeed feel that it needed correction. In the volume referred to I said, what I have always repeated, that his position in the fort north of the river was almost the only one from which he could survey and guide the whole field. My duty was simply to perform faithfully the part assigned me. The fortune of war brought it about that Hood attacked the Twenty-third Corps line, instead of turning it, as would have been wiser strategy for him. In the latter event no doubt General Stanley would have been in the critical place, and mine would have been comparatively insignificant. It is also true that General Schofield *could* have ordered me to report to General Stanley as my senior, as he ordered portions of the Fourth Corps to report to me; but *he did not*, and I have tried to narrate history as it was, not as it might have been.

Jacob D. Cox,
Major General, U.S.V.

REPLY BY COLONEL STONE

I shall make no other reply to General Stanley's criticism than to quote from the official report.

General Schofield, whose report is dated December 31, 1864, says: "General J. D. Cox deserves a very large share of the credit for the brilliant victory at Franklin. The troops were placed in position and entrenched under his immediate direction, and *the greater portion of the line engaged was under his command during the battle.*"

Of the sixty-two regiments in "the line engaged" only twenty-four belonged to the Twenty-third Corps that day. The rest were of the Fourth Corps, of which General Stanley was commander.

General Kimball, a division commander in the Fourth Corps, whose report is dated December 5, says that he sent a regiment to report to General Ruger *at the request of General Cox.* This shows that he then recognized General Cox as in command.

General Opdycke, commanding a brigade of the Fourth Corps, states in his report that about 4:00 P.M. General Cox sent him a request to have his brigade ready, and adds, "I got no other orders till after the battle."

General Ruger, commanding a division in the Twenty-third Corps, states in his report that he was ordered to report to General Cox.

General Wagner, of the Fourth Corps, makes no mention of reporting to any one after reaching his final position.

These are all the commanders of all the troops engaged, except General Cox's own division.

On December 2, General Cox made a full and detailed report, in which he says:

> About noon (of November 30) General Kimball, commanding the first division, Fourth Corps, *reported to me by order of the commanding general.* . . . About 1:00 P.M., General Wagner, commanding Second Division of the Fourth Corps, *reported to me his division* . . . and informed me that he was under orders to keep out two brigades until the enemy should make advance in line in force, when he was to retire, skirmishing, and become a reserve to the line established by me. . . . Captain Bridges (Fourth Corps artillery) *was ordered by the commanding general to report to me with three batteries.* . . . About 2:00 P.M. the enemy . . . came into full view. . . . The fact was reported to the commanding general, as well as the disposition of our own troops as they were, and his orders received in reference to holding the position.

In a subsequent report, covering the same ground, under date of January 10, 1865, General Cox says: "At 2:00 P.M. . . . . General Wagner *presented orders to report to me.* . . . At 3:00 P.M. . . . . the order was reiterated to General Wagner to withdraw his brigade. . . . He was at that time in person near the Carter house, my headquarters."

I leave these quotations to speak for themselves. Nothing was further from my intention than to do even a seeming injustice to General Stanley—one of the most gallant, capable, and experienced soldiers in the army. The value of his services during the retreat from Pulaski to Nashville is inestimable. His conduct that day, and all days, was that of a brave, resolute, able commander.

As to the distance between the fort to which General Schofield retired and the battleground, I may add that from careful measurement on the maps, from personal observation within a few years, and from the estimates of residents of Franklin, I see no reason to doubt the correctness of my statement that it was "some two miles, by the road." Of course, in an air line it is much less.

Henry Stone,
Brevet Colonel, U.S.V.

PART 10

Fireside and Field of Battle

46

"Little Jim," the Pride of the Regiment
Harry M. Kieffer, Drummer Boy,
One Hundred Fiftieth Pennsylvania

THE PET-MAKING disposition was quite natural, and therefore very general among the men of all commands. Pets of any and all kinds, whether chosen from the wild or the domestic animals, were everywhere in great esteem, and happy was the regiment which possessed a tame crow, squirrel, coon, or even a kitten.

Our own regiment had a pet of great value and high regard in "Little Jim," of whom some incidental mention has already been made. As Little Jim enlisted with the regiment, and was honorably mustered out with it at the close of the war, after three years of as faithful service as so little a creature as he could render to the flag of his country, some brief account of him here may not be amiss.

Little Jim, then, was a small rat terrier of fine blooded stock, his immediate maternal ancestor having won a silver collar in a celebrated rat pit in Philadelphia. Late in 1859, while yet a pup, he was given by a friend to John C. Kensill, with whom he was mustered into the United States service "for three years, or during the war," on Market Street, Philadelphia, Pennsylvania, August 1862. Around his neck was a silver collar with the inscription, "Jim Kensill, Co. F, One Hundred Fiftieth Regt. P.V."

He soon came to be a great favorite with the boys, not only of his own company, but of the entire regiment as well, the men of the different companies thinking quite as much of him as if he belonged to each of them individually, and not to Sergeant Kensill alone. On the march he would often be caught up from the roadside where he was trotting along, and given a ride on the arms of the men, who would pet and talk to him as if he were a child and not a dog. In winter quarters, however, he would not sleep anywhere except on Kensill's arm and underneath the blankets; nor was he ever known to spend a night away from home. On first taking the field, rations were scarce with us, and for several days fresh meat could not be had for poor Jim, and he nearly starved. Gradually, however, his master taught him to take a hardtack between his fore paws and, holding it there, to munch and crunch at it till he had consumed it. He soon learned to like hardtack, and grew fat on it, too. On the march to Chancellorsville he was lost for two whole days, to the great grief of the men. When his master learned that he had been seen with a neighboring regiment, he started off in search of him at once. As soon as Jim heard his owner's sharp whistle, he came bounding and barking to his side, overjoyed to be at home again, albeit he had lost his collar, which his thievish captors had cut from his neck in order the better to lay claim to him.

He was a good soldier, too, being no coward and caring not a wag of his tail for the biggest shells the Johnnies could toss over at us. He was with us under our first shell fire at "Clarke's Mills," a few miles below Fredericksburg, in May, 1863, and ran after the very first shell that came screaming over our heads. When the shell had buried itself in the ground, Jim went up close to it, crouching down on all fours, while the boys cried, "Rats! Rats! Shake him, Jim! Shake him, Jim!" Fortunately that first shell did not explode, and when others came that did explode, Jim, with true military instinct, soon learned to run after them and bark, but to keep a respectful distance from them.

On the march to Gettysburg he was with us all the way; but when we came near the enemy his master sent him back to William Wiggins, the wagoner, as he thought too much of Jim to run the risk of losing him in battle. It was a pity Jim wasn't with us out in front of the seminary the morning of the first day, when the fight opened; for as soon as the cannon began to boom the rabbits began to run in all directions, as if scared out of their poor little wits; and there would have been fine sport for Jim, had he been there.

In the first day's fight, Jim's owner, Sergeant John C. Kensill, while bravely leading the charge for the recapture of the One Hundred Forty-ninth Pennsylvania Regiment's battle flags was wounded and left for dead on the field, with a bullet through his head. He, however, so far recovered from his wound that in October following he rejoined the regiment, which was then lying down along the Rappahannock. In looking for the regiment, on his return from a northern hospital, Sergeant Kensill chanced to pass the wagon train, and saw Jim busy at a bone under a wagon. Hearing a familiar whistle, Jim at once looked up, saw his master, left his bone, and came leaping and barking in greatest delight to his owner's arm.

On the march he was sometimes sent back to the wagon. Once he came near being killed. To keep him from following the regiment, or from straying away in search of it, the wagoner had tied him to the rear axle of his wagon with a strong cord. In crossing a stream, in his anxiety to get his team over safely, the wagoner forgot all about poor little Jim, who was dragged and slashed through the waters in a most unmerciful way. After getting over, the teamster, looking back, found poor Jim under the rear of the wagon, being dragged along by the neck, and more dead than alive. He was then put on the sick list for a few days, but with this single exception never had a mishap of any kind.

His master having been honorably discharged before the close of the war because of wounds, Jim was left in the regiment in care of Wiggins, the wagoner. When the regiment was mustered out of service at the end of the war, Little Jim was mustered out too. He stood up in rank with the boys, and wagged his tail for joy that peace had come and that his discharge papers were regularly made out, the same as those of the men, and that they read thus:

> To all whom it may concern. Know ye, that *Jim Kensill,* Private, Co. F, One Hundred Fiftieth Regiment, Penna. Vols., who was enrolled on the twenty-second day of August, one thousand eight hundred and sixty-two, to serve three years or during the war, is hereby DISCHARGED from the service of the United States, this twenty-third day of June, 1865, at Elmira, New York, by direction of the Secretary of War.
>
> (No objection to his being reenlisted is known to exist) Said *Jim Kensill* was born in Philadelphia, in the State of Pennsylvania, is six years of age, six inches high, dark complexion, black eyes, black-and-tan hair, and by occupation when enrolled a rat-terrier.
>
> Given at Elmira, New York, this twenty-third day of June, 1865.
>
> James R. Reid,
>
> Capt. Tenth U.S. Inf'y, A.C.M.

Before parting with him, the boys bought him a silver collar, which they had suitably inscribed, and which, having honorably earned in the service of his country in war, he proudly wore in peace to the day of his death.

47

They Followed the Army: The Anguish of Runaway Slaves
John Walton, Lieutenant, Twenty-fifth Ohio Infantry

ON THE NIGHT of February 25, 1865, the Twenty-fifth Ohio Volunteers were ordered to prepare to enter Charleston in the morning. We were encamped on the Ashley river within sight of St. Michael's Church spire. We had been marching for many days along the Savannah and Charleston Railroad,

Contrabands Following the Federal Army (*St. Nicholas*)

occasionally encountering small parties of rebel cavalry, outriders upon the flank of the army then hastily evacuating the Palmetto City. Night had closed around us when we reached our camping place near the river, and it was not until I had eaten such supper as the colonel's cook had prepared that I was enabled to start for [Brigadier General John P.] Hatch's headquarters to report the incidents of the day, that being one of my duties as adjutant of the regiment. Hatch and his staff had taken possession of a deserted plantation house, about two miles away, on the river road, and the ride along the quiet highway, between rows of magnolia trees, was very pleasant in the cool air of the bright, clear night. About a mile to my left I could see the campfires of the One Hundred Fifty-seventh New York, and further up the river the lights of other camps; but for more than a mile the road was deserted, and I encountered no living thing, until I became aware of sounds in front, which rose and fell upon my ears like the wail of crying children.

I touched my horse with my spurs and rode rapidly forward in the direction of the sounds, which became louder as I advanced, until, upon turning a short bend in the road, my ears were greeted with a scream of such hopeless and bitter agony that my horse shied so quickly as to almost throw me into the hedge. I dismounted at once, and leading my horse, went forward to a scene, the like of which, although for five years I had encountered distress in every special kind of misery, I had never seen, and to think of which fills my heart with pain, after all these years.

On the grass by the side of the road lay the dead body of an old colored woman, and sitting by her side was a colored girl, whose age was about twenty-six years, holding tightly in her arms a little Negro child aged about ten or eleven years, rocking herself backward and forward, both moaning and crying in a perfect abandonment of grief. It was some time before I could arouse the girl sufficiently to get her to tell me their story, and it was very difficult for me to understand the mixture of French *patois* and Negro dialect in which she told me, between many outbursts of pitiful grief, the cause of their mighty trouble.

They had been slaves, living near Beaufort, and when our division marched up the coast, the old mother with her two daughters, like thousands of others of that unhappy race, had followed in the wake of the army ever after to be "Loose an' free." Their sole possessions, the girl told me, consisted of an extra cotton dress for each, which they had tied in a bundle and carried with them.

Their privations had been great, sleeping under the trees each night, almost the whole night without food, always dreading capture and return into slavery, trudging along in the rear of the army, their minds filled with hope of a blessed rest at last in that land where all were free. Each day the feeble old woman became weaker and less able to endure the fatigue of the endless journey, until that evening they sat down to rest within sight of the steeples of the great city where I found them. She said that her mother had been very weak and ill during the day, and they all were suffering from hunger, the child crying for something to eat, and a number of soldiers passing she begged that they would give her a trifle of food for her sick mother and starving sister. They had laughed at her and insulted her, and one cowardly brute had struck her, while another took their bundle of clothing, being all they had in the world, and all went laughing down the road.

This left them poor indeed, and she told me that she cried aloud at their desolation and tore her hair in her utter helplessness. She said that she did not know how it was, but when she noticed her mother again she was lying dead, as I found her—"loose an' free," indeed.

PART 11

The War in 1865

48

The Victory at Fort Fisher
John W. Ames, Brevet Brigadier General, U.S.V.

WHEN, AS A school boy, I used to read that "then Caesar crossed his entire army into cis-Alpine Gaul and went into winter quarters," I felt the relief of winter quarters greatly. It was the end of a chapter, and consequently of the day's lesson, and release, for twenty-four hours, at least, from wearisome soldiering in a dead language. In later days of actual warfare and the wearisome campaigns of autumn, I learned a new significance in winter quarters. Know that winter quarters are more blessed to receive than to read about. Then Virginia roads are quagmires impassable; then flood, and frost, and snow, and ice, combine to form a danger more formidable than the enemy: artillery can not move; baggage, commissary, and ammunition-wagons must halt; human nature—even horse and mule nature—must avoid the exposure of an American winter, and seek for shelter. Winter quarters, then, are quarters of some transient permanence, of some comfort, of certain plenty and warmth. Earthworks shelter from the weather; chimneys are built, and fires crackle with the luxuriance of forests of free fuel. The Commissary Department becomes systematized into great efficiency by the fixed point of its delivery; mails, and news, and parcels from the North begin to flow more surely and steadily to the army as the route becomes worn smooth by custom, and sutlers practice extortion in newer and broader fields. But, greater than all, leaves of absence and furloughs are granted, and granted liberally. What sight of land is, after a long sea voyage; what recovery is to a sick man; what pardon is to a criminal—this, or something like this, a leave of absence is to a soldier. Blessed were the fifteen days in which to leave desolation and the army behind, and look once more upon inhabited houses, fields unravaged, fair cities, womanhood, friends, home! Back again then with new uniforms, and new resolves, and new hearts and hopes.

Out of the slime and pestilence of Dutch Gap Canal, and beyond the field of unburied dead at New Market Heights, came visions of the rude comforts

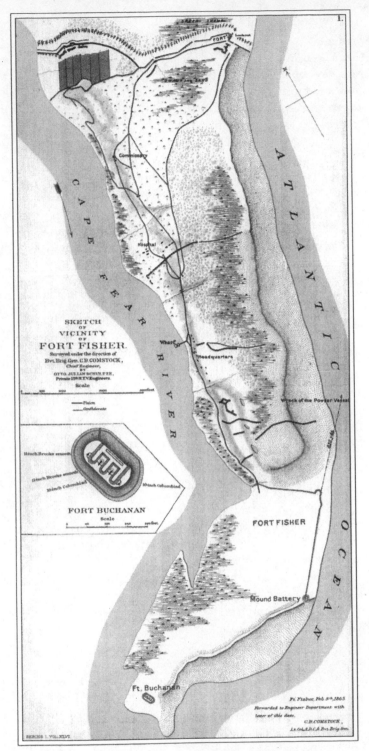

Sketch of Vicinity of Fort Fisher (*Atlas; Official Records*)

of the winter log camps, and the sweet and blessed prospect of the week's run to the North. And, in spite of the fine weather of the first days of December 1864, the dreams and hopes of many blossomed into fruition and fact. From the Weldon Railroad to the cavalry out-posts at Chaffin's Bluff—along the whole of the vast entrenched line—there began now to be daily departures northward.

But all leave applications from one or two brigades of the Army of the James seemed unaccountably to come to naught in official pigeon holes, or to be returned with the hackneyed "exigencies of the service." And just as this striking proof of official ill-will toward the excluded brigades became fairly noticeable, the explanation came in the embarkation of these troops on the first Fort Fisher expedition. Then the sea tossing and the winter quarters off Cape Hatteras; the failure and the return; the debarkation at the old landing place, and the march by night through ice, and mud, and water to the desolate old camping grounds.

One day to shake off the sea, to scour the salt rust off musket barrels, to drain the water out of the camp hollows, to build up again the fallen huts and chimneys; another to write in due form, with the necessary military persiflage, the inevitable application for a leave; then to lobby it through, waiting in general's ante-chambers, and button holing the beleaguered adjutant with explanations of its real necessity. Two days only of actual foothold on the firm earth, when all aspirations for the sweet North are rudely nipped by blank refusal of all applications, and the substitution of the ruder order to "march in two hours."

This came on the third of January, 1865, and to the same troops that had landed from the first expedition late on the last night of the old year. All granted leaves—if any had been granted—were countermanded, and before sunset we were again marching over the now frozen ground toward the landing at Bermuda. In the interval, [Major General Benjamin] Butler had been relieved from command of the Army of the James, but so promptly were we pushed forward and embarked that we only fairly learned our new commander's name when we were on board the transports. It is worthy of remark that we went at once on board of the seagoing steamers, so that the delay of the transhipment at Old Point was avoided at the outset.

On the fifth, we passed Fortress Monroe with hardly a pause, and in the night steamed out through the gates of the Chesapeake into the stormy sea.

Winter reigned in triumph on the ocean, and for a week, at least, after passing Capes William and Henry, the wind blew in a prolonged and furious gale. All the terrors of Hatteras were in the ascendant, and our winter quarters were stormy and comfortless. An age of misery was compressed into a week of seasickness, as we almost vainly strove to buffet our way round the cape of storms. Cloudy skies, angry seas! this was the only prospect we could see, in the few and far between intervals of our escapes from the nauseous cabin to the quarterdeck.

But the seemingly endless struggle had its end at last. On the night of the eleventh, we had conquered the cape, and were running smoothly into the familiar offing of Beaufort harbor. Here we rendezvoused simply, not now needing the refitting that the former expedition required. [Major General Alfred H.] Terry only waited to find his whole force about him, and sailed before noon of the twelfth. It was a grand and inspiriting sight to see the long lines of vessels; the placid beauty of sea and sky banished seasickness and roused our hopes. The transport vessels sailed in a single line, each in the wake of its predecessor; the naval fleet formed two lines, one on each side of the transports—the three together stretching away to the southward with a perspective convergence somewhere at the horizon: a grand display of naval beauty, and symmetry, and power.

It is but a short sail from Beaufort to the mouth of Cape Fear River; we finished the run early in the night, and lay to for daylight. The navy meanwhile got herself into position, and turned her iron muzzles toward the fort—"her guns all shotted and her tompions out." The daylight found all ready, and wind and weather fairly beautiful—mild, balmy, and soft as spring.

This time—taught by the experience of a former effort—all the boats of the naval and transport vessels were put into the service of disembarking the infantry, while a few of the ironclads and monitors drew near the great serrated mass of Fort Fisher, and opened a majestic and leisurely cannonade to cover the landing and smother any effort from the fort to thwart our purpose. The boats, on approaching the line of surf, threw out small anchors and grapnels, and then let themselves wash shoreward on the wave that was rushing to break on the beach. When the undertow began to recede, one of the sailors jumped into the water and held the boat's stern against the seaward wash, while the armed passengers climbed over the sides into the knee-deep water, carrying knapsacks and the sacred ammunition high up on fixed bayonets, and ran for the shore, chased by the crested advance of the succeeding billow. No time to hesitate, after once leaving the boat; those who paused a moment, to square themselves for the run, or to settle their top-heavy muskets, were likely to pay for it in the souse of the approaching wave. On the dry, warm sand of the beach we emptied the water out of our shoes and wrung it out of the saturated lower garments, leaving them in the bright sunlight to dry, while we sat and watched the continued disembarking. This was exciting and amusing sport. The troops were evidently not of those who pass their summers at Newport or Long Branch, and they consequently brought to the disembarking an ignorance of the manners and customs of ocean waves that made the scene delightful and ludicrous. "Jump now," cautioned Jack, when the undertow was running out and the water at its shoalest [*sic*]; but many jumped so carefully and slowly that they were only fairly over the boat's side when the next wave had deepened the water to their necks or eyes. The presence of the unexpected is irritating to the actor in any such scene, but vastly amusing to the spectator. To step carefully into knee-deep water and find it suddenly somewhere over head and ears is unpleasant to experience, but very funny to see; or funnier still the complaisant pause of one unsuspicious of the coming rush of the liquid wall behind him, and the sudden upsetting of dignity and all hope of a dry landing by the blow of a wave that breaks about him and rolls him in toward the shore in its mass of foaming suds. The laughter grew into a roar that rivaled the noise of the breaking waves, and the landing became a scene of merriment that would have done no discredit to the jolliest of picnics. A picnic it was, too, in the feast of oysters furnished by the salt pool behind the beach; in the delight of being on firm earth, after one week off Hatteras; in the bright sunshine and beautiful weather; the grand naval display, with its holiday of bunting; the smooth and shelving beach; the rolling waves, and the swimming boats.

Before the troops were all landed, small fires of driftwood were crackling everywhere, coffee was boiling, and oysters roasting. By the middle of the afternoon, every infantryman was on shore, and from basking on the beach we were roused to the serious business of our presence on that coast. Regiments were gathered out of the chaos, rolls were called, and work began. The fort seemed close at hand, though really four miles away; but we were in such full view, and made so much martial display with regimental colors and the glitter of burnished musket barrels in the sunlight, that we wondered at the silence of the enemy and his apparent indifference to our proceedings. But with all our parade before him not a shot was bowled at us over the smooth beach from the sullen, silent walls.

The beach was perhaps two hundred yards wide, then came about two hundred more of the salt marshy pool, beyond which were the tall pines of the forest, with its undergrowth of the tangled vines and thorny bushes. With as broad a front as the beach gave us room for, we finally put the column of [Brigadier General Charles J.] Paines's division in march toward the fort—skirmishers in advance. About a mile of progress brought us to the head of the salt pool, and to the hour of sunset, as well. Here we turned away from the sea and marched to the right, into the darkness of the forest and the coming night. It was a low forest, full of the alternate grassy hammocks and wet places of marsh, with a tangled mass of vines and bushes. Our column front became strung out to a single file, winding with difficulty among trees and thickets, turning away from the deeper pools and fallen logs. It was hard to keep trace of the leader or to hold on to the points of compass, but we struggled on in the darkness, till, exhausted with the hard tramp, dripping with perspiration, and torn with thorns, we at last felt the sand growing firmer and drier under our feet. The line of struggling men, too, began to close up somewhat more compactly. At last, a gleam of open water through the trees, and the line soon compacted itself into a halt. We were on the bank of Cape Fear River.

The Cape Fear flows nearly parallel with the coastline of the ocean for some twenty miles or more above its mouth. At the point where we struck it—three miles above Fort Fisher—it was about a mile across from sea to river.

Our line was made as straight as the swampiness of the ground permitted, and faced toward Wilmington. A mile farther down, the division under [Brigadier General Adelbert] Ames was facing toward the fort and entrenching. At the order to entrench, we fell to, with coffee cups for shovels, and very soon had a mass of the soft sand put into semblance of an earthwork. But at midnight our left was thrown somewhat farther back, where a higher part of the river bank gave a more defensible position; and here an allowance of shovels—landed wisely by some how-to-do-it quartermaster—was dealt out, and the new line of earthworks soon became really formidable. Logs were gathered and staked into position for a revetment, and the sand was soon banked against it. A buzz of industry all along the line, lasting through the whole night, and by morning we had a line too formidable and too well protected by abatis to be rashly attacked. Strolling up and down the length of the growing line in the chill moonlight, from the placid expanse of the broad, baylike river to where the surf was breaking on the sea beach, we found a universal industry. Even the landing boats were still at work, ferrying through the surf, and piling the beach with stores of ammunition and provisions. Batteries of artillery were landed in the morning, and during the forenoon were got into position on the new lines.

So far we had let the fort severely alone, paying our whole attention to the establishment of a permanent foothold on the peninsula, and securing it against the possible attack of the enemy, and the chances of starvation. The position also gave us an outlook over the river, but the ship channel was too near the western shore of the broad river to be under the command of our field guns. The warmth and brightness of the next day—the fourteenth—atoned for the coldness of the night, soothing many of the night laborers into comfortable sleep under the blaze of sunlight. The whole day was taken up with the further landing of provisions, ammunition, and artillery, and in completing and improving the lines. Weariness and a feeling of security in the finished works made the day for the troops one of comparative rest. We relapsed into lazy criticism, which, though this time favorable to the steps so far taken, inclined to discredit the theory of an intended assault upon the fort. It was argued that, in occupying the peninsula, we were cutting off the fort from the land of its friends, and effectually extinguishing the Wilmington blockade-running. What more could the fall of Fort Fisher accomplish? This was fallacious reasoning, however, which hardly satisfied its authors, and which the next day's work disproved.

Next morning it fell to my lot to have charge of the picket line. My instructions from General Terry were to take charge of the pickets from the ocean on the right over to the river bank, thence down the river bank to the picket line of General Ames' division, and, in case of an advance by that division, to fill up the gap in the river picket line.

The warmth of spring was in the balmy air, and the tramp from the beautiful beach, through the resinous pines, was thoroughly enjoyable. No sign of any enemy in the Wilmington front; nothing but the beauty of the thorn bushes, the brightness of the sunshine, and the peaceful chirrup of birds. But from below came the gradually increasing thunder of the great naval guns opening their

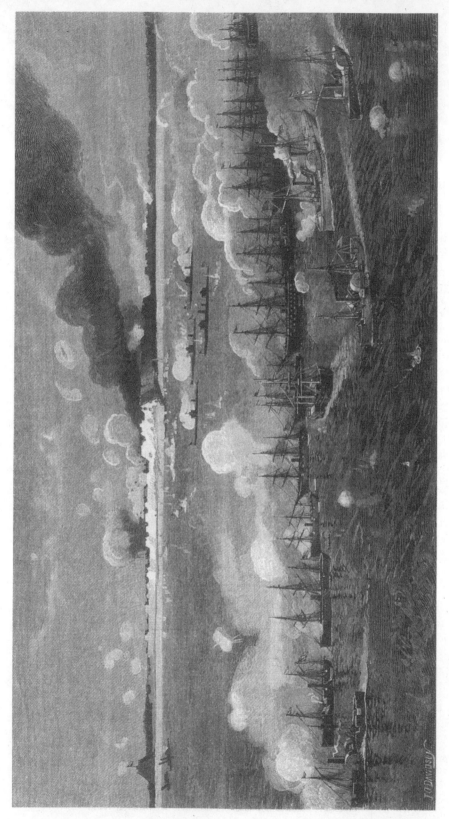

The Naval Bombardment of Fort Fisher (*Century*)

iron shower once more upon the doomed fort. Turning down the river bank, I passed across the end of our new entrenchments with the garrison of colored troops, and on down the narrowing peninsula. The river bank was six feet or more above the water, and the soil almost wholly white sea sand. The pines dwindled into shrubs, with thorn thickets in marshy places; and these again into bare, grassless ridges of sand, and shallow pools of water. A country road on the river bank ran apparently to the fort, though it was of older date, as several shabby Southern houses—one or two with some faint trace of small fields, as if agriculture had once spaded up the sand—stood along it. Strolling down the sandy road, I could see the masts of the naval fleet, the notched ridge of Fort Fisher, and then the hulls of vessels and squat turrets of the monitors, rise alternately above the lowland; while on the right the placid expanse of river reflected the glare of sunshine. Near the farther shore were several steam tugs busy moving to and fro between the various defenses of the river's mouth. But most attractive to the eye was the grandeur and beauty of the great naval fleet, her flags lazily flapping in the soft air, and her black guns putting forth their strength of destruction against the sandy fortress.

The uproar of the cannonade kept sea and shore in a tremor, which was fainter or stronger as lighter or heavier guns were discharged. And occasionally a jar like an earthquake shook the ground as the enormous guns of the iron-clads, lying very near the shore, gave tongue. The huge projectile itself was quite visible, leaping from the rolling masses of smoke at the gun's muzzle, through its deliberate rush to the end of its flight—an explosion near the fort, or silent burial in the soft sand. The noise of its slow passage through the air was a deep, hoarse roar that drowned the shriller scream of the smaller missiles.

From the constant noise and jar of the firing and the screaming of the flying shells, the volumes of gunpowder smoke, the movement of troops on the shore, it was evident, that, for better or worse, the mettle of Fort Fisher was to be put to a genuine test. The navy had got to work in terrible earnest, and had apparently extinguished the feeble effort of the fort to reply. But, though silent and sullen, the Rebel flags still fluttered, and the walls loomed huge and formidable through the smoke clouds. Once before the impregnable aspect alone of the great sand pile had driven off her foes, but now a new commander had brought back the same troops, and his reputation depended on his not blenching at a horrid front. A trial was to be made, and at once.

On approaching still nearer, I began to pass lines of men in battle array, but seated on the ground while waiting the order to advance. They were chatting and laughing indifferently, behaving, as troops before a battle always do behave, as far as my observation goes—that is, doing anything except indulging in the heroics of a grand moment or the prayers of an awful one. Passing down still nearer, and where now and then a *wide* shot from the ships exploded over their shore allies, I reached a low line of rifle pits, where were more soldiers, still busy with cards or luncheon, and indifferent to the coming moment. From near the end of this line of works, another rifle pit line ran over toward the sea, and at right-angles with the road and the first line. At the angle was a square, enclosed redoubt of sand, Rebel built. The nearer end of the hostile fort—where it touched the river—was perhaps eight hundred feet from this redoubt. The peninsula here was very low—merely a beach—and less than half a mile from sea to river. In the sand redoubt I found General Terry, the commander of our troops, with his staff, and General Ames, the latter just about to push on with his division to the assault.

With this grand war drama about to open before my eyes, it was impossible to resist the excitement of the moment, or the desire to see the opening of the assault; so I prolonged my duties at the lower extremity of my line of river pickets.

A brigade—that of [Brigadier General N. Martin] Curtis, the same that had thrown its skirmishers on the slope of the fort on the former expedition—now led the way. The skirmishers had crept up as close to the fort as the naval fire permitted, and were now lying in hastily scraped holes in the sand, and the brigade line was behind the low bank of a ditch, a little in their rear.

A signal flag fluttered in the redoubt, and the hail of naval shells swung obediently away from the nearer end of the fort and concentrated on the great angle farther down. Then, amid shouts of command, and with a cheer, Curtis's men rose from their ditch and rushed forward; and the skirmish line seemed to reach the stockade of logs at the edge of the ditch.

At the same time a band of men in naval uniform, brilliantly led by officers conspicuous in gold-banded caps, dashed forward from the left of Curtis's line of infantry. All of this advance movement was met by a fierce rattle of musketry, and the angry crash of canister from field pieces, which fired through the portholes of the stockade. The sullen and hitherto silent walls now swarmed with gray uniforms.

Before this discharge the naval party—which bore the brunt of it, being more directly in its front—melted away into a few figures of men flying through the sulphurous smoke, and a few more lying motionless on the beach. But the infantry brigade was only checked, and was soon returning the fire of the fort, from the hastily extemporized shelter of sand holes. "Put in [Colonel Galusha] Pennypacker's brigade," I heard General Terry say to his adjutant; and the new line soon moved forward and joined the rest. Under their increased fire, another move forward was made, which brought the assault to the log stockade at the scrap of the ditch.

The log work was originally a formidable defense, consisting of a close fence of upright tree trunks, of six or eight inches in diameter and eight or ten feet in height. Outside of this, torpedoes had been buried in the soft sand. But the rain of naval shells had cut the wires connecting the latter with the electric batteries in the fort, and had breached and shattered the logs so that the volunteer axe men had little trouble in cutting a passage for the assault. Enough of *debris,* however, remained to break up such symmetry of brigade formation as the hurried advance and the enemy's fire had left. As the troops neared the fort, the line of naval fire, and the resistance of the enemy, as well as the natural obstacles of the ground, narrowed their objective point to the upper, or river end, of the fort wall. And this narrowing of course compressed the wings of each brigade to its center, and the two brigades themselves together. In the crash and uproar of the battle, and the enthusiasm of the advance, the men shouldered their way forward with little regard to the regimental formation. The result was a crowd of men pouring through the log obstacles into the ditch, cheering and impetuous, but with no longer any visible military formation. Such a crowding together would have been a terrible exposure to the hostile fire, and fatal to the assault, under the ordinary circumstances; but, from where I stood, two causes seemed to operate in our favor.

In a scientifically built fort, the ditch is, of course, no place for the attacking party: a bastion, or flank wall, is always arranged to enfilade it; and, in the present instance, the bastion was duly placed and properly armed to rake and harrow with lead and iron all points of the ditch. But the immense scale of Fort Fisher had removed this threatening bastion more than a quarter of a mile from the present point of attack; so the navy could rain shells upon it during the whole of the assault, without endangering our troops in the ditch. Practically, the naval fire silenced the flanking bastion—not wholly, of course, but the scattering fire from it was a small matter to the men who had just passed through a far deadlier one.

The second apparent cause of safety was the vertical immensity of the fort. The great height of the work, and its width of parapet—several times the length of the muskets leveled over it—gave a wide space at its foot which was below any possible line of fire coming from its top.

Partially sheltered, then, at the very foot of the fort, both from direct fire and enfilading bastion, our troops gathered in the ditch, and, reassured by their safety, began with wild cheers to swarm up the green slope of the fort itself. It was an exciting moment. Regimental pride—nothing shows a soldier's spirit more strongly—animated the broken mass of men, in the rough clamber up the slope; and a rush of color bearers led the way, in the ambition to be first on the parapet.

A fierce outburst of musketry greeted the first heads that rose above the level of the fort; and at least one flag and its bearer rolled down the slope into the ditch. But the fort wall once gained, the assaulters are as much protected by it as the garrison; and so our men made some sort of foothold on the slope, and delivered over the parapet as fierce a fire as they received. They were thus burning powder close in each other's faces. Burrowing for foothold, and firing steadily over the bank, the character of the battle changed from the wild, dashing assault to a steady deliberation of attack, until the inspiration of the hitherto unbroken success, and regimental rivalry, once more urged the men forward another step, which turned the wavering balance against the rebels.

Like a vessel divided into bulkhead compartments, Fort Fisher is divided into many separate compartments by traverses. These are earth walls standing at right angles with the fort, and rising some eight feet or more higher than the parapet. Their object is to protect the gunners from a flank fire. Between the traverses are the gun platforms and guns, with separate *ramps* and stairs from the parade ground inside. Each compartment mounts one or two large *barbette* guns, besides holding two or three hundred infantrymen.

The assault was directed only against the two compartments nearest the river end of the fort; but the Rebel fire was delivered not only from the troops in these compartments, but from all the rest in range, and from the tops of the traverses on the left.

The soldierly ambition of one or two color bearers is the cause of their discovery of ragged hollows on the tops of the two nearest traverses; and, with a simultaneous rush, they push upward, and plant their flags above the heads of the Rebel troops. A dozen or more men follow them, and fill the shell hollows, from which they open fire downward upon the Rebels in the two compartments. This was the grandest and most stirring moment of the fight. The regimental flags floating in the battle smoke, close above the heads of the Rebel garrison, and the daring of the men, who, though few in numbers, were able to disconcert the defenders with the plunging fire from their elevated position on the traverses—it was almost hand-to-hand business! This new fire from above checked the direct fire of the Rebels; and the slackening was at once taken advantage of by the assaulting troops, who sprang on the parapet, with ringing cheers, and poured over it to the gun platforms, among the now passive Rebels. The first two compartments were thus surrendered. And presently, one or two hundred unarmed Rebels came filing down the outer slope of the fort, through the ditch and stockade, and across the sandy plain, running and crowding, under the whizzing of shells and bullets, back toward the sandy road—two or three armed Federals in charge. These were prisoners of war—the garrison of the captured compartments. The garrison of the third compartment, which soon fell into our hands, escaped into the fourth.

Hitherto the attack had been against a small part of the fort, but directed full in front. The capture of the first three compartments changed the direction of attack toward the left, and still more narrowed the objective to the depth of the traverses. In an ordinary case, the capture of any part of a fort would have given the victors command of the whole interior—in other words, would have been its immediate fall—unless, indeed, the garrison was strong enough to retake it. Here, however, the victors found the interior untenable, both because of a fire opened from an interior rifle pit line, and because the great siege guns mounted on the other face of the fort were reversed and brought into play against the captured flank. And this fire grew more effective, as further captures unmasked more guns. As fast, then, as our troops captured any part of the wall, they had to abandon its interior themselves, and, still clinging with insecure foothold on the outside of the slope, to edge their way along, delivering a left oblique fire, scrambling over on reaching the shelter of a traverse, climbing up this higher perch, and, at last, delivering over it a downward and direct fire that was beautifully effective.

Slowly and obstinately the Rebels yielded traverse after traverse, compartment after compartment, to the dash, enthusiasm, and soldierly spirit of their enemies. The courage of the first assault was admirably supplemented by the persistent, bulldog tenacity of the assaulting troops all through the long afternoon. Wounded men only came straggling back over the sands; and these spoke exultingly, in spite of their pain and loss of blood.

The roar of naval fire—as its area of action became lessened by the continued success—gradually gave way to the deadlier crash of musketry. The shouting too lessened, as the work became hotter, and both sides settled to the business. With the slackening of the naval fire, the great bastion at the angle grew freer to offer resistance; the reversed guns of the inlet face of the fort, and the rifle pit line inside, found more area to play upon. So the work grew harder and the progress slower. The Rebels gained by the concentration—their artillery swelling a louder and louder roar, as our naval fire grew faint. Then they turned assaulters, and dashed at the nearest traverse in our hands. Then came a time when, for hours, the battle made no progress either way. Here, perhaps, the wavering balance might have been turned against the jaded assaulters by a leader of nerve, with a soldierly eye for the supreme moment. The ring of the old "Rebel yell," with an attack of real force and obstinacy, might have thrown back the assaulters with an impetus that should carry them entirely away from the fort— into defeat. But it was not to be, though anxiety and doubt clouded the brilliancy of the first success for a time, and the soldiers lost their elation, and with it not a little of their fighting force.

Somewhere about four o'clock in the afternoon, when the obstinate fight looked dubious, a distant sound of startling omen came to my ears: a sound of firing from the north. Absorbed as I was in the terrible game in front, I was alive enough to the responsibility of my position, as commander of the picket line, to hear this sound, which was probably inaudible to all other ears at Fort Fisher. An outburst of musketry from the north was to me an attack from Wilmington upon my northern picket line—an attempt to force our northern line of works across the peninsula. And this, too, coming at the critical hour when the assault at the fort had slackened to a standstill, and the exhausted men were losing heart.

Turning to the northward with reluctant haste and anxious foreboding, I ran ankle deep through the loose sand, which was dotted and spattered with grape-shot and bullets—too full of the new danger to *dodge* the whirring missiles; past skirmish holes, rifle pit lines, and sand redoubts; out of fire at last, and among extemporized hospitals and busy surgeons, and the *corral* of rebel prisoners; and so, hot and breathless, up the country road. But no more firing sounded from the north; it was absolutely still in that direction. This was so reassuring that I slackened my pace as I came among pines; and, presently, coming upon the idle groups of Negro soldiers lolling about the rear of their unscathed breastworks, I knew, at last, that [Major General Robert F.] Hoke had made no impression upon them.

However, the picket line might be broken, and the works therefore unguarded; so I hurried on the left group of pickets, next the river bank. The first station was unbroken—indeed almost unconscious of any attack; the second reported firing, but had seen no enemy; and so the report grew, until, near the middle of the line, I got exaggerated particulars, and found the break in the line. The last group had seen a line of Rebels—or they said so—and had returned their fire and held their station pit, although the next two or three—in among the thickets of a swamp—had been captured, and were still occupied by Rebels. This last report seemed more than doubtful, though, if true, the stations were unapproachable, hidden as they were in swamp and thicket, without certainty of capture. But from the beach end of the line the way was clearer. Hastening back to the works, and passing rapidly down among the lazy coffee boilers, till the firm beach and rolling wave line were reached, a squad was soon got together, and we began to trace up the picket line once more—the same story growing more distinct till it ended at the broken line again. But it was now an easy matter to skirmish through the swamp; and we soon found a line of three or four deserted picket stations. These we regarrisoned, and left behind us a continuous chain of pickets.

This was the whole of Hoke's attack from the north—if indeed it was an attack at all, and not a mere escapade by a small squad of cavalrymen. But it was militarily correct in every respect, except force, and could hardly have come at a wiser moment. But its feebleness was so striking that it did us good service in showing how little we had to fear from that quarter, and that it was possible to reinforce the troops at the fort from the idle defenders of the north line. And so—thanks to General Hoke—fresh men aided the tired soldiers in the fight; and freshening musketry told of the tightening of the Federal grip upon Fort Fisher.

The darkness of night had come upon us while busy in the swamp jungles, and prolonged our work until a late hour, before the line was made whole again, and the details and reliefs properly arranged and provided for. And it was still later when, at last, we got back to the lines and could rest, watching the belated moon rising over the water. And still the angry crash of musketry came swelling up from the fort; and the constant flashing glimmered like heat lightning.

Presently came an order to collect shovels to be sent to the fort; and, as we busied ourselves about it, there was a new sound from below—a sound like a distant cheer—and again the same sound from the water, as if the sailors on the fleet were cheering. The musketry, too, had lulled—was now, at last, silent; and the heat lightning glimmered no more. What was it? At once, the southern sky seemed full of rockets and many colored lights; and, as the showers of red, white, and blue stars fell into the sea, we knew that the navy was proclaiming *Victory!*

Victory—and we proclaimed it, too, bursting into full-throated sympathy, in the contagion of rejoicing, till sea and shore, and the tall, solemn pines, echoed back wilder and heartier cheering than had ever before disturbed a midnight at Federal Point. Our men wanted to leap their breastworks and march on Wilmington at once, midnight as it was, in the fullness of their joy and soldierly ardor.

And so fell Fort Fisher, and with it many an English blockade runners house, and the ephemeral prosperity of Nassau. Our navy gained a fleet of ships that had been tossing perilously off the dangerous mouth of the Cape Fear for four years; and the South lost her supply of foreign arms and clothing and medicines, her active foreign sympathy and her export trade in cotton, and Wilmington— her only mart—was closed at last.

49

The Conference at City Point
William T. Sherman, General, U.S.A.

We arrived (at City Point) during the afternoon of March 27 (1865), and I found [Lieutenant General Ulysses S.] Grant and staff occupying a neat set of log huts on a bluff overlooking the James River. The General's family was with him. We had quite a long and friendly talk, when he remarked that the President, Mr. [Abraham] Lincoln, was near by, in a steamer lying at the dock, and he proposed that we should call at once. We did so, and found Mr. Lincoln on board the "Ocean Queen." We had met in the early part of the war, and he recognized me, and received me with a warmth of manner and expression that was most grateful. We then sat some time in the after-cabin, and Mr. Lincoln made many inquiries about the events which attended the march from Savannah to Goldsboro, and seemed to enjoy the numerous stories about "our bummers," of which he had heard much.

When in lively conversation, his face brightened wonderfully, but if the conversation flagged, his face assumed a sad and sorrowful expression.

General Grant and I explained to him that my next move from Goldsboro would bring my army—increased to 80,000 men by [Major Generals John M.] Schofield's and [Alfred H.] Terry's reenforcements—in close communication with General Grant's army, then investing [General Robert E.] Lee in Richmond, and that, unless Lee could effect his escape and make junction with [General Joseph E.] Johnston in North Carolina, he would soon be shut up in Richmond, with no possibility of supply, and would have to surrender. Mr. Lincoln was extremely interested in this view of the case, and when we explained that Lee's only chance was to escape, join Johnston, and, being then between me in North Carolina and Grant in Virginia, he could choose which to fight. Mr. Lincoln seemed unusually impressed with this, but General Grant explained that at the very moment of our conversation General Sheridan was passing his cavalry across the James River from the north to the south; that he would with this cavalry so extend his left below Petersburg as to reach the South Shore Road, and that, if Lee should "let go" his fortified lines, he, Grant, would follow him so close that he could not possibly fall on me alone in North Carolina. I, in like manner, expressed the fullest confidence that my army in N. Carolina was willing to cope with Lee and Johnston combined till Grant could come up, but we both agreed that one more bloody battle was likely to occur before the close of the war.

Mr. Lincoln repeatedly inquired as to General Schofield's ability in my absence, and seemed anxious that I should return to N. Carolina, and more than once exclaimed: "Must more blood be shed? Cannot this last bloody battle be avoided?" We explained that we had to presume that General Lee was a real general; that he must see that Johnston alone was no barrier to my progress; and that, if my army of 80,000 veterans should reach Burkesville, he in Richmond was lost, and that we were forced to believe he would not await that inevitable conclusion, but make one more desperate effort.

I think we were with Mr. Lincoln an hour or more, and then returned to General Grant's quarters, where Mrs. Grant had prepared for us some coffee or tea. During this meal Mrs. Grant inquired if we had seen Mrs. Lincoln. I answered, No; I did not know she was on board. "Now," said Mrs. Grant, "you are a pretty pair," etc., and went on to explain that we had been guilty of a piece of unpardonable rudeness. But the General said: "Never mind, we will repeat the visit tomorrow, and can then see Mrs. Lincoln."

The next morning a good many officers called to see me, among them [Major Generals George G.] Meade and [Edward O. C.] Ord, also Admiral [David D.] Porter. The latter inquired as to the *Russia,* in which I had come up from Morehead City, and explained that she was a "slow tub," and he would send me back in the steamer *Bat,* Captain [John] Barnes, U.S. Navy, because she was very fleet, and could make seventeen knots an hour. Of course I did not object, and fixed that afternoon to start back.

Meantime we had to repeat our call on Mr. Lincoln on board the *Ocean Queen,* then anchored out in the stream at some distance from the wharf. Admiral Porter went along, and we took a tug at the wharf, which conveyed us off to the *Ocean Queen.* Mr. Lincoln met us all in the same hearty manner as on the previous occasion, and this time we did not forget Mrs. Lincoln. General

Grant inquired for her, and the President explained that she was not well, but he stepped to the stateroom, and returned to us, asking us to excuse her. We all took seats in the after-cabin, and the conversation became general. I explained to Mr. Lincoln that Admiral Porter had given me the *Bat,* a very fast vessel, to carry me back to Newbern, and that I was ready to start back then. It seemed to relieve him, as he was afraid that something might go wrong at Goldsboro in my absence. I had no such fears, and the most perfect confidence in General Schofield, and doubt not I said as much.

I ought not and must not attempt to recall the words of that consultation. Of course none of us then foresaw the tragic end of the principal figure of that group, so near at hand; and none of us saw the exact manner in which the war would close; but I know that I felt, and believe the others did, that the end of the war was near.

The imminent danger was that Lee, seeing the meshes closing surely around him, would not remain passive, but would make one more desperate effort, and General Grant was providing for it by getting General Sheridan's cavalry well to his left flank so as to watch the first symptoms, and to bring the rebel army to bay till the infantry could come up. Meantime I asked two weeks' delay and the *status quo,* when we would have our wagons loaded, and would start from Goldsboro for Burkesville *via* Raleigh. Though I cannot attempt to recall the words spoken by any one of the persons present on that occasion, I know we talked generally about what was to be done when Lee's and Johnston's armies were beaten and dispersed. On this point Mr. Lincoln was very full. He said that he had long thought of it; that he hoped the end could be reached without more bloodshed, but in any event he wanted us to get the deluded men of the rebel armies disarmed and back to their homes; that he contemplated no revenge, no harsh measures, but quite the contrary; and that their sufferings and hardships in the war would make them the more submissive to law.

I cannot say that Mr. Lincoln or anybody else used this language at the time, but I know I left his presence with the conviction that he had in his mind, or that his cabinet had, some plan of settlement ready for application the moment Lee and Johnston were defeated.

In Chicago about June or July of that year, when all the facts were fresh in my mind, I told them to George P. A. Healy, the artist, who was casting about for a subject for an historical painting, and he adopted this interview. Mr. Lincoln was then dead, but Healy had a portrait, which he himself had made at Springfield some five or six years before. With this portrait, some existing photographs, and the strong resemblance in form of Mr. [Leonard] Swett, of Chicago, to Mr. Lincoln he made the picture of Mr. Lincoln seen in this group. For General Grant, Admiral Porter, and myself he had actual sittings, and I am satisfied the four portraits in this group of Healy's are the best extant. The original picture, life-size, is, I believe, now in Chicago, the property of Mr. McCaig; but Healy afterwards, in Rome, painted ten smaller copies, about eighteen by twenty-four inches, one of which I now have, and it is now within view. I think the likeness of Mr. Lincoln by far the best of the many I have seen elsewhere, and those of General Grant, Admiral Porter, and myself equally good and faithful. I think Admiral Porter gave Healy a written description of our relative positions in that interview, also the dimensions, shape, and furniture of the cabin of the *Ocean Queen;* but the rainbow is Healy's—typical, of course, of the coming peace. In this picture I seem to be talking, the others attentively listening. Whether Healy made this combination from Admiral Porter's letter or not, I cannot say; but I thought that he caught the idea from what I told him had occurred when saying "that if Lee would only remain in Richmond till I could reach Burkesville we would have him between our thumb and fingers," suiting the action to the word.

It matters little what Healy meant by his historic group, but it is certain that we four sat pretty much as represented, and were engaged in an important conversation during the forenoon of March 28, 1865, and that we parted never to meet again.

50

Lee at Appomattox

Edward Porter Alexander, Brigadier General, C.S.A.

LOOKING BACK at the situation of the Confederate Army of Northern Virginia at the opening of the spring campaign of 1865, it is hard to conceive that any man in it could have failed to realize that its career must soon be brought to a close. To defend Richmond and Petersburg, it was stretched out from the Chickahominy, on the left, to Five Forks, on the right, crossing two rivers, a distance by its shortest roads of over thirty miles, to hold which there were only about 50,000 men of all arms, and there were, virtually, no more men left where those came from.

In front of us, in many places within pistol shot, lay the enemy with about 130,000 men, and with no end of men left at home to be had if needed. Had [Lieutenant General Ulysses S.] Grant chosen, he could have gotten twice as many, for the United States at that time had nearly a million men in arms. And, indeed, up through the Carolinas were marching [Major General William T.] Sherman and [Major General John] Schofield, almost unopposed, with nearly ninety thousand more to come upon our flank. Yet the army never seemed to realize at all the drawing near of the inevitable result.

Brigadier General Edward
Porter Alexander
(*Century*)

When the Confederate peace commissioners went to the Fort Monroe conference, I recollect a sort of indignant apprehension that they might be led to discuss something less than our absolute independence, and nothing else, I am sure, would have been easily accepted by the army.

It was developed at that conference that by returning to the Union we might not only secure favorable political conditions, but possibly, also, four hundred millions in government bonds as compensation for slavery. Perhaps we may be called monumental idiots in not realizing our desperate situation and in refusing such liberal terms. But, if so, we have paid the penalty of our folly, and is it not now best for all that our cause was *lost*—not *compromised?*

While I cannot recall the faintest conscious doubt of the final success of our cause, one circumstance makes it evident that subconsciousness which seems to feel the "haps in the air that a moment may bring" had begun to absorb some idea of what was coming.

The circumstance was this: I had some 700 dollars in [the] bank in Richmond. One warm day in March, as the air began to feel springlike and balmy, without any conscious thought, I got a friend going into Richmond to draw my

Confederate money and invest it in gold. He brought me a ten-dollar gold piece, which I put in my pocket, and thus I saved that much from the wreck.

General Lee himself was not yet entirely without hope, and on March 25 actually left his own lines and made a furious and bloody, but unsuccessful, assault upon the enemy's strongly fortified position at Fort Stedman, apparently in the belief that he could still cope with the whole Federal army if he could get them out of their entrenchments. This desperate sortie was thoroughly characteristic of General Lee.

When he first assumed command of the army, he came from West Virginia, where there had been no fighting, and some of the Richmond papers assailed him bitterly as vacillating and timid. In conversation on the subject, at the time, with Colonel [Joseph C.] Ives of President [Jefferson] Davis's staff, during a ride along the lines, I asked his estimate of Lee. His reply was impressive. Stopping his horse and turning to face me, he said: "Lee is the most audacious officer in either army, Confederate or Federal. He will fight quicker and longer, and take more desperate chances, than any other general this country has ever seen, and you will live to see it." It was a remarkable prediction to have been made before Lee had ever fought a battle. Many of our subsequent battles recalled it to my mind, but none of them more forcibly than this brave effort to destroy a veteran army of nearly thrice his numbers.

My command at this time included, with the field artillery north of the Appomattox, the heavy batteries and torpedo defenses of the James River. The enemy's fleet of ironclads occupied the river a short distance below, and would frequently steam up and exchange shots with our long-range guns.

In the latter part of March a lot of torpedoes were prepared to be set adrift at night, arranged to float with the current down among the enemy's vessels, then settle a few feet under water, anchor themselves promiscuously about, and wait for something to run against them. As it would be impossible to guess how many there were and where they had settled, they would tend to discourage navigation in our direction.

On April 2 I went down into the swamp, where arrangements were being made to launch the torpedoes that night, and spent the whole day in having them filled with powder and made ready. About sundown I returned to my camp for dinner, and there first heard of the events of the previous twenty-four hours at Petersburg. [Major General George] Pickett's division had been captured at Five Forks, the lines at Petersburg were broken, A. P. Hill and many other officers were killed—among them Willie Pegram, the brilliant young colonel of artillery, loved and admired throughout the army.

Our men had fought everywhere as well as ever they fought before, and at many points had driven the enemy back with severe losses; but the thin ranks had been overrun at some places, and, as a whole, the integrity of our system of defense was gone. [Lieutenant General James] Longstreet had arrived with [Major General Charles W.] Field's division from the north side of the James,

and had checked the enemy's advance into town, but the position could no longer be held. About an hour later orders were received to withdraw everything
during the night across the James, abandoning Richmond, and to move southward to Amelia Court House, where we would unite with the forces to be withdrawn from Petersburg.

My command was stretched over many miles, and we had a busy night getting it on the road, spiking and abandoning the heavy guns, and arming as infantry the men who had served them. With heavy hearts we left our beautiful
lines, prepared with such care for many months, only to be walked over by the
enemy in the morning, without receiving a single shot.

About midnight I rode into Richmond. The scenes there that night I cannot attempt to describe. Troops, trains, and artillery were coming in from the
lines and crossing the river by the bridge, while at the same time the city was
being evacuated by the government and all its employees, from the president
and Congress down to the mechanics in the armories and workshops. In short,
about the whole male population was leaving, and a few of the females—all who
were able to. I had friends and relatives in each class, and made hasty visits to
their houses to see if I could render any help. The one thing needful for those
who were to remain was to see that they had a few days' provisions on hand;
for with the morning would come the enemy, and the little remaining value of
Confederate money would pass away like the morning cloud and the early dew.
After seeing what was possible to be done in this line, and taking a hospitable
cup of genuine coffee at a house where several weeping ladies were being left
by their husbands, I rode down to the bridge to see our batteries as they came
by and give them final directions. By that time the city was lighted up with
conflagrations, and six miles southeast, at Drewry's Bluff, could be seen the
burning of our little fleet of gunboats. The thundering explosions of their magazines were the most tremendous sounds I ever heard, the atmospheric conditions being particularly favorable for transmission in our direction.

I think no person in Richmond went to bed that night. Close by the bridge,
the Richmond and Danville freight depot, filled with quartermaster and commissary supplies, was burning, and no one was trying to put it out, or even looking on; but a few people were carrying off such things as they wished. A very
dissipated-looking old Irishwoman was rolling out bales of blankets and pack-
ing them into a little coal-cellar under her house. She packed the cellar full, but
before daylight the fire reached her, and took house, blankets, and all. I helped
myself to a new saddle and bridle, and my faithful small darky Charley tied on
a side of bacon, which, during the next few days, well repaid all the trouble it
cost. That was the last issue of Confederate rations in which I ever participated. I do not know to what extent the fires were originally set, if at all, by military order, but I imagine that perhaps orders were given to burn the ordnance
storehouses and workshops, and I believe that the fires were purposely spread
by a class which always turns up, ready to take advantage of opportunities for

plunder. There was no lack of such characters in Richmond that night. Bands of them roamed the business streets, plundering unprotected stores. I was told that a jeweler shot dead one man who broke into his store, and officers of the rear-guard who left the city after daybreak reported one man left hanging on a lamp post and two or three other dead bodies lying in the streets. This was probably the work of a provost guard which was about, though I did not see it.

Shortly after daybreak the last of the guns passed, and I went with them, crossing the canal on a bridge already on fire from a burning canal boat which had floated or been pushed underneath. About sunrise we took our last look back from the hills at the smoking and deserted city, which had been defended so long and so well.

We marched all day, and bivouacked at dark near Tomahawk Church, about sixteen miles from Richmond. But while the command rested and slept I was sent upon a reconnaissance of some roads, which kept me in the saddle during the whole night. Early on the fourth the march was resumed, and crossing the Appomattox on a railroad bridge, I camped at night near Amelia Court House, utterly exhausted by sixty hours' incessant work and movement. That night was my last night in a tent, as our headquarters wagon was sent off next morning with a train which was captured and burned by the Federal cavalry, leaving us nothing but the clothes we wore, and not our best clothes at that.

At Amelia Court House, on the fifth, we joined General Lee and the troops who had come from Petersburg. We had expected to receive rations at this place, but there had been some mistake, and we had to accept the commissary's apologies in their place.

There was here a hurried sort of reorganization of corps, necessary from the death of A. P. Hill, the scattered and more or less broken condition of many divisions, and the joining of the local troops from Richmond under [Lieutenant General Richard S.] Ewell.

Much of the artillery and the trains were started from Amelia Court House off to the right toward Lynchburg, while what was left of the army, with a few selected batteries and battalions of artillery, stripped of all trains and impedimenta, was to make a break to pass Burkeville and secure our line to retreat to North Carolina, where we would unite with Johnston. About noon I started with General Lee, who went with the head of the column. Only a few miles out, near Jetersville, we struck a considerable body of enemy, and preparations were rapidly made to give battle. Our cavalry were feeling them in front, and for a while Lee seemed to contemplate an attack with all his force. Then suddenly orders were changed, and Longstreet, with his corps, was turned off to the right, and ordered to march with all haste to Rice's Station, where we were to take and hold position until the rest of the army could concentrate upon us. It was a long and weary all-night march, only about sixteen miles, but equal to double that distance under favorable conditions. There were several false alarms along the lines during the night, and in one of them two of our brigades fired on each other, killing several men—among them one of our finest artillery officers, Major Frank Smith, who had commanded heavy batteries on the James.

Riding ahead of the guns and infantry with my staff, we arrived near Rice's about dawn, when we turned out in the woods to get an hour's sleep, and to boil and eat a very tough old hen which we had secured as we came along.

By sunrise we were again in the saddle to examine the locality and select a line of battle on which the troops, as they arrived, were posted. But many of those expected never arrived. The enemy had intercepted our line of march, and a very sharp engagement took place at Sailor's [Sayler's] Creek, where Ewell, Custis Lee, [Major General Joseph B.] Kershaw, and about 7,000 men were captured, after a fight severe and bloody, but successful on our part until those engaged were surrounded and overwhelmed. General Lee was evidently much worried at the news brought to him of this disaster, and rode back to see if it were possible to save anything. But the enemy was now close to our line of march everywhere; they broke in at various places, got among our trains, and captured and burned many. Among the commands captured in this way was my own splendid old artillery battalion, now commanded by Colonel [Frank] Huger. It was peacefully climbing a long hill by a narrow road, when [Major General George A.] Custer, with a brigade of cavalry, came charging down upon them. Three of the leading guns were unlimbered, and fired two or three rounds of canister upon the Federals when they swarmed over everything. Captain O. B. Taylor, of the leading battery, was called on to surrender, but answered with defiance and orders to his cannoneers to continue firing, whereupon he was shot dead. Huger was captured after shooting through the cheek a major who first invited him to surrender, in the ceremonious and complimentary language customary on such occasions. A second invitation coming from a cavalryman, who came up and held a carbine to his head, was accepted. But the major bore no malice, and that night came to thank Huger for a delightful "furlough wound." Custer and Huger had been friends at West Point, and having captured him, Custer took him along all day, as he said, "to let you see how I am going to take you fellows in."

Meanwhile at Rice's Station we skirmished a little, but having a fairly good position, the enemy evidently proposed to turn it in preference to attacking. So when night came, it being impossible now to make the trip directly south to Johnston, we abandoned our lines and changed our course toward Lynchburg. That night march was something fearful. Floundering through rain, mud, and darkness, with worn-out and starving horses dragging heavy guns over a narrow road blocked with troops and trains, we were moving all night, and scarcely advanced a mile an hour. And there was nothing in the prospects for the morrow to cheer one up.

Day by day, death, wounds, and capture were robbing us heavily of comrades with whom we had been through many campaigns, and now our army was reduced to little more than a collection of fragments, out of food and nearly out of ammunition. The enemy was ahead of us and around us, in numbers that could not be counted. Yet the morale of the men was not impaired, and no one seemed to feel any doubt but that somehow we should still come out all right. Certainly, during all the business beginning at Fort Stedman on March 25, including Five Forks, the Petersburg lines, the defense of Fort Gregg, Sailor's Creek, and all skirmishes up to the final fight at Appomattox Court House on the 9th, the plain, hard solid fighting of the men was simply wonderful, in view of their surroundings. Up to the very last minute, before the flag of truce stopped the firing, it was as unflinching fighting as it had ever been, and it was not without some successes on a scale proportioned to the numbers engaged.

On the morning of April 7 [Major General William] Mahone captured over a thousand of the enemy's infantry, and on the afternoon of the same day our cavalry brought in [Colonel John I.] Gregg of the Federal cavalry and many of his men. And, to anticipate a little in my narrative, on the morning of the ninth itself, our cavalry captured and sent in a section of artillery with horses, harness, and everything complete, down to the red blankets on the horses. I issued them promptly to James N. Lamkin's battery, which had served mortars in the lines about Petersburg, but had been very ambitious to get field guns. I had promised Lamkin that he should have them, and we considered it a melancholy sort of joke that these came just in time to enable me to make good my word.

About daylight on the seventh we passed through Farmville, and crossed the Appomattox to the north bank, burning the bridges behind us as the enemy's cavalry entered the town. We shelled his pursuing columns across the river for a while, and he shelled us back, and then we continued our retreat. Each day it became more slow and painful, as the animals approached the limits of endurance. At last we had to abandon ordnance-wagons and the caissons, and even some guns, which would mire down and could not be extricated. We would cut down wheels and axles and leave them in the road. The march was kept up until late at night, when I and my staff rode off into a pine thicket and hid, lest stragglers should steal our horses while we lay on the saddle-blankets and slept, with the saddles for pillows.

April 8 was but a repetition of the seventh, except that we were less interrupted by the enemy's cavalry, which had left our flank, and was being pushed forward to get ahead of us at Appomattox.

Soon after sunrise, on the morning of the 9th, I came up with General Lee, halted, with his staff, by the roadside, a mile and a half from the village. [Major General John B.] Gordon, who was in advance, was already engaged, and the increasing sound of cannon and musketry told that the enemy was in heavy force.

The progress of the column was stopped, and trains were parked in the fields, while guns and infantry moved forward to the sound of the firing. General Lee called me to him, and, walking off from the group, sat down on a log and said: "The enemy seems to be across our road in force this morning. What have we got to do?"

Now, our artillery had not been seriously engaged during the retreat, and was never in better humor for a fight. The cannoneers, for some days before, beginning, perhaps, to appreciate the situation, had called out along the road, "Don't let us surrender any of this ammunition! We have been saving ammunition all the war! We did not save it to be surrendered!"

I told General Lee of this, and said that I could show up near forty guns with one hundred rounds apiece, if he wished to give battle. He replied that the force in front of us was too great, that while he had, perhaps, fifteen thousand infantry, half of them were mere fragments of different commands, unorganized and largely without arms or ammunition, and that he could scarcely concentrate an effective force of eight thousand men, which was too small to accomplish any valuable results. I was not unprepared to hear this decision, for the last forty-eight hours had made apparent the desperate condition to which we were reduced, and I had views on the matter, which I was glad of so favorable an opportunity to express. So I spoke up:

"Then general, we have choice of but two courses: to surrender, or to order the army to disperse, and, every man for himself, to take the woods and make his way either to Johnston's army in Carolina, or to his home, taking his arms, and reporting to the governor of his State. And of these alternatives that latter is the best. For if there is any hope for the Confederacy it is in delay. But, if this army is surrendered to-day, the Confederacy is gone. The morale of this army has sustained both the people at home and the other armies. Our surrender would demoralize all, and Grant turning one hundred thousand men, released from duty here, against Johnston, Taylor, and Kirby Smith, they will all go, one after the other, like a row of bricks. Then, if there is any hope from Europe, we stand a chance by delay; but we destroy it whenever the news of the surrender of this army crosses the water. Or if there is any chance for the separate State governments to make any terms whatever with the Federal government, we stand these chances by delay, and we lose them by a surrender. Intimations, too, have been given that each State may make terms for itself, while the Confederacy will not be recognized. But even suppose there are none of these chances, suppose there is nothing left but to submit to whatever the enemy chooses to inflict, even then there is one thing the men who have fought under you for three years have the right to ask of you. You care little for military reputation. But we are your men, and your fame is very precious to us. The record of this army as yet is without a blot, and now its last hour has come. Grant is called 'Unconditional Surrender Grant,' and it has been their boast that our fate was to be that of the armies at Fort Donelson and Vicksburg. But the men who have fought under you so long have the right to ask you to spare us the mortification of your asking Grant for terms, and being told, 'Unconditional surrender.' Save us from that!"

I was never in my life so wrought up upon any subject as upon this. Words came to me, and both my argument and my appeal seemed to me unanswerable. For no one could deny the importance of *terms* to prevent vindictive trials and punishments, and there seemed no other chance to secure them. General Lee listened to me quietly until I had quite finished, and then said:

"Suppose I were to adopt your suggestion, how many do you suppose would get away?"

I replied: "I think two thirds of us could get away. We should be like rabbits and partridges in the bushes, and they could not scatter like that to catch us."

"Well," he said, "I have less than 16,000 infantry with arms in their hands. Even if two thirds of these got away it would be too small a force to accomplish any useful result, either with Johnston or with governors of the States. But few would go to Johnston, for their homes have been overrun by the enemy, and the men will want to go first and look after their families. As to any help from Europe, I have never believed in it. I appreciate that the surrender of this army is, indeed, the end of the Confederacy. But that result is now inevitable, and must be faced. And, as Christian men, we have no right to choose a course from pride or personal feelings. We have simply to see what we can do best for our country and people. Now, if I should adopt your suggestion and order this army to disperse, the men, going homeward, would be under no control, and, moreover, would be without food. They are already demoralized by four years of war, and would supply their wants by violence and plunder. They would soon become little better than bands of robbers. A state of society would result, throughout the South, from which it would require years to recover. The enemy's cavalry, too, would pursue to catch at least the general officers, and would harass and devastate sections that otherwise they will never visit. Moreover," he said, "as to myself, I am too old to go to bushwhacking, and even if it were right to order the army to disperse, the only course for me to pursue would be to surrender myself to General Grant. But," he added, "I can tell you for your comfort that Grant will not demand an 'unconditional surrender.' He will give us honorable and liberal terms, simply requiring us not to take up arms again until exchanged." He then went on to tell me that he was in correspondence with Grant, and expected to meet him in our rear at 10:00 A.M., when he would accept the terms that had been indicated.

My recollection of this conversation is very vivid. When I had finished making my appeal, I did not believe that he could refuse it, for he prized highly the affection of his men, and he had, moreover, all the fighting instincts of a soldier. But he showed me the situation from a plane to which I had not risen, and when he finished speaking I had not a word to say. I had before that fully intended, for myself, not to be surrendered, but to take to the bushes on the first sign of a flag of truce. Many other officers and men had similar intentions. But after my talk with Lee I and all my friends determined to stay and see it out. And I think nobody did run away, except a few of the cavalry out on the flank, who took a professional pride in getting around the enemy, and could not resist the opportunity. And they all came back and surrendered as soon as they got news of the terms given us, and heard also that rations would be issued immediately after the ceremony.

Soon after this conversation I was ordered by Longstreet to select a line of battle for his corps, and form the artillery and infantry upon it, that Gordon, who was being forced in, might fall back upon him. I accordingly selected a line about a thousand yards on our side of the village of Appomattox, and put about five thousand infantry of Field's, Mahone's, and [Major General Cadmus] Wilcox's divisions in position upon it, and crammed it full of artillery, making the last line of battle ever formed by the Army of Northern Virginia.

Meanwhile Lee had ridden to the rear to meet Grant, leaving Longstreet in command. When Lee had been gone over half an hour, Fitzhugh Lee, commanding the cavalry, sent word to Longstreet that he had found an opening through which the army could escape. Longstreet called Colonel John C. Haskell, commanding one of our battalions of artillery, who was riding a mare celebrated for her beauty and swiftness, and said to him: "Lee has gone to the rear to surrender the army; ride after him, and kill your mare, but overtake him and tell him what Fitzhugh Lee has reported." Haskell immediately dashed down the road at the utmost speed, and after going about three miles passed the rear guard, and turning a bend in the road, found Lee, with his staff, dismounted by the side of the road, awaiting an answer to a communication he had sent in to the Federal lines for Grant. Going at full speed, Haskell passed the group a short distance before he could stop his horse. Lee came forward to meet him as he turned back, saying: "What is it? What is the matter?" and then, without waiting for an answer, said: "You have killed your beautiful mare! What did you do it for?" Haskell gave his message, and Lee questioned him about the situation, and finally told him to tell Longstreet to exercise his own judgment as to what he should do. Meanwhile, however, Fitzhugh Lee had found that the supposed opportunity to get through the enemy's line did not exist, and one of Longstreet's staff was sent to follow Haskell and report. Haskell's mare did not die, but was sold after the surrender to a Federal officer for a high price.

While this was going on the situation at the front was growing more critical. Gordon found his short line threatened by an overwhelming force of infantry, while large bodies of cavalry were enveloping his flanks. He called upon Longstreet for help, and Longstreet sent his inspector general, Major R. M. Sims, to suggest a flag of truce to the Federal commander in his front, to ask a suspension of hostilities pending Lee's interview with Grant.

Gordon requested Sims to bear the message, but cautioned him not to let our men know of his errand. Sims rode out to the left flank, where a line of our cavalry, dismounted behind a fence, were exchanging a hot fire with the enemy along the edge of a wood some two hundred yards off. Then, putting spurs to his horse, he galloped rapidly across to the enemy's line. He had in his haversack a white towel, and as he drew near the enemy he pulled it out and displayed it. As soon as it was recognized (which was not until he was quite near), the enemy ceased firing, and [Lieutenant Colonel E. W.] Whitaker came to meet him. Sims asked to be taken to Sheridan, but was told that Custer was near and in command of that part of the field, and it was decided to see him. Going a short distance to the rear, they came upon Custer moving at a gallop, with a brigade of cavalry, to envelop our left flank. Custer presented a striking appearance with his long sandy-colored hair on his shoulders, a red cravat with streaming ends, a large scarf pin, and brilliant stones in his hat and shoulder straps. He asked what was wanted, and Sims gave his message: that Gordon requested a truce pending a meeting between Grant and Lee.

Custer said: "We will do no such thing. We have your people now where we want you, and will listen to no terms but unconditional surrender."

Sims replied: "Well, sir, we will never submit to that, but you will allow me to carry your message back to General Gordon."

To this Custer assented. During this interview Sims had been followed and joined by Major [G. Campbell] Brown of Gordon's staff, and the two officers returned together, escorted by Whitaker and another officer.

Gordon was found at the court house, where the street was now filled with stragglers and wounded, and he requested Brown and the two Federal officers to go over to the right and endeavor to find Sheridan and secure a suspension of hostilities from him. Meanwhile the opposing forces on the left seemed to find out that something like a truce was going on, and without any general order the firing on each side was gradually discontinued. At this stage of the proceedings Custer undertook a little game of bluff on his own responsibility. Accompanied by an orderly, and waving the orderly's white handkerchief, he left his lines and galloped across to ours, approaching them at a point occupied by the Rockbridge Artillery of Hardaway's battalion, under the immediate command of Major W. H. Gibbes.

As the Federals rode up they were surrounded by the cannoneers and some infantry skirmishers, who, not exactly appreciating the situation, and covetous of good boots, actually dismounted the orderly and were about to swap boots with him, and even proposed a like trade to Custer, when he called out to Gibbes: "Gibbes, I appeal to you for protection." Gibbes at once recognized him, having known him as a cadet at West Point, and, on his request, took him to Gordon. As other parts of the line were still firing, Gordon sent Major W. W. Parker of the artillery to order a cessation of fire. A battery called Johnson's from Richmond, Virginia, commanded by Captain John. W. Wright, was the last to receive the order, and fired the last gun. Gordon referred Custer to Longstreet, and Gibbes conducted him. Custer, with much assurance in his manner, told Longstreet that he had come from Sheridan to demand the immediate and unconditional surrender of the army. Longstreet, who was generally imperturbable, made no reply until Custer had sharply repeated his demand, when he said coolly that Lee was in communication with Grant on the subject, and that pending their conference neither he (Longstreet) had the right to surrender, nor Custer or Sheridan to make such a demand. Custer answered: "Sheridan and I are independent here today, and have our troops in position to crush you out at once, and unless you make an immediate and unconditional surrender we will pitch in."

General Lee Departing the McLean House after the Surrender
(*Harper's New Monthly Magazine*)

At this Longstreet blazed out angrily to the effect that they might "pitch in" as soon as they pleased, but that he (Custer) had best get back into his own lines immediately, or his authorized presence and his arrogant errand would not be overlooked. Custer made no reply except to ask a safe conduct back. Longstreet shortly directed his assistant adjutant general, Colonel Osman Latrobe, to send some one with Custer, and Gibbes and an orderly escorted him back.

Meanwhile Sheridan and Gordon had met near Appomattox Court House, and a suspension of hostilities had been agreed upon until the next meeting between Lee and Grant.

After some delay Lee had received a message from Grant that he had left the rear of our army and was passing along his own lines around to our front. Lee accordingly returned, and passing through our line of battle, dismounted close in front, in an apple orchard, near a house said to be the home of [Samuel] Sweeney, celebrated as a minstrel and banjo player before the war. Here he was left standing alone for a few minutes, having sent his staff off on various errands, and as he expressed a desire to sit down, I had some rails brought from a fence near by, and a seat piled for him under one of the apple-trees, a short distance from the road. He sat there for perhaps two hours, close in front of Longstreet's line of battle, until [Lieutenant Colonel Orville E.] Babcock of Grant's staff came from Appomattox to escort him there to meet Grant.

I made my bivouac in that orchard that night. Relic hunters had already begun to cut limbs from the apple-tree under which Lee sat, and within twenty-four hours it was literally dug up by the roots, and not a chip of it was left. I have always regretted since that I did not appreciate how I should come to value some memorial of the event, and myself secure a piece of the tree as a memento; for I have since tried in vain to get a piece even as big as a toothpick. I think it was carried off entirely by Confederates who, standing in our last line of battle, saw Lee sitting under the tree awaiting Grant's messenger. I have never even heard of more than one piece of it since. One of my sisters, "refugeeing" through Carolina, first heard the story of the surrender from a Texan who had been present and seen Lee under the tree, and had cut himself a walking-stick from it, and was now footing it for home.

We learned after the surrender that Sheridan complained of some movements of our troops after the flag was sent in. I do not know what was the occasion of the complaint, but some half-hour after the firing had ceased, the captain of a battery pointed out to me a Federal cavalry regiment moving around our left flank, and begged permission to fire a shot at them. Knowing, however, Lee's intention to surrender, I refused permission. It was about one o'clock when Babcock came from the enemy's line, and Lee, with [Lieutenant Colonel Charles] Marshall, rode with him back to Appomattox, and then the whole army knew what was taking place.

I think it was after 3:00 P.M. when we saw Lee returning. We wished to express to him in some way our sympathy and affection, and I ordered all the cannoneers to be brought from the guns and formed in line along the road, with instructions to uncover in silence as he rode by. He had hardly reached the line, however, when someone started a cheer, which was taken up by others, and then both infantry and artillery broke their lines and crowded about his horse in the road. The general stopped and made a short address. Briefly, it was about as follows:

"I have done for you all that it was in my power to do. You have done all your duty. Leave the result to God. Go to your homes and resume your occupations. Obey the laws and become as good citizens as you were soldiers."

There was not a dry eye in the crowd that heard him, and even he seemed deeply moved. The men crowded around to try and shake his hand or touch his horse, and some appealed to him to get us all exchanged and try it again; but he made no reply to such remarks. Then he rode on to his camp, and the crowd broke up, and then ranks were formed once more and marched off to bivouac, and the Army of Northern Virginia was an army no longer, but a lot of captives awaiting their paroles. But it had written its name in history, and no man need be ashamed of its record, though its last chapter is a story of disaster. And surely those qualities in its commander for which men are loved and admired by friend and foe shone out here with no less luster than on any other field.

My story would be very incomplete did I not refer to the manner in which our exceedingly liberal treatment by Grant was regarded. It was, in the first place, a great surprise, for Grant had never before given any terms to an opponent. Now he seemed anxious to give us everything we could ask for. We knew our inferiority in force and our desperate condition too well to ascribe it to any hesitation to give us battle again. The generosity of his terms could only be ascribed to a policy of conciliation deliberately entered upon. Of course we were sore and mortified, so much so that we had not much to say to anyone; but it put everybody in some sort of hope that, after all, defeat might not mean utter destruction. And (to anticipate in my narrative for a few days) I participated in a conversation with Senator E. B. Washburne, who was with the Federal army at Appomattox, in which he declared emphatically that President Lincoln's policy would be entirely on the same line. Mr. Washburne was asked what Lincoln intended to do with the Southern States. He replied very impressively that he had had a long, confidential talk with Mr. Lincoln on the subject since the capture of Richmond, and while he was not at liberty to go into details, he would say that the liberality of Mr. Lincoln's plans would surprise both the North and the South, and he ventured the prediction that within a year Lincoln would be as popular at the South as at the North. I understood him to imply that Mr. Lincoln intended to give money to the South, probably as compensation for the slaves.

Grant's policy of conciliation was followed by everyone in his army, even to the teamsters along the roads. Several old acquaintances hunted me up, and, while delicately avoiding all disparagement of Confederate currency, hinted that as a paroled prisoner I might find it convenient to have some variety in my

"I Have Done for You All That It Was in My Power to Do" (*McClure's*)

pocket-book, and that it would be a great personal favor if I would let them lend me some of the surplus greenbacks with which they were burdened. Such offers, too, were not confined to those who had been special friends. Afterward, in riding forty miles through the troops and trains of the Federal army, I met with not a single word or look which did not seem inspired with kind feeling and a disposition to spare us all the mortification possible.

I think no one who was not at that surrender can fully appreciate the calamity wrought to the South by the assassination of President Lincoln. For Wilkes Booth slew also the kindly and generous sentiment which already inspired the army, and which would doubtless soon have pervaded the whole country.

But to return to camp on the night of April 9. The only event of the evening was the arrival of some Federal rations. There was no demonstration over it;

but many events have been honored with salutes and hurrahings to make men hoarse which never gave one half the internal satisfaction that these rations did.

I think the full moral effect of the surrender was hardly felt until the next morning, being obscured by the excitement attendant upon it. The next day seemed to usher in a new life in a new world. We had lived through the war. There was nobody trying to shoot us, and nobody for us to shoot at. Our guns were gone, our country was gone, our very entity seemed to be destroyed. We were no longer soldiers, and had no orders to obey, nothing to do, and nowhere to go.

Looked at merely as a business proceeding, the simple method of paroling the Confederate army and taking charge of its surrendered property was admirably short and effective. Arms were stacked, and guns harnessed up and drawn out along the roads, and the Federal officers came and removed them. Our own captains signed parole papers for their men, colonels for regimental officers, generals for their staffs and regimental commanders. My parole read: "The bearer, E. P. Alexander, Brig. Gen. of Artillery of the Army of Northern Virginia, a paroled prisoner of war, has permission to go home and there remain undisturbed until exchanged."

And then came the general breaking up: the partings with Lee, Longstreet, and the other generals under whom we had fought; with comrades with whom we had shared four years of march, bivouac, and battle; and with the private soldiers, whose enduring courage and devotion no man could know without love and admiration. And not without emotion could we say goodbye even to the guns themselves, and to the poor brutes that had drawn them over so many miles of road and upon so many fields of battle. The fate of our artillery horses was pitiable. We had been out of forage for I do not know how many days, and the horses were rapidly giving out before the surrender. The limit of their endurance now seemed to have been reached, and when they finally pulled the guns to the place of surrender, several hours' delay occurring in their removal, numbers of them lay down and actually died from starvation, harnessed to their guns.

I have omitted a remarkable coincidence which I came upon at Appomattox, and which is worthy of mention.

When I first joined the Army of Northern Virginia in 1861, I found a connection of my family, Wilmer McLean, living on a fine farm through which ran Bull Run, with a nice farm-house about opposite the center of our line of battle along that stream. General [Pierre G. T.] Beauregard made his headquarters at this house during the first affair between the armies—the so-called battle of Blackburn's Ford, on July 18. The first hostile shot which I ever saw fired was aimed at this house, and about the third or fourth went through the kitchen, where our servants were cooking dinner for the headquarters staff.

I had not seen or heard of McLean for years, when, the day after the surrender, I met him at Appomattox Court House, and asked with some surprise what he was doing there. He replied, with much indignation: "What are you doing here? These armies tore my place on Bull Run all to pieces, and kept running

Richmond after the War (*McClure's*)

over it backward and forward till no man could live there, so I just sold out and came here, two hundred miles away, hoping I should never see a soldier again. And now, just look around you! Not a fence-rail is left on the place, the last guns trampled down all my crops, and Lee surrenders to Grant in my house." McLean was so indignant that I felt bound to apologize for our coming back, and to throw all the blame for it upon the gentleman on the other side.

51

My Negotiations with General Sherman
Joseph E. Johnston, General, C.S.A.

When general [Robert E.] Lee was appointed general in chief, late in the winter of 1865, a large number of members of Congress, including Senator [Louis] Wigfall of Texas (who is my authority for the statement), urged the president to replace me in the military service. This was done by the following telegrams, received together:

Richmond, February 22, 1865.

General J. E. Johnston: The Secretary of War directs that you report by telegraph to General R. E. Lee, Petersburg, Va.
(Signed) S. Cooper, Adjt. and Inspt. General.

Head-Quarters, February 22, 1865.

General J. E. Johnston: Assume command of the Army of Tennessee and all troops in South Carolina, Georgia, and Florida. Assign General [Pierre G. T.] Beauregard to duty under you as you may select. Concentrate all available forces and drive back [Major General William T.] Sherman.
(Signed) R. E. Lee.

Mr. [Jefferson] Davis explains (volume 2, page 631) that he assented to this assignment "with the understanding that General Lee would supervise and control the operations."[1] This evidently is a mistake. It has been known, since

---

1. Johnston refers here and elsewhere to Jefferson Davis's *The Rise and Fall of the Confederate Government* (New York, 1881).

the first military organization, that no one absent from an army can "control its operations."

After learning that this assignment was not disagreeable to General Beauregard, I accepted it, with no other hope than that of contributing to obtain favorable terms of peace; the only one that a rational being could then entertain. For the result of the war was evident to the dullest, although General Lee's matchless skill and resolution were still maintaining his position against the great Federal power.

The troops placed under my control that might be united to oppose General Sherman's forces, which were not less than 65,000 (instead of being 30,500, as Mr. Davis asserts), amounted, when concentrated at Bentonville, to not more than 18,500, including 4,000 cavalry. The cavalry, under [Lieutenant General Wade] Hampton, was observing the march of the Federal army, and harassing it as much as possible. The infantry was in four bodies, at long distances from each other: [Lieutenant General William J.] Hardee's troops, hurrying from Charleston toward Cheraw (6,500 of whom crossed the Cape Fear); [Major General Robert F.] Hoke's division of above 5,000 near Goldsboro; and 3,950 of the Army of Tennessee at Charlotte and Goldsboro, under [Lieutenant Generals Alexander P.] Stewart, D. H. Hill, and [Major General Carter L.] Stevenson.

The Federal army was moving from Winnsboro toward Cheraw, in two columns, occasionally half a day's march apart, and within the quadrilateral at the angles of which were the four bodies of Confederate troops.

My immediate object was to unite these four bodies in front of one of General Sherman's columns, in the hope of attacking it to advantage by striking its head. My ultimate object was to join General Lee when he should abandon Richmond, so that he might fall upon Sherman with our united forces. Later on, however, I learned from him that he could only leave his position by marching to the West. As General Sherman's course from Cheraw made it uncertain whether he would take the road through Raleigh, or that through Goldsboro, the troops of the Army of Tennessee were directed to Smithfield, intermediate between the two routes. With about 1,800 of these troops, under General D. H. Hill, and Hoke's division, General [Braxton] Bragg attacked a much superior force under [Major] General J. D. Cox near Kinston, on the 8th of March. The enemy was driven from the field, and pursued by Generals Hill and Hoke with their accustomed vigor. But General Bragg stopped the pursuit. General Cox halted in the first good position, which he entrenched. General Bragg attacked him in it, on the tenth, and was easily repulsed—so easily that his loss in men and material was trifling. But the prestige of victory was left to the enemy, in exchange for the 1,500 prisoners and three field-pieces they lost on the 8th. In action with the left Federal column, General Hardee lost about 500 men, inflicting upon the enemy at least an equal loss.

On the march, encounters of cavalry were frequent. In all those reported to me, General Hampton had the advantage.

From Fayetteville, General Sherman's right column took the direct road to Goldsboro, and the other that by Averysboro. The Confederate forces, assembled near Bentonville, attacked the column on March 19, drove it from the field and pursued it a mile, into woods and thickets so dense as to stop the pursuit, by making order and control impossible.

Although all the Federal forces were united before us next morning, we held our position that day and the next against five times our number and were able to carry off our wounded—which was a very slow operation, as we had no ambulances and very few wagons. This action had a happy effect upon our troops and the neighboring people.

General Sherman writes of this action (page 305, volume 2)[2] that Johnston's army struck the head of [Major General Henry] Slocum's column, knocking back [Brigadier General William P.] Carlin's division; but when the rest of the Fourteenth and the Twentieth corps came up he repulsed all of Johnston's attacks. This a mistake. The Federal troops began the action, making two attacks,

The Last Southern Hurrah at Bentonville (*Life of Sherman*)

---

2. William T. Sherman, *Memoirs of General W. T. Sherman* (New York, 1875).

each of half an hour's duration. Both attacks were repelled. After these repulses, at about 3:00 P.M., the Confederate troops assailed the Federals and drove them from the field, which ended the fighting, excepting an occasional Federal cannon-shot. He reports the Confederate loss as four to three, compared with the Federal, although the former had the advantage in all the fighting, and in most of it were covered by breastworks. The statement that the right wing buried 100 Confederates and took 1,287 prisoners is inconsistent with the fact that its men were fully exposed and that ours were under shelter, nor did his men approach our position until the twenty-second—hours after it had been evacuated. And, again, only 653 of our men were missing at the end of the affair.

General Sherman had a great accession to his forces at Goldsboro; where he remained until April 10. The Confederate troops were in bivouac during that time—a day's march north-west.

On April 5, the press dispatches informed us that General Lee had abandoned the lines he had been holding with such admirable courage and conduct.

On the tenth, the Federal army commenced its march toward Raleigh. The Confederate troops moved in the same direction. Having the advantage of a day's march, they reached Raleigh the next afternoon, when I received, by telegraph, orders to report to the president at Greensboro without delay.

I reached the station there early in the morning of the 12th, and was General Beauregard's guest in the boxcar in which he lodged. It was conveniently near the president's quarters. His Excellency sent for us in an hour or two. We found him with three members of his cabinet—Messrs. [Judah P.] Benjamin, [Stephen R.] Mallory, and [John H.] Reagan. We were told that [Major General John C.] Breckenridge was on his way from Virginia, and that Mr. George Davis was unwell. We had supposed that the president wished to obtain information from us of the military condition of that department, but it soon appeared that we were to receive, not to give information. For those present were told, with very little preface, that, in two or three weeks, the president would have in the field a larger army, calling out the many thousands who had abandoned the service, and all those enrolled by the conscript bureau, who could not be brought into it by the military force used for the purpose by that bureau. It was suggested that men who had left the army when our cause was not desperate, and those who under similar circumstances could not be forced into it, would scarcely return to it, or enter it, in its present hopeless condition, upon a mere invitation. The fact that we had not arms enough for the soldiers who stood by their colors made this scheme inexpressibly wild. But no opinions were asked and we were dismissed. Before leaving the room, we were told that General Breckenridge's arrival that evening was certain, and that he was expected to bring positive intelligence of the fate of the Army of [Northern] Virginia.

General Breckenridge came as expected, and reported that General Lee had capitulated on April 9. After this intelligence, General Beauregard and I carefully considered the state of our affairs. We found ourselves compelled to admit that the military resources of the South were exhausted, and that the Confederacy was overthrown. Subsequently, in conversation with General Breckenridge, I endeavored to convince him of this fact, and represented that the president had but one power of government left in his hands—that of terminating hostilities—which it was his duty to exercise by making peace without delay. I offered to suggest to him the necessity of immediately opening negotiations to arrange the terms of peace between the two sections, should an opportunity be given me. He promised to make one for me next morning.

Later in the evening Mr. Mallory found me, and sought to convince me of the necessity of the course that I had endeavored to impress upon General Breckenridge, and desired me to urge upon the president the need of doing promptly all in his power to end the war. This he thought peculiarly the duty of the ranking military officer. After maintaining that it belonged rather to his constitutional advisers, I told him of the agreement made with General Breckenridge.

General Beauregard and I were summoned to the president's quarters next morning (April 13), I supposed at General Breckenridge's suggestion. We were desired to compare the military condition of the Confederacy with that of the United States. As spokesman, I said that we had an army of 20,000 infantry and artillery, and 5,000 mounted troops; against which the United States could bring three: that in Virginia of 180,000, as we were informed; that in North Carolina of 110,000, and that in Alabama of 60,000, making odds against us of at least fifteen to one. Then we had neither money nor credit, and no arms except those in the hands of our soldiers, nor ammunition excepting that in their cartridge boxes, nor shops to repair arms or fix ammunition; and that therefore the only effect of our keeping the field would be the devastation of our country and the ruin of the people, and this, too, without inflicting harm on the enemy. I asserted further that it would be the highest of human crimes to continue the war. General Beauregard assented decidedly to this view.

The members of the cabinet were then desired by the president to express their opinions as to the possibility of our continuing the war. General Breckenridge and Messrs. Mallory and Reagan concurred with the military officers—that we had been overcome in arms, and that it was necessary to make peace. But Mr. Benjamin entertained the opposite opinion, which he asserted in a speech enthusiastically warlike.

The president then remarked that it was idle to suggest to him negotiation with the government of the United States, for it was known, from the result of an attempt that he had lately made, that no terms offered by him would be considered, nor would his authority to treat be acknowledged by Mr. [Abraham] Lincoln. I reminded him that, as he knew from his military reading, peace had been occasionally established by the generals of belligerent powers agreeing upon general terms, which, accepted by the two governments, became the basis of treaties. I suggested that he should permit me to propose negotiations for that object of General Sherman. Mr. Davis opposed this idea; but, in arguing against it, he brought himself to assent to the first plan—that he should propose negotiation to Mr. Lincoln. He sketched a letter appropriate to be addressed by me to General Sherman, asking him to meet me to arrange the terms of an armistice, to enable the civil authorities to agree upon terms of permanent peace. I urged that this course should be taken at once, by his dictating this letter to Mr. Mallory, who was a good penman, and my signing and sending it to General Sherman. It was prepared immediately, and was in these words:

> The results of the recent campaign in Virginia have changed the relative military condition of the belligerents. I am therefore induced to address you, in this form, the inquiry whether, in order to stop the further effusion of blood and devastation of property, you are willing to make a temporary suspension of active operations, and to communicate to [Lieutenant General Ulysses S.] Grant, commanding the Armies of the United States, the request that he will take like action in regard to other armies, the object being to permit the civil authorities to enter into the needful arrangements to terminate the existing war.

This letter was immediately dispatched to General Hampton, commanding the Confederate cavalry (who was near Hillsboro), to be forwarded by him to General Sherman—to whom it was delivered on the fourteenth.

I left Greensboro that evening to rejoin the army, which was marching from Raleigh toward Greensboro.

In the morning of the sixteenth, near Greensboro, I received General Sherman's assent to the proposed meeting. Supposing that the president was waiting in Greensboro to be ready to negotiate should General Sherman agree to the armistice, I went to the town to obtain any instructions he might have for me. There I learned that Mr. Davis was on his way to Charlotte. So, after requesting General Hampton by telegraph to arrange the time and place of meeting, I went to his head-quarters, a few miles east of Hillsboro. There he informed me that the meeting was to be at noon of the seventeenth, on the Raleigh road, at a house midway between the pickets of the two armies.

The meeting occurred, as appointed, at the house of a Mr. [James] Bennett. As soon as the door of the room assigned us was closed, and we without witnesses, General Sherman showed me a telegram which he said was brought by a courier who overtook him after he left the railroad station. It was from Mr. [Edwin M.] Stanton, announcing the assassination of the president of the United States. I remarked, after reading the dispatch, that no greater misfortune could have befallen the South than that event.

From his account of this interview, it is evident that General Sherman's memory confounds, I think, occurrences in Raleigh with those in Mr. Bennett's house. The idea that the Confederates could be suspected of such a crime never entered my mind, and the amount of sensibility ascribed to me is unnatural; nor is General Sherman capable of the rudeness of speaking to me in such terms of my president as he attributes to himself. He informed me that an armistice to give opportunity for negotiation by the two governments would be useless, because the government of the United States did not acknowledge the existence of a Southern Confederacy, and, consequently, it could not recognize any civil officers authorized to make treaties, and, therefore, he could not transmit or receive any proposition to the president of the United States by one calling himself president of the Southern Confederacy. But, after expressing, with an air and manner carrying conviction and sincerity, an earnest wish to avert from the Southern people the devastation inevitable from war, General Sherman offered me such terms as those of Appomattox Court House.

I replied that General Lee's capitulation was unavoidable; but that, in my position, the armies being four days' march apart, it could be easily avoided; and I proposed that, instead of a suspension of hostilities, we should agree upon general terms of pacification, as our official positions empowered us to do, and as other generals had done; quoting among other precedents the termination of the war in 1797 by General Bonaparte and the Archduke Charles, the overtures having been made by the victorious general—Bonaparte.

On my repeating Bonaparte's sentiment, that if his overtures should save the life of one man, he would value the civic crown so won above any honor merely military, General Sherman evidently, as he said, appreciated that sentiment, and added that to put an end to bloodshed and devastation, and restore the union, and with it the prosperity of the South, were objects of ambition to him. He regarded joint resolutions of Congress, and proclamations by the president of the United States, as proving conclusively that the restoration of the Union was the object of the war, and he believed that the men of the Union army had been fighting for that object. A long conversation with Mr. Lincoln at City Point, but a short time before, impressed upon him the opinion that the president then so considered it.

In a short time we agreed upon the terms as written out by General Sherman on April 19, excepting that he would not consent to include Mr. Davis in the amnesty clause. The afternoon was consumed in efforts to dispose of this question in a manner that would be satisfactory to the Southern president and Southern people. No conclusion had been reached at sunset, when the discussion was suspended, to be resumed at ten o'clock next morning.

On returning to General Hampton's quarters, I telegraphed to General Breckenridge, secretary of war, to join me, in the hope that his confidential relations with Mr. Davis might enable him to suggest terms satisfactory to the president and people. General Breckenridge and Mr. Reagan came to General Hampton's quarters early next morning. I explained to them the subjects of the discussion between General Sherman and myself the day before, the terms proposed, and the only one not agreed to—that including the Confederate president in the clause giving general amnesty. I stated that I desired assistance of the Secretary of War in making that clause a satisfactory one. Mr. Reagan asked if the terms discussed had been reduced to writing. I replied that they had not. He proposed to write them out. With that object I carefully repeated them to him.

As the United States acknowledged only the military officers of the Confederacy, General Breckenridge and I rode to the place of meeting without Mr. Reagan.

When we met, I explained to General Sherman my reason for asking General Breckenridge's presence, and asked his admission as a major general, not as Secretary of War, to which he assented. I then presented to General Sherman, as my proposition, the terms discussed the day before, as written out by Mr. Reagan, which included general amnesty, and reminded him that he had already accepted all but one clause. After listening to General Breckenridge, who addressed him six or eight minutes in advocacy of these terms, General Sherman, with my paper before him, wrote very rapidly the agreement which we signed, and which follows. He wrote so rapidly that I was convinced that he had decided to agree to these terms before coming to the meeting. His paper only differs from mine in style and the addition of the article to establish the Federal courts, which seemed to me superfluous.

The terms agreed upon were [partially as follows]:

1. The contending armies now in the field to maintain the *status quo,* until notice is given by the commanding general of any one to its opponent, and reasonable time—say, forty-eight hours—allowed.

2. The Confederate armies now in existence to be disbanded and conducted to their several state capitals, there to deposit their arms and public property in the state arsenal; and each officer and man to execute and file an agreement to cease from acts of war, and to abide the action of the state and federal authority. The number of arms and munition of war to be reported to the chief of ordnance at Washington City, subject to the future action of the Congress of the United States, and, in the meantime, to be used solely to maintain peace and order within the borders of the states respectively.

5. The people and inhabitants of all the states to be guaranteed, so far as the executive can, their political rights and franchises, as well as their rights of person and property, as defined by the Constitution of the United States and of the states respectively.

6. The executive authority of the government of the United States not to disturb any of the people by reason of the late war, so long as they live in peace and quiet, abstain from acts of armed hostility, and obey the laws in existence at the place of their residence.

7. In general terms—the war to cease; a general amnesty, so far as the executive of the United States can command, on condition of the disbandment of the Confederate armies, the distribution of the arms, and the resumption of peaceful pursuits by the officers and men hitherto composing said armies. Not being fully empowered by our respective principals to fulfill these terms, we individually and officially pledge ourselves to promptly obtain the necessary authority, and to carry out the above program.

W. T. Sherman, Major-General,
Commanding Army of the United States in North Carolina.

J. E. Johnston, General,
Commanding Confederate States Army in North Carolina.

Four copies were made, one for each president, and one for each signer. General Sherman then returned to his army and I to mine; and each of us announced, publicly, the suspension of hostilities.

Soon after my arrival at Greensboro, Colonel Archer Anderson, adjutant general of the army, delivered to me two notes, of different dates, from the president. In the first I was informed that the sum of $39,000, in silver, subject to my order, was in the hands of the treasury agent, Mr. J. N. [Hendren]; which I was directed to use as the military chest of the army. In the other, which was of later date, I was directed to send this money to him in Charlotte. As the faithful soldiers around me had been without pay many months, and were in great need of money, I thought and felt that its best use would be its distribution among them without regard to rank—generals and privates sharing equally, the sick in hospitals being included. The sum divided was $37,800; $1,200 having been taken by the commissary-general. I also urged the Secretary of War, in writing, to procure the application of a portion of the specie in the possession of the Administration to the payment of a part of the very large arrears due the troops. The letter was carried by Colonel A. P. Mason, who was instructed to wait for an answer. One was promised by telegraph; but it never came. Mr. Davis asserts (page 691, vol. ii) that it is more than doubtful if he wrote the notes above mentioned. I assert that *he* does not doubt it. Colonel Anderson's evidence of the distribution of the silver proves that he wrote the first note, which he denies. His denial of the writing of that note invalidates his denial of the other. It was duty, in such a case, as Mr. Davis well knows, to call the attention of the War Department to the great needs of the troops committed to me.

When I assumed command in North Carolina, there were very large supplies of provision for man and horse in the railroad depots. But the War Department prohibited their use by the troops serving there, on the ground that they were necessary to the army before Richmond; although those troops could not have consumed them in six or eight months. The wagons of the Army of Tennessee arrived in Augusta in the beginning of March; and Colonel W. E. Moore, chief commissary of the army, was instructed to use one hundred of them to form a line of depots between Washington, Georgia, and Charlotte, for the general object of collecting supplies, and for the possible march of our troops along the line, should General Lee leave his position before Richmond. About the March 20, Colonel Moore reported that more than 700,000 rations had been collected in the fine depots of the line. The meeting of General Sherman and myself on April 17 suggested, among the troops, the idea that peace was to be made, or that they were to be surrendered. So, many of them left the army to plant their crops, but many more to escape becoming prisoners of war. Such as could lay hands on them rode off with the horses and mules belonging to the batteries and trains.

In the afternoon of the April 24 I received from the president, who was then in Charlotte, notice by telegraph that he had ratified the terms of pacification agreed upon by General Sherman and me on the eighteenth. Within an hour thereafter a courier brought me from General Hampton two communications from General Sherman—one giving notice of the rejection of the terms above mentioned by the president of the United States, and the other announcing the termination of the armistice forty-eight hours after noon of that day. These facts were communicated to the administration without delay; and I proposed that, to prevent further devastation of our country by the marching of armies, our army should be disbanded. A reply dated 11:00 P.M., April 24, we received early next morning. It suggested that the infantry might be disbanded then, to reassemble at a place named. I was directed to bring with me all the cavalry, a few light field pieces, and all other men who could be mounted on serviceable beasts. I declined to obey this order; giving as my reason, that it provided for the performance of but one of the three important duties I had to perform—securing the safety of the president and cabinet, but not that of the people and of the army, and I suggested the immediate escape of the high civil officers under a proper escort.

The confident belief that it would be a high crime to continue the war governed me in this instance, as it had prompted me to urge the civil authorities of the South to end the war.

The arrangement ordered would have put the great bodies of Union troops in motion, everywhere spreading suffering and ruin among our people, without serving the object of the president's escape as well as an escort of a few picked men would have done.

I determined, therefore, to make another effort to bring about a pacification—within the extent of my command, at least—in the confidence that it would spread fast to the West and South. In that hope I proposed another armistice to General Sherman, and another arrangement, on the basis of the military clause in the agreement of the 18th. General Sherman sent a favorable reply very promptly; so that I was able to set out early on the twenty-sixth to meet him at Bennett's, as before, after reporting to the Administration that I was about to do so.

My proposition to General Sherman had been reported to the president, or secretary of war, when made to him.

We met at Mr. Bennett's about noon; and, as General Sherman was anxious to restore tranquility to the country, we soon agreed upon terms, and established peace within the limits of our commands, which were the same. We believed that they would produce a general pacification. They were:

1. All acts of war on the part of the troops under General Johnston's command to cease from this date.

2. All arms and public property to be deposited at Greensboro, and delivered to an ordnance officer of the United States Army.

3. Rolls of all the officers and men to be made in duplicate; one copy to be retained by the commander of the troops, and the other to be given to officer to be designated by General Sherman. Each officer and man to give his individual obli-

gation in writing not to take up arms against the Government of the United States until properly released from this obligation.

4. The side arms of officers, and their private horses and baggage, to be retained by them.

5. This being done, all the officers and men will be permitted to return to their homes, not to be disturbed by the United States authorities, so long as they observe their obligation and the laws in force where they may reside.

W. T. Sherman, Major-General,
Commanding United States Forces in North Carolina.

J. E. Johnston, General,
Commanding Confederate Forces in North Carolina.

U. S. Grant, Lieutenant-General.

Approved:

SUPPLEMENTAL TERMS.

1. The field transportation to be loaned to the troops for their march to their homes, and for subsequent use in their industrial pursuits. Artillery horses may be used in field transportation if necessary.

2. Each brigade or separate body to retain a number of arms equal to one-seventh of its effective strength, which, when the troops reach the capitals of their States, will be disposed of as the general commanding the department may direct.

3. Private horses, and other private property of both officers and men, to be retained by them.

4. The commanding general of the Military Division of West Mississippi, Major General [Edward R. S.] Canby, will be requested to give transportation by water from Mobile or New Orleans to the troops from Arkansas and Texas.

5. The obligations of officers and soldiers to be signed by their immediate commanders.

6. Naval forces within the limits of General Johnston's command to be included in the terms of this convention.

J. M. Schofield, Major General,
Commanding United States Forces in North Carolina.

J. E. Johnston, General,
Commanding Confederate Forces in North Carolina.

General Sherman assured me that he would transfer from the department all the troops except a small number sufficient to maintain order. He did this by an order issued the next day. Several of the leading officers of his army accompanied General Sherman on this occasion, and their conversation made the clear impression on my mind that they regretted the rejection of the terms of the 18th.

I announced this pacification to the Governors of the States immediately concerned, by telegraph, as follows:

The Disaster in Virginia, the capture by the enemy of all our workshops for the preparation of ammunition and repairing of arms, the impossibility of recruiting our little army, opposed to more than ten times its number, or of supplying it except by robbing our own citizens, destroyed all hope of successful war. I have made, therefore, a convention with Major-General Sherman, to terminate hostilities in North and South Carolina, Georgia, and Florida. I made this convention to spare the blood of this gallant little army, to prevent further sufferings of our people by the devastation and ruin inevitable from the marches of invading armies, and to avoid the crime of waging a hopeless war.

The general terms of agreement were published to the army on the twenty-seventh.

Before the Confederate army came to Greensboro, most of the provisions in depot there had been wasted or consumed by fugitives from the Army of Northern Virginia, or by the poor people of the neighborhood. That at Charlotte had been consumed by our cavalry encamped near by and stragglers. The depots established in South Carolina had been emptied in like manner. The consumers, acting upon the opinion, probably, that as there was no longer a government, they might, as well as any others, divide this property, which was sorely needed by most of them.

The only means of feeding the troops on the way to their homes was by distribution of a little cloth and a stock of cotton-yarn to serve them in lieu of currency. But the quantity of these articles on hand was utterly inadequate. General Sherman, however, prevented the great suffering that otherwise would have occurred along the homeward routes of the troops by giving us 200,000 rations, on no other condition than our transporting this provision from the coast to our camps.

The business of preparing and signing the necessary papers was concluded on May 2. They imposed on the members of the Confederate army an obligation not to take up arms against the United States, and secured them the protection of the Government. The three corps, and as many little bodies of cavalry, were then ordered to march to their homes, each under its former commander. I took leave of those admirable soldiers in Order No. 22.

Comrades: In terminating our official relations, I earnestly exhort you to observe faithfully the terms of pacification agreed upon, and to discharge the obligations of good and peaceful citizens, as well as you have performed the duties of thorough soldiers in the field. By such a course you will best secure the comfort of your families and kindred, and restore tranquility to our country.

You will return to your homes with the admiration of our people, won by the courage and noble devotion you have displayed in this long war. I shall always remember with pride the loyal support and generous confidence you have given me.

I now part with you with deep regret, and bid you farewell with feelings of cordial friendship, and with earnest wishes that you may have hereafter all the prosperity and happiness to be found in the world.

Official.   J. E. Johnston, General.
Kinlock Talconess, A.A.G.

Surrender of Johnston's Army (*Life of Sherman*)

The large bodies of Federal Troops stationed in the South proved by their conduct that they regarded the restoration of the Union as the object of the war, and treated the people around them as fellow-citizens, as they would have done those of Northern States if stationed among them. This inspired in the South a more kindly feeling for the Northern people and the Federal Government than had existed for ten years before. For it was imagined that those who did not fight were still more friendly than the invaders of our country; and a strong expectation grew that the Southern States would soon enter the Union.

Very few apprehended such "reconstruction" as that soon imposed.

The example of pacification set in North Carolina was followed quickly in the other military departments.

The report of an interview with Mr. Davis, published in the "Globe-Democrat" of St. Louis, about the middle of February, indicates that his memory had failed. For, according to it, he asserted that, on the April 24, 1865, immediately after he approved the agreement of April 18 and received intelligence of its rejection by the United States Government, he ordered me to execute a plan of his to prosecute the war, which I disobeyed, although commanding a large army; a part of which (36,000 men) was paroled at Greensboro. The proofs that he was conscious, at that time, of his utter inability to wage war, are, that at Greensboro, April 13, after discussing the subject with four of his cabinet and two generals, he agreed with five of the six, that the military resources of the Confederacy were exhausted, and the endeavor to obtain peace an absolute necessity. And then—on the 24th, the date of the disobeyed order—he ratified the terms of a convention based on the fact that he had not the power to continue the war; and, but the day before, he wrote to Mrs. Davis in a tone and in terms of utter hopelessness. All the members of his cabinet advocated the ratification of the agreement of April 18.

These letters have been published. As to my "large army," General Brecken-ridge testified that, on the eighteenth it had 14,770 men, and was rapidly dimin-ishing. If Mr. Davis had projected war, he would not have ordered the disband-ing of the infantry, who were far more important than cavalry. The object of the order was evidently to strengthen his cavalry guard. He asserted that I had the advantage in cavalry. I had but 1,000 left; General Sherman nearly 6,000, and [Major General James H.] Wilson, in Georgia, nearly 20,000, as they reported. As to the testimony of the numbers paroled, two-thirds of those mentioned by Mr. Davis were men who *ought* to have been in the ranks, but who had quitted them, and were eager to get the protection given by parole. They were like the 53,000 paroled under the same terms of pacification in South Carolina and Georgia.

52

The Last Days of the Confederate Government
Stephen R. Mallory, Secretary of the Navy, C.S.A.

APRIL 2, 1865, though a clear, beautiful day in Richmond, will ever be remembered as the darkest in her history. The temperature wooed the people abroad, a pleasant air swept the foliage and flowers of the capitol grounds, the sun beamed upon its bronze group of conscript fathers, gossiping idlers lounged upon its shaded seats, and the church bells pealed their invitations as cheerily as ever to the piously inclined, who sought their several places of worship. The old city had never, during the war, worn an aspect more serene and quiet, and yet at that very moment the hours of the Confederacy, of which she was the honored capital, were being numbered by the dread arbitrament of blood.

Rumors spoke of a fight somewhere near Petersburg; but this had long been an everyday affair, and they attracted but little attention.

As usual, the president's face was closely scrutinized as he entered St. Paul's, alone, and quietly sought his pew; but its expression varied not from that cold, stern sadness which four years of harassing mental labor had stamped upon it; and as he raised his head after a brief interval from its devotional position, and

Confederate Secretary of the Navy Stephen R. Mallory (*McClure's*)

turned his furrowed brow to Doctor [Charles] Minnegerode, the cold, calm eyes, the sunken cheek, the compressed lip, were all as impenetrable as an iron mask. Not a devotee in all that congregation seemed more gravely attentive than he to the morning service, or responded to its sublime exhortations more fervently; and yet his head was agonized, and his brain sorely perplexed by [General Robert E.] Lee's dispatches of the early hours of the day, telling of [Lieutenant General Ulysses S.] Grant's overwhelming charge through his center, of heavy losses, of his inability to reestablish his lines, and suggesting the abandonment of Richmond. The dull, booming sounds of distant guns were mingled with the impressive words of the service, forming strange and startling responses to its invocations for peace on earth and goodwill to men.

A messenger from the War Department enters the church, steals behind the president, whispers a few words in his ear, and withdraws. All eyes are again fixed upon Mr. [Jefferson] Davis's face as he follows the messenger the whole length of the aisle; but Lee's later dispatches, telling of new and heavy losses, and urging immediate withdrawal from the capital, are not betrayed by one line of that pale, careworn visage.

The members of the cabinet, with the exception of Mr. [Judah P.] Benjamin, were similarly called out of church by special messenger at their several places of worship, and the faces of all were scanned for information as they withdrew; but though all were fully impressed with the momentous crisis, familiarity with adversity had given to each an inevitable immobility of expression, and they betrayed no evidence of the emotions which filled their breasts.

Mr. Benjamin having completed his plain and unexceptionable toilet, and scanned the latest foreign papers, pursued his way from his residence on Main Street beyond Adams Street to the State Department, with his usual happy, jaunty air; his pleasant smile, his mild Havana, and the very twirl of his slender, gold-headed cane contributing to give, to casual observers, expression to that careless confidence of the last man outside the ark, who assured Noah of his belief that "it would not be such a hell of a shower, after all." But he talked with friends in passing; friends with observing, detective eyes, and they did not fail to see, under that smile, which bore no resemblance to mirth or contentment, that the astute secretary was painfully "exercised."

The disastrous news and warnings of Lee, first whispered to officials only, soon reached the ears of the people, who saw, in the rapid preparations of the several departments, the immediate withdrawal of the government from Richmond.

There was no confusion, no noise, no undue excitement; for this contingency had long been anticipated, and to a large extent provided for.

In few words, calmly, solemnly, the president expressed to his cabinet and other high officials, gathered around him at his office, his views of the situation and of the measures which it demanded; and each at once entered upon his allotted duty.

Citizens gathered here and there in groups, gazed sadly, silently, as if upon the closing scene of some deplorable drama; and in the boxes of government records and papers on their way to the depot, recognized evidences of the last day of the Confederacy.

Women, the gentle, loving women of Old Virginia (Heaven bless them!), clad in deepest black, for all Virginia's daughters mourned the loss of kindred in the war; the noble women who had cheered their husbands, brothers, sons, and lovers to the field in a cause cherished by them as sacred, who for it had sacrificed everything but honor, and who were ready to surrender life itself to save it, wept in the streets at this evidence of the hopelessness of the cause.

Prominent citizens interchanged views as to the means of protecting the people against the license of the conquering soldiers on the morrow; but so great was the general gloom, arising from the overwhelming conviction that the Confederacy was lost, that considerations of personal safety or peril failed to arouse attention. His Honor, Mayor [Joseph] Mayo, in his white cravat and irrepressible ruffles, his spotless waistcoat and his blue, brass-buttoned coat, was upon this, as upon all occasions of special interest to his people, foremost in their behalf. The African church had at an early hour poured its crowded congregation into the streets, and American citizens of African descent were shaking hands and exchanging congratulations upon all sides. Many of them walked the streets with eager faces, parted lips, and hurried strides, gazing anxiously into the distance as if to catch the first glimpse of their coming friends.

By the arrangements of the secretary of war, the Danville train of cars, assigned to the president and those who were to accompany him, was to leave Richmond at 8:30 P.M., and before this hour the heads of departments and their chief assistants were ready at the depot. There were reasons for delay, however, and the cars did not leave until 11:00 P.M. In the meantime, hundreds were leaving the doomed city by every practicable means, some on foot, others on horseback, and on carriages, carts, and wagons. The Danville depot was filled by an eager crowd seeking transportation on the train; and the ingenious efforts of many to obtain it, and their shifts and devices to circumvent Colonel Carrington and Major Richardson, who had charge of the train, occasioned no little amusement of those already aboard. The order had been given to admit no one whose services were not indispensable to the operations of the government, which it

Confederate President Jefferson Davis (*McClure's*)

was hoped might be reestablished "somewhere south" and some artful dodgers contrived to "ring in," upon the ground of their vast importance to some great public interest, claims which, when unsupported by the name of some head of a department, were never received without opposition and argument highly entertaining to all but the claimant themselves. Exceptions were made in favor of ladies, for crinoline in the South is not circumscribed by man's arbitrary rules, and many gained admittance to the train.

Members of the Home Guard, embracing many of the best citizens of Richmond of wealth and professional distinction, were on duty in charge of the depot and train. They fully appreciated the fatal significance of the movement; they knew the impending perils to themselves, their families, and property, not only from the Negro troops which were expected to enter the city on the following morning as victors, but from the rabble who stood ready to plunder during the night; and yet they performed their duties as assiduously and strictly, under the last order they would ever receive from the Confederate government, as if triumphs and disasters were crowding upon every fleeting moment. At 11:00 P.M. the president, who, with the secretary of war and other members of the government, had been seated during the preceding hour in the office of the railroad president in anxious expectation of better news from Lee, took his seat in the cars, and the train moved in gloomy silence over the James River. A commanding view of the riverfront of the city was thus afforded, and as the fugitives receded from its flickering lights, many and sad were the commentaries they made upon the Confederate cause.

Heads of departments, chief clerks, books and records; Adjutant General [Samuel] Cooper with the material and personnel of his office, all the essential means for conducting the government, were here; and so able and expert were these agents, that a few hours only, and a half-dozen log cabins, tents, and even wagons, would have sufficed for putting it in fair working order. Its functions, to be sure, were considerably curtailed by Grant's recent operations and the consequent exodus from Richmond.

The James River squadron, with its ironclads, which had lain like chained and sulky bulldogs under the command of Rear Admiral Raphael Semmes to prevent the ascent of the enemy's ships, would, in the classic flash of the times, "go up" before morning, the order having already been given; and the naval operations of the Confederacy east of the Mississippi would cease.

The postmaster general's arrangements—and they had all been guided by wisdom, energy, and ability—were in sad confusion. By the untiring perseverance of his chief subordinates, who were qualified in a remarkable degree for their duties, he had long kept up mail communication between Richmond and such portions of the country as remained to the Confederacy, embracing the Trans-Mississippi Department. But latterly the enemy had so broken up his routes, and dispersed his contractors and agents, that very little was left of his postal system beyond his records and clerks. A glance at Judge [John H.] Reagan, postmaster general, was sufficient to show his deep anxieties. Silent and somber, his eyes as bright and glistening as beads, but evidently seeing nothing around them, now whittling a stick down to the little end of nothing without ever reaching a satisfactory point, he sat chewing and ruminating in evident perplexity. The Confederate States did not embrace a truer, bigger-hearted man or a more conscientious public servant than the postmaster general, and the solution of the problem of keeping up the mails while the enemy had all the lines of communication was evidently bothering him.

Mr. [George A.] Trenholm, Secretary of the Treasury, suffering from a painful attack of neuralgia, was accompanied by a portion of his family; and, as usual with men of his practical sense and knowledge of the fitness of things, he was provided with abundant supplies for the inner man, which his companions shared. The coin of his department he had put in charge of the corps of midshipmen, placed at his command by the Secretary of the Navy for this purpose, under the immediate orders of Commander W. H. Parker. These young aspirants for nautical fame, embracing the sons of Breckenridge, Semmes, and other prominent men, guarded this treasure from Richmond to Augusta, and thence back to Abbeville, for thirty days, when they delivered it to the agent of the Treasury Department, Judge Crump, and were disbanded by the government. Exclusive of the specie belonging to the Virginia banks, and loaned for a special purpose, and the return of which the president had ordered, the sum thus removed was under 300,000 dollars, while it was supposed by many of those who followed it, resolved to be "in at the death," to amount to millions. Under all the circumstances, this coin was felt to be a very troublesome elephant. The president would not sanction its use or distribution for any purpose but that of paying men in the ranks, many of whom were destitute and nearly naked; but its limited amount did not permit this disposition to be made of it. Cabinet officers and other high functionaries of the government were without money, and many of them had not been paid for months. Confederate notes were worthless, and it was thought by some that their right to receive a portion of their salaries in coin was not fairly considered by the president. He was unchangeable, however, as he usually was when convinced of being right, and the specie finally reached Washington, Georgia, in six wagons. But this is a digression, and we will return to the train.

Silence reigned over the fugitives. All knew how the route to Danville approached the enemy's lines, all knew the activity of his large mounted force, and the chance between a safe passage of the Dan and a general "gobble" by [Major General Philip H.] Sheridan's cavalry seemed somewhat in favor of the "gobble."

But apart from the consideration of personal peril, which was generally disregarded, the terrible reverses of the last twenty-four hours were impressed upon the minds and hearts of all as fatal to their cause. There were many even in that small gathering who, to save it, would have cheerfully played the part of Curtius—men who preferred death in any form to its failure and to the grim specters of anarchy, tyranny, and terrorism, which rose behind this utter annihilation of their long cherished hopes and convictions. Painful images of the gigantic efforts, the bloody sacrifices of the South all fruitless now, and bitter reflections upon trials yet to come, were passing through the minds of all, and were reflected, more or less distinctly, upon every face. The progress of the train was slow, and its interruption frequent, and it was not until the bright beams of the morning sun shone into the cars, as they drew their slow length along, at the rate of about ten miles an hour, that any relief from the general gloom was felt, and even then all attempts to dispel it seemed ill timed and out of place.

Mr. Benjamin's deep olive complexion seemed to have become a shade or two darker within the last twenty-four hours, but his Epicurean philosophy was ever in command, and his hope and good humor inexhaustible. In the pleasantest of humble voices he playfully called attention to the "serious family" around him as he discussed a sandwich; and with a "never-give-up-the-ship" sort of air, referred to other great national causes which had been redeemed from far gloomier reverses than ours. A few mercenary spirits of the South had devoted themselves during the terrible struggle specially and successfully to Mammon, but of the Confederates generally it might be said that poverty was the "badge of all their tribe," a badge worn rather with pride than humiliation. Mr. Benjamin was not an exception to the general rule; and he who had long commanded ample wealth to satisfy every want of his genial and refined hospitality, had been for nearly two years restricting himself in the use of what are regarded as the ordinary essentials of daily diet, and was now playfully boasting of the ingenious devices by which he made "both ends meet," and exhibiting his coat and pantaloons, both made of the old shawl which had carried him through three winters, as evidences of his adroit economy.

Ex-Governor [Francis] Lubbock of Texas, on the president's staff with the rank of colonel, evidently regarded himself as *ex officio* bound to "make an effort." An earnest, enthusiastic, big-hearted man was Colonel Lubbock, who had seen much of life, knew something of men, less of women, but a great deal about horses, with a large stock of Texas anecdotes, which he disposed of in a style earnest and demonstrative.

The other members of the president's staff present were Colonels John Taylor Wood and William Preston Johnston (son of the late Albert Sidney Johnston), both gentlemen of high character, cultivated minds, and pleasing address. They were quiet, but professed to be confident, saw much to deplore but no reason for despair or for an immediate abandonment of the fight. As the morning advanced our fugitives recovered their spirits, a process which was doubtless aided somewhat by Mr. Trenholm, the astute secretary of the treasury, whose well-filled hampers and stock of "old Peach" seemed inexhaustible; and by the time the train reached Danville at 5:00 P.M. all shadows seemed to have departed.

A large number of the people of Danville were assembled at the depot as the train entered it, and the president was cordially greeted; but there was that in the cheers that told as much of sorrow as of joy. In that spirit of hospitality as universal in Virginia as the dews of heaven, the people of Danville opened their houses and provided as far as practicable for the accommodation of the members of the government. The president, with the secretaries of the treasury and the navy, found quarters prepared for them at the home of Colonel [William] Sutherlin, who, though an invalid, and not in the Confederate service, seemed to consider the credit of his town involved in hospitality to the fugitives. Secretary Benjamin, the attorney general, postmaster general, adjutant general, and others were in like manner cared for.

All confidently looked for news from or of Lee on the following day, April 4, and many were the speculations as to its probable character, more or less based upon a thousand rumors. The secretary of war, with the chief of the Engineer Corps, [Major General Jeremy F.] Gilmer, Quartermaster General [Brigdier General Alexander R.] Lawton, Commissary General [Brigadier General Isaac M.] St. John, with a handful of men, had left Richmond on horseback about three hours after the president, expecting to join him at Danville.

The fourth and the succeeding four days passed without bringing a word from Lee or Breckenridge, or of the operations of the army; and the anxiety of the president and his followers was intense. "No news is good news," said the over-hopeful Mr. Benjamin; but the apothegm failed to convince. Some asserted, upon the faith of a very reliable gentleman "just in," that Lee had gained a glorious victory, held his army well in hand, and was steadily pursuing Grant. Others declared that Lee was too busy fighting to send couriers, and that the wires were down. The president was not deceived by these follies; but though he looked for disaster, he was wholly unprepared for Lee's capitulation. In the meantime, Danville had received from Richmond a large addition to her population; and fugitives were constantly arriving with startling rumors of military events, not one of which, however, involved Lee's defeat. Adequate accommodation for these refugees could not be found, and they were herding as best they could. Many, including ladies, and in one instance a bridal party, were living in cars switched off upon a side track, receiving commissary rations and cooking them as circumstances permitted.

Beyond a spasmodic effort of [Brigadier General Josiah] Gorgas to open his irrepressible Ordnance Bureau, there was no effort to organize departments, for this could be done only under the protection of an army, a protection that seemed very uncertain. Thus were passed five days. To a few, a very few, they were days of hope; to many they were days of despondency, if not of despair; and to all, days of intense anxiety.

The navy people—captains, commanders, lieutenants, surgeons, engineers, *et cetera*—usually congregated at the naval store, where Paymaster Semple, the efficient bureau officer, had accumulated, as he had at several other depots, not only abundant supplies for his own branch of service, but sufficient to extend to the army frequent and valuable aid. At any hour of the day after 9:00 A.M., these officers, Captain Lee of the Navy Department among them, might be seen perched around the store upon the beef and bread barrels, some abstractedly shaping strands of cord or marline into fancy forms, which changed from running bowlines to hangmen's knots or Turk's heads, or were laid up hawser-fashion and unlaid, to be spliced and knotted or to become something else. Others were overhauling their trunks and bags, putting their traps in order at intervals, calling attention to some quaint cup, curious case, or odd-looking box or other strange relic of distant lands, by brief allusions to its history, and to "my first cruise in the China seas," or to "my cruise with old Perry to Japan," or to "my last cruise in the Mediterranean with old Buchanan." Others were writing letters upon desks improvised of provision or clothing boxes, upon sheets of paper borrowed from this one, with pens borrowed from another one, and with an inkstand which served all the writers, however distant, at the same time.

They were generally grave and silent; and without ships or boats or duties, all adrift upon dry land, they presented a pretty fair illustration of "fish out of water." They doubtless felt that, should the Southern people rise at once and flock to their leading armies, there would still be fields of labor and fame for any soldier; but with all Confederate ports, bays, and waters in the hands of the enemy, their occupation as naval men was gone.

Among the junior officers of the Confederate service, embracing such men as [Commander John N.] Maffitt, [Lieutenant John] Wilkinson, [Lieutenant Hunter] Davidson, [Lieutenant] John Brooke, [Lieutenant] Robert Minor, [Lieutenant] Murdaugh, [Lieutenant John W.] Dunnington, [Lieutenant James I.] Waddell, Shepherd, [Captain Joseph] Fry, [Lieutenant J. R.] Eggleston, and others, were many who were justly regarded in the old navy as not the least of its bright particular stars. To such men, with talent, education, energy, and professional experience and ability, all aided by vigorous manhood, the future will accord an honorable support, if not wealth and distinction, in any career to which they may devote themselves. Not so the senior officers. They, in obedience to what they regarded as the highest dictates of honor and duty, left the old navy, followed their respective States into secession, and shared their fortunes; and now, after forty or fifty years of honorable service, they find themselves, in their old age, without the means of supporting their families and without heart or vigor to enter upon a new career. No class of men who embarked in the Confederate cause is more entitled to consideration, respect, and sympathy for stern adherence to principle.

The plans of the Confederate government for obtaining fighting ships from Europe were well devised, but met with determined opposition. The depredations of the *Alabama* and the *Florida,* both built by the Lairds at Birkenhead, had brought down upon the British government the concentrated indignation of the United States; and from their public journals and Congressional debates, no less than from the remonstrances of Mr. Adams, John Bull, though with evident reluctance, was compelled to choose between offending the United

States and the Confederates. They were both capital customers, but he had to decide, and it did not take him long to do it and in his characteristic way. The portly old sea dog jammed his hat down upon his head, thrust his hands into his pockets, expanded his chest, puffed out his cheeks, dilated his eyes, turned red in the face, and with, well-stimulated passion swore roundly at the "so-called Confederate Government," and turned Mr. Mason out in the cold. Lord John Russell adroitly patted him upon the back, and kept the dogged old fellow in this humor by telling him to go ahead and seize all rams and all other suspicious water animals, and that though the foreign enlistment act would not justify it he would appeal to Parliament to make an act to suit the case.

It is but fair to say, however—and the whole story will at no distant day be made public—that while the results of the actions of the British and French governments upon the subject were the same to the Confederacy, their conduct was widely and characteristically different; and that while John Bull put his foot squarely down and said to the "so-called Confederate Government," "Don't come here to get any more ships and kick up a row; damn me, I'll not stand it," France, the government of the emperor, fair and false to both sides, exhibited about as much good faith and sincerity as might be expected from any professional Jeremy Diddler.

But *revenons a nos moutons.*

In the afternoon of April 9, a courier from Lee's army, one of three to whom the message had been committed, reached Danville with intelligence of Lee's surrender. It fell upon the ears of all like a tire bell in the night. The president received the unexpected blow about 4:00 P.M. at his office, where several members of his cabinet and staff were assembled. They carefully scanned the message as it passed from hand to hand, looked at each other gravely and mutely, and for some moments a silence, more eloquent of great disaster than words could have been, prevailed. The importance of prompt action, however, was evident, and in a short time preparations for moving south, before the enemy's cavalry could intervene and prevent escape, were in rapid progress. The hour of departure for Greensboro, North Carolina, was fixed for 8:00 P.M. that evening; but, as usual, there was delay. Nothing seemed to be ready or in order, and the train, with the president, did not leave until nearly eleven o'clock. Much rain had fallen, and the depot could be reached only through mud knee deep. With the utter darkness, the crowding of quartermasters' wagons, the yells of their contending drivers, the curses, loud and deep, of soldiers, organized and disorganized, determined to get upon the train in defiance of the guard, the mutual shouts of inquiry and response as to missing individuals or luggage, the want of baggage arrangements, and the insufficient and dangerous provision made for getting horses into their cars, the crushing of the crowd, and the determination to get transportation at any hazard, together with the absence of any recognized authority, all seasoned by *sub rosa* rumors that the enemy had already cut the Greensboro road, created a confusion such as it was never before the fortune of old Danville to witness.

At 10:00 P.M., cabinet officers and other chiefs of the government, each seated upon or jealously guarding his baggage, formed near the cars a little silent group by themselves in the darkness, lighted only by Mr. Benjamin's inextinguishable cigar. It was nearly 11:00 P.M. when the president took his seat and the train moved off. The night was intensely dark, with a silent rain, the road in wretched condition, and the progress was consequently very slow. Upon reaching Greensboro it was found that a body of Federal cavalry had cut the road at a point which the train had passed but five minutes before. It was a lucky escape, but "a miss is as good as a mile" was the brief commentary of the president upon it.

No provision had been made for the accommodation of the president and staff, or for his cabinet; and to their surprise they found it impracticable to obtain these essentials important alike to peasant and potentate, board and lodging. Greensboro had been a flourishing town, and there were many commodious and well-furnished residences in and about it; but their doors were closed and their "latch-strings pulled in" against the members of a retreating government. The president was not well, and Colonel Wood of his staff provided him with a bed at the limited and temporary quarters of his family; and the staff and Cabinet, with other prominent gentlemen, took up their quarters in a dilapidated, leaky passenger car. Here they ate, slept, and lived during their stay in Greensboro, a Negro boy cooking their rations in the open air near by. Mr. Trenholm, who was very ill, and who found quarters at the large and elegant mansion of Governor [John M.] Morehead, was the only exception.

Offhand, generous hospitality has ever been regarded as characteristic of the South, and had such a scene as this been predicted of any of its people, it would have encountered universal unbelief. This pitiable phase of human nature was a marked exception to the conduct of the people upon this eventful journey, who, from Greensboro to Washington, Georgia, received the president and his companions with uniform kindness, courtesy, and hospitality. The "cabinet car" was, however, during these dreary days at Greensboro a very agreeable resort. Like true men of the world, its distinguished hosts did the honors to their visitors with a cheerfulness and good humor, seasoned by a flow of good spirits, which threw a charm around the wretched shelter and made their situation seem rather a matter of choice than of necessity. The navy store supplied bread and bacon, and by the active foraging of Paymaster Semple and others of the party, biscuits, eggs, and coffee were added; and with a few tin cups, spoons, and pocket knives, and a liberal use of fingers and capital appetites, they managed to get enough to eat, and slept as best they could.

The times were "sadly out of joint" just then, and so was the Confederate government.

The curious life of the fleeing Confederate government in its cabinet car at Greensboro continued for nearly a week, and was not all discomfort. Indeed, the difficulties of their position were minimized by the spirit with which these men encountered every trial. Here was the astute "minister of justice," a grave and most exemplary gentleman, with a piece of half-broiled "middling" in one hand and a hoecake in the other, his face beaming unmistakable evidence of the condition of the bacon. There was the clever secretary of state busily dividing his attention between a bucket of stewed dried apples and a haversack of hard-boiled eggs. Here was a postmaster general sternly and energetically running his bowie knife through a ham as if it were the chief business of life; and there was the secretary of the navy courteously swallowing his coffee scalding hot that he might not keep the venerable adjutant general waiting too long for the coveted tin cup! All personal discomforts were not only borne with cheerful philosophy, but were made the constant texts for merry comment, quaint anecdotes, or curious story. State sovereignty, secession, foreign intervention and recognition, finance and independence, the ever recurring and fruitful themes of discussion, gave place to the more pressing and practical questions of dinner or no dinner, and how, when, and where it was to be had, and to schemes and devices for enabling a man of six feet to sleep upon a car seat four feet long.

On April 11, in obedience to an invitation from the president, Generals [Joseph E.] Johnston and [Pierre G. T.] Beauregard reached Greensboro for a conference upon the military situation.

"Joe" Johnston, as he was universally known in the army, had more of the *air militaire* than any other officer of the Confederate service. Of medium height, about five feet eight, and weighing about 150 pounds, he had a well-formed and developed figure; a clean; elastic step; an erect, manly, graceful carriage; and an impressive air of command. Bronzed by the sun and hardened by exposure, he seemed in the best condition to meet any possible demand upon his physique; while his grave, handsome face and bright eye, telling of intellectual power and cultivation, were frequently lighted up by a flashing, sunny smile, which betrayed, in spite of an habitual expression of firmness and austerity, a genial nature and a ready appreciation of humor. The Confederate armies included many educated and efficient men in high grades, gentlemen of Christian faith and practice, and of military genius, experience, and capacity; but, in the judgment of those who served under him, there was none who could be more truthfully designated as a soldier *sans peur et sans reproche* than "Old Joe."

The views of Generals Johnston and Beauregard of the military situation of the Confederacy have already been referred to. On April 15, at Greensboro, General Johnston fully and frankly expressed to a member of the cabinet, an old personal friend, his conviction that all further resistance to the Federal forces east of the Mississippi would but augment the sufferings and desolation of the country without the slightest prospect of achieving independence. He sustained his opinions by reference to the relative positions, power, and resources of the belligerents.

"What, in your judgement," said his friend, "do the best interests of our people require of the government?"

"We must stop fighting at once," said General Johnston, "and secure peace upon the best terms we can obtain."

"Can we secure terms?"

"I think we can," he replied. "At all events, we should make the effort at once, for we are at the end of our row."

"General Johnston," said his friend, "your position as the chief of this army and as military commander of this department demands from you a frank statement of your views to the President. You believe that our cause is hopeless, and that further resistance with the means at our command would not only be useless, but unjustifiable, and that we should lay down our arms and secure the best terms we can get for our people. I will, if you please, state all this to the President; but I think *you* had better do so at once, and explicitly."

"General Beauregard and I have been requested to meet the President this evening," he replied, "and I will give him my opinions very explicitly. You will not find me reticent upon them."

At 8:00 P.M. that evening the Cabinet, with the exception of Mr. Trenholm, whose illness prevented his attendance, joined the president at his room. It was a small apartment, some twelve by sixteen feet, containing a bed, a few chairs, and a table with writing materials, and was situated on the second floor of the small dwelling of Mrs. John Taylor Wood, and a few minutes after 8:00 P.M. the two generals entered.

The uniform habit of President Davis in cabinet was to consume some little time in general conversation before entering upon the business of the occasion. At such times he not infrequently introduced some anecdote or interesting episode, generally some reminiscence of his early life in the army, the Mexican War, or his Washington experiences, and his manner of relating, and his application of them was at all times most happy and pleasing. Few men seized more readily upon the aspects of any transaction, or turned them to better account; and his powers of mimicry whenever he condescended to exercise them were inimitable.

Upon this occasion, at a time when the cause of the Confederacy was hopeless; when its soldiers were disbanding and returning to their homes; when its government, stripped of nearly all its power could not hope to exist beyond a few days more; and when the enemy, more powerful and exultant than ever, was advancing upon all sides; true to his habit, the president introduced several subjects of conversation unconnected with the condition of the country and then, turning to General Johnston, he said, in his usual, quiet, grave way, when entering upon matters of business:

"I have requested you and General Beauregard, General Johnston, to join us this evening, that we may have the benefit of your views upon the situation of the country. Of course we all feel the magnitude of the moment. Our late disasters are terrible; but I do not think we should regard them as fatal. I think we can whip the enemy yet, if our people will turn out. We must look at matters calmly, however, and see what is left for us to do. Whatever can be done must be done at once. We have not a day to lose."

A pause ensued, General Johnston not seeming to deem himself expected to speak, when the president said, "We should like to have your views, General Johnston."

Upon this, the general, without preface or introduction, his words translating the expression that his face had worn since he entered the room, said in his terse, concise, demonstrative way, as if seeking to condense thoughts that were crowding for utterance:

"My views are, sir, that our people are tired of the war, feel themselves whipped, and will not fight. Our country is overrun, its military resources greatly diminished, while the enemy's military power and resources were never greater and may be increased to any extent desired. We cannot place another large army in the field, and, cut off as we are from foreign intercourse, I do not see how we could maintain it in fighting condition if we had it. My men are daily deserting in large numbers, and are stealing my artillery teams to aid their escapes to their homes. Since Lee's surrender they regard the war as at an end. If I march out of North Carolina her people will all leave my ranks. It will be the same as I proceed south through South Carolina and Georgia, and I shall expect to retain no man beyond the by-road or cow path that leads to his home. My small force is melting away like snow before the sun, and I am hopeless of recruiting it."

The tone and manner, almost spiteful, in which General Johnston jerked out these brief, decisive sentences, pausing at every period, left no doubt as to his own convictions. When he ceased speaking, a pause of some two or three minutes ensued. Whatever was thought of his statements, and their importance was fully understood, they elicited neither comment nor inquiry. The president, who, during their delivery, had sat with his eyes fixed upon a scrap of paper, which he was folding and refolding abstractedly, had listened without a change of position or expression. He now broke the silence by saying in a low, even tone: "What do you say, General Beauregard?"

"I concur in all General Johnston has said," he replied.

Another silence, more eloquent of the full appreciation of the condition of the country than words could have been, succeeded, during which the president's manner was unchanged. After a brief pause, he said, without variation of tone or expression, and without raising his eyes from the slip of paper between his fingers: "Well, General Johnston, what do you propose? You speak of obtaining terms. You know, of course, that the enemy refuses to treat with us. How do you propose to obtain terms?"

"I think the opposing generals in the field may arrange them."

"Do you think Sherman would treat with you?"

"I have no reason to think otherwise. Such a course would be perfectly legitimate and in accordance with military usage."

"We can easily try it, sir; if we can accomplish any good for the country, heaven knows I am not particular as to form. How will you reach Sherman?"

"I would address him a brief note proposing an interview to arrange terms of surrender and peace, embracing, of course, a cessation of hostilities during the negotiations."

"Well, sir, you can adopt this course, though I confess I am not sanguine as to ultimate results."

The member of the cabinet before referred to as conversing with General Johnston, who was anxious that his views should be promptly carried out, immediately seated himself at the writing table, and, taking up a pen, offered to act as the general's amanuensis. At the request of the latter, however, the president dictated the letter to General Sherman, which was written at once upon a half sheet of letter, folded as note paper, and signed by General Johnston, who took it and said he would send it to General Sherman early in the morning; and in few minutes the conference broke up.

This note, which was a brief proposition for the suspension of hostilities and a conference with a view to agreeing upon terms of peace, has been published with other letters which passed between the two generals.

On or about April 16 the president, his staff, and the cabinet left Greensboro to proceed still further south, with plans unformed, clinging to the hope that Johnston and Sherman would secure peace and the quiet of the country, but still all doubtful as to the result, and still more doubtful as to the consequences of failure. It was evident to every dispassionate mind that no further military stand could be made, and that Mr. Davis should secure his safety by leaving the country in the event of the failure of these negotiations; and hence it was deemed expedient that he should place himself further south, to be ready to cross the Mississippi and get into Mexico, or to leave the coast of Florida for the Bahamas or Cuba. But it was no less evident that Mr. Davis was extremely reluctant to quit the country at all, and that he would make no effort to leave it so long as he could find an organized body of troops, however small, in the field. He shrank from the idea of abandoning any body of men who might still be found willing to strike for the cause, and gave little attention to the question of his personal safety.

In leaving Greensboro, Mr. Reagan, Mr. [John C.] Breckinridge, and Mr. Mallory rode with Mr. Davis and his three aides on horseback; and Mr. Trenholm, Mr. George Davis, and Mr. Benjamin, the other three members of the cabinet, were in ambulances with General Cooper and other officers. The roads were bad from recent rains and [from] great use of them without repairs. The route lay through Jamestown, High Point, and Lexington, and at the latter place, which they reached at nine o'clock at night, they remained all night. Mr. Davis and a portion of his cabinet stopped at the house of Mr. Barringer, where they were most cordially and hospitably received, and where Mrs. Barringer, a most interesting lady of cultivation and refinement, evinced all the warmth and kindness of a true daughter of the South. Mr. Davis was very moody and unhappy, and this was the first day on which I had noticed in him any evidence of an abandonment of hope.

The party left Lexington during the forenoon of the next day, rode slowly to keep with the wagons and ambulances, crossed the head-waters of the Pee Dee, and reached Salisbury that evening. Salisbury had been occupied by the enemy, and much of the town, including the valuable depot and railroad buildings, had been destroyed. Mr. Davis went to the house of a private friend, where he remained all night, and on the following afternoon the party again started south, stopping that night at the little town of Concord. On the following day they rode into Charlotte.

Here the Confederate government had several public establishments, many local officers, and arrangement had been made for the accommodation of Mr. Davis and his Cabinet at private houses. They were received and treated with the utmost kindness and courtesy. Upon all sides, however, the proofs of the hopelessness of the cause were evident. In the course of an hour after reaching Charlotte, and before the party had separated for their several quarters, a dispatch was received from Mr. Breckenridge, who had, with Mr. Reagan returned to Johnston's camp at Greensboro, announcing to Mr. Davis the assassination of Mr. [Abraham] Lincoln.

I was not with Mr. Davis when he received it, but meeting him a few minutes afterwards, and having in the meantime heard of the dispatch, I expressed my utter disbelief of the assassination. He replied that it sounded to him like a canard, but that in revolutionary times events no less startling were constantly occurring. I expressed my deep regret, and, among other views, my conviction of Mr. Lincoln's moderation, his sense of justice, and my apprehension that the South would be accused of instigating his death. To this Mr. Davis replied, sadly: "I certainly have no special regard for Mr. Lincoln; but there are a great many men of whose end I would much rather have heard than his. I fear it will be disastrous to our people, and I regret it deeply."

The party remained at Charlotte about one week. While here, Mr. Davis received the propositions agreed upon between Johnston and Sherman for peace, submitted them to his cabinet, and called upon the members present for written opinions upon the subject. These were called for about 10:00 P.M. in the evening, when the terms were received, and the cabinet met him at ten next morning, all present except Mr. Breckinridge, who had approved them, and who was then with Johnston; and Mr. Trenholm, who was sick at a private house in Charlotte. No comparison or interchange of opinion had been had, and yet their views were nearly identical as to the condition of the country, the character of the terms, and the policy of accepting them, and Mr. Trenholm, when called upon, concurred in the views of his colleagues. They were thus returned to Johnston approved. Three days afterwards Mr. Davis received a dispatch from Johnston announcing that the government of the United States disapproved Sherman's course, and that no other terms than those offered by Grant to Lee could be given. Johnston accepted these terms within the time agreed upon, and surrendered his army.

No other course now seemed open to Mr. Davis but to leave the country, as he had announced his willingness to do, and his immediate advisers urged him to do so with the utmost promptness. Troops began to come into Charlotte, however, escaping from Johnston's surrender, and there was much talk among them of crossing the Mississippi and continuing the war. Portions of [Lieutenant General Wade] Hampton's, [Brigadier General Basil W.] Duke's, [Brigadier General George G.] Dibrell's, and [Brigadier General Samuel W.] Ferguson's commands of the cavalry were hourly coming in. They seemed determined to get across the river and fight it out, and whenever they encountered Mr. Davis they cheered and sought to encourage him. It was evident that he was greatly affected by the constancy and spirit of these men, and that he became indifferent to his own safety, thinking only of gathering together a body of troops to make head against the foe and so arouse the people to arms. His friends, however, saw the urgent expediency of getting further south as rapidly as possible, and after a week's stay at Charlotte they started with an escort of some two or three hundred cavalry, and two days afterwards reached Yorkville, South Carolina, traveling slowly and not at all like men escaping from the country. At Yorkville, Colonel [William] Preston and other gentlemen had arranged for the accommodation of Mr. Davis and his party at private houses, and here they remained one night and a part of the next day. The cavalry escort scouted extensively and kept Mr. Davis advised of the position of the enemy's forces, to avoid which was a matter of some difficulty. With this view the party from Yorkville rode over to a point below Clinton, on the Lawrenceville and Columbus Railroad, and thence struck off to Cokesboro, on the Greenville Railroad. Here the party received the kindest attention at private houses. On the evening of his arrival, Mr. Davis received news by a scout that the enemy's cavalry in considerable force was but ten miles off, and that he was pressing stock upon all sides, and it was deemed advisable to make but a brief stay.

At 2:00 A.M. Mr. Davis was aroused by another scout, who announced that he had left the enemy only ten miles off, and that they would be in the town in two or three hours. Preparations were made with such forces as could be mustered, consisting of fragments of different cavalry commands to give him a proper reception, and four hours were thus passed without further alarm. At 6:30 A.M. the party rose out of Cokesboro toward Abbeville, expecting an encounter at any moment, and prepared to fight, but Abbeville was safely reached without seeing an enemy. From all that could be learned here, however, it was evident that the hostile cavalry was making diligent efforts to capture Mr. Davis and his party.

The escort was here collected, or so much of it as was left, and upon conversing with its officers, Mr. Davis was candidly apprised by some of them that they could not depend upon their men fighting, that they regarded the struggle as over. The officers themselves, and a few men, were ready to do anything in their power to secure his safety; but he became satisfied that the escort was almost useless. He was again urged by his friends to push on south for Florida or west for the Mississippi to secure escape from the country; but the idea of personal safety, when the country's condition was before his eyes, was an unpleasant one to him, and he was ever ready to defer its consideration.

The party had traveled through the country from Charlotte with greater publicity than Dan Rice's caravan enjoyed, and the enemy knew every foot of its progress and where it stopped every night. Wherever Mr. Davis went, he found the people of towns and hamlets at their doors, or outside their gates, ready to greet him and to offer flowers and strawberries, prayers and kind wishes; for the straggling soldiers, passing every day, regularly heralded his progress.

The party left Abbeville at 11:00 P.M. the same night for Washington, Georgia, a distance of some forty-five miles, and by riding briskly reached the Savannah River at daylight. This they crossed upon a pontoon bridge and reached Washington about 10:00 A.M. An hour before leaving Abbeville, it was learned that a strong party of Federal cavalry was *en route* for the pontoon bridge, and might reach and destroy it before Mr. Davis and his party could cross; but nothing interrupted our progress except the loss of an hour in determining at the junction of two roads which was the right one. The night was very dark and cold, and at times a slight rain fell. In approaching the river through a swampy country I rode in advance of the party with Colonel William Preston Johnston and a single guide. The party consisted of some twenty wagons, several ambulances, and about 150 mounted men. In passing a small cabin, about twenty yards from the road, where a light shone dimly, I encountered a horseman in the middle of the road, his horse standing still with his head turned toward me. I was alongside of him and in contact with his horse before I was aware of his presence. Seeing him dressed in dark clothes with a band of gold lace shining upon his cap, I supposed at first glance that it was General Duke of the cavalry, who was of the party, and whom I had seen with gold lace on his cap. The horseman, however, asked in a hurried manner, "What troops are these coming up? What party is this?" Another glance showed me he was a Federal officer, and I at once feared that his party had reached the bridge, and that he was reconnoitering far in advance. I could have captured him, but reflecting that the road was almost impassable, and that any delay might prevent us from reaching Washington, I replied evasively and invited him to accompany me. He withdrew to the side of the road, however, and there I left him.

At Washington we heard crude statements of cavalry parties of Federals upon all sides. Having previously announced to Mr. Davis my determination not to leave the country, and not to cross the Mississippi with him, for I regarded all designs and plans for continuing the war as wrong, I here handed him a brief note of resignation, took my leave of him, and, joining [Brigadier General Louis T.] Wigfall and wife, started for Atlanta and La Grange, where my wife and children were, and where I resolved to await the action of the government.

In taking leave of Mr. Davis, I told him that I would accompany him if he would determine to go to South Florida and thence leave the country, for I believed I could aid him materially; but up to 4:00 P.M. of the day he reached Washington he was still unable to determine his future course. At about this hour he found that Mrs. Davis and family, who had left Washington the day before, were some twenty miles off, and that he could join them by using the railroad, take leave of them the same night, and return to Washington; and this he seemed inclined to do when I bade him goodbye.

I have since learned from Judge Reagan, who was with him, that he did not take this course, but left Washington on horseback with his staff next morning. His capture has been published and commented upon very fully.

I proceeded to Atlanta, was detained there six hours, and thence joined my family a La Grange, Georgia, where some days later I was taken prisoner.

During the ride from Greensboro, North Carolina, to Washington, Georgia, I saw a great deal of the people throughout the route, and still more of our disbanded troops returning to their homes from the armies of Lee and Johnston. All were glad that the "war was over," and yet all regretted defeat.

There never was a cause which more thoroughly united a population than that of the Confederacy. Tears frequently streamed down the faces of the people as Mr. Davis passed and bowed to them, and all hearts overflowed with sympathy for him.

PART 12

Postscript

An Interview with General Longstreet
Henry W. Grady

IF YOU SHOULD happen to find yourself in this little mountain town—and you could not well find yourself in a cooler place—and you were to drop in at the dingy post office—and you could not well drop in at a dingier one—you would, in all probability, meet with a surprise when you inquired for your letters. Instead of the hurried, pert, and inquisitive apparition that pops up at the call hole of the average country post office when a strange voice is heard, you would be confronted with a deliberate and noble face. Through the little window you would see a large, well-shaped head, a pair of brave, frank gray eyes, a strong, expressive mouth, massive jaws, silken moustache and whiskers almost as white and worn as "Burnsides," the whole fine in tone and fibre, aristocratic in every detail, and carrying a singular impression of power and dignity; you would then be looking into the eyes of the most accomplished soldier on the Southern side of the later war, the man that led the Southern troops in the first real battle of that gigantic struggle. [General Robert E.] Lee's most trusted and best loved lieutenant, the "bulldog" of the Army of Virginia—General James Longstreet. You would watch him with interest, remark his striking likeness to King William of Prussia, thank him for his courteous reply to your inquiries, and then step out and inquire about him.

General Longstreet is a Georgian. It is true that he was born just across the line in South Carolina, but his family is Georgian and his home has been in Georgia. The Longstreets have always been considerable people of intelligence and authority. They have been distinguished in the pulpit, on the bench and in letters. Judge [James] Longstreet is the author of the *Georgia Scenes,* the best character sketch book probably ever produced in this country. General Longstreet was born in 1820, and entered the West Point Academy when he was 18 years of age. In 1842 he graduated and entered the army. He served with distinction in the Mexican War and won two brevet promotions. He was made captain for "gallant conduct" after the battle of Churubusco, breveted major for gallantry at El Molino del Rey, and was "distinguished" in General [Winfield] Scott's official report of the assault on Chapultepec.

It will be seen, therefore, that he has had nothing but military training and no experience save that gained on the battlefield or in camp. He is a soldier by instinct, education, practice and habit. There is no man whose opinions on the conduct of the war have more weight with thoughtful and competent people. Of unusually strong, broad mind, having devoted his leisure to the study of war as a science and his business hours to the prosecution of war as a fact, being so thoroughly military in his habits that the soldier always rose above the partisan and gave him clear-eyed rather than jaundiced vision, his opinions are entitled to weight. Beyond this he was the most intimate friend, probably, that General Lee ever had, and he had the luck, or ill luck, of being the chief actor in at least two of the decisive battles of the war.

I had the pleasure of a long and easy talk with General Longstreet concerning the conduct of that war—its decisive battles, its leading actors, its blunders and its brilliant points. These views, commenting upon the work in the field, I

Lieutenant General James Longstreet (*Century*)

forward to the *Times* as a sort of supplement to the criticism of [Major General Robert] Toombs on the work in the council chamber, which I sent you a short time since. Said General Longstreet, erect, military and precise in his manner, but courteous always: "I was paymaster in the United States army when the trouble between the States began. I had the rank of major and was stationed in New Mexico. I viewed from my distant point of observation the agitation of the Southern leaders with impatience. I was devoted to the Union and failed to see any cause for breaking it up when secession was accomplished. I held on. I had determined to remain where I was if secession was peacefully accomplished, of which, however, I had little hope. My relatives in Georgia wrote me urgently to come on at once, saying that 'all the good officers were being taken up.' I replied that if there was going to be any war it would last for several years, and that in that time every soldier would find his level, and so that it mattered little whether he commenced at the top or bottom. At length [Fort] Sumter was fired upon, and then I knew that war was inevitable and felt that my place was with my people. I resigned my commission and came home. I was at once made brigadier general, and may I say that I led the Southern troops into the first battle they ever fought and commanded in the first field of victory that the Southern flag ever floated over. This was the affair at Blackburn's Ford, usually known as Bull Run. [Brigadier General Daniel] Tyler attempted to force a passage, but my brigade repulsed him handsomely."

"Were you much elated over this victory?"

"I was proud of it, of course, but I did not join in the wild delight that followed it. I never had any doubt that our people would make good fighters, but I knew that the issue must at last be put upon organization. Individual bravery amounts to nothing in a protracted war. Everything depends upon organization. As I feared it would be, the Southern armies were never properly organized or disciplined. The Northern armies were moved like machines and handled like machines. A spring was touched, the whole mass moved regularly and promptly. With us it was different. There never was a better army than the Army of [Northern] Virginia, but it lacked the machinelike harmony of the Northern armies. We had too much individuality in the ranks and inefficiency at Richmond. The government was to blame, I think, for the lack of organization."

"Did the Southern troops display more valor than the Northern troops?"

"I cannot say that they did. As I said before, individual bravery amounts to very little in a battle. Men must be fought in blocks and masses, just as parts of a machine. Nearly everything depends upon the commander. If the men have confidence in him and in his movements, they will stand by him to the end. They will actually come to feel safer in following him, no matter where he leads, than in breaking away from him. A good general can take an army of Chinamen and whip an army of Englishmen, if the latter are improperly handled. No matter how brave men are, they will not fight if they feel that they are in doubtful and unskillful hands. This principle explains the wonderful victories of the French under the first Napoleon. If a general can only inspire his men with the feeling that he knows what he is about, he will have good fighters. He can put them anywhere on any field, and in the face of any fire!

"I was once dining with Horace Greeley," said the General, becoming a bit discussive, "and he asked me if it was not necessary to swear at your men and 'whoop them up,' as the saying goes. I replied that I thought not. There is nothing like quiet assurances and confidences. A general need never be noisy, and I think quiet troops are the best fighters. I once sent out a brigade to occupy a certain point. As it was mounting a little crest, it came full upon immense masses of Federals. The men were panic-stricken, and thought I had made a mistake in ordering them forward. They halted irresolute, and then dropped down upon the ground. It was very important that they should advance and a make a feint, at least. I therefore rode quietly through their ranks on the crest, and there halting my horse, adjusted my glasses and calmly surveyed the scene in front. I turned carelessly around, and as I expected, there was my brigade at my back, every man in position ready for anything—confident and assured.

"At another time, in the heat of the battle of Chattanooga, [Brigadier General Henry L.] Benning, of Georgia, one of the bravest men I ever saw, came charging up to me in great agitation. He was riding a captured artillery horse, without any saddle, with the blind bridle on, and was using a rope trace as a whip. His hat was gone and he was much disordered. 'General,' he said, 'my brigade is utterly destroyed and scattered.' 'Is that so?' I asked quietly; 'utterly destroyed, you say?' 'Yes, sir,' he replied; 'gone all to pieces!' His great heart was nearly breaking. I approached him and said quietly: 'Don't you think you could find one man, General?' 'One man,' he said in astonishment; 'I suppose I could. What do you want with him?' 'Go and get him,' I said, still quietly, laying my hand on his arm, 'and bring him here. Then you and I and he will charge together. This is sacred, General, and we may as well die here as anywhere.' He looked at me curiously a moment, then laughed and, with an oath, lashed his horse with his rope trace and was off like a flash. In a few moments he swept by me at the head of a command that he had gathered together somehow or other and he was into the fight again."

"But were not the Southern troops, in defending their own soil, inspired by stronger motives than the Northern troops, who were intruders?"

"I think not. The sentiment in favor of the Union and the memories that cling about the old flag were just as strong, if not stronger, than the love of the soil of the States and the feeling aroused in defending homes. There were thousands of men in every State who turned against their native States in deference to this love of the Union, and joined with the Federals in invading their own homes. It is impossible to overestimate the love that the Federals had for the Union and the old flag. It was a love that was born with the Revolution and cemented with the blood of our fathers. I remember myself that after the battle at Chickamauga [Major General John C.] Breckenridge made a speech congrat-

ulating his men at being able for the first time in their lives to sleep on the battlefield, and he said that they had to thank me for it. The next day some one
remarked that I must feel very proud of this. I replied that the war and all connected with it filled me with inexpressible sadness, and that I felt just as if I was
being congratulated over whipping my own brother. The truth is, the soldiers
on both sides were nerved by lofty and desperate emotions, and I knew from
the first that there would be heroism displayed by both armies, and that the
struggle must be prolonged and strenuous."

"What were the decisive battles of the war?"

"It is my opinion that we were whipped when we failed at Gettysburg. After
that we had only a chance. After [General Braxton] Bragg's failure to follow up
the advantage at Chattanooga I felt that only a miracle could save us, and you
know a soldier does not rely to any great extent on miracles. You see, as regards
Gettysburg, we had staked a great deal on the invasion of which it was the turning point. It had been decided that we must make an offensive campaign. I did
not favor the invasion of Pennsylvania. My idea was to hurry the army, then
concentrating at Jackson for the purpose of succoring Vicksburg, forward to
Tullahoma, where Bragg was confronting [Major General William Starke] Rosecrans, who might have been easily crushed, and with our grand army we could
have swept through Tennessee and Kentucky and pierced Ohio. By sending this
great force, with the prestige of victory, through Tennessee and Kentucky we
would have won over both of those doubtful States. I found, however, that General Lee had his head very much set on invading Pennsylvania. I agreed to his
plans, only making one point, viz: that we should never attack the Federals, but
force them to attack us. I remembered Jackson's saying: 'We sometimes fail to
drive the enemy from a position. They always fail to drive us!'

"The invasion was made. Its wise plan was changed by the Battle of Gettysburg and we were forced back across the river. I felt then that we were beaten. I
considered it simply a question of time. Once after this was there a chance (a
bare chance) of saving the Confederacy. This was after the battle of Chickamauga, which was in many respects the most brilliant victory of the war. The
enemy was more thoroughly put to rout here than before or since. If there ever
was an occasion that demanded pursuit pell-mell this was the time. The Federals were rushing back on Chattanooga in the utmost confusion. It was a bright
moonlit night and our people were anxious to pursue. We might actually have
entered Chattanooga with the flying Federals and thus recovered the key to
Georgia and East Tennessee. General Bragg declined to follow up his advantage.
The enemy rallied, reformed, and Bragg was driven back to Missionary Ridge.
I had a talk with Mr. [Jefferson] Davis shortly after Chickamauga. I told him
that there was no hope for the triumph of our arms. He was very much discouraged and finally grew petulant. He said he never remembered having seen such
a movement as I proposed at Chickamauga. I replied that if his memory would

carry him as far back as the First Manassas he would see such a movement. He replied very tartly and we had some sharp words. These were arranged, however, and we parted on good terms."

"You say, General, that organization was the deficiency of the military system of the Confederacy. What was the fault of its operations?"

"Chiefly this—the failure to concentrate troops. The government, moved doubtless by a desire to protect our soil as much as possible, kept our troops scattered, and thus made them inefficient. There was scarcely a time when we had a really grand army at any one point. The policy of the Federals, and especially General Grant's policy, was to mass everything available at one single point, and then drive straight at it. Of course our government disliked to leave any section of the Confederacy at the mercy of the Federals. Therefore our men were scattered over our whole extent of territory. I do not think that our best generals even comprehended the necessity of concentration of forces. They relied too much on the valor of their men. They seemed to forget that where good, cautious generals commanded on each side, numbers must triumph over valor. There was a notable instance of this at Fort Donelson. General Albert Sidney Johnston, one of the loftiest souls that ever lived, had about 45,000 men. Of this force 15,000 were at Donelson, 15,000 at Columbus and 15,000 in the front of [Major General Don Carlos] Buell. Grant, having a force of about 30,000 men, fell upon Donelson and captured it. Had Johnston either concentrated his forces at Donelson or in front of Buell, he could have crushed either Grant or Buell. As it was, General Grant told me afterwards that he was as badly whipped at Donelson as the Confederates were, if the Confederates had only known it, and been able to act upon their knowledge."

"Who do you think the best general on the Southern side of the war?"

"I am inclined to think that General Joe Johnston was the ablest and most accomplished man that the Confederate armies produced. He never had the opportunity accorded to many others, but he showed wonderful power as a tactician and a commander. I do not think that we had his equal for handling an army and conducting a campaign. General Lee was a great leader—wise, deep and sagacious. His moral influence was something wonderful. But he lost his poise in certain occasions. No one who is acquainted with the facts can believe that he would have fought the battle of Gettysburg had he not been under great excitement, or that he would have ordered the sacrifice of Pickett and his Virginians on the day after the battle. He said to me afterwards, 'Why didn't you stop all that thing that day?' At the Wilderness when our lines had been driven in, and I was just getting to the field, General Lee put himself at the head of one of my brigades, and leading it into action my men pressed him back, and I said to him that if he would leave my command in my own hands I would reform the lines. His great soul rose masterful within him when a crisis or disaster threatened. This tended to disturb his admirable equipoise. I loved General Lee as a brother while he lived and I revere his memory. He was a great man, a born leader, a wise general, but I think Johnston was the most accomplished and capable commander that we had."

"Who was the greatest general on the Northern side?"

"Grant—incomparably the greatest. He possessed an individuality that impressed itself upon all that he did. [Major General George B.] McClellan was a skillful engineer, but never rose above the average conclusions of his council. [Major General William T.] Sherman never fought a great battle, and displayed no extraordinary power. But Grant was great. He understood the terrible power of concentration and persistency. How stubbornly he stuck to Vicksburg and to Richmond. He concentrated all his strength, trained his energies to a single purpose, and then delivered terrible sledge hammer blows against which strategy and tactics and valor could avail nothing. He knew that majorities properly handled must triumph in war as in politics, and he always gathered his resources together before striking."

"What was the most desperate battle of the war?"

"Gettysburg—as far as my observation extended. There was never any fighting done anywhere to surpass the battle made by my men on July 2. I led 12,000 men into that charge. Over one-third of this number were killed or wounded. These veterans charged the whole Federal army, entrenched on a crest, harassed on each flank until the line was stretched, and at last I found myself charging 50,000 entrenched men, in the face of a volcano of artillery, with a single line of battle. My two divisions encountered and drove back the Third Corps, the Fifth Corps, the Sixth Corps, the Second Corps, one division of the Twelfth and the Pennsylvania Reserves. As they broke line after line they encountered new ones and felt the steady shock of fresh troops. The Federals contend that the bulk of Lee's army was in this charge, and put the strength of the attacking column at 45,000 men, when it was only my 12,000, with 2,000 of these knocked out of ranks before they had hardly started up the slope. I do not think the records of the war can show anything to approach this work."

"Did you agree with Lee as to the necessity of the surrender at Appomattox?"

"I did. For some time I had felt that we were fighting against hope. I kept my lips closed and fought ahead in silence. For the week proceeding the surrender I fought almost without ceasing. I was covering General Lee's retreat, while [Major General John B.] Gordon opened a way for him in front. I had [Major General Charles W.] Field's division, all that was left. The Federals pressed upon us relentlessly and we fell back, fighting night and day, inch by inch, covering the slow retreat of our wagon trains. Our lines were never once broken or disordered. My men fought with the finest regularity and heroism. Wherever I placed a brigade, there it would stand until I ordered it away. I was among my men constantly, so that I knew little of the general situation. Early in the morning General Lee sent for me, and I at once went to him. He was in deep concern. He stated to me that his retreat had been cut off and it was impossible for him to escape from the circle that had been drawn about him. 'If that is the case, General,' I replied, 'you should surrender the army. If escape is impossible, not another life should be sacrificed.' General Lee then began to talk about the distress and trouble that a surrender would bring upon his country and his people. 'That cannot be put against the useless shedding of these brave men's blood. If you are satisfied that you cannot save the army, it should be surrendered. The people will know that you have done all that man can do.' He then told me that he had discovered that there were heavy masses of infantry in front and that he could not hope to cut through. It was a terrible moment for General Lee. Having fought for years with high and lofty purposes, having won victory after victory and made a record for his army not equaled in our history, it was hard that he must surrender everything. I cannot tell you how my heart went to him." (But the moistened eyes and the fine voice, grown husky, as General Longstreet went over this story, did tell me). "I left General Lee and went back to my men. I ordered firing stopped. I stood quietly awaiting events. Suddenly a horse came clattering down my front. I looked up and saw a smart-looking officer, with yellow hair streaming behind him, hurrying forward to where I stood. He was in great excitement, and urged his horse to where I stood. Then he wrenched him suddenly to his haunches, and said, in a somewhat violent tone: 'In the name of General Phil Sheridan, I demand the instant surrender of this army!' I was not in a humor for trifling just then, but I replied as calmly as I could: 'I am not the commander of this army, and if I were I should not surrender to you,' meaning, of course, that I would treat with the proper authority. 'I make the demand,' he rejoined, 'simply for the purpose of preventing further bloodshed.' 'If you wish to prevent any further shedding of blood don't shed any more; we have already stopped,' I said, still keeping cool. He reiterated his demand for an immediate and unconditional surrender. I then notified him that he was outside of his lines, and that if he was not more courteous I would remind him of this fact in a way that might be unpleasant to him. I then explained that General Grant and General Lee were then engaged in a conference that would probably settle everything. He grew pleasant then, and after awhile galloped off. He was a brave and spirited young fellow, but my old veterans were not in the mood to humor him when he dashed up to us that day. The surrender fell with more crushing effect on my troops than on any in the army. They were in fine condition and were flushed with victory. We had thrown back the Federals day after day as they pressed on us—punishing them when they came too near and stunning them when they charged us seriously. Enveloped for six or eight days in the continual smoke of battle, we had little idea of what was going on elsewhere, and when we surrendered 4,000 bayonets to General Grant we surrendered also 1,600 Federal prisoners that had been plucked out of his army during our retreat. Still, we all had the most perfect confidence in General Lee's ability and heroism and we knew that he had done all mortal man could do."

"Did you say to General Lee when parting with him that you regretted you had gone into the war?"

"No, sir; I said that before I drew my sword again I would be sure that it was necessary. I did not believe, and I do not now believe, that the war was justified on either side. It is a terrible thing and should be resorted to only in absolute self-defense—just as killing in private life. Besides, I had fought all the time, knowing that our plans were wrong and believing that we could not succeed. I saw our forces scattered over a vast country and along an endless line of sea coast, while General Grant, with the true genius of war, massed his energies upon point after point and crushed us inexorably. Still I did not, and do not regret my services. I fought for my people. I fought steadily, uncomplainingly, as best I knew how, and there never was an hour that I would not have gladly laid my life down to have assured the success of our cause. No, sir; I regret nothing. I only did my duty. The war was a grievous error—an error of both sections and for which both sections have deeply atoned. As for me, I only did my duty in a humble way, as a man and a soldier, and the same reverent, devoted sentiment that impelled me to draw my sword filled my heart when I sheathed it forever."

Colonel P. W. Alexander, who as "P.W.A." was the best known of Southern war correspondents, lately gave me a reminiscence of General Longstreet. He says that right before the battle of the Wilderness he slept in the same room with the general. After he had gone to bed General Longstreet came in. He undressed and then kneeled by his bedside and engaged in the most earnest prayers. While his words were not audible it could be seen that he was very much affected, was literally "wrestling with prayer." He remained upon his knees for a full half hour, Colonel Alexander watching him by the starlight that crept through an open window. By the way, it is a notable fact that the South—lavish, reckless, imperious in all her ways—sent her armies to the field under the leadership of God-fearing, God-seeking men, while the decorous and straight-laced North did no such thing. It may be that the land of sentiment believed in prayer, while the land of cold reason put its trust in artillery, and preferred that its leaders should look to the condition of their troops rather than indulge in petitions to the Divine Arbiter, that, after all, is said to give victory to the side having the most men and the heaviest guns.

Lee, Jackson, and Longstreet were men of prayer, in the fullest sense of the word. Bragg was baptized in the presence of his army. [Lieutenant General Richard] Ewell became a devout Christian. Albert Sidney Johnston never went into battle without going down upon his knees to the Lord of Hosts. Gordon was a devout and prayer-loving man. Neither General Grant, or Sherman, or Sheridan, or [Benjamin F.] Butler—but, then, it is important, after all, to look after the artillery.

General Longstreet was a leader great in details. He never went into camp without seeing personally that his men were properly disposed. His orders to his troops were unique and in vivid contrast to the fine rhetoric and stirring

The Grand Review in Washington (*Life of Sherman*)

appeals usual in such papers. He filled his orders with practical hints and advice. As for instance: "Remember though the fiery noise of battle is most terrifying and seems to threaten universal ruin it is not so destructive as it seems, and few soldiers are slain after all. The Commanding General desires to particularly impress this fact. Let officers and men even under the most formidable fire preserve a quiet demeanor; keep cool; obey orders; fire low. Remember while you are doing this and driving the enemy before you, your comrades are supporting you on either side and are in turn edging on you." He had the most wonderful influence over his men. They would follow him anywhere. General Toombs once said that Longstreet was the only Southern general capable of leading an army of 70,000 men into Pennsylvania.

Since the war, General Longstreet has been living in comparative quiet. Some years ago he wrote a letter advising the South to accept the situation and make the best of it, that subjected him to considerable abuse. Latterly, however, this has died away, and he is restored to his old place in the hearts of his people, since the wisdom of his advice having been passed, he is allowed credit for purity of motive in giving it. He lived in New Orleans for some years, and was unlucky in a commercial business. He removed to Gainesville, Georgia, some years ago, where he bought a sheep farm and a large summer hotel. He was made postmaster, without having applied, upon the death of the old postmaster. His hotel is managed by his son and nephew. His salary is about $2,000 and he is allowed an assistant. His health is good, but his right arm is paralyzed, the effect of old wounds. He is quiet, self-possessed and kindly—a great favorite with the townspeople. He has a charming family, a fair competency, a peaceful home, and will probably end a life stormy, potent and terrible to the highest degree in a placid and grateful contentment.

Chapter 1: "Recollections of the John Brown Raid" first appeared in the July 1883 issue of *The Century Magazine*. At the time of the raid, Alexander R. Boteler (1815–92) was a United States congressman from the Virginia district embracing Harper's Ferry.

Chapter 2: "Mob Violence in Baltimore" first appeared in the September 1885 issue of the *Magazine of American History* under the title "Baltimore in 1861." At the time of which he wrote, John C. Robinson (1817–97) was a captain in the Regular Army, assigned to the command of Fort McHenry, near Baltimore.

Chapter 3: "The First Battle of the War: Big Bethel" first appeared in the December 28, 1878, issue of the Philadelphia *Weekly Times* and was submitted by Major General John B. Magruder's brother, Colonel Allan B. Magruder, from the deceased general's unpublished memoirs. At the Battle of Big Bethel, John B. Magruder (1807–71) was a colonel commanding the Hampton Division, which defended the Virginia Peninsula.

Chapter 4: "With Generals Bee and Jackson at First Manassas" first appeared in the February 26, 1881, issue of the Philadelphia *Weekly Times* under the title "First Battle of Bull Run." At First Manassas, William Mack Robbins was a company-grade officer in the Fourth Alabama Infantry.

Chapter 5: "Folly and Fiasco in West Virginia" first appeared in the March 11, 1882, issue of the Philadelphia *Weekly Times* under the title "Garnett in West Virginia." William B. Taliaferro (1822–98) was a colonel commanding the Twenty-third Virginia Infantry during the West Virginia Campaign.

Chapter 6: "Missouri's Unionists at War" first appeared in the June 28, October 11, and November 29, 1879, issues of the Philadelphia *Weekly Times* under the title "Missouri's Union Record." Montgomery Blair (1813–83) was postmaster general in the Lincoln administration and the brother of Major General Frank P. Blair Jr. His recollections must be read with the understanding that the Blair family's break in the fall of 1861 with John C. Frémont, whom they had championed for command in Missouri, was particularly bitter. The proximate cause of their breach was the arrest of Frank P. Blair Jr. by Frémont on charges of insubordination. The Blairs held Frémont responsible for the death of their favorite, Nathaniel Lyon, at Wilson's Creek; questioned his military competence; and had come to distrust his radical politics.

Chapter 7: "Avenging First Bull Run: The Port Royal Expedition" first appeared in the October 1885 issue of the *Magazine of American History* as "The Port Royal Expedition, 1861: The First Union Victory of the Civil War." Brigadier General Egbert L. Viele (1825–1902) commanded a Union brigade in the expedition.

Chapter 8: "Life in the White House with President Lincoln" first appeared in the November 1890 issue of *The Century Magazine* under the title "Life in the White House in the Time of Lincoln." John Hay (1838–1905) was private secretary to President Lincoln and later served as secretary of state in the administration of President Theodore Roosevelt.

Chapter 9: "Reminiscences of General Grant" first appeared in the October 1885 issue of *The Century Magazine.* Major General James Harrison Wilson (1837–1925) was the only member of Grant's staff elevated to a line command; he ended the war as commander of Federal cavalry in the Western Theatre. Although his debt to Grant was great, his recollections are nonetheless reliable.

Chapter 10: "The Real Stonewall Jackson" first appeared in the April 1894 issue of *The Century Magazine.* Daniel Harvey Hill (1821–89) was a Confederate lieutenant general and the brother-in-law of Thomas J. Jackson.

Chapter 11: "Recollections of Nathan Bedford Forrest" first appeared in the May 4, 1878, issue of the Philadelphia *Weekly Times.* Confederate Major General Dabney H. Maury (1822–1900) was associated with Forrest in several Western campaigns.

Chapter 12: "In the Air above Yorktown" first appeared in the November 1876 issue of *The Galaxy* under the title "War Memoirs, Yorktown and Williamsburg." During the Peninsular campaign, George A. Custer (1839–76) was a lieutenant in the Fifth United States Cavalry, serving as an aide de camp on the staff of the commander of the Army of the Potomac, Major General George B. McClellan.

Chapter 13: "Our First Battle, Bull Pasture Mountain [McDowell]" first appeared in the April 1886 issue of the *Magazine of American History.* Alfred E. Lee (1838–1905) was a private in the Eighty-second Ohio Infantry during the time of which he wrote. Lee rose through the ranks to become a captain and assistant adjutant general on the staff of Brigadier General James S. Robinson during the Carolinas campaign of 1865.

Chapter 14: "An Undeserved Stigma: Fitz John Porter at Second Bull Run" first appeared in the December 1882 issue of *The North American Review* under the title "An Undeserved Stigma." Ulysses S. Grant (1822–85), retired commanding general of the United States Army and two-term president, was a private citizen at the time he wrote "An Undeserved Stigma." The article caused a nationwide sensation and stirred renewed congressional activity to gain relief for the cashiered Fitz John Porter.

Chapter 15: "A Witness to Mutiny at Antietam" first appeared in the August 1894 issue of *Harper's New Monthly Magazine* under the title "Chapters in Journalism." George W. Smalley (1833–1916) was an army reporter for the New York *Tribune* during the years 1862–63. His account of Antietam was regarded by many fellow war correspondents as the single greatest journalistic exploit of the Civil War. After the war he became one of America's most distinguished foreign correspondents.

Chapter 16: "The Reserve at Antietam" first appeared in the September 1886 issue of *The Century Magazine.* As a captain, Thomas M. Anderson (1836–1917) commanded the Twelfth United States Infantry at Antietam.

Chapter 17: "My Story of Fredericksburg" first appeared in the January 1913 issue of *Hearst's Magazine*. Joshua L. Chamberlain (1828–1914) was the lieutenant colonel of the Twentieth Maine Volunteer Infantry at Fredericksburg. A consummate self-promoter who wrote and spoke widely of his war experiences, Chamberlain later served as governor of Maine and president of Bowdoin College.

Chapter 18: "Lee at Fredericksburg" first appeared in the August 1886 issue of *The Century Magazine*. Major J. Horace Lacy served on the staff of Major General Gustavus W. Smith, Confederate secretary of war *ad interim*, at the time of which he wrote.

Chapter 19: "Desperation and Heroism at the Battle of Valverde" first appeared in the November 22, 1864, issue of the Philadelphia *Weekly Times* under the title "Battle of Valverde." Lieutenant Franklin Cook led a company of the Fifth United States Infantry at Valverde. Both the department commander, Colonel Edward R. S. Canby, and the commander on the field, Colonel Benjamin S. Roberts, commended Cook for gallantry.

Chapter 20: "The Shiloh Campaign" first appeared serially in the January and February 1886 issues of the *North American Review*. A heavily revised and very much condensed version, which eliminated nearly half the text, including many of the most controversial passages, appeared in the original *Battles and Leaders of the Civil War*. General Pierre G. T. Beauregard (1818–93) was second in command of the Confederate Army of the Mississippi until the death of General Albert S. Johnston on the first day of the Battle of Shiloh, when he assumed army command. Beauregard's article must be read in the context of his long feud with Jefferson Davis, which began when the Confederate president relieved him from command in the summer of 1862, after the loss of Corinth.

Chapter 21: "The Great Locomotive Chase" first appeared in the September 1903 issue of *McClure's Magazine* under the title "Andrews' Railroad Raid." Private Jacob Parrott of Company K, Thirty-third Ohio Infantry, participated in the raid. (Although not a member of Andrews's raiding party, one Frank C. Dougherty appeared as coauthor of the article.)

Chapter 22: "The Attack on Corinth" first appeared in the June 1922 issue of *The Palimpsest*. Clinton H. Parkhurst (1844–1933) was a sergeant in the Sixteenth Iowa Volunteer Infantry at Corinth. His account of the Battle of Corinth is one of the better portrayals of Civil War combat from the common soldier's perspective.

Chapter 23: "Losing a Division at Stones River" first appeared in the January 1886 issue of *The United Service* under the title "The Battle of Stones River." It was incorporated into Johnson's book *A Soldier's Reminiscences in Peace and War*, published later that year. As a brigadier general, Richard W. Johnson (1827–97) commanded a division in the Army of the Cumberland at Stones River. Although Johnson went on to serve competently until the war's end, many held him responsible for the near Union defeat on December 31, 1862. Particularly galling to Johnson was the verdict of Henry M. Cist, who in his widely read *The Army of the Cumberland* (New York, 1882) charged that Johnson's division had been poorly placed and ill-disposed to meet an attack. "All this was criminal negligence," averred Cist, "a failure in the performance of duty for which some one should have suffered." Johnson's article was a response to Cist.

Chapter 24: "When the Rappahannock Ran Red" first appeared in the May 1913 issue of *Hearst's Magazine*. As a captain at Chancellorsville, James R. O'Beirne commanded the color company of the Thirty-seventh New York Infantry and was cited for distinguished service by both his brigade and regimental commanders. For gallantry earlier in the war at Fair Oaks, he earned the Congressional Medal of Honor. O'Beirne ended the war a brevet brigadier general.

Chapter 25: "The Campaign and Battle of Gettysburg" first appeared in the July 1876 issue of the *Atlantic Monthly* under the title "Campaign and Battle of Gettysburg, June and July 1863." It is a much fuller—and in many respects markedly different—account of Major General Oliver Otis Howard's controversial service at Gettysburg than that found in the *Autobiography of Oliver Otis Howard,* published thirty-two years later. Howard (1830–1909) commanded the Eleventh Corps of the Army of the Potomac at Gettysburg.

Chapter 26: "Gettysburg: A Reply to General Howard" first appeared in the December 1876 issue of *The Galaxy.* Major General Winfield S. Hancock (1824–86) commanded the Second Corps of the Army of the Potomac at Gettysburg. Hancock claimed to have written the article reluctantly and only to refute General Howard's account of the battle.

Chapter 27: "Why Lee Lost at Gettysburg" first appeared in the September 22, 1877, issue of the Philadelphia *Weekly Times.* As a brigadier general, Henry Heth (1825–99) commanded a division in A. P. Hill's corps of the Confederate Army of Northern Virginia and touched off the Battle of Gettysburg on July 1, 1863, when he advanced against John Buford's Federal cavalry contrary to orders.

Chapter 28: "Lincoln at Gettysburg" first appeared in the November 1909 issue of *The Century Magazine.* A prominent attorney, Isaac Wayne MacVeagh (1833–1917) was chairman of the Republican State Committee of Pennsylvania during the war. He later became attorney general in President James A. Garfield's administration.

Chapter 29: "A Winter at Vicksburg" first appeared in the January 3, 1885, issue of the Philadelphia *Weekly Times.* Major General Dabney H. Maury (1822–1900) commanded a Confederate division during the first months of the Vicksburg campaign.

Chapter 30: "Defending Port Hudson" first appeared in the July 10, 1880, issue of the Philadelphia *Weekly Times* under the title "The Siege of Port Hudson." During the siege, P. F. de Gournay, then a lieutenant colonel, was elevated from command of the Twelfth Louisiana Artillery Battalion to command of the left wing of heavy artillery batteries guarding the river approaches to Port Hudson.

Chapter 31: "From Tullahoma to Chattanooga" first appeared in the May 1887 issue of *The Century Magazine* under the title "The Campaign for Chattanooga." It was an expanded version of an article that appeared in the March 6, 1882, number of the *National Tribune* as "The Chattanooga Campaign." Major General William Starke Rosecrans (1819–1902) commanded the Union Army of the Cumberland in the Chickamauga campaign. Defeated soundly at Chickamauga, Rosecrans was relieved of command and finished out the war in comparative obscurity. The *Century* and *National Tribune* articles constituted his principal public defense of his actions during the campaign.

Chapter 32: "Chickamauga" first appeared in the March 13, 1886, issue of the Philadelphia *Weekly Times*. At Chickamauga, Benjamin F. Sawyer was lieutenant colonel of the Twenty-fourth Alabama Infantry.

Chapter 33: "Holding Burnside in Check in East Tennessee" first appeared serially in the May 20 and July 22, 1882, issues of the Philadelphia *Weekly Times,* under the titles, respectively, "Holding Burnside in Check" and "Burnside against Jones." During the time of which he wrote, Major General Samuel Jones (1819–87) commanded the Confederate Department of Western Virginia and East Tennessee. His direction of the department was controversial and, rightly or wrongly, led to his reassignment in March 1864 as commander of the then relatively quiet Department of South Carolina, Georgia, and Florida.

Chapter 34: "Charging with Sheridan up Missionary Ridge" first appeared in the March 1914 issue of *Hearst's Magazine.* Michael V. Sheridan was a lieutenant and member of his brother Major General Philip H. Sheridan's staff during the Chattanooga campaign.

Chapter 35: "The Forgotten Fight on Tunnel Hill" first appeared as part of Green B. Raum's serialized memoirs, "With the Western Army," in the April 24, May 1, and May 22, 1902, issues of the *National Tribune.* As a brigadier general in the Chattanooga campaign, Colonel Green B. Raum (1829–1909) commanded the Second Brigade of Brigadier General John E. Smith's Second Division of the Seventeenth Army Corps, a part of Major General William T. Sherman's Union Army of the Tennessee. Raum's often discursive narrative has been condensed here.

Chapter 36: "Grant's Conduct of the Wilderness and Spotsylvania Campaigns" first appeared as a published address in the *Annual Report of the American Historical Association for the Year 1908* under the title "Grant's Conduct of the Wilderness Campaign." During the 1864 Virginia campaigns, Brigadier General Edward Porter Alexander (1835–1910) commanded the artillery of Lieutenant General James Longstreet's corps, Army of Northern Virginia.

Chapter 37: "Lee's Response to Grant's Overland Campaign of 1864" first appeared as a published address in the *Annual Report of the American Historical Association for the Year 1908* under the title "Lee's Conduct of the Wilderness Campaign." William R. Livermore (1843–1919) was a cadet at the U.S. Military Academy during the Civil War and later became a respected military scholar.

Chapter 38: "Grant and Sheridan in 1864: A Study in Contrasts" first appeared in the November 17, 1888, issue of *The Ohio Soldier* under the title "Grant's Stoicism and Sheridan's Enthusiasm." The nineteenth president of the United States, Brigadier General Rutherford B. Hayes (1822–93) commanded first a brigade, and later a division, in the Federal Army of West Virginia during Major General Philip H. Sheridan's 1864 Shenandoah Valley campaign.

Chapter 39: "A Tough Tussle with Sheridan" first appeared in the November 3, 1888, issue of *The Ohio Soldier* under the title "An Incident of Sheridan's Campaign in the Valley." During the 1864 Shenandoah Valley campaign, Lieutenant Colonel Jacob Weddle commanded the First West Virginia Infantry, Second Brigade, First Division, of Brevet Major General George Crook's Union Army of West Virginia.

Chapter 40: "Boys in Battle at New Market" first appeared in the January 1889 issue of *The Century Magazine* under the title "The West Point of the Confederacy, Boys in Battle at New Market, Virginia, May 15, 1864." A seventeen-year old Virginia Military Institute cadet at the time of New Market, John S. Wise later became a distinguished attorney and wrote *The End of An Era*, one of the more poignant Confederate memoirs. Wise presented a revised version of his *Century* article in *The End of an Era*. Wise tended to embellish and romanticize events; nonetheless, his account of the Battle of New Market is generally reliable.

Chapter 41: "Fighting for Petersburg" first appeared in the May 5, 1883, issue of the Philadelphia *Weekly Times*. Thomas T. Roche was a member of Company K, Sixteenth Mississippi Infantry during the campaign. His last name also appeared as Roach in unit muster rolls.

Chapter 42: "A Terrible Day: The Battle of Atlanta, July 22, 1864," first appeared in the April 16, 1885, issue of the *National Tribune* under the title "A Terrible Day." At Atlanta, Brevet Major General John W. Fuller (1827–91) commanded the Fourth Division, Sixteenth Corps, of Major General James B. McPherson's Union Army of the Tennessee.

Chapter 43: "The March to the Sea, an Armed Picnic" first appeared in the June 11 and 18, 1885, issues of the *National Tribune,* as part of the serialized "Military Memoirs" of William P. Carlin (1829–1903). During the March to the Sea, Carlin commanded the First Division, Fourteenth Corps, of the Union Army of Georgia, a part of Major General William T. Sherman's Grand Army.

Chapter 44: "The Red River Expedition" first appeared in the October 25 and November 1, 1879, issues of the Philadelphia *Weekly Times*. Captain William S. Burns (b. 1833) was acting assistant adjutant general on the staff of Major General Andrew J. Smith, who commanded a detachment of the Sixteenth and Seventeenth corps of the Federal Army of the Tennessee during the Red River campaign.

Chapter 45: "A Question of Command at Franklin" first appeared in the February 1889 issue of *The Century Magazine*. Major General David S. Stanley (1828–1902) commanded the Federal Fourth Army Corps at Franklin; Brigadier General Jacob D. Cox (1828–1900) commanded the Federal Twenty-third Army Corps there. Henry Stone (?–1896) served on the staff of the commander of the Department of the Cumberland, Major General George H. Thomas, during the Franklin and Nashville campaigns with the rank of captain. Mercurial by nature, Stanley occasionally played loose with the truth; Cox was a more sober and reliable commentator of events in which he played a part.

Chapter 46: "'Little Jim,' the Pride of the Regiment" first appeared in the October 1883 issue of *St. Nicholas Magazine* as "Recollections of a Drummer Boy, Chapter VII." Harry M. Kieffer (1845–   ) was a drummer boy in the One Hundred Fiftieth Pennsylvania Volunteer Infantry Regiment. First published in *St. Nicholas,* Kieffer's embellished but very popular war reminiscences were reprinted as *The Recollections of a Drummer Boy* (Boston, 1888).

Chapter 47: "They Followed the Army: The Anguish of Runaway Slaves" first appeared in the October 29, 1887, issued of *The Ohio Soldier* under the title "They Followed the

Army." Lieutenant John Walton served as adjutant of the Twenty-fifth Ohio Infantry during Carolina campaigns of 1865.

Chapter 48: "The Victory at Fort Fisher" first appeared in the October 1872 issue of *The Overland Monthly*. As a colonel, John W. Ames (?–1878) commanded a Union brigade in the assault on Fort Fisher.

Chapter 49: "The Conference at City Point" first appeared in the March 1891 issue of *The North American Review* under the title "Unpublished Letters of General Sherman." The text is that of a letter General William T. Sherman (1820–91) wrote to Isaac N. Arnold on November 28, 1872. As a major general, Sherman commanded all Federal armies in the Western Theatre during the final year of the war.

Chapter 50: "Lee at Appomattox" first appeared in the April 1902 issue of *The Century Magazine*. During the Appomattox campaign, Brigadier General Edward Porter Alexander (1835–1910) commanded the artillery of Lieutenant General James Longstreet's corps, Army of Northern Virginia. "Lee at Appomattox" is of particular value as Alexander did not treat the Appomattox campaign in his classic *Military Memoirs of a Confederate* (New York, 1907); it also differs in many respects from the account Alexander gave in his posthumously published *Fighting for the Confederacy* (Chapel Hill, N.C., 1989).

Chapter 51: "My Negotiations with General Sherman" first appeared in the August 1886 issue of *The North American Review*. General Joseph E. Johnston (1807–91) commanded the Confederate Army of Tennessee in the closing weeks of the war. His article was explicitly intended as a rebuttal to President Davis's uncomplimentary appraisal of his leadership during the last days of the war, as set forth in Davis's *Rise and Fall of the Confederate Government* (New York, 1881).

Chapter 52: "The Last Days of the Confederate Government" first appeared in the December 1900 issue of *McClure's Magazine*, published posthumously with the permission of Stephen R. Mallory's daughter. Mallory (1813–73) was secretary of the navy of the Confederacy.

Chapter 53: "An Interview with General Longstreet" first appeared in the August 2, 1879, issue of the Philadelphia *Weekly Times* under the title "General Longstreet: His Reminiscences of the Struggle between the States." Politically liberal, Henry W. Grady (1850–89) became co-proprietor of the Atlanta *Constitution* in 1880 and was a leading architect of the New South.

In 1879, Philadelphia *Weekly Times* publisher Alexander K. McClure engaged Grady, then the Georgia correspondent for the New York *Herald,* to travel to General James Longstreet's home and interview him for the "Annals of the War" series. As McClure proudly recalled, the article contained Longstreet's "first public defense" of his actions at Gettysburg and "presented in brief the statements given in his elaborate book," the subsequently published *From Manassas to Appomattox* (Philadelphia, 1896). For more on Grady's interview of Longstreet, which occurred on July 23, 1879, see A. K. McClure, *Recollections of Half a Century* (Salem, Mass., 1902), pages 398–403.

MAP AND ILLUSTRATION CREDITS

Maps and illustrations are from the following sources:

Atlas to Accompany the Official Records of the Union and Confederate Armies. Washington, D.C., 1891–95. (Cited in map captions as *Atlas.*)

Century Magazine.

Forbes, Ida B. *General Wm. T. Sherman, His Life and Battles, or, From Boy-hood, to His "March to the Sea."* Illustrated by Edwin Forbes. New York, 1886. (Cited in illustration captions as *Life of Sherman.*)

Johnson, Rossiter. *Campfire and Battlefield.* New York, 1898. (Cited in illustration captions as *Campfire and Battlefield.*)

Harper's New Monthly Magazine.

Knox, Thomas W. *Camp-fire and Cotton-field; Southern Adventure in Time of War.* New York, 1865.

Magazine of American History.

McClure's Magazine.

National Tribune.

St. Nicholas Magazine.

Townsend, Luther T. *History of the Sixteenth Regiment, New Hampshire Volunteers.* Washington, 1897. (Cited in illustration captions as *History of 16th New Hampshire.*)

U.S. Army Military History Institute Photographic Archives, Carlisle Barracks, Pennsylvania.

The War of the Rebellion: A Compilation of the Official Records of the Union and Confederate Armies. Washington, D.C., 1880–1901. (Cited in map captions as *Official Records.*)

INDEX

Author's note: In preparing the index for *Battles and Leaders of the Civil War, Volume 5*, I have deviated a bit from standard indexing practice. As indexable items (names, places, concepts) often recur frequently in the same article—sometimes appearing on every page—I generally have cited only their first appearance in an article, except where the references to them differ significantly in nature.

PETER COZZENS is a foreign service officer with the U.S. Department of State. His books include the trilogy *No Better Place to Die: The Battle of Stones River; This Terrible Sound: The Battle of Chickamauga;* and *The Shipwreck of Their Hopes: The Battles for Chattanooga;* as well as *General John Pope: A Life for the Nation; The Darkest Days of the War: The Battles of Iuka and Corinth;* and *Eyewitness to the Indian Wars, 1865–1890: The Struggle for Apacheria.*

The University of Illinois Press
is a founding member of the
Association of American University Presses.

University of Illinois Press
1325 South Oak Street
Champaign, IL 61820-6903
www.press.uillinois.edu